Equality in Law between Men and Women
in the European Community

United Kingdom

# Equality in Law between Men and Women in the European Community

*Series Editors*

**MICHEL VERWILGHEN**
*Professeur ordinaire à la Faculté de Droit*
*Université catholique de Louvain*

**FERDINAND VON PRONDZYNSKI**
*Professor of Law and Dean of the Law School*
*University of Hull*

European Commission

# Equality in Law
# between Men and Women
# in the European Community

# United Kingdom

*by*

CHRISTOPHER McCRUDDEN

*Fellow and Tutor in Law*
*Lincoln College, Oxford*

**MARTINUS NIJHOFF PUBLISHERS**
DORDRECHT/BOSTON/LONDON

OFFICE FOR OFFICIAL PUBLICATIONS OF THE EUROPEAN COMMUNITIES
LUXEMBOURG

A C.I.P. Catalogue record for this book is available from the Library of Congress.


ISBN (this volume)   0-7923-1828-5 (Martinus Nijhoff Publishers)
                     92-826-4478-2 (Office for Official Publications of the EC)

This study was commissioned by the Equal Opportunities Unit of Directorate-General V (Employment, Industrial Relations and Social Affairs) of the European Commission. It does not, however, express the Commission's official views. The responsibility for the views expressed lies with the authors.


A French version of this text has been published by the Office for Official Publications of the European Communities and Les Editions Juridiques Bruylant, Brussels.

Published by
Office for Official Publications of the European Communities, L-2985 Luxembourg
ISBN (this volume) 92-826-4478-2          Catalogue number CE-97-92-012-EN-C
and
Martinus Nijhoff Publishers,
P.O. Box 163, 3300 AD Dordrecht, The Netherlands
ISBN (series) 0-7923-1842-0                    ISBN (this volume) 0-7923-1828-5


Sold and distributed for the Office for Official Publications of the European Communities by the distributors listed on the inside back cover.


Kluwer Academic Publishers incorporates the publishing programmes of D. Reidel, Martinus Nijhoff, Dr W. Junk and MTP Press.


Sold and distributed in the USA and Canada
by Kluwer Academic Publishers,
101 Philip Drive, Norwell, MA 02061, U.S.A.


In all other countries sold and distributed
by Kluwer Academic Publishers Group,
P.O. Box 322, 3300 AH Dordrecht, The Netherlands

*Printed in Belgium*

# PREFACE

I would like to thank the following for their help in the production of the Commentary part of this volume in various ways. Particular thanks are due to Vicki Chapman, Solicitor and Legal Officer of the Child Poverty Action Group and Linda Luckhaus, University of Warwick, for extensive help in the writing of chapter 5 on social security. The following also read the manuscript and commented on it most helpfully: Dr Mark Freedland, St John's College, Oxford; Professor Bob Hepple, University College, London; Lord Lester, QC; Beverley Jones, Chief Legal Officer, Equal Opportunities Commission for Northern Ireland; Vareena Jones, Principal Legal Officer of the Equal Opportunities Commission; Professor Ferdinand von Prondzynski, University of Hull; and Michael Rubenstein, editor of the *Industrial Relations Law Reports* and joint editor of the *Equal Opportunities Review.* Those mentioned bear no responsibility, of course, for any remaining errors and omissions.

The United Kingdom legislation and other texts reprinted in Section I: Legislation of the Sources part of this volume are United Kingdom Crown copyright, and are reproduced by permission of Her Majesty's Stationery Office.

With the exception of the extracts from the judgments of the Court of Appeal in *Secretary of State for Social Security* v. *Thomas*, which have been taken from a transcript, the texts reprinted in Section II: Cases of the Sources part have been reproduced either from the *Industrial Relations Law Reports* by permission of the editor, Michael Rubenstein, or from the now discontinued *British Equal Opportunities Cases*, Volume 1 (1976-1986) by permission of the publishers, CCH Editions Limited.

The book attempts to state accurately the legal position in the United Kingdom as developed in legislation and jurisprudence up to 1 January 1992. Developments since that date have not been included in either the Commentary or the Sources parts of this volume.

Christopher McCrudden
Lincoln College, Oxford
1 October 1993

# TABLE OF CONTENTS

*Page*

Preface . . . . . . . . . . . . . . . . . . . . . . . . . . . . . . . . . . . . . . . . . . . . . . . v
Table of contents . . . . . . . . . . . . . . . . . . . . . . . . . . . . . . . . . . . . vii
Foreword . . . . . . . . . . . . . . . . . . . . . . . . . . . . . . . . . . . . . . . . . . . . xiii
Notice to the reader . . . . . . . . . . . . . . . . . . . . . . . . . . . . . . . . . . . xvii
Abbreviations . . . . . . . . . . . . . . . . . . . . . . . . . . . . . . . . . . . . . . . . . xix
Table of legislation etc. . . . . . . . . . . . . . . . . . . . . . . . . . . . . . . . . xxi
Table of cases . . . . . . . . . . . . . . . . . . . . . . . . . . . . . . . . . . . . . . . . xxxiii

## COMMENTARY ON EQUALITY LAW

1    GENERAL . . . . . . . . . . . . . . . . . . . . . . . . . . . . . . . . . . . . . . . . 3

1.1    Introduction . . . . . . . . . . . . . . . . . . . . . . . . . . . . . . . . . . . . . . 3
       1.1.1    Introduction to national legal system . . . . . . . . . . . . . . . 3
       1.1.2    Economic and social context . . . . . . . . . . . . . . . . . . . . 3

1.2    Sources . . . . . . . . . . . . . . . . . . . . . . . . . . . . . . . . . . . . . . . . . 4
       1.2.1    International standards . . . . . . . . . . . . . . . . . . . . . . . . . . 4
                1.2.1.1    Human rights . . . . . . . . . . . . . . . . . . . . . . . . . 4
                1.2.1.2    Treaties on special questions . . . . . . . . . . . . . 5
       1.2.2    European Community law . . . . . . . . . . . . . . . . . . . . . . 6
                1.2.2.1    Direct effect of Community law . . . . . . . . . . . 6
                1.2.2.2    Retrospective implementation . . . . . . . . . . . . 8
       1.2.3    Constitutional law . . . . . . . . . . . . . . . . . . . . . . . . . . . 9
       1.2.4    Legislation . . . . . . . . . . . . . . . . . . . . . . . . . . . . . . . .10
                1.2.4.1    Prior legislation . . . . . . . . . . . . . . . . . . . . . . 10
                1.2.4.2    Present legislation . . . . . . . . . . . . . . . . . . . . 11

2    BASIC CONCEPTS . . . . . . . . . . . . . . . . . . . . . . . . . . . . . . . . .13

2.1    Equality and discrimination . . . . . . . . . . . . . . . . . . . . . . . . . .13

2.2    Direct discrimination . . . . . . . . . . . . . . . . . . . . . . . . . . . . . . .13
       2.2.1    Definition . . . . . . . . . . . . . . . . . . . . . . . . . . . . . . . . .13
                2.2.1.1    Reason . . . . . . . . . . . . . . . . . . . . . . . . . . . . . 14
                2.2.1.2    Detriment . . . . . . . . . . . . . . . . . . . . . . . . . . 16
                2.2.1.3    Comparator . . . . . . . . . . . . . . . . . . . . . . . . . 16
       2.2.2    Extended definition . . . . . . . . . . . . . . . . . . . . . . . . . . 17
                2.2.2.1    Marital status . . . . . . . . . . . . . . . . . . . . . . . 17
                2.2.2.2    Family status . . . . . . . . . . . . . . . . . . . . . . . . 17
                2.2.2.3    Pregnancy . . . . . . . . . . . . . . . . . . . . . . . . . . 17
                2.2.2.4    Sexual harassment . . . . . . . . . . . . . . . . . . . . 19
                2.2.2.5    Physical attributes . . . . . . . . . . . . . . . . . . . . 19
                2.2.2.6    Dress codes . . . . . . . . . . . . . . . . . . . . . . . . . .19

2.3    Indirect discrimination . . . . . . . . . . . . . . . . . . . . . . . . . . . . . .20
       2.3.1    Definition . . . . . . . . . . . . . . . . . . . . . . . . . . . . . . . . .20
       2.3.2    Suspect criteria . . . . . . . . . . . . . . . . . . . . . . . . . . . . . 21
       2.3.3    Disproportionate impact . . . . . . . . . . . . . . . . . . . . . . . 24
       2.3.4    Objective justification . . . . . . . . . . . . . . . . . . . . . . . . . 29

2.4    Victimization . . . . . . . . . . . . . . . . . . . . . . . . . . . . . . . . . . . . .31

**3      EQUAL PAY** ........................................ .33

3.1    Principle ........................................ .33

3.2    Exceptions ........................................ .33
       3.2.1    Size ................................ 33
       3.2.2    Work done outside the jurisdiction ..................... 33
       3.2.3    Health and safety ........................... 33
       3.2.4    National security ........................... 33
       3.2.5    Religion, religious schools .................... 34
       3.2.6    Retirement age ........................... 34
       3.2.6    Other exceptions ........................... 34

3.3    Personal scope of principle ........................... 35
       3.3.1    Employees ............................... 35
       3.3.2    Independent contractors .................... 35
       3.3.3    Home workers ........................... 35
       3.3.4    Public sector ........................... 35
       3.3.5    Domestic employees ........................ 36
       3.3.6    Non-employed population .................... 36

3.4    Activities covered ................................ 36

3.5    Definition of remuneration ........................... 37
       3.5.1    Article 119 of the EEC Treaty ................ 37
       3.5.2    Fringe benefits ........................... 38
       3.5.3    Contributions by employer .................. 38
       3.5.4.   Contributions by employee .................. 38
       3.5.5    Post-employment benefits ................... 39
       3.5.6    Pensions ............................... 39
       3.5.7    Collective agreements ..................... 40

3.6    Comparator ........................................ 41
       3.6.1    Same establishment ....................... 41
       3.6.2    Contemporaneous employment ................. 41
       3.6.3    Hypothetical male ........................ 42
       3.6.4    Different establishment/same employer .......... 42
       3.6.5    Cross-industry comparisons ................. 43

3.7    Woman does same work as man ......................... 43
       3.7.1    Identical work ........................... 43
       3.7.2    Similar work ........................... 43
       3.7.3    Night-work ............................. 44

3.8    Equal value ........................................ 44
       3.8.1    Job evaluation ........................... 46
       3.8.2    Job classification ........................ 46
              3.8.2.1    Factors ........................ 48
              3.8.2.2    Weightings ..................... 48
              3.8.2.3    Traditional male/female attributes ........ 48
       3.8.3    Higher value ........................... 49
       3.8.4    Proportionate pay ........................ 49

3.9    Legitimate reason for pay differential ................. 49
       3.9.1    Material difference ...................... 49
       3.9.2    Economic benefits/market forces ............. 50
       3.9.3    Night-work ............................. 51
       3.9.4    Part-time work ........................... 51
       3.9.5    Red circles ........................... 52
       3.9.5    Other reasons ........................... 53

3.10   Levelling up/down ................................ 54

| | | |
|---|---|---|
| 4 | EQUAL TREATMENT | 55 |
| 4.1 | Principle | 55 |
| 4.2 | Exceptions | 55 |
| | 4.2.1 Exclusions | 55 |
| |     4.2.1.1 Size | 55 |
| |     4.2.1.2 Work done outside the jurisdiction | 55 |
| |     4.2.1.3 Health and safety | 55 |
| |     4.2.1.4 National security | 58 |
| |     4.2.1.5 Religion, religious schools | 59 |
| |     4.2.1.6 Retirement age | 59 |
| | 4.2.2 Sex as a determining factor | 61 |
| |     4.2.2.1 Lists | 61 |
| |     4.2.2.2 Genuine occupational qualification | 61 |
| |     4.2.2.3 Authenticity | 63 |
| |     4.2.2.4 Security | 64 |
| |     4.2.2.5 Religion | 65 |
| |     4.2.2.6 Decency and privacy | 65 |
| |     4.2.2.7 Single-sex establishments | 67 |
| 4.3 | Territorial scope | 68 |
| 4.4 | Personal scope | 69 |
| | 4.4.1 Employees | 69 |
| | 4.4.2 Independent contractors | 69 |
| | 4.4.3 Home workers | 70 |
| | 4.4.4 Public sector | 70 |
| | 4.4.5 Domestic employees | 71 |
| | 4.4.6 Persons without a contract of employment | 71 |
| | 4.4.7 Others | 71 |
| 4.5 | Activities covered | 71 |
| 4.6 | Comparator | 74 |
| 4.7 | Hiring | 74 |
| | 4.7.1 Recruitment methods | 74 |
| | 4.7.2 Advertisements | 74 |
| | 4.7.3 Job title | 75 |
| | 4.7.4 Job description | 75 |
| | 4.7.5 Selection arrangements | 75 |
| | 4.7.6 Terms on which a job is offered | 75 |
| | 4.7.7 Refusal or deliberate omission to offer a job | 75 |
| 4.8 | Working conditions | 75 |
| | 4.8.1 Relation to pay | 76 |
| | 4.8.2 Education and training | 76 |
| | 4.8.3 Access to benefits, facilities, services, promotion | 77 |
| 4.9 | Exclusion, dismissal or other detriment | 78 |
| 4.10 | Instructions to discriminate | 78 |
| 4.11 | Pressure to discriminate | 78 |
| 4.12 | Discrimination by an employer or a trade union | 79 |
| 4.13 | Discriminatory practices | 80 |
| 4.14 | Special treatment | 80 |
| | 4.14.1 Protective legislation | 80 |
| |     4.14.1.1 Pregnancy and maternity | 80 |
| |     4.14.1.2 Parental leave and similar measures | 82 |
| |     4.14.1.3 Difficult or unpleasant working conditions | 82 |
| |     4.14.1.4 Health and safety | 82 |
| | 4.14.2 Positive action | 82 |
| |     4.14.2.1 Definition | 82 |
| |     4.14.2.2 Areas | 83 |
| |     4.14.2.3 Means | 86 |
| |     4.14.2.4 Constitutional or legal problems | 87 |

5        SOCIAL SECURITY . . . . . . . . . . . . . . . . . . . . . . . . . 89

5.1      Definition of social security . . . . . . . . . . . . . . . . . . . . . . . . . . . . . . 89
         5.1.1   Statutory social security . . . . . . . . . . . . . . . . . . . . . . . . . . . 89
         5.1.2   Occupational social security  . . . . . . . . . . . . . . . . . . . . . 90
         5.1.3   Social assistance . . . . . . . . . . . . . . . . . . . . . . . . . . . . . . 91

5.2      Social security Directives and other legislation  . . . . . . . . . . . . . . . . . . 91
         5.2.1   Article 119 of the EEC Treaty . . . . . . . . . . . . . . . . . . . . . . . 91
         5.2.2   Directive 75/117/EEC . . . . . . . . . . . . . . . . . . . . . . . . . . 91
         5.2.3   Directive 76/207/EEC . . . . . . . . . . . . . . . . . . . . . . . . . . 91
         5.2.4   Directive 79/7/EEC . . . . . . . . . . . . . . . . . . . . . . . . . . . . 91
         5.2.5   Directive 86/378/EEC . . . . . . . . . . . . . . . . . . . . . . . . . . 95

5.3      Problematic concepts  . . . . . . . . . . . . . . . . . . . . . . . . . . . . . . . . 96
         5.3.1   Breadwinner . . . . . . . . . . . . . . . . . . . . . . . . . . . . . . . . . 96
         5.3.2   Sole breadwinner  . . . . . . . . . . . . . . . . . . . . . . . . . . . . . 96
         5.3.3   Head of household  . . . . . . . . . . . . . . . . . . . . . . . . . . . 97
         5.3.4   Cohabitant . . . . . . . . . . . . . . . . . . . . . . . . . . . . . . . . 97
         5.3.5   Living alone . . . . . . . . . . . . . . . . . . . . . . . . . . . . . . . . 97
         5.3.6   Dependant . . . . . . . . . . . . . . . . . . . . . . . . . . . . . . . . 97

5.4      Exceptions . . . . . . . . . . . . . . . . . . . . . . . . . . . . . . . . . . . . . . . 98
         5.4.1   Retirement age  . . . . . . . . . . . . . . . . . . . . . . . . . . . . . 98
         5.4.2   Sex as a determining factor . . . . . . . . . . . . . . . . . . . . . . . 98

5.5      Levelling up/down . . . . . . . . . . . . . . . . . . . . . . . . . . . . . . . . . 99

5.6      Part-time work . . . . . . . . . . . . . . . . . . . . . . . . . . . . . . . . . . 100

6        ENFORCEMENT OF THE PRINCIPLE . . . . . . . . . . . . . . . . . . . 101

6.1      Court or tribunal procedure  . . . . . . . . . . . . . . . . . . . . . . . . . . . . . 103
         6.1.1   Acquiring the evidence  . . . . . . . . . . . . . . . . . . . . . . . . . 107
                 6.1.1.1   Prescribed forms  . . . . . . . . . . . . . . . . . . . . . . 107
                 6.1.1.2   Obligation to furnish all relevant evidence . . . . . . . . 108
                 6.1.1.3   Annual information to works councils . . . . . . . . . . . 110
                 6.1.1.4   Information to trade unions for bargaining . . . . . . . . 110
         6.1.2.  Burden of proof  . . . . . . . . . . . . . . . . . . . . . . . . . . . . . 111
         6.1.3   Costs  . . . . . . . . . . . . . . . . . . . . . . . . . . . . . . . . . . . 113
         6.1.4   Legal aid . . . . . . . . . . . . . . . . . . . . . . . . . . . . . . . . . 113
         6.1.5   Remedies . . . . . . . . . . . . . . . . . . . . . . . . . . . . . . . . . 114
                 6.1.5.1   Nullity/annulment . . . . . . . . . . . . . . . . . . . . . . 114
                 6.1.5.2   Termination of discriminatory conduct . . . . . . . . . . 114
                 6.1.5.3   Declaration  . . . . . . . . . . . . . . . . . . . . . . . . . 115
                 6.1.5.4   Compensation  . . . . . . . . . . . . . . . . . . . . . . . 115
                 6.1.5.5   Recommendation  . . . . . . . . . . . . . . . . . . . . . 117
                 6.1.5.6   Positive enforcement order . . . . . . . . . . . . . . . . . 119
                 6.1.5.7   Positive action plan . . . . . . . . . . . . . . . . . . . . . 120
                 6.1.5.8   Criminal sanctions  . . . . . . . . . . . . . . . . . . . . 120
         6.1.6   Class actions  . . . . . . . . . . . . . . . . . . . . . . . . . . . . . . 120
         6.1.7   Exclusion of judicial redress . . . . . . . . . . . . . . . . . . . . . . 121
         6.1.8   Time-limits  . . . . . . . . . . . . . . . . . . . . . . . . . . . . . . . 121

6.2      Courts and tribunals  . . . . . . . . . . . . . . . . . . . . . . . . . . . . . . . 121
         6.2.1   Special labour court or tribunal . . . . . . . . . . . . . . . . . . . . 122
                 6.2.1.1   Equality officer  . . . . . . . . . . . . . . . . . . . . . . . 122
                 6.2.1.2   Arbitration officer  . . . . . . . . . . . . . . . . . . . . . 124
                 6.2.1.3   Equal opportunities agency  . . . . . . . . . . . . . . . . 125
                 6.2.1.4   Conciliation procedures . . . . . . . . . . . . . . . . . . . 125
         6.2.2   Specialized training for judges  . . . . . . . . . . . . . . . . . . . 125
         6.2.3   Specialization within the system  . . . . . . . . . . . . . . . . . 125

6.3     Enforcement agency ..................................... 126
        6.3.1   Type ......................................... 126
                6.3.1.1   Labour inspectorate ..................... 126
                6.3.1.2   Equal opportunities agency ................ 126
        6.3.2   Functions .................................... 127
                6.3.2.1   Advice ............................... 127
                6.3.2.2   Research ............................. 127
                6.3.2.3   Legal aid ............................. 127
        6.3.3   Remedies .................................... 128
                6.3.3.1   Notice ............................... 128
                6.3.3.2   Injunction ............................ 129
                6.3.3.3   Compensation ......................... 130

6.4     Collective agreements ................................. 130
        6.4.1   Equal pay clause .............................. 130
        6.4.2   Automatic nullity ............................. 130
        6.4.3   Collective redress ............................ 132
        6.4.4   Agency monitoring ............................ 132
        6.4.5   Contract compliance .......................... 132

## SOURCES OF EQUALITY LAW

SECTION I. LEGISLATION ...................................... 135

§1      Equal pay ........................................... 136

        Equal Pay Act 1970 (1970 c. 41) ......................... 136

§2      Equal treatment ...................................... 144

        Sex Discrimination Act 1975 (1975 c. 65) .................. 144
        Code of Practice for the Elimination of Discrimination on
           the Grounds of Sex and Marriage and the Promotion of
           Equality of Opportunity in Employment (1985) ............. 198
        Sex Discrimination Act 1986 (1986 c. 59) ................... 211
        Employment Act 1989 (1989 c. 38) ......................... 215

§3      Equal pay and equal treatment enforcement: further provisions ...... 221

        Sex Discrimination (Formal Investigations) Regulations 1975
           (SI 1975 No 1993) .................................. 221
        Sex Discrimination (Questions and Replies) Order 1975
           (SI 1975 No 2048) .................................. 225
        Industrial Tribunals (Non-discrimination Notices Appeals)
           Regulations 1977 (SI 1977 No 1094) .................... 229
        Industrial Tribunals (Rules of Procedure) Regulations 1985
           (SI 1985 No 16) .................................... 238

§4      Equality in social security ............................. 266

        Social Security Act 1980 (1980 c. 30), Sch. 1, Part I ............ 266
        Health and Social Security Act 1984 (1984 c. 48), s. 11 ........... 269
        Social Security Act 1986 (1986 c. 50), s. 37 .................. 271
        Social Security Act 1989 (1989 c. 24), Sch. 5, Part I ............ 272

SECTION II. CASES ........................................... 281

§1      Equal pay ........................................... 282

A       House of Lords
        Hayward v. Cammell Laird Shipbuilders Ltd (No 2) .............. 282
        Leverton v. Clwyd County Council ......................... 293
        Pickstone v. Freemans plc ............................... 306
        Rainey v. Greater Glasgow Health Authority ................. 318

B        Court of Appeal

         Bromley *v.* H. & J. Quick ................................ 326

C        Lower Court or Tribunal

         Jenkins *v.* Kingsgate (Clothing Productions) Ltd (No 2) .......... 338

§2       Equal treatment ...................................... 347

A        House of Lords

         Duke *v.* GEC Reliance ................................ 347
         James *v.* Eastleigh Borough Council ...................... 356

B        Court of Appeal

         Baker *v.* Cornwall County Council ....................... 379
         Briggs *v.* NE Education & Library Board .................. 388
         Hampson *v.* Department of Education & Science .............. 407
         Meer *v.* London Borough of Tower Hamlets ................. 411
         Skyrail Oceanic Ltd *v.* Coleman ....................... 420
         Strathclyde Regional Council *v.* Porcelli .................. 425
         Wallace *v.* SE Education & Library Board .................. 436
         West Midlands PTE *v.* Singh ........................... 439

C        Lower Court or Tribunal

         Balgobin & Francis *v.* London Borough of Tower Hamlets ......... 447
         Clarke & Powell *v.* Eley (IMI) Kynoch Ltd ................. 454
         Home Office *v.* Holmes ............................... 464
         Horsey *v.* Dyfed CC ................................. 470
         Page *v.* Freight Hire (Tank Haulage) Ltd ................. 476
         Price *v.* Civil Service Commission ...................... 483
         Snowball *v.* Gardner Merchant Ltd ...................... 488
         Webb *v.* Emo Air Cargo (UK) Ltd ....................... 491

§3       Equality in social security ............................ 500

         Court of Appeal

         Secretary of State for Social Security *v.* Thomas .............. 500


Documentation ............................................ 525
Index .................................................. 533

# FOREWORD

Since the Second World War several international organizations have been endeavouring to promote the principle of equal opportunities between women and men, in law as well as in practice. This objective has also been pursued in a number of countries within the framework of domestic law. The intention has been to pursue a social objective and to achieve a change in the patterns of social conduct. In this context it has been felt that where the law visibly adopts the principle of equality this may contribute to the transformation of attitudes.

It has generally been accepted that equal opportunities ought to be pursued in the working environment in particular. In part this is because employment equality is a concept which can be more easily addressed by legal means than can other aspects of equality, but it is also true that a better distribution of wealth and income between the sexes and the abandonment of separate gender roles in the labour market can provide a powerful impetus to the realization of equal opportunities in society more generally.

To some extent these initiatives have been successful. Progress has been made in a relatively short space of time, although perhaps in limited areas of the equal opportunities agenda. But the impact has been restricted, and much effort still needs to be made in order to improve both law and social practice.

\* \* \*

Within the European Community also there has been a steady growth of interest in the issue of equality between women and men. Article 119 of the Treaty instituting the European Economic Community, signed in Rome on 25 March 1957, provides for equal pay for women and men workers who perform equal work. The main Directive advancing the idea of equal pay, Directive 75/117/EEC, will soon be celebrating its twentieth birthday.

But it is not enough to enact Directives. It is also necessary to analyse and control the implementation of these texts in the Member States of the European Community. The Commission of the European Communities has obviously understood this, since in its Action Programme for 1982-1985 it placed particular emphasis on the need to follow up the implementation of the Equality Directives. In pursuit of this the Commission established a number of expert networks to consider the equality agenda from a variety of viewpoints. One of these networks was the Network of Experts on the Implementation of the Equality Directives, consisting of experts from each of the Member States of the Community.

These experts have drawn up a series of reports on various aspects of their remit, and have been able to offer advice to the Commission on desirable courses of action to be followed. The network has also met regularly to discuss the reports and to update the Commission and each other on important developments in each of the Member States. Some of the network's consolidated reports have been published by the European Commission, and indeed the information contained in network documentation has been used in conferences of legal practitioners and other interested persons organized under the auspices of the Commission. However, the national reports written by network members remain unpublished and are unavailable to the general public.

In fact these reports form an excellent source of legislative and jurisprudential information from the Member States in matters of equality. They shed light on the progress made and the work which remains to be done if we are to achieve equality both in law and in practice. The experts therefore expressed the desire to see their work published and widely disseminated in the European Community and internationally, so that it can be used to assist not only legal practitioners but also other groups and persons seeking to achieve the objective of equal opportunities.

However, the reports drawn up for the network could not necessarily have been published in the form in which they were produced. Their authors had drawn up working documents, rather than studies designed for publication. Furthermore network members were, at any rate initially, given significant discretion as to how the work should be produced. From 1986 onwards a common format based on agreed schemas was devised to give network reports greater homogeneity, and this also prompted a growing desire to produce a more extensive collection of knowledge in this field.

The European Commission therefore decided to promote the progressive publication of an encyclopædia on equality in law between women and men in the European Community. This was to consist of volumes which were no longer to be only administrative documents intended for Commission use, but were to present a high level of scientific and formal quality.

There is no need to discuss at length the importance and interest of such a publication, which forms a natural part of the Commission's programme of action regarding the promotion of equality of opportunity. In fact it represents an excellent method of consolidating Community knowledge of existing legal provisions in order to ensure their better implementation. It represents also the desire to extend and develop the traditional means of disseminating information, in such a way as to sensitize the public more effectively.

The plans for such an encyclopædia were formulated by experts attending the Spanish Presidency seminar on equal opportunities in Toledo in April 1989.

It was with much pleasure that the coordinators of this major project have been able to witness the gradual production of the volumes in this collection. Nevertheless, in spite of all the care take by the experts involved in this work, the encyclopædia is neither exhaustive, perfect nor definitive, since the law continues to evolve. However, it is hoped that it will prove useful to all those — judges, tribunal members, lawyers, civil servants, teachers and researchers — who are interested in this subject.

* * *

The present volume, pertaining to United Kingdom law, is an integral part of the encyclopædia. It was therefore prepared on the basis of a structure common to all volumes in the series, in order to allow for a comparative reading of the law in each Member State on equality between women and men. The texts reflect the position as at 1 January 1992.

The first part of the volume — the Commentary — is based on a detailed plan common to all the national volumes, drawn up in such a way as to allow the reader to adopt a comparative approach. This plan draws both on the characteristics of the legal systems in use in the States linked to the Roman-Germanic legal tradition and in those following the common law tradition. One result of this is that certain headings may not be relevant to the position in each Member State.

The rest of the volume contains legislative texts in force in British law (at the time of finalization of the manuscript) which implement the principles laid down in the EC Equality Directives, as well as the most significant court and tribunal decisions applying those texts.

* * *

The coordinators wish to express their gratitude to all those who have lent their assistance and support to the encyclopædia project, and to show particular appreciation to certain of them.

We need to record our gratitude to the authors, without whom this work would not have been produced. The essential quality of the encyclopædia lies in the work of its main authors; they spared no effort in the assembling of the necessary documentation and in drawing up an intelligible and useful commentary.

A particular word of thanks is due to the staff of the Equal Opportunities Unit of DG V of the European Commission. Since the project was discussed in the initial stages a large number of officials have been associated with it and have provided active assistance and support to the coordinators. It has been a pleasure to collaborate with the Unit.

Similarly, the coordinators would like to express their sincere thanks to the officials of the Office for Official Publications of the European Communities, whose patient and expert supervision made it possible to convert the manuscripts into publishable texts of a very high quality.

We express particular gratitude to the publishing houses which accepted the burden of the present work, which is hardly lightweight as it numbers some thirty volumes!

May this work assembled with the active participation of so many eminent and committed collaborators contribute to progress in the law, to the common good and to the promotion of formal and actual equality between the women and men of Europe.

| | |
|---|---|
| Ferdinand von PRONDZYNSKI | Michel VERWILGHEN |
| Professor of Law and | Professeur ordinaire |
| Dean of the Law School | à la Faculté de Droit |
| University of Hull | Université catholique de Louvain |
| United Kingdom | Belgium |

# NOTICE TO THE READER

The editors of the encyclopædia wish to draw the attention of the reader to certain characteristics of the collection.

1. Each volume of the encyclopædia is published in two languages, English and French. The volumes have been edited so as to ensure that they have, as far as possible, the same content and structure in their English and French versions, although the language and terminology may occasionally differ as a result of normal usage in English and French respectively.

2. The authors of the Commentary section of each volume have worked according to a common schema agreed in the European Commission's Network of Experts on the Implementation of the Equality Directives. This allows the collection as a whole to follow a uniform structure. However, the Sources section in each volume is structured according to the domestic law framework, which varies from Member State to Member State.

3. The materials contained in the Sources section of each volume have (except where the original language is English or French) been translated into the two languages of the encyclopædia. These translations are not official, though every effort has been made to provide translated versions which are of high quality and accuracy. In the event of any doubt, it will be necessary for the reader to refer to legal sources in the original language; these are the only sources of guaranteed accuracy.

4. Equality in law between women and men within the European Community is a subject affected by rapid change, in EC law as well as in the law of each Member State. The formal sources evolve so quickly that information supplied in these volumes may have to be updated from that contained in the published encyclopædia. As far as possible major legislative and jurisprudential changes which occurred during the preparation of the volumes have been indicated in footnotes. The editors hope to be able to produce regular updates at a later stage.

5. References to laws, regulations and judicial decisions follow the normal usage of the Member State from which they originate.

# ABBREVIATIONS

| | |
|---|---|
| AC | Law Reports, Appeal Cases |
| ACAS | Advisory Conciliation and Arbitration Service |
| AG | Attorney-General |
| All ER | All England Law Reports |
| art.(s) | article(s) |
| ASTMS | Association of Scientific, Technical and Managerial Staffs |
| BEQ | British Equal Opportunities Cases |
| c. | chapter (in Act numbers, e.g. 1975 c. 65) |
| CA | Court of Appeal |
| Ch. | Law Reports, Chancery Division |
| ChD | Supreme Court of England & Wales, Chancery Division |
| CMLR | Common Market Law Reports |
| Cmnd | Command Paper |
| CRE | Commission for Racial Equality |
| Ct of Sess. | Court of Session (Scotland) |
| DHSS | Department of Health & Social Security |
| EAT | Employment Appeals Tribunal |
| EC | European Community/ies |
| ECHR | European Convention of Human Rights, or |
| | European Court of Human Rights (Strasbourg) |
| ECJ | European Court of Justice (Luxembourg) |
| ECR | European Court Reports |
| EEC | European Economic Community |
| EHRR | European Human Rights Reports |
| EOC | Equal Opportunities Commission |
| EOR | Equal Opportunities Review |
| EPCA | Employment Protection (Consolidation) Act 1978 |
| EqPA | Equal Pay Act 1970 |
| GOQ | Genuine occupational qualification |
| HC | High Court, or |
| | House of Commons Paper |
| HL | House of Lords |
| HL (E) | House of Lords (England) |
| HL (Sc.) | House of Lords (Scotland) |
| ICA | Invalid Care Allowance |
| ICR | Industrial Cases Reports |
| IRLR | Industrial Relations Law Reports |
| IT | Industrial Tribunal |
| J/JJ | Justice/Justices |
| LBC | London Borough Council |
| LC | Lord Chancellor |
| LJ/LJJ | Lord Justice/Lords Justices |
| MR | Master of the Rolls (principal judge, Court of Appeal for England and Wales) |
| NALGO | National and Local Government Officers' Association |
| NCIP | Non-Contributory Invalid Pension |
| NE | North-East(ern) |
| NI | Northern Ireland |
| NICA | Northern Ireland Court of Appeal |
| NIHC | Northern Ireland High Court |
| NIIT | Northern Ireland Industrial Tribunal |

| | |
|---|---|
| NIJB | Northern Ireland Judgments Bulletin |
| OJ C | Official Journal of the European Communities, C Series  (Information and Notices) |
| OJ L | Official Journal of the European Communities, L Series (Legislation) |
| P | President (of the Supreme Court of England and Wales, Family Division) |
| para.(s) | paragraph(s) |
| plc | public limited company |
| Pt | Part |
| PTE | Passenger Transport Executive |
| QB | Law Reports, Queen's Bench Division |
| QBD | Supreme Court of England and Wales, Queen's Bench Division |
| QC | Queen's Counsel |
| R. | Rex or Regina |
| r./rr. | rule/rules |
| reg.(s) | regulation(s) |
| RSC | Rules of the Supreme Court |
| RUC | Royal Ulster Constabulary |
| s./ss | section/sections |
| SC | United States Supreme Court Reports |
| Sc. | Scotland or Scottish |
| Sch. | Schedule |
| SDA | Sex Discrimination Act, or Severe Disablement Allowance |
| SE | South-East(ern) |
| Sess. | see Ct of Sess. |
| SI | Statutory Instrument |
| SOGAT | Society of Graphical and Allied Trades |
| SSAT | Social Security Appeal Tribunal |
| subpara.(s) | subparagraph(s) |
| subs./ss | subsection/s |
| subsubs./ss | subsubsection/s |
| SW | South-West(ern) |
| TURU | Trade Union Research Unit |
| UK | United Kingdom |
| US Sup. Ct | United States Supreme Court |
| VC | Vice-Chancellor (principal judge, Supreme Court of England and Wales, Chancery Division) |
| WLR | Weekly Law Reports |

# TABLE OF LEGISLATION, ETC.

[Numbers in bold type refer to pages at which a provision is reprinted verbatim.]

## Treaties and International Instruments

**Council of Europe**
European Convention for the Protection of Human Rights and Fundamental
Freedoms 1950 . . . . . . . . . . . . . . . . . . . . . . . . . . . . . . . . . . . . . . 4, 87
art. 14 . . . . . . . . . . . . . . . . . . . . . . . . . . . . . . . . . . . . . . . . . . .5
European Social Charter 1961 . . . . . . . . . . . . . . . . . . . . . . . . . . . . . . . 4
European Social Charter 1961, Additional Protocol 1988 . . . . . . . . . . . . . . . . . 4

**European Communities**
Treaty establishing the European Economic Community
art. 48(4) . . . . . . . . . . . . . . . . . . . . . . . . . . . . . . . . . . . . . . . 500-523
art. 119 . . . . . . . . 6, 30, 37-40, 52, 54, 61, 76, 91, 122, 131, 282-292, 293-305,
306-317, 318-325, 326-337, 338-346, 347-355, 500-523
art. 177 . . . . . . . . . . . . . . . . . . . . . . . . . . . 306-317, 347-355, 500-523
art. 189 . . . . . . . . . . . . . . . . . . . . . . . . . . . . . . . . . . . 6, 347-355

**International Labour Organization**
Discrimination (Employment and Occupation) Convention 1958 (No 111) . . . . . . . . . . .5
Equal Remuneration Convention 1951 (No 100) . . . . . . . . . . . . . . . . . . . . . . .5
Night Work (Women) Convention 1948 (No 89), Protocol 1990 . . . . . . . . . . . . . . . .5
Night Work Convention 1990 (No 171) . . . . . . . . . . . . . . . . . . . . . . . . . . .5
Night Work Recommendation 1990 (No 178) . . . . . . . . . . . . . . . . . . . . . . . . .5

**United Nations**
Convention on the Elimination of All Forms of Discrimination against Women
1979 . . . . . . . . . . . . . . . . . . . . . . . . . . . . . . . . . . . . . . . . . .5
art. 4(1) . . . . . . . . . . . . . . . . . . . . . . . . . . . . . . . . . . . . . . . 87
Convention on the Political Rights of Women 1953 . . . . . . . . . . . . . . . . . . . . .5
International Covenant on Civil and Political Rights 1966 . . . . . . . . . . . . . . . . 4
International Covenant on Economic, Social and Cultural Rights 1966 . . . . . . . . . . . 4
Universal Declaration of Human Rights 1948 . . . . . . . . . . . . . . . . . . . . . . . 4

## European Communities Secondary Legislation, etc.

**Directives**
75/117/EEC: Council Directive of 10 February 1975 on the approximation of the
laws of the Member States relating to the application of the principle of equal
pay for men and women
OJ L45, 19.2.75, p. 32 . . . . . . . . . . . . . . . . . . . . 6, 37, 43, 76, 91, 326-337
art. 1 . . . . . . . . . . . . . . . . . . . . . . . . . 282-292, 293-305, 306-317, 338-346
76/207/EEC: Council Directive of 9 February 1976 on the implementation of the
principle of equal treatment for men and women as regards access to
employment, etc.
OJ L39, 14.2.76, p. 40 . . . . . . . . . . 6, 8, 24, 60, 76, 91, 97, 347-355, 500-523
arts 1, 2 . . . . . . . . . . . . . . . . . . . . . . . . . . . . . . . . . . . . . . . 91
art. 6 . . . . . . . . . . . . . . . . . . . . . . . . . . . . . . . . . . . . . . . . 115
art. 9(2) . . . . . . . . . . . . . . . . . . . . . . . . . . . . . . . . . . . . . . . 64

79/7/EEC: Council Directive of 19 December 1978 on the progressive implementation of the principle of equal treatment for men and women in matters of
social security
  OJ L6, 10.1.79, p. 24 . . . . . . . . . . . . . . . . . . . . . . . 6, 12, 89, 91-94, 97, 266
  arts 1, 2 . . . . . . . . . . . . . . . . . . . . . . . . . . . . . . . . . . . . . . . . . . . . . . . . . . . 500-523
  art. 3 . . . . . . . . . . . . . . . . . . . . . . . . . . . . . . . . . . . . . . . . . . . . . . . . . 94, 500-523
  arts 4, 5 . . . . . . . . . . . . . . . . . . . . . . . . . . . . . . . . . . . . . . . . . . . . . . . . . . . 500-523
  art. 7 . . . . . . . . . . . . . . . . . . . . . . . . . . . . . . . . . . . . . . . . . . . . . . . . . 91, 500-523
  art. 7(1) . . . . . . . . . . . . . . . . . . . . . . . . . . . . . . . . . . . . . . . . . . . . . . . . . . . 500-523
  art. 7(1)(a) . . . . . . . . . . . . . . . . . . . . . . . . . . . . . . . . 92, 93, 347-355, 500-523
  art. 7(2) . . . . . . . . . . . . . . . . . . . . . . . . . . . . . . . . . . . . . . . . . . . . . . . . . . . 500-523
  art. 8 . . . . . . . . . . . . . . . . . . . . . . . . . . . . . . . . . . . . . . . . . . . . . . . . . . . . . 500-523
  art. 8(1) . . . . . . . . . . . . . . . . . . . . . . . . . . . . . . . . . . . . . . . . . . . . . . . . . . . 500-523
86/378/EEC: Council Directive of 24 July 1986 on the implementation of the
principle of equal treatment for men and women in occupational social
security schemes
  OJ L225, 12.8.86, p. 40 . . . . . . . . . . . . . . . . . . . . . . . . . 6, 12, 20, 34, 95, 96
  art. 1 . . . . . . . . . . . . . . . . . . . . . . . . . . . . . . . . . . . . . . . . . . . . . . . . . . . . . . . . 95
  art. 2(1) . . . . . . . . . . . . . . . . . . . . . . . . . . . . . . . . . . . . . . . . . . . . . . . . . . . . . 95
  arts 2(2), 4 . . . . . . . . . . . . . . . . . . . . . . . . . . . . . . . . . . . . . . . . . . . . . . . . . . 95
  art. 9 . . . . . . . . . . . . . . . . . . . . . . . . . . . . . . . . . . . . . . . . . . . . . . . . . . . . . . . . 96
86/613/EEC: Council Directive of 11 December 1986 on the application of the
principle of equal treatment as between men and women engaged in an
activity, including agriculture, in a self-employed capacity, and on the
protection of self-employed women during pregnancy and motherhood
  OJ L359, 19.12.86, p. 56 . . . . . . . . . . . . . . . . . . . . . . . . . . . . . . . . . . . . . . . . . 6

**Regulations**
1612/68: Council Regulation (EEC) of 15 October 1968 on the freedom of
movement for workers within the Community
  arts 7(1), 7(4) . . . . . . . . . . . . . . . . . . . . . . . . . . . . . . . . . . . . . . . . . . . 500-523

**Other**
Commission Communication to the Council on the new Community action
  programme on the promotion of equal opportunities for women (1982-85) . . . . . . 6
Commission Communication to the Council on equal opportunities for women
  (medium-term Community programme 1986-1990) . . . . . . . . . . . . . . . . . . . . . . 6
Council Resolution of 21 January 1974 concerning a social action programme . . . . . . . . 6

# United Kingdom Statutes

Armed Forces Act 1981
  (1981 c. 55) . . . . . . . . . . . . . . . . . . . . . . . . . . . . . . . . . . . . . . . . . 136, 144
Companies Act 1985
  (1985 c. 6) . . . . . . . . . . . . . . . . . . . . . . . . . . . . . . . . . . . . . . . . . . . . . . . . . . 68
Continental Shelf Act 1964 (1964 c. 29)
  s. 1(7) . . . . . . . . . . . . . . . . . . . . . . . . . . . . . . . . . . . . . . . . . . . . . . . . . . . . . 68
County Courts Act 1984
  (1984 c. 28) . . . . . . . . . . . . . . . . . . . . . . . . . . . . . . . . . . . . . . . . . . . . . . . . . 144
Courts and Legal Services Act 1990 (1990 c. 41)
  ss 64, 65 . . . . . . . . . . . . . . . . . . . . . . . . . . . . . . . . . . . . . . . . . . . . . . . . . . . . 69
Criminal Justice Act 1982
  (1982 c. 48) . . . . . . . . . . . . . . . . . . . . . . . . . . . . . . . . . . . . . . . . . . . . . . . . . 144
Education Reform Act 1988
  (1988 c. 40) . . . . . . . . . . . . . . . . . . . . . . . . . . . . . . . . . . . . . . . . . . . . . . . . . . 73
Education (Scotland) Act 1980
  (1980 c. 44) . . . . . . . . . . . . . . . . . . . . . . . . . . . . . . . . . . . . . . . . . . . . . . . . . 144

Employment and Training Act 1973 (1973 c. 50)
  s. 2 . . . . . . . . . . . . . . . . . . . . . . . . . . . . . . . . . . . . . . . . . . . . . . . . . . . . . . . . . . . . 84
  s. 8 . . . . . . . . . . . . . . . . . . . . . . . . . . . . . . . . . . . . . . . . . . . . . . . . . . . . . . . . . . . . 73
Employment and Training Act 1981
  (1981 c. 57) . . . . . . . . . . . . . . . . . . . . . . . . . . . . . . . . . . . . . . . . . . . . . . . . . . . . 144
Employment Act 1980
  (1980 c. 42) . . . . . . . . . . . . . . . . . . . . . . . . . . . . . . . . . . . . . . . . . . . . . . . . . . . . 144
  s. 11 . . . . . . . . . . . . . . . . . . . . . . . . . . . . . . . . . . . . . . . . . . . . . . . . . . . . . . . . . . . 81
  s. 12 . . . . . . . . . . . . . . . . . . . . . . . . . . . . . . . . . . . . . . . . . . . . . . . . . . . . . . . . . . . 81
  s. 13 . . . . . . . . . . . . . . . . . . . . . . . . . . . . . . . . . . . . . . . . . . . . . . . . . . . . . . . . . . . 81
Employment Act 1989
  (1989 c. 38) . . . . . . . . . . . . . . . . . . . . . . . . . . . . . 10, 12, 58, 61, 144, 211, **215**
  s. 1 . . . . . . . . . . . . . . . . . . . . . . . . . . . . . . . . . . . . . . . . . . . . . . . . . . . . . 10, **215**
  s. 1(1) . . . . . . . . . . . . . . . . . . . . . . . . . . . . . . . . . . . . . . . . . . . . . . . . . . . . 10, 11
  s. 2 . . . . . . . . . . . . . . . . . . . . . . . . . . . . . . . . . . . . . . . . . . . . . . . . . . . . . 11, **216**
  s. 3 . . . . . . . . . . . . . . . . . . . . . . . . . . . . . . . . . . . . . . . . . . . . . . . . . . . . . . 356-378
  s. 4 . . . . . . . . . . . . . . . . . . . . . . . . . . . . . . . . . . . . . . . . . . . . . . . . . . . . . 58, **217**
  s. 5 . . . . . . . . . . . . . . . . . . . . . . . . . . . . . . . . . . . . . . . . . . . . . . . . . . 59, 67, **217**
  s. 6 . . . . . . . . . . . . . . . . . . . . . . . . . . . . . . . . . . . . . . . . . . . . . . . . . . . . 11, **218**
  s. 7 . . . . . . . . . . . . . . . . . . . . . . . . . . . . . . . . . . . . . . . . . . . . . . . . . . . . . . . . . 76
  s. 8 . . . . . . . . . . . . . . . . . . . . . . . . . . . . . . . . . . . . . . . . . . . . . . . . . . 83, 84, **219**
  s. 16 . . . . . . . . . . . . . . . . . . . . . . . . . . . . . . . . . . . . . . . . . . . . . . . . . . . . . . . . . 39
  s. 20 . . . . . . . . . . . . . . . . . . . . . . . . . . . . . . . . . . . . . . . . . . . . . . . . . . . . . . . . 104
  Sch. 1 . . . . . . . . . . . . . . . . . . . . . . . . . . . . . . . . . . . . . . . . . . . . . . . . . . . . . . . . 58
Employment Protection Act 1975
  (1975 c. 71) . . . . . . . . . . . . . . . . . . . . . . . . . . . . . . . . . . . . . . . . . . . . . . . 136, 144
  ss 3, 10 . . . . . . . . . . . . . . . . . . . . . . . . . . . . . . . . . . . . . . . . . . . . . . . . . . 293-305
  ss 17, 18 . . . . . . . . . . . . . . . . . . . . . . . . . . . . . . . . . . . . . . . . . . . . . . . . . . . . 110
  s. 34 . . . . . . . . . . . . . . . . . . . . . . . . . . . . . . . . . . . . . . . . . . . . . . . . . . . . 491-499
Employment Protection (Consolidation) Act 1978
  (1978 c. 44) . . . . . . . . . . . . . . . . . . . . . . . . . . . . . . . 136, 144, 211, 464-469
  ss 31A, 33, 45, 45(1), 46, 47, 48, 56, 56A(1) . . . . . . . . . . . . . . . . . . . . . . . 81
  s. 60 . . . . . . . . . . . . . . . . . . . . . . . . . . . . . . . . . . . . . . . . . . . . . . . . . 18, 491-499
  Sch. 9, para. 1 . . . . . . . . . . . . . . . . . . . . . . . . . . . . . . . . . . . . . . . . . . . . . . . 238
  Sch. 9, para. 7 . . . . . . . . . . . . . . . . . . . . . . . . . . . . . . . . . . . . . . . . . . . . . . . 110
Employment Subsidies Act 1978 (1978 c. 6)
  s. 1 . . . . . . . . . . . . . . . . . . . . . . . . . . . . . . . . . . . . . . . . . . . . . . . . . . . . . . . . . 84
Enterprise and New Towns (Scotland) Act 1990 (1990 c. 35)
  s. 17 . . . . . . . . . . . . . . . . . . . . . . . . . . . . . . . . . . . . . . . . . . . . . . . . . . . . . . . . . 85
Equal Pay Act 1970
  (1970 c. 41) . . . . . . . . . . . . . . . . . . . . . . . . . . . . . . . . . 21, 38, 43, **136**, 144
  s. 1 . . . . . . . . . . . . . . . . . . . . . . . . . . . . . . . . . . . . . 26, 33, 54, **136**, 293-305
  s. 1(1) . . . . . . . . . . . . . . . . . . . . . . . . . . . . . . . . . . . . . . . 36, 130, 293-305
  s. 1(2) . . . . . . . . . . . . . . . . . . . . . . . . . . . . . . . . . . . . . . 282-292, 338-346
  s. 1(2)(a) . . . . . . . . . . . . . . . . . . . . . . . . . . . . . . . . . . . . . . . . . . . . . . . 306-317
  ss 1(2)(a)(i), (ii) . . . . . . . . . . . . . . . . . . . . . . . . . . . . . . . . . . . . . . . . . . . 282-292
  s. 1(2)(b) . . . . . . . . . . . . . . . . . . . . . . . . . . . . . . . . 293-305, 306-317, 326-337
  ss 1(2)(b)(i), (ii) . . . . . . . . . . . . . . . . . . . . . . . . . . . . . . . . . . . . . . . . . . . 282-292
  s. 1(2)(c) . . . . . . . . . . . . . . . . . . . . . . . . . . . . . . . . . 46, 48, 293-305, 306-317
  ss 1(2)(c)(i), (ii) . . . . . . . . . . . . . . . . . . . . . . . . . . . . . . . . . . . . . . . . . . 282-292
  s. 1(3) . . . . . . . . . . 49, 76, 123, 282-292, 293-305, 318-325, 338-346, 407-410
  s. 1(4) . . . . . . . . . . . . . . . . . . . . . . . . . . . . . . . . . . . 43, 44, 293-305, 306-317
  s. 1(5) . . . . . . . . . . . . . . . . . . . . . . . . . . . . . . . . **44, 45**, 293-305, 326-337
  s. 1(6) . . . . . . . . . . . . . . . . . . . . . . . . . . . . . . . . . . . . . . . . . . . . . . . . . . . 293-305
  s. 1(6)(a) . . . . . . . . . . . . . . . . . . . . . . . . . . . . . . . . . . . . . . . . . . . . . . . . . . . . 35
  s. 1(6)(c) . . . . . . . . . . . . . . . . . . . . . . . . . . . . . . . . . . . . . . . . . . . . . . . . . . . . 41
  s. 1(8) . . . . . . . . . . . . . . . . . . . . . . . . . . . . . . . . . . . . . . . . . . . . . . . . . . . . . . 35
  s. 1(9) . . . . . . . . . . . . . . . . . . . . . . . . . . . . . . . . . . . . . . . . . . . . . . . . . . 36, 124

**Equal Pay Act 1970 continued**

s. 2 . . . . . . . . . . . . . . . . . . . . . . . . . . . . . . . . . . . . . . . . . . . . . . . . . . . . **139**
ss 2(1), 2(1A) . . . . . . . . . . . . . . . . . . . . . . . . . . . . . . . 114, 115, 120
s. 2(4) . . . . . . . . . . . . . . . . . . . . . . . . . . . . . . . . . . . . . . . . . . . . . . 121
s. 2(5) . . . . . . . . . . . . . . . . . . . . . . . . . . . . . . . . . . . . . . 115, 120, 122
s. 2A . . . . . . . . . . . . . . . . . . . . . . . . . . . . . . . **140**, 293-305, 306-317
s. 2A(1) . . . . . . . . . . . . . . . . . . . . . . . . . . . . . 124, 293-305, 326-337
s. 2A(1)(a) . . . . . . . . . . . . . . . . . . . . . . . . . . . . . 293-305, 326-337
s. 2A(1)(b) . . . . . . . . . . . . . . . . . . . . . . . . . . . . . . . . . . . . . 326-337
s. 2A(2) . . . . . . . . . . . . . . . . . . . . . . . . . . . . . . . . . . . 46, 326-337
ss 2A(2)(a), (b), 2A(3) . . . . . . . . . . . . . . . . . . . . . . . . . . . . . 326-337
s. 3 . . . . . . . . . . . . . . . . . . . . . . . . . . . . . . . . . . . . . . . . . 40, 136
s. 3(4) . . . . . . . . . . . . . . . . . . . . . . . . . . . . . . . . . . . . . . . 282-292
s. 4 . . . . . . . . . . . . . . . . . . . . . . . . . . . . . . . . . . . . . . . . . . . 136
s. 5 . . . . . . . . . . . . . . . . . . . . . . . . . . . . . . . . . . . . . . . . . . **141**
s. 6 . . . . . . . . . . . . . . . . . . . . . . . . . . . . . . . . . . . . . . . . . . **142**
s. 6(1)(b) . . . . . . . . . . . . . . . . . . . . . . . . . . . . . . . . . . . . . . . . 34
s. 6(1A) . . . . . . . . . . . . . . . . . . . . . . . . . . . . . . . . . . . . . . 347-355
s. 6(1A)(b) . . . . . . . . . . . . . . . . . . . . . . . . . . . . . 34, **34**, 347-355
s. 6(2) . . . . . . . . . . . . . . . . . . . . . . . . . . . . . . . . . . . . . . . . . . 34
s. 7 . . . . . . . . . . . . . . . . . . . . . . . . . . . . . . . . . . . . . . . . . . **142**
s. 7(1) . . . . . . . . . . . . . . . . . . . . . . . . . . . . . . . . . . . . **36, 124**
s. 7(2) . . . . . . . . . . . . . . . . . . . . . . . . . . . . . . . . . . . . . . 36, 125
s. 8 . . . . . . . . . . . . . . . . . . . . . . . . . . . . . . . . . . . . . . . . . . . 136
s. 9(1) . . . . . . . . . . . . . . . . . . . . . . . . . . . . . . . . . . . . . . . . . **143**
s. 10 . . . . . . . . . . . . . . . . . . . . . . . . . . . . . . . . . . . . . . . . . . 136
s. 11 . . . . . . . . . . . . . . . . . . . . . . . . . . . . . . . . . . . . . . . . . . **143**

**Equal Pay Act (Northern Ireland) 1970**

(1970 c. 32) . . . . . . . . . . . . . . . . . . . . . . . . . . . . . 18, 143, 436-438

**European Communities Act 1972**

(1972 c. 68) . . . . . . . . . . . . . . . . . . . . . . . . . . . . . . . . . 3, 282-292
s. 2 . . . . . . . . . . . . . . . . . . . . . . . . . . . . . . . . . . 306-317, 338-346
s. 2(1) . . . . . . . . . . . . . . . . . . . . . . . . . . . . . . . . . 306-317, 338-346
s. 2(2) . . . . . . . . . . . . . . . . . . . . . . . . . . . . . . . . . . . . . . . 306-317
s. 2(4) . . . . . . . . . . . . . . . . . . . . . . . 306-317, 338-346, 347-355
s. 3(1) . . . . . . . . . . . . . . . . . . . . . . . . . . . . . . . . . . . . . . . 500-523

**Fair Employment (Northern Ireland) Act 1976**

(1976 c. 25) . . . . . . . . . . . . . . . . . . . . . . . . . . . . . . . . . . . . . 122
s. 16(2) . . . . . . . . . . . . . . . . . . . . . . . . . . . . . . . . . . . . . . 356-378

**Health and Safety at Work, etc., Act 1974 (1974 c. 37)**

Part I . . . . . . . . . . . . . . . . . . . . . . . . . . . . . . . . . . . . . . . 56, 58
s. 2 . . . . . . . . . . . . . . . . . . . . . . . . . . . . . . . . . . . . . . . . 476-482

**Health and Social Security Act 1984**

(1984 c. 48) . . . . . . . . . . . . . . . . . . . . . . . . . . . . . . . . . . . . . . 12
s. 11 . . . . . . . . . . . . . . . . . . . . . . . . . . . . . . . . . . . . . . . . . **269**

**Legal Aid Act 1988**

(1988 c. 34) . . . . . . . . . . . . . . . . . . . . . . . . . . . . . . . . . . . . . 144

**Legal Aid (Scotland) Act 1986**

(1986 c. 47) . . . . . . . . . . . . . . . . . . . . . . . . . . . . . . . . . . . . . 144

**Local Government Act 1988 (1988 c. 9)**

Part II . . . . . . . . . . . . . . . . . . . . . . . . . . . . . . . . . . . . . . . . 132

**Local Government and Housing Act 1989 (1989 c. 42)**

s. 7 . . . . . . . . . . . . . . . . . . . . . . . . . . . . . . . . . . . . . . . . . . . 70

**Oil and Gas Enterprise Act 1982**

(1982 c. 23) . . . . . . . . . . . . . . . . . . . . . . . . . . . . . . . . . . . . . 144

**Old Age and Widows' Pension Act 1940**

(1940 c. 13) . . . . . . . . . . . . . . . . . . . . . . . . . . . . . . . . . . . 347-355

Police Act 1964
    (1964 c. 48) . . . . . . . . . . . . . . . . . . . . . . . . . . . . . . . . . . . . . . . 64
Race Relations Act 1976
    (1976 c. 74) . . . . . . . . . . . . . . . . . . . . . . . . . . . . . . . . . . . . . 64, 144
    s. 1 . . . . . . . . . . . . . . . . . . . . . . . . . . . . . . . . . . . . . . . . . . . 470-475
    s. 1(1)(a) . . . . . . . . . . . . . . . . . . . . . . . . . . . . 13, 411-419, 438-446
    s. 1(1)(b) . . . . . . . . . . . . . . . . . . . . . 20, 407-410, 411-419, 454-463
    s. 1(1)(b)(ii) . . . . . . . . . . . . . . . . . . 388-406, 407-410, 411-419
    ss 3(1), 4(2)(b), 47 . . . . . . . . . . . . . . . . . . . . . . . . . . . . . . . . . 438-446
    s. 57(4) . . . . . . . . . . . . . . . . . . . . . . . . . . . . . . . . . . . . . . . . 117
Sex Discrimination Act 1975
    (1975 c. 65) . . . . . . . . . . . . . . . . . . . . . . 8, 10, 11, 38, 136, 144
    Part I (ss 1-5) . . . . . . . . . . . . . . . . . . . . . . . . . . . . . . . . . . . . **146**
    s. 1 . . . . . . . . . . . . . . . . . . . . . . **146**, 356-378, 464-469, 470-475, 476-482
    s. 1(1) . . . . . . . . . . . . . . . . . . . . . . . . . . . . . . . . . 388-406, 470-475
    s. 1(1)(a) . . . . . . . . . . . . . . . . . . . . . . **13**, 56, 57, 356-378, 420-424
                                       425-435, 447-453, 454-463, 491-499
    s. 1(1)(b) . . . . . . . . . . . . . . . 20, 112, 318-325, 338-346, 356-378
                                      388-406, 454-463, 464-469, 483-487
    s. 1(1)(b)(i) . . . . . . . . . . . . . . . . . . . 388-406, 454-463, 483-487
    s. 1(1)(b)(ii) . . . . . . . . . . . . . . . . . . 318-325, 356-378, 388-406
                                      407-410, 454-463, 464-469, 483-487
    s. 1(1)(b)(iii) . . . . . . . . . . . . . . . . 388-406, 454-463, 464-469, 483-487
    s. 1(2) . . . . . . . . . . . . . . . . . . . . . . . . . . . . . . . . . . . . . . . . 470-475
    s. 2 . . . . . . . . . . . . . . . . . . . . . . . . . . . . . 13, **146**, 491-499
    s. 2(2) . . . . . . . . . . . . . . . . . . . . . . . . . . . . . . . . . **17**, 491-499
    s. 3 . . . . . . . . . . . . . . . . . . . . . . . . . . . . . . . . . **147**, 470-475
    s. 3(1) . . . . . . . . . . . . . . . . . . . . . . . . . . . . . . . . . . . . . . 388-406
    s. 3(1)(a) . . . . . . . . . . . . . . . . . . . . . . . . . . . . . . . . . **17**, 420-424
    s. 3(1)(b) . . . . . . . . . . . . . . . . . . . . . . . . . . . . . . . . . . . . **17, 20**
    s. 3(1)(b)(ii) . . . . . . . . . . . . . . . . . . . . . . . . . . . . . . . . . . 388-406
    s. 4 . . . . . . . . . . . . . . . . . . . . . . . . . . . . . . . . . . . . . . . **147**
    s. 4(1) . . . . . . . . . . . . . . . . . . . . . . . . . . . . . . . . . . . . . . . **31**
    s. 5 . . . . . . . . . . . . . . . . . . . . . . . . . . . . . . . . . . . . . . . **148**
    s. 5(3) . . . . . . . . 16, 356-378, 388-406, 420-424, 425-435, 470-475, 491-499
    Part II (ss 6-21) . . . . . . . . . . . . . . . . . . . . . . . . . . . . . . . 84, **148**
    s. 6 . . . . . . . . . . . . . 70, 71, 73, 83, **148**, 379-387, 464-469, 476-482, 483-487
    s. 6(1) . . . . . . . . . . . . . . . . . . . . . . . . . . . . . . . . . . . . . . . . 66
    s. 6(1)(a) . . . . . . . . . . . . . . . . . . . . . . . . . . . . . . . . . . . . . . 74
    s. 6(1)(b) . . . . . . . . . . . . . . . . . . . . . . . . . . . . . . . . . . 59, 75-77
    s. 6(1)(c) . . . . . . . . . . . . . . . . . . . . . . . . . . . . . . . . . 75, 379-387
    s. 6(2) . . . . . . . . . . . . . . . . . . . 59, 76, 347-355, 388-406, 464-469
    s. 6(2)(a) . . . . . . . . . . . . . . . . . . . . . . . . . . 66, 75-77, 379-387
    s. 6(2)(b) . . . . . . . . 78, 388-406, 420-424, 425-435, 464-469, 476-482, 491-499
    s. 6(3) . . . . . . . . . . . . . . . . . . . . . . . . . . . . . . . . . . . . . . . 55
    s. 6(4) . . . . . . . . . . . . . . . . . . . . . . . . . . 59, 60, 347-355, 356-378
    ss 6(4A), (4B) . . . . . . . . . . . . . . . . . . . . . . . . . . . . . . . . . . **60**
    s. 6(4C) . . . . . . . . . . . . . . . . . . . . . . . . . . . . . . . . . . . . . . 61
    s. 6(5) . . . . . . . . . . . . . . . . . . . . . . . . . . . . . . . . . . . . . 75, 76
    s. 6(6) . . . . . . . . . . . . . . . . . . . . . . . . . . . . . . . . . . . . . . . 77
    s. 6(7) . . . . . . . . . . . . . . . . . . . . . . . . . . . . . . . . . . . . . . . 76
    s. 7 . . . . . . . . . . . . . . . . . . . . . . . . . . 61, 70, 73, **150**, 476-482
    s. 7(2) . . . . . . . . . . . . . . . . . . . . . . . . . . . . . . . . . . . . . . . 61
    s. 7(2)(a) . . . . . . . . . . . . . . . . . . . . . . . . . . . . . . . . . . **63, 64**
    s. 7(2)(b) . . . . . . . . . . . . . . . . . . . . . . . . . . . . . . . . . . . . . 65
    s. 7(2)(d) . . . . . . . . . . . . . . . . . . . . . . . . . . . . . . . . . . 64, 66
    s. 7(2)(f) . . . . . . . . . . . . . . . . . . . . . . . . . . . . . . . . . . . . . 10
    ss 7(3), (4) . . . . . . . . . . . . . . . . . . . . . . . . . . . . . . . . . . . . 63

**Sex Discrimination Act 1975** continued

s. 8 . . . . . . . . . . . . . . . . . . . . . . . . . . . . . . . . . . . . . . . . . . . . . . . . . . . . . . . . . . 144, **152**
ss 8(3), (4) . . . . . . . . . . . . . . . . . . . . . . . . . . . . . . . . . . . . . . . . . . . . . . . . . 75, 76
s. 8(5) . . . . . . . . . . . . . . . . . . . . . . . . . . . . . . . . . . . . . . . . . . . . . . . . . . . . . . . 76
s. 9 . . . . . . . . . . . . . . . . . . . . . . . . . . . . . . . . . . . . . . . . . . . . . . . . . . . 69, 73, **152**
s. 10 . . . . . . . . . . . . . . . . . . . . . . . . . . . . . . . . . . . . . . . . . . . . . . . . . . . . . 68, **153**
s. 10(4) . . . . . . . . . . . . . . . . . . . . . . . . . . . . . . . . . . . . . . . . . . . . . . . . . . **35, 70**
s. 11 . . . . . . . . . . . . . . . . . . . . . . . . . . . . . . . . . . . . . . . . . . . . . . . . . . . . 72, **154**
ss 11(1), (4) . . . . . . . . . . . . . . . . . . . . . . . . . . . . . . . . . . . . . . . . . . . . . . . 347-355
s. 11(4) . . . . . . . . . . . . . . . . . . . . . . . . . . . . . . . . . . . . . . . . . . . . . . . . . . . 347-355
s. 12 . . . . . . . . . . . . . . . . . . . . . . . . . . . . . . . . . . . . . . . . . . . . . . . 79, 85, **155**
s. 13 . . . . . . . . . . . . . . . . . . . . . . . . . . . . . . . . . . . . . . . . . . . . . . . . . . . . 72, **156**
s. 14 . . . . . . . . . . . . . . . . . . . . . . . . . . . . . . . . . . . . . . . . . . . . . . . . 66, 76, **156**
s. 15 . . . . . . . . . . . . . . . . . . . . . . . . . . . . . . . . . . . . . . . . . . . . . . . . . . . . 73, **157**
ss 15(1), (2), (4), (5) . . . . . . . . . . . . . . . . . . . . . . . . . . . . . . . . . . . . . . . . . . 73
s. 16 . . . . . . . . . . . . . . . . . . . . . . . . . . . . . . . . . . . . . . . . . . . . . . . . . . . . . . **157**
s. 17 . . . . . . . . . . . . . . . . . . . . . . . . . . . . . . . . . . . . . . . . . . . . . . . . . . 64, **157**
ss 18, 19 . . . . . . . . . . . . . . . . . . . . . . . . . . . . . . . . . . . . . . . . . . . . . . . . 64, **159**
s. 20 . . . . . . . . . . . . . . . . . . . . . . . . . . . . . . . . . . . . . . . . . . . . . . . . . . . . . . **159**
s. 21 . . . . . . . . . . . . . . . . . . . . . . . . . . . . . . . . . . . . . . . . . . . . . . . . . . . . . . **160**
Part III (ss. 22-36) . . . . . . . . . . . . . . . . . . . . . . . . . . . . . . . . . . . . . . . . . . . 144
s. 29 . . . . . . . . . . . . . . . . . . . . . . . . . . . . . . . . . . . . . . . . . . . . . . . 77, 356-378
s. 29(1) . . . . . . . . . . . . . . . . . . . . . . . . . . . . . . . . . . . . . . . . . . . . . . . . . 356-378
Part IV (ss 37-42) . . . . . . . . . . . . . . . . . . . . . . . . . . . . . . . . . . . . . . . . . . . **160**
s. 37 . . . . . . . . . . . . . . . . . . . . . . . . . . . . . . . . . . . . . . . . . . . . . . . . . . 80, **160**
s. 38 . . . . . . . . . . . . . . . . . . . . . . . . . . . . . . . . . . . . . . . . . . . . . . 74, 129, **160**
ss 38(1)-(4) . . . . . . . . . . . . . . . . . . . . . . . . . . . . . . . . . . . . . . . . . . . . . . . . 74
s. 38(5) . . . . . . . . . . . . . . . . . . . . . . . . . . . . . . . . . . . . . . . . . . . . . . . . . . . 75
ss 39-40 . . . . . . . . . . . . . . . . . . . . . . . . . . . . . . . . . . . . . . . . . . . . 78, 129, **161**
s. 40 . . . . . . . . . . . . . . . . . . . . . . . . . . . . . . . . . . . . . . . . . . . . . . 78, 129, **161**
s. 41 . . . . . . . . . . . . . . . . . . . . . . . . . . . . . . . . . . . . . . . . . . . . . . 73, 79, **161**
ss 41(1), (3) . . . . . . . . . . . . . . . . . . . . . . . . . . . . . . . . . . . . . . . . . . . . . . 447-453
s. 42 . . . . . . . . . . . . . . . . . . . . . . . . . . . . . . . . . . . . . . . . . . . . . . . . . . . 79, **162**
Part V (ss 43-52) . . . . . . . . . . . . . . . . . . . . . . . . . . . . . . . . . . . . . . . . . . . . **162**
s. 43 . . . . . . . . . . . . . . . . . . . . . . . . . . . . . . . . . . . . . . . . . . . . . . . . . . 67, **162**
s. 46 . . . . . . . . . . . . . . . . . . . . . . . . . . . . . . . . . . . . . . . . . . . . . . 66, 67, **163**
s. 47 . . . . . . . . . . . . . . . . . . . . . . . . . . . . . . . . . . . . . . . . . . . . . . . . . . 83, **164**
s. 48 . . . . . . . . . . . . . . . . . . . . . . . . . . . . . . . . . . . . . . . . . . . . . . . . . . 85, **164**
s. 48(1) . . . . . . . . . . . . . . . . . . . . . . . . . . . . . . . . . . . . . . . . . . . . . . . . . . . 84
ss 48(2), (3) . . . . . . . . . . . . . . . . . . . . . . . . . . . . . . . . . . . . . . . . . . . . . . . . 85
s. 49 . . . . . . . . . . . . . . . . . . . . . . . . . . . . . . . . . . . . . . . . . . . . . . . . . . 85, **165**
s. 50 . . . . . . . . . . . . . . . . . . . . . . . . . . . . . . . . . . . . . . . . . . . . . . . . . . . . . **166**
s. 51 . . . . . . . . . . . . . . . . . . . . . . . . . . . . . . . . . . . . . . 11, 55, 58, 80, **166**
s. 51(1) . . . . . . . . . . . . . . . . . . . . . . . . . . . . . . . . . . . . . . . . . . . . . . . . 476-482
s. 51A . . . . . . . . . . . . . . . . . . . . . . . . . . . . . . . . . . . . . . . . 11, **167**, 356-378
s. 52 . . . . . . . . . . . . . . . . . . . . . . . . . . . . . . . . . . . . . . . . . . . . . . . . . . 59, **167**
ss 52(1)-(3) . . . . . . . . . . . . . . . . . . . . . . . . . . . . . . . . . . . . . . . . . . . . . . . . 58
s. 52A . . . . . . . . . . . . . . . . . . . . . . . . . . . . . . . . . . . . . . . . . . . . . . . . . . . . **168**
Part VI (ss 53-61) . . . . . . . . . . . . . . . . . . . . . . . . . . . . . . . . . . . . . . . . . . . **168**
s. 53 . . . . . . . . . . . . . . . . . . . . . . . . . . . . . . . . . . . . . . . . . . . . . . . . . . . . . **168**
s. 53(1) . . . . . . . . . . . . . . . . . . . . . . . . . . . . . . . . . . . . . . . . . . . . . . . . . . 126
s. 54 . . . . . . . . . . . . . . . . . . . . . . . . . . . . . . . . . . . . . . . . . . . . . . . . . . . . . **168**
s. 54(1) . . . . . . . . . . . . . . . . . . . . . . . . . . . . . . . . . . . . . . . . . . . . . . . . . . 127
s. 55 . . . . . . . . . . . . . . . . . . . . . . . . . . . . . . . . . . . . . . . . . . . . **169**, 476-482
s. 56 . . . . . . . . . . . . . . . . . . . . . . . . . . . . . . . . . . . . . . . . . . . . . . . . . . . . . **169**
s. 56A . . . . . . . . . . . . . . . . . . . . . . . . . . . . . . . . . . . . . . . . 86, **169**, 198
s. 56A(1) . . . . . . . . . . . . . . . . . . . . . . . . . . . . . . . . . . . . . . . . . . . . . . 86, 127
s. 56A(10) . . . . . . . . . . . . . . . . . . . . . . . . . . . . . . . . . . . . . . . . . . . . . . . . . 86

**Sex Discrimination Act 1975** continued
s. 57 . . . . . . . . . . . . . . . . . . . . . . . . . . . . . . . . . . . . . . . . . . . . . . . **171**
s. 57(1) . . . . . . . . . . . . . . . . . . . . . . . . . . . . . . . . . . . . . . . . . . . . · 128
s. 58 . . . . . . . . . . . . . . . . . . . . . . . . . . . . . . . . . . . . . . . . . . . . . . . **171**
s. 58(3) . . . . . . . . . . . . . . . . . . . . . . . . . . . . . . . . . . . . . . . . . . . . . . 221
s. 59 . . . . . . . . . . . . . . . . . . . . . . . . . . . . . . . . . . . . . . . . . . . . . . . **172**
s. 59(1) . . . . . . . . . . . . . . . . . . . . . . . . . . . . . . . . . . . . . . . . . . . · · 221
s. 60 . . . . . . . . . . . . . . . . . . . . . . . . . . . . . . . . . . . . . . . . . 128, **173**
s. 61 . . . . . . . . . . . . . . . . . . . . . . . . . . . . . . . . . . . . . . . . . . . . . . . **174**
Part VII (ss 62-76) . . . . . . . . . . . . . . . . . . . . . . . . . . . . . . . . . . . . . **175**
s. 62 . . . . . . . . . . . . . . . . . . . . . . . . . . . . . . . . . . . . . . . . . . . . . . . **175**
ss 62(1)-(2) . . . . . . . . . . . . . . . . . . . . . . . . . . . . . . . . . . . . . . . . . . 121
s. 63 . . . . . . . . . . . . . . . . . . . . . . . . . . . . . . . . . . . . . . . **175**, 347-355
s. 64 . . . . . . . . . . . . . . . . . . . . . . . . . . . . . . . . 108, **176**, 347-355
ss 64(1), (2) . . . . . . . . . . . . . . . . . . . . . . . . . . . . . . . . . . . . . . . . . . 125
s. 64(4) . . . . . . . . . . . . . . . . . . . . . . . . . . . . . . . . . . . . . . . . . . . . . 108
s. 65 . . . . . . . . . . . . . . . . . . . . . . . . . . 120, **176**, 454-463, 347-355
s. 65(1) . . . . . . . . . . . . . . . . . . . . . . . . . . . . . . . . . . . . . . . . . . . . . 114
s. 65(1)(a) . . . . . . . . . . . . . . . . . . . . . . . . . . . . . . . . . . . . . . . 114, 115
s. 65(1)(b) . . . . . . . . . . . . . . . . . . . . . . . . . . . . . . . . . . . . . . . . · · 114
s. 65(1)(c) . . . . . . . . . . . . . . . . . . . . . . . . . . . . . . . . . 114, 117, 119
s. 65(2) . . . . . . . . . . . . . . . . . . . . . . . . . . . . . . . . . . . . . . . . . . . . . 115
s. 65(3) . . . . . . . . . . . . . . . . . . . . . . . . . . . . . . . . . . . . . . . . . . . . . 117
s. 66 . . . . . . . . . . . . . . . . . . . . . . . . . . . . . . . . . . . . . . . **177**, 347-355
s. 66(3) . . . . . . . . . . . . . . . . . . . . . . . . . . . . . . 117, 356-378, 454-463
s. 66(4) . . . . . . . . . . . . . . . . . . . . . . . . . . . . . . . . . . . . . . . . . . . . . 116
s. 67 . . . . . . . . . . . . . . . . . . . . . . . . . . . . . . . . . . . . . . . . . 128, **177**
s. 67(2) . . . . . . . . . . . . . . . . . . . . . . . . . . . . . . . . . . . . . . . . . . · · 221
s. 68 . . . . . . . . . . . . . . . . . . . . . . . . . . . . . . . . . . . . . . . . . 129, **179**
ss 69, 70 . . . . . . . . . . . . . . . . . . . . . . . . . . . . . . . . . . . . . . . . . . . **179**
ss 71, 72 . . . . . . . . . . . . . . . . . . . . . . . . . . . . . . . . . . . . . . 129, **180**
s. 73 . . . . . . . . . . . . . . . . . . . . . . . . . . . . . . . . . . . . . . . . . . . . . . . **181**
s. 74 . . . . . . . . . . . . . . . . . . . . . . . . . . . . . . . . . . . 107, **182**, 225
s. 74(1)(a) . . . . . . . . . . . . . . . . . . . . . . . . . . . . . . . . . . . . . . . 379-387
s. 74(2) . . . . . . . . . . . . . . . . . . . . . . . . . . . . . . . . . . . . . . . . . . . **107**
s. 74(2)(a) . . . . . . . . . . . . . . . . . . . . . . . . . . . . . . . . . . . . . . . . . . 108
s. 75 . . . . . . . . . . . . . . . . . . . . . . . . . . . . . . . . . . . . . . . . 114, **183**
s. 75(1) . . . . . . . . . . . . . . . . . . . . . . . . . . . . . . . . . . . . . . . . . . . . . 113
ss 75(2), (3) . . . . . . . . . . . . . . . . . . . . . . . . . . . . . . . . . . . . . . . . . 114
s. 76 . . . . . . . . . . . . . . . . . . . . . . . . . . . . . . . . . . . . . . . . . . . . . . . **184**
ss 76(1), (5), (6b) . . . . . . . . . . . . . . . . . . . . . . . . . . . . . . . . . . . . . . 122
Part VIII (ss 77-87) . . . . . . . . . . . . . . . . . . . . . . . . . . . . . . . . . . · · **185**
s. 77 . . . . . . . . . . . . . . . . . . . . . . . . . . . . . . . . . . 130, 131, **185**
s. 77(2) . . . . . . . . . . . . . . . . . . . . . . . . . . . . . . . . . . . . . . . . . . . . . 130
ss 77(3), (4) . . . . . . . . . . . . . . . . . . . . . . . . . . . . . . . . . . . . . . . . . 121
ss 80, 81 . . . . . . . . . . . . . . . . . . . . . . . . . . . . . . . . . . . . . . . . . . . **186**
s. 81(4) . . . . . . . . . . . . . . . . . . . . . . . . . . . . . . . . . . . . . . . . . . . . . 225
s. 82 . . . . . . . . . . . . . . . . . . . . . . . . . . . . . . . . . . . . . . . . . 69, **187**
s. 82(1) . . . . . . . . . . . . . . . . . . . . . . . . . . . . . . . . . . . . . . . . . . . . . 221
s. 82(1A) . . . . . . . . . . . . . . . . . . . . . . . . . . . . . . . . . . . . . . . . . . . . . 73
s. 83 . . . . . . . . . . . . . . . . . . . . . . . . . . . . . . . . . . . . . . . . . . . . . . . **189**
s. 84 . . . . . . . . . . . . . . . . . . . . . . . . . . . . . . . . . . . . . . . . . . . . . . . **190**
s. 85 . . . . . . . . . . . . . . . . . . . . . . . . . . . . . . . . . . . . . . . 65, 70, **190**
s. 86 . . . . . . . . . . . . . . . . . . . . . . . . . . . . . . . . . . . . . . . . . . 70, **190**
s. 87 . . . . . . . . . . . . . . . . . . . . . . . . . . . . . . . . . . . . . . . . . . . . . . · **192**
Sch. 1 . . . . . . . . . . . . . . . . . . . . . . . . . . . . . . . . . . . . . . . . . . . . . . 144
Sch. 2 . . . . . . . . . . . . . . . . . . . . . . . . . . . . . . . . . . . . . . . . 144, 221
Sch. 3 . . . . . . . . . . . . . . . . . . . . . . . . . . . . . . . . . . . . . . . . . . . **192**

Sex Discrimination Act 1975 continued
    Sch. 3, para. 1 ......................................... **192**
    Sch. 3, para. 2 .................................... 126, **192**
    Sch. 3, para. 3 ......................................... **193**
    Sch. 3, para. 3(5) ....................................... 126
    Sch. 3, para. 4 ......................................... **193**
    Sch. 3, para. 5 .................................... 127, **193**
    Sch. 3, paras 6, 7 ...................................... **194**
    Sch. 3, para. 8 .................................... 127, **194**
    Sch. 3, paras 9-13 ..................................... **195**
    Sch. 3, para. 14 ................................... 127, **195**
    Sch. 3, para. 15 ....................................... **196**
    Sch. 4 ................................................ **196**
    Sch. 4, paras 3, 5 ..................................... **196**
    Sch. 5, 6 .............................................. 144

Sex Discrimination Act 1986
    (1986 c. 59) ...................... 12, 136, 144, **211**, 347-355
    s. 1 ................................................ 55, 211
    s. 1(1) ................................................. 71
    s. 2 .................................................. 211
    s. 2(1) ................................................. 60
    s. 3 .................................................. 211
    s. 4 .................................................. 211
    s. 5 ................................................. **211**
    s. 6 ........................... 40, 130, **131**, 211, **212**
    ss 6(3), (3)(a) ........................................ 131
    s. 7 .................................................. 211
    s. 7(2)(ba) ............................................. 71
    s. 8 .............................................. 211, **213**
    s. 9 ............................................. 40, **213**
    s. 9(1)-(3) ........................................... 211
    s. 10 ............................................ 211, **214**

Sex Disqualification (Removal) Act 1919
    (1919 c. 71) ........................................... 10

Social Security Act 1975
    (1975 c. 14) ........................................... 92
    s. 14 .............................................. 500-523
    s. 14(6) ............................................... 98
    ss 15(1), 15A, 16(1), 21, 22, 24 .................... 500-523
    s. 27 "pensionable age" ............................. 500-523
    s. 27(1) ........................................... 356-378
    ss 28-32, 35 ....................................... 500-523
    s. 36 .......................................... **269**, 500-523
    ss 36(4)(d), 36(7) ................................. 500-523
    s. 37 ......................................... 98, 271, 500-523
    ss 37(1), (2), (5), (6) ............................ 500-523
    ss 37A(5), 38, 39 .................................. 500-523
    s. 39(1)(b) ............................................ 98
    s. 45A ................................................. 98
    s. 101(5A) ............................................ 101
    s. 101A ............................................... 102
    s. 108(1)(b) ....................................... 500-523

Social Security Act 1980 (1980 c. 30)
    s. 14 ................................................. 102
    Sch. 1 ........................................... 12, **266**
    Sch. 1, Part I ................................... 97, **266**
    Sch. 1, paras 1, 3-7 ................................. **266**

Social Security Act 1986
  (1986 c. 50) . . . . . . . . . . . . . . . . . . . . . . . . . . . . . . . . . . . . . . . . . . . . 12
  s. 24(4) . . . . . . . . . . . . . . . . . . . . . . . . . . . . . . . . . . . . . . . . . . . . . . . 81
  s. 37 . . . . . . . . . . . . . . . . . . . . . . . . . . . . . . . . . . . . . . . . . . . . 92, 271
  ss 46(1), (2), 47 . . . . . . . . . . . . . . . . . . . . . . . . . . . . . . . . . . . . . . . . 81
  ss 48(4), (5) . . . . . . . . . . . . . . . . . . . . . . . . . . . . . . . . . . . . . . . . . . 82
Social Security Act 1989
  (1989 c. 24) . . . . . . . . . . . . . . . . . . . . . . . . . . . . 12, 95, 136, 144
  Sch. 5 . . . . . . . . . . . . . . . . . . . . . . . . . . . . . . . . . . . . 20, 34, 272
  Sch. 5, Part I . . . . . . . . . . . . . . . . . . . . . . . . . . . . . . . . . . 61, 272
  Sch. 5, paras 1, 2 . . . . . . . . . . . . . . . . . . . . . . . . . . . . . . . . . . 272
  Sch. 5, para. 3 . . . . . . . . . . . . . . . . . . . . . . . . . . . . . . . . . 99, 274
  Sch. 5, para. 4 . . . . . . . . . . . . . . . . . . . . . . . . . . . . . . . . 102, 274
  Sch. 5, para. 5 . . . . . . . . . . . . . . . . . . . . . . . . . . . . . . . . . . . 275
  Sch. 5, para. 6 . . . . . . . . . . . . . . . . . . . . . . . . . . . . . . . . . . . 276
  Sch. 5, para. 7 . . . . . . . . . . . . . . . . . . . . . . . . . . . . . . . . . 34, 277
  Sch. 5, para. 7(a) . . . . . . . . . . . . . . . . . . . . . . . . . . . . . . . . . . 90
  Sch. 5, paras 7(b), (e) . . . . . . . . . . . . . . . . . . . . . . . . . . . . . . . 90
  Sch. 5, para. 8 . . . . . . . . . . . . . . . . . . . . . . . . . . . . . . . . 102, 278
  Sch. 5, paras 9, 10 . . . . . . . . . . . . . . . . . . . . . . . . . . . . . . . . 278
  Sch. 5, paras 10, 12 . . . . . . . . . . . . . . . . . . . . . . . . . . . . . . . 279
Social Security Pensions Act 1975
  (1975 c. 60) . . . . . . . . . . . . . . . . . . . . . . . . . . . . . . . . . 34, 60, 92
Trade Union and Labour Relations Act 1974
  (1974 c. 52) . . . . . . . . . . . . . . . . . . . . . . . . . . . . . . . . . . 347-355
  s. 29(1) . . . . . . . . . . . . . . . . . . . . . . . . . . . . . . . . . . . . . . . 131
  Sch. 1, Part III, para. 21 . . . . . . . . . . . . . . . . . . . . . . . . . . . . . 229
Transport Act 1985
  (1985 c. 67)
  s. 93(7)(a) . . . . . . . . . . . . . . . . . . . . . . . . . . . . . . . . . . . 356-378
Wages Act 1986
  (1986 c. 48) . . . . . . . . . . . . . . . . . . . . . . . . . . . . . . . . . . . . . 136

# United Kingdom Secondary Legislation

County Court Rules 1981 (SI 1981 No 1687)
  Order 14, r. 8(1) . . . . . . . . . . . . . . . . . . . . . . . . . . . . . . . 438-446
Education (Modification of Enactments Relating to Employment) Order 1989
  (SI 1989 No 901) . . . . . . . . . . . . . . . . . . . . . . . . . . . . . . . . . . 73
Equal Pay (Amendment) Regulations 1983
  (SI 1983 No 1794) . . . . . . . . . . . . . . . . . . . 45, 136, 293-305, 306-317
  reg. 2 . . . . . . . . . . . . . . . . . . . . . . . . . . . . . . . . . . . . . . 306-317
Income Support (Transitional) Regulations 1987
  (SI 1987 No 1969) . . . . . . . . . . . . . . . . . . . . . . . . . . . . . . . . . 96
Industrial Tribunals Complementary Rules of Procedure 1985: see Industrial
  Tribunals (Rules of Procedure) Regulations 1985 (SI 1985 No 16), Sch. 2
Industrial Tribunals (England and Wales) Regulations 1965
  (SI 1965 No 1101) . . . . . . . . . . . . . . . . . . . . . . . . . . . . . . . . 125
Industrial Tribunals (Interest) Order 1990
  (SI 1990 No 479) . . . . . . . . . . . . . . . . . . . . . . . . . . . . . . . . . 115
Industrial Tribunals (Non-discrimination Notices Appeals) Regulations 1977 (SI
  1977 No 1094) . . . . . . . . . . . . . . . . . . . . . . . . . . . 12, 129, 229
  regs 1, 2 . . . . . . . . . . . . . . . . . . . . . . . . . . . . . . . . . . . . . . 229
  regs 3, 4 . . . . . . . . . . . . . . . . . . . . . . . . . . . . . . . . . . . . . . 231
  Sch., rr. 1-3 . . . . . . . . . . . . . . . . . . . . . . . . . . . . . . . . . . . . 231
  Sch., rr. 4, 5 . . . . . . . . . . . . . . . . . . . . . . . . . . . . . . . . . . . . 232
  Sch., rr. 6-8 . . . . . . . . . . . . . . . . . . . . . . . . . . . . . . . . . . . . 233

Industrial Tribunals (Non-discrimination Notices Appeals) Regulations 1977
    continued
        Sch., rr. 9, 10 . . . . . . . . . . . . . . . . . . . . . . . . . . . . . . . . . . . . . . . . **234**
        Sch., rr. 11, 12. . . . . . . . . . . . . . . . . . . . . . . . . . . . . . . . . . . . . . **235**
        Sch., r. 13 . . . . . . . . . . . . . . . . . . . . . . . . . . . . . . . . . . . . . . . . . **236**
Industrial Tribunals Rules of Procedure 1985: see Industrial Tribunals (Rules of
    Procedure) Regulations 1985 (SI 1985 No 16),  Sch. 1
Industrial Tribunals (Rules of Procedure) (Equal Value Amendment) Regulations
    1983 (SI 1983 No 1807) . . . . . . . . . . . . . . . . . . . . . . . . . . . . . . . . . . . . 45
Industrial Tribunals (Rules of Procedure) Regulations 1985
    (SI 1985 No 16) . . . . . . . . . . . . . . . . . . . . . . . . . . . . . . 12, 103, **238**
        reg. 1 . . . . . . . . . . . . . . . . . . . . . . . . . . . . . . . . . . . . . . . . . . . . . **238**
        reg. 2 . . . . . . . . . . . . . . . . . . . . . . . . . . . . . . . . . . . . . . . . . . . . . **239**
        reg. 3 . . . . . . . . . . . . . . . . . . . . . . . . . . . . . . . . . . . . . . . . . . . . . **241**
        reg. 3(2) . . . . . . . . . . . . . . . . . . . . . . . . . . . . . . . . . . . . . . . 306-317
        reg. 4 . . . . . . . . . . . . . . . . . . . . . . . . . . . . . . . . . . . . . . . . . . . . . **241**
        Sch 1: Industrial Tribunals
            Rules of Procedure 1985 . . . . . . . . . . . . . . . . . . . . . . . . . . . . **241**
        Sch. 1, r. 1 . . . . . . . . . . . . . . . . . . . . . . . . . . . . . . . . . . . . . . . . **241**
        Sch. 1, rr. 1(1), (2) . . . . . . . . . . . . . . . . . . . . . . . . . . . . . . . . . . 103
        Sch. 1, r. 2 . . . . . . . . . . . . . . . . . . . . . . . . . . . . . . . . . . . . 103, **242**
        Sch. 1, r. 3 . . . . . . . . . . . . . . . . . . . . . . . . . . . . . . . . . . . . . . . . **242**
        Sch. 1, r. 3(1) . . . . . . . . . . . . . . . . . . . . . . . . . . . . . . . . . . . . . . 103
        Sch. 1, r. 4 . . . . . . . . . . . . . . . . . . . . . . . . . . . . . . . . . . . . 109, **243**
        Sch. 1, r. 4(1) . . . . . . . . . . . . . . . . . . . . . . . . . . . . . . . . . . . . . . 108
        Sch. 1, r. 4(1)(b)(ii) . . . . . . . . . . . . . . . . . . . . . . . . . . . . . . . 438-446
        Sch. 1, r. 4(3), (4) . . . . . . . . . . . . . . . . . . . . . . . . . . . . . . . . . . 110
        Sch. 1, r. 5 . . . . . . . . . . . . . . . . . . . . . . . . . . . . . . . . . . . . . . . . **244**
        Sch. 1, r. 5(1) . . . . . . . . . . . . . . . . . . . . . . . . . . . . . . . . . . . . . . 104
        Sch. 1, rr. 6, 7 . . . . . . . . . . . . . . . . . . . . . . . . . . . . . . . . . . . . . . **245**
        Sch. 1, r. 7(6) . . . . . . . . . . . . . . . . . . . . . . . . . . . . . . . . . . . . . . 104
        Sch. 1, r. 8 . . . . . . . . . . . . . . . . . . . . . . . . . . . . . . . . . . . . . . . . **246**
        Sch. 1, r. 8(1) . . . . . . . . . . . . . . . . . . . . . . . 104, 438-446, 488-490
        Sch. 1, r. 8(2)-(4) . . . . . . . . . . . . . . . . . . . . . . . . . . . . . . . . . . . 104
        Sch. 1, r. 9 . . . . . . . . . . . . . . . . . . . . . . . . . . . . . . . . . . . . . . . . **247**
        Sch. 1, rr. 9(1)-9(6), (8) . . . . . . . . . . . . . . . . . . . . . . . . . . . . . . 105
        Sch. 1, r. 10. . . . . . . . . . . . . . . . . . . . . . . . . . . . . . . . . . . . . . . . **248**
        Sch. 1, r. 11. . . . . . . . . . . . . . . . . . . . . . . . . . . . . . . . . . . . 113, **249**
        Sch. 1, r. 11(1), (2). . . . . . . . . . . . . . . . . . . . . . . . . . . . . . . . . . . 113
        Sch. 1, r. 12. . . . . . . . . . . . . . . . . . . . . . . . . . . . . . . . . . . . . . . . **251**
        Sch. 1, r. 13. . . . . . . . . . . . . . . . . . . . . . . . . . . . . . . . . . . . . . . . **252**
        Sch. 1, r. 14. . . . . . . . . . . . . . . . . . . . . . . . . . . . . . . . . . . 120, **252**
        Sch. 1, r. 15. . . . . . . . . . . . . . . . . . . . . . . . . . . . . . . . . . . 121, **252**
        Sch. 1, rr. 16, 17 . . . . . . . . . . . . . . . . . . . . . . . . . . . . . . . . . . . . **253**
        Sch 2: Industrial Tribunals Complementary
            Rules of Procedure 1985 . . . . . . . . . . . . . . . . . . . **255**, 293-305, 306-317
        Sch. 2, r. 4 . . . . . . . . . . . . . . . . . . . . . . . . . . . . . . . . . . . 109, **255**
        Sch. 2, r. 4(1A), (1B) . . . . . . . . . . . . . . . . . . . . . . . . . . . . . 109, 110
        Sch. 2, r. 4(2A) . . . . . . . . . . . . . . . . . . . . . . . . . . . . . . . . . . . . . 109
        Sch. 2, r. 7A . . . . . . . . . . . . . . . . . . . . . . . . . . . . . . . . . . . . . . . **256**
        Sch. 2, r. 7A(1) . . . . . . . . . . . . . . . . . . . . . . . . . . . . . . . . . 105, 122
        Sch. 2, r. 7A(3), (4) . . . . . . . . . . . . . . . . . . . . . . . . . . . . . . . . . . 123
        Sch. 2, r. 7A(5) . . . . . . . . . . . . . . . . . . . . . . . . . . . . . . . . . 123, 124
        Sch. 2, r. 7A(6) . . . . . . . . . . . . . . . . . . . . . . . . . . . . . . 106, 123, 124
        Sch. 2, r. 7A(7), (8) . . . . . . . . . . . . . . . . . . . . . . . . . . . . . . 106, 123
        Sch. 2, r. 7A(9)-(13) . . . . . . . . . . . . . . . . . . . . . . . . . . . . . . . . . 106
        Sch. 2, r. 8 . . . . . . . . . . . . . . . . . . . . . . . . . . . . . . . . . . . . . . . . **258**
        Sch. 2, r. 8(2A)-8(2D) . . . . . . . . . . . . . . . . . . . . . . . . . . . . . . . . 107

Industrial Tribunals (Rules of Procedure) Regulations 1985 continued
Sch. 2, r. 8(2E) ........................................... 105, 107
Sch. 2, r. 9 ................................................. 260
Sch. 2, r. 11................................................. 261
Sch. 2, r. 12................................................. 262
Sch. 2, r. 12(2A) ........................................... 105
Sch. 2, r. 17................................................. 264
National Health Service (Charges for Drugs and Appliances) Regulations
(SI 1980 No 1503)
reg. 7 .................................................. 356-378
Police Federation Regulations 1969
(SI 1969 No 1787) ........................................ 10
Race Relations Code of Practice Order 1983
(SI 1983 No 1801) ....................................... 438-446
Sex Discrimination and Equal Pay (Offshore Employment) Order 1987
(SI 1987 No 930) ......................................... 11, 68
art. 2..................................................... 153
Sex Discrimination (Amendment) Order 1988
(SI 1988 No 249) ......................................... 12, 59
art. 2..................................................... 167
Sex Discrimination (Formal Investigation) Regulations 1975
(SI 1975 No 1993) ........................................ 12, 221
regs 1, 2 ................................................. 221
regs 3-6.................................................. 222
Sch. 1.................................................... 222
Sch. 2.................................................... 223
Sex Discrimination (Formal Investigations) (Amendment) Regulations 1977
(SI 1977 No 843) ......................................... 221
Sex Discrimination (Northern Ireland) Order 1976
(SI 1976 No 1042) ..................................... 11, 388-406
art. 3(1)................................................. 388-406
art. 3(1)(a).............................................. 436-438
art. 3(1)(b).............................................. 388-406
art. 3(1)(b)(i)-(iii)..................................... 388-406
art. 5(1)................................................. 388-406
art. 5(1)(b)(ii)......................................... 388-406
art. 7.................................................... 388-406
art. 8(1)(c)............................................. 436-438
art. 8(2)................................................ 388-406
art. 8(2)(a)............................................. 436-438
art. 8(2)(b)............................................. 388-406
art. 76(5)............................................... 388-406
Sex Discrimination (Questions and Replies) Order 1975
(SI 1975 No 2048) ................................... 12, 107, 225
arts 1-3 ................................................ 225
art. 4................................................... 226, 108
arts 5, 6................................................ 226
Schs 1, 2 ............................................... 227
Sex Discrimination (Questions and Replies) (Amendment) Order 1977
(SI 1977 No 844) ..................................... 107, 225
Sex Discrimination Act 1975 (Exemption of Police Federation Constitutional and
Electoral Arrangements) Order 1989 (SI 1989 No 2420) .............. 10
Sex Discrimination Act 1975 (Exemption of Special Treatment for Lone Parents)
Order 1989 (SI 1989 No 2140) ............................ 84
Sex Discrimination Code of Practice Order1985
(SI 1985 No 387) ........................................ 198
Social Security (Credits) Regulations
(SI 1975 No 336) ....................................... 500-523

Social Security (Invalid Care Allowance) Regulations 1976 (SI 1976 No 409)
    reg. 10 ...............................................500-523
    reg. 27 ...............................................500-523
Social Security (Overlapping Allowance) Regulations 1979
    (SI 1979 No 597) ......................................500-523
Social Security (Severe Disablement Allowance) Regulations 1984
    (SI 1984 No 1303)
    reg. 4 ................................................500-523

## United Kingdom Codes of Practice

ACAS Code of Practice 2: Disclosure of Information to Trade Unions for
    Collective Bargaining Purposes ................................. 111
EOC Code of Practice for the Elimination of Discrimination on the grounds of Sex
    and Marriage and the Promotion of Equality of Opportunity in Employment
    (1985)...........................................86, **198**
    Introduction (paras 1-10) ...................................  **199**
    paras 1, 2...............................................  **199**
    para. 3...............................................  **55,  199**
    paras 4, 5...............................................  **199**
    paras 6-10 ..............................................  **200**
    Part I (paras 11-32) ......................................  **200**
    para. 11...............................................  **200**
    para. 12...............................................  **201**
    para. 13...............................................  74, **201**
    para. 14...............................................  **201**
    para. 15...............................................  63, **201**
    paras 16, 17 ............................................  63, **202**
    para. 18...............................................  **202**
    para. 19...............................................  75, **202**
    para. 20...............................................  **203**
    para. 21...............................................  75, **203**
    para. 22...............................................  **203**
    para. 23...............................................  75, **203**
    para. 24...............................................  **204**
    para. 25...............................................  77, **204**
    paras 26, 27 ............................................  **205**
    para. 28...............................................  77, **205**
    para. 29...............................................  **22,  206**
    para. 30...............................................  **206**
    para. 31...............................................  31, **206**
    para. 32...............................................  **206**
    Part II (paras 33-43) ......................................  **207**
    para. 33...............................................  **207**
    para. 34...............................................  82, **207**
    paras 35-40 ............................................  82, **208**
    para. 41...............................................  **208**
    paras 42, 43 ............................................  **209**
Race Relations Code of Practice ..................................438-446

# TABLE OF CASES

[Numbers in bold type refer to pages at which extracts are reprinted verbatim.]

## Numerical Table of Cases
### before the Court of Justice of the European Communities

80/70    Defrenne v. Belgian State [1971] ECR 445 . . . . . . . . . . . . . . . . . . . . . 37
152/73   Sotgiu v. Deutsche Bundespost [1974] ECR 153 . . . . . . . . . . . . . . . . 508
43/75    Defrenne v. Sabena (No 2) [1976] ECR 455 . . . . . . . . . . . . . . . . . . . 6, 8
129/79   Macarthys Ltd v. Smith [1980] ECR 1275, [1980] 3 WLR 929, [1981]
         1 All ER 111, [1980] ICR 672, [1980] IRLR 210 . . . . . . . . 7, 42, 298, 340
69/80    Worringham v. Lloyds Bank Ltd [1981] ECR 767, [1981] 1 WLR
         950, [1981] 2 All ER 434, [1981] ICR 558, [1981] IRLR 178 . . . 6, 8, 37-39
96/80    Jenkins v. Kingsgate (Clothing Productions) Ltd [1981] ECR 911,
         [1981] 1 WLR 972, [1981] ICR 592, [1981] IRLR 228 . . . . . . . 7, 23, 286
                                                                        298, 322, 338-346
19/81    Burton v. British Railways Board [1982] ECR 555, [1982] QB 1080,
         [1982] 3 WLR 387, [1982] 3 All ER 537, [1982] ICR 329, [1982]
         IRLR 116 . . . . . . . . . . . . . . . . . . . . . . . . . . . . . . 6, 76, 511, 517
61/81    Commission of the European Communities v. United Kingdom [1982]
         ECR 2601, [1982] IRLR 333 . . . . . . . . . . . . . . 45, 306, 310, 314, 326
165/82   Commission of the European Communities v. United Kingdom [1983]
         ECR 3431 . . . . . . . . . . . . . . . . . . . . . . . . . . . . . . . . . 12, 55, 71
14/83    von Colson & Kamann v. Land Nordrhein-Westfalen [1984] ECR
         1891 . . . . . . . . . . . . . . . . . . . . . . . . . . . . . . . . . . . 312, 353, 354
143/83   Commission of the European Communities v. Denmark [1985] ECR
         427, [1986] 1 CMLR 43 . . . . . . . . . . . . . . . . . . . . . . . . . . . . . . 43
152/84   Marshall v. Southampton & SW Hampshire Area Health Authority,
         [1986] ECR 723, [1986] QB 401, [1986] 2 WLR 780, [1986] 2 All ER
         584, [1986] ICR 335, [1986] IRLR 140 . . . . . . . . . . . . 7, 12, 34, 59, 60
                                                                        351-354, 512, 518
170/84   Bilka-Kaufhaus GmbH v. Weber von Hartz [1986] ECR 1607, [1987]
         ICR 110, [1987] IRLR 317 . . . . . 7, 23, 30, 37, 39, 52, 298, 323, 401, 409
222/84   Johnston v. Chief Constable of the Royal Ulster Constabulary, [1986]
         ECR 1651, [1987] QB 129, [1986] 3 WLR 1038, [1987] ICR 83,
         [1986] IRLR 263 . . . . . . . . 6, 12, 24, 59, 63, 64, 334, 508, 510, 512, 520
262/84   Beets-Proper v. Van Lanschot Bankiers [1986] ECR 773 . . . . . . . . . . . 511
150/85   Drake v. Chief Adjudication Officer [1986] ECR 1995, [1987] QB
         166, [1986] 3 All ER 65 . . . . . . . . . . . . . . . . . . . . 92, 99, 271, 505
192/85   Newstead v. Department of Transport [1987] ECR 4753, [1988] 1 All
         ER 129, [1988] IRLR 66 . . . . . . . . . . . . . . . . . . . . . . . . . . . . . 38
237/85   Rummler v. Dato-Druck GmbH [1986] ECR 2101, [1987] ICR 774,
         [1987] IRLR 32 . . . . . . . . . . . . . . . . . . . . . . . . . . . 47, 48, 330
384/85   Borrie Clarke v. Chief Adjudication Officer [1987] ECR 2865 . . 94, 99, 506
157/86   Murphy v. Bord Telecom Eireann [1988] ECR 673,
         [1988] IRLR 267 . . . . . . . . . . . . . . . . . . . . . . . . . . . . . . 49, 310
48, 106 & 107/88
         Achterberg-te Riele v. Sociale Verzekeringsbank Amsterdam [1989]
         ECR 1963 . . . . . . . . . . . . . . . . . . . . . . . . . . . . . . . . . . . . . 94
109/88   Handels- og Kontorfunktionaerernes Forbund i Danmark v. Dansk
         Arbejdsgiverforening [1989] ECR 3199, [1989] IRLR 532 . . . . . . . . . 7, 24
171/88   Rinner-Kühn v. FWW Spezial-Gebäudereinigung GmbH & Co. KG
         [1989] ECR 2743, [1989] IRLR 493 . . . . . . . . . . . . . . . 7, 23, 38, 52
C-177/88 Dekker v. Stichting Vormingscentrum voor Jonge Volwassenen (VJV-
         Centrum) Plus [1990] ECR I-3941, [1991] IRLR 27 . . . . . . . . . . . . . . 18

179/88    Handels- og Kontorfunktionaerernes Forbund i Danmark v. Dansk
          Arbejdsgiverforening [1990] ECR I-3979, [1991] IRLR 31 . . . . . . . . . . . 18
C-262/88  Barber v. Guardian Royal Exchange Assurance Group [1990] ECR I-
          1889, [1990] 2 All ER 660, [1990] IRLR 240 . . . . . . . . . . . . . . 7, 8, 38-40
                                                                        42, 61, 96, 516, 517
C-33/89   Kowalska v. Freie und Hansestadt Hamburg [1990] ECR I-2591,
          [1990] IRLR 447 . . . . . . . . . . . . . . . . . . . . . . . . . . . . . . 23, 52, 131
C-106/89  Marleasing SA v. La Comercial Internacional de Alimentación [1990]
          ECR I-4135 . . . . . . . . . . . . . . . . . . . . . . . . . . . . . . . . . . . . . . 9
C-184/89  Nimz v. Freie und Hansestadt Hamburg [1991] ECR I-297 . . 24, 52, 54, 131
C-188/89  Foster v. British Gas plc [1990] ECR I-3313, [1990] IRLR 353 . . . . . . . . 8
C-213/89  R. v. Secretary of State for Transport, ex parte Factortame Ltd [1990]
          ECR I-2433, [1990] 3 WLR 818, [1990] CMLR 573 . . . . . . . . . . . . . . . 3
C-31/90   Johnson v. Chief Adjudication Officer [1991] ECR I-3723 . . . . . . . 93, 94
C-243/90  R. v. Secretary of State for Social Security, ex parte Smithson
          [1992] ECR I-467 . . . . . . . . . . . . . . . . . . . . . . . . . . . . . . . . 94
C-63 & C-64/91
          Jackson & Cresswell v. Chief Adjudication Officer
          [1992] ECR I-4737 . . . . . . . . . . . . . . . . . . . . . . . . . . . 91, 94, 97
C-9/91    R. v. Secretary of State for Social Security, ex parte EOC . . . . . . . . . . . 93

## Alphabetical Table of Cases

Abdulaziz, Cabales & Balkandali v. United Kingdom (1985) 7 EHRR 471
   (ECHR) . . . . . . . . . . . . . . . . . . . . . . . . . . . . . . . . . . . . . . . . . 5
Achterberg-te Riele v. Sociale Verzekeringsbank Amsterdam, Joined Cases 48, 106
   & 107/88, [1989] ECR 1963 (ECJ) . . . . . . . . . . . . . . . . . . . . . . . . . 94
AG v. Guardian Newspapers Ltd [1987] 1 WLR 1248, [1987] 3 All ER 316
   (HL) . . . . . . . . . . . . . . . . . . . . . . . . . . . . . . . . . . . . . . . . . . 5
AG v. Guardian Newspapers Ltd (No 2) [1988] 3 WLR 776, [1988] 3 All ER 545
   (HL) . . . . . . . . . . . . . . . . . . . . . . . . . . . . . . . . . . . . . . . . . . 5
Ainsworth v. Glass Tubes & Components Ltd [1977] ICR 347, [1977] IRLR 74
   (EAT) . . . . . . . . . . . . . . . . . . . . . . . . . . . . . . . . . . . . . . . . . 41
Albion Shipping Agency v. Arnold [1982] ICR 22, [1981] IRLR 525 (EAT) . . . . 42, 51
Aldridge v. British Telecom plc [1989] ICR 790, [1990] IRLR 11 (EAT) . . . 41, 107, 123
Alexander v. Home Office [1988] 1 WLR 968, [1988] 2 All ER 118, [1988] ICR
   685, [1988] IRLR 190 (CA) . . . . . . . . . . . . . . . . . . . . . . . . . . . . 116
Armagh District Council v. Fair Employment Agency [1984] IRLR 234 (NICA) . . . . 372
Arnold v. Beecham Group Ltd [1982] ICR 744, [1982] IRLR 307 (EAT) . . . . . . . . . 45
Ashmore v. British Coal Corporation [1990] IRLR 26 (CA) . . . . . . . . . . . . . . . . 121
Automotive Products Ltd v. Peake [1978] QB 233 (CA) . . . . . . . . 476, 478, 481, 482
Aziz v. Trinity Street Taxis Ltd [1989] QB 463, [1988] 3 WLR 79, [1988] 2 All
   ER 860, [1988] ICR 534, [1988] IRLR 204 (CA) . . . . . . . . . . . . . . . . . . . 31

Baker v. Cornwall County Council [1990] ICR 452, [1990] IRLR 194 (CA) . . 112, **379**
Balfour v. Eastern Health & Social Services Board, 32/81SD, unreported (NIIT) . . . . . 66
Balgobin & Francis v. London Borough of Tower Hamlets [1987] ICR 829,
   [1987] IRLR 401 (EAT) . . . . . . . . . . . . . . . . . . . . . . . . . . 19, 79, **447**
Barber v. Guardian Royal Exchange Assurance Group, Case C-262/88, [1990]
   ECR I-1889, [1990] 2 All ER 660, [1990] IRLR 240 (ECJ) . . . . . . . . 7, 8, 38-40
                                                                        42, 61, 96, 516, 517
Barclays Bank plc v. Karpur [1989] IRLR 136 (HL) . . . . . . . . . . . . . . . . . . . 122
Bebb v. Law Society [1914] 1 Ch 286 (CA) . . . . . . . . . . . . . . . . . . . . . . . . . 9
Beets-Proper v. Van Lanschot Bankiers, Case 262/84, [1986] ECR 773 (ECJ) . . . . . 511
Belgian Linguistics Case (Merits), ECHR, Series A, Vol. 6, judgment of 23 July
   1968 . . . . . . . . . . . . . . . . . . . . . . . . . . . . . . . . . . . . . . . . . . 87
Beneviste v. University of Southampton [1989] ICR 617, [1989] IRLR 122 (CA) . . . . 49
Bick v. Royal West of England Residential School for the Deaf [1976] IRLR 326
   (IT) . . . . . . . . . . . . . . . . . . . . . . . . . . . . . . . . . . . . . . . . . . 17

Bilka-Kaufhaus GmbH v. Weber von Hartz, Case 170/84, [1986] ECR 1607,
  [1987] ICR 110, [1987] IRLR 317 (ECJ) . . . . . . . . . . . . . . 7, 23, 30, 37, 39, 52
                                                              298, 323, 401, 409
Bohon-Mitchell v. Council for Legal Education [1978] IRLR 525 (IT) . . . . . . . . . . . 28
Borrie Clarke v. Chief Adjudication Officer, Case 384/85, [1987] ECR 2865
  (ECJ) . . . . . . . . . . . . . . . . . . . . . . . . . . . . . . . . . 94, 99, 506
Bracebridge Engineering Ltd v. Darby [1990] IRLR 3 (EAT) . . . . . . . . . . . . . . . . 19
Bradford Metropolitan Council v. Arora [1991] IRLR 165 (CA) . . . . . . . . . . . . . . 117
Brennan v. Dewhurst (J H) [1984] ICR 52, [1983] IRLR 357 (EAT) . . . . . . . . . . . . 74
Briggs v. NE Education & Library Board [1990] IRLR 181
  (NICA) . . . . . . . . . . . . . . . . . . . . . . . . . 22, 23, 27, 29, 30, 66. 388
Brindley v. Tayside Health Board [1976] IRLR 364 (IT) . . . . . . . . . . . . . . . . . . 74
British Airways Engineering Overhaul Ltd v. Francis [1981] ICR 279 (EAT) . . . . . . 31
British Gas plc v. Sharma [1991] IRLR 101 (EAT). . . . . . . . . . . . . . . . . . 112, 119
British Judo Association v. Petty [1981] ICR 660, [1981] IRLR 484 (EAT) . . . . . . . . 73
British Leyland v. Powell [1978] IRLR 57 (EAT). . . . . . . . . . . . . . . . . . . . . . 44
British Library v. Palyza [1984] ICR 504, [1984] IRLR 306 (EAT). . . . . . . . . . . . 109
British Railways Board v. Natarajan [1979] 2 All ER 794, [1979] ICR 326 (EAT) . . . 109
British Railways Board v. Paul [1988] IRLR 20 (EAT) . . . . . . . . . . . . . . . . . . . 121
Bromley v. Quick (H & J) Ltd [1988] ICR 623, [1988] IRLR 249 (CA). . . . 45, 297, 326
Brown & Royle v. Cearns & Brown Ltd (1986) 6 EOR 27 (IT) . . . . . . . . . . . . . . . 49
Brunt v. NIES [1979] NI Judgments Bulletin No 2. . . . . . . . . . . . . . . . . 437, 438
Burton v. British Railways Board, Case 19/81, [1982] ECR 555, [1982] QB 1080,
  [1982] 3 WLR 387, [1982] 3 All ER 537, [1982] ICR 329, [1982] IRLR
  116 (ECJ) . . . . . . . . . . . . . . . . . . . . . . . . . 6, 76, 511, 517
Byrne v. Financial Times Ltd [1991] IRLR 417 (EAT) . . . . . . . . . . . . . . . . . . 109

Calder v. James Finlay Corporation Ltd [1989] ICR 157 (EAT) . . . . . . . . . . . . . . 122
Capper Pass Ltd v. Lawton [1977] 2 All ER 11, [1976] IRLR 366 (EAT). . . . . . . 43, 44
Carrington v. Helix Lighting Ltd [1990] IRLR 6 (EAT). . . . . . . . . . . . . . . . . . . 109
Chattopadhyay v. Headmaster of Holloway School [1982] ICR 132, [1981] IRLR
  487 (EAT) . . . . . . . . . . . . . . . . . . . . . . . . . . . . . 112, 384, 442
Chiu v. British Aerospace plc [1982] IRLR 56 (EAT) . . . . . . . . . . . . . . . . . . . 16
City of Los Angeles Department of Water & Power v. Manhart (1978) 98 SC 1370
  (US Sup. Ct) . . . . . . . . . . . . . . . . . . . . . . . . . . . . . . . . . . . 422
Clark v. Bexley Health Authority & Secretary of State, unreported (IT) . . . . . . . . . . 53
Clarke & Powell v. Eley (IMI) Kynoch Ltd [1982] IRLR 131 (IT) . . . . . . . . . . . . 454
Clarke & Powell v. Eley (IMI) Kynoch Ltd [1983] ICR 165, [1982] IRLR 482
  (EAT) . . . . . . . . . . . . . . . . . . . . 21, 22, 24, 25, 29, 395, 412, 454
Clarke v. Chief Adjudication Officer, Case 384/85 (ECJ): see Borrie Clarke v. ...
Clay Cross (Quarry Services) Ltd v. Fletcher [1978] 1 WLR 1429, [1979] 1 All
  ER 474, [1979] ICR 1, [1978] IRLR 361 (CA) . . . . . . . . . . . . . . 26, 50, 291
Clymo v. Wandsworth London Borough Council [1989] ICR 250, [1989] IRLR
  241 (EAT) . . . . . . . . . . . . . . . . . . . 22, 29, 77, 392, 394, 397, 398, 400
Cobb v. Secretary of State for Employment [1989] ICR 506, [1989] IRLR 464
  (EAT) . . . . . . . . . . . . . . . . . . . . . . . . . . . . . . . . . . . . 23, 30
Commission of the European Communities v. Denmark, Case 143/83, [1985] ECR
  427, [1986] 1 CMLR 43 (ECJ) . . . . . . . . . . . . . . . . . . . . . . . . . . 43
Commission of the European Communities v. United Kingdom, Case 61/81,
  [1982] ECR 2601, [1982] IRLR 333 (ECJ) . . . . . . . . . . . 45, 306, 310, 314, 326
Commission of the European Communities v. United Kingdom, Case 165/82,
  [1983] ECR 3431 (ECJ). . . . . . . . . . . . . . . . . . . . . . . . 12, 55, 71
Conway v. Queen's University Belfast [1981] IRLR 43 (NICA). . . . . . . . . . . . . . 111
Cornelius v. University College of Swansea [1987] IRLR 141 (CA) . . . . . . . . . . . . 31
CRE v. Imperial Society of Teachers of Dancing [1983] ICR 473, [1983] IRLR
  315 (EAT). . . . . . . . . . . . . . . . . . . . . . . . . . . . . . . . . . . . 78
Cresswell v. Chief Adjudication Officer, Case C-64/91 (ECJ): see Jackson &
  Cresswell

Daley v. Allied Suppliers [1983] ICR 90 (EAT) . . . . . . . . . . . . . . . . . . . . . . . . . 69
Darragh v. Jones, 5/83 EP, unreported (NIIT) . . . . . . . . . . . . . . . . . . . . . . . . 31, 44
De Souza v. AA [1986] ICR 514, [1986] IRLR 103 (CA) . . . . . . 19, 78, 79, 399. 489
Defrenne v. Belgian State, Case 80/70, [1971] ECR 445 (ECJ) . . . . . . . . . . . . . . . 37
Defrenne v. Sabena (No 2), Case 43/75, [1976] ECR 455 (ECJ) . . . . . . . . . . . . . . 6, 8
Dekker v. Stichting Vormingscentrum voor Jonge Volwassenen (VJV-Centrum)
    Plus, Case C-177/88, [1990] ECR I-3941, [1991] IRLR 27 (ECJ) . . . . . . . . . . 18
Denneby v. Sealink UK Ltd [1987] IRLR 120 (EAT) . . . . . . . . . . . . . . . . . . . . . . 105
Department of the Environment v. Fox [1979] ICR 736, [1980] 1 All ER 58
    (EAT) . . . . . . . . . . . . . . . . . . . . . . . . . . . . . . . . . . . . . . . . . . . . . . . . . . . 70
Dhatt v. McDonald's Hamburger Ltd [1988] ICR 591 (EAT) . . . . . . . . . . . . . . . . 16
Dibro Ltd v. Hore [1990] IRLR 129 (EAT) . . . . . . . . . . . . . . . . . . . . . . . . . . 45, 46
Dick v. University of Dundee, S/3814/81, unreported (IT) . . . . . . . . . . . . . . . . . . . 27
Din v. Carrington Viyella Ltd (Jersey Kapwood Ltd) [1982] ICR 256, [1982]
    IRLR 281 (EAT) . . . . . . . . . . . . . . . . . . . . . . . . . . . . . . . . . . . . . . . . . . . . . 14
Donley v. Gallagher, unreported (NIIT) . . . . . . . . . . . . . . . . . . . . . . . . . . . . . . . 18
Dornan v. Belfast City Council [1990] IRLR 179 (NICA) . . . . . . . . . . . . . . . . . . 112
Drake v. Chief Adjudication Officer, Case 150/85, [1986] ECR 1995, [1987] QB
    166, [1986] 3 All ER 65 (ECJ) . . . . . . . . . . . . . . . . . . . . . . 92, 99, 271, 505
Dugdale v. Kraft Foods Ltd [1976] 1 WLR 1288, [1977] 1 All ER 454, [1977]
    ICR 48, [1976] IRLR 368 (EAT) . . . . . . . . . . . . . . . . . . . . . . . . . . . . . . . . 44
Duke v. GEC Reliance [1988] AC 618, [1988] 1 All ER 626, [1988] ICR 339,
    [1988] IRLR 118 HL (E) . . . . . . . . . . . . . . . . . . . . . . . 7-9, 59, 312, 347, 500
Durrant v. North Yorkshire Area Health Authority [1979] IRLR 401 (EAT) . . . . . . . 341
Eaton Ltd v. Nuttall [1977] 1 WLR 549, [1977] 3 All ER 1131, [1977] ICR 872,
    [1977] IRLR 71 (EAT) . . . . . . . . . . . . . . . . . . . . . . . . . . . . . . . . . . . . 45, 331

Edwards v. Bairstow [1956] AC 14 (HL) . . . . . . . . . . . . . . . 299, 327, 334, 437
Eke v. Commissioners for Customs & Excise [1981] IRLR 334 (EAT) . . . . . . . . . . 77
Electrolux Ltd v. Hutchinson [1977] ICR 252, [1976] IRLR 410 (EAT) . . . . . . . . . . 44
Enderby v. Frenchay Health Authority & Secretary of State for Health (1988) 24
    EOR 42 (IT); [1991] IRLR 44 (EAT) . . . . . . . . . . . . . . . 21, 29, 51, 53, 54, 80
England v. Bromley London Borough Council [1978] ICR 1 (EAT) . . . . . . . . . . . . 331
EOC for NI v. Board of Governors, Royal School Dungannon, unreported
    (NIIT) . . . . . . . . . . . . . . . . . . . . . . . . . . . . . . . . . . . . . . . . . . . . . . . . . . . 65
EOC for NI's Application, re [1989] IRLR 64 (NIHC) . . . . . . . . . . . . . . . . . . . . . 16

Fair Employment Agency v. Craigavon Borough Council [1980] IRLR 316
    (NICA) . . . . . . . . . . . . . . . . . . . . . . . . . . . . . . . . . . . . . . . . . . . . . . . . . . 111
Finnegan v. Clowney Youth Training Programme Ltd [1990] IRLR 299 (HL) . . . . . . . 8
Fletcher v. Clay Cross (Quarry Services) Ltd [1979] ICR 1, [1978] IRLR 361
    (CA) . . . . . . . . . . . . . . . . . . . . . . . . . . . . . . . . . . . . . . . . . 320, 342, 345
Forex Neptune (Overseas) Ltd v. Miller [1987] ICR 170 (EAT) . . . . . . . . . . . . . . . 53
Foster v. British Gas plc [1988] ICR 584, [1988] IRLR 354 (CA) . . . . . . . . . . . . . . 8
Foster v. British Gas plc, Case C-188/89, [1990] ECR I-3313, [1990] IRLR 353
    (ECJ) . . . . . . . . . . . . . . . . . . . . . . . . . . . . . . . . . . . . . . . . . . . . . . . . . . . . 8
Fox v. Lloyds Bank (1989) unreported (IT) . . . . . . . . . . . . . . . . . . . . . . . . . . . . 53
Francis v. British Airways Engineering Overhaul Ltd [1982] IRLR 10 (EAT) . . . . . . 393
Fullarton Fabrication (Irvine) Ltd v. Cairney (1987) 2 BEQ 137 . . . . . . . . . . . . . . . 53

Garland v. British Rail Engineering Ltd, also reported as Roberts v. Cleveland
    Area Health Authority, [1979] 1 WLR 754, [1979] 2 All ER 1163, [1979]
    ICR 558, [1979] IRLR 244 (CA) . . . . . . . . . . . . . . . . . . . . . . . . . . . . 59, 349
Garland v. British Rail Engineering Ltd, Case 12/81, [1982] ECR 359, [1983] 2
    AC 751, [1982] 2 WLR 918, [1982] 2 All ER 402, [1982] ICR 420, [1982]
    IRLR 257 (ECJ and HL) . . . . . . . . . . . . . . . . . . . . . 7, 38, 39, 316, 352
Gibson v. NE Education & Library Board, 2/81 EP . . . . . . . . . . . . . . . . . . . . . . . 38
Gill & Coote v. El Vinos Ltd [1983] QB 425, [1983] 2 WLR 155, [1983] 1 All ER
    398 (CA) . . . . . . . . . . . . . . . . . . . . . . . . . . . . . . . . . . . . . . . . . . . . . . . . . 16

Greater Glasgow Health Board v. Carey [1987] IRLR 484 (EAT) . . . . . . . . . . . . . . 22
Greater Manchester Police Authority v. Lea [1990] IRLR 372 (EAT) . . . . . . . . . . . . 27
Greencroft Social Club & Institute v. Mullen [1985] ICR 796 (EAT) . . . . . . . . . . . . 27
Greene v. Broxtowe District Council [1977] 1 All ER 694, [1977] ICR 241
    (EAT) . . . . . . . . . . . . . . . . . . . . . . . . . . . . . . . . . . . . . . . . . . . . . . . . . . . 45
Grieg v. Community Industry [1979] ICR 356, [1979] IRLR 158
    (EAT) . . . . . . . . . . . . . . . . . . . . . . . . . . . . . . . . . . 14, 16, 56, 74, 437, 478
Griggs v Duke Power Co. (1971) 401 US 424 (US Sup. Ct) . . . . . . . . . . . 29, 343-345
                                                                      347, 395, 457, 459
Grimes v. Southern Education & Library Board, unreported (NIIT) . . . . . . . . . . . . . . 17
Gunning v. Mirror Group Newspapers Ltd [1986] ICR 145, [1986] IRLR 27
    (CA) . . . . . . . . . . . . . . . . . . . . . . . . . . . . . . . . . . . . . . . . . . . . . . . . . . . . 69

Hadmor Productions Ltd v. Hamilton [1982] IRLR 102 (HL) . . . . . . . . . . . . . . . . 410
Hammersmith & Queen Charlotte's Special Health Authority v. Cato [1988] ICR
    132 (EAT) . . . . . . . . . . . . . . . . . . . . . . . . . . . . . . . . . . . . . . . . . 7, 39, 61
Hampson v. DES [1988] IRLR 87 (EAT) . . . . . . . . . . . . . . . . . . . . . . . . . . . . . 409
Hampson v. DES [1989] ICR 179, [1989] IRLR 72 (CA) . . 30, 400-402, 405, 406, 407
Handels- og Kontorfunktionaererernes Forbund i Danmark v. Dansk
    Arbejdsgiverforening, Case 109/88, [1989] ECR 3199, [1989] IRLR 532
    (ECJ) . . . . . . . . . . . . . . . . . . . . . . . . . . . . . . . . . . . . . . . . . . . . . . . . . 7, 24
Handels- og Kontorfunktionaererernes Forbund i Danmark v. Dansk
    Arbejdsgiverforening, also reported as Hertz v. Aldi Marked K/S, Case
    179/88, [1990] ECR I-3979, [1991] IRLR 31 (ECJ) . . . . . . . . . . . . . . . . . . . . 18
Handley v. Mono (H) Ltd [1979] ICR 147 (EAT) . . . . . . . . . . . . . . . . . . . . . . . . 341
Hasley v. Fair Employment Agency [1989] IRLR 106 (NICA) . . . . . . . . . . . . . . . . 41
Haughton v. Olau Line (UK) Ltd [1986] 1 WLR 504, [1986] 2 All ER 47, [1986]
    ICR 357, [1986] IRLR 465 (CA) . . . . . . . . . . . . . . . . . . . . . . . . . . . . . . . . . 68
Hayes v. Malleable Working Men's Club [1985] ICR 703, [1985] IRLR 367
    (EAT) . . . . . . . . . . . . . . . . . . . . . . . . . . . . . . . . . . . . . . . . 18, 492-496
Hayward v. Cammell Laird Shipbuilders Ltd [1984] IRLR 463 (IT); [1986] IRLR
    287 (EAT); [1987] IRLR 186 (CA) . . . . . . . . . . . . . . . . . . . . . . . . 282, 287
Hayward v. Cammell Laird Shipbuilders Ltd (No 2) [1988] AC 894, [1988] 2
    WLR 1134, [1988] 2 All ER 257, [1988] ICR 464, [1988] IRLR 257
    HL (E) . . . . . . . . . . . . . . . . . . . . . . . . . . . . . . . . . 36, 282, 293, 299
Hertz v. Aldi Marked K/S: see Handels- og Kontorfunktionaererernes Forbund i
    Danmark v. Dansk Arbejdsgiverforening, Case 179/88 (ECJ)
Home Office v. Holmes [1985] 1 WLR 71, [1984] 3 All ER 549, [1984] ICR 678,
    [1984] IRLR 299 (EAT) . . . . . . . . . . . . . . . . . . 22, 23, 29, 392-394, 397, 464
Horsey v. Dyfed County Council [1982] ICR 755, [1982] IRLR 395 (EAT) . . . . . . . . .
    . . . . . . . . . . . . . . . . . . . . . . . . . . . . . . . . . . 14, 16, 17, 74, 76, 470
Hugh-Jones v. St John's College, Cambridge [1979] ICR 848 (EAT) . . . . . . 10, 67, 69
Hurley v. Mustoe [1981] ICR 490, [1981] IRLR 208 (EAT) . . . . . . 14, 16, 17, 23, 473
Hussein v. Saints Complete House Furnishers [1979] IRLR 343 (IT) . . . . . . . . . . . . 28
Hutchinson v. Westward Television Ltd [1977] ICR 279, [1977] IRLR 69 (EAT) . . . 122

International Brotherhood of Teamsters Ltd v. United States (1977) 431 US 324 . . . . 116
Irish Bank Officials Association v. Banks' Staff Relations Committee, unreported
    (NIIC) . . . . . . . . . . . . . . . . . . . . . . . . . . . . . . . . . . . . . . . . . . . . . . . . . . 38
Irvine v. Prestcold Ltd [1981] ICR 777 (CA) . . . . . . . . . . . . . . . . . . . . . . . . . . . 116
Irving v. Post Office [1987] IRLR 289 (CA) . . . . . . . . . . . . . . . . . . . . . . . . . . . . 79

Jackson & Cresswell v. Chief Adjudication Officer, Joined Cases C-63 & C-64/91
    [1992] ECR I-4737 . . . . . . . . . . . . . . . . . . . . . . . . . . . . . . . . . . 91, 94, 97
Jalota v. Imperial Metal Industry (Kynoch) Ltd [1979] IRLR 313 (EAT) . . . . . 444, 445
James v. Eastleigh Borough Council [1990] 1 QB 61,
    [1989] IRLR 318 (CA) . . . . . . . . . . . . . . . . . . . . 356, 357, 365, 371, 498, 506

James v. Eastleigh Borough Council [1990] 2 AC 751, [1990] 3 WLR 55, [1990]
    2 All ER 607, [1990] ICR 554, [1990] IRLR 288, HL (E) . . . . . . . . 15, **356**, 506
Jenkins v. Kingsgate (Clothing Productions) Ltd (No 2) [1981] 1 WLR 1485,
    [1981] ICR 715, [1981] IRLR 388 (EAT) . . . . . . 7, 52, 300, 323, **338**, 360, 374
Jenkins v. Kingsgate (Clothing Productions) Ltd, Case 96/80, [1981] ECR 911,
    [1981] 1 WLR 972, [1981] ICR 592, [1981] IRLR 228 (ECJ)
                                            7, 23, 286, 298, 322, 338-346
Jeremiah v. Ministry of Defence [1980] QB 87, [1979] 3 WLR 857, [1979] 3 All
    ER 833, [1980] ICR 13 (CA) . . . . . . . . . . . . . . . . . . . . . . . . . . 14, 16, 56, 57
Johnson v. Chief Adjudication Officer, Case C-31/90, [1991] ECR I-3723 (ECJ) . 93, 94
Johnston v. Chief Constable of the Royal Ulster Constabulary, Case 222/84,
    [1986] ECR 1651, [1987] QB 129, [1986] 3 WLR 1038, [1987] ICR 83,
    [1986] IRLR 263 (ECJ) . . . . . . . 6, 12, 24, 59, 63, 64, 334, 508, 510, 512, 520
Jones v. Chief Adjudication Officer [1990] IRLR 533 (CA) . . . . . . . . . . 24, 29, 30, 93


Kearns v. Trust House Forte Catering Ltd (1978 15 June) unreported (EAT) . . . . . . . 341
Kerr v. Haslett (J & J), unreported (NIIT) . . . . . . . . . . . . . . . . . . . . . . . . . . . . . 19
Khanna v. Ministry of Defence [1981] ICR 653, [1981] IRLR 331 (EAT)
                                                77, 112, 384, 442
Kidd v. DRG (UK) Ltd [1985] ICR 405, [1985] IRLR 190 (EAT) . . . . . . . . 23, 28, 30
King v. Great Britain-China Centre [1991] IRLR 513 (CA) . . . . . . . . . . . . . . . . 112
Knight v. AG [1979] ICR 194 (EAT) . . . . . . . . . . . . . . . . . . . . . . . . . . . . . 69, 70
Kowalska v. Freie und Hansestadt Hamburg, Case C-33/89, [1990] ECR I-2591,
    [1990] IRLR 447 (ECJ) . . . . . . . . . . . . . . . . . . . . . . . . . . . . 23, 52, 131


Labour Party v. Turner [1987] IRLR 101 (CA) . . . . . . . . . . . . . . . . . . . . . . . . . 28
Lambeth LBC v. CRE [1990] IRLR 231 (CA) . . . . . . . . . . . . . . . . . . . . . . . . 63, 83
Lawson v. Britfish Ltd [1987] ICR 726, [1988] IRLR 53 (EAT) . . . . . . . . . . . . . . 41
Leverton v. Clwyd County Council [1987] 1 WLR 65, [1987] ICR 158 (EAT) . 109, 294
Leverton v. Clwyd County Council [1989] AC 706, [1989] 2 WLR 47, [1989] 1
    All ER 78, [1989] ICR 33, [1989] IRLR 28 (HL) . . . . . . . . . . . 41, 42, 51, **293**
Lillis v. Ford Motor Co. Ltd, unreported (NIIT) . . . . . . . . . . . . . . . . . . . . . . . . 15
Lindsay v. United Kingdom (1979) 15 Decisions & Reports 247 . . . . . . . . . . . . . . . 87
London Borough of Barking & Dagenham v. Camara [1988] ICR 865, [1988]
    IRLR 373 (EAT) . . . . . . . . . . . . . . . . . . . . . . . . . . . . . . . . . . . . . . . . . 112


Macarthys Ltd v. Smith, Case 129/79, [1980] ECR 1275, [1980] 3 WLR 929,
    [1981] 1 All ER 111, [1980] ICR 672, [1980] IRLR 210 (ECJ) . . . 7, 42. 298, 340
McAuley v. Eastern Health & Social Services Board [1991] IRLR 467 (NICA) . . 46, 47
McLean v. Paris Travel Service Ltd [1976] IRLR 202 (IT) . . . . . . . . . . . . . . . . . . 17
McPherson v. Rathgael Centre for Children & Young People [1991] IRLR 206
    (NICA) . . . . . . . . . . . . . . . . . . . . . . . . . . . . . . . . . . . . . . . . . . . . . . . . . 49
McQuade v. Lobster Pot Restaurant, unreported (NIIT) . . . . . . . . . . . . . . . . . . . 18


Maidment v. Cooper & Co. (Birmingham) Ltd [1978] ICR 1094, [1978] IRLR 462
    (EAT) . . . . . . . . . . . . . . . . . . . . . . . . . . . . . . . . . . . . . . . . . . . . . . . . . . 49
Malone's Application, re [1988] NI Judgments Bulletin . . . . . . . . . . . . . . . . . . . . . 9
Mandla v. Lee [1983] 2 AC 548, [1983] 2 WLR 620, [1983] ICR 385, [1983] 1
    All ER 1062, [1983] IRLR 209 (HL) . . . . . . . . . . . . . . . . . . . . . . . . . 25, 398
Marleasing SA v. La Comercial Internacional de Alimentación, Case C-106/89,
    [1990] ECR I-4135 (ECJ) . . . . . . . . . . . . . . . . . . . . . . . . . . . . . . . . . . . . 9
Marshall v. Southampton & SW Hampshire Area Health Authority (No 2) [1990]
    IRLR 481 (CA) . . . . . . . . . . . . . . . . . . . . . . . . . . . . . . . . . . . . . . . . 7, 115
Marshall v. Southampton & SW Hampshire Area Health Authority, Case 152/84,
    [1986] ECR 723, [1986] QB 401, [1986] 2 WLR 780, [1986] 2 All ER 584,
    [1986] ICR 335, [1986] IRLR 140 (ECJ) . . . 7, 12, 34, 59, 60, 351-354, 512, 518
Martin v. Choc Box, unreported (NIIT) . . . . . . . . . . . . . . . . . . . . . . . . . . . . . . 18

Mateer v. GEC Turbine Generators Ltd, unreported (NIIT) . . . . . . . . . . . . . . . . . 17
Meer v. London Borough of Tower Hamlets [1988] IRLR 399 (CA) . . . . . . . . 22, **411**
Ministry of Defence v. Jeremiah [1978] ICR 984 (EAT) . . . . . . . . . . . . . . . . . . . 117
Ministry of Defence v. Jeremiah [1980] QB 87, [1979] IRLR 436 (CA) . . . . . . 360, 373
                                                        374, 399, 428, 477, 478
Mitchell v. Sun Alliance, unreported (NIIT). . . . . . . . . . . . . . . . . . . . . . . . . . . . 31
Moberly v. Commonwealth Hall (University of London) [1977] IRLR 176
    (EAT). . . . . . . . . . . . . . . . . . . . . . . . . . . . . . . . . . . . . . . . . . . . . 437, 438
Murphy v. Bord Telecom Eireann, Case 157/86, [1988] ECR 673, [1988] IRLR
    267 (ECJ) . . . . . . . . . . . . . . . . . . . . . . . . . . . . . . . . . . . . . . . . . . 49, 310


Nagle v. Fielden [1966] 2 QB 633 (CA) . . . . . . . . . . . . . . . . . . . . . . . . . . . . 9, 10
National Coal Board v. Sherwin [1978] ICR 790, [1978] IRLR 122 (EAT) . 44, 51, 298
National Vulcan Engineering Insurance Group Ltd v. Wade [1979] QB 132,
    [1978] 3 WLR 214, [1978] 3 All ER 121, [1978] ICR 800,
    [1978] IRLR 225 (CA) . . . . . . . . . . . . . . . . . . . . . . . . . . . . . . . . . 50, 111
Neale v. Hereford & Worcester County Council [1985] IRLR 281 (CA). . . . . . . . . 450
Neil v. Ford Motor Co. [1984] IRLR 339 (IT) . . . . . . . . . . . . . . . . . . . . . . . . . . 46
Neil v. Northern Ireland Civil Service, unreported (NIIT) . . . . . . . . . . . . . . . . . . 23
Nelson v. Tyne & Wear PTE [1978] ICR 1183 (EAT). . . . . . . . . . . . . . . . . . . . 118
Newstead v. Department of Transport, Case 192/85, [1987] ECR 4753, [1988] 1
    All ER 129, [1988] IRLR 66 (ECJ) . . . . . . . . . . . . . . . . . . . . . . . . . . . . 38
Nimz v. Freie und Hansestadt Hamburg, Case C-184/89, [1991]
    ECR I-297 (ECJ) . . . . . . . . . . . . . . . . . . . . . . . . . . . . 24, 52, 54, 131
Noble v. David Gold & Son (Holdings) Ltd [1980] ICR 543, [1980] IRLR 252
    (CA) . . . . . . . . . . . . . . . . . . . . . . . . . . . . . . . . . . . . . . . . . . . . . 16, 423
Noone v. NW Thames Regional Health Authority [1988] ICR 813, [1988] IRLR
    195 (CA) . . . . . . . . . . . . . . . . . . . . . . . . . . . . . . . . . . . . 112, 116, 119
Norway's Application, in re (No 2) [1988] 3 WLR 603 (CA) . . . . . . . . . . . . . . . . 408


O'Brien v. Sim-Chem Ltd [1980] 1 WLR 1011, [1980] 3 All ER 132, [1980] ICR
    573, [1980] IRLR 373 (HL) . . . . . . . . . . . . . . . . . . . . . . . . . . . . . . . . . 45
O'Kelly v. Trusthouse Forte plc [1983] IRLR 369 (HL) . . . . . . . . . . . . . . . . . . . 327
Ojutiku v. Manpower Services Commission [1982] ICR 661, [1982] IRLR 418
    (CA). . . . . . . . . . . . . . . . . . . . . . . . . . . 30, 401, 404, 408-410, 460-462
Orphanos v. QMC [1985] AC 761, [1985] 2 WLR 703, [1985] 2 All ER 233,
    [1985] IRLR 349 (HL) . . . . . . . . . . . . . . . . . . . . . . . . . . . . . . . . . 28, 117
Outlook Supplies Ltd v. Parry [1978] 2 All ER 707, [1978] ICR 388, [1978] IRLR
    12 (EAT) . . . . . . . . . . . . . . . . . . . . . . . . . . . . . . . . . . . . . . . . . . . . . . 53
Owen & Briggs v. James [1981] IRLR 133 (EAT); [1982] ICR 618, [1982] IRLR
    502 (CA) . . . . . . . . . . . . . . . . . . . . . . . . . . . . . . . . . . . . . . . . . . 15, 443
Oxford v. DHSS [1977] ICR 884, [1977] IRLR 225 (EAT) . . . . . . . . . . . 108, 111, 442


Page v. Freight Hire (Tank Haulage) Ltd [1981] 1 All ER 394, [1981] ICR 299
    (EAT) . . . . . . . . . . . . . . . . . . . . . . . . . . . . . . . . . . . . . . . . . . . . 57, **476**
Panesar v. Nestlé Co. Ltd [1980] IRLR 60 (EAT); [1980] IRLR 64 (CA) . . . . . . . . 405
                                                            455, 459-462
Peake v. Automotive Products Ltd [1977] IRLR 105 (EAT); [1978] QB 233,
    [1977] 3 WLR 853, [1978] 1 All ER 106, [1977] ICR 968, [1977] IRLR
    365 (CA) . . . . . . . . . . . . . . . . . . . . . . . . . . 14, 56, 57, 77, 372, 373
Pearse v. City of Bradford Metropolitan Council [1988] IRLR 379 (EAT) . . . . . . . . 28
Perera v. Civil Service Commission [1980] ICR 699, [1980] IRLR 233 (EAT) . . . . . 109
Perera v. Civil Service Commission (No 2) [1982] ICR 350, [1982] IRLR 147
    (EAT) . . . . . . . . . . . . . . . . . . . 22, 26, 27, 77, 397, 414, 417, 419
Perera v. Civil Service Commission (No 2) [1983] ICR 428, [1983] IRLR 166
    (CA) . . . . . . . . . . . . . . . . . . . . . . . . . . . . . 22, 26, 27, 77, 413-419

Pickstone v. Freemans plc [1989] AC 66, [1988] 3 WLR 265, [1988] 2 All ER
    803, [1988] ICR 697, [1988] IRLR 357, HL(E) .......... 7, 8, 41, 54, **306**
                                                          507, 508, 513
Pointon v. University of Sussex [1979] IRLR 119 (CA) ..................... 49
Porcelli v. Strathclyde Regional Council [1985] ICR 177, [1984] IRLR 467 (EAT);
    see also Strathclyde Regional Council v. Porcelli ..................... 488
Prestcold Ltd v. Irvine [1980] ICR 610, [1980] IRLR 267 (EAT); [1981] ICR 777
    (CA) ........................................................ 77, 118
Preston v. Rodgers (JCJ), Edenmore Hotel, 9/82 EP, unreported (NIIT) ......... 44
Price v. Civil Service Commission [1977] 1 WLR 1417, [1978] 1 All ER 1228,
    [1978] ICR 27, [1977] IRLR 291 (EAT) ......... 23, 25, 26, 74, 396-398, **483**
Price v. Rhondda Urban District Council [1923] 2 Ch 372 (ChD) ............... 9


Queen v. ...: see R. v. ...
Quinnen v. Hovells [1984] ICR 525, [1984] IRLR 227 (EAT) .............. 35, 69


R. v. Birmingham City Council, ex parte EOC [1989] AC 1155, [1989] 2 WLR
    520, [1989] 1 All ER 769, [1989] IRLR 173 (HL) ............ 9, 15, 16, 359
                                       360, 363, 365, 369, 372, 373, 498
R. v. Boardman [1975] AC 421 (HL) ..................................... 443
R. v. CAC, ex parte Hy-Mac Ltd [1979] IRLR 461 (CA) ..................... 40
R. v. CAC, ex parte Norwich Union (1988) 22 EOR 41 (QBD) ................ 40
R. v. CRE, ex parte Westminster City Council [1985] ICR 827 (CA) ......... 14, 363
R. v. Henn [1981] AC 850 (HL) ........................................ 507
R. v. Home Secretary, ex parte Brind [1991] AC 696 (HL) .................. 5
R. v. Kilbourne [1973] AC 729 (HL) .................................... 443
R. v. Moloney [1985] AC 905 (HL) ..................................... 368
R. v. Secretary of State for Education & Science, ex parte Keating (1985) 84 LGR
    469 (QBD) ........................................................ 360, 374
R. v. Secretary of State for Employment, ex parte EOC [1991] IRLR 493 (HC) ...... 30
R. v. Secretary of State for Social Security, ex parte EOC, Case C-9/91 (ECJ) ...... 93
R. v. Secretary of State for Social Security, ex parte Smithson, Case C-243/90
    [1992] ECR I-467 (ECJ) ............................................. 94
R. v. Secretary of State for Transport, ex parte Factortame Ltd, Case C-213/89,
    [1990] ECR I-2433, [1990] 3 WLR 818, [1990] CMLR 573 (ECJ and HL) ..... 3
R. v. Secretary of State, ex parte Schaffter [1987] IRLR 53 (HC) .............. 28


Rainey v. Greater Glasgow Health Authority [1985] IRLR 414 (Ct of Sess.) ...... 324
Rainey v. Greater Glasgow Health Authority [1987] AC 224, [1986] 3 WLR 1017,
    [1987] 1 All ER 65, [1987] ICR 129, [1987] IRLR 26, HL (Sc.) ..... 21, 30, 51
                                               298, 318, 401, 409, 410
Rasul v. CRE [1978] IRLR 203 (EAT) ................................... 109
Raval v. DHSS [1985] ICR 685, [1985] IRLR 370 (EAT) .................... 25
Read v. Tiverton District Council & Bull [1977] IRLR 202 (IT) ............... 79
Ready Mixed Concrete (South East) Ltd v. Minister of Pensions & National
    Insurance [1968] 2 QB 497 .......................................... 69
Record Production Chapel of the Daily Record & Sunday Mail of SOGAT 82 v.
    Turnbull & EOC (1984, 16 April) unreported (Scottish EAT) ............. 80
Reed Packaging Ltd v. Boozer [1988] ICR 391, [1988] IRLR 333 (EAT) ...... 53, 291
Rice v. Fon-A-Car [1980] ICR 133 (EAT) ............................. 70, 73
Rinner-Kühn v. FWW Spezial-Gebäudereinigung GmbH & Co. KG, Case
    171/88, [1989] ECR 2743, [1989] IRLR 493 (ECJ) ............. 7, 23, 38, 52
Roberts v. Birds Eye Walls Ltd [1991] IRLR 19 (EAT) ..................... 40
Roberts v. Cleveland Area Health Authority [1978] ICR 370, [1977] IRLR 401
    (EAT) ........................................................ 347, 349, 352
Roberts v. Cleveland Area Health Authority (CA), also reported as Garland v.
    British Rail Engineering Ltd, [1979] 1 WLR 754, [1979] 2 All ER 1163,
    [1979] ICR 558, [1979] IRLR 244 (CA) ............................. 59, 349

Roberts v. Tate & Lyle Food & Distribution Ltd [1983] IRLR 240 (EAT) . . . . . 350, 353
Rolls Royce v. Doughty [1987] ICR 932, [1987] IRLR 447 (EAT) . . . . . . . . . . . . . . 8
Rosedale Mouldings Ltd v. Sibley [1980] IRLR 387 (EAT) . . . . . . . . . . . . . . . . . 490
Rummler v. Dato-Druck GmbH, Case 237/85, [1986] ECR 2101, [1987] ICR
774, [1987] IRLR 32 (ECJ) . . . . . . . . . . . . . . . . . . . . . . . . . . . . . 47, 48, 330

Saunders v. Richmond-upon-Thames LBC [1978] ICR 75, [1977] IRLR 362
(EAT) . . . . . . . . . . . . . . . . . . . . . . . . . . . . . . . . . . . . . . . . . . . . . 74
Schmidt v. Austicks Bookshops Ltd [1978] ICR 85 (EAT) . . . . . . . . . . . . . . . . . 19
Science Research Council v. Nassé [1980] AC 1028, [1979] 3 WLR 762, [1979] 3
All ER 673, [1979] ICR 921, [1979] IRLR 465 (HL) . . . . . . . . . . . . . . 108, 444
Scott v. Beal College (1985) 3 EOR 38 (IT) . . . . . . . . . . . . . . . . . . . . . . . . . . . . . 49
Secretary of State for Scotland v. Henley (1983, 19 May) unreported (Scottish
EAT) . . . . . . . . . . . . . . . . . . . . . . . . . . . . . . . . . . . . . . . . . . . . . . . 65
Secretary of State for Social Security v. Thomas, idem v. Cooze, idem v. Beard,
idem v. Murphy, Morley v. Secretary of State for Social Security [1990]
IRLR 436 (CA) . . . . . . . . . . . . . . . . . . . . . . . . . . . . . . . . 7, 92, **500**
Seide v. Gillette Industries Ltd [1980] IRLR 427 (EAT) . . . . . . . . . . . . . . . 472, 474
Selvarajan v. Inner London Education Authority [1980] IRLR 313 (EAT) . . . . . . . . . 109
Sheffield Metropolitan District Council v. Siberry [1989] ICR 208 (EAT) . . . . . . . . . 105
Sheikh v. Anderton [1989] 2 WLR 1102, [1989] 2 All ER 684, [1989] ICR 373
(CA) . . . . . . . . . . . . . . . . . . . . . . . . . . . . . . . . . . . . . . . . . . . . . 64, 69
Shields v. Coomes (E) (Holdings) Ltd [1978] 1 WLR 1408, [1979] 1 All ER 456,
[1978] ICR 1159, [1978] IRLR 263 (CA) . . . . . . . 44, 50, 53, 321, 344, 423, 478
Short v. Poole Corporation [1926] 1 Ch 66 (CA) . . . . . . . . . . . . . . . . . . . . . . . . . 9
Showboat Entertainment Centre Ltd v. Owens [1984] 1 WLR 384, [1984] ICR 65,
[1984] 1 All ER 836, [1984] IRLR 7 (EAT) . . . . . . . . . . . . . . . . . . . . . . . 16
Simon v. Brimham Associates [1987] IRLR 307 (CA) . . . . . . . . . . . . . . . . . . 16, 74
Singh v. Rowntree Mackintosh Ltd [1979] IRLR 199 (Sc EAT) . . . . 401, 408, 459, 460
Sisley v. Britannia Security Systems Ltd [1983] ICR 628, [1983] IRLR 404
(EAT) . . . . . . . . . . . . . . . . . . . . . . . . . . . . . . . . . . . . . . . . . . . . . . 65
Skyrail Oceanic Ltd v. Coleman [1981] ICR 864, [1981] IRLR 398 (CA) . . . . . . 14, 116
**420**, 473, 475, 517
Snowball v. Gardner Merchant Ltd [1987] ICR 719, [1987] IRLR 397 (EAT) . . . . . . 16
19, **488**
Snoxell v. Vauxhall Motors Ltd [1978] 1 QB 11, [1977] 3 WLR 189, [1977] 3 All
ER 770, [1977] ICR 700, [1977] IRLR 123 (EAT) . . . . . . . . . . . . . . . . . 50, 53
Sorbie v. Trust House Forte Hotels Ltd [1976] IRLR 371 (EAT) . . . . . . . . . . . . . . 54
Sotgiu v. Deutsche Bundespost, Case 152/73, [1974] ECR 153 (ECJ) . . . . . . . . . . . 508
Steel v. Union of Post Office Workers [1978] 1 WLR 64, [1978] 2 All ER 504,
[1978] ICR 181, [1977] IRLR 288 (EAT) . . . . . . . . . . . . . . . . . 24, 29, 77, 401
405, 408, 455, 459, 460
Stockton-on-Tees Borough Council v. Brown [1989] AC 20, [1988] 2 WLR 935,
[1988] ICR 410, [1988] 2 All ER 129 (HL) . . . . . . . . . . . . . . . . . . . . . . . . 18
Strathclyde Regional Council v. Porcelli [1986] ICR 564, [1986] IRLR 134 (Ct of
Sess.): see also Porcelli v. Strathclyde Regional Council . . . . 14, 16, 19, **425**, 451
Sun Alliance & London Insurance Ltd v. Dudman [1978] ICR 551 (EAT) . . . . . . . . . 53

Tanna v. Post Office [1981] ICR 374 (EAT) . . . . . . . . . . . . . . . . . . . . . . . . . . . . 69
Tennant Textile Colours Ltd v. Todd [1989] IRLR 3 (NICA) . . . . . . . . . . 107, 123, 124
Thomas v. National Coal Board [1987] ICR 757, [1987] IRLR 451 (EAT) . . . . . . 41, 42
44, 51
Thorndyke v. Bell Fruit (North Central) Ltd [1979] IRLR 1 (IT) . . . . . . . . . . . . . 23, 27
Timex Corporation v. Hodgson [1982] ICR 63, [1981] IRLR 530 (EAT) . . . . . . . . . . 63
Todd v. Eastern Health & Social Services Board & DHSS, unreported (NIIT) . . . . . . 18
Tottenham Green Under-Fives Centre v. Marshall [1989] ICR 214, [1989] IRLR
147 (EAT) . . . . . . . . . . . . . . . . . . . . . . . . . . . . . . . . . . . . . . . . . . . . 63
Tottenham Green Under-Fives Centre v. Marshall (No 2) [1991] IRLR 162
(EAT) . . . . . . . . . . . . . . . . . . . . . . . . . . . . . . . . . . . . . . . . . . . . . . 63

Training Commission v. Jackson, *The Independent*, 25 January 1990 . . . . . . . . . . . . 23
Trico Folberth Ltd v. Groves [1976] IRLR 327 (IT) . . . . . . . . . . . . . . . . . . . . . . 102
Turley v. Allders Department Stores Ltd [1980] ICR 66, [1980] IRLR 4 (EAT)18, 492-497
Turton v. MacGregor Wallcoverings Ltd [1977] IRLR 249 (EAT) . . . . . . . . . . . . . . 23

United Biscuits Ltd v. Young [1978] IRLR 15 (EAT) . . . . . . . . . . . . . . . . . . . . . 53

Virdee v. ECC Quarries Ltd [1978] IRLR 295 (IT) . . . . . . . . . . . . . . . . . . . . . . 108
von Colson & Kamann v. Land Nordrhein-Westfalen, Case 14/83, [1984] ECR
      1891 (ECJ) . . . . . . . . . . . . . . . . . . . . . . . . . . . . . . . . . . . 312, 353, 354

Waddington v. Leicester Council for Voluntary Services [1977] 1 WLR 544,
      [1977] 2 All ER 633, [1977] ICR 266, [1977] IRLR 32 (EAT) . . . . . . . 44, 50, 53
Wallace v. SE Education & Library Board [1980] IRLR 193 (NICA) . . . . . . . . 111, 112
                                                                                                436, 442
Watches of Switzerland Ltd v. Savell [1983] IRLR 141 (EAT) . . . . . . . . . . . 21, 25, 29
Webb v. Emo Air Cargo (UK) Ltd [1990] ICR 442, [1990] IRLR 124 (EAT) . . . 18, **491**
Webster v. Hoover plc (1989) unreported (IT) . . . . . . . . . . . . . . . . . . . . . . . . . . 53
Weinberger v. Wiesenfeld (1975) 95 SC 1225 (US Sup. Ct) . . . . . . . . . . . . . . . . 422
West Midlands PTE v. Singh [1988] 1 WLR 730, [1988] 2 All ER 873, [1988]
      ICR 614, [1988] IRLR 186 (CA) . . . . . . . . . . . . . . . . . . . . . 77, 109, 112, **439**
Wileman v. Minilec Engineering Ltd [1988] IRLR 144 (EAT) . . . . . . . . . . . . . . . . . 19
Williams v. Dyfed County Council [1986] ICR 449 (EAT) . . . . . . . . . . . . . . . . . . 109
Winton v. Northern Ireland Electricity (1989) unreported (NIIT) . . . . . . . . . . . . . . . 53
Wong v. Greater London Council, 542/79, unreported (EAT) . . . . . . . . . . . . . . . . . 27
Worringham v. Lloyds Bank Ltd, Case 69/80, [1981] ECR 767, [1981] 1 WLR
      950, [1981] 2 All ER 434, [1981] ICR 558, [1981] IRLR 178 (ECJ) . . . 6, 8, 37-39
Wright v. Civil Service Commission, No 9324/79/B, unreported (IT) . . . . . . . . . . . . 28

# COMMENTARY

# ON EQUALITY LAW

# 1 GENERAL

## 1.1 INTRODUCTION

### 1.1.1 INTRODUCTION TO NATIONAL LEGAL SYSTEM

The United Kingdom is a unitary State made up of Great Britain (comprising England, Scotland and Wales) together with Northern Ireland. A basic component of the constitutional structure is the concept of parliamentary sovereignty, under which Parliament is the supreme law-making institution whose actions may not be challenged in any national court. This doctrine is now, however, subject to the EC law requirement that EC law overrides national law, and this has been given effect in UK law by virtue of the European Communities Act 1972.[1]

The United Kingdom has three separate legal systems, that of England and Wales, that of Scotland, and that of Northern Ireland. For the purposes of this Commentary, the law of England and Wales is discussed, having for all intents and purposes the same content as in the other legal systems, unless specific differences are noted.

The judicial system comprises a number of courts which are used for general civil and criminal business, together with a number of specialist tribunals.

### 1.1.2 ECONOMIC AND SOCIAL CONTEXT

A snapshot of the British labour force in the early 1990s shows that it is roughly 58 per cent male and 42 per cent female. Excluding the self-employed, there are nearly 10 million women workers compared with nearly 12 million male workers. A significant proportion of women employees work part-time and the vast majority of those who work part-time are women. Women are segregated horizontally and vertically from men at work, i.e. women are found predominantly in certain types of occupations and infrequently found in other types of occupations, and in those occupations where there are women, they tend to be disproportionately represented in lower level, low-paid jobs. Women's pay is substantially below men's, being about 75 per cent of the average gross hourly earnings of

---

1    See further *R. v. Secretary of State for Transport*, ex parte *Factortame Ltd*, Case C-213/89, [1990] ECR I-2433, [1990] 3 WLR 818, [1990] CMLR 573 (ECJ and HL) and §1.2.2 below.

full-time employees. With overtime included the percentage of male pay earned by women falls to about 66 per cent. These differences appear to be due to a variety of factors of which discrimination and inequality of opportunity are two elements. The extent to which these are causal factors is, however, controversial.

## 1.2         SOURCES

### 1.2.1         INTERNATIONAL STANDARDS

#### 1.2.1.1         Human rights

*United Nations*

Under the auspices of the United Nations a number of general treaties have been promulgated which have aspects of relevance to equality between men and women. The United Kingdom is a party to the following: the Universal Declaration of Human Rights, 1948, the International Covenant on Economic, Social and Cultural Rights, 1966, which entered into force on 3 January 1976, and the International Covenant on Civil and Political Rights, 1966, which entered into force on 23 March 1976. None of these treaties has, however, been incorporated into United Kingdom domestic law.

*International Labour Organization*

See §1.2.1.2 below.

*Council of Europe*

A number of general treaties have been promulgated under the auspices of the Council of Europe, aspects of which are of relevance to equality between men and women. Those to which the United Kingdom is a party include, in particular, the European Convention for the Protection of Human Rights and Fundamental Freedoms, 1950 (ECHR), which entered into force on 3 September 1953, and the European Social Charter, 1961, which entered into force on 26 February 1965. (The Additional Protocol to the Social Charter, opened for signature from May 1988, prohibits discrimination in employment on grounds of sex.) Neither of these treaties has been incorporated into United Kingdom domestic law.

Attempts to use the ECHR in domestic courts as a source from which legal argument may be derived have met with mixed success. There has also been considerable discussion of the relationship between British courts and the ECHR, in particular the domestic application of the Convention in the

United Kingdom. See, for example, *AG* v. *Guardian Newspapers Ltd*;[1] *AG* v. *Guardian Newspapers Ltd (No 2)*;[2] *R*. v. *Home Secretary, ex parte Brind*.[3] Aspects of United Kingdom immigration policies have been held contrary to the non-discrimination requirement in art. 14 ECHR by the European Court of Human Rights in *Abdulaziz, Cabales & Balkandali* v. *United Kingdom*.[4]

### 1.2.1.2          Treaties on special questions

*United Nations*

Two treaties to which the United Kingdom is a party have been promulgated under the auspices of the United Nations, aspects of which are specifically aimed at the issues of equality between men and women: the Convention on the Political Rights of Women, 1953, which entered into force on 7 July 1954, and the Convention on the Elimination of All Forms of Discrimination against Women, 1979, which entered into force on 3 September 1981. Neither of these treaties has been incorporated into United Kingdom domestic law.

*International Labour Organization*

The International Labour Organization has sponsored a number of treaties with aspects specifically aimed at the issues of equality between men and women, in particular the Equal Remuneration Convention, 1951 (No 100), which entered into force on 23 May 1953, and the Discrimination (Employment and Occupation) Convention, 1958 (No 111), which entered into force on 15 June 1960. Neither of these treaties has been incorporated into United Kingdom domestic law. The United Kingdom is a party to Convention No 100 but not to Convention No 111. The relationship between equal treatment for men and women and prohibitions on night-working has given rise to the Night Work Convention, 1990 (No 171), the Night Work Recommendation, 1990 (No 178) and the 1990 Protocol to the Night Work (Women) Convention, 1948 (No 89).

*Council of Europe*

See §1.2.1.1 above.

---

1    [1987] 1 WLR 1248, [1987] 3 All ER 316 (HL).
2    [1988] 3 WLR 776, [1988] 3 All ER 545 (HL).
3    [1991] AC 696 (HL). See also DREMCZEWSKI, *European Human Rights Convention in Domestic Law* (1983), pp. 269-322.
4    (1985) 7 EHRR 471 (ECHR).

**1.2.2          EUROPEAN COMMUNITY LAW**

The starting point for setting out EC law on this issue is the Treaty establishing the European Economic Community, in particular art. 119, which entrenches the principle of equal pay. Following on from the Council Resolution of 21 January 1974 concerning a social action programme, several Directives were passed in the 1970s: Council Directive of 10 February on the approximation of the laws of the Member States relating to the application of the principle of equal pay for men and women (75/117/EEC); Council Directive of 9 February 1976 on the implementation of the principle of equal treatment for men and women as regards access to employment, etc. (76/207/EEC); and Council Directive of 19 December 1978 on the progressive implementation of the principle of equal treatment for men and women in matters of social security (79/7/EEC).

Between 1980 and 1988 a further series of Equality Directives was passed following the Commission Communication to the Council, presented on 14 December 1981, on the new Community action programme on the promotion of equal opportunities for women (1982-85), and the Commission Communication to the Council, transmitted on 20 December 1985, on equal opportunities for women (medium-term Community programme 1986-90). These Directives were: Council Directive of 24 July 1986 on the implementation of the principle of equal treatment for men and women in occupational social security schemes (86/378/EEC); and Council Directive of 11 December 1986 on the application of the principle of equal treatment as between men and women engaged in an activity, including agriculture, in a self-employed capacity (86/613/EEC).

**1.2.2.1          Direct effect of Community law**

The concept of the direct effect of Community law has been examined and clarified in a significant number of decisions by the European Court of Justice (ECJ). In addition to the direct applicability of regulations, provided for in the Treaty (art. 189), the Court has extended the principle of direct effect to some Treaty articles and directives. The provisions must be clear, precise and unconditional: see in particular the cases of *Defrenne* v. *Sabena (No 2)*,[1] *Worringham* v. *Lloyds Bank Ltd*,[2] *Johnston* v. *RUC*,[3] *Burton* v. *British Railways Board*,[4] *Marshall* v. *Southampton & SW Hampshire Area*

---

[1]   Case 43/75, [1976] ECR 455 (ECJ).
[2]   Case 69/80, [1981] ECR 767, [1981] 1 WLR 950, [1981] 2 All ER 434, [1981] ICR 558, [1981] IRLR 178 (ECJ).
[3]   Case 222/84, [1986] ECR 1651, [1987] QB 129, [1986] 3 WLR 1038, [1987] ICR 83, [1986] IRLR 263 (ECJ).
[4]   Case 19/81, [1982] ECR 555, [1982] QB 1080, [1982] 3 WLR 387, [1982] 3 All ER 537, [1982] ICR 329, [1982] IRLR 116 (ECJ).

*Health Authority ,*[1] *Bilka-Kaufhaus GmbH* v. *Weber von Hartz,*[2] *Macarthys Ltd* v. *Smith,*[3] *Jenkins* v. *Kingsgate (Clothing Productions) Ltd,*[4] *Garland* v. *British Rail Engineering Ltd,*[5] *Rinner-Kühn* v. *FWW Spezial-Gebäudereinigung GmbH & Co. KG,*[6] *Handels- og Kontorfunktionaerernes Forbund i Danmark* v. *Dansk Arbejdsgiverforening,*[7] *Barber* v. *Guardian Royal Exchange Assurance Group.*[8] In the remaining part of this section, aspects of the domestic courts' decisions on direct effect will briefly be considered.

## Conditions of direct effect

The conditions under which the Directives have direct effect in UK law have been considered by a number of domestic courts: see *Marshall* v. *Southampton & SW Hampshire Area Health Authority (No 2),*[9] *Hammersmith & Queen Charlotte's Special Health Authority* v. *Cato,*[10] *Duke* v. *GEC Reliance,*[11] *Pickstone* v. *Freemans plc,*[12] *Jenkins* v. *Kingsgate (Clothing Productions) Ltd (No 2),*[13] *Secretary of State for Social Security* v. *Thomas.*[14]

## Vertical/horizontal direct effect

An individual may rely on the Directive against an organ of the State whether it acts as an employer or as a public authority: see *Marshall* v. *Southampton & SW Hampshire Area Health Authority,*[15] and *Johnston*

---

1   Case 152/84, [1986] ECR 723, [1986] QB 401, [1986] 2 WLR 780, [1986] 2 All ER 584, [1986] ICR 335, [1986] IRLR 140 (ECJ).
2   Case 170/84, [1986] ECR 1607, [1987] ICR 110, [1987] IRLR 317 (ECJ).
3   Case 129/79, [1980] ECR 1275, [1980] 3 WLR 929, [1981] 1 All ER 111, [1980] ICR 672, [1980] IRLR 210, (1980) 1 BEQ 402 (ECJ).
4   Case 96/80, [1981] ECR 911, [1981] 1 WLR 972, [1981] ICR 592, [1981] IRLR 228 (ECJ).
5   Case 12/81, [1982] ECR 359, [1983] 2 AC 751, [1982] 2 WLR 918, [1982] 2 All ER 402, [1982] ICR 420, [1982] IRLR 257 (ECJ and HL).
6   Case 171/88, [1989] ECR 2743, [1989] IRLR 493 (ECJ).
7   Case 109/88, [1989] ECR 3199, [1989] IRLR 532 (ECJ).
8   Case C-262/88, [1990] ECR I-1889, [1990] 2 All ER 660, [1990] IRLR 240 (ECJ).
9   [1990] IRLR 481 (CA).
10  [1988] ICR 132 (EAT).
11  [1988] AC 618, [1988] 1 All ER 626, [1988] ICR 339, [1988] IRLR 118 HL (E).
12  [1989] AC 66, [1988] 3 WLR 265, [1988] 2 All ER 803, [1988] ICR 697, [1988] IRLR 357 HL (E).
13  [1981] 1 WLR 1485, [1981] ICR 715, [1981] IRLR 388 (EAT).
14  [1990] IRLR 436 (CA).
15  Case 152/84, [1986] ECR 723, [1986] QB 401, [1986] 2 WLR 780, [1986] 2 All ER 584, [1986] ICR 335, [1986] IRLR 140 (ECJ).

v. *RUC.*[1] In two cases, domestic courts have held that the lack of horizontal
direct effect had the effect that EC law could not be relied on in domestic
courts: *Duke* v. *GEC Reliance*,[2] and *Finnegan* v. *Clowney Youth Training
Programme Ltd*,[3] but see also *Pickstone* v. *Freemans plc.*[4]

### Effect against public/private employer

The issue of what constitutes an organ of the state has been considered
by UK domestic courts in *Foster* v. *British Gas plc*[5] and *Rolls Royce*
v. *Doughty*,[6] but these interpretations have now been overtaken by the ECJ
decision in *Foster* v. *British Gas plc*[7] in which the Court takes a liberal
approach to what constitutes a state body.

### 1.2.2.2     Retrospective implementation

There are two possible meanings of the idea of retrospective effect. The
first concerns the effect of a judicial decision on actions which occurred prior
to that decision. The general principle is that, within the constraints of time-
limits for the initiation of a case, decisions are retrospective. In two cases,
however, the ECJ has decided that interpretations of EC equality law which
it arrived at should have prospective effect only: *Defrenne* v. *Sabena
(No 2)*,[8] and *Barber* v. *Guardian Royal Exchange Assurance Group.*[9] There
have been no decisions of UK courts following this approach. In
*Worringham* v. *Lloyds Bank Ltd*[10] the ECJ refused the Bank's request that the
effects of the judgment be limited in respect of pay for periods prior to the
judgment.

A second meaning of retrospection concerns the effect of EC legislation
on the interpretation of domestic legislation enacted earlier than the EC
legislation. In *Duke* v. *GEC Reliance*[11] the House of Lords held that the SDA
1975 should not be construed in accordance with the provisions of the Equal
Treatment Directive, which was not enacted until 1976. This was also the

---

1    Case 222/84, [1986] ECR 1651, [1987] QB 129, [1986] 3 WLR 1038, [1987] ICR 83,
     [1986] IRLR 263 (ECJ).
2    [1988] AC 618, [1988] 1 All ER 626, [1988] ICR 339, [1988] IRLR 118 HL (E).
3    [1990] IRLR 299 (HL).
4    [1989] AC 66, [1988] 3 WLR 265, [1988] 2 All ER 803, [1988] ICR 697, [1988]
     IRLR 357 HL (E).
5    [1988] ICR 584, [1988] IRLR 354 (CA).
6    [1987] ICR 932, [1987] IRLR 447 (EAT).
7    Case C-188/89, [1990] ECR I-3313, [1990] IRLR 353 (ECJ).
8    Case 43/75, [1976] ECR 455 (ECJ).
9    Case C-262/88, [1990] ECR I-1889, [1990] 2 All ER 660, [1990] IRLR 240 (ECJ).
10   Case 69/80, [1981] ECR 767, [1981] 1 WLR 950, [1981] 2 All ER 434, [1981] ICR
     558, [1981] IRLR 178 (ECJ).
11   [1988] AC 618, [1988] 2 All ER 626, [1988] ICR 339, [1988] IRLR 118 HL (E).

approach adopted in *Finnegan* v. *Clowney Youth Training Programme Ltd.*[1] This approach does not seem compatible, however, with the decision by the ECJ in *Marleasing SA* v. *La Comercial Internacional de Alimentación*[2] in which the ECJ held that a national court is obliged to interpret national law as far as possible in accordance with rules laid down by Community law, whether prior or subsequent.

### 1.2.3 CONSTITUTIONAL LAW

The constitutional law of the United Kingdom is a combination of common law (judicially created traditions and standards) and statute law. Prior to the enactment of domestic legislation, there were some attempts to argue that the common law provided protection to those discriminated against on grounds of sex, but these were unsuccessful (*Bebb* v. *Law Society*,[3] *Price* v. *Rhondda Urban District Council*,[4] *Short* v. *Poole Corporation*[5]) in all but one case (*Nagle* v. *Fielden*[6]).

Since the enactment of the domestic legislation, there have been attempts to use the judicial review procedure — in which the applicant argues that a public body is acting *ultra vires*, unreasonably, or contrary to natural justice — to enforce anti-discrimination standards, including both those of domestic and European law. In *Re Malone's Application*[7] judicial review was refused because the issue in dispute, an allegation by a clerk that discriminatory retirement ages were being applied by a university, was not a 'public law' issue. In *R.* v. *Birmingham City Council,* ex parte *EOC*,[8] however, an application for judicial review was successful and a declaration was granted to the effect that the Council was acting *ultra vires* in breach of anti-discrimination law requirements. Several of the cases mentioned subsequently arise from judicial review, and the process is becoming increasingly important as a mechanism for enforcement.

There is no one overriding written constitutional document, nor a Bill of Rights enforceable in the domestic courts. There are therefore no formal judicially enforceable constitutional constraints on the ambit of the equality legislation; but nor, on the other hand, are there any enforceable constitutional underpinnings for this legislation.

---

1   [1990] IRLR 299 (HL).
2   Case C-106/89, [1990] ECR I-4135 (ECJ).
3   [1914] 1 Ch 286 (CA).
4   [1923] 2 Ch 372 (Ch D).
5   [1926] 1 Ch 66 (CA).
6   [1966] 2 QB 633 (CA).
7   [1988] NIJB.
8   [1989] AC 1155, [1989] 2 WLR 520, [1989] 1 All ER 769, [1989] IRLR 173 (HL).

## 1.2.4          LEGISLATION

### 1.2.4.1          Prior legislation

Before the legislation of the 1970s, 1980s, and 1990s (see §1.2.4.2), the United Kingdom had little legislation prohibiting discrimination against women or providing for equality in the occupational sphere. The one major exception to this was the Sex Disqualification (Removal) Act 1919 which provided, in part, and subject to a number of exceptions, that:

> ... a person shall not be disqualified by sex or marriage from the exercise of any public function, or from being appointed to or holding any civil or judicial office or post, or from entering or assuming or carrying on any civil profession or vocation, or from admission to any incorporated society ... .

A study of the Act concluded, however, that 'the most remarkable thing about [the Act] is how little it has been relied upon as a means of establishing the unlawfulness of sex discrimination in employment'.[1] The Act was cited in *Nagle* v. *Fielden*[2] as a source of public policy. For an unsuccessful attempt to rely on this Act see *Hugh-Jones* v. *St John's College, Cambridge.*[3]

Of more practical importance is the effect of the equality legislation passed since the 1970s (see §1.2.4.2) on other statutory provisions, including prior statutory provisions. In general, under UK law, the effect of subsequent legislation is generally to repeal prior inconsistent legislation. However, the SDA 1975 preserved the legality of some discriminatory legislation which might otherwise have been impliedly repealed, and of actions carried out under it if required by that legislation. In addition, s. 7(2)(f) allowed an exception where 'the job needs to be held by a man because of restrictions imposed by the laws regulating the employment of women'. The Employment Act 1989 amended the SDA 1975 and repealed s. 7(2)(f). The Sex Discrimination Act 1975 (Exemption of Police Federation Constitutional and Electoral Arrangements) Order 1989[4] preserves the effect of specified provisions of the Police Federation Regulations 1969[5] by disapplying s. 1(1) of the 1989 Act.

The Employment Act 1989 now provides in general for the overriding of some legislative provisions requiring direct discrimination as respects employment or training (s. 1). The Act applies to any provision of an Act passed before the SDA 1975, or an instrument approved or made by or under such an Act (including one approved or made after the passing of the SDA

1    CREIGHTON, 1979, p. 68.
2    [1966] 2 QB 633 (CA).
3    [1979] ICR 848 (EAT).
4    SI 1989 No 2420.
5    SI 1969 No 1787.

1975). The Act provides that such a provision shall be of no effect in so far as it imposes a requirement to do an act which would be rendered unlawful by any of the provisions of the SDA 1975 prohibiting discrimination in employment or vocational training. Where such legislation is alleged to be indirectly discriminatory, the employer may argue that the statutory requirements are justifiable in the circumstances.

The Act repeals certain specific discriminatory enactments and preserves others. In addition, s. 2 provides that the Secretary of State has power to repeal statutory provisions which he considers require discrimination as respects employment or training. Where it appears to the Secretary of State that a provision of an Act passed before the Employment Act 1989, or an instrument approved or made by or under such an Act (including one approved or made after the passing of the 1989 Act), requires the doing of something which would (within the meaning of the SDA 1975) constitute such an act of discrimination, he may by order make such provision (whether by amending, repealing or revoking the relevant provision or otherwise) as he considers appropriate for removing any such requirement.

Section 6 of the Act further empowers the Secretary of State to exempt particular acts of discrimination required by or under statute from the general overriding provision of s. 1(1) and thus the application of the SDA 1975. The Secretary of State may by order make such provision as he considers appropriate for disapplying the previous provisions of the 1989 Act in the case of any provision to which it appears to him that that s. 1(1) would otherwise apply.

In addition, the SDA 1975, as amended by the 1989 Act, provides in ss 51 and 51A that certain acts which would otherwise be discriminatory are not to be regarded as discriminatory if done to comply with a number of prior statutory provisions. These include certain provisions relating to pregnancy, maternity, health and safety and are considered further below (see §§4.2.1.3, 4.14).

## 1.2.4.2      Present legislation

As regards equal treatment, the principal Act is the Sex Discrimination Act, passed in 1975.[1] A number of subsidiary pieces of legislation were required to put various parts of the Act into full effect and these were also passed in 1975: the Sex Discrimination (Formal Investigations) Regulations

---

[1]    The Northern Ireland equivalent is the Sex Discrimination (Northern Ireland) Order 1976 (SI 1976 No 1042).

1975,[1] the Sex Discrimination (Questions and Replies) Order 1975,[2] and the Sex Discrimination and Equal Pay (Offshore Employment) Order 1987.[3]

The Industrial Tribunals (Non-discrimination Notices Appeals) Regulations 1977[4] and the Industrial Tribunals (Rules of Procedure) Regulations 1985[5] effected various changes in the procedures for adjudicating sex discrimination cases. In 1986, following *Marshall*[6] and the second infringement decision against the UK relating to equality law by the ECJ,[7] the Sex Discrimination Act 1986 was passed. Following *Johnston* v. *RUC*[8] the Sex Discrimination (Amendment) Order 1988[9] was passed. The Employment Act 1989 also substantially amended the SDA 1975, particularly concerning protective legislation.

As regards the implementation of the Social Security Directives, Sch. 1 to the Social Security Act 1980 was designed to implement the 1979 Directive. The Health and Social Security Act 1984 further replaced various discriminatory benefits, as did the Social Security Act 1986. The Social Security Act 1989 sought to implement the 1986 Directive.

---

1   SI 1975 No 1993.
2   SI 1975 No 2048.
3   SI 1987 No 930.
4   SI 1977 No 1094.
5   SI 1985 No 16.
6   *Marshall* v. *Southampton & SW Hampshire Area Health Authority,* Case 152/84, [1986] ECR 723, [1986] QB 401, [1986] 2 WLR 780, [1986] 2 All ER 584, [1986] ICR 335, [1986] IRLR 140 (ECJ).
7   *Commission of the European Communities* v. *United Kingdom,* Case 165/82, [1983] ECR 3431 (ECJ).
8   Case 222/84, [1986] ECR 1651, [1987] QB 129, [1986] 3 WLR 1038, [1987] ICR 83, [1986] IRLR 263 (ECJ).
9   SI 1988 No 249.

# 2  BASIC CONCEPTS

## 2.1  EQUALITY AND DISCRIMINATION

There are eight basic concepts which are used in UK law relating to equality between men and women. In the area of equal pay, there are the four concepts of 'like work', 'work rated as equivalent', 'work of equal value' and 'discrimination'. In the area of equal treatment and social security, there are the four concepts of 'equality of opportunity', 'direct discrimination', 'indirect discrimination' and 'equal treatment'. This section will discuss in greater detail the ideas of 'direct' and 'indirect' discrimination. It should also be noted that in general there is a symmetry between restrictions on discrimination against men and women. Thus, for example, the SDA 1975, s. 2 provides that the provisions of the Act 'relating to sex discrimination against women, are to be read as applying equally to the treatment of men, and for that purpose shall have effect with such modifications as are requisite'. Where protection is asymmetrical, this is noted below.

## 2.2  DIRECT DISCRIMINATION

### 2.2.1  DEFINITION

The definition of discrimination in the SDA 1975 provides in part that:

> A person discriminates against a woman in any circumstances relevant for the purposes of any provision of this Act if ... on the ground of her sex he treats her less favourably than he treats or would treat a man ... .[1]

There is a similar definition of discrimination against married persons (see below). Although not referred to as such in the legislation, these definitions of discrimination have come to be termed 'direct discrimination'. These definitions of direct discrimination are similar to the definition of direct discrimination in the Race Relations Act 1976,[2] and references to interpretations of one are regularly used in the elucidation of the similar concept in the other Act.

The definition has three main parts. One element relates to the reason why the action complained about was carried out: for the action complained of to be direct discrimination it must have been done 'on the ground of [the

---

[1]  SDA 1975, s. 1(1)(a).
[2]  Race Relations Act 1976, s. 1(1)(a).

complainant's] sex'. A second element relates to the detriment suffered by the person: for the action complained of to be direct discrimination it must have amounted to 'less favourable treatment'. The third element relates to the comparator involved: for the action complained of to be direct discrimination it must have been treatment less favourable than that which was or would have been accorded a person of the opposite sex ('... he treats or would treat a man'). These three elements will now be examined in greater detail.

## 2.2.1.1    Reason

*Intentional*

Although in one of the first cases under the SDA 1975 an approach was taken by the Court of Appeal which appeared to restrict direct discrimination to a situation in which the respondent had a hostile motive,[1] this approach is no longer followed. In *Grieg* v. *Community Industry*,[2] the Employment Appeal Tribunal (EAT) concluded that:

> ... subject to express exceptions, it is not an answer to say that what was done was done with good motives or was done, even objectively, in the best interests of the person concerned or in the best interests of the business with which that case is involved.

Subsequently, the Court of Appeal itself reconsidered the position in *Jeremiah* v. *Ministry of Defence*[3] and held that a hostile motive was not required.[4]

The idea of a discriminatory intention therefore goes much beyond the idea of discriminatory motive. In particular, it includes acting on the basis of stereo-typed assumptions. It is less favourable treatment 'on the ground of ... sex', for example, to act on the assumption that the husband is the primary source of income for the household;[5] or that women with children are unreliable.[6] It is also less favourable treatment 'on the ground of ... sex' for an employer to withdraw an appointment because of objections by other employees to the appointment of a woman. In *R*. v. *CRE*, ex parte *Westminster City Council*[7] the Court of Appeal upheld the decision of the

---

1    *Peake* v. *Automotive Products Ltd* [1978] QB 233, [1977] 3 WLR 853, [1978] 1 All ER 106, [1977] ICR 968, [1977] IRLR 365 (CA).
2    [1979] ICR 356, [1979] IRLR 158 (EAT).
3    [1980] QB 87, [1979] 3 WLR 857, [1979] 3 All ER 833, [1980] ICR 13 (CA).
4    See also *Porcelli* v. *Strathclyde Regional Council* [1986] ICR 564, [1986] IRLR 134 (Ct of Sess.); *Din* v. *Carrington Viyella Ltd (Jersey Kapwood Ltd)* [1982] ICR 256, [1982] IRLR 281 (EAT).
5    *Skyrail Oceanic Ltd* v. *Coleman* [1981] ICR 864, [1981] IRLR 398 (CA); *Horsey* v. *Dyfed County Council* [1982] ICR 755, [1982] IRLR 395 (EAT).
6    *Hurley* v. *Mustoe* [1981] ICR 490, [1981] IRLR 208 (EAT).
7    [1985] ICR 827 (CA).

CRE to issue a non-discrimination notice. The notice recorded that the Council, by its Assistant Director of Cleansing, had unlawfully discriminated against a black employee by withdrawing his appointment as a temporary refuse collector following pressure from white workmen. The majority accepted that it was open to the CRE to reach the decision it did. If the Council official believed that the real ground of the objection was racial, he was obliged to evaluate the ostensible objection with care, and his failure to do so showed that he was acting in a way in which he would not have acted had the employee been white. And if the official had withdrawn the appointment because he was afraid of industrial action on a racially motivated objection to the transfer, then the CRE was able to make a finding of unlawful discrimination.[1] For an employer's decision to be directly discriminatory, it is not necessary that the gender factor be the sole reason for the employer's decision, provided it is an important factor in an employer's decision.[2]

*Unintentional*

Two important cases decided by the House of Lords clarify further the scope of the definition of direct discrimination. In *R.* v. *Birmingham City Council,* ex parte *EOC*[3] the House of Lords held that the Council had unlawfully discriminated by providing fewer grammar school places for girls than boys. Thus a girl who achieved the same academic standard as a boy was less likely to be awarded a school place at a grammar school than a boy. The Council set a higher pass mark for girls than boys in the grammar school entrance examination. Lord Goff held that whatever may have been the intention or motive of the Council, it was because of their sex that the girls in question received less favourable treatment than the boys and so were the subject of discrimination.

In *James* v. *Eastleigh Borough Council*[4] the House of Lords held that the Council discriminated unlawfully in charging a man aged 61 admission to a Council swimming pool while allowing his wife of the same age free admission, due to the Council policy of not charging admission to those who had reached the state pension age, which is 65 for men and 60 for women. The House of Lords adopted a broad interpretation of the words 'on the grounds of', regarding the relevant issue as whether the complainant would have received the same treatment from the respondent *but for* his or her sex, even where there is no discriminatory intention or motive.

---

1    See also *Lillis* v. *Ford Motor Co. Ltd* , unreported (NIIT).
2    See *Owen & Briggs* v. *James* [1982] ICR 618, [1982] IRLR 502 (CA).
3    [1989] AC 1155, [1989] 2 WLR 520, [1989] 1 All ER 769, [1989] IRLR 173 (HL).
4    [1990] 2 AC 751, [1990] 3 WLR 55, [1990] 2 All ER 607, [1990] ICR 554, [1990] IRLR 288 HL (E).

### 2.2.1.2 Detriment

The idea of less favourable treatment involves a comparison (either actual or hypothetical) between the treatment accorded to a woman and that accorded to a man, and *vice versa*. In *Chiu* v. *British Aerospace plc*,[1] for example, the plaintiff failed to establish direct discrimination because the industrial tribunal found that he had not shown that other employees had been treated differently from him in similar circumstances.

The element of 'less favourable treatment' also involves a requirement that the treatment must in some way be unfavourable. Giving a person of one sex less choice than a person of another sex constitutes less favourable treatment. A non-employment case illustrates these points. In *Gill & Coote* v. *El Vinos Ltd*[2] two women sought to be served at a bar; they were refused service. The management required that women (but not men) be served at the tables provided and not at the bar counter itself. The women sued and the management argued that this treatment was not less favourable, just different. The plaintiffs succeeded; the denial of something which was clearly in demand by both men and women was 'less favourable treatment'.[3]

### 2.2.1.3 Comparator

Section 5(3) of the SDA 1975 provides that 'a comparison of the case of persons of different sex ... must be such that the relevant circumstances in the one case are the same, or not materially different, in the other'. So, for example, the treatment accorded a woman on the basis of her physical strength is to be compared with the treatment accorded a man of similar physical strength.[4] The treatment of a woman with children is to be compared with the treatment of a man with children.[5]

---

1   [1982] IRLR 56 (EAT).
2   [1983] QB 425, [1983] 2 WLR 155, [1983] 1 All ER 398 (CA).
3   See further *R.* v. *Birmingham City Council*, ex parte *EOC* [1989] AC 1155, [1989] 2 WLR 520, [1989] 1 All ER 769, [1989] IRLR 173 (HL); *Simon* v. *Brimham Associates* [1987] IRLR 307 (CA); *Snowball* v. *Gardner Merchant Ltd* [1987] ICR 719, [1987] IRLR 397 (EAT); *Porcelli* v. *Strathclyde Regional Council* [1986] ICR 564, [1986] IRLR 134 (Ct of Sess.); *Jeremiah* v. *Ministry of Defence* [1980] QB 87, [1979] 3 WLR 857, [1979] 3 All ER 833, [1980] ICR 13 (CA).
4   *Noble* v. *David Gold & Son (Holdings) Ltd* [1980] ICR 543, [1980] IRLR 252 (CA).
5   *Hurley* v. *Mustoe* [1981] ICR 490, [1981] IRLR 208 (EAT). See also *Grieg* v. *Community Industry* [1979] ICR 356, [1979] IRLR 158 (EAT); *Horsey* v. *Dyfed County Council* [1982] ICR 755, [1982] IRLR 395 (EAT); *Showboat Entertainment Centre Ltd* v. *Owens* [1984] 1 WLR 384, [1984] ICR 65, [1984] 1 All ER 836, [1984] IRLR 7 (EAT); *Dhatt* v. *McDonald's Hamburger Ltd* [1988] ICR 591 (EAT); Re *EOC for NI's Application* [1989] IRLR 64 (NIHC).

**2.2.2          EXTENDED DEFINITION**

**2.2.2.1          Marital status**

There are two provisions relevant to the prohibition of discrimination on the grounds of marital status. Neither provision separately, nor taken together, prohibits discrimination on grounds of marital status to the extent that other forms of sex discrimination are prohibited. The first provision is in the SDA 1975, s. 1(2) which provides that:

> If a person treats or would treat a man differently according to the man's marital status, his treatment of a woman is for the purposes of subsection (1)(a) [direct discrimination] to be compared to his treatment of a man having the like marital status.

Secondly, the SDA 1975, s. 3(1) provides:

> A person discriminates against a married person of either sex ... if-
> (a)    on the ground of his or her marital status he treats that person less favourably than he treats or would treat an unmarried person of the same sex, ... .

There is an equivalent provision prohibiting indirect discrimination against married persons.[1] The effect of these provisions is that discrimination against single people because they are not married is not unlawful.[2]

**2.2.2.2          Family status**

This ground is covered only indirectly under sex or marital status (see §2.2.2.1 above). So for example in *Grimes* v. *Southern Education & Library Board* (NIIT) it was held to be discrimination on grounds of marital status when a married woman failed to secure promotion and a less qualified female candidate was chosen instead, where the decision not to promote the married woman was based on a presumption that married women with young children would experience difficulties. See also *Mateer* v. *GEC Turbine Generators Ltd* (NIIT).

**2.2.2.3          Pregnancy**

The SDA 1975, s. 2(2) provides that 'no account shall be taken of special treatment afforded to women in connection with pregnancy or childbirth'. However, the question which this section considers is whether less favourable treatment on grounds of pregnancy is unlawfully

---

1    SDA 1975, s. 3(1)(b). See *Hurley* v. *Mustoe* [1981] ICR 490, [1981] IRLR 208 (EAT); *Horsey* v. *Dyfed County Council* [1982] ICR 755, [1982] IRLR 395 (EAT).
2    *Bick* v. *Royal West of England Residential School for the Deaf* [1976] IRLR 326 (IT); *McLean* v. *Paris Travel Service Ltd* [1976] IRLR 202 (IT).

discriminatory. Dismissal on the ground of pregnancy is specifically deemed unfair under the Employment Protection (Consolidation) Act 1978 (EPCA), s. 60.[1] The woman must, however, first serve a qualifying period of two years' service before she enjoys protection. For that reason, some women have sought protection under the SDA 1975, which provides for no such qualifying period. There is no specific protection accorded to women on the grounds of pregnancy under the Act. The question has arisen, therefore, whether the general prohibition against discrimination on grounds of sex protects pregnant women from discrimination.

In *Turley* v. *Allders Department Stores Ltd*,[2] the EAT held that to dismiss a woman because she is pregnant is not within the definition of unlawful discrimination; the woman lay member of the tribunal dissented. In subsequent cases, however, the EAT held that the *Turley* case was in effect wrongly decided. In *Hayes* v. *Malleable Working Men's Club*[3] industrial tribunals were instructed by the EAT to regard *Turley* as 'confined to its own restricted (and assumed) facts' — the ultimate ignominy for any case and, in effect, its death knell. The EAT remitted the claims to a freshly constituted industrial tribunal for re-hearing. The EAT concluded that both direct and indirect discrimination would be relevant. In *Webb* v. *Emo Air Cargo (UK) Ltd*,[4] the EAT again held that *Turley* should not be followed and held that discrimination on grounds of pregnancy could be unlawful sex discrimination. However, the Tribunal held that the treatment of pregnant women should be compared with that accorded men with sickness. In *Todd* v. *Eastern Health & Social Services Board & DHSS* (NIIT) a similar approach was adopted in a case under the Equal Pay Act (Northern Ireland) 1970, as amended.

The sickness comparison was not followed in Northern Ireland. In several cases industrial tribunals in Northern Ireland regarded pregnancy not as the same as sickness, but as a unique gender characteristic.[5] Unfavourable treatment based on pregnancy was held to amount to sex discrimination. This limitation appears now to be unnecessary and inappropriate under EC law: see *Dekker* v. *Stichting Vormingscentrum voor Jonge Volwassenen (VJV-Centrum) Plus*.[6]

---

1    See also *Stockton-on-Tees Borough Council* v. *Brown* [1989] AC 20, [1988] 2 WLR 935, [1988] ICR 410, [1988] 2 All ER 129 (HL).
2    [1980] ICR 66, [1980] IRLR 4 (EAT).
3    [1985] ICR 703, [1985] IRLR 367 (EAT).
4    [1990] ICR 442, [1990] IRLR 124 (EAT).
5    *Donley* v. *Gallagher; McQuade* v. *Lobster Pot Restaurant; Martin* v. *Choc Box.*
6    Case C-177/88, [1990] ECR I-3941, [1991] IRLR 27 (ECJ), *Handels- og Kontorfunktionaerernes Forbund i Danmark* v. *Dansk Arbejdsgiverforejning*, Case 179/88, [1990] ECR I-3979; reported as *Hertz* v. *Aldi Marked K/S* [1991] IRLR 31 (ECJ).

## 2.2.2.4        Sexual harassment

In *Porcelli* v. *Strathclyde Regional Council*[1] the Court of Session (Inner House) held that if the form of any unfavourable treatment or any material part of it which was meted out included a significant element of a sexual character to which a man would not be vulnerable, the treatment was on grounds of the woman's sex. The weapon used was based upon the sex of the victim. If the form of treatment would not have been used against an equally disliked man, and the treatment of the woman was different in a material respect from that which would have been inflicted on a male colleague, then the action was unlawful direct sex discrimination.

Where an employer failed to protect women employees from sexual harassment by another employee this was held not to be unlawful discrimination by the employer if he would have treated complaints on other issues not related to gender in the same way: *Balgobin & Francis* v. *London Borough of Tower Hamlets*.[2] A woman alleging sexual harassment may also be examined as to her reputation and attitude as to sexual matters, as this is regarded as being relevant both to issues of credibility and extent of detriment.[3] However, a single act of sexual harassment may amount to sex discrimination.[4]

## 2.2.2.5        Physical attributes

There is no case law or statutory provision dealing explicitly with this issue.

## 2.2.2.6        Dress codes

In *Schmidt* v. *Austicks Bookshops Ltd*[5] the EAT held that to allow men but not women to wear trousers was not unlawful discrimination. However, this decision has been heavily criticized,[6] and may well not reflect current approaches. In *Kerr* v. *Haslett (J & J)* (NIIT), for example, a dress code was held to be discriminatory against men.

---

1    [1986] ICR 564, [1986] IRLR 134 (Ct of Sess.).
2    [1987] ICR 829, [1987] IRLR 401 (EAT).
3    *Snowball* v. *Gardner Merchant Ltd* [1987] ICR 719, [1987] IRLR 397 (EAT).
4    *Bracebridge Engineering Ltd* v. *Darby* [1990] IRLR 3 (EAT). See also *Wileman* v. *Minilec Engineering Ltd* [1988] IRLR 144 (EAT), and *De Souza* v. *AA* [1986] ICR 514, [1986] IRLR 103 (CA).
5    [1978] ICR 85 (EAT).
6    See, for example, HEPPLE, Encyclopedia IB-802.

## 2.3          INDIRECT DISCRIMINATION

### 2.3.1          DEFINITION

The SDA 1975 provides in s. 1(1)(b) that:

> A person discriminates against a woman in any circumstances relevant for the purposes of any provision of this Act if-
>
> ...
>
> (b)    he applies to her a requirement or condition which applies or would apply equally to a man but-
>> (i)    which is such that the proportion of women who can comply with it is considerably smaller than the proportion of men who can comply with it, and
>> (ii)   which he cannot show to be justifiable irrespective of the sex of the person to whom it is applied, and
>> (iii)  which is to her detriment because she cannot comply with it.

This definition of discrimination has come to be termed 'indirect discrimination'.

The SDA 1975 provides in s. 3(1) that with regard to discrimination against married persons in the employment field:

> A person discriminates against a married person of either sex in any circumstances relevant for the purposes of any provision of [this Act] if-
>
> ...
>
> (b)    he applies to that person a requirement or condition which he applies or would apply equally to an unmarried person but-
>> (i)    which is such that the proportion of married persons who can comply with it is considerably smaller than the proportion of unmarried persons of the same sex who can comply with it, and
>> (ii)   which he cannot show to be justifiable irrespective of the marital status of the person to whom it is applied, and
>> (iii)  which is to that person's detriment because he cannot comply with it.[1]

The Social Security Act 1989 (Sch. 5) seeks to implement the 1986 Directive. Every employment-related benefit scheme shall comply with the principle of 'equal treatment'. The principle of equal treatment is that persons of one sex shall not, on the basis of sex, be treated less favourably than persons of the other sex in any respect relating to an employment-related scheme. Where any provision of the scheme imposes on both male and female members a requirement or condition which is such that the proportion of persons of the one sex ('the sex affected') who can comply with it is considerably smaller than the proportion of persons of the other sex who can

---

1     The Race Relations Act 1976, s. 1(1)(b) contains a similar definition of indirect discrimination with regard to ethnic minority groups.

do so, and which is not justifiable irrespective of the sex of the members, the imposition of that requirement or condition shall be regarded as less favourable treatment of persons of the sex affected. If any question arises whether a condition or requirement is or is not justifiable irrespective of the sex of the members, it shall be for those who assert that it is so justifiable to prove that fact.

As regards equal pay, the decision of the EAT in *Enderby* v. *Frenchay Health Authority & Secretary of State for Health*[1] holds that the Equal Pay Act 1970 (EqPA) and EC law empower applicants to contest a pay practice as indirectly discriminatory, though in several respects it appears to take a restrictive view of what constitutes indirect sex discrimination in this context (see below). The concept of indirect discrimination has been applied to a limited extent with regard to the permitted defences under the EqPA. A number of cases have held that an indirectly discriminatory policy or practice cannot amount to a 'material difference' and 'material factor' defence.[2]

## 2.3.2        SUSPECT CRITERIA

The United Kingdom definition thus requires, first, that the applicant identify a suspect criterion. The relevant terms of the statute which this section will consider are 'requirement or condition which applies or would apply equally to a man'. In a number of early cases under the legislation, the need to identify a condition or requirement was liberally interpreted by the courts and tribunals. In *Clarke & Powell* v. *Eley (IMI) Kynoch Ltd*[3] the EAT held that the purpose of the legislation is to eliminate practices which have a disproportionately adverse impact on women, and the words 'condition or requirement' should not therefore be given a narrow meaning excluding cases which fell within the mischief with which the Act was designed to deal. In *Watches of Switzerland Ltd* v. *Savell*[4] the applicant complained that the defects in the company's promotions procedures were such that the effect was that women were less likely to be promoted. The condition or requirement specified by the applicant was that in order to be promoted she had to satisfy the vague, subjective and unadvertised promotion procedure of the company. The EAT held that this formulation could amount to a condition or requirement.

Subsequently, however, a stricter approach was adopted and in two cases the Court of Appeal held that a condition or requirement exists only

---

1     [1991] IRLR 44 (EAT).
2     See *Rainey* v. *Greater Glasgow Health Authority* [1987] AC 224, [1986] 3 WLR 1017, [1987] 1 All ER 65, [1987] ICR 129, [1987] IRLR 26, HL (Sc.). See also §3.9 below.
3     [1983] ICR 165, [1982] IRLR 482 (EAT).
4     [1983] IRLR 141 (EAT).

where it amounts to a 'complete bar if not met'.[1] Therefore, if an employer expresses a preference for certain attributes which operate with a discriminatory impact but do not amount to a complete bar on selection if not met, the employer may not be acting unlawfully.

In *Clymo* v. *Wandsworth London Borough Council*[2] the EAT held that if an employee was engaged to work in a full-time capacity, then it was not open to that person to argue that this constituted the applying of a requirement or condition to the person because the obligation to work full-time was 'part and parcel' of the job. In *Briggs* v. *NE Education & Library Board*,[3] however, the Northern Ireland Court of Appeal interpreted the phrase more widely, holding that even if the nature of the job requires it to be full-time that does not preclude full-time work being regarded as a 'condition or requirement'.

*Breadwinner, head of family:* The definition of indirect discrimination may, in certain circumstances, prohibit discrimination on the grounds of being the 'breadwinner' or 'head of the family'.

*Full-time/part-time work:* The Equal Opportunities Commission (EOC) Code of Practice specifies in para. 29:

> In an establishment where part-timers are solely or mainly women, unlawful indirect discrimination may arise if, as a group, they are treated less favourably than other employees without justification.

The Code recommends that where part-time workers do not enjoy *pro rata* pay or benefits with full-time workers, the arrangements should be reviewed to ensure that they are justified without regard to sex.

In the domestic courts the issue has been considered extensively.[4] In *Clymo* v. *Wandsworth London Borough Council*,[5] however, the EAT held that a requirement that an employee work full-time was not discriminatory.[6]

---

1   *Perera* v. *Civil Service Commission No 2* [1982] ICR 350, [1982] IRLR 147 (EAT); [1983] ICR 428, [1983] IRLR 166 (CA) and *Meer* v. *London Borough of Tower Hamlets* [1988] IRLR 399 (CA).
2   [1989] ICR 250, [1989] IRLR 241 (EAT).
3   [1990] IRLR 181 (NICA).
4   *Clarke & Powell* v. *Eley (IMI) Kynoch Ltd* [1983] ICR 165, [1982] IRLR 482 (EAT) (employees must work full-time in order to avoid redundancy: unlawful); *Home Office* v. *Holmes* [1985] 1 WLR 71, [1984] 3 All ER 549, [1984] ICR 678, [1984] IRLR 299 (EAT) (in some circumstances employers must accommodate a desire to work part-time).
5   [1989] ICR 250, [1989] IRLR 241 (EAT).
6   But see *Briggs* v. *NE Education & Library Board* [1990] IRLR 181 (NICA). See also *Greater Glasgow Health Board* v. *Carey* [1987] IRLR 484 (EAT).

This issue has also been considered on a number of occasions in the ECJ, in particular in *Jenkins* v. *Kingsgate (Clothing Productions) Ltd*,[1] *Bilka-Kaufhaus GmbH* v. *Weber von Hartz*,[2] *Rinner-Kühn* v. *FWW Spezial-Gebäudereinigung GmbH & Co KG*,[3] and *Kowalska* v. *Freie und Hansestadt Hamburg*.[4] The implications of the *Rinner-Kühn* case have yet to be fully explored in the United Kingdom context. Some regard the decision as casting doubt on the continued validity of those parts of employment protection legislation for which there is a weekly hours of work qualification, including unfair dismissal, redundancy pay, and statutory maternity pay. Some of these issues are to be explored in a forthcoming judicial review.

*Working hours:* See the following cases: *Home Office* v. *Holmes*,[5] *Kidd* v. *DRG (UK) Ltd*,[6] *Cobb* v. *Secretary of State for Employment*,[7] and *Briggs* v. *NE Education & Library Board*.[8]

*Marital status:* Relevant cases include *Hurley* v. *Mustoe*,[9] *Kidd* v. *DRG (UK) Ltd*,[10] and *Training Commission* v. *Jackson*.[11]

*Family status:* See *Thorndyke* v. *Bell Fruit (North Central) Ltd*.[12]

*Pregnancy:* See §2.2.2.3 above.

*Mobility requirement:* There is no case law or statutory provision dealing explicitly with this issue.

*Strength:* There is no case law or statutory provision dealing explicitly with this issue.

*Age limits:* Age limits have been considered to be discriminatory in a number of cases, including *Price* v. *Civil Service Commission*,[13] and *Turton* v. *MacGregor Wallcoverings Ltd*.[14]

---

1   Case 96/80, [1981] ECR 911, [1981] 1 WLR 972, [1981] ICR 592, [1981] IRLR 228 (ECJ).
2   Case 170/84, [1986] ECR 1607, [1987] ICR 110, [1987] IRLR 317 (ECJ).
3   Case 171/88, [1989] ECR 2743, [1989] IRLR 493 (ECJ).
4   Case C-33/89, [1990] ECR I-2591, [1990] IRLR 447 (ECJ).
5   [1985] 1 WLR 71, [1984] 3 All ER 549, [1984] ICR 678, [1984] IRLR 299 (EAT).
6   [1985] ICR 405, [1985] IRLR 190 (EAT).
7   [1989] ICR 506, [1989] IRLR 464 (EAT).
8   [1990] IRLR 181 (NICA).
9   [1981] ICR 490, [1981] IRLR 208 (EAT).
10   [1985] ICR 405, [1985] IRLR 190 (EAT).
11   *The Independent*, 25 January 1990.
12   [1979] IRLR 1 (IT).
13   [1977] 1 WLR 1417, [1978] 1 All ER 1228, [1978] ICR 27, [1977] IRLR 291 (EAT).
14   [1977] IRLR 249 (EAT). See also *Neil* v. *Northern Ireland Civil Service* (NIIT).

*Minimum height:* There is no case law or statutory provision dealing explicitly with this issue. However, in Northern Ireland the police removed a minimum height requirement so as to comply with the Equal Treatment Directive following the *Johnston* case.[1]

*Seniority:* In a number of cases seniority requirements have been held to be indirectly discriminatory: see *Clarke & Powell v. Eley (IMI) Kynoch Ltd*[2] and *Steel v. Union of Post Office Workers*.[3] This relatively strict approach was questioned following the ECJ decision in *Handels- og Kontorfunktionaerernes Forbund i Danmark v. Dansk Arbejdsgiverforening* apparently holding that seniority requirements in pay were to be scrutinized on a less strict basis than other requirements.[4] In *Nimz v. Freie und Hansestadt Hamburg*,[5] the ECJ held however that seniority requirements had to be objectively justified by the employer where they had a disproportionate effect on women.

*Preference for existing employees:* There is no case law or statutory provision dealing explicitly with this issue.

### 2.3.3      DISPROPORTIONATE IMPACT

Having established a 'requirement or condition' which is applied equally to all persons, a complainant alleging indirect discrimination must show that the proportion of persons of one gender who can comply with it is considerably smaller than the proportion of persons not of that gender who can comply with it. In *Jones v. Chief Adjudication Officer*[6] the Court of Appeal summarized the process of reasoning necessary to establish adverse impact. Mustill LJ set out seven points. For ease of illustration he assumed that the complaint stemmed from the failure of a woman to satisfy a relevant positive qualification for selection, and that only one such qualification was in issue:[7]

1.   Identify the criterion for selection;
2.   Identify the relevant population, comprising all those who satisfy all the other criteria for selection ... ;
3.   Divide the relevant population into groups representing those who satisfy the criterion and those who do not;
4.   Predict statistically what proportion of each group should consist of women;
5.   Ascertain what are the actual male/female balances in the two groups;

---

1    *Johnston v. RUC*, Case 222/84, [1986] ECR 1651, [1987] QB 129, [1986] 3 WLR 1038, [1987] ICR 83, [1986] IRLR 263 (ECJ).
2    [1983] ICR 165, [1982] IRLR 482 (EAT).
3    [1978] 1 WLR 64, [1978] 2 All ER 504, [1978] ICR 181, [1977] IRLR 288 (EAT).
4    Case 109/88, [1989] ECR 3199, [1989] IRLR 532 (ECJ).
5    Case C-184/89, [1991] ECR I-297 (ECJ).
6    [1990] IRLR 533 (CA).
7    *Loc. cit.* (p. 537).

6.   Compare the actual with the predicted balances;
7.   If women are found to be under-represented in the first group and over-
     represented in the second, it is proved that the criterion is discriminatory.

Three issues arise from this element of the definition: (i) what is the
meaning of 'can comply'? (ii) what is the meaning of 'considerably smaller'?
and (iii) to what extent must the disparate impact be shown to be the result of
a discriminatory intention? We shall discuss the first issue, before turning to
consider various aspects of the second and third questions below.

*'Can comply'*

A liberal approach has been taken, in general, to the meaning of 'can
comply'. The House of Lords (in a race discrimination case) has held that it
means 'can in practice' or 'can consistently with the customs or values of the
particular group'.[1] In *Price* v. *Civil Service Commission*[2] the EAT interpreted
the phrase in the sex discrimination context to allow the tribunal to take into
account 'the current or usual behaviour of women as observed in practice'.

In *Clarke & Powell* v. *Eley (IMI) Kynoch Ltd*[3] the EAT held that the
point of time at which the proportion of men and of women who 'can comply'
with the requirement is considered must be the same point in time, i.e. the
date the applicant alleges she suffered a detriment. In *Watches of Switzerland
Ltd* v. *Savell*,[4] however, the EAT held that the fact that she might satisfy the
condition in future meant that she could comply with it.

*Statistical evidence*

British courts and tribunals have decided few of the issues which may
arise with respect to the use of statistics. What are the proper sources of
statistics? What is the relevant geographic area of these statistics? What is
the proper time frame for the statistics? How much disproportionate impact
is 'considerable'? On what basis is one to decide between conflicting
conclusions based on different statistical tests each of which is equally
appropriate? Should the primary focus be on the percentage of the minority
actually hired, or on isolating and eliminating single exclusionary criteria in
the overall hiring process? Nor, in the industrial tribunals, is a consistent
approach taken when answers are attempted. The deficiencies of the
adversarial process are particularly evident, so that the sophistication of the
approach taken by industrial tribunals is apparently considerably influenced

---

1   *Mandla* v. *Lee* [1983] 2 AC 548, [1983] 2 WLR 620, [1983] ICR 385, [1983] 1 All
    ER 1062, [1983] IRLR 209 (HL).
2   [1977] 1 WLR 1417, [1978] 1 All ER 1228, [1978] ICR 27, [1977] IRLR 291 (EAT).
3   [1983] ICR 165, [1982] IRLR 482 (EAT).
4   [1983] IRLR 141 (EAT). See also *Raval* v. *DHSS* [1985] ICR 685, [1985] IRLR 370
    (EAT).

by the sophistication of the evidence presented by the parties. Those cases in which these issues have been discussed will be noted below.

In *Price* v. *Civil Service Commission*[1] Phillips J indicated the broad acceptability of sophisticated statistical evidence provided that there was evidence from the statistician and the opportunity for him to be cross-examined on the proper analysis and inferences to be drawn from the statistics. Since then the courts appear to have become concerned that sophisticated statistical evidence should not become the norm. In *Clay Cross (Quarry Services) Ltd* v. *Fletcher*[2] the Court of Appeal stressed the need to avoid 'legalism' (per Lawton LJ) in the interpretation of the EqPA and reiterated its desire to return to as uncomplicated a construction of the Act as possible because of the function of industrial tribunals. In that case the Court so construed the Act as not to require complicated statistical evidence and contrasted its preferred approach with that of an equivalent American case.

A second reason is the difficulty of obtaining statistical information of the type which would be required. In Great Britain employers are not required to collect statistics of the racial and gender composition of their workforce.[3] Without such a requirement, such statistics are often unavailable. Establishing a *prima facie* case of indirect discrimination thus assumes the use of statistical evidence to establish that the use of a criterion has had an adverse impact on a minority group or women, but, since there is no requirement that employers collect or analyse relevant statistics, the means to do so may often not be available. The effect of this omission is to make it time-consuming, expensive and on occasion almost impossible to make an indirect discrimination case, due to the absence of relevant statistics. This was recognized in *Perera* v. *Civil Service Commission (No 2)* where the EAT stated that it considered it:

> ... most undesirable that, in all cases of indirect discrimination, elaborate statistical evidence should be required before the case can be found proved. The time and expense involved in preparing and proving statistical evidence can be enormous, as experience in the United States has demonstrated. It is not good policy to require such evidence to be put forward ... .[4]

Nevertheless, the degree of adverse impact necessary to establish a *prima facie* case is likely to continue to be an important issue in litigation. In *Price* v. *Civil Service Commission*[5] the EAT was not prepared to decide whether the proportion was considerably smaller and the case was remitted

---

1    [1977] 1 WLR 1417, [1978] 1 All ER 1228, [1978] ICR 27, [1977] IRLR 291 (EAT).
2    [1978] 1 WLR 1429, [1979] 1 All ER 474, [1979] ICR 1, [1978] IRLR 361 (CA).
3    In Northern Ireland, however, monitoring is now required of the religious composition of the workforce, and, in the same context, of its gender composition.
4    [1982] ICR 350, [1982] IRLR 147 (EAT); [1983] ICR 428, [1983] IRLR 166 (CA).
5    [1977] 1 WLR 1417, [1978] 1 All ER 1228, [1978] ICR 27, [1977] IRLR 291 (EAT).

to the industrial tribunal for further statistical evidence. In the industrial tribunal, the Civil Service Commission conceded that the age ban was such that the proportion of women who could comply with it was considerably smaller than the proportion of men who could comply with it, and that it was to the applicant's detriment. The EAT indicated, however, that it should not be made too difficult to establish a *prima facie* case of indirect discrimination, since 'compliance with subpara. (i) is only a preliminary step, which does not lead to finding that an act is one of discrimination unless the person acting fails to show that it is justifiable'. In *Dick* v. *University of Dundee*[1] the industrial tribunal apparently held that the 'considerably smaller' proportion test had been satisfied on the basis of statistics which showed (i) that the number of female employees complying with the condition (being a full-time employee) was 60 per cent but the number of male employees working full-time was 88 per cent, and (ii) that the number of male employees who were not able to comply with the condition was only 12 per cent of the total male working force whereas the number of such female employees was 40 per cent of the whole female workforce. In *Perera* v. *Civil Service Commission (No 2)*[2] the EAT held that a condition or requirement that an applicant be under 32 was indirectly discriminating against the plaintiff. On taking one group as the relevant pool, 22 of the whites were under 32, whereas none of the non-whites were. On taking another group as the relevant pool, 110 of the 136 whites were under 32, whereas none of the 26 blacks were. In *Greater Manchester Police Authority* v. *Lea*[3] the Authority, in order to help those who were unemployed, did not appoint those who were either in receipt of occupational pensions or had taken voluntary redundancy. The applicant, a man, argued successfully that he had been indirectly discriminated against in this respect. He argued in support that 99.4 per cent of women and 95.3 per cent of men could comply with the relevant condition. The EAT held that this was a sufficiently smaller proportion to amount to a *prima facie* case of indirect discrimination. In an unreported decision, *Wong* v. *Greater London Council*,[4] the EAT decided that if a requirement or condition excluded all of one racial group then, as none could comply, the 'considerably smaller' test did not apply because nil was not a proportion. In *Greencroft Social Club & Institute* v. *Mullen*,[5] however, the EAT refused to follow *Wong*, saying that it ran counter to the spirit of the legislation.

1    IT Case S/3814/81, unreported.
2    [1982] ICR 350, [1982] IRLR 147 (EAT); [1983] ICR 428, [1983] IRLR 166 (CA).
3    [1990] IRLR 372 (EAT).
4    EAT 542/79, unreported.
5    [1985] ICR 796 (EAT). See also *Thorndyke* v. *Bell Fruit (North Central) Ltd* [1979] IRLR 1 (IT); *Briggs* v. *NE Education & Library Board* [1990] IRLR 181 (NICA).

*Relevant pools*

The approach so far to what constitutes the relevant pool is to regard it as largely a question of 'fact' for the tribunals and the EAT will not 'lightly interfere' with the tribunal's choice.[1] A relatively broad approach was taken in an early case. In *Hussein* v. *Saints Complete House Furnishers*[2] general population statistics were successfully relied on by the applicant. In *Bohon-Mitchell* v. *Council for Legal Education*[3] qualified population statistics were held sufficient. In *Price* v. *Civil Service Commission*[4] the EAT held that the appropriate pool was all suitably qualified men and women who could apply for the post in question. In *Wright* v. *Civil Service Commission*,[5] however, the pool was restricted by an industrial tribunal to those who fulfilled the necessary qualifications for promotion by those already employed by the employer. In *Kidd* v. *DRG (UK) Ltd*[6] the industrial tribunal had to consider a requirement to work full-time. The tribunal chose to look only at households with young children who required so much care that looking after them could not be combined with full-time employment; it ignored the fact that most such children live in households headed by married couples. Thus the comparison between the proportions of men and women who could comply with the requirement to work full-time became very restrictive. The decision was, however, upheld on appeal.[7] In *Pearse* v. *City of Bradford Metropolitan Council*[8] the EAT held that the correct pool for comparison was all those who had the appropriate qualifications to apply for the vacant post, regardless of whether they were actually eligible to apply.[9]

*Impact on the individual*

The third element to be demonstrated by a complainant in establishing a claim of indirect discrimination — after proving the existence and application of a requirement or condition and its disparate impact — is that of detriment, i.e. that the requirement or condition was to the detriment of the person to whom it was applied because he or she could not comply with it. For example, in a challenge to the provisions of a superannuation pension fund, the Court of Appeal held in *Labour Party* v. *Turner*[10] that a requirement or condition that it was necessary to have a spouse in order to

---

1   *Kidd* v. *DRG (UK) Ltd* [1985] ICR 405, [1985] IRLR 190 (EAT).
2   [1979] IRLR 343 (IT).
3   [1978] IRLR 525 (IT).
4   [1977] 1 WLR 1417, [1978] 1 All ER 1228, [1978] ICR 27, [1977] IRLR 291 (EAT).
5   Unreported, No 9324/79/B (IT).
6   [1985] ICR 405, [1985] IRLR 190 (EAT).
7   [1985] ICR 405, [1985] IRLR 190 (EAT).
8   [1988] IRLR 379 (EAT).
9   See also *R.* v. *Secretary of State, ex parte Schaffter* [1987] IRLR 53 (HC); *Orphanos* v. *QMC* [1985] AC 761, [1985] 2 WLR 703, [1985] 2 All ER 233, [1985] IRLR 349 (HL).
10  [1987] IRLR 101 (CA).

or condition that it was necessary to have a spouse in order to ensure that survivor's benefits would be received under the scheme was not indirectly discriminatory because it could not be said that a member 'could not comply' prior to the employee's retirement. Pension schemes dealt with future benefits and the member might well be able to comply in the future. There was nothing to stop a divorced or single woman marrying in the future.[1]

*Intention*

In *Enderby* v. *Frenchay Health Authority & Secretary of State for Health*[2] the EAT held that it was not enough for an applicant to show disparate impact on members of one sex. What must be shown is that the disparate impact is because of sex, which has been interpreted by some as importing the need to show an intention to discriminate. This appears contrary to a long line of authority which holds that it is effect, not intent, which counts.[3]

## 2.3.4 OBJECTIVE JUSTIFICATION

It is a defence to a claim of indirect discrimination that the requirement or condition complained of is nevertheless justifiable irrespective of sex. In the early cases under the SDA 1975 tribunals and courts adopted a relatively strict interpretation of this defence (from the point of view of the respondent), equating it with necessity rather than mere administrative convenience. Thus, drawing on the 'business necessity' test laid down in a leading United States case,[4] the EAT held that:

> ... a practice which would otherwise be discriminatory is not to be permitted unless it can be shown to be justifiable, and it cannot be justifiable unless its discriminatory effect is justified by the need, not the convenience, of the business or enterprise.[5]

For this purpose it would be relevant to consider whether the employer could find some other non-discriminatory method of achieving his or her objective.

---

1     See also *Clarke & Powell* v. *Eley (IMI) Kynoch Ltd* [1983] ICR 165, [1982] IRLR 482 (EAT); *Watches of Switzerland Ltd* v. *Savell* [1983] IRLR 141 (EAT); *Home Office* v. *Holmes* [1985] 1 WLR 71, [1984] 3 All ER 549, [1984] ICR 678, [1984] IRLR 299 (EAT); *Clymo* v. *Wandsworth London Borough Council* [1989] ICR 250, [1989] IRLR 241 (EAT); *Briggs* v. *NE Education & Library Board* [1990] IRLR 181 (NICA).

2     [1991] IRLR 44 (EAT).

3     See, for example, *Jones* v. *Chief Adjudication Officer* [1990] IRLR 533 (CA).

4     *Griggs* v. *Duke Power Company* (1971) 401 US 424 (US Sup. Ct).

5     *Steel* v. *Union of Post Office Workers* [1978] 1 WLR 64, [1978] 2 All ER 504, [1978] ICR 181, [1977] IRLR 288 (EAT).

Subsequent decisions significantly diluted this interpretation. The Court of Appeal ruled that it is not for an employer to prove that a requirement was necessary for the good of his or her business: if a person produces reasons for doing something which would be 'acceptable to right-thinking people as sound and tolerable reasons for so doing, then he has justified his conduct'.[1] Following this approach, in *Kidd* v. *DRG (UK) Ltd*[2] the EAT accepted that in the circumstances of the case the employer's requirement to work full-time was justifiable. There was evidence that this was marginally to the advantage of the respondents and on that basis the tribunal was entitled to find that the requirement was justified.

However, following the decision of the ECJ in *Bilka-Kaufhaus GmbH* v. *Weber von Hartz*,[3] British courts and tribunals have reverted to a somewhat stricter approach, and in *Rainey* v. *Greater Glasgow Health Authority*[4] the House of Lords adopted the EC law test laid down in *Bilka* as the appropriate standard also for interpreting the British justifiability defence in the SDA 1975. The ECJ held that a practice which excludes a far greater number of women than men would breach art. 119 of the EEC Treaty 'unless the undertaking shows that the exclusion is based on objectively justified factors unrelated to any discrimination on grounds of sex'. To demonstrate objective justification, the employer must show that the means chosen for achieving this objective 'correspond to a real need on the part of the undertaking, are appropriate with a view to achieving the objective in question and are necessary to that end'.

In *Hampson* v. *DES*[5] the Court of Appeal reinterpreted *Ojutiku*, holding that there was no significant difference between it and the test laid down in *Rainey*.[6]

In *Jones* v. *Chief Adjudication Officer*[7] the Court of Appeal considered the role of proportionality in the context of proof of objective justification of legislation found to be *prima facie* indirectly discriminatory:

> What the court does not have to decide is whether it represents a sensible and moderate way of giving effect to a general legislative policy. These general questions fall within the purview of the national legislature and of the national constitutional court, if the Member State possesses one, and are not the concern of European law. What the national court must do is to identify with precision those

---

1   *Ojutiku* v. *Manpower Services Commission* [1982] ICR 661, [1982] IRLR 418 (CA).
2   [1985] ICR 405, [1985] IRLR 190 (EAT).
3   Case 170/84, [1986] ECR 1607, [1987] ICR 110, [1987] IRLR 317 (ECJ).
4   [1987] AC 224, [1986] 3 WLR 1017, [1987] 1 All ER 65, [1987] ICR 129, [1987] IRLR 26 HL (Sc.).
5   [1989] ICR 179, [1989] IRLR 72 (CA).
6   See further *Briggs* v. *NE Education & Library Board* [1990] IRLR 181 (NICA); *Cobb* v. *Secretary of State for Employment* [1989] ICR 506, [1989] IRLR 464 (EAT).
7   [1990] IRLR 533 (CA). See further *R.* v. *Secretary of State for Employment*, ex parte *EOC*, [1991] IRLR 493 (HC).

features of the measure under attack which discriminate against members of one sex either directly or indirectly by their terms or indirectly by their effect. The court must then consider whether those features are the unavoidable consequence of a justifiable policy, not in itself of a sexual discriminatory nature.

## 2.4 VICTIMIZATION

The SDA 1975, s. 4 provides that in certain circumstances discrimination by way of victimization is unlawful. The Act provides that:

(1)  A person ... discriminates against another person ... in any circumstances relevant for the purposes of any provision of this Act if he treats the person victimised less favourably than in those circumstances he treats or would treat other persons, and does so by reason that the person victimised has

(a)  brought proceedings against the discriminator or any other person under [the equality legislation], or

(b)  given evidence or information in connection with proceedings brought by any person against the discriminator or any other person under [the equality legislation], or

(c)  otherwise done anything under or by reference to [the equality legislation] in relation to the discriminator or any other person, or

(d)  alleged that the discriminator or any other person has committed an act which (whether or not the allegation so states) would amount to a contravention of ... or give rise to a claim under [equality legislation],

or by reason that the discriminator knows the person victimised intends to do any of those things, or suspects the person victimised has done, or intends to do, any of them.

This prohibition against discrimination does not apply to treatment of a person by reason of any allegation made by him if the allegation was false and not made in good faith.

It has been held that the appropriate comparison is between the reactions of the employer to the actions of someone who made a complaint under the legislation, and those of the employer to the actions of someone who did not complain.[1] However, the complainant must establish that the less favourable treatment was related to this particular legislation. If similar treatment would have been accorded to someone who took proceedings under other legislation, then it is not unlawful victimization.[2]

---

[1]  *Aziz* v. *Trinity Street Taxis Ltd* [1989] QB 463, [1988] 3 WLR 79, [1988] 2 All ER 860, [1988] ICR 534, [1988] IRLR 204 (CA).

[2]  *Cornelius* v. *University College of Swansea* [1987] IRLR 141 (CA). See further *British Airways Engineering Overhaul Ltd* v. *Francis* [1981] ICR 279 (EAT); *Mitchell* v. *Sun Alliance*, unreported (NIIT); *Darragh* v. *Jones & Abernethy*, unreported (NIIT). See also EOC Code of Practice, para. 31 for recommendations.

# 3   EQUAL PAY

## 3.1      PRINCIPLE

In principle, where a man and a woman, working in the same employment, are doing like work, work rated as equivalent, or work of equal value, then the Equal Pay Act 1970, as amended (EqPA), requires (s. 1) that their contractual terms and conditions (including pay) should be the same, unless there is a material difference or a material factor which justifies unequal treatment. There are, however, a number of important exceptions and qualifications to this general principle.

## 3.2      EXCEPTIONS

### 3.2.1      SIZE

There is no requirement that an establishment be of any particular size before it is included in the coverage of the legislation.

### 3.2.2      WORK DONE OUTSIDE THE JURISDICTION

The Act applies only in the case of contracts under which a woman is employed at an establishment in Great Britain. Employment is to be regarded as being at an establishment in Great Britain unless the employee does his or her work wholly or mainly outside Great Britain. Great Britain includes such of the territorial waters of the United Kingdom as are adjacent to Great Britain. There is an exception to this provision in the case of employment on board a ship registered at a port of registry in Great Britain, or employment on aircraft or hovercraft registered in the UK and operated by a person who has his principal place of business, or is ordinarily resident, in Great Britain. See §4.3 for further details and discussion.

### 3.2.3      HEALTH AND SAFETY

There is no exception in the Act for acts done in furtherance of health and safety.

### 3.2.4      NATIONAL SECURITY

There is no exception in the Act for acts done in furtherance of national security.

### 3.2.5        RELIGION, RELIGIOUS SCHOOLS

There is no exception in the Act for acts done in relation to religion or religious schools.

### 3.2.6        RETIREMENT AGE

The Act, with two major exceptions, does not operate in relation to terms in a contract of employment related to death or retirement, or any provision made in connection with death or retirement.[1] The EqPA does, however, apply, firstly, to the terms relating to membership of an occupational pension scheme (defined by the Social Security Pensions Act 1975) which is also an employment-related benefit scheme (defined by the Social Security Act 1989, Sch. 5, para. 7) so far as those terms relate to any matter in respect of which the scheme has to comply with the equality provisions of European law.[2]

The second exception is that discrimination in compulsory *retirement* ages between men and women is unlawful. As regards the public sector, this was established so far as EC law is concerned by the ECJ in *Marshall* v. *Southampton & SW Hampshire Area Health Authority*.[3] As regards the private sector, the principle established in *Marshall* was extended to the private sector by the Sex Discrimination Act 1986, which provides that the Equal Pay Act:

> ... shall not operate in relation to terms related to death or retirement, or to any provision made in connection with death or retirement *other than* a term or provision which, in relation to retirement, affords access to opportunities for promotion, transfer or training or provides for a woman's dismissal or demotion.[4]

There is, however, no change in the differential age at which there is access to a state pension which continues to be 60 for women and 65 for men. This has occasioned considerable difficulty in numerous situations (see further §4.2.1.6).

### 3.2.7        OTHER EXCEPTIONS

The Act does not operate in relation to terms which afford special treatment to women in connection with pregnancy or childbirth,[5] nor does it

---

1   EqPA, s. 6(1A)(b). For this purpose, retirement includes retirement, whether voluntary or not, on grounds of age, length of service or incapacity (EqPA, s. 6(2)).
2   Council Directive 86/378/EEC; see Social Security Act 1989, Sch. 5.
3   Case 152/84, [1986] ECR 723, [1986] QB 401, [1986] 2 WLR 780, [1986] 2 All ER 584, [1986] ICR 335, [1986] IRLR 140 (ECJ).
4   EqPA, s. 6(1A)(b) (emphasis added).
5   EqPA, s. 6(1)(b).

operate in relation to terms affected by compliance with the laws regulating the employment of women.

## 3.3        PERSONAL SCOPE OF PRINCIPLE

### 3.3.1        EMPLOYEES

For the purposes of the EqPA, 'employed' has an extended meaning in comparison with general labour law. It means 'employed under a contract of service or of apprenticeship or a *contract personally to execute any work or labour*' (s. 1(6)(a): emphasis added). On this phrase, see *Quinnen* v. *Hovells.*[1]

### 3.3.2        INDEPENDENT CONTRACTORS

To the extent that they are covered by the extended definition of 'employed' above, independent contractors are covered by the provisions of the Act. See further §4.4.2.

### 3.3.3        HOME WORKERS

The effect of the provisions described above is that home workers may be included in the coverage of the Act, if they fall within the definitions, and if they are able to find a relevant male comparator. The position with regard to home workers is further clarified explicitly by a provision in the SDA 1975, s. 10, that:

> Where work is not done at an establishment it shall be treated for the relevant purposes as done at the establishment from which it is done or (where it is not done from any establishment) at the establishment with which it has the closest connection.[2]

See further §4.4.3.

### 3.3.4        PUBLIC SECTOR

The EqPA covers employees in the public sector in much the same way that it covers the private sector. The Act applies to service for a Minister of the Crown or government department (other than service of a person holding a statutory office, or service on behalf of the Crown for purposes of a person holding a statutory office or purposes of a statutory body) as it applies to employment by a private person.[3]

---

[1]     [1984] ICR 525, [1984] IRLR 227 (EAT). See further §4.4.1.
[2]     SDA 1975, s. 10(4).
[3]     EqPA, s. 1(8).

However, conditions of service in the armed forces are excluded from the coverage of the EqPA.[1] The Act provides, as an alternative, that neither the Secretary of State nor the Defence Council shall make or recommend the making of:

> ... any instrument relating to the terms and conditions of service of members of the naval, military or air forces of the Crown, if the instrument has the effect of making a distinction, as regards pay, allowances or leave, between men and women who are members of those forces, not being a distinction fairly attributable to differences between the obligations undertaken by men and those undertaken by women ... .[2]

This prohibition is not enforceable by an individual through a judicial process. Instead, either the Secretary of State or the Defence Council may refer to the Central Arbitration Committee for their advice any question whether a provision made or proposed to be made ought to be regarded as making a distinction not permitted.[3]

### 3.3.5 DOMESTIC EMPLOYEES

Domestic employees are covered by the legislation to the same extent as other employees. See further §4.4.5.

### 3.3.6 NON-EMPLOYED POPULATION

The non-employed population is not covered by the legislation.

## 3.4 ACTIVITIES COVERED

In cases of like work (§§3.7.1, 3.7.2), work rated as equivalent or work of equal value (§3.8), s. 1(1) of the EqPA specifies that the implied equality clause operates to make the woman's contract of employment not less favourable than the man's: where a term of the woman's contract is or becomes less favourable to her than a term of a similar kind in the man's contract; and where the woman's contract does not include a term corresponding to a term which benefits a man under his contract. In *Hayward* v. *Cammell Laird Shipbuilders Ltd (No 2)*[4] the woman was doing work of equal value to several comparators. The employer argued that although the woman received lower basic pay and overtime rates than the comparators, when the terms and conditions of her contract were considered as a whole, they were not less favourable than those of the male comparators. The House

---

1     EqPA, s. 1(9).
2     EqPA, s. 7(1).
3     EqPA, s. 7(2).
4     [1988] AC 894, [1988] 2 WLR 1134, [1988] 2 All ER 257, [1988] ICR 464, [1988] IRLR 257 HL (E).

of Lords held that the appropriate comparison was between each term in a contract. Therefore the woman was entitled to equality in respect of basic pay, the specific term in her contract which was less favourable. Thus, if any term of the woman's contract is less favourable than a term of a similar kind in the man's contract, the term of the woman's contract is treated as modified so as to make it not less favourable, irrespective of whether she is as favourably treated as the man when the whole of his contract and the whole of her contract are considered.

## 3.5        DEFINITION OF REMUNERATION

The EqPA applies to terms and conditions of employment which are included in the individual contract or employment and not just 'pay' or 'remuneration' (as in art. 119 of the EEC Treaty and the Equal Pay Directive). Equality is required, in the circumstances to be considered subsequently, between the terms of the man's and the woman's contract of employment. This includes pay, but goes beyond it. What is included in the terms of the contract of employment is potentially very wide and depends in any particular situation on the construction of the contract. The following have, however, been held to be included as terms of a contract: basic pay, benefits in kind such as the use of a car, cash bonuses, and sickness benefits.

### 3.5.1        ARTICLE 119 OF THE EEC TREATY

There has been considerable interpretation of the meaning of 'pay' for the purposes of art. 119 of the EEC Treaty in references from British courts to the ECJ. For the purposes of this provision, 'pay' means the 'ordinary basic or minimum wage or salary and any other consideration, whether in cash or in kind, which the worker receives directly or indirectly, in respect of his employment from his employer'.[1] The ECJ has held that 'pay' includes: the conditions for admission to an occupational pension scheme, where the benefits paid to employees constitute consideration received by the worker from the employer in respect of employment,[2] contributions paid by an employer in the name of employees to a retirement benefits scheme, where the contributions are included in the calculation of the employee's gross salary and directly determine the calculation of other advantages linked to salary,[3] (but not contributions paid to a social security scheme not affecting

---

1    See *Defrenne* v. *Belgian State*, Case 80/70, [1971] ECR 445 (ECJ).
2    *Bilka-Kaufhaus GmbH* v. *Weber von Hartz*, Case 170/84, [1986] ECR 1607, [1987] ICR 110, [1987] IRLR 317 (ECJ).
3    *Worringham* v. *Lloyds Bank Ltd*, Case 69/80, [1981] ECR 767, [1981] 1 WLR 950, [1981] 2 All ER 434, [1981] ICR 558, [1981] IRLR 178 (ECJ).

gross pay[1]), travel facilities accorded to employees after retirement,[2] benefits the employee receives from an employer under national sick pay legislation,[3] benefits paid by an employer to a worker in connection with compulsory redundancy, whether paid under a contract of employment, by virtue of legislative provisions or on a voluntary basis, and pensions paid under a contracted-out private occupational scheme.[4]

### 3.5.2      FRINGE BENEFITS

Provided the fringe benefits in question are included in the contract of employment (expressly or impliedly) then they will be covered by the EqPA 1970. Otherwise they will fall to be considered under the SDA 1975, or art. 119 of the EEC Treaty. For example, a female outdoor pursuits instructor was held to have less favourable terms and conditions than a male employee employed on like work due to not being provided accommodation free of charge.[5] In *Irish Bank Officials Association* v. *Banks' Staff Relations Committee*, the Northern Ireland Industrial Court held that loan applications were included within the principle of equal pay.

### 3.5.3      CONTRIBUTIONS BY EMPLOYER

In *Worringham* v. *Lloyds Bank Ltd*[6] the ECJ held that a contribution to a retirement benefits scheme which is paid by an employer in the name of employees by means of an addition to the gross salary and which therefore helps to determine the amount of that salary constitutes 'pay' within the meaning of art. 119 of the EEC Treaty.

### 3.5.4      CONTRIBUTIONS BY EMPLOYEE

The decision in *Newstead* v. *Department of Transport*[7] that employee contributions to a pension scheme do not fall under art. 119 may have been overruled by the ECJ in *Barber* v. *Guardian Royal Exchange Assurance*

---

1    *Newstead* v. *Department of Transport*, Case 192/85, [1987] ECR 4753, [1988] 1 All ER 129, [1988] IRLR 66 (ECJ).
2    *Garland* v. *British Rail Engineering Ltd*, Case 12/81, [1982] ECR 359, [1983] 2 AC 751, [1982] 2 WLR 918, [1982] 2 All ER 402, [1982] ICR 420, [1982] IRLR 257 (ECJ and HL).
3    *Rinner-Kühn* v. *FWW Spezial-Gebäudereinigung GmbH & Co. KG*, Case 171/88, [1989] ECR 2743, [1989] IRLR 493 (ECJ).
4    *Barber* v. *Guardian Royal Exchange Assurance Group*, Case C-262/88, [1990] ECR I-1889, [1990] 2 All ER 660, [1990] IRLR 240 (ECJ).
5    *Gibson* v. *NE Education & Library Board* (2/81 EP).
6    Case 69/80, [1981] ECR 767, [1981] 1 WLR 950, [1981] 2 All ER 434, [1981] ICR 558, [1981] IRLR 178 (ECJ).
7    Case 192/85, [1987] ECR 4753, [1988] 1 All ER 129, [1988] IRLR 66 (ECJ).

*Group*,[1] in which the Court appears to have held that all aspects of a private occupational pension scheme are covered by art.119.

### 3.5.5       POST-EMPLOYMENT BENEFITS

In *Garland* v. *British Rail Engineering Ltd*[2] all employees, both male and female, were given certain non-contractual travel concessions on British Rail for themselves, their spouses and children. However, on retirement, female employees were no longer granted travel facilities for their families, only for themselves. Retired male employees continued to be granted facilities for themselves, their wives and children. The ECJ held that the facilities were pay within art. 119 of the EEC Treaty irrespective of whether the facilities were contractual or not. In *Hammersmith & Queen Charlotte's Special Health Authority* v. *Cato*,[3] the EAT held that a contractual redundancy payment constituted pay for the purposes of art. 119.

Following these cases, the UK Government announced that it would legislate to equalize statutory redundancy payment provisions between men and women. In the Employment Act 1989, s. 16 does this. The Act provides that where there is a 'normal retiring age' of less than 65 for the job in question which is the same for men and women, the entitlement to statutory redundancy payments is restricted to that age. In other cases, women's entitlement to the redundancy payment is extended to age 65, the same as for men.

The ECJ held subsequently in *Barber* v. *Guardian Royal Exchange Assurance Group*[4] that the benefits paid by an employer to a worker in connection with compulsory redundancy fall within the concept of pay, whether they are paid under a contract of employment, or on the basis of legislative provisions, or on the basis of an *ex gratia* payment.

### 3.5.6       PENSIONS

In *Bilka-Kaufhaus GmbH* v. *Weber von Hartz*[5] the ECJ held that occupational pensions which were based on negotiations between an employer and his employees and which were not covered directly by state legislation were 'pay' within the meaning of art. 119 of the EEC Treaty. In *Worringham* v. *Lloyds Bank Ltd*[6] the ECJ held that it was not necessary for

---

1    Case C-262/88, [1990] ECR I-1889, [1990] 2 All ER 660, [1990] IRLR 240 (ECJ).
2    Case 12/81, [1982] ECR 359, [1983] 2 AC 751, [1982] 2 WLR 918, [1982] 2 All ER 402, [1982] ICR 420, [1982] IRLR 257 (ECJ and HL).
3    [1988] ICR 132 (EAT).
4    Case C-262/88, [1990] ECR I-1889, [1990] 2 All ER 660, [1990] IRLR 240 (ECJ).
5    Case 170/84, [1986] ECR 1607, [1987] ICR 110, [1987] IRLR 317 (ECJ).
6    Case 69/80, [1981] ECR 767, [1981] 1 WLR 950, [1981] 2 All ER 434, [1981] ICR 558, [1981] IRLR 178 (ECJ).

them to decide whether rights and benefits of a worker under a pension scheme constituted 'pay' for the purposes of art. 119. However, in *Barber* v. *Guardian Royal Exchange Assurance Group*[1] the ECJ held that a pension paid under a contracted-out private occupational scheme does constitute 'pay'. In *Roberts* v. *Birds Eye Walls Ltd*[2] the EAT held, following *Barber,* that art. 119 prohibits an employer from reducing a woman's occupational pension from age 60 on grounds that she will be in receipt of state pension, but not reducing a man's pension until age 65.

### 3.5.7      COLLECTIVE AGREEMENTS

The EqPA 1970, as amended by the SDA 1975, originally included provisions requiring the amendment of any provisions in collective agreements and formal pay structures which applied specifically to men only or to women only. Any party to the agreement or the Secretary of State for Employment was able to refer the agreement or pay structure to an adjudicatory body established under statute — the Central Arbitration Committee (CAC) — for amendment. Although the CAC treated the provisions relating to collective agreements as 'enabling them to test for anything amounting to sex discrimination in pay structures or provisions in collective agreements',[3] this approach was disapproved of by the High Court.[4] The provisions became 'to all intents and purposes defunct'.[5] There were last-minute attempts to revive them. In its last decision under EqPA s. 3, the CAC held that it had jurisdiction to amend a collective agreement which indirectly discriminated against women, applying EC law. The agreement had excluded part-time permanent staff from a mortgage allowance scheme. However, this decision was subsequently quashed: *R.* v. *CAC,* ex parte *Norwich Union.*[6] The jurisdiction was abolished in the SDA 1986, s. 9.

The SDA 1986, s. 6 now provides that discriminatory provisions in collective agreements are rendered void, though no clear mechanism is explicitly provided in the Act by which this 'voidness' may be established without the need for an individual complaint being made before an industrial tribunal. See §6.4 below, for a fuller discussion.

---

1     Case C-262/88, [1990] ECR I-1889, [1990] 2 All ER 660, [1990] IRLR 240 (ECJ).
2     [1991] IRLR 19 (EAT).
3     DAVIES & FREEDLAND, *Labour Law,* 2nd ed., 1986, p. 380.
4     *R.* v. *CAC,* ex parte *Hy-Mac Ltd* [1979] IRLR 461 (CA).
5     DAVIES & FREEDLAND, *loc. cit.*
6     (1988) 22 EOR 41 (QBD).

## 3.6　　　　COMPARATOR

The choice of the relevant comparator is that of the applicant, not the employer or the tribunal.[1] There is no requirement that the comparator selected by the applicant should be representative of a group.[2] The applicant may choose which comparator with whom to compare her job.[3] The number of comparators permitted is, however, subject to judicial supervision.[4] The applicant is not prevented from claiming work of equal value with a man only because there is another man with whom she does like work.[5]

### 3.6.1　　　SAME ESTABLISHMENT

A comparison of the work of the applicant and that of a comparator is required under the EqPA only when the comparator is employed in the 'same employment' as the comparator.[6] This is regarded as being the case in two circumstances in which the applicant and the comparator are working in the same establishment: first, where the applicant is employed by the same employer as the comparator in the same establishment. Once this is established, then the comparison is valid. There is no further requirement to establish that the applicant and comparators are employed on the same terms and conditions.[7] This will be the case, second, where the applicant is employed at the same establishment as the comparator though by a different employer from the comparator, provided the employers are associated. Employers are 'associated' if one is a company (not just a government agency, *Hasley* v. *Fair Employment Agency*[8]) of which the other (directly or indirectly) has control or if both are companies of which a third person (directly or indirectly) has control.[9]

### 3.6.2　　　CONTEMPORANEOUS EMPLOYMENT

Under EC law, as applied in the United Kingdom, the principle of equal pay is not confined to situations in which men and women are contemporaneously doing equal work. It also applies where it is established

---

1　*Ainsworth* v. *Glass Tubes & Components Ltd* [1977] ICR 347, [1977] IRLR 74 (EAT).
2　*Thomas* v. *National Coal Board* [1987] ICR 757, [1987] IRLR 451 (EAT).
3　*Ainsworth* v. *Glass Tubes & Components Ltd* [1977] ICR 347, [1977] IRLR 74 (EAT); *Aldridge* v. *British Telecom plc* [1989] ICR 790, [1990] IRLR 11 (EAT).
4　*Leverton* v. *Clwyd County Council* [1989] AC 706, [1989] 2 WLR 47, [1989] 1 All ER 78, [1989] ICR 33, [1989] IRLR 28 (HL).
5　*Pickstone* v. *Freemans plc* [1989] AC 66, [1988] 3 WLR 265, [1988] 2 All ER 803, [1988] ICR 697, [1988] IRLR 357 HL (E).
6　EqPA, s. 1(6)(c).
7　*Lawson* v. *Britfish Ltd* [1987] ICR 726, [1988] IRLR 53 (EAT).
8　[1989] IRLR 106 (NICA).
9　EqPA, s. 1(6)(c).

that a woman has received less pay than a man who was employed immediately prior to her employment and who did equal work for the employer.[1] However, a change in an employer's trading position leading to reduced profitability is capable of constituting a defence to a woman's claim for equal pay for her male predecessor, provided the employer can show that he was not taking advantage of the complainant's sex to get the work done at a rate less than that for which a man would have worked.[2]

### 3.6.3    HYPOTHETICAL MALE

Comparisons are confined to parallels which may be drawn on the basis of concrete appraisals of work actually performed by employees of a different sex within the same establishment. There is therefore no possibility of comparisons being drawn with 'hypothetical' men under UK law, and such a comparison has been held by the ECJ not to be possible under EC law[3]. The extent of this prohibition is however uncertain and the absence of a named comparator has not prevented the ECJ upholding an applicant's claim in *Barber* v. *Guardian Royal Exchange Assurance Group*.[4]

### 3.6.4    DIFFERENT ESTABLISHMENT/SAME EMPLOYER

Comparisons are allowed where the applicant and the comparator are in different establishments: first, where the applicant is employed by the same employer as the comparator, though in another establishment, provided common terms and conditions of employment are observed either generally or for employees of the relevant classes;[5] and second, where the applicant and the comparator are employed by different employers in different establishments, provided common terms and conditions are observed either generally or for employees of the relevant classes, and the employers are associated. In *Leverton* v. *Clwyd County Council*[6] the House of Lords held that for there to be common terms and conditions it was not necessary for the applicant and the comparator to have broadly similar terms and conditions. The test was whether there were terms and conditions of employment applied generally at both establishments, even though these may vary for particular groups of employees.

---

1    *Macarthys Ltd* v. *Smith,* Case 129/79, [1980] ECR 1275, [1980] 3 WLR 929, [1981] 1 All ER 111, [1980] ICR 672, [1980] IRLR 210 (ECJ).
2    *Albion Shipping Agency* v. *Arnold* [1982] ICR 22, [1981] IRLR 525 (EAT).
3    *Macarthys Ltd* v. *Smith,* Case 129/79, [1980] ECR 1275, [1980] 3 WLR 929, [1981] 1 All ER 111, [1980] ICR 672, [1980] IRLR 210 (ECJ).
4    Case C-262/88, [1990] ECR I-1889, [1990] 2 All ER 660, [1990] IRLR 240 (ECJ).
5    *Leverton* v. *Clwyd County Council* [1989] AC 706, [1989] 2 WLR 47, [1989] 1 All ER 78, [1989] ICR 33, [1989] IRLR 28 (HL).
6    [1989] AC 706, [1989] 2 WLR 47, [1989] 1 All ER 78, [1989] ICR 33, [1989] IRLR 28 (HL). See also *Thomas* v. *National Coal Board* [1987] ICR 757, [1987] IRLR 451 (EAT).

**3.6.5          CROSS-INDUSTRY COMPARISONS**

There is no provision either for intra-industry or cross-industry comparisons under British law, although the position under EC law is uncertain. As regards equity across enterprises, Szyszczak[1] and Hepple[2] have argued that comparisons wider than those currently allowed for under the British equal pay legislation may well be necessary in order to comply with the Equal Pay Directive. Except where the previous provisions apply, the EqPA does not permit cross-industry comparisons.

**3.7          WOMAN DOES SAME WORK AS MAN**

**3.7.1          IDENTICAL WORK**

In the British statutory scheme established in 1970, the contracts of employment of a considerable number of employees had a new 'equality clause' incorporated into them which modified contrary terms and conditions of employment. Under this clause equal pay was guaranteed where men and women are doing work which is either 'like work' or 'work rated as equivalent'. One situation where 'like work' takes place is where the work the woman does is 'of the same ... nature' as the man's.[3]

**3.7.2          SIMILAR WORK**

The second circumstance in which 'like work' will be found is where the work of the man and the woman is work 'of a broadly similar nature'. This has been interpreted as requiring consideration of the type of work involved and the skill and knowledge required to do it.[4] A broad judgment ought to be adopted.

If it is work of a broadly similar nature, a second question must be considered: are any differences between the things she does and the things the men do 'of practical importance in relation to terms and conditions of employment'?[5] If not, then like work is established. This second limb of the test has been interpreted as meaning that only differences of a kind which one would expect to find reflected in the terms and conditions of employment should be seen as 'of practical importance' sufficient to defeat a

---

1    In McCRUDDEN, 1987.
2    *Encyclopedia*, 1B-905; see also *Commission of the European Communities* v. *Denmark*, Case 143/83, [1985] ECR 427, [1986] 1 CMLR 43 (ECJ).
3    EqPA, s. 1(4).
4    *Capper Pass Ltd* v. *Lawton* [1977] 2 All ER 11, [1976] IRLR 366 (EAT) (finding like work between female cooks working in the kitchen of a directors' dining room, and a male assistant chef in the works canteen).
5    EqPA, s. 1(4).

claim. Trivial differences, or differences not likely to be reflected in terms and conditions of employment, ought to be ignored.[1] In comparing the applicant's work with that of the man 'regard shall be had to the frequency or otherwise with which any such differences occur in practice as well as to the nature and extent of the differences'.[2] In *Darragh* v. *Jones*[3] the applicant's claim for equal pay with a male employee was dismissed. The male comparator had lengthy experience in Post Office work; this was a difference of practical importance. In *Preston* v. *Rodgers (JCJ), Edenmore Hotel*[4] a female bar attendant was employed on like work with the male comparator despite different stock duties having been assigned to each.

### 3.7.3      NIGHT-WORK

In *Dugdale* v. *Kraft Foods Ltd*[5] the EAT held that a man and a woman were doing like work despite the fact that the woman did not work night-shifts or Sunday mornings. The time at which work is performed did not constitute a difference of practical importance in relation to terms and conditions of employment. However, in *Thomas* v. *National Coal Board* [6] the EAT held that the degree of risk and the additional responsibility due to night-work amounted to differences of practical importance and justified unequal pay.

### 3.8      EQUAL VALUE

There are two ways in which the concept of work of equal value is relevant under UK domestic law. First, the Act provides that a woman employed on 'work rated as equivalent' with that of a man must be treated equally. Two employees are 'rated as equivalent' if her job and his job have been given an equal value:

> ... in terms of the demand made on a worker under various headings (for instance effort, skill, decision), on a study undertaken with a view to evaluating in those terms the jobs to be done by all or any of the employees in an undertaking or group of undertakings, or would have been given an equal value but for the evaluation

---

1    *Capper Pass Ltd* v. *Lawton* [1977] 2 All ER 11, [1976] IRLR 366 (EAT).
2    EqPA, s. 1(4). See *Shields* v. *Coomes (E) (Holdings) Ltd*  [1978] 1 WLR 1408, [1979] 1 All ER 456, [1978] ICR 1159, [1978] IRLR 263 (CA); *British Leyland* v. *Powell* [1978] IRLR 57 (EAT); *Capper Pass Ltd* v. *Lawton* [1977] 2 All ER 11, [1976] IRLR 366 (EAT); *Electrolux Ltd* v. *Hutchinson* [1977] ICR 252, [1976] IRLR 410 (EAT); *Waddington* v. *Leicester Council for Voluntary Services* [1977] 1 WLR 544, [1977] 2 All ER 633, [1977] ICR 266, [1977] IRLR 32 (EAT).
3    5/83 EP NIIT.
4    9/82 EP NIIT.
5    [1976] 1 WLR 1288, [1977] 1 All ER 454, [1977] ICR 48, [1976] IRLR 368 (EAT). See also *National Coal Board* v. *Sherwin* [1978] ICR 790, [1978] IRLR 122 (EAT).
6    [1987] ICR 757, [1987] IRLR 451 (EAT).

being made on a system setting different values for men and women on the same demand under any heading.[1]

The job evaluation scheme must be 'analytical' in order to comply with these provisions, i.e. the jobs of each worker covered by the study must have been valued in terms of the demand made on the worker under various headings.[2] Once a job evaluation study has been undertaken and has resulted in a conclusion that the job of a woman is of equal value with that of a man, then the man and the woman should be paid the same. It is not necessary for the pay structure to have been adjusted as a result of the job evaluation study for the woman to be able to proceed under this head of claim.[3] Subsequently, the EAT held that there is no complete job evaluation study until the study has been accepted by the employers and employees as valid and regulating their relationship.[4] However, in the light of *Dibro Ltd* v. *Hore*[5] this holding may be restricted in future cases (see §§ 3.8.1, 3.8.2 below).

Secondly, as a result of *Commission of the European Communities* v. *United Kingdom*[6] new British legislation was passed in the latter part of 1983, providing that in addition to the 'like work' and 'work rated as equivalent' elements of the 'equality clause' incorporated into the individual contract of employment, an additional 'work of equal value' element would henceforth be included.[7]

Unlike under 'work rated as equivalent', where the employer is required to implement a job evaluation scheme which has been (in legal terms) voluntarily introduced by the employer, the new head of 'equal value' provides that a woman may claim to be doing work of equal value to a man, and ensure that their jobs are evaluated, where the employer has not voluntarily carried out a job evaluation scheme. Except where the particular man with whom the woman seeks to compare herself is employed on like work, or work rated as equivalent, or where there is an existing valid non-discriminatory analytical job evaluation scheme, the woman may call in aid the legal process to require that a job evaluation scheme be carried out

---

1    EqPA, s. 1(5).

2    See *Bromley* v. *Quick (H & J) Ltd* [1988] ICR 623, [1988] IRLR 249 (CA).

3    *O'Brien* v. *Sim-Chem Ltd* [1980] 1 WLR 1011, [1980] 3 All ER 132, [1980] ICR 573, [1980] IRLR 373 (HL).

4    *Arnold* v. *Beecham Group Ltd* [1982] ICR 744, [1982] IRLR 307 (EAT). See also *Greene* v. *Broxtowe District Council* [1977] 1 All ER 694, [1977] ICR 241 (EAT); *Eaton Ltd* v. *Nuttall* [1977] 1 WLR 549, [1977] 3 All ER 1131, [1977] ICR 872, [1977] IRLR 71 (EAT).

5    [1990] IRLR 129 (EAT).

6    Case 61/81, [1982] ECR 2601, [1982] IRLR 333 (ECJ).

7    Equal Pay (Amendment) Regulations 1983 (SI 1983 No 1794); Industrial Tribunals (Rules of Procedure) (Equal Value Amendment) Regulations 1983 (SI 1983 No 1807). It should be noted, however, that the House of Lords, in passing the regulations, added a rider to the effect that it did not regard the legislation as giving full effect to European law requirements.

evaluating her job and the job she is arguing is of equal value to hers, in terms of the demands made on her. The EqPA specifies that the demands are to be assessed 'for instance under such headings as effort, skill and decision'.[1] Thus, where an applicant makes an equal value complaint to an industrial tribunal, unless there is an existing non-discriminatory analytical job evaluation scheme which covers the applicant's job and the comparator's job (see §3.8.1 below), the tribunal is required to refer the issue to an independent expert (see §6.1 below). The expert is required to draw up a report, using a non-discriminatory analytical job evaluation scheme, determining whether the applicant and the comparator are doing work of equal value (see §3.8.2 below).

**3.8.1        JOB EVALUATION**
**3.8.2        JOB CLASSIFICATION**

In UK law the term 'job classification' is not used, while 'job evaluation' now has an important legal role. Job evaluation is relevant in the context of equal pay cases in a number of situations. First, it may ground a claim under the 'work rated as equivalent' head if a job evaluation has been carried out by an employer. Second, it is the method adopted under the legislation for estimating whether two jobs are of equal value under the new head of claim (see §3.8.2.1 below). Third, a tribunal is not permitted even to begin the process of determining whether any work is of equal value to another if, *inter alia*, 'it is satisfied that there are no reasonable grounds for determining that the work is of equal value ... '.[2] Without prejudice to the generality of this provision, a tribunal is required to discontinue hearing a case on this ground where an existing analytical job evaluation study has given the claimant's job a value different from that of her male comparator, unless it is discriminatory. A job evaluation study does not apply to employees unless they are employees in the undertaking or group of undertakings to which the study related.[3] This includes where a job evaluation scheme came into existence after the initiation of proceedings provided that it relates to facts and circumstances existing at the time when the proceedings were instituted.[4]

The concern that job evaluation schemes may themselves be sexually biased is thus explicitly taken into account with respect to job evaluation studies. What 'discrimination' in such a situation means has been the subject of some litigation. In *Neil* v. *Ford Motor Co.*[5] an industrial tribunal held that there was no presumption that a voluntary scheme discriminated on the grounds of sex. The burden of proof, the tribunal asserted, lay on the employees to show that there were reasonable grounds for believing that it did discriminate. The tribunal adopted a particularly narrow test for

---

1    EqPA, s. 1(2)(c).
2    EqPA, s. 2A(2).
3    *McAuley* v. *Eastern Health & Social Services Board* [1991] IRLR 467 (NICA).
4    *Dibro Ltd* v. *Hore* [1990] IRLR 129 (EAT).
5    [1984] IRLR 339 (IT).

determining whether discrimination could be inferred: whether there is good reason to suppose that any comparative value set by the system on any demand or characteristic would have been given a more favourable value had those determining values not consciously or subconsciously been influenced by consideration of the sex of those on whom the demands would chiefly be made. The tribunal added that there would be sufficient reason for such a supposition if it had found that a traditionally female attribute was undervalued. In *McAuley* v. *Eastern Health & Social Services Board*[1] the applicants argued that the respondents could not show that the bench-mark job ranking order was not based on intentional or unintentional discrimination. In particular, it was argued that an inference should be drawn from statistical evidence which established the female preponderance of ancillary workers in the employment of the respondents in the bottom three grades. However, the industrial tribunal and the Northern Ireland Court of Appeal were not prepared to make an inference of discrimination. The statistical evidence could be explained in ways other than discrimination being at work. Those carrying out the job evaluation scheme, in the person of the employer's expert, impressed the tribunal, and the unions concerned had failed to press the question of discrimination in negotiations at national level enabling the respondents to argue successfully that the scheme was broadly 'acceptable'. There has been little European case law on the issue, but see *Rummler* v. *Dato-Druck GmbH*.[2]

Studies carried out by the Trade Union Research Unit[3] and for the EOC[4] on reports by independent experts for tribunals note a number of characteristics of the approach taken by experts. The independent experts' studies normally only covered those jobs in dispute, and their named comparator jobs. The experts generally devised their own schemes and did not use any proprietary job evaluation schemes. (A number of the experts appear to regard themselves as developing a body of alternative knowledge about how to conduct non-discriminatory job evaluation.) It was usual for the experts to interview applicant and comparator, line managers and supervisors, union representatives, legal representatives, and any experts advising the parties. It was also usual for the experts to observe the applicant and comparator at work. The time spent in interviews and observations varied from one and a half to seven days. In addition, written descriptions were commonly sought from comparators, applicants and the employer. Both parties were always asked to comment on a summary of the information received, although this was commonly no more than the written submissions of the parties.

---

1    [1991] IRLR 467 (NICA).

2    Case 237/85, [1986] ECR 2101, [1987] ICR 774, [1987] IRLR 32 (ECJ).

3    TURU, 1988.

4    BOWEY, 1989, summarized in (1989) 24 EOR 18. An earlier commentary on independent experts' reports up to 1986 is provided in BEDDOE, 1986.

### 3.8.2.1        Factors

The EqPA, s. 1(2)(c) specifies that the method by which equal value is to be assessed is by comparing whether the woman's work is of equal value to the man's, 'in terms of the demands made on her (for instance under such headings as effort, skill and decision)'. This has been interpreted as requiring an analytical scheme based on breaking down the jobs into component elements or 'factors', evaluating what each factor scores, comparing the scores of the same factors in each job and then comparing the overall score for each job.

All the schemes devised by the experts were factor-based schemes. There were, however, variations among experts as to both the number and categories of factors used. Of the 21 reports analysed in the EOC study, for example, in each report the expert used at least three headings or factors, and none used more than 10. In every case 'skill and knowledge' was included. All but four assessed 'mental effort'. All but eight assessed 'physical effort'. Six factor headings (physical effort, mental effort, skill and knowledge, working conditions, responsibility for things, responsibility for people) accounted for all but five of the 197 factors and sub-factors used in the 21 reports. A scoring system was adopted by all the experts for the measurement of relative demands under each factor. Factor scales were almost always simple verbal (not numerical) scales. Most of the experts employed scoring systems based around a simple low/moderate/high scale, with or without additional levels such as medium/high or medium/low.

### 3.8.2.2        Weightings

Equal weighting of factors was generally adopted by the independent experts. There is no decision under UK law as to whether equal weightings attached to factors are necessary or permissible. The only restriction appears to be that where weightings are used they must be neither directly nor indirectly discriminatory.

### 3.8.2.3        Traditional male/female attributes

EOC guidance on job evaluation ('Job evaluation schemes free of sex bias') stresses the need to avoid the adoption of factors or their weighting which results in traditional 'male' attributes being preferred to traditional 'female' attributes. There have, however, been no appellate decisions on this issue. For discussion by the ECJ, see, however, *Rummler* v. *Dato-Druck GmbH*.[1]

---

1    Case 237/85, [1986] ECR 2101, [1987] ICR 774, [1987] IRLR 32 (ECJ).

**3.8.3          HIGHER VALUE**

Since *Murphy* v. *Bord Telecom Eireann*[1] it is now accepted that if a woman succeeds in establishing that her work is of higher value than that of a man, she has established 'equal value' for the purposes of the Act. The extent to which strict equality in demands is required before the applicant succeeds has been the subject of differing approaches in the industrial tribunals.[2]

**3.8.4          PROPORTIONATE PAY**

In order to succeed, the woman must establish that her work is at least of equal value to that of an appropriate male comparator. She will not succeed if she establishes that she is doing work of less value to that of a male comparator even if her pay is discriminatorily less than would be justified by the difference in value.[3]

**3.9          LEGITIMATE REASON FOR PAY DIFFERENTIAL**

**3.9.1          MATERIAL DIFFERENCE**

Where a woman's work falls into one of the first two categories ('like work' or 'work rated as equivalent'), equal pay is required to be paid, unless the employer proves that any variation between a man's and woman's contract of employment is 'genuinely due to a *material factor* which is not the difference of sex'.[4] In a case where the applicant has claimed 'work of equal value', the employer may show that there is a 'genuine material factor which is not the difference of sex'. The 'material factor' defence was introduced in the same legislation which provided for equal pay for work of equal value.

To succeed in establishing a material difference or material factor defence, the employer must show that the variation in the woman's terms is genuinely due to the difference or factor, i.e. the variation in pay is due to the difference or factor. Thus, where a difference or factor has in the past contributed to the variation but no longer operates to do so, the variation is no longer justified.[5] Nor is it a defence to an equal pay claim for the employer to show that the reason the applicant is paid less than her comparator is a genuine error.[6]

---

1    Case 157/86, [1988] ECR 673, [1988] IRLR 267 (ECJ).
2    Compare *Brown & Royle* v. *Cearns & Brown Ltd* (1986) 6 EOR 27 (IT) (strict equality) with *Scott* v. *Beal College* (1985) 3 EOR 38 (IT) (broad brush approach).
3    *Pointon* v. *University of Sussex* [1979] IRLR 119 (CA); *Maidment* v. *Cooper & Co. (Birmingham) Ltd* [1978] ICR 1094, [1978] IRLR 462 (EAT).
4    EqPA, s. 1(3) (emphasis added).
5    *Beneviste* v. *University of Southampton* [1989] ICR 617, [1989] IRLR 122 (CA).
6    *McPherson* v. *Rathgael Centre for Children & Young People* [1991] IRLR 206 (NICA).

The courts have also been careful to scrutinize the employer's justification in other ways. If the tribunal finds that the material difference or material factor alleged is merely a pretext for unlawful discrimination, or if unlawful discrimination was a causal element in the variation, the employer will not succeed. In particular, employers have not been permitted to rely on material differences or material factors that have their roots in direct discrimination in the past.[1] In *National Vulcan Engineering Insurance Group Ltd* v. *Wade*[2] the Court of Appeal held that the variation in pay was genuinely due to the assessment of the skill, capacity and experience of each employee under a grading system and this amounted to a genuine material difference.

### 3.9.2         ECONOMIC BENEFITS/MARKET FORCES

Employers have pointed to market forces as reasons for differences in remuneration. Some employers have argued, for example, that it is necessary to maintain a balance between the internal wage structure and the external wage structure. The employer is, in effect, claiming that external job-for-job comparison should be used to limit the results of internal factor comparison, which otherwise would conclude that two 'different' jobs generally compensated differently should instead be paid equal wages. Such arguments have had a mixed response in British tribunals and courts.

Interpreting the 'material difference' defence, the Court of Appeal in *Clay Cross (Quarry Services) Ltd* v. *Fletcher*[3] confined the defence to the 'personal equation of the woman as compared to that of the man', such as much longer length of service, or superior skill or qualification, or greater output or productivity, or 'red circling'. The court would not consider in its analysis any extrinsic forces that led to the man being paid more. An employer could not avoid his obligation under the Act by saying, 'I paid him more because he asked for more', or 'I paid her less because she was willing to work for less'. If any such excuses were permitted, the court held, 'the Act would be a dead letter. Those are the very reasons why there was unequal pay before the statute. They are the very circumstances in which the statute was intended to operate'.

Since that case, however, the authority of this rejection of the 'market forces' argument has been weakened, even in the context of 'material

---

1    *Snoxell* v. *Vauxhall Motors Ltd* [1978] 1 QB 11, [1977] 3 WLR 189, [1977] 3 All ER 770, [1977] ICR 700, [1977] IRLR 123 (EAT). See also *Shields* v. *Coomes (E) (Holdings) Ltd* [1978] 1 WLR 1408, [1979] 1 All ER 456, [1978] ICR 1159, [1978] IRLR 263 (CA).
2    [1979] QB 132, [1978] 3 WLR 214, [1978] 3 All ER 121, [1978] ICR 800, [1978] IRLR 225 (CA). See also *Waddington* v. *Leicester Council for Voluntary Services* [1977] 1 WLR 544, [1977] 2 All ER 633, [1977] ICR 266, [1977] IRLR 32 (EAT).
3    [1978] 1 WLR 1429, [1979] 1 All ER 474, [1979] ICR 1, [1978] IRLR 361 (CA).

difference' claims. In *Rainey* v. *Greater Glasgow Health Authority*[1] the House of Lords upheld an employer's market forces defence. A Health Board argued that the almost £3,000 difference between a male prosthetist and a woman claimant was justified because she had been recruited directly into the National Health Service, whereas he had been transferred in at the higher rate that he had previously enjoyed in the private sector. Although all of the prosthetists at the higher rate were men, and all but one at the lower rate were women, the majority of the court upheld the differential because it was essential to recruit from the private sector at higher rates in order to staff the service. In *Enderby* v. *Frenchay Health Authority & Secretary of State for Health*[2] the EAT held that if the material factor defence put forward by the respondent — market forces — is found to have played a part in creating the difference in pay, this constitutes a complete defence even where the employer is unable to establish that the factor did not justify the whole of the difference.

### 3.9.3      NIGHT-WORK

In *National Coal Board* v. *Sherwin*[3] an employer argued that the fact that the men were employed on night-work, while the women were not, constituted a genuine material difference. While the tribunal accepted that although the fact that the men and the women worked at different times could constitute a material difference, in the circumstances of the case the variation between the men's and the women's pay was greater than could be justified by the fact that the men worked permanently on the night-shift. Since then, however, in *Thomas* v. *National Coal Board*,[4] it was held that the risk and additional responsibility of unsupervised night-work amounted to a material factor. In *Leverton* v. *Clwyd County Council*[5] the House of Lords held that a tribunal had not erred in finding that differences in hours and holiday entitlements amounted to a material factor defence in an equal value case.

### 3.9.4      PART-TIME WORK

One of the most difficult issues in the implementation of equal pay legislation arises when the courts consider an employer's attempt to justify unequal pay by relying on factors which, though apparently neutral, have a disparate impact on women. Such a defence, in other words,

---

1    [1987] AC 224, [1986] 3 WLR 1017, [1987] 1 All ER 65, [1987] ICR 129, [1987] IRLR 26 HL (Sc.). See further *Albion Shipping Agency* v. *Arnold* [1982] ICR 22, [1981] IRLR 525 (EAT).
2    [1991] IRLR 44 (EAT).
3    [1978] ICR 790, [1978] IRLR 122 (EAT).
4    [1987] ICR 757, [1987] IRLR 451 (EAT).
5    [1989] AC 706, [1989] 2 WLR 47, [1989] 1 All ER 78, [1989] ICR 33, [1989] IRLR 28 (HL).

disproportionately disadvantages women as a group. There has been a series of cases in which female part-time workers have sought pay equal to that received by male full-time workers. The EAT held in *Jenkins* v. *Kingsgate (Clothing Productions) Ltd (No 2)*[1] that any difference in pay must be 'objectively justified'. The tribunal therefore held that to show a 'material difference', an employer must show that the lower pay for part-time workers is reasonably necessary to achieve some justifiable objective other than a gender-related objective — for example, greater efficiency. It would not be enough to show that the employer intended to achieve this legitimate objective; the employer would have to show that the different objective was actually achieved. Since then the ECJ's important decision in *Bilka-Kaufhaus GmbH* v. *Weber von Hartz*[2] has clarified the appropriate test even further both in the context of part-time workers and more generally. The ECJ laid down that, under EC law, the relevant test is: (i) whether there are objective grounds justifying the difference, (ii) whether the practice is 'necessary', and (iii) whether the difference claimed to be justified is proportionate to the objective pursued.

Since then, the issue has been considered again by the ECJ in *Rinner-Kühn* v. *FWW Spezial-Gebäudereinigung GmbH & Co KG*,[3] in which a German statutory provision provided that the employer must continue to pay a worker who after having entered into employment is unable to continue working because of illness. However, workers whose employment did not exceed 10 hours per week, or 45 per month, were excluded. A considerably larger proportion of women than men were excluded by this provision. The ECJ held that the legislation must be justified and that the Government must 'establish that the means selected correspond to an objective necessary for its social policy and are appropriate and necessary for the attainment of that objective'. In *Kowalska* v. *Freie und Hansestadt Hamburg*[4] the applicant, a woman worker who worked part-time, argued that her employer was in breach of art. 119 of the EEC Treaty in failing to afford her severance payments on a non-discriminatory basis on her retirement. The collective agreement governing her right to severance payments stipulated that only full-time workers were entitled to such payments, where a considerably smaller proportion of men worked part-time than women. Failing to provide an objective justification, the ECJ held, indicated a breach of art. 119.

### 3.9.5 RED CIRCLES

Employers have in the past raised a wide range of issues under the material difference defence. British courts have allowed an employer to

---

1 [1981] 1 WLR 1485, [1981] ICR 715, [1981] IRLR 388 (EAT).
2 Case 170/84, [1986] ECR 1607, [1987] ICR 110, [1987] IRLR 317 (ECJ).
3 Case 171/88, [1989] ECR 2743, [1989] IRLR 493 (ECJ).
4 Case C-33/89, [1990] ECR I-2591, [1990] IRLR 447 (ECJ). See also *Nimz* v. *Freie und Hansestadt Hamburg*, Case C-184/89, [1991] ECR I-297 (ECJ).

justify lower pay to women because of factors personal to the particular men or women being compared. Unequal pay has been held to be justified by a number of personal differences such as: a different performance rating, where the rating was based on a system of performance appraisals; seniority, where employees receive periodic pay increases based on their tenure with the employer; and 'red circling', the procedure whereby the position of an employee is re-evaluated and, as a result, downgraded, but his or her wages are temporarily fixed until the wages appropriate to the downgraded position are equivalent to his or her wages. In order to decide whether red circling constitutes a defence in the circumstances of a particular case, relevant considerations include whether the wage protection is temporary or permanent, whether it had its origin in sex discrimination, whether employees of both sexes outside the red circle are treated the same, whether the protected group of employees is closed, and whether the red circling was done in consultation with all employees.[1] In *Outlook Supplies Ltd* v. *Parry*[2] the EAT discussed further how long red circling could reasonably be continued. In considering whether a red circle is a defence, it is relevant to take into account the time which has elapsed since the protection was introduced and whether the continuation of the protection was reasonable.

**3.9.6      OTHER REASONS**

There is also considerable debate in the United Kingdom, at the time of writing, about the extent to which, and under what circumstances, other reasons may be adduced as material factor defences: for example, the fact that the relevant men and women are in different collective bargaining units or separate pay structures may constitute a justification for a variation in pay between them. In some cases,[3] industrial tribunals and the EAT have accepted an employer's justification based on these grounds, while in others[4] differently constituted tribunals have rejected an employer's argument based

---

1    See, for example, *Snoxell* v. *Vauxhall Motors Ltd* [1978] 1 QB 11, [1977] 3 WLR 189, [1977] 3 All ER 770, [1977] ICR 700, [1977] IRLR 123 (EAT); *Sun Alliance & London Insurance Ltd* v. *Dudman* [1978] ICR 551 (EAT); *Shields* v. *Coomes (E) (Holdings) Ltd* [1978] 1 WLR 1408, [1979] 1 All ER 456, [1978] ICR 1159, [1978] IRLR 263 (CA). See also *Fullarton Fabrication (Irvine) Ltd* v. *Cairney* (1987) 2 BEQ 137; *United Biscuits Ltd* v. *Young* [1978] IRLR 15 (EAT) (facts supporting a red circle must be presented to the tribunal); *Forex Neptune (Overseas) Ltd* v. *Miller* [1987] ICR 170 (EAT) (demotion can amount to a genuine material factor defence); *Reed Packaging Ltd* v. *Boozer* [1988] ICR 391, [1988] IRLR 333 (EAT).

2    [1978] 2 All ER 707, [1978] ICR 388, [1978] IRLR 12 (EAT).

3    *Clark* v. *Bexley Health Authority & Secretary of State,* unreported (IT); *Enderby* v. *Frenchay Health Authority and Secretary of State for Health,* (1988) 24 EOR 42 (IT); *Reed Packaging Ltd* v. *Boozer* [1988] ICR 391, [1988] IRLR 333 (EAT); *Waddington* v. *Leicester Council for Voluntary Services* [1977] 1 WLR 544, [1977] 2 All ER 633, [1977] ICR 266, [1977] IRLR 32 (EAT).

4    *Webster* v. *Hoover plc* (1989) unreported (IT); *Fox* v. *Lloyds Bank* (1989) unreported (IT); *Winton* v. *Northern Ireland Electricity* (1989) unreported (NIIT).

on similar grounds. In *Enderby* v. *Frenchay Health Authority & Secretary of State for Health*[1] the EAT has now held that collective bargaining and a collective agreement are relevant to the issues of justification and may constitute such a justification provided that there is no 'gender tainting' of the bargaining agreement.

The extent to which an occupational category or job is gender dominated, though not explicitly considered on the face of the legislation, is relevant in a number of circumstances: first, as we have seen above, in providing evidence from which an inference may be drawn of the operation of a discriminatory job-evaluation scheme; second, in providing evidence from which an inference may be drawn that a material factor is one which is tainted with discrimination. In a third situation, however, it has been determined to be irrelevant. In *Pickstone* v. *Freemans plc*[2] the House of Lords held that merely because a woman did 'like work' with some men did not preclude a successful claim that she was doing work of equal value to a man other than those with whom she was doing 'like work'.

## 3.10      LEVELLING UP/DOWN

The EqPA, s. 1 provides that where there is like work, work rated as equivalent, or work of equal value, then the terms of the individual's contract of employment shall be not less favourable than that of the man, thus requiring levelling up.[3] In *Nimz* v. *Freie und Hansestadt Hamburg*[4] the ECJ held that art. 119 of the EEC Treaty required levelling up of arrangements in favour of the indirectly discriminated-against group.

---

1    [1991] IRLR 44 (EAT).
2    [1989] AC 66, [1988] 3 WLR 265, [1988] 2 All ER 803, [1988] ICR 697, [1988] IRLR 357 HL (E).
3    *Sorbie* v. *Trust House Forte Hotels Ltd* [1976] IRLR 371 (EAT).
4    Case C-184/89, [1991] ECR I-297 (ECJ).

# 4   EQUAL TREATMENT

## 4.1      PRINCIPLE

In principle, men and women have the right to equal treatment, in the
sense that they may not be unlawfully discriminated against, directly or
indirectly. This general principle is, however, subject to a number of
exceptions.

## 4.2      EXCEPTIONS

### 4.2.1      EXCLUSIONS

#### 4.2.1.1      Size

Although the SDA 1975 (s. 6(3)) originally included exceptions for
small employers, the SDA 1986, s. 1 repealed these exceptions after
infringement proceedings taken by the European Commission.[1] However, the
EOC Code of Practice includes the following advice with regard to small
businesses (para. 3):

> The Code has to deal in general terms and it will be necessary for employers to
> adapt it in a way appropriate to the size and structure of their organisations. Small
> businesses, for example, will require much simpler procedures than organisations
> with complex structures and it may not always be reasonable for them to carry out
> all the Code's detailed recommendations. In adapting the Code's recommendations,
> small firms should, however, ensure that their practices comply with the Sex
> Discrimination Act.

#### 4.2.1.2      Work done outside the jurisdiction

See §4.3 below.

#### 4.2.1.3      Health and safety

The SDA 1975, s. 51 provided for certain exceptions from the coverage
of the SDA 1975 for certain acts done for purposes of the protection of
women. It provided that nothing in the parts of the SDA prohibiting
discrimination in employment or vocational training rendered unlawful any

---

[1]   *Commission of the European Communities* v. *United Kingdom*, Case 165/82, [1983]
ECR 3431 (ECJ).

act done by a person in relation to a woman if it was necessary in order to comply with a requirement of a relevant statutory provision (within the meaning of Part I of the Health and Safety at Work etc. Act 1974) and if it was done by that person for the purpose of the protection of the woman in question (or any class of women that included that woman).

In *Peake* v. *Automotive Products Ltd*[1] Mr Peake complained that his employer permitted women employed by the same employer on the same shift as himself to leave work five minutes early each day. This practice, he argued, constituted unlawful direct discrimination against him. The EAT proceeded on the basis that the arrangements were made in the interests of safety and that the trade union had approved them. The employer argued that the practice was 'a sensible practical way to go about it wholly free of any intention to discriminate ... and that what was done was not in the least done on the grounds of sex'. The EAT rejected this argument. The Court of Appeal, however, reversed the judgment of the EAT. The approach taken by the two courts diverged considerably. Lord Denning in the Court of Appeal interpreted the less favourable treatment element of the definition as not obliterating 'the differences between men and women', or doing away with 'the chivalry and courtesy which we expect mankind to give woman-kind'. He continued that 'when a working rule is made differentiating between men and women in the interests of safety, there is no discrimination contrary to s. 1(1)(a) of the statute'.

In *Grieg* v. *Community Industry*,[2] however, the EAT distinguished Lord Denning's 'safety or good administration' exception in *Peake*:

> We read what is said in that case about sensible administrative arrangements as applicable to a case where a person is already employed and where a question arises whether there has been a benefit or a detriment. We do not read the judgment of the Master of the Rolls as intending to cover other situations than that with which the Court was dealing and it seems to us that different considerations do apply or may apply when one is considering a refusal of employment.

Subsequently, the Court of Appeal itself reconsidered Peake in *Jeremiah* v. *Ministry of Defence*.[3] In that case, one part of a factory produced colour bursting shells, where the work was dirty and required the use of protective clothing and the taking of showers at the end of the day. Those who worked in the shop got 4p per hour extra for such work, termed 'obnoxious pay'. The Ministry's practice was not to require women to work in the colour bursting shell shop, on the grounds that they did not want to have to take showers at the end of the day. Women had not asked to work in these

---

1   [1978] QB 233, [1977] 3 WLR 853, [1978] 1 All ER 106, [1977] ICR 968, [1977] IRLR 365 (CA).
2   [1979] ICR 356, [1979] IRLR 158 (EAT).
3   [1980] QB 87, [1979] 3 WLR 857, [1979] 3 All ER 833, [1980] ICR 13 (CA).

shops nor was there evidence that they would be willing to do so. Mr Jeremiah argued that he was being unlawfully discriminated against because if he volunteered for overtime, he was required to work on occasion in the colour bursting shop, whereas women were not so required. The Court of Appeal held that this was direct discrimination, despite their previous holding in *Peake*.

Lord Denning in effect overruled one of the grounds for his own decision in *Peake,* when he said:

> Turning to that case again, I think we were under a disadvantage, because Mr Peake appeared in person: and we were not referred to some of the relevant parts of the statute. There were two grounds for the decision. Now on reconsideration, I think the only sound ground was that the discrimination was *de minimis* ... In these circumstances, the other ground [about chivalry and administrative practice] should no longer be relied upon.

Brandon LJ was more cautious in overturning the 'safety and administrative practices ground ' in *Peake*:

> I do not find it necessary to express any opinion one way or the other ... because it seems to me that, even assuming that the first ground of the decision was correct and is binding on this court, it has no application to the facts of this case.

He did, however, consider the judgment of Shaw LJ in *Peake* to be 'unpersuasive' in holding that 'hostility' must be present before s. 1(1)(a) could be found to have been breached.

Industrial tribunals continued to hold that aspects of the Court of Appeal decision in *Peake* were still good law, however, in particular the 'interests of safety' aspect. The continued use of this part of Lord Denning's judgment came before the EAT in *Page* v. *Freight Hire (Tank Haulage) Ltd.*[1] Mrs Page was employed by the respondents as a heavy goods vehicle driver. One of the jobs she was asked to do involved hauling chemicals between chemical plants. One of these chemicals was DMF made by ICI. Subsequently, a senior manager of ICI informed the respondents that because of the danger to women of child-bearing age from the chemical, Mrs Page must not be used to haul that chemical again and she was taken off that job. The industrial tribunal held that the respondents had not acted unlawfully. Relying on the Court of Appeal decision in *Peake*, the tribunal held that it was an answer for an employer to show that what had been done was done in the interests of safety. The EAT, however, allowed Mrs Page's appeal against the decision. After reviewing the decision of Lord Denning in the *Jeremiah* case, the EAT concluded that he was saying that not only good administration but also the interests of safety were no longer to be put

---

[1]    [1981] 1 All ER 394, [1981] ICR 299 (EAT).

forward as a justification for what was otherwise discrimination on the grounds of sex. The EAT continued:

> It seems to us that in this legislation ... the exceptions to the provisions which define what is a breach of the Sex Discrimination Act are to be found in the sections of the Act itself ....

However, the company argued further that s. 51 of the SDA 1975, which relieved persons from liability under the SDA because they were required to comply with the Health and Safety at Work etc. Act 1974, rendered their actions lawful in this case. The applicant argued that for this exception to apply an employer had to show that his or her action was the only course available to him or her. The EAT rejected this argument, holding that the employer was entitled to act as he did on the basis of a direction from the manufacturers of the chemical and a written warning.

The Employment Act 1989, s. 4 provided that without prejudice to the operation of s. 51 of the SDA 1975, nothing in the provisions of the SDA 1975 rendered unlawful any act done by a person in relation to a woman if it was necessary for that person to do that act in order to comply with any requirement of any of the provisions specified in Sch. 1 to the Employment Act 1989 (which was concerned with the protection of women at work).

The Employment Act 1989 amended s. 51, removing most of the restrictions on the employment of women (for example, on heavy work in mines or quarries) except those justified on health and safety grounds (see §1.2.4.1 above). An employer may claim that it is necessary to do a discriminatory act to comply with a requirement under the Health and Safety at Work etc. Act 1974. For such a claim to succeed he is required to demonstrate that it was done 'for the purpose of the protection of the woman in question or of any class of women that included that woman'.

### 4.2.1.4    National security

The SDA 1975, s. 52(1) allows discrimination for the purpose of safeguarding national security. SDA 1975, s. 52(2) further provides that a certificate purporting to be signed by or on behalf of a government minister and certifying that an act specified in the certificate was done for the purpose of safeguarding national security is conclusive evidence that it was done for that purpose. By s. 52(3), such a certificate must be received in evidence and deemed to be a certificate complying with this requirement unless the contrary is proved.

These restrictions on the coverage of the Act so far as issues concerning national security were involved were disapplied to an extent after the ECJ decision in *Johnston* v. *RUC*.[1] SDA 1975, s. 52 is disapplied in cases alleging discrimination under the employment and vocational training provisions of the SDA 1975 in so far as a certificate purporting to be signed by or on behalf of a Minister of the Crown and certifying that an act specified in the certificate was done for the purpose of safeguarding national security is no longer conclusive evidence that it was done for that purpose.

### 4.2.1.5 Religion, religious schools

There is no exception as such for religious schools. The Employment Act 1989, s. 5 provides, however, for a specific exemption for discrimination in connection with certain educational appointments which will affect religious schools. It provides that nothing in the employment or vocational training provisions of the SDA 1975 shall render unlawful any act done by a person in connection with the employment of another person as the head teacher or principal of any educational establishment if it was necessary for that person to do that act in order to comply with any requirement of any instrument relating to the establishment that its head teacher or principal should be a member of a particular religious order.

The section further provides that nothing in the employment or vocational training provisions of the SDA 1975 shall render unlawful any act done by a person in connection with the employment of another person as a professor in any university if the professorship in question is, in accordance with any Act or instrument relating to the university, either a canon professorship or one to which a canonry is annexed.

### 4.2.1.6 Retirement age

As originally enacted, s. 6(4) of the SDA 1975 provided that the provisions of s. 6 prohibiting discrimination against applicants[2] and employees[3] did not apply to provisions in relation to death or retirement. In *Roberts* v. *Cleveland Area Health Authority*[4] differences in normal retirement ages between men and women were held to be excluded from the coverage of the SDA. In *Duke* v. *GEC Reliance*[5] the House of Lords adopted a similar approach. In *Marshall* v. *Southampton & SW Hampshire Area Health Authority*,[6] however, Miss Marshall complained of sex discrimination

---

1    Case 222/84, [1986] ECR 1651, [1987] QB 129, [1986] 3 WLR 1038, [1987] ICR 83, [1986] IRLR 263 (ECJ): Sex Discrimination (Amendment) Order 1988 (SI 1988 No 249).
2    SDA 1975, s. 6(1)(b).
3    SDA 1975, s. 6(2).
4    [1979] 1 WLR 754, [1979] 2 All ER 1163, [1979] ICR 558, [1979] IRLR 244 (CA).
5    [1988] AC 618, [1988] 1 All ER 626, [1988] ICR 339, [1988] IRLR 118, HL (E).
6    Case 152/84, [1986] ECR 723, [1986] QB 401, [1986] 2 WLR 780, [1986] 2 All ER 584, [1986] ICR 335, [1986] IRLR 140 (ECJ).

arising from her dismissal at the age of 62 after she had reached normal retirement age for a woman but before that of a man. The ECJ decided that the 1976 Directive prohibited discrimination as regards age limits for compulsory retirement; but since the Directive was not horizontally directly effective, this prohibition applied only to State organs. The SDA 1986 extended the principle in *Marshall* to private sector employers, and to voluntary redundancy schemes, early retirement schemes, and so forth, as regards dismissal of employees.

The SDA 1986, s. 2(1) amended the SDA 1975, which now provides that the exception in s. 6(4) does not prevent the application of the provisions of s. 6 prohibiting discrimination against applicants and employees to provisions in relation to retirement in so far as the section renders it unlawful for a person to discriminate against a woman:

(a)  in such of the terms on which he offers her employment as make provision in relation to the way he will afford her access to opportunities for promotion, transfer or training or as provide for her dismissal or demotion; or

(b)  in the way he affords her access to opportunities for promotion, transfer or training or by refusing or deliberately omitting to afford her access to any such opportunities; or

(c)  by dismissing her or subjecting her to any detriment which results in her dismissal or consists in or involves her demotion.[1]

As regards occupational pension schemes, the Social Security Pensions Act 1975 required employers to provide equal access, though it was permissible to offer different benefits under these schemes. Hepple[2] states that the 1986 amendment sought to retain this position. The SDA now provides, therefore, that the exception for death and retirement does not prevent the application of the provisions of s. 6 prohibiting discrimination against applicants and employees in so far as the section renders it unlawful for a person to discriminate against a woman:

(a)  in such of the terms on which he offers her employment as make provision in relation to the way in which he will afford her access to any benefits, facilities or services under an occupational pension scheme; or

(b)  in the way he affords her access to any such benefits, facilities or services; or

(c)  by refusing or deliberately omitting to afford her access to any such benefits, facilities or services; or

(d)  by subjecting her to any detriment in connection with any such scheme; ... .[3]

However, an act of discrimination is rendered unlawful only to the extent that the act relates to a matter in respect of which an occupational pension scheme has to comply with the principle of equal treatment in

---

1    SDA 1975, s. 6(4A).

2    *Encyclopedia*, para. IB-809.

3    SDA 1975, s. 6(4B).

accordance with Part I of Sch. 5 to the Social Security Act 1989. The effect of these provisions is that, according to Hepple,[1] occupational pensions and redundancy payments are outside the purview of the Act. In *Hammersmith & Queen Charlotte's Special Health Authority* v. *Cato*[2] the EAT held that a contractual payment which followed the statutory redundancy payments scheme by reducing payments for women over the age of 59 but not for men contravened art. 119 of the EEC Treaty. However, the Employment Act 1989 gave women the right to statutory redundancy payments at the same age as men under domestic law. In *Barber* v. *Guardian Royal Exchange Assurance Group*[3] the ECJ held that it is contrary to art. 119 for a man who has been made compulsorily redundant to be entitled to claim only a deferred pension payable at the normal retirement age when a woman in the same position is entitled to an immediate retirement payment, due to the application of a condition to the pension provision which varies access to the benefits according to the sex of the beneficiary in the same way as is provided for by the national statutory pension scheme. See further §§3.2.6, 5.2.4, 5.4.1.

In the application of the provisions of s. 6 prohibiting discrimination against applicants and employees to discrimination against married persons of either sex, Part I of Sch. 5 to the Social Security Act 1989 shall be taken to apply to less favourable treatment of married persons on the basis of their marital status as it applies in relation to less favourable treatment of persons on the basis of sex, and references to persons of either sex shall be construed accordingly.[4]

### 4.2.2 SEX AS A DETERMINING FACTOR

### 4.2.2.1 Lists

The principal listing of situations in which sex is permitted to be a determining factor is contained in the 'genuine occupational qualification' exception (see §4.2.2.2 below).

### 4.2.2.2 Genuine occupational qualification

SDA 1975, s. 7 provides that the principal provisions of the SDA prohibiting discrimination in employment do not apply to any employment where being a man or a woman is a genuine occupational qualification (GOQ) for the job. Section 7(2) of the SDA 1975 provides that sex is a genuine occupational qualification in a number of situations.

---

[1]   *Loc. cit.*
[2]   [1988] ICR 132 (EAT).
[3]   Case C-262/88, [1990] ECR I-1889, [1990] 2 All ER 660, [1990] IRLR 240 (ECJ).
[4]   SDA 1975, s. 6(4C).

(1) The essential nature of the job calls for a man for reasons of physiology (excluding physical strength or stamina) or, in a dramatic performance or other entertainment, for reasons of authenticity, so that the essential nature of the job would be materially different if carried out by a woman.

(2) The job needs to be held by a man to preserve decency or privacy because it is likely to involve physical contact with men in circumstances where they might reasonably object to its being carried out by a woman, or the holder of the job is likely to do his work in circumstances where men might reasonably object to the presence of a woman because they are in a state of undress or are using sanitary facilities.

(3) The job is likely to involve the holder of the job doing his work, or living, in a private home and needs to be held by a man because objection might reasonably be taken to allowing to a woman the degree of physical or social contact with a person living in the home, or the knowledge of intimate details of such a person's life, which is likely, because of the nature or circumstances of the job or of the home, to be allowed to, or available to, the holder of the job.

(4) The nature or location of the establishment makes it impracticable for the holder of the job to live elsewhere than in premises provided by the employer, and the only such premises which are available for persons holding that kind of job are lived in, or normally lived in, by men and are not equipped with separate sleeping accommodation for women and sanitary facilities which could be used by women in privacy from men, and it is not reasonable to expect the employer either to equip those premises with such accommodation and facilities or to provide other premises for women.

(5) The nature of the establishment, or of part of it within which the work is done, requires the job to be held by a man because it is, or is part of, a hospital, prison or other establishment for persons requiring special care, supervision or attention, and those persons are all men (disregarding any woman whose presence is exceptional), and it is reasonable, having regard to the essential character of the establishment or that part, that the job should not be held by a woman.

(6) The holder of the job provides individuals with personal services promoting their welfare or education, or similar personal services, and those services can most effectively be provided by a man.

(7) The job needs to be held by a man because it is likely to involve the performance of duties outside the United Kingdom in a country whose laws or customs are such that the duties could not, or could not effectively, be performed by a woman.

(8) The job is one of two to be held by a married couple.

The GOQ exception applies where only some of the duties of the job fall within (1) to (7) as well as where all of them do.[1] However, the exceptions in paras (1), (2), (3), (4), (5), or (7) do not apply in relation to the filling of a vacancy at a time when the employer already has male employees who are capable of carrying out the duties falling within that paragraph, whom it would be reasonable to employ on those duties, and whose numbers are sufficient to meet the employer's likely requirements in respect of those duties without undue inconvenience.[2]

Where sex is a GOQ for the job, employers may lawfully discriminate in the arrangements they make for determining who should be offered employment, or by refusing or deliberately omitting to offer that employment, or in the way they afford access to opportunities for promotion or transfer to, or training for such employment. The GOQ defence does not apply however where the conduct complained of is discrimination in the terms on which employment is offered, or in the way employers afford access to any other benefits, facilities, or services offered.[3]

The EOC's Code of Practice advises employers on the ambit of the GOQ defence.[4]

On the general principles which should apply to the interpretation of the GOQ defence, see *Tottenham Green Under-Fives Centre* v. *Marshall*,[5] *Lambeth LBC* v. *CRE*,[6] and *Tottenham Green Under-Fives Centre* v. *Marshall (No 2)*.[7] On the effect of EC law on the interpretation of these provisions, see *Johnston* v. *RUC*.[8]

### 4.2.2.3 Authenticity

*Actors/Models*

We have seen that the exception for genuine occupational qualifications includes an exception for circumstances where:

> ... the essential nature of the job calls for a man for reasons of physiology (excluding physical strength or stamina) or, in a dramatic performance or other

---

1    SDA 1975, s. 7(3).
2    SDA 1975, s. 7(4).
3    See further *Timex Corporation* v. *Hodgson* [1982] ICR 63, [1981] IRLR 530 (EAT).
4    See EOC Code, paras 15-17.
5    [1989] ICR 214, [1989] IRLR 147 (EAT).
6    [1990] IRLR 231 (CA).
7    [1991] IRLR 162 (EAT).
8    Case 222/84, [1986] ECR 1651, [1987] QB 129, [1986] 3 WLR 1038, [1987] ICR 83, [1986] IRLR 263 (ECJ).

entertainment, for reasons of authenticity, so that the essential nature of the job would be materially different if carried out by a woman ... .[1]

with the limitations noted above.

### 4.2.2.4        Security

*Police*

In *Johnston* v. *RUC*[2] the ECJ held that in certain circumstances it was open to a Member State to restrict policing duties to armed men. However, it held that art. 9(2) of the Equal Treatment Directive required the Member State to reassess such a decision periodically to see whether the exception should be maintained and that exceptions were subject to the principle of proportionality which limited the exception to what was appropriate and necessary for achieving what is aimed at.

The SDA 1975, s. 17 provides that regulations made under the Police Act 1964 shall not treat men and women differently except (a) as to requirements relating to height, uniform or equipment, or allowances in lieu of uniform or equipment, or (b) so far as special treatment is accorded to women in connection with pregnancy or childbirth, or (c) in relation to pensions to or in respect of special constables or police cadets.[3]

Where employment discrimination is prohibited, and for the purposes of the employment discrimination provisions of the Act, the holding of the office of constable shall be treated as employment by the chief officer of police as respects any act done by him in relation to a constable or that office, and by the police authority as respects any act done by them in relation to a constable or that office.

*Prison officers*

There are two relevant provisions of the SDA 1975. First, s. 18 specifies that nothing in the employment discrimination provisions of the Act renders unlawful any discrimination between male and female prison officers as to requirements relating to height. Second, the genuine occupational qualification provisions of the Act discussed above provide (s. 7(2)(d)) that a GOQ operates where the nature of the establishment, or of part of it within which the work is done, requires the job to be held by a man because it is, or is part of, a prison or other establishment for persons requiring special care,

---

1    SDA 1975, s. 7(2)(a).
2    Case 222/84, [1986] ECR 1651, [1987] QB 129, [1986] 3 WLR 1038, [1987] ICR 83, [1986] IRLR 263 (ECJ).
3    See also *Sheikh* v. *Anderton* [1989] 2 WLR 1102, [1989] 2 All ER 684, [1989] ICR 373 (CA) on the position of special constables under the Race Relations Act 1976.

supervision or attention, and those persons are all men (disregarding any woman whose presence is exceptional), and it is reasonable, having regard to the essential character of the establishment or that part, that the job should not be held by a woman. In *Secretary of State for Scotland* v. *Henley*[1] the EAT held that being a man was not a GOQ within the meaning of this section for the post of governor in an all-male prison.

*Armed forces and other military or semi-military corps*

The SDA 1975, s. 85 specifies that the Act does not apply in relation to service in the naval, military or air forces of the Crown. Nor does the Act render unlawful discrimination in admission to the Army Cadet Force, Air Training Corps, Sea Cadet Corps or Combined Cadet Force, or any other cadet training corps for the time being administered by the Ministry of Defence. Nor does the Act apply to employment in the case of which the employee may be required to serve in support of the naval, military or air forces of the Crown.

### 4.2.2.5    Religion

*Clergy, members of religious orders*

The SDA 1975, s. 19 specifies that nothing in the employment discrimination provisions of the Act applies to employment for purposes of an organized religion where the employment is limited to one sex so as to comply with the doctrines of the religion or avoid offending the religious susceptibilities of a significant number of its followers.

### 4.2.2.6    Decency and privacy

The genuine occupational qualification provisions of the SDA 1975 specify that a GOQ operates where the job needs to be held by a man to preserve decency or privacy because it is likely to involve physical contact with men in circumstances where they might reasonably object to its being carried out by a woman, or the holder of the job is likely to do his work in circumstances where men might reasonably object to the presence of a woman because they are in a state of undress or are using sanitary facilities.[2] In *EOC for NI* v. *Board of Governors, Royal School Dungannon* (NIIT), being a man was held to be a genuine occupational qualification for the post of headmaster of a boys' boarding school on the grounds that such a GOQ was necessary to preserve decency and privacy.

---

[1]    (1983, 19 May) unreported (Scottish EAT).
[2]    SDA 1975, s. 7(2)(b). See further *Sisley* v. *Britannia Security Systems Ltd* [1983] ICR 628, [1983] IRLR 404 (EAT).

## Physical education teachers

Except to the extent that other provisions provide for an exception which is relevant, there is no exception in the Act relating to physical education teachers.[1]

## Hospitals

The genuine occupational qualification provisions of the SDA 1975 specify that a GOQ operates where the nature of the establishment, or of part of it within which the work is done, requires the job to be held by a man because it is, or is part of, a hospital, and those persons are all men (disregarding any woman whose presence is exceptional), and it is reasonable, having regard to the essential character of the establishment or that part, that the job should not be held by a woman.[2] See *Balfour* v. *Eastern Health & Social Services Board*[3] where the applicability of the exception was regarded as not proven by a hospital and in which a male staff nurse successfully claimed unlawful discrimination against the hospital.

## Midwives

Until 1 September 1983 SDA 1975, s. 6(1) did not apply to employment as a midwife, s. 6(2)(a) did not apply to promotion, transfer or training as a midwife, and s. 14 did not apply to training as a midwife.

## Embarrassment

In addition to the provisions concerning genuine occupational qualifications discussed above, SDA 1975, s. 46 provides that nothing in the employment discrimination provisions shall render unlawful sex discrimination in the admission of persons to 'communal accommodation' if the accommodation is managed in a way which, given the exigencies of the situation, comes as near as may be to fair and equitable treatment of men and women. Account shall be taken of whether and how far it is reasonable to expect that the accommodation should be altered or extended, or that further alternative accommodation should be provided; and the frequency of the demand or need for use of the accommodation by men as compared with women.

The SDA 1975, s. 46 further provides that nothing in the employment discrimination provisions of the SDA 1975 shall render unlawful sex discrimination against a woman, or against a man, as respects the provision of any benefit, facility or service if the benefit, facility or service cannot

---

1     See *Briggs* v. *NE Education & Library Board* [1990] IRLR 181 (NICA).

2     SDA 1975, s.7(2)(d).

3     32/81SD, unreported (NIIT).

properly and effectively be provided except for those using communal accommodation, and in the relevant circumstances the woman or, as the case may be, the man could lawfully be refused the use of the accommodation by virtue of the previously described provision.

However, neither exception described above is a defence to an act of sex discrimination under the employment discrimination provisions unless such arrangements as are reasonably practicable are made to compensate for the detriment caused by the discrimination. In s. 46 'communal accommodation' means residential accommodation which includes dormitories or other shared sleeping accommodation which for reasons of privacy or decency should be used by men only, or by women only (but which may include some shared sleeping accommodation for men, and some for women, or some ordinary sleeping accommodation). It also includes residential accommodation all or part of which should be used by men only, or by women only, because of the nature of the sanitary facilities serving the accommodation.

### 4.2.2.7    Single-sex establishments

The Employment Act 1989, s. 5 provides for certain exemptions for discrimination in connection with certain educational appointments. It provides that nothing in the provisions of the 1975 Act shall render unlawful any act done by a person in connection with the employment of another person as the head, a fellow or any other member of the academic staff of any college in a university if it was necessary to do that act in order to comply with any requirement of any instrument relating to the college that the holder of the position in question should be a woman. However, that exception does not apply in relation to instruments taking effect after the commencement of the 1989 Act. The Secretary of State may by order provide that these provisions shall not have effect in relation to any educational establishment or university specified in the order.

In addition, SDA 1975, s. 43 specifies that nothing in the employment discrimination provisions of the Act shall be construed as affecting any provision for conferring benefits on persons of one sex only (disregarding any benefits to persons of the opposite sex which are exceptional or are relatively insignificant), being a provision which is contained in a charitable instrument, or rendering unlawful an act which is done in order to give effect to such a provision. A 'charitable instrument' means an enactment or other instrument so far as it relates to charitable purposes, and in Scotland includes the governing instrument of an endowment or of an educational endowment.[1]

---

[1]    See further *Hugh-Jones* v. *St John's College, Cambridge* [1979] ICR 848 (EAT).

## 4.3      TERRITORIAL SCOPE

The SDA 1975, s. 10 specifies that for the purposes of the employment discrimination provisions of the Act, employment is to be regarded as being at an establishment in Great Britain unless the employee does his work wholly or mainly outside Great Britain. This does not apply to employment on board a ship registered at a port of registry in Great Britain, or employment on aircraft or hovercraft registered in the United Kingdom and operated by a person who has his principal place of business, or is ordinarily resident, in Great Britain, but for the purposes of the Act such employment is to be regarded as being at an establishment in Great Britain unless the employee does his work wholly outside Great Britain. In the case of employment on board a ship registered at a port of registry in Great Britain (except where the employee does his work wholly outside Great Britain, and outside any area added by Order: see below) the ship shall for the purposes of the Act be deemed to be the establishment.[1] 'Great Britain' includes such of the territorial waters of the United Kingdom as are adjacent to Great Britain. In relation to employment concerned with exploration of the sea bed or subsoil or the exploitation of their natural resources, Her Majesty may by Order in Council provide that Great Britain includes any area for the time being designated under s. 1(7) of the Continental Shelf Act 1964, except an area or part of an area in which the law of Northern Ireland applies.

The Sex Discrimination & Equal Pay (Offshore Employment) Order 1987[2] provides (in part) that in relation to employment concerned with exploration of the sea bed or subsoil or the exploitation of their natural resources, s. 10 of the SDA 1975 shall have effect as if the reference to Great Britain included (a) any area for the time being designated under s. 1 (7) of the Continental Shelf Act 1964, except an area or part of an area in which the law of Northern Ireland applies; and (b) in relation to employment concerned with the exploration or exploitation of the Frigg Gas Field, a part of the Norwegian sector of the Continental Shelf. However, the Order has no application to employment which is concerned with the exploration or exploitation of the Frigg Gas Field unless the employer is (a) a company registered under the Companies Act 1985; (b) an overseas company which has established a place of business within Great Britain from which it directs the offshore operations in question, or (c) any other person who has a place of business within Great Britain from which he directs the offshore operations in question.

---

1     See, for example, *Haughton* v. *Olau Line (UK) Ltd* [1986] 1 WLR 504, [1986] 2 All ER 47, [1986] ICR 357, [1986] IRLR 465 (CA).

2     SI 1987 No 930.

## 4.4     PERSONAL SCOPE

### 4.4.1     EMPLOYEES

The SDA 1975, s. 82 specifies that 'employment' means employment under a contract of service or of apprenticeship or a contract personally to execute any work or labour. On the meaning of 'contract of service' in general labour law, see *Ready Mixed Concrete (SE) Ltd* v. *Minister of Pensions & National Insurance*.[1] In *Gunning* v. *Mirror Group Newspapers Ltd*[2] the Court of Appeal held that the correct test for determining whether there was 'a contract personally to execute any work or labour' was whether the sole or dominant purpose of the contract was the execution of any work or labour by the contracting party personally.[3] In *Hugh-Jones* v. *St John's College, Cambridge*[4] the EAT held that a research fellowship could amount to employment. Although there was no contract of service, there was a contract to execute work or labour since these words included the doing of research, following a course of study in preparation for research or even in some circumstances working outside the University. In *Knight* v. *AG*[5] it was held that a Justice of the Peace is not 'employed'.

The Courts and Legal Services Act 1990, ss 64 and 65, extend the protection of the SDA 1975 to barristers (advocates in Scotland), to cover discrimination in professional relationships between barristers, and between barristers (advocates in Scotland) and those instructing them.

### 4.4.2     INDEPENDENT CONTRACTORS

SDA 1975, s. 9 specifies that certain discrimination against contract workers is prohibited. This section applies to any work for a person ('the principal') which is available for doing by individuals ('contract workers') who are employed not by the principal but by another person, who supplies them under a contract made with the principal. It is unlawful for the principal, in relation to work to which this section applies, to discriminate against a woman who is a contract worker in the terms on which he allows her to do that work, or by not allowing her to do it or continue to do it (unless being a man is a genuine occupational qualification), or by subjecting her to any other detriment, or in the way he affords her access to any benefits, facilities or services or by refusing or deliberately omitting to afford her access to them. This last prohibition does not apply to benefits, facilities or

---

1     [1968] 2 QB 497.
2     [1986] ICR 145, [1986] IRLR 27 (CA).
3     See also *Sheikh* v. *Anderton* [1989] 2 WLR 1102, [1989] 2 All ER 684, [1989] ICR 373 (CA); *Quinnen* v. *Hovells* [1984] ICR 525, [1984] IRLR 227 (EAT); *Tanna* v. *Post Office* [1981] ICR 374 (EAT); *Daley* v. *Allied Suppliers* [1983] ICR 90 (EAT).
4     [1979] ICR 848 (EAT).
5     [1979] ICR 194 (EAT).

services of any description if the principal is concerned with the provision (for payment or not) of benefits, facilities or services of that description to the public, or to a section of the public to which the woman belongs, unless that provision differs in a material respect from the provision of the benefits, facilities or services by the principal to his contract workers.[1]

### 4.4.3    HOME WORKERS

The SDA 1975, s.10(4) provides that where work is not done at an establishment it shall be treated for the relevant purposes as done at the establishment from which it is done or (where it is not done from any establishment) at the establishment with which it has the closest connection.

### 4.4.4    PUBLIC SECTOR

The SDA 1975, s. 85 specifies that the Act applies to an act done by or for purposes of a Minister of the Crown or government department, or to an act done on behalf of the Crown by a statutory body, or a person holding a statutory office, as it applies to an act done by a private person. The employment discrimination provisions of the Act also apply to service for purposes of a Minister of the Crown or government department, other than service of a person holding a statutory office, or service on behalf of the Crown for purposes of a person holding a statutory office or purposes of a statutory body, as they apply to employment by a private person. A 'statutory body' means a body set up by or in pursuance of an enactment, and 'statutory office' means an office so set up; but service 'for purposes of' a Minister of the Crown or government department does not include service in any Ministerial office.[2]

The SDA 1975, s. 86 applies to government appointments outside the scope of employment relationships (such as appointments by a Minister of the Crown or government department to an office or post where s. 6 does not apply in relation to the appointment). In making the appointment, and in making the arrangements for determining who should be offered the office or post, the Minister of the Crown or government department shall not do an act which would be unlawful under s. 6 if the Crown were the employer for the purposes of this Act.

The Local Government and Housing Act 1989 provides in s. 7 that every appointment of a person to a paid office or employment under a local authority or parish or community council 'shall be made on merit', subject to the exception in s. 7 of the SDA 1975 where discrimination is permitted in

---

1    See *Rice* v. *Fon-A-Car* [1980] ICR 133 (EAT) for a definition of 'contract worker'.
2    See further *Knight* v. *AG* [1979] ICR 194 (EAT); *Department of the Environment* v. *Fox* [1980] 1 All ER 58, [1979] ICR 736 (EAT).

relation to employment where the sex of the employee is a genuine occupational qualification (see §4.2.2.2 above).

### 4.4.5 DOMESTIC EMPLOYEES

Employment for the purposes of a private household used to be exempt from the SDA 1975, but this provision was replaced by the SDA 1986, s. 1(1), following the ECJ decision in *Commission of the European Communities* v. *United Kingdom*.[1] Domestic employees are covered by the provisions of the Act in the same way as other employees. However, a new genuine occupational qualification exception, added in the 1986 Act, is likely to be particularly relevant to some such employment relationships. The GOQ defence now specifies that the Act does not apply if the job is likely to involve the holder of the job doing his work, or living, in a private home and needs to be held by a man because objection might reasonably be taken to allowing to a woman the degree of physical or social contact with a person living in the home, or the knowledge of intimate details of such a person's life, which is likely, because of the nature or circumstances of the job or of the home, to be allowed to, or available to, the holder of the job.[2]

### 4.4.6 PERSONS WITHOUT A CONTRACT OF EMPLOYMENT

See §§4.4.1 to 4.4.5 above.

### 4.4.7 OTHERS

There are no other relevant statutory provisions.

### 4.5 ACTIVITIES COVERED

SDA 1975, s. 6 prohibits discrimination against applicants and employees. It is unlawful for a person, in relation to employment, to discriminate against a woman (a) in the arrangements he makes for the purpose of determining who should be offered that employment, (b) in the terms on which he offers her that employment (excluding any provision for the payment of money which, if the woman in question were given the employment, would be included (directly or otherwise) in the contract under which she was employed), or (c) by refusing or deliberately omitting to offer her that employment.

It is unlawful for a person, in the case of a woman employed by him, to discriminate against her in the way he affords her access to opportunities for promotion, transfer or training, or to any other benefits, facilities or services,

---

1    Case 165/82, [1983] ECR 3431 (ECJ).
2    SDA 1975, s. 7(2)(ba).

or by refusing or deliberately omitting to afford her access to them. However, this prohibition does not apply to benefits, facilities or services of any description if the employer is concerned with the provision (for payment or not) of benefits, facilities or services of that description to the public, or to a section of the public comprising the woman in question, unless (a) that provision differs in a material respect from the provision of the benefits, facilities or services by the employer to his employees, or (b) that provision of the benefits, facilities or services to the woman in question is regulated by her contract of employment, or (c) the benefits, facilities or services relate to training.

It is unlawful for a person, in relation to employment by him, to discriminate against a woman by dismissing her, or subjecting her to any other detriment.

SDA 1975, s. 11 makes it unlawful for a firm, in relation to a position as partner in the firm, to discriminate against a woman (a) in the arrangements they make for the purpose of determining who should be offered that position (unless being a man is a genuine occupational qualification), or (b) in the terms on which they offer her that position, or (c) by refusing or deliberately omitting to offer her that position (unless being a man is a genuine occupational qualification).

In a case where the woman already holds a position, it is unlawful for a firm to discriminate (a) in the way they afford her access to any benefits, facilities or services, or by refusing or deliberately omitting to afford her access to them, or (b) by expelling her from that position, or subjecting her to any other detriment.

The prohibition on discrimination applies in relation to persons proposing to form themselves into a partnership as it applies in relation to a firm. The dismissal of a person from employment or the expulsion of a person from a position as partner includes (a) the termination of that person's employment or partnership by the expiration of any period (including a period expiring by reference to an event or circumstance), not being a termination immediately after which the employment or partnership is renewed on the same terms, and (b) the termination of that person's employment or partnership by any act of his (including the giving of notice) in circumstances such that he is entitled to terminate it without notice by reason of the conduct of the employer or, as the case may be, the conduct of the other partners.

SDA 1975, s. 13 makes it unlawful for an authority or body which can confer an authorization or qualification which is needed for, or facilitates, engagement in a particular profession or trade to discriminate against a woman (a) in the terms on which it is prepared to confer on her that authorization or qualification, or (b) by refusing or deliberately omitting to grant her application for it, or (c) by withdrawing it from her or varying the terms on which she holds it.[1]

Where an authority or body is required by law to satisfy itself as to his good character before conferring on a person an authorization or qualification which is needed for, or facilitates, his engagement in any profession or trade then, without prejudice to any other duty to which it is subject, that requirement shall be taken to impose on the authority or body a duty to have regard to any evidence tending to show that he, or any of his employees, or agents (whether past or present), has practised unlawful discrimination in, or in connection with, the carrying on of any profession or trade.

SDA 1975, s. 15(1) makes it unlawful for an employment agency to discriminate against a woman (a) in the terms on which the agency offers to provide any of its services, or (b) by refusing or deliberately omitting to provide any of its services, or (c) in the way it provides any of its services.[2]

By virtue of s. 15(2) it is also unlawful for a local education authority or an education authority to do any act in the performance of its functions under s. 8 of the Employment and Training Act 1973 which constitutes discrimination. Section 15 does not apply, however, if the discrimination only concerns employment which the employer could lawfully refuse to offer the woman.[3] In addition, an employment agency or local education authority or an education authority shall not be subject to any liability under s. 15 if it proves (a) that it acted in reliance on a statement made to it by the employer to the effect that, by reason of the operation of subs. (4), its action would not be unlawful, and (b) that it was reasonable for it to rely on the statement.[4]

The Education (Modification of Enactments Relating to Employment) Order 1989[5] varies ss 6, 7, 9, 41 and 82(1A) of the SDA 1975 to take account of the requirement contained in the Education Reform Act 1988 for local education authorities to delegate financial management of schools and institutions to their governing bodies.

---

1  See *British Judo Association* v. *Petty* [1981] ICR 660, [1981] IRLR 484 (EAT).
2  See *Rice* v. *Fon-A-Car* [1980] ICR 133 (EAT).
3  SDA 1975, s. 15(4).
4  SDA 1975, s. 15(5).
5  SI 1989 No 901.

## 4.6          COMPARATOR

As discussed above (§2.2.1.3), a comparison of the case of persons of different sex or marital status must be such that the relevant circumstances in the one case are the same, or not materially different, in the other.[1]

## 4.7          HIRING

### 4.7.1          RECRUITMENT METHODS

It is unlawful for a person to discriminate against an applicant 'in the arrangements he makes for the purpose of determining who should be offered ... employment'.[2] The EOC Code of Practice makes various recommendations concerning recruitment methods (see EOC Code, para. 13[3]).

### 4.7.2          ADVERTISEMENTS

SDA 1975, s. 38 prohibits discriminatory advertisements. It is unlawful to publish or cause to be published an advertisement which indicates, or might reasonably be understood as indicating, an intention by a person to do any act which is or might be unlawful by virtue of the employment discrimination provisions of the SDA 1975.[4] However, this prohibition does not apply to an advertisement if the intended act would not in fact be unlawful.[5] Use of a job description with a sexual connotation (such a 'waiter', 'salesgirl', 'postman' or 'stewardess') shall be taken to indicate an intention to discriminate, unless the advertisement contains an indication to the contrary.[6] The publisher of an advertisement made unlawful by s. 38(1) shall not be subject to any liability under that subsection in respect of the publication of the advertisement if he proves that the advertisement was published in reliance on a statement made to him by the person who caused it to be published to the effect that the publication would not be unlawful, and that it was reasonable for him to rely on the statement.[7] A person who knowingly or

---

1    See, for example, *Grieg* v. *Community Industry* [1979] ICR 356, [1979] IRLR 158 (EAT); *Horsey* v. *Dyfed County Council* [1982] ICR 755, [1982] IRLR 395 (EAT).

2    SDA 1975, s. 6(1)(a).

3    See further *Brindley* v. *Tayside Health Board* [1976] IRLR 364 (IT); *Price* v. *Civil Service Commission* [1977] 1 WLR 1417, [1978] 1 All ER 1228, [1978] ICR 27, [1977] IRLR 291 (EAT); *Brennan* v. *Dewhurst* (JH) [1984] ICR 52, [1983] IRLR 357 (EAT); *Saunders* v. *Richmond-upon-Thames LBC* [1978] ICR 75, [1977] IRLR 362 (EAT); *Simon* v. *Brimham Associates* [1987] IRLR 307 (CA).

4    SDA 1975, s. 38(1).

5    SDA 1975, s. 38(2).

6    SDA 1975, s. 38(3).

7    SDA 1975, s. 38(4).

recklessly makes such a statement which in a material respect is false or misleading commits an offence, and shall be liable on summary conviction to a fine.[1]

The EOC Code of Practice makes various recommendations concerning advertising (see EOC Code, para. 19).

**4.7.3      JOB TITLE**
**4.7.4      JOB DESCRIPTION**

See §4.7.2 above.

**4.7.5      SELECTION ARRANGEMENTS**

It is unlawful to discriminate in the arrangements made for the purpose of determining who should be offered employment (see EOC Code of Practice recommendations, paras 21 and 23).

**4.7.6      TERMS ON WHICH A JOB IS OFFERED**

It is unlawful (SDA 1975, s. 6(1)(b)) for a person to discriminate against an applicant '... in the terms on which he offers [the applicant] that employment ... '. Subject to SDA 1975, s. 8(3), this provision does not apply to any provision for the payment of money which would be included in the contract under which the applicant was employed if she was given the job.[2] Section 8(3) provides that where a person offers a woman employment on certain terms, and if she accepted the offer then, by virtue of an equality clause, any of those terms would fall to be modified, or any additional term would fall to be included, the offer shall be taken to contravene s. 6(1)(b).[3]

**4.7.7      REFUSAL OR DELIBERATE OMISSION TO OFFER A JOB**

It is unlawful (SDA 1975, s. 6(1)(c)) for a person to discriminate against an applicant by refusing or deliberately omitting to offer the applicant that employment.

**4.8      WORKING CONDITIONS**

It is unlawful (SDA 1975, s. 6(2)(a)) for a person, in the case of a woman employed by him at an establishment in Great Britain, to discriminate against her in the way he affords her access to opportunities for promotion, transfer or training, or to any other benefits, facilities or services,

---

1      SDA 1975, s. 38(5).
2      SDA 1975, s. 6(5).
3      But see SDA 1975, s. 8(4): see §4.8.1.

or by refusing or deliberately omitting to afford her access to them. However, by virtue of s. 6(7), this prohibition does not apply to benefits, facilities or services of any description if the employer is concerned with the provision (for payment or not) of benefits, facilities or services of that description to the public, or to a section of the public comprising the woman in question, unless (a) that provision differs in a material respect from the provision of the benefits, facilities or services by the employer to his employees, or (b) that provision of the benefits, facilities or services to the woman in question is regulated by her contract of employment, or (c) the benefits, facilities or services relate to training.

### 4.8.1　　　RELATION TO PAY

SDA 1975, s. 6(5) specifies that the prohibition of discrimination in terms and conditions of employment under s. 6(1)(b) does not apply to benefits consisting of the payment of money when the provision of those benefits is regulated by the woman's contract of employment. By SDA 1975, s. 8(3), where a person offers a woman employment on certain terms, and if she accepted the offer then, by virtue of an equality clause, any of those terms would fall to be modified, or any additional term would fall to be included, the offer shall be taken to contravene s. 6(1)(b). By s. 8(4), where a person offers a woman employment on certain terms, and the previous provision would apply but for the fact that, on her acceptance of the offer EqPA, s. 1(3) would prevent the equality clause from operating, the offer shall be taken not to contravene s. 6(1)(b). By s. 8(5), an act does not contravene s. 6(2) if it contravenes a term modified or included by virtue of an equality clause, or it would contravene such a term but for the fact that the equality clause is prevented from operating by EqPA, s. 1(3). The remedy in such a case is under the EqPA.

In *Burton* v. *British Railways Board*[1] the ECJ held that where female employees over the age of 55, but male employees over the age of 60, were allowed to take voluntary redundancy, and thus men were prevented from gaining access to voluntary redundancy payment at the same age as women, this case came within the scope of the Equal Treatment Directive as regards 'working conditions including conditions governing dismissal', but not art. 119 of the EEC Treaty or the Equal Pay Directive. See, however, §4.2.1.6.

### 4.8.2　　　EDUCATION AND TRAINING

The opportunities given for training must not be discriminatory (SDA 1975, s. 6(2)(a)).[2] SDA 1975, s. 14, as amended by s. 7 of the Employment Act 1989, makes it unlawful, in the case of a woman seeking or undergoing

---

1　　Case 19/81, [1982] ECR 555, [1982] QB 1080, [1982] 3 WLR 387, [1982] 3 All ER 537, [1982] ICR 329, [1982] IRLR 116 (ECJ).

2　　See *Horsey* v. *Dyfed County Council* [1982] ICR 755, [1982] IRLR 395 (EAT).

training which would help fit her for any employment, for any person who provides, or makes arrangements for the provision of, facilities for such training to discriminate against her (a) in the terms on which that person affords her access to any training course or other facilities concerned with such training, or (b) by refusing or deliberately omitting to afford her such access, or (c) by terminating her training, or (d) by subjecting her to any detriment during the course of her training.

### 4.8.3 ACCESS TO BENEFITS, FACILITIES, SERVICES, PROMOTION

It is unlawful to discriminate in the terms on which employment is offered or in affording access to any benefits, facilities or services.[1] The EOC Code of Practice, para. 28 recommends that terms of employment, benefits, facilities and services should all be reviewed to ensure that there is no unlawful discrimination. For example, part-time work, domestic leave, company cars and benefits for dependants should be available to both male and female employees in the same or not materially different circumstances.

'Benefits, facilities and services' include matters to which the employee is not contractually entitled: for example, a concession enabling some employees to leave before other employees,[2] or the refusal to investigate complaints of unfair treatment.[3] The 'facilities' claimed must actually exist.[4] If the employee is contractually entitled to the benefit, then a complaint must be taken under the EqPA 1970 and not under the SDA 1975.[5]

It is also unlawful for employers to discriminate in the way they afford access to opportunities for promotion, transfer or training.[6] As regards promotion etc., see the EOC Code of Practice recommendations, para. 25.[7]

---

1   SDA 1975, ss 6(1)(b), 6(2)(a), 29.
2   *Peake* v. *Automotive Products* [1978] QB 233, [1977] 3 WLR 853, [1978] 1 All ER 106, [1977] ICR 968, [1977] IRLR 365 (CA).
3   *Eke* v. *Commissioners for Customs & Excise* [1981] IRLR 334 (EAT).
4   *Clymo* v. *Wandsworth London Borough Council* [1989] ICR 250, [1989] IRLR 241 (EAT).
5   SDA 1975, s. 6(6).
6   SDA 1975, s. 6(2)(a).
7   See further *Steel* v. *Union of Post Office Workers* [1978] 1 WLR 64, [1978] 2 All ER 504, [1978] ICR 181, [1977] IRLR 288 (EAT); *Khanna* v. *Ministry of Defence* [1981] ICR 653, [1981] IRLR 331 (EAT); *West Midlands PTE* v. *Singh* [1988] 1 WLR 730, [1988] 2 All ER 873, [1988] ICR 614, [1988] IRLR 186 (CA); *Perera* v. *Civil Service Commission (No 2)* [1982] ICR 350, [1982] IRLR 147 (EAT); [1983] ICR 428, [1983] IRLR 166 (CA); *Prestcold Ltd* v. *Irvine* [1980] ICR 610, [1980] IRLR 267 (EAT); [1981] ICR 777 (CA).

**4.9**              **EXCLUSION, DISMISSAL OR OTHER DETRIMENT**

It is unlawful to discriminate either in dismissals or by treating an
employee unfavourably in any other way.[1] What constitutes 'any other
detriment' has occasioned considerable case law. In *De Souza* v. *AA*[2] the
Court of Appeal held that before an employee can be said to have been
subjected to a detriment, it must be found that by reason of the acts
complained of a reasonable worker would or might take the view that he had
been thereby disadvantaged in the circumstances in which he had thereafter
to work. In order for an employee to be said to have been subjected to a
detriment, however, it is not necessary that the result of the discrimination
complained of was either dismissal or other disciplinary action by the
employer, or some action by the employee such as leaving the employment
on the basis of constructive dismissal or seeking a transfer. If the
discrimination was such that a reasonable employee could justifiably
complain about his or her working conditions or environment, it could
contravene the relevant statutory provisions whether or not the working
conditions were so bad as to be able to amount to constructive dismissal or
even if the employee was prepared to work on and put up with the
harassment.

**4.10**             **INSTRUCTIONS TO DISCRIMINATE**

SDA 1975, s. 39 makes it unlawful for a person who has authority over
another person, or in accordance with whose wishes that other person is
accustomed to act, to instruct him to do any act which is unlawful by virtue
of the employment discrimination provisions of the SDA 1975, or to procure
or attempt to procure the doing by him of any such act.[3]

**4.11**             **PRESSURE TO DISCRIMINATE**

SDA 1975, s. 40 makes it unlawful to induce, or attempt to induce, a
person to do any act which contravenes the employment discrimination
provisions of the SDA 1975 by providing or offering to provide him with any
benefit, or subjecting or threatening to subject him to any detriment. An offer
or threat is not prevented from being included because it is not made directly
to the person in question, if it is made in such a way that he is likely to hear
of it.[4]

---

1    SDA 1975, s. 6(2)(b).
2    [1986] ICR 514, [1986] IRLR 103 (CA).
3    See *CRE* v. *Imperial Society of Teachers of Dancing* [1983] ICR 473, [1983] IRLR
     315 (EAT).
4    *Loc. cit.*

**4.12**         **DISCRIMINATION BY AN EMPLOYEE OR**
                 **A TRADE UNION**

While the main responsibility for eliminating discrimination and
providing equal opportunity is that of the employer, individual employees at
all levels have responsibilities too. SDA 1975, s. 41 provides that anything
done by a person in the course of his employment shall be treated for the
purposes of this Act as done by his employer as well as by him, whether or
not it was done with the employer's knowledge or approval. Anything done
by a person as agent for another person with the authority (whether express
or implied, and whether precedent or subsequent) of that other person shall
be treated for the purposes of this Act as done by that other person as well as
by him. In proceedings brought under the SDA 1975 against any person in
respect of an act alleged to have been done by an employee of his it shall be
a defence for that person to prove that he took such steps as were reasonably
practicable to prevent the employee from doing that act, or from doing in the
course of his employment acts of that description.[1] SDA 1975, s. 42 provides
that a person who knowingly aids another person to do an act made unlawful
by this Act shall be treated for the purpose of this Act as himself doing an
unlawful act. An employee or agent for whose act the employer or principal
is liable (or would be so liable but for the operation of the exception) under
the vicarious liability provisions is deemed to aid the doing of the act by the
employer or principal.[2] A person does not knowingly aid another to do an
unlawful act if he acts in reliance on a statement made to him by that other
person that, by reason of any provision of this Act, the act which he aids
would not be unlawful, and it is reasonable for him to rely on the statement.
A person who knowingly or recklessly makes such a statement which in a
material respect is false or misleading commits an offence, and shall be liable
on summary conviction to a fine.

SDA 1975, s. 12 prohibits discrimination by trade unions and other
similar bodies (defined as 'an organization of workers, an organization of
employers, or any other organization whose members carry on a particular
profession or trade for the purposes of which the organization exists'). This
section makes it unlawful for a trade union, in the case of a woman who is
not a member of the organization, to discriminate against her (a) in the terms
on which it is prepared to admit her to membership, or (b) by refusing, or
deliberately omitting to accept, her application for membership.

It is also unlawful for a trade union, in the case of a woman who is a
member of the organization, to discriminate against her (a) in the way it

---

1    See *De Souza* v. *AA* [1986] ICR 514, [1986] IRLR 103 (CA); *Irving* v. *Post Office*
     [1987] IRLR 289 (CA); *Balgobin* v. *London Borough of Tower Hamlets* [1987] ICR
     829, [1987] IRLR 401 (EAT).
2    See *Read* v. *Tiverton District Council & Bull* [1977] IRLR 202 (IT).

affords her access to any benefits, facilities or services, or by refusing or deliberately omitting to afford her access to them, or (b) by depriving her of membership, or varying the terms on which she is a member, or (c) by subjecting her to any other detriment. In the formal investigation carried out by the EOC into SOGAT, the EOC decided that there was a duty on trade unions as well as employers to ensure non-discriminatory access to the benefits of collective bargaining.[1] For further application of these principles see *Record Production Chapel of the Daily Record & Sunday Mail of SOGAT 82 v. Turnbull & EOC.*[2]

## 4.13          DISCRIMINATORY PRACTICES

SDA 1975, s. 37 provides that certain discriminatory practices are made unlawful. A 'discriminatory practice' means the application of a requirement or condition which results in an act of discrimination which is unlawful by virtue of the employment discrimination provisions of the SDA 1975 read together with the prohibition of indirect discrimination, or which would be likely to result in such an act of discrimination if the persons to whom it is applied were not all of one sex. A person acts in contravention of this section if and so long as he applies a discriminatory practice, or he operates practices or other arrangements which in any circumstances would call for the application by him of a discriminatory practice. There are two substantial limitations in the ambit of this provision. It applies only to indirect discrimination. Second, proceedings in respect of a contravention of this section shall be brought only by the EOC in accordance with the formal investigation provisions of the Act (see §6.3.3 below).

## 4.14          SPECIAL TREATMENT

### 4.14.1          PROTECTIVE LEGISLATION

See also §§1.2.4.1, 2.2.2.3 and 4.2.1.3 above.

### 4.14.1.1          Pregnancy and maternity

The SDA 1975, s. 51, as amended by the Employment Act 1989, provides that nothing in the parts of the SDA prohibiting discrimination in employment or vocational training renders unlawful any act done by a person in relation to a woman, if it was necessary for that person to do it in order to comply with a requirement of an existing statutory provision having effect for the purpose of protecting women as regards pregnancy or maternity. In

---

1   See also *Enderby* v. *Frenchay Health Authority & Secretary of State for Health* [1991] IRLR 44 (EAT).

2   (1984, 16 April) unreported (Scottish EAT).

addition, there are various statutory provisions providing for pregnancy and maternity relevant for employment.

*Right to time off for antenatal care*

Section 31A of the Employment Protection (Consolidation) Act 1978, inserted by s. 13 of the Employment Act 1980, provides a right to paid time off for antenatal care. An employee who has made an appointment for antenatal care on the advice of a doctor or midwife has the right not to be refused unreasonably paid time off during working hours to keep the appointment.

*Right to return after pregnancy*

The Employment Protection (Consolidation) Act 1978, ss 33, 45 to 48 and 56, as modified by ss 11 and 12 of the Employment Act 1980, provide that a woman has the right to return to work in the job in which she was originally employed and on terms and conditions not less favourable than those which would have been applicable to her if she had not been absent.[1] The qualifying period is two years. The Employment Act 1980 imposed significant restrictions on the exercise of this right, in particular in providing relief against the right to return to work to small employers with no more than five employees.[2]

*Maternity pay provisions*

A new scheme providing for statutory maternity pay was introduced by the Social Security Act 1986. To be entitled to statutory maternity pay, a pregnant woman worker must (a) be in continuous employment for 26 weeks preceding the 14th week before the expected week of confinement, and (b) have normal weekly earnings during the last eight weeks of that period at a level not less than the lower earnings limit for national insurance contributions, and (c) have reached the start of the 11th week before the expected week of confinement.[3] She must also have furnished her employer with notice of her pregnancy and intended absence three weeks in advance and in writing, if requested.[4] The period of entitlement is 18 weeks not commencing before the 11th week or after the sixth week before the expected week of confinement.[5]

The scheme creates two rates of entitlement. The higher rate is set at nine-tenths of a woman's normal weekly earnings for a period of six weeks

---

1     Employment Protection (Consolidation) Act 1978, s. 45(1).
2     Employment Act 1980, s. 12, adding new EPCA 1978, s. 56A(1).
3     Social Security Act 1986, s. 46(1) and (2).
4     Social Security Act 1986, s. 24(4).
5     Social Security Act 1986, s. 47.

followed by 12 weeks at a flat-rate payment. Qualification for this higher rate is dependent on two years' continuous employment.[1] The lower rate, a flat-rate payment for 18 weeks, is payable to all who qualify for statutory maternity pay but not at the higher rate.[2]

### 4.14.1.2          Parental leave and similar measures

Only women are entitled to take advantage of statutory parental leave measures: see §4.14.1.1 above.

### 4.14.1.3          Difficult or unpleasant working conditions
### 4.14.1.4          Health and safety

See §§1.2.4.1, 2.2.2.3, 4.2.1.3 and 4.14.1.1 above.

### 4.14.2          POSITIVE ACTION

### 4.14.2.1          Definition

The legal position under the law of the United Kingdom of these various types of 'positive action' is complicated and in significant respects uncertain. It is useful to view the relationship between 'positive action' and the legal regime established to deal with discrimination in four different ways.

First, some type of positive action may be imposed on an employer as a primary duty. The primary duties imposed on employers under the SDA 1975 are simply stated: not to discriminate directly, not to discriminate indirectly. These duties will be referred to as the 'anti-discrimination principle'. Secondly, positive action may be dealt with in the legislation as a remedy which may be imposed by some legal authority (court, tribunal or agency) for breach of the anti-discrimination principle. The types of positive action which may be imposed as a remedy are highly restricted in the SDA 1975, as we shall see subsequently. Thirdly, some types of positive action may be permitted without restriction because adherence to the anti-discrimination principle is not a legal duty at all. Some types of positive action may, fourthly, be permitted but not required of an employer — a power available to an employer consistent with but going beyond the anti-discrimination principle. The EOC Code of Practice has made a number of recommendations to encourage good employment practices which follow this fourth type of approach (see paras 34-40).

---

1    Social Security Act 1986, s. 48(4) and (5).
2    Social Security Act 1986, s. 48(4).

*Affirmative action*

The legal regime in the United Kingdom goes beyond this approach in permitting positive action which is inconsistent with the anti-discrimination principle, involving the creation of a power which is an exception to the anti-discrimination principle. The SDA 1975 allows certain steps to redress the effects of previous unequal opportunities.

*Reverse discrimination*

Unless specifically permitted, however, such action is regarded as reverse discrimination and is unlawful under the SDA 1975.[1]

### 4.14.2.2    Areas

*Training bodies*

SDA 1975, s. 47 permits discriminatory training by bodies which would otherwise be unlawful. It provides that nothing in the employment discrimination provisions renders unlawful any act done in relation to particular work by any person in, or in connection with, affording women only, or men only, access to facilities for training which would help to fit them for that work, or encouraging women only, or men only, to take advantage of opportunities for doing that work, where it reasonably appears to that person that at any time within the 12 months immediately preceding the doing of the act there were no persons of the sex in question doing that work in Great Britain (or an area within Great Britain), or the number of persons of that sex doing the work in Great Britain (or an area within Great Britain) was comparatively small.

The section further specifies that the employment discrimination provisions do not render unlawful any act done by any person in, or in connection with, affording persons access to facilities for training which would help to fit them for employment, where it reasonably appears to that person that those persons are in special need of training by reason of the period for which they have been discharging domestic or family responsibilities to the exclusion of regular full-time employment. In these circumstances training may be confined to persons who have been discharging domestic or family responsibilities, or persons may be specially selected for training, or both. However, this provision does not apply in relation to any discrimination which is rendered unlawful by SDA 1975, s. 6.

The Employment Act 1989, s. 8 grants a power to the Secretary of State to exempt from the coverage of the employment discrimination provisions discrimination in favour of lone parents in connection with training. The

---

1    *Lambeth LBC* v. *CRE* [1990] IRLR 231 (CA).

Secretary of State may by order provide with respect to any specified arrangements made under s. 2 of the Employment and Training Act 1973 (functions of the Secretary of State as respects employment and training), or any specified class or description of training for employment provided otherwise than in pursuance of that section, or any specified scheme set up under s. 1 of the Employment Subsidies Act 1978 (schemes for financing employment), that this section shall apply to such special treatment afforded to or in respect of lone parents in connection with their participation in those arrangements, or in that training or scheme, as is specified or referred to in the order. Where this section applies to any treatment afforded to or in respect of lone parents, neither the treatment so afforded nor any act done in the implementation of any such treatment shall be regarded for the purposes of the SDA 1975 as giving rise to any discrimination falling within the provisions prohibiting discrimination against married persons for purposes of Part II of that Act. An order may specify or refer to special treatment afforded as mentioned in that subsection whether it is afforded by the making of any payment or by the fixing of special conditions for participation in the arrangements, training or scheme in question, or otherwise, and whether it is afforded by the Secretary of State or by some other person. Any class or description of training for employment specified in such an order by virtue of that paragraph may be framed by reference to the person, or the class or description of persons, by whom the training is provided. The Sex Discrimination Act 1975 (Exemption of Special Treatment for Lone Parents) Order 1989[1] made under the Employment Act 1989 provides that with respect to employment training, s. 8 of the 1989 Act:

> ... shall apply to any special treatment afforded
> (a)  by the making of any payment in connection with the participation of a lone parent in employment training, to a person having the care of a child of that lone parent, or
> (b)  by the fixing of any special condition for the participation of lone parents in employment training.

The Employment Act 1989, s. 8 makes it lawful to discriminate by providing facilities exclusively for single parents.

*Employers*

SDA 1975, s. 48(1) permits certain types of positive action by employers which would otherwise be unlawful. The section specifies that nothing in the employment discrimination provisions shall render unlawful any act done by an employer in relation to particular work in his employment, being an act done in, or in connection with, affording his female employees only, or his male employees only, access to facilities for training which would help to fit them for that work, or encouraging women

---

1    SI 1989 No 2140.

only, or men only, to take advantage of opportunities for doing that work, where at any time within the 12 months immediately preceding the doing of the act there were no persons of the sex in question among those doing that work or the number of persons of that sex doing the work was comparatively small.

The Enterprise and New Towns (Scotland) Act 1990, s. 17 imposes a duty on Scottish Enterprise and Highlands and Islands Enterprise in exercising its functions to promote the use of s. 48 among employers.

*Trade unions*

SDA 1975, s. 48(2) permits certain types of positive action by trade unions which would otherwise be unlawful. It provides that nothing in s. 12 shall render unlawful any act done by an organization to which that section applies in, or in connection with affording female members of the organization only, or male members of the organization only, access to facilities for training which would help to fit them for holding a post of any kind in the organization, or encouraging female members only, or male members only, to take advantage of opportunities for holding such posts in the organization, where at any time within the 12 months immediately preceding the doing of the act there were no persons of the sex in question among persons holding such posts in the organization or the number of persons of that sex holding such posts was comparatively small.

SDA 1975, s. 48(3) provides that nothing in the employment discrimination provisions shall render unlawful any act done by an organization to which s. 12 applies in, or in connection with, encouraging women only, or men only, to become members of the organization where at any time within the 12 months immediately preceding the doing of the act there were no persons of the sex in question among those members or the number of persons of that sex among the members was comparatively small.

SDA 1975, s. 49 further provides that if an organization to which s. 12 applies comprises a body the membership of which is wholly or mainly elected, nothing in s. 12 shall render unlawful a provision which ensures that a minimum number of persons of one sex are members of the body by reserving seats on the body for persons of that sex, or by making extra seats on the body available (by election or co-option or otherwise) for persons of that sex on occasions when the number of persons of that sex in the other seats is below the minimum, where in the opinion of the organization the provision is in the circumstances needed to secure a reasonable lower limit to the number of members of that sex serving on the body; and nothing in the employment discrimination provisions of the Act shall render unlawful any act done in order to give effect to such a provision. However, s. 49 shall not be taken as making lawful discrimination in the arrangements for determining the persons entitled to vote in an election of members of the body, or otherwise to choose the persons to serve on the body, or discrimination in any arrangements concerning membership of the organization itself.

### 4.14.2.3          Means

*Measures to correct imbalance*

Without the exceptions in the SDA 1975, it is likely that the prohibition on direct discrimination would render unlawful the seeking out of qualified applicants from the under-represented community by more intensive advertising to that community, by greater encouragement to members of that community to apply for jobs, or by provision of training specifically to members of that group.

*Code of Practice*

The EOC is empowered to produce a Code of Practice for the elimination of discrimination on the grounds of sex and marriage and the promotion of equality of opportunity in employment,[1] and one was issued in 1985. The EOC issued this Code of Practice for the following purposes: for the elimination of discrimination in employment, to give guidance as to what steps it is reasonably practicable for employers to take to ensure that their employees do not in the course of their employment act unlawfully contrary to the SDA 1975, and for the promotion of equality of opportunity between men and women in employment.

The Code gives guidance to employers, trade unions and employment agencies on measures which can be taken to achieve equality. The chances of success of any organization will clearly be improved if it seeks to develop the abilities of all employees, and the Code shows the close link which exists between equal opportunity and good employment practice.

A failure on the part of any person to observe any provision of a code of practice shall not of itself render him liable to any proceedings; but in any proceedings under the SDA before an industrial tribunal any code of practice issued under SDA 1975, s. 56A shall be admissible in evidence, and if any provision of such a code appears to the tribunal to be relevant to any question arising in the proceedings it shall be taken into account in determining that question.[2]

---

[1]     SDA 1975, s. 56A(1).
[2]     SDA 1975, s. 56A(10).

## Training

There are no relevant statutory provisions other than those discussed above.

### 4.14.2.4 Constitutional or legal problems

There are no provisions of constitutional or basic law with actual or potential implications for positive action measures. However, a number of international conventions to which the United Kingdom is a party are relevant, and, indeed, appear to go much further in permitting a measure of preference to be accorded certain groups, for example, the Convention on the Elimination of All Forms of Discrimination against Women, 1979, art. 4(1). In addition, the European Convention on Human Rights appears to permit such actions.[1]

---

1　See *Belgian Linguistics Case (Merits)*, ECHR, Series A,Vol. 6, judgment of 23 July 1968; *Lindsay* v. *United Kingdom* (1979) 15 Decisions & Reports 247.

# 5   SOCIAL SECURITY

## 5.1   DEFINITION OF SOCIAL SECURITY

### 5.1.1   STATUTORY SOCIAL SECURITY

There is no simple distinction between social security and social assistance in the United Kingdom scheme; it is indeed an issue of considerable controversy how to categorize particular benefits, as we shall see below.

In the United Kingdom, the state social security scheme can be divided into three main categories. First, there are non-means-tested non-contributory benefits, which broadly speaking are the benefits paid to those with disabilities and benefits for children. These are paid out of general taxation and entitlement depends on certain conditions as to past residence in the country. The main non-contributory non-means-tested benefits within the scope of Council Directive of 19 December 1978 on the progressive implementation of the principle of equal treatment for men and women in matters of social security (79/7/EEC) are severe disablement allowance, invalid care allowance, attendance allowance and mobility allowance.

Second, there are non-means-tested contributory benefits. These are paid out of the national insurance fund. Contributions to the fund are paid by employees and their employers, the self-employed and those who pay voluntary contributions. Generally, entitlement to benefit depends on the claimant's contribution record. Contributions to the fund are either paid or credited. An employed earner does not have to pay contributions if he or she earns less than a lower earnings limit. The main contributory non-means-tested benefits within the scope of Directive 79/7/EEC are unemployment benefit, sickness benefit, invalidity benefit and industrial injury benefit (although this is not dependent on past contributions but on the employee's status as an employed earner).

The third main category is means-tested poverty-related benefits, which are funded out of general taxation. In 1988 the means-tested benefits system underwent a major overhaul, and the main benefits were replaced. Income support and the Social Fund replaced supplementary benefit; family credit replaced family income supplement; in addition there is housing benefit and community charge benefit. Income support is intended to be the safety net of the welfare state. It is payable to individuals whose financial resources are less than their financial needs. Where people are married (or living together as husband and wife) and/or have dependent children, they are treated as one unit and their financial resources and needs are added together (the aggregation principle), in order to determine whether their resources are less than their needs and hence whether they are entitled to benefit. Where a couple is married or held to be living together, only one of them can claim and hence gain direct access to the benefit. It is payable to claimants who are not in full-time work, and whose partner is not in full-time work. Full-time work for this purpose is currently 24 hours per week. Claimants claiming income support have to be available for work unless they come into one of the categories of people who do not have to be available. These categories relate to age, parenthood, child care, responsibility for others as carers, illness, disability, and include some students and people on training courses. Housing benefit and community charge benefit are paid to help people with their rent and community charge. They are both national schemes but are run by the local authority and are calculated in a way similar to the calculation for income support.

### 5.1.2      OCCUPATIONAL SOCIAL SECURITY

The Social Security Act 1989, Sch. 5, para. 7(a) defines the meaning of 'employment-related benefit scheme' as:

> ... any scheme or arrangement which is comprised in one or more instruments or agreements and which has, or is capable of having, effect in relation to one or more descriptions or categories of employment so as to provide service-related benefits to or in respect of employed or self-employed earners-
> (i)    who have qualifying service in an employment of any such description or category, or
> (ii)   who have made arrangements with the trustees or managers of the scheme to enable them to become members of the scheme,
> but does not include a limited scheme.

A 'limited scheme' means any personal scheme for employed earners to which the employer does not contribute; any scheme which has only one member, other than a personal scheme for an employed earner to which his employer contributes; and any contract of insurance which is made for the benefit of employed earners only and to which the employer is not a party.[1] 'Service-related benefits' means benefits, in the form of pensions or otherwise, payable in money or money's worth in respect of termination of service; retirement, old age or death; interruptions of service by reason of sickness or invalidity; accidents, injuries or diseases connected with employment; unemployment; or expenses incurred in connection with children or other dependants. It includes, in the case of a member who is an employed earner, any other benefit so payable to or in respect of the member in consequence of his employment.[2]

---

1    Social Security Act 1989, Sch. 5, para. 7(b).
2    Social Security Act 1989, Sch. 5, para. 7(e).

**5.1.3 SOCIAL ASSISTANCE**

See §5.1.1 above.

**5.2 SOCIAL SECURITY DIRECTIVES AND OTHER LEGISLATION**

**5.2.1 ARTICLE 119 OF THE EEC TREATY**

**5.2.2 DIRECTIVE 75/117/EEC**

See §3.5 above.

**5.2.3 DIRECTIVE 76/207/EEC**

See §4.2.1.6 above.

In two cases currently before the ECJ[1] it will be argued that income support and its predecessor, supplementary benefit, are covered by this Directive when being paid to a woman who is either working part-time or training. In both cases the claimants are arguing that failure to allow the deduction of child care costs from part-time earnings or training allowance indirectly discriminates against women in breach not only of Directive 79/7/EEC (see §5.2.4 below) but also Directive 76/207/EEC, as it creates a barrier to equal access to employment[2] and to vocational training.[3]

The UK Government will be arguing that Directive 76/207/EEC does not apply to income support or supplementary benefit as arts 1 and 2 directly exclude matters of social security from its scope. The claimants are arguing that the words in arts 1 and 2 are not words of exclusion but simply an indication that the guarantee of equal access to social security will be made good later. The words are not an indication that it is permissible to prevent equal access to employment by arrangements within the social security system.

**5.2.4 DIRECTIVE 79/7/EEC**

The 1979 Directive applies the principle of equal treatment for men and women to matters of social security. However, art. 7 of the Directive permits Member States to exclude from its scope (a) the determination of pensionable age for the purposes of granting old-age and retirement pensions

---

[1] *Jackson & Cresswell* v. *Chief Adjudication Officer,* Joined Cases C-63 & C-64/9, [1992] ECR I-4737 (judgment delivered after the closing date for the manuscript of this Commentary).

[2] *Cresswell.*

[3] *Jackson.*

and the possible consequences thereof for other benefits; (b) advantages in respect of old-age pension schemes granted to persons who have brought up children; the acquisition of benefit entitlements following periods of interruption of employment due to the bringing up of children; (c) the granting of old-age or invalidity benefit entitlements by virtue of the derived entitlements of a wife; (d) the granting of increases of long-term invalidity, old-age, accidents at work and occupational disease benefits for a dependent wife; (e) the consequences of the exercise, before the adoption of the Directive, of a right of option not to acquire rights or incur obligations under a statutory scheme.

As a result of the 1979 Directive, various changes were introduced into the United Kingdom benefits system. In particular, various discriminatory elements which were introduced in the Social Security Act 1975 and the Social Security Pensions Act 1975 were amended. Steps were taken to equalize treatment of married men and women in respects of adult and child dependency additions. Three means were adopted. The first was to equalize up by, for example, granting spouse additions with short-term contributory benefits to married women on the same terms as those previously enjoyed by married men. The second approach was to abolish the addition altogether, as happened to the child dependency addition with short term contributory benefits. The third approach was to equalize the conditions of access while at the same time adding new, more restrictive, conditions applicable to both men and women claimants, for example, the introduction of a spouse's earnings rule, restricting entitlement for men and women claimants to the child dependency addition with long-term contributory benefits. The rules excluding married and cohabiting women from entitlement to supplementary benefit were abolished. In addition, the non-contributory invalidity pension and its housewives counterpart were repealed, and replaced by severe disablement allowance. Lastly, in anticipation of the decision of the European Court of Justice in *Drake* v. *Chief Adjudication Officer*,[1] the Social Security Act 1986, s. 37 extended invalid care allowance to carers who were married women, and those living with a man as his wife, on equal terms with men and single women carers.

The 1979 Directive excluded from the scope of the Directive 'the determination of pensionable age for the purpose of granting old-age and retirement pensions and the possible consequences thereof for other benefits'.[2] The exception of pensionable ages in the 1979 Directive was narrowly construed in *Secretary of State for Social Security* v. *Thomas*.[3] The case was heard with four others. All the cases concerned women who had given up work when aged between 60 and 65 because they were ill or had to care for a disabled person, and had claimed either severe disablement

---

1     Case 150/85, [1986] ECR 1995, [1987] QB 166, [1986] 3 All ER 65 (ECJ).

2     Article 7(1)(a).

3     [1990] IRLR 436 (CA).

allowance or invalid care allowance. Benefit had been refused because they (unlike a man of the same age) were over pensionable age. Both benefits were clearly within the scope of the Directive. Article 7(1)(a) allows Member States to maintain different pension ages for men and women, but the question in this case concerned the scope of the phrase 'and the possible consequences thereof for other benefits'. The Court of Appeal accepted that as these benefits are income replacement benefits, it is necessary to have an upper age limit but rejected the argument that it was appropriate to have a discriminatory one. The Court held that the onus must fall on the Secretary of State to show that the designation of different age limits for men and women, when defining the qualifications for the benefits in issue, was a necessary consequence of Parliament's having defined the qualifications for entitlement to old-age and retirement benefits by reference to different age limits for men and women, but held further that the Secretary of State had failed to discharge that onus. The case has been appealed to the House of Lords.

In *Jones* v. *Chief Adjudication Officer*[1] the Court of Appeal held that the 1979 Directive did not render unlawful as indirectly discriminatory a provision of UK social security law which aims to prevent double payments being made for the same contingency.

Several other issues are pending before the ECJ in cases referred from UK courts. In *R.* v. *Secretary of State for Social Security,* ex parte *EOC*[2] the issue before the ECJ is whether art. 7(1)(a) permits Member States to derogate from the principle of equal treatment (a) by requiring men to pay national insurance contributions for five years longer than women in order to be entitled to the same basic pension; and (b) by requiring men who continue in gainful employment up to the age of 65 to continue to pay national insurance contributions up to that age, when women over the age of 60 are not required to pay national insurance contributions whether or not they remain in gainful employment after that age, where a Member State preserves different pensionable ages for men and women for the purpose of granting old-age and retirement pensions, and where national insurance contributions fund a range of benefits including State retirement pensions.

A different issue arises in *Johnson* v. *Chief Adjudication Officer.*[3] Prior to December 1984 the UK abolished the non-contributory invalidity pension (NCIP) which required married or cohabiting women to fulfil an additional test of being incapable of normal household duties and replaced it with a new benefit, the severe disablement allowance. However, the new benefit ensured that persons formally entitled to NCIP would automatically be entitled to severe disablement allowance. The ECJ held in *Clarke* v. *Chief Adjudication*

---

1    [1990] IRLR 533 (CA).
2    Case C-9/91 (ECJ).
3    Case C-31/90, [1991] ECR I-3723 (ECJ).

*Officer*[1] that the effect of Directive 79/7/EEC is to give equal access to severe disablement allowance for men and women, and that the transitional regulations perpetuated the discrimination inherent in NCIP. Therefore, any woman who can show that she would have been entitled to NCIP without the additional household duties test is entitled to severe disablement allowance.

On 24 June 1987 the ECJ delivered its judgment in *Clarke*. In August of that year Mrs Johnson claimed severe disablement allowance. She had previously been in receipt of NCIP but, on moving in with her partner, had lost entitlement. Her claim for severe disablement allowance was rejected on the basis of the domestic time-limit for claiming benefits which meant that her claim in August 1987 could only be backdated to August 1986, when she did not fulfil the conditions for entitlement to severe disablement allowance. She needed to go back to 1984 to be entitled via the transitional regulations which passported NCIP claimants on to severe disablement allowance. The opinion of the Advocate-General was delivered on 5 February 1991. He said that while the domestic time-limit is not of itself discriminatory, when combined with the transitional regulations it produced a discriminatory effect in breach of Directive 79/7/EEC.

The *Johnson* case also raises the issue of the personal scope of the Directive. Mrs Johnson had left the labour market to care for her daughter, then aged six. When her daughter reached 16, Mrs Johnson attempted to return to work and signed on as unemployed. However, she was prevented from returning because of a back condition. The UK Government argued before the ECJ that, in light of the Court's decision in *Achterberg-te Riele* v. *Sociale Verzekeringsbank Amsterdam*,[2] Mrs Johnson was not within the personal scope of the Directive as she was not a worker and had not ceased to be a worker as a result of the materialization of one of the risks listed in art. 3.

It is being argued in two further cases[3] that both supplementary benefit and income support are 'statutory schemes', which provide protection against the listed risks, or alternatively that they are 'social assistance' intended to supplement or replace such schemes. The UK Government is arguing that the means-tested benefits are outside the scope of the Directive. Their argument is that the means-tested benefits, and in particular income support, cannot be seen as statutory schemes providing protection against the risks listed in art. 3, or as social assistance.

In *R.* v. *Secretary of State for Social Security*, ex parte *Smithson*[4] Mrs Smithson was not entitled to a higher pensioner premium because she

---

1    Case 384/85, [1987] ECR 2865 (ECJ).
2    Joined Cases 48, 106 & 107/88, [1989] ECR 1963 (ECJ).
3    *Jackson & Cresswell* v. *Chief Adjudication Officer*, Joined Cases C-63 & C-64/91, [1992] ECR I-4737: see §5.2.3 above.
4    Case C-243/90, [1992] ECR I-467 (ECJ).

was not in receipt of invalidity benefit whereas if she had been a man she would have been so entitled, due to her age (67). This is because a man in her position could choose not to be treated as retired and claim invalidity benefit up to the age of 70 where a woman cannot after 65.

See also §§3.2.6 and 4.2.1.6 above.

**5.2.5      DIRECTIVE 86/378/EEC**

The United Kingdom sought to implement the 1986 Directive in the Social Security Act 1989. That Act does not come into force until the beginning of 1993 (or for certain sections, 1999). The 1986 Directive, art. 1 provides that the principle of equal treatment shall be applied to 'occupational social security schemes'. These are defined as:

> ... schemes not governed by Directive 79/7/EEC whose purpose is to provide workers, whether employees or self-employed, in an undertaking or group of undertakings, area of economic activity or occupational sector or group of such sectors with benefits intended to supplement the benefits provided by statutory social security schemes or to replace them, whether membership of such schemes is compulsory or optional.[1]

The Directive does not apply to individual contracts, schemes having one member, insurance contracts to which the employer is not a party (in the case of salaried workers), or the optional provisions of occupational schemes offered to participants individually to guarantee them additional benefits, or a choice of date on which the normal benefits will start, or a choice of several benefits.[2] It applies to occupational schemes which provide protection against the following risks: sickness, invalidity, old age, including early retirement, industrial accidents and occupational diseases, and unemployment. It also applies to occupational schemes which provide for other social benefits, in cash or in kind, and in particular survivor's benefits and family allowances, if such benefits are accorded to employed persons and thus constitute a consideration paid by the employer to the worker by reason of the latter's employment.[3]

The 1986 Directive allows Member States to defer the compulsory application of the Directive with regard to (a) the determination of pensionable age for the purposes of granting old-age or retirement pensions, and the possible implications for other benefits, either until the date on which such equality is achieved in statutory schemes, or (at the latest) until such equality is required by a directive; (b) survivors' pensions until a directive

---

1      Directive 86/378/EEC, art. 2(1).
2      Directive 86/378/EEC, art. 2(2).
3      Directive 86/378/EEC, art. 4.

requires the principle of equal treatment in statutory social security schemes in that regard; (c) the requirement of equal treatment in setting levels of worker contribution to take account of the different actuarial factors for up to 13 years from 1986.[1]

However, the ECJ decision in *Barber* v. *Guardian Royal Exchange Assurance Group*[2] calls into question the wide exceptions permitted under this Directive and it is currently unclear to what extent the Directive will survive in its present form.

## 5.3       PROBLEMATIC CONCEPTS

### 5.3.1       BREADWINNER

In all UK means-tested benefits, men and women (whether married or not married but living together as husband and wife) have both their requirements and resources aggregated.

Since 1983 either partner of the couple could be the claimant. However, it is still in practice much more frequently the case that the man is the claimant for the couple, and many women may not therefore have direct access to benefits. This fact has given rise to the argument that the aggregation principle may be indirectly discriminatory in some circumstances.

In 1988, when the UK Government overhauled the existing means-tested scheme, transitional regulations were introduced to cushion the impact of the new scheme and ensure that those who would be worse off as a result of the change did not suffer an immediate reduction in benefit.[3] However, to claim transitional protection the claimant for income support purposes had to have been the claimant for supplementary benefit. In practice this was often the man. If subsequently the man left or died the woman would have to make a fresh claim in her own right and would lose that transitional protection. These transitional regulations are currently being challenged before the Social Security Commissioner as indirectly discriminatory on these grounds.[4]

### 5.3.2       SOLE BREADWINNER

Under the old supplementary benefit scheme certain work-related expenses could be deducted from part-time earnings before these were taken into account against benefit. In particular, reasonable child care costs could

---

1    Directive 86/378/EEC, art. 9.
2    Case C-262/88, [1990] ECR I-1889, [1990] 2 All ER 660, [1990] IRLR 240 (ECJ).
3    Income Support (Transitional) Regulations 1987 (SI 1987 No 1969).
4    CIS/375/1990 and CIS/8/1990.

be deducted. Under the new income support scheme child care costs can no longer be deducted from part-time earnings. For single parents this causes particular difficulties. As the vast majority of single parents are women it is being argued in two cases that the disproportionate impact on women is indirectly discriminatory and in breach of both Directive 76/207/EEC and Directive 79/7/EEC (see §§5.2.3 and 5.2.4 above.) This issue has been considered by the Social Security Commissioner in two cases, but neither supplementary benefit nor income support has been held to be included under the scope of either Directive. In *Jackson*, the Social Security Commissioner considered supplementary benefit was not covered by either of the Directives, but that if it was found by the independent social security appeal tribunal (SSAT) that the provision was discriminatory, then it was not objectively justifiable. In *Cresswell*, the Commissioner held that income support is also not covered by either Directive. Both cases were appealed to the Court of Appeal and have now been referred to the ECJ on the question of the scope of the Directive.[1]

**5.3.3        HEAD OF HOUSEHOLD**
**5.3.4        COHABITANT**

See §5.3.1 above.

**5.3.5        LIVING ALONE**

There is, to the writer's knowledge, no relevant law on this issue.

**5.3.6        DEPENDANT**

A number of the non-means-tested benefits involve increases (a special allowance) for persons dependent on the claimant. As Ogus and Barendt put it:

> The traditional rules on dependency allowances assumed stereotyped family relationships in which the husband/father is the primary or only breadwinner, while the wife/mother assumes domestic responsibilities and her earnings, if any, are inessential additions to the family income.[2]

The 1979 Directive prompted the Government to make fundamental changes. The husband's entitlement to claim for a wife, and a wife's entitlement to claim for a husband were largely equalized,[3] except in the case of category A or C retirement pensions. A woman cannot claim an increase of category C retirement pension for her husband in the same way as a husband can for his

---

1    *Jackson & Cresswell* v. *Chief Adjudication Officer*, Joined Cases C-63 & C-64/91,
      [1992] ECR I-4737; see §5.2.3 above.
2    *The Law of Social Security*, p. 339.
3    Social Security Act 1980, Sch.1, Part 1.

wife.[1] A woman claiming a dependency increase to a category A retirement pension for a husband has to satisfy an additional condition: immediately prior to entitlement to that pension she must have been in receipt of a dependency increase for him as an addition to unemployment benefit, sickness benefit or invalidity benefit. If there is any break in her entitlement she loses it completely.[2]

In the case of unemployment benefit and sickness benefit, different rates are payable in respect of spouses depending on whether the claimant is over pensionable age (65 for men and 60 for women).[3]

## 5.4     EXCEPTIONS

### 5.4.1     RETIREMENT AGE

The condition of eligibility for a retirement pension is that the claimant has attained pensionable age. 'Pensionable age' is 60 for women and 65 for men. The consequences of this have been of considerable importance in a number of situations discussed above (see, for example, §§ 3.2.6, 4.2.1.6 and 5.2.4).

### 5.4.2     SEX AS A DETERMINING FACTOR

A number of aspects of both statutory social security and social assistance were directly discriminatory against married women during the 1970s and 1980s. There were a number of discriminatory elements which had long persisted in these schemes. Child and adult dependency additions to non-contributory and contributory benefits were withheld from married women unless their husbands were incapable of self support. Married men were not likewise restricted. Married and cohabiting women were automatically excluded from entitlement to the means-tested supplementary benefit and family income supplement. Only the male partner could claim. Two non-contributory non-means-tested benefits were introduced during the 1970s which explicitly excluded married and cohabiting women from entitlement. These two benefits were invalid care allowance, for those caring for people with severe disabilities, and non-contributory invalidity pension, for the long-term incapacitated who had insufficient contributions to qualify them for the contributory invalidity pension. Under s. 37 of the Social Security Act 1975, invalid care allowance was payable to a person who was engaged in caring for a severely disabled person provided that the carer was not in gainful employment. The statute was, however, discriminatory in the

---

1     Social Security Act 1975, s. 39(1)(b).
2     Social Security Act 1975, s. 45A.
3     Social Security Act 1975, s. 14(6).

sense that a woman was not entitled if, for example, she was married and living with her husband. In 1977, a version of a non-contributory invalidity pension was introduced in which married and cohabiting women initially excluded could subsequently gain entitlement to the pension if they could show they were incapable of performing normal household duties. These directly discriminatory elements have now been removed.[1] As regards single women, the only directly discriminatory elements now remaining are that the pensionable age for women is five years earlier than that for men, and that the benefits payable as maternity benefits (statutory maternity pay and state maternity allowance) are confined to women. There are a number of aspects which, it may be argued, give rise to indirect discrimination such as the differential treatment accorded to part-time workers.

Survivors' benefit is still paid solely to widows. Entitlement to the three main widows' benefits depend upon a widow's late husband's contribution record. In one case[2] it was unsuccessfully argued before the Social Security Commissioner that the overlapping benefit rules which prevented invalid care allowance being paid to a widow indirectly discriminated against women. The Commissioner held that the difference between the claimant and any man who is entitled to invalid care allowance is that the claimant will lose her invalid care allowance for a reason which can never apply to a man but that is not the result of discrimination; it results from the fact that she starts from a different position from that of any man.

## 5.5 LEVELLING UP/DOWN

The Social Security Act 1989, Sch. 5, para. 3 states, as regards occupational social security schemes, that any provision of an employment-related benefit scheme which does not comply with the principle of equal treatment will be overridden and compulsorily 'levelled up', so that the more favourable treatment given to the one sex will also be given to the other. Anyone who benefits as a result will be required to pay the contributions which are appropriate to the more favourable treatment and to bear any other burden which it involves. However, the Act also gives such a person the option to elect to receive the less favourable treatment and pay the contributions and comply with the other conditions incidental to it.

Following the ECJ's decision in Drake,[3] the UK Government levelled up entitlement to invalid care allowance by allowing married and cohabiting women access to the benefit in the same way as men and single women. In 1984, when the Government replaced the old discriminatory invalidity

---

1   See *Drake* and *Clarke*, discussed in § 5.2.4 above.

2   R(S) 2/89.

3   *Drake* v. *Chief Adjudication Officer*, Case 150/85, [1986] ECR 1995, [1987] QB 166, [1986] 3 All ER 65 (ECJ).

pension with severe disablement allowance, this was a form of levelling down, in that those previously entitled to severe disablement allowance were automatically entitled to the new benefit but conditions of entitlement to the new benefit for those who qualified after that date are much stricter.

## 5.6        PART-TIME WORK

See §§2.3.2 and 3.9.4 above. A considerable difficulty for part-time workers, the vast majority of whom are women, is access to insurance-based benefits, because of the level of the lower earning limit. Part-time workers are more likely to have lower earnings, therefore access to benefits which are related to minimum earnings rules will adversely affect part-time workers and hence women. The conditions of entitlement to unemployment benefit, which require contributions to have been paid in one of the last two complete tax years before the relevant benefit year in order to satisfy the first conditions, are also likely to discriminate against those who are more likely to have had periods of part-time work when they would not have paid sufficient contributions to meet requirements, and these are more likely to be women than men.

# 6   ENFORCEMENT OF THE PRINCIPLE

The arrangements for enforcing the principle of equal pay and equal treatment in Britain are complex, and involve a mix of types of enforcement procedures. Individual complaints relating to equal pay and equal treatment in employment may be brought by an aggrieved person before an industrial tribunal. This has become the primary method of legal enforcement in practice. In addition, an employer may apply to an industrial tribunal for an order declaring the rights of the employer and the employees where a dispute arises in relation to the effect of an equality clause, but this has seldom occurred in practice.[1] The Secretary of State for Employment may refer to a tribunal any question concerning whether a woman's employer is contravening an equality clause, if it is not reasonable to expect her to take steps herself to have the question determined. This power has never been exercised.

There are additional methods by which both equal pay and equal treatment are further enforced. An equality agency, the Equal Opportunities Commission (EOC), has the power to initiate formal investigations, issue non-discrimination notices, and take proceedings in certain circumstances in industrial tribunals and courts. In a number of cases the EOC has also taken judicial review of the decisions of public bodies (see §1.2.3 above).

As regards the enforcement of the principle in social security, we have seen that several pieces of legislation have been enacted which aim to implement European equality law requirements in the sphere of social security. In many cases the first mechanism for securing rights provided under social security legislation is a claim made to an adjudication officer.[2] Decisions by an adjudication officer may be appealed to an independent social security appeal tribunal (SSAT) on questions of fact and law. The applicant has three months from the date of the adjudication officer's original decision in which to appeal. There is a right to a written statement of reasons. Applicants may be accompanied to the tribunal hearing by a representative. Hearings before the SSAT are usually in public. The tribunal usually consists of three people, a chairperson who is a lawyer, and two non-legal persons. The tribunal's decision and the grounds for the decision must be in writing. There are no strict rules of procedure in the hearing of an appeal.[3]

---

1   See, however, *Trico Folberth Ltd* v. *Groves* [1976] IRLR 327 (IT).
2   Social Security Act 1975, s. 101(5A).
3   OGUS & BARENDT, *The Law of Social Security*, 3rd ed., 1988, pp. 571-576.

Both the applicant and the Department of Social Security have a further right of appeal to a Social Security Commissioner on questions of law. Leave to appeal must be granted by either the chairperson of the tribunal or by a Commissioner within six weeks of being sent the decision.[1] A decision can be reached by the Commissioner on the basis of the written submissions without an oral hearing, but one is seldom refused if requested. The hearing is generally in public. If an oral hearing takes place, representation is permitted before the Commissioner. A decision is given in writing.[2]

An appeal may be made against a decision of a Commissioner to the Court of Appeal (the Court of Session in Scotland).[3] An appeal is only on a point of law and leave must be obtained. The application for leave to appeal must be made in writing within three months of the Commissioner's decision, to the Commissioner or failing that to the Court of Appeal itself. There is no legal aid for hearings before either the SSAT or the Commissioner.[4]

The Social Security Act 1989, Sch. 5, para. 4 provides a special procedure for the modification of occupational pension schemes by the Occupational Pensions Board to conform to the principle of equal treatment. On an application made in respect of an employment-related benefit scheme, other than a public service scheme, by persons competent to make such an application, the Occupational Pensions Board (the 'Board') may make an order modifying, or authorizing the modification of, the scheme, for the purpose of making provision implementing the principle of equal treatment. In relation to any employment-related benefit scheme, the persons competent to make an application to the Board are the trustees or managers of the scheme; any person other than the trustees or managers who has power to alter the rules of the scheme; any person who is an employer of persons in service in an employment to which the scheme applies; and such other persons as regulations may specify, in relation to any category of schemes into which the scheme falls, as being proper persons to make an application for the purposes of this paragraph in respect of a scheme of that category. The Board shall not entertain an application for an order by them unless they are satisfied that the modification of the scheme in question cannot be achieved otherwise than by means of such an order; or can only be achieved in accordance with a procedure which is liable to be unduly complex or protracted, or involves the obtaining of consents which cannot be obtained, or can only be obtained with undue delay or difficulty. Under Sch. 5, para. 8 of the 1989 Act, a county court, on the application of any person interested, shall have jurisdiction to determine any question arising as to whether any provision of an employment-related benefit scheme does or does not comply with the principle of equal treatment.

---

1   Social Security Act 1975, s. 101A.
2   OGUS & BARENDT, *op. cit.*, pp. 580-583.
3   Social Security Act 1980, s. 14.
4   OGUS & BARENDT, *op. cit.*, pp. 587-588.

In addition, in some cases it is possible to challenge decisions made by government bodies through judicial review of the decision before the High Court.

## 6.1          COURT OR TRIBUNAL PROCEDURE

Unless otherwise stated, this section discusses litigation in industrial tribunals: see Industrial Tribunals (Rules of Procedure) Regulations 1985.[1] Where an individual is claiming a breach of equal pay or equal treatment requirements, proceedings are instituted by the applicant presenting to the Secretary of the Tribunals an originating application, which is in writing and sets out the name and address of the applicant, the names and addresses of the person against whom relief is sought, and the grounds on which relief is sought. Where the Secretary of the Tribunals is of the opinion that the originating application does not seek or on the facts stated cannot entitle the applicant to a relief which a tribunal has power to give, he may give notice to that effect to the applicant stating the reasons for his opinion and informing him that the application will not be registered unless he states in writing that he wishes to proceed with it.[2]

Upon receiving an originating application the Secretary of the Tribunal enters particulars of it in the Register, sends a copy of it to the respondent, and informs the parties in writing of the case number of the originating application entered in the Register and of the address to which notices and other communications to the Secretary of the Tribunals shall be sent. Every copy of the originating application sent by the Secretary of the Tribunals is accompanied by a written notice which includes information about the means and time for entering an appearance, the consequences of failure to do so, and the right to receive a copy of the decision. The Secretary of the Tribunals also notifies the parties that in all cases under the provisions of any enactment providing for conciliation the services of an Advisory Conciliation and Arbitration Service (ACAS) conciliation officer are available to them.[3]

A respondent shall within 14 days of receiving the copy of an originating application enter an appearance to the proceedings by presenting to the Secretary of the Tribunals a written notice of appearance setting out his full name and address and stating whether or not he intends to resist the application and, if so, setting out sufficient particulars to show on what grounds. Upon receipt of a notice of appearance the Secretary of the Tribunals sends a copy of it to any other party.[4]

---

[1]   SI 1985 No 16.
[2]   Industrial Tribunals Rules of Procedure 1985, rr. 1(1), 1(2).
[3]   Industrial Tribunals Rules of Procedure 1985, r. 2.
[4]   Industrial Tribunals Rules of Procedure 1985, r. 3(1).

The President or a Regional Chairman fixes the date, time and place of the hearing of the originating application and the Secretary of the Tribunals, not less than 14 days (or such shorter time as may be agreed by him with the parties) before the date so fixed, sends to each party a notice of hearing which includes information and guidance as to attendance at the hearing, witnesses and the bringing of documents (if any), representation by another person and written representations.[1]

The Employment Act 1989, s. 20 provides for regulations to be made to give an industrial tribunal chairman discretion to require a deposit of up to £150 from either party as a condition of proceeding, if the chairman considers that his or her case has no reasonable prospect of success. These regulations have not yet been made.

At any hearing of or in connection with an originating application a party and any person entitled to appear may appear before the tribunal and may be heard in person or be represented by counsel or by a solicitor or by a representative of a trade union or an employers' association or by any other person whom he desires to represent him.[2] The tribunal conducts the hearing in such manner as it considers most suitable to the clarification of the issues before it and generally to the just handling of the proceedings; it seeks to avoid formality in its proceedings and it is not bound by any enactment or rule of law relating to the admissibility of evidence in proceedings before the courts of law. At the hearing of the originating application a party and any other person entitled to appear are entitled to give evidence, to call witnesses, to question any witnesses and to address the tribunal.[3]

If a party fails to appear or to be represented at the time and place fixed for the hearing, the tribunal may, if that party is an applicant, dismiss, or, in any case, dispose of the application in the absence of that party or may adjourn the hearing to a later date: provided that before deciding to dismiss or disposing of any application in the absence of a party the tribunal shall consider any representations submitted by that party. A tribunal may require any witness to give evidence on oath or affirmation.[4]

A decision of a tribunal may be taken by a majority and, if the tribunal is constituted of two members only, the chairman has a second or casting vote. The decision of a tribunal, which may be given orally at the end of a hearing or reserved, is recorded in a document signed by the chairman. The tribunal gives reasons, which are in full form, for its decision. The reasons for the decision of the tribunal are recorded in a document signed by the chairman. The clerk to the tribunal transmits any decision to the Secretary of

---

1    Industrial Tribunals Rules of Procedure 1985, r. 5(1).
2    Industrial Tribunals Rules of Procedure 1985, r. 7(6).
3    Industrial Tribunals Rules of Procedure 1985, rr. 8(1), 8(2).
4    Industrial Tribunals Rules of Procedure 1985, rr. 8(3), 8(4).

the Tribunals who enters it in the Register and sends a copy of the entry to each of the parties and to the persons entitled to appear who did so appear. The Register is kept at the Office of the Tribunals and is open to the inspection of any person without charge at all reasonable hours.[1]

In equal value cases the procedure is different in a number of significant respects. The first major difference is that there are three preliminary stages unique to equal value cases. The first preliminary stage is where a tribunal is required, before proceeding to hear the parties on the claim, to invite them to apply for an adjournment for the purpose of seeking to reach a settlement of the claim.[2] A second preliminary stage may take place involving consideration of the genuine material factor defence. On the application of either party, a tribunal may hear evidence and permit the parties to address it on this issue.[3] Third, the tribunal is required to dismiss the claim without determining whether any work is of equal value where there are no reasonable grounds to justify the applicant's claim,[4] including where an existing non-discriminatory job evaluation scheme has given the claimant's job a value different from that of her male comparator.

If the claim is not dismissed as a result of a preliminary hearing, the tribunal, before considering the question of equal value, requires an expert to prepare a report with respect to the question.[5] An industrial tribunal is not entitled to require an expert's report prior to ruling on the employer's defence that there are no reasonable grounds for the claim.[6]

Where a tribunal has received the report of an expert, it sends a copy of the report to each of the parties and fixes a date for the hearing of the case to be resumed at least 14 days after the date on which the report is sent to the parties. Upon the resuming of the hearing of the case the report may be admitted as evidence in the case unless the tribunal has exercised its power not to admit the report on one of the following grounds: that the expert has not complied with one or more of the requirements imposed on him; or that the conclusion contained in the report is one which, taking due account of the information supplied and representations made to the expert, could not reasonably have been reached; or that for some other material reason (other than disagreement with the conclusion that the applicant's work is or is not of equal value or with the reasoning leading to the conclusion) the report is unsatisfactory. In any of these circumstances the tribunal may, if it thinks fit,

---

1    Industrial Tribunals Rules of Procedure 1985, rr. 9(1) to 9(6) and 9(8).
2    Industrial Tribunals Complementary Rules of Procedure 1985, r. 12(2A).
3    Industrial Tribunals Complementary Rules of Procedure 1985, r. 8(2E).
4    See, for example, *Dennehy* v. *Sealink (UK) Ltd* [1987] IRLR 120 (EAT).
5    Industrial Tribunals Complementary Rules of Procedure 1985, r. 7A(1).
6    *Sheffield Metropolitan District Council* v. *Siberry* [1989] ICR 208 (EAT).

determine not to admit the report, and in such a case another expert's report is commissioned.[1]

In forming its view on whether or not to admit the expert's report, the tribunal takes account of any representations of the parties and may in that connection permit any party to give evidence upon, to call and question any witness upon any relevant matter. The tribunal may, at any time after it has received the report of an expert, require that expert (or, if that is impracticable, another expert) to explain any matter contained in his report or, having regard to such matters as may be set out in the requirement, to give further consideration to the question. The expert makes his reply in writing to the tribunal, giving his explanation or, as the case may be, setting down any conclusion which may result from his further consideration and his reasons for that conclusion. Where the tribunal has received a reply from the expert, it sends a copy of the reply to each of the parties and allows the parties to make representations, and the reply is treated as information furnished to the tribunal and is given such weight as the tribunal thinks fit.[2]

Where a tribunal has determined not to admit a report, that report is treated for all purposes connected with the proceedings as if it had not been received by the tribunal and no further account is taken of it, and the requirement on the expert to prepare a report lapses.[3]

The tribunal may, and shall upon the application of a party, require the attendance of an expert who has prepared a report in connection with an equal value claim in any hearing relating to that claim. Where an expert attends in compliance with such requirement any party may cross-examine the expert on his report and on any other matter pertaining to the question on which the expert was required to report. At any time after the tribunal has received the report of the expert, any party may, on giving reasonable notice of his intention to do so to the tribunal and to any other party to the claim, call one witness to give expert evidence on the question on which the tribunal has required the expert to prepare a report; and where such evidence is given, any other party may cross-examine the person giving that evidence upon it. Generally, no party may give evidence upon, or question any witness upon, any matter of fact upon which a conclusion in the report of the expert is based. A tribunal may, however, permit a party to give evidence upon, to call witnesses and to question any witness upon any such matters of fact if either the matter of fact is relevant to and is raised in connection with the defence of genuine material factor, or the report of the expert contains no conclusion on the question of whether the applicant's work and the work of the comparator are of equal value and the tribunal is satisfied that the absence of that conclusion is wholly or mainly due to the refusal or

---

1    Industrial Tribunals Complementary Rules of Procedure 1985, rr. 7A(6) to 7A(8).
2    Industrial Tribunals Complementary Rules of Procedure 1985. rr. 7A(9) to 7A(12).
3    Industrial Tribunals Complementary Rules of Procedure 1985, r. 7A(13).

deliberate omission of a person required by the tribunal to furnish information or to produce documents to comply with that requirement.[1] In *Tennant Textile Colours Ltd* v. *Todd*,[2] the Northern Ireland Court of Appeal held that after the independent expert's report had been submitted to the tribunal, the parties were able to make submissions contradicting the findings of fact contained in the report.

Lastly, a tribunal may, on the application of a party, hear evidence upon and permit the parties to address it upon the defence of genuine material factor before it requires an expert to prepare a report. Where the tribunal so proceeds, it shall be without prejudice to further consideration of that issue after the tribunal has received the report.[3]

### 6.1.1        ACQUIRING THE EVIDENCE

### 6.1.1.1        Prescribed forms

SDA 1975, s. 74 provides help for aggrieved persons in obtaining information, in that it provides a special procedure for questioning a potential respondent. With a view to helping a person ('the person aggrieved') who considers he may have been discriminated against in contravention of this Act to decide whether to institute proceedings and, if he does so, to formulate and present his case in the most effective manner, the Secretary of State has prescribed forms by which the person aggrieved may question the respondent on his reasons for doing any relevant act, or on any other matter which is or may be relevant, and forms by which the respondent may if he so wishes reply to any questions. The Sex Discrimination (Questions and Replies) Order 1975[4] came into operation on 29 December 1975. The Secretary of State has prescribed the period within which questions must be duly served in order to be admissible and prescribed the manner in which a question, and any reply by the respondent, may be duly served.

SDA 1975, s. 74(2) provides that where the person aggrieved questions the respondent

    (a)   the question and any reply by the respondent ... shall ... be admissible as evidence in the proceedings;

    (b)   if it appears to the court or tribunal that the respondent deliberately and without reasonable excuse omitted to reply within a reasonable period or that his reply is evasive or equivocal, the court or tribunal may draw any inference

---

1    Industrial Tribunals Complementary Rules of Procedure 1985, rr. 8(2A) to 8(2D).
2    [1989] IRLR 3 (NICA). See also *Aldridge* v. *British Telecom plc* [1989] ICR 790, [1990] IRLR 11 (EAT).
3    Industrial Tribunals Complementary Rules of Procedure 1985, r. 8(2E).
4    SI 1975 No 2048 (amended by Sex Discrimination (Questions & Replies) (Amendment) Order 1977 (SI 1977 No 844)).

from that fact that it considers it just and equitable to draw, including an inference that he committed an unlawful act.

In proceedings before a tribunal, a question shall only be admissible as evidence in pursuance of s. 74(2)(a) of the SDA 1975 (a) where it was served before a complaint had been presented to a tribunal, if it was so served within the period of three months beginning when the act complained of was done; (b) where it was served when a complaint had been presented to a tribunal, either if it was so served within the period of 21 days beginning with the day on which the complaint was presented or if it was so served later with leave given, and within a period specified, by a direction of a tribunal.[1]

### 6.1.1.2    Obligation to furnish all relevant evidence

The tribunal has wide powers to require further particulars (to make the complainant's application or the respondent's notice of appearance more specific), to require the attendance of witnesses and to grant discovery and the inspection of documents. A tribunal, on the application of a party to the proceedings, or, if it thinks fit, of its own motion, may require a party to furnish in writing to the person specified by the tribunal further particulars of the grounds on which he relies and of any relevant facts and contentions. The tribunal may grant to the person making the application such discovery or inspection (including the taking of copies) of documents as might be granted by a county court. The tribunal may also require the attendance of any person (including a party to the proceedings) as a witness, wherever such person may be within Great Britain, and may, if it does so require the attendance of a person, require him to produce any document relating to the matter to be determined.[2] However, anything communicated to a conciliation officer (see §6.2.1.4 below) in connection with the performance of his functions under SDA 1975, s. 64 shall not be admissible in evidence in any proceedings before an industrial tribunal except with the consent of the person who communicated it to that officer.[3]

In *Science Research Council* v. *Nasse*[4] an applicant alleging discrimination in promotion sought discovery of confidential reports on himself and two other people who had been promoted, and discovery of notes made by a local review board. The House of Lords held that there was no public interest immunity for disclosure in respect of private confidential documents. The test for deciding whether discovery should be ordered was

---

1    Sex Discrimination (Questions & Replies) Order 1975 (SI 1975 No 2048), art. 5. See further *Oxford* v. *DHSS* [1977] ICR 884, [1977] IRLR 225 (EAT); *Virdee* v. *ECC Quarries Ltd* [1978] IRLR 295 (IT).

2    Industrial Tribunals Rules of Procedure 1985, r. 4(1).

3    SDA 1975, s. 64(4).

4    [1980] AC 1028, [1979] 3 WLR 762, [1979] 3 All ER 673, [1979] ICR 921, [1979] IRLR 465 (HL).

whether it was necessary for the fair disposal of the proceedings. In *West Midlands PTE* v. *Singh*[1] the Court of Appeal ordered discovery of details of the ethnic origins of applicants for and appointees to posts within a band of grades comparable to that for which he had applied. Such evidence may have a probative effect as indicating intention in the particular case in issue. It is likely that a similar approach would be taken to the discovery of statistics of sex composition. In *Leverton* v. *Clwyd County Council* [2] the applicant sought an order for discovery in order to identify an appropriate comparator, in a case in which she claimed equal value with clerical workers. She based her claim on a joint employer/union report which drew the employer's attention to the low levels of pay for nursery nurses compared with those for clerical workers. The EAT held that she was entitled to the order on the basis that she had established a *prima facie* case on the basis of the joint report.[3]

The ordinary rules relating to obtaining further and better particulars and the discovery and inspection of documents apply in cases of equal pay complaints before industrial tribunals as they apply in other cases before the tribunal.[4] Within the constraints of relevance, most information can be required by either side from the other, though confidentiality will sometimes successfully be used to prevent disclosure of otherwise relevant evidence. There are, however, special rules relating to access to information by the independent expert.[5] The expert has no authority to require any information to be produced, but may apply to the tribunal for an order to require any person to furnish relevant information. The expert cannot, however, obtain an order requiring a person to give oral evidence. Nor does there appear to be any power to order an employer to permit the independent expert access to the place of work.

There are additional powers available to a tribunal for use only in proceedings involving an equal value claim. A tribunal may, on the application of an expert who has been required by the tribunal to prepare a report, require any person whom the tribunal is satisfied may have information which may be relevant to the question or matter on which the expert is required to report to furnish, in writing, such information as the

---

1   [1988] 1 WLR 730, [1988] 2 All ER 873, [1988] ICR 614, [1988] IRLR 186 (CA).
2   [1987] 1 WLR 65, [1987] ICR 158 (EAT).
3   On discovery, see further *Williams* v. *Dyfed County Council* [1986] ICR 449 (EAT); *Selvarajan* v. *Inner London Education Authority* [1980] IRLR 313 (EAT); *Rasul* v. *CRE* [1978] IRLR 203 (EAT); *Perera* v. *Civil Service Commission* [1980] ICR 699, [1980] IRLR 233 (EAT); *British Railways Board* v. *Natarajan* [1979] 2 All ER 794, [1979] ICR 326 (EAT); *British Library* v. *Palyza* [1984] ICR 504, [1984] IRLR 306 (EAT); *Carrington* v. *Helix Lighting Ltd* [1990] IRLR 6 (EAT); *Byrne* v. *Financial Times Ltd*, [1991] IRLR 417 (EAT).
4   Industrial Tribunals Rules of Procedure 1985, r. 4; Industrial Tribunals Complementary Rules of Procedure 1985, r. 4.
5   Industrial Tribunals Complementary Rules of Procedure 1985, rr. 4(1A), 4(1B) and 4(2A).

tribunal may require. A tribunal may also require any person to produce any documents which are in the possession, custody or power of that person and which the tribunal is satisfied may contain matter relevant to the question on which the expert is required to report. Any information so required to be furnished or document so required to be produced shall be furnished or produced, at or within such time as the tribunal may appoint, to the Secretary of the Tribunals who shall send the information or document to the expert.[1] A tribunal shall not make such a requirement of a conciliation officer who has acted in connection with the complaint, or if it is satisfied that the person so required would have good grounds for refusing to comply with the requirement if it were a requirement made in connection with a hearing before the tribunal.[2]

Any person who without reasonable excuse fails to comply with any requirement shall be liable on summary conviction to a fine.[3] If a requirement is not complied with, a tribunal, before or at the hearing, may dismiss the whole or part of the originating application, or, as the case may be, strike out the whole or part of the notice of appearance, and, where appropriate, direct that a respondent shall be debarred from defending altogether. However, a tribunal shall not so dismiss or strike out or give such a direction unless it has sent notice to the party who has not complied with the requirement giving him an opportunity to show cause why such should not be done.[4]

### 6.1.1.3        Annual information to works councils

See §6.1.1.4 below.

### 6.1.1.4        Information to trade unions for bargaining

Sections 17 and 18 of the Employment Protection Act 1975 provide for the disclosure of information by employers to trade unions for the purpose of collective bargaining. The Act places a general duty on an employer to disclose at all stages of collective bargaining information requested by representatives of independent trade unions. The unions must be recognized by the employer for collective bargaining purposes. The information to be disclosed is that without which a trade union representative would be impeded to a material extent in bargaining and which it would be in accordance with good industrial relations practice to disclose for the purpose of collective bargaining. There are various exceptions to this duty which need not be discussed here. If the trade union considers that an employer has failed to disclose to its representatives information which the employer was

---

1    Industrial Tribunals Complementary Rules of Procedure 1985, r. 4(1A).
2    Industrial Tribunals Complementary Rules of Procedure 1985, r. 4(1B).
3    EPCA 1978, Sch. 9, para. 7; Industrial Tribunals Rules of Procedure 1985, r. 4(3).
4    Industrial Tribunals Rules of Procedure 1985, r. 4(4).

required to disclose, it may make a complaint to the Central Arbitration Committee (CAC).

A Code of Practice has been issued by ACAS on this provision which indicates that equal opportunities issues are one of the matters about which it may be relevant to require disclosure of information.[1] In two complaints the CAC has upheld a complaint by a union seeking information relevant for equal opportunity bargaining.

### 6.1.2    BURDEN OF PROOF

In equal pay cases the legal burden of proof that an equality clause operates lies in general with the applicant, except where the employer claims that any variation is genuinely due to a material factor which is not the difference of sex, in which case the legal onus of proof lies on the employer to establish this defence. In *National Vulcan Engineering Insurance Group Ltd* v. *Wade*[2] the Court of Appeal held that the burden of proving a genuine material difference under the Equal Pay Act was the ordinary burden in civil cases, i.e. on the balance of probabilities.

The legal burden of proof of direct discrimination in equal treatment cases lies with the plaintiff. In a number of early cases the EAT held that the evidential burden might be envisaged as shifting to the employer once the complainant had made out a possible case, so that a finding of no case to answer should be reserved only for the exceptional or frivolous case.[3] The Northern Ireland Court of Appeal has pursued this line of development to a significant extent in a number of cases.[4] In the *Craigavon* case the Lord Chief Justice held that:

> ... once discrimination (in the sense of unfair preference) is proved, the fact that the successful candidate was of a different [gender] from the unsuccessful but apparently better qualified candidate is itself evidence of [sex] discrimination.

Since then, however, the British EAT has been more sceptical of the value of formal shifts in the onus of evidential proof. In *Khanna* v. *Ministry of Defence*[5] the EAT preferred that 'concepts of shifting evidential burdens [should be] avoided'. That approach was 'more likely to obscure than to

---

1    See ACAS, Code of Practice 2: *Disclosure of Information to Trade Unions for Collective Bargaining Purposes.*
2    [1979] QB 132, [1978] 3 WLR 214, [1978] 3 All ER 121, [1978] ICR 800, [1978] IRLR 225 (CA).
3    *Oxford* v. *DHSS* [1977] ICR 884, [1977] IRLR 225 (EAT).
4    *Wallace* v. *SE Education & Library Board* [1980] IRLR 193 (NICA); *Conway* v. *Queen's University Belfast* [1981] IRLR 43 (NICA); *Fair Employment Agency* v. *Craigavon Borough Council* [1980] IRLR 316 (NICA).
5    [1981] ICR 653, [1981] IRLR 331 (EAT).

illuminate the right answer'. The proper approach was to look at all the evidence and:

> ... to take into account the fact that direct evidence of discrimination is seldom going to be available and that, accordingly, in these cases the affirmative evidence of discrimination will normally consist of inferences to be drawn from the primary facts. If the primary facts indicate that there has been discrimination of some kind, the employer is called on to give an explanation and, failing clear and specific explanation being given by the employer to the satisfaction of the industrial tribunal, an inference of unlawful discrimination from the primary facts will mean the complaint succeeds.

The concept of a shifting evidential burden of proof was regarded as 'rather nebulous'.[1]

Although this approach was questioned by the EAT in *London Borough of Barking & Dagenham* v. Camara,[2] the *Khanna* approach has subsequently been given strong support by the English Court of Appeal in *Baker* v. *Cornwall County Council*,[3] holding that the tribunal 'should be prepared to draw the inference that the discrimination was on such grounds unless the alleged discrimination can satisfy the tribunal that there was some other innocent explanation'. In *Dornan* v. *Belfast City Council*[4] the Northern Ireland Court of Appeal also endorsed *Khanna*, *Chattopadhyay* and *Wallace*, to similar effect.

Subsequently, in *British Gas plc* v. *Sharma*[5] the EAT interpreted *Khanna* and *Noone* more restrictively, as requiring tribunals, having looked at the whole of the evidence, to decide whether there are primary facts which in the absence of an explanation point to discrimination. If there is no acceptable or adequate explanation then it is open to the tribunal to find by inference that there was discrimination (though they are not bound to do so). But in *King* v. *Great Britain-China Centre*[6] the Court of Appeal held that it was not only open to the tribunal to make such an inference, it was 'legitimate' to do so.

There is a mixed legal burden of proof included in the SDA 1975 definition of indirect discrimination.[7] The plaintiff is required to prove that she (or he) has been subjected to a condition or requirement which is such that a considerably smaller proportion of women (or men) can comply with it

---

1    See also *Chattopadhyay* v. *Headmaster of Holloway School* [1982] ICR 132, [1981] IRLR 487 (EAT).
2    [1988] ICR 865, [1988] IRLR 373 (EAT).
3    [1990] ICR 452, [1990] IRLR 194 (CA).
4    [1990] IRLR 179 (NICA). See also *Noone* v. *NW Thames Regional Health Authority* [1988] ICR 813, [1988] IRLR 195 (CA); *West Midlands PTE* v. *Singh* [1988] 1 WLR 730, [1988] 2 All ER 873, [1988] ICR 614, [1988] IRLR 186 (CA).
5    [1991] IRLR 101 (EAT).
6    [1991] IRLR 513 (CA).
7    SDA 1975, s. 1(1)(b).

than can males (or females), and that this has been to her (or his) detriment. The employer then has the legal onus to establish that this condition or requirement is nevertheless justifiable, irrespective of sex.

### 6.1.3 COSTS

The rules relating to legal costs in industrial tribunals differ from those applicable in the ordinary courts in Britain. In the tribunals each side is responsible ordinarily for its own costs.[1]

A tribunal does not normally make an award in respect of the costs or expenses incurred by a party to the proceedings but where in its opinion a party (and if he is a respondent whether or not he has entered an appearance) has in bringing or conducting the proceedings acted frivolously, vexatiously or otherwise unreasonably the tribunal may make an order that that party shall pay to another party either a specified sum in respect of the costs or expenses incurred by that other party or the whole or part of those costs or expenses as taxed (if not otherwise agreed). The tribunal may also make an order that that party shall pay to the Secretary of State the whole, or any part, of any allowances (other than allowances paid to members of tribunals or assessors) paid by the Secretary of State to any person for the purposes of, or in connection with, his attendance at the tribunal.[2]

Where the tribunal has on the application of a party to the proceedings postponed the day or time fixed for or adjourned the hearing, the tribunal may make orders against or, as the case may require, in favour of that party as respects any costs or expenses incurred or any allowances paid as a result of the postponement or adjournment.[3]

### 6.1.4 LEGAL AID

Full legal aid is not available before the industrial tribunals, only coming into effect at the stage of appeal before the EAT and beyond. However, where, in relation to proceedings or prospective proceedings either under the EqPA 1970 or the SDA 1975, an individual who is an actual or prospective complainant or claimant applies to the EOC for assistance, the EOC considers the application and may grant it if they think fit to do so on the ground that the case raises a question of principle, or that it is unreasonable, having regard to the complexity of the case or the applicant's position in relation to the respondent or another person involved or any other matter, to expect the applicant to deal with the case unaided, or by reason of any other special consideration.[4]

---

1  Industrial Tribunals Rules of Procedure 1985, r. 11.
2  Industrial Tribunals Rules of Procedure 1985, r. 11(1).
3  Industrial Tribunals Rules of Procedure 1985, r. 11(2).
4  SDA 1975, s. 75(1).

Assistance by the EOC under the SDA 1975, s. 75 may include giving advice; procuring or attempting to procure the settlement of any matter in dispute; arranging for the giving of advice or assistance by a solicitor or counsel; arranging for representation by any person including all such assistance as is usually given by a solicitor or counsel in the steps preliminary or incidental to any proceedings, or in arriving at or giving effect to a compromise to avoid or bring to an end any proceedings, or any other form of assistance which the EOC may consider appropriate.[1] In so far as expenses are incurred by the EOC in providing the applicant with assistance under this section, the recovery of those expenses constitutes a first charge for the benefit of the EOC on any costs or expenses which (whether by virtue of a judgment or order of a court or tribunal or an agreement or otherwise) are payable to the applicant by any other person in respect of the matter in connection with which the assistance is given, and so far as relates to any costs or expenses, on his rights under any compromise or settlement arrived at in connection with that matter to avoid or bring to an end any proceedings.[2]

## 6.1.5       REMEDIES

Under the EqPA 1970, s. 2(1) and s. 2(1A) the industrial tribunal may (a) make a declaration of rights, (b) make an award of payment of arrears of remuneration, and (c) make an award of damages. Under the SDA 1975 an industrial tribunal may ('as it considers it just and equitable'[3]) make one of the following orders: first, an order declaring the rights of the respondent and complainant 'in relation to the act to which the complaint relates';[4] secondly, an order requiring the respondent to pay damages;[5] thirdly, the tribunal may make a recommendation (not an order) that the respondent take, within a specified period, 'action appearing to the tribunal to be practicable for the purpose of obviating or reducing the adverse effect on the complainant of any act of discrimination to which the complaint relates'.[6]

### 6.1.5.1        Nullity/annulment

See §6.4.2 below.

### 6.1.5.2        Termination of discriminatory conduct

See §6.3.3 below on EOC enforcement remedies.

---

1    SDA 1975, s. 75(2).
2    SDA 1975, s. 75(3).
3    SDA 1975, s. 65(1).
4    SDA 1975, s. 65(1)(a).
5    SDA 1975, s. 65(1)(b).
6    SDA 1975, s. 65(1)(c).

## 6.1.5.3　　Declaration

A declaration is an order declaring the rights of the complainant and the respondent in relation to the act to which the complaint relates. Declarations are available under both the EqPA[1] and the SDA 1975.[2]

### 6.1.5.4　　Compensation

Arrears of remuneration and damages are available under the EqPA.[3] No payment of damages may be awarded in respect of a time earlier than two years before the date on which proceedings were instituted.[4] There is no upper limit to the award that may be made. From 1 April 1990 applicants are entitled to interest on industrial tribunal awards.[5]

Under the SDA 1975, however, one of the most important limitations on the award of damages in general is that the award may not in total amount to more than £10,000.[6] There are two main heads of damages: special damages, which are for 'pecuniary losses such as lost pay, fringe benefits and expenses, calculated to date of hearing'[7] and general damages, which are 'damages not accurately quantifiable in money terms, for which damages can be awarded although they involve an element of guess work by the tribunal. This will include loss of opportunities for future earnings, benefits etc.'.[8]

It is arguable that EC law requires a different approach to remedies for direct and indirect sex discrimination to that adopted in British legislation. The adequacy of UK statutory compensation limits and the extent to which they conform to the requirements of the 1976 Equal Treatment Directive have been considered in *Marshall* v. *Southampton & SW Hampshire Area Health Authority (No 2)*.[9] The Court of Appeal held that art. 6 of the Directive, which requires Member States to provide adequate remedies, does not have direct effect so that it could not be relied upon to award compensation in excess of the limit laid down by the SDA 1975. The terms of art. 6 are not 'sufficiently clear and unconditional' to be capable of being directly effective. This decision is on appeal to the House of Lords.

---

1　EqPA 1970, s. 2(1A).
2　SDA 1975, s. 65(1)(a).
3　EqPA 1970, s. 2(1).
4　EqPA 1970, s. 2(5).
5　Industrial Tribunals (Interest) Order 1990 (SI 1990 No 479).
6　SDA 1975, s. 65(2).
7　HEPPLE, *Encyclopedia*, para. IB-813.
8　HEPPLE, *loc. cit.*
9　[1990] IRLR 481 (CA).

*Front pay*

There is a specific limitation to the award of general damages. When assessing compensation under that head where there has been discrimination in promotions the tribunal can only estimate how long the complainant will remain at her present grade and award compensation within the statutory limits on the basis of that estimate.[1] It cannot order a specific payment to be continued until the person discriminated against achieves an equivalent position to that which she had been discriminatorily denied.[2] There is, in other words, no equivalent to the American remedy of 'front pay' by which a person wrongfully denied a promotion and remaining in a lower paid job receives by way of compensation the difference between the two salaries until she is promoted.[3]

*Damages for injury to feelings*

In addition to damages which are available for any monetary loss which is attributable to the discrimination, the SDA 1975 stipulates that 'for the avoidance of doubt',[4] a damages award may also include compensation for injury to feelings whether or not the tribunal has awarded compensation under any other head. The extent of awards under this head has varied considerable and there have been conflicting judicial approaches. In *Noone* v. *NW Thames Regional Health Authority*[5] the Court of Appeal held that an award of £3,000 was appropriate in this case as an 'injury to feelings' award. In *Alexander* v. *Home Office*[6] the Court of Appeal laid down the principles upon which awards for injuries to feelings should be based, including that though such awards should be restrained, they should not be minimal.

*Aggravated and exemplary damages*

In *Alexander* v. *Home Office* the Court of Appeal held that damages should reflect compensation for the consequences of the discrimination. Both aggravated and exemplary damages might also be awarded, however, where the circumstances of the discrimination were such that the resulting sense of injury was heightened by the manner in which, or the motive for which, the discrimination was carried out (aggravated damages) or as a punishment for anti-social behaviour towards the person discriminated against (exemplary damages), and in *Noone* v. *NW Thames Regional Health Authority*,[7] the Court of Appeal also saw no reason why exemplary damages should not be

---

1   *Skyrail Oceanic Ltd* v. *Coleman* [1981] ICR 864, [1981] IRLR 398 (CA).
2   *Irvine* v. *Prestcold Ltd* [1981] ICR 777 (CA).
3   *International Brotherhood of Teamsters* v. *United States* (1977) 431 US 324.
4   SDA 1975, s. 66(4).
5   [1988] ICR 813, [1988] IRLR 195 (CA).
6   [1988] 1 WLR 968, [1988] 2 All ER 118, [1988] ICR 685, [1988] IRLR 190 (CA).
7   [1988] ICR 813, [1988] IRLR 195 (CA).

awarded. In *Bradford Metropolitan Council* v. *Arora*[1] the Court of Appeal held that exemplary damages may be appropriate and necessary in employment discrimination cases where compensatory damages are inadequate to punish the discriminator for outrageous conduct.

### Damages for indirect discrimination

It is important to distinguish the remedy available for an individual proving a breach of the direct discrimination provisions from that available to an individual proving indirect discrimination. In both cases an individual who succeeds in a claim of discrimination may obtain damages. In the case of indirect discrimination, however, no award of damages or compensation can be made if the respondent proves that the requirement or condition in question was not applied with the intention of treating the claimant unfavourably 'on the ground of [her] sex'.[2] In *Orphanos* v. *QMC*,[3] a case involving a claim of indirect discrimination, Lord Fraser interpreted the equivalent provision in the Race Relations Act (s. 57(4)) to mean, firstly, that only that discrimination which was at one and the same time both direct and indirect discrimination would be subject to a damages award, and secondly that 'intention' was to be interpreted as directed at 'the subjective intention of the discriminator'. On this test the College was held not to have discriminated intentionally.

### 6.1.5.5      Recommendation

The tribunal may only make a recommendation 'for the purpose of obviating or reducing the adverse effect on the complainant of any act of discrimination'.[4] The effect of this restriction is that the tribunal is not able to make general recommendations about discriminatory employment practices which may have been in issue in the litigation.[5] Thus remedies are individual in character. Nor may the tribunal recommend that the employer engage in any of the practices which are permitted to him under the provisions in the Act and which allow a limited degree of affirmative, or 'positive' action.

The limited recommendations which may be made by the industrial tribunal are not specifically enforceable. If not complied with, but only if the non-compliance was 'without reasonable justification', the tribunal may make an order of damages or increase an already existing order of damages subject to a maximum.[6] Where a recommendation has not been complied with in an indirect discrimination case, even the limited sanction of increasing the

---

1   [1991] IRLR 165 (CA).
2   SDA 1975, s. 66(3).
3   [1985] AC 761, [1985] 2 WLR 703, [1985] 2 All ER 233, [1985] IRLR 349 (HL).
4   SDA 1975, s. 65(1)(c).
5   *Ministry of Defence* v. *Jeremiah* [1978] ICR 984 (EAT).
6   SDA 1975, s. 65(3).

damages (or providing them in the first place) as a substitute does not apply. In *Nelson* v. *Tyne & Wear PTE*[1] the question of what constituted a 'reasonable justification' arose for detailed consideration. An earlier industrial tribunal had found sex discrimination against a number of women for promotion and had recommended that:

> ... [the employers] within 6 months of the ... decision give serious consideration, without regard to sex and having regard to the principles of the [Sex Discrimination] Act of 1975, to each of the applicants for promotion to depot clerk either full-time or as part of their duties as cash clerk; in the latter case on the same basis, including ... wages, as the male cash clerks on depot duties.

The women subsequently complained that their employer had failed to comply with the recommendation. The employer argued that he had reasonable justification for not doing so. The tribunal agreed with the employer's argument. The EAT summarized the industrial tribunal's approach as follows:

> [It was] much concerned with the practical, industrial realities, and although properly insistent that sex discrimination be eliminated, realized that it could not be done at the drop of a hat; that problems of industrial relations, of getting over difficulties with the unions, or of dealing with past undertakings and considerations, all in the real world, needed to be taken into account in ending the discrimination which they had found established ... .

The EAT agreed with this approach:

> Industrial tribunals, of course, ought to be careful, having found discrimination established, not, by too mild orders, to allow it to continue unchecked for too long in the future. On the other hand it would be most unreasonable not to take into account practical realities and not to allow a period of time to sort out the difficulties consequent upon the finding, and would not be in the interests of the cause of eliminating sex discrimination. ... [It] is obviously not possible by order to end [the discrimination] instantly in every case. In some cases it is. In many cases it is bound to take a little while to ease the orders through the practical realities of industrial relations before it can be an accomplished fact.

The women lost their appeal.

The limitations on damages awards has led complainants to seek an expanded role for recommendations, but without success. In *Prestcold Ltd* v. *Irvine*[2] the industrial tribunal found sex discrimination against a woman when she was not promoted by her employer. The tribunal made a damages award but went further, making a recommendation as well. The recommendation was:

---

1    [1978] ICR 1183 (EAT).
2    [1980] ICR 610, [1980] IRLR 267 (EAT); [1981] ICR 777 (CA).

> That the complainant be seriously considered as the most suitable candidate for the position of service administration manager as soon as it falls vacant, and that she be given opportunities for career development meanwhile, and that in the alternative she should continue to receive the difference in salary ... until she has been promoted either to that job or to a job of equivalent status.

The employer argued on appeal to the EAT that the tribunal had no power to make such a recommendation and the EAT agreed. Firstly, SDA 1975, s. 65(1)(c) specifies that the recommendation must be that a respondent take action 'within a specified period'.

> It seems to us that a respondent must know, from the time he receives the recommendation, the period within which he should act if he is to observe the recommendation. Accordingly, in our judgment, the recommendation must state precisely on its face the period. The respondent cannot know the period from the beginning, if it is defined only by reference to an event such as a retirement or death neither of which can necessarily be forecast with certainty. In our judgment, the period specified in the recommendation must be stated either by reference to an express number of years, months or days or by reference to a date itself stated in the recommendation.

Secondly, the action to be taken by the employer must be such action as appears 'to be practicable for the purpose of obviating or reducing the adverse effect on the complainant of any act of discrimination to which the complaint relates'. The EAT held that the words 'action appearing ... to be practicable':

> seem to us to indicate the taking of steps other than the payment of wages for the purpose of obviating or reducing the adverse effect of the discrimination. ... Accordingly we hold that the power to make a recommendation ... does not include a recommendation that wages should be paid.

The Court of Appeal agreed.[1]

In *British Gas plc* v. *Sharma*[2] the EAT held that tribunals did not have the power to make a recommendation that the employer promote the respondent to the next suitable vacancy.

### 6.1.5.6 Positive enforcement order

Where an applicant has been successful in establishing her claim in an equal pay case, the tribunal makes an order amending the applicant's contract of employment by adding or deleting one or more terms so as to make the

---

[1] See further *Noone* v. *NW Thames Regional Health Authority* [1988] ICR 813, [1988] IRLR 195 (CA).

[2] [1991] IRLR 101 (EAT).

terms of the woman's contract not less favourable the man's (i.e. requiring levelling up the women's wages to the man's), and requiring payment of back pay. The tribunal may not make an award of back pay which relates to the contravention of an equality clause earlier than two years before the claim was commenced.[1] The SDA 1975 does not permit an industrial tribunal to require that an employer remedy his discrimination by entering into a contract of employment, by promoting a particular person, or by reinstating or re-engaging her. The legislation only allows recommendations to be made that such action be taken by the employer.[2]

### 6.1.5.7    Positive action plan

No such remedy may be awarded by an industrial tribunal.

### 6.1.5.8    Criminal sanctions

No such remedy may be awarded by an industrial tribunal.

### 6.1.6    CLASS ACTIONS

There is no provision permitting class actions representing a group of similarly situated applicants, but there are provisions whereby applications made by a number of different applicants may be joined and heard together by the tribunal and independent expert, though both are required to reach a decision on each individual's case.

A tribunal may at any time either upon the application of any person or, where appropriate, of its own motion, direct any person against whom any relief is sought to be joined as a party to the proceedings, and give such consequential directions as it considers necessary. A tribunal may likewise, either upon such application or of its own motion, order that any respondent named in the originating application or subsequently added, who shall appear to the tribunal not to have been, or to have ceased to be, directly interested in the subject of the originating application, be dismissed from the proceedings. Where there are numerous persons having the same interest in an originating application, one or more of them may be cited as the person or persons against whom relief is sought, or may be authorized by the tribunal, before or at the hearing, to defend on behalf of all the persons so interested.[3]

Where there are pending before the industrial tribunals two or more originating applications, then, if at any time upon the application of a party or of its own motion it appears to a tribunal that some common question of law or fact arises in both or all the originating applications, or the relief

---

1    EqPA 1970, ss. 2(1), 2(1A) and 2(5).
2    SDA 1975, s. 65.
3    Industrial Tribunals Rules of Procedure 1985, r. 14.

claimed therein is in respect of or arises out of the same set of facts, or for some other reason it is desirable, the tribunal may order that some or all of the originating applications shall be considered together, and may give such consequential directions as may be necessary. However, the tribunal may not make an order without sending notice to all parties concerned giving them an opportunity to show cause why such an order should not be made.[1]

A procedure has grown up, where a claim has been made by substantial numbers of individual women in a work force (usually on equal pay issues), of the tribunal ordering that representative sample cases should be chosen for trial from large numbers of applications concerning similar issues, and staying the other cases pending decision on the sample cases. In *Ashmore* v. *British Coal Corporation*[2] the Court of Appeal upheld an industrial tribunal's decision to strike out an equal pay claim where the applicant sought to have the case re-listed after it had been stayed, where the issue in the case had been determined in the sample cases.

### 6.1.7 EXCLUSION OF JUDICIAL REDRESS

SDA 1975, s. 77(3) provides that a term in a contract which purports to exclude or limit any provision of the SDA 1975 or the EqPA 1970 is unenforceable by any person in whose favour the term would otherwise operate. This limitation does not apply to a contract settling a complaint, where the contract is made with the assistance of a conciliation officer.[3] No proceedings, whether civil or criminal, shall lie against any person in respect of an act by reason that the act is unlawful by virtue of a provision of the SDA 1975. This does not preclude the making of an order of *certiorari*, *mandamus* or prohibition:[4] see also §4.2.1.4.

### 6.1.8 TIME-LIMITS

It has been held by the EAT that there is no time-limit for an applicant bringing an equal pay complaint to an industrial tribunal (although a reference by the Secretary of State for Employment must be brought within six months of the person on whose behalf it is brought leaving the relevant employment).[5] However, it has been argued that this decision is wrongly decided. Another case on this issue is currently on appeal to the EAT.

A woman shall not be entitled, in proceedings brought in respect of a failure to comply with an equality clause (including proceedings before an industrial tribunal), to be awarded any payment by way of arrears of

---

1  Industrial Tribunals Rules of Procedure 1985, r. 15.
2  [1990] IRLR 26 (CA).
3  SDA 1975, s. 77(4).
4  SDA 1975, ss. 62(1) and 62(2).
5  EqPA, s. 2(4). See *British Railways Board* v. *Paul* [1988] IRLR 20 (EAT).

remuneration or damages in respect of a time earlier than two years before the date on which the proceedings were instituted.[1]

Under s. 76(1) of the SDA 1975, however, an industrial tribunal may not consider a complaint unless it is presented to the tribunal before the end of the period of three months beginning when the act complained of was done. An act of discrimination may be an act 'extending over a period', i.e. a continuing act of discrimination. In that case, the act is treated as done at the end of the period.[2] There is an unresolved issue as to whether the domestic time-limit applies to a case brought under art. 119 of the EEC Treaty in domestic tribunals.

A court or tribunal may nevertheless consider any such complaint, claim or application which is out of time if, in all the circumstances of the case, it considers that it is just and equitable to do so.[3]

## 6.2         COURTS AND TRIBUNALS

### 6.2.1        SPECIAL LABOUR COURT OR TRIBUNAL

Sex discrimination and equal pay cases dealing with employment issues are heard before the ordinary industrial tribunals, except in Northern Ireland where there are circumstances in which they may be held before a specialized wing of the industrial tribunal system, the Fair Employment Tribunal. These circumstances are where a complaint raises issues of both sex discrimination and religious discrimination under the Fair Employment Act 1976, as amended.

### 6.2.1.1        Equality officer

In equal value cases only, the tribunal is required, unless a preliminary hearing has determined that the applicant cannot proceed, to select an independent expert to draw up a report as to whether the applicant and the comparator are doing work of equal value.[4] The parties to the case have no say in the choice of expert. The costs of the expert are payable by the Secretary of State for Employment. Independent experts are appointed by ACAS on a part-time basis. The criteria for appointment are experience in job evaluation, an understanding of the legislation and industrial experience, and the necessary time to undertake cases. As we have seen (§6.1 above),

---

1    EqPA, s. 2(5).
2    SDA, s. 76(6)(b). See, for example, *Calder* v. *James Finlay Corporation Ltd* [1989] ICR 157 (EAT); *Barclays Bank plc* v. *Kapur* [1989] IRLR 136 (HL).
3    SDA 1975, s. 76(5). See further *Hutchinson* v. *Westward Television Ltd* [1977] ICR 279, [1977] IRLR 69 (EAT).
4    Industrial Tribunals Complementary Rules of Procedure 1985, r. 7A(1).

once the tribunal refers the question of equal value to an independent expert it is required to adjourn the hearing pending receipt of the expert's report.[1]

The expert is required to take account of all information supplied and all such representations made to him as have a bearing on the question; before drawing up his report, to produce and send to the parties a written summary of the said information and representations and invite the representations of the parties upon the material contained therein; to make his report to the tribunal in a document which shall reproduce the summary and contain a brief account of any representations received from the parties upon it, and any conclusion; and to take no account of the difference of sex and at all times act fairly.[2]

Although the legislation requires that the expert produces a report within 42 days,[3] all experts have taken considerably longer – up to two years in one case which was unaffected by appeals or other procedural reasons for delays. Although 16 experts are currently appointed to the panel of experts, in practice most of the work has fallen on the small number of independent experts who are no longer in full-time employment. The delays in respect of experts' reports is now a cause for serious concern. The President of the EAT has said in one case that:

> the present restrictions on procedure imposed by the rules gave rise to delays which were properly described as scandalous and amounted to a denial of justice to women seeking remedy through the judicial process.[4]

After drawing up the report, the expert then refers back to the industrial tribunal. The tribunal decides whether or not to accept the expert's report, and if so, whether there is any defence which, despite the equal value of the jobs, nevertheless justifies the inequality in pay. The onus is on the employer to demonstrate the reasons why the man and the woman are not being paid the same, by establishing that a non-discriminatory 'genuine material factor' is operating.[5]

When the tribunal receives this report from the expert, a hearing is reconvened to consider it. The expert's report is to be admitted as evidence in the case unless the tribunal decides not to admit it.[6] If the report is not admitted, another report must be commissioned.[7] If it is admitted, the

---

1  Industrial Tribunals Complementary Rules of Procedure 1985, r. 7A(4).
2  Industrial Tribunals Complementary Rules of Procedure 1985, r. 7A(3).
3  Industrial Tribunals Complementary Rules of Procedure 1985, r. 7A(5).
4  Wood J in *Aldridge* v. *British Telecom plc* [1989] ICR 790, [1990] IRLR 11 (EAT).
5  EqPA 1970, s. 1(3).
6  *Tennant Textile Colours Ltd* v. *Todd* [1989] IRLR 3 (NICA).
7  Industrial Tribunals Complementary Rules of Procedure 1985, rr. 7A(6), 7A(7) and 7A(8).

tribunal must then decide whether to accept the independent expert's assessment of equal value, and whether any defence has been established by the employer. In *Tennant Textile Colours Ltd* v. *Todd*,[1] the Northern Ireland Court of Appeal held, in considering the weight that the industrial tribunal should attach to an independent expert's report, that the findings of fact in the report are not binding, and do not prevent either party from contesting the conclusions.

If, on the application of one or more of the parties made not less than 42 days after a tribunal has notified an expert of the requirement to prepare a report, the tribunal forms the view that there has been or is likely to be undue delay in receiving that report, the tribunal may require the expert to provide in writing to the tribunal an explanation for the delay or information as to his progress and may, in consideration of any such explanation or information as may be provided and after seeking representations from the parties, revoke, by notice in writing to the expert, the requirement to prepare a report, and another expert's report is then commissioned.[2]

### 6.2.1.2    Arbitration officer

The EqPA 1970, s. 2A(1) provides that where an agricultural wages order made before or after the commencement of the Equal Pay Act contains any provision applying specifically to men only or to women only, the order may be referred by the Secretary of State to the CAC to declare what amendments need to be made in the order, so as to remove that discrimination between men and women. When the CAC has declared the amendments needing to be so made, it is the duty of the Agricultural Wages Board, by a further agricultural wages order coming into operation not later than five months after the date of the CAC's decision, either to make those amendments in the order referred to the CAC or otherwise to replace or amend that order so as to remove the discrimination.

Conditions of service in the armed forces are excluded from the coverage of the conventional enforcement procedures of the EqPA, s. 1(9). The Act provides, as an alternative, that neither the Secretary of State nor the Defence Council shall make or recommend the making of:

> ... any instrument relating to the terms and conditions of service of members of the naval, military or air forces of the Crown, if the instrument has the effect of making a distinction, as regards pay, allowances or leave, between men and women who are members of those forces, not being a distinction fairly attributable to differences between the obligations undertaken by men and those undertaken by women.[3]

---

1   [1989] IRLR 3 (NICA).
2   Industrial Tribunals Complementary Rules of Procedure 1985, r. 7A(5).
3   EqPA, s. 7(1).

This prohibition is not enforceable by an individual through a judicial process. Instead, either the Secretary of State or the Defence Council may refer to the CAC for their advice any question whether a provision made or proposed to be made ought to be regarded as making a distinction not permitted.[1]

### 6.2.1.3       Equal opportunities agency

See §6.3.1.2 below.

### 6.2.1.4       Conciliation procedures

In all equal pay cases ACAS has the role of attempting to conciliate between the two parties to the case. If this is successful, then the agreement is registered officially with the industrial tribunal. Unless conciliation is successful, or either party withdraws, the case will proceed to an tribunal hearing.

After an individual has made a complaint to a tribunal (and sometimes even before such a complaint, if requested) an officer of ACAS may attempt to 'conciliate'. SDA 1975, s. 64(1) provides that an ACAS officer has a duty to endeavour to promote a settlement of the complaint without its being determined by a tribunal if (a) he is requested to by the complainant or the employer concerned; or (b) in the absence of such a request, the conciliation officer considers that there is a reasonable prospect of success. There is provision in SDA 1975, s. 64(2) for a conciliation officer to attempt conciliation in a complaint before it is made to a tribunal in the same way as when a complaint has been made.

### 6.2.2       SPECIALIZED TRAINING FOR JUDGES

An industrial tribunal is composed of three members: a legally qualified chairman, a panel member appointed from a panel representative of employers, and a panel member chosen from a panel representative of employees.[2] In all sex discrimination cases, including equal pay, there is a convention that at least one of the panel members will be a woman. Recently, some limited training has been available for industrial tribunal members on anti-discrimination law from the Central Office of Industrial Tribunals.

### 6.2.3       SPECIALIZATION WITHIN THE SYSTEM

In practice there is a degree of informal specialization in sex discrimination cases by some chairmen of industrial tribunals in some regions.

---

1    EqPA 1970, s. 7(2).
2    Industrial Tribunals (England & Wales) Regulations 1965 (SI 1965 No 1101).

## 6.3        ENFORCEMENT AGENCY

### 6.3.1        TYPE

#### 6.3.1.1        Labour inspectorate

There is no labour inspectorate with a role in enforcing the equality legislation.

#### 6.3.1.2        Equal opportunities agency

The SDA 1975, s. 53(1) established a body of Commissioners named the Equal Opportunities Commission (EOC), consisting of at least eight, but not more than 15 individuals each appointed by the Secretary of State on a full-time or part-time basis. The EOC has the duty to work towards the elimination of discrimination, to promote equality of opportunity between men and women generally, and to keep under review the working of the SDA 1975 and the EqPA 1970 and, when they are so required by the Secretary of State or otherwise think it necessary, draw up and submit to the Secretary of State proposals for amending them. There is an equivalent separate Commission in Northern Ireland.

*Autonomous agency*

The EOC is not an emanation of the Crown, and shall not act or be treated as the servant or agent of the Crown. Accordingly neither the EOC nor a Commissioner or member of its staff is entitled to any status, immunity, privilege or exemption enjoyed by the Crown. The Commissioners and members of the staff of the EOC as such are not civil servants. The EOC's property is not property of, or held on behalf of, the Crown.[1] The Secretary of State may terminate the appointment of a Commissioner if satisfied that without the consent of the EOC he failed to attend the meetings of the EOC during a continuous period of six months beginning not earlier than nine months before the termination; or he is an undischarged bankrupt, or has made an arrangement with his creditors, or is insolvent; or he is by reason of physical or mental illness, or for any other reason, incapable of carrying out his duties.[2]

The Secretary of State may pay, or make such payments towards the provision of, such remuneration, pensions, allowances or gratuities to or in respect of the Commissioners or any of them as, with the consent of the

---

[1]    SDA 1975, Sch. 3, para. 2.
[2]    SDA 1975, Sch. 3, para. 3(5).

Minister for the Civil Service, he may determine.[1] The EOC may, after consultation with the Secretary of State, appoint such officers and servants as it thinks fit, subject to the approval of the Minister for the Civil Service as to numbers and as to remuneration and other terms and conditions of service.[2] The Secretary of State shall pay to the EOC with the consent of the Minister for the Civil Service and the Treasury such sums as the Secretary of State thinks fit for enabling the EOC to meet other expenses.[3]

*Situated within ministry*

The EOC is not situated within a ministry.

*Government department*

The Government department with overall responsibility for equality matters is the Home Office. For specifically employment discrimination and equality issues, the Department of Employment has special responsibility.

### 6.3.2 FUNCTIONS

### 6.3.2.1 Advice

In addition to providing advice on a more informal and targeted basis, the EOC may issue codes of practices containing such practical guidance as the EOC thinks fit for either or both of the following purposes, namely the elimination of discrimination in the field of employment, and the promotion of equality of opportunity in that field between men and women[4] (see further §4.14.2.3 above). The EOCs have both produced extensive and important recommendations for reform of the legislation.

### 6.2.2.2 Research

The EOC may (and does) undertake or assist (financially or otherwise) the undertaking by other persons of any research, and any educational activities, which appear to the EOC necessary or expedient for the purposes for which it was established.[5]

### 6.3.2.3 Legal aid

See §6.1.4 above.

---

1   SDA 1975, Sch. 3, para. 5.
2   SDA 1975, Sch. 3, para. 8.
3   SDA 1975, Sch. 3, para. 14.
4   SDA 1975, s. 56A(1).
5   SDA 1975, s. 54(1).

## 6.3.3          REMEDIES

The EOC has power to mount a formal investigation, without any need to have first received a complaint.[1] Investigations may be of two types: one type is an investigation into a named person in which the EOC investigates whether the employer is contravening an equality clause; a second type is a general investigation in which there is no allegation by the EOC of a breach of an equality clause. The first type of investigation may lead either to recommendations or a non-discrimination notice, or both. The second type of investigation may lead only to recommendations being made.

In addition to what may be required by the EOC (see §6.3.3.1 below) if, in the light of any of their findings in a formal investigation, it appears to the EOC necessary or expedient, it may recommend to any person changes in policies or procedures with a view to promoting equality of opportunity between the men and women who are affected by any of his activities.[2] These powers of recommendation are not restricted to circumstances where the EOC has made findings of unlawful discrimination. Though the EOC may not require it, the EOC is empowered to recommend a degree of affirmative action. No legal sanctions are available, however, for failure to accept these recommendations.

### 6.3.3.1          Notice

Where a formal investigation by the EOC has disclosed unlawful discrimination (including indirect discrimination), the EOC is empowered to issue a non-discrimination notice requiring the respondent not to commit any such discrimination and, where compliance with that requirement involves changes in any of his practices or other arrangements, to inform the EOC that he has effected those changes and what those changes are. The EOC cannot technically prescribe what changes in practice are to occur. It is for the respondent to tell the EOC what changes he will make though the EOC can tell the respondent to take such steps as may reasonably be required for the purpose of communicating that information to other persons concerned. A non-discrimination notice may also require the person to provide the EOC with information 'reasonably required'in order to verify that the terms of the notice have been complied with.[3]   A period of five years after the notice has become final is the statutory maximum time for which the EOC may impose these requirements. Within this constraint the notice may specify the time at which and the manner and form in which the information is to be furnished to the EOC. The EOC is empowered to make a further investigation at any time within five years to ascertain whether the recipient has complied with its terms.

---

1     SDA 1975, s. 57(1).
2     SDA 1975, s. 60.
3     SDA 1975, s. 67.

Whereas the remedies available before the industrial tribunal are individual and damages-based, and thus give little scope for general remedial requirements to be imposed on an employer, the remedies available to the EOC after a formal investigation suffer from the opposite deficiency. They are solely general in character, permitting a wide range of practices to be commented on, but allow no remedy to any individuals whom the EOC has discovered to have been discriminated against individually.

A person served with a non-discrimination notice may appeal against any requirement of the notice.[1] If there is an employment issue, the appeal is to an industrial tribunal which may quash the requirement if it is unreasonable, if it is based on an incorrect finding of fact, or for any other reason, and may substitute other requirements. An appeal against a non-discrimination notice must be made to an industrial tribunal not later than six weeks after a non-discrimination notice is served on any person. Where the court or tribunal considers a requirement in respect of which an appeal is thought to be unreasonable because it is based on an incorrect finding of fact or for any other reason, the court or tribunal shall quash the requirement. On quashing a requirement the court or tribunal may direct that the non-discrimination notice shall be treated as if, in place of the requirement quashed, it had contained a requirement in terms specified in the direction. See further the Industrial Tribunals (Non-discrimination Notices Appeals) Regulations 1977[2] which came into operation on 5 August 1977.

### 6.3.3.2    Injunction

Where the EOC has reasonable cause to believe that the person intends not to comply with a requirement in a non-discrimination notice, the EOC may apply to a county court for an order requiring him to comply with it. This is not an injunction, however, and non-compliance with it is not contempt. A small fine is the only remaining sanction. As we have seen, an injunction from the county court is only available where, after a non-discrimination notice (or a finding by a tribunal) has become final, it appears that 'unless restrained he is likely to do one or more' unlawful discriminatory acts in the future.[3]

SDA 1975, s. 72 provides that proceedings in respect of a contravention involving discriminatory practices, discriminatory advertisements and pressure to discriminate (SDA 1975, ss 38, 39, or 40) may be brought only by the EOC. If it appears to the EOC that a person has done an act which by virtue of ss 38, 39 or 40 was unlawful, and that unless restrained he is likely to do further acts which by virtue of any of those sections are unlawful, the

---

1    SDA 1975, s. 68.
2    SI 1977 No 1094.
3    So-called 'persistent discrimination': SDA 1975, s. 71.

EOC may apply to a county court for an injunction, restraining him from doing such acts; and the court, if satisfied that the application is well-founded, may grant the injunction or order in the terms applied for or more limited terms. The EOC shall not allege that the person to whom the proceedings relate has done an act which is unlawful under the SDA 1975 and within the jurisdiction of an industrial tribunal unless a finding by an industrial tribunal that he did that act has become final. The EOC may also take preliminary action in the industrial tribunal before taking injunction proceedings in the county court against a discriminator.

### 6.3.3.3      Compensation

No compensation is payable to individuals on the basis of formal investigations by the EOC.

## 6.4            COLLECTIVE AGREEMENTS

### 6.4.1          EQUAL PAY CLAUSE

Under the EqPA 1970, s. 1(1), if the terms of a contract under which a woman is employed at an establishment in Great Britain do not include (directly or by reference to a collective agreement or otherwise) an equality clause they shall be deemed to include one.

### 6.4.2          AUTOMATIC NULLITY

Under the SDA 1975, s. 77 a term of a contract is void where its inclusion renders the making of the contract unlawful by virtue of the Act, or it is included in furtherance of an act rendered unlawful by the Act, or it provides for the doing of an act which would be rendered unlawful by the Act.

Section 77(2) excludes from the above any contractual terms which constitute, further or provide for unlawful discrimination against a party to the contract, but instead renders such terms unenforceable. On the application of any person interested in such a contract, a county court may make such order as it thinks just for removing or modifying any term made unenforceable by that subsection; but such an order shall not be made unless all persons affected have been given notice of the application (except where under rules of court notice may be dispensed with) and have been afforded an opportunity to make representations to the court.

SDA 1986, s. 6 provides that without prejudice to the generality of the provisions of SDA 1975, s. 77 (with respect to the validity and revision of contracts), that section shall apply, as it applies in relation to the term of a contract, to

(a)   any term of a collective agreement, including an agreement which was not intended, or is presumed not to have been intended, to be a legally enforceable contract;

(b)   any rule made by an employer for application to all or any of the persons who are employed by him or who apply to be, or are, considered by him for employment;

(c)   any rule made by an organisation, authority or body for application to all or any of its members or prospective members or to all or any of the persons on whom it has conferred authorisations or qualifications or who are seeking the authorisations or qualifications which it has power to confer.

This provision applies whether the agreement was entered into, or the rule made, before or after the coming into force of SDA 1986, s. 6.

By SDA 1986, s. 6(3)(a) a term or rule is deemed to provide for the doing of an act which would be rendered unlawful by the SDA 1975 if it provides for the inclusion in any contract of employment of any term which by virtue of an equality clause would fall either to be modified or to be supplemented by an additional term, and that clause would not be prevented from operating in relation to that contract by the material factors defence.

Nothing in SDA 1975, s. 77 affects the operation of any term or rule in so far as it provides for the doing of a particular act in the circumstances where the doing of that act would not be, or be deemed by virtue of s. 6(3) of the SDA 1986 to be, rendered unlawful by the 1975 Act.

A 'collective agreement' for the purposes of SDA 1975, s. 77 means any agreement relating to one or more of the matters mentioned in s. 29 (1) of the Trade Union and Labour Relations Act 1974 (meaning of trade dispute), being an agreement made by or on behalf of one or more employers or one or more organizations of employers or associations of such organizations with one or more organizations of workers or associations of such organizations.

It is unclear whether these provisions of national law have been overtaken by EC law. In *Kowalska* v. *Freie und Hansestadt Hamburg*[1] the ECJ held that a collective agreement which was indirectly discriminatory against women was in breach of art. 119 of the EEC Treaty. In *Nimz* v. *Freie und Hansestadt Hamburg*[2] the ECJ held that where there is discrimination in a provision of a collective agreement, the national court is required to disapply that provision without requesting or awaiting its prior removal by collective negotiation or any other procedure, and to apply to members of the group which is disadvantaged by that discrimination the same arrangements as are applied to other employees.

---

1   Case C-33/89, [1990] ECR I-2591, [1990] IRLR 447 (ECJ).
2   Case C-184/89, [1991] ECR I-297 (ECJ).

### 6.4.3          COLLECTIVE REDRESS

Except to the extent stated above, there are no provisions for collective legal redress.

### 6.4.4          AGENCY MONITORING

The EOC has engaged in monitoring collective agreements on occasion, but not on a continuous basis.

### 6.4.5          CONTRACT COMPLIANCE

Central government does not engage in contract compliance policies in the context of gender equality issues. During the 1980s, however, a number of local government bodies embarked on such policies. The effect of Part II of the Local Government Act 1988 was to limit severely the power of local government in Britain to use contract compliance. Local authorities are now required to exercise a number of functions in relation to proposed or subsisting public supply of works contracts without reference to matters which are non-commercial for the purposes of this section.

The following decisions are subject to the prohibition: the inclusion or exclusion of any lists of persons from whom tenders are invited; where the authorities considering whether to enter into a public works or supplies contract, decisions such as the inclusion or exclusion of persons from a group of persons from whom tenders are invited, accepting or not accepting a submission for a contract, selecting the person whom to award a contract and withholding or giving approval to the selection of sub-contractors; and in the case of existing contracts, the selection and giving or withholding approval of sub-contractors and decisions to terminate the contract.

The Act lists eight matters designated non-commercial. Most importantly, for the purposes of restricting contract compliance in the area of equality between men and women, the Act specifies that 'the terms and conditions of employment of the contractor's workforce or the composition of or arrangements for the promotion, transfer or training or the other opportunities' are all regarded as 'non-commercial' considerations.

# SOURCES

# OF EQUALITY LAW

# SECTION I

# LEGISLATION

## Contents

§1 **Equal Pay**

Equal Pay Act 1970 (1970 c. 41)                                    136

§2 **Equal Treatment**

Sex Discrimination Act 1975 (1975 c. 65)                           144
Code of Practice for the Elimination of Discrimination on
   the Grounds of Sex and Marriage and the Promotion of
   Equality of Opportunity in Employment (1985)               198
Sex Discrimination Act 1986 (1986 c. 59)                           211
Employment Act 1989 (1989 c. 38)                                   215

§3 **Equal Pay and Equal Treatment Enforcement:**
   **Further Provisions**

Sex Discrimination (Formal Investigations) Regulations 1975
   (SI 1975 No 1993)                                           221
Sex Discrimination (Questions and Replies) Order 1975
   (SI 1975 No 2048)                                           225
Industrial Tribunals (Non-discrimination Notices Appeals)
   Regulations 1977 (SI 1977 No 1094)                          229
Industrial Tribunals (Rules of Procedure) Regulations 1985
   (SI 1985 No 16)                                             238

§4 **Equality in Social Security**

Social Security Act 1980 (1980 c. 30), Sch. 1, Part I              266
Health and Social Security Act 1984 (1984 c. 48), s. 11           269
Social Security Act 1986 (1986 c. 50), s. 37                      271
Social Security Act 1989 (1989 c. 24), Sch. 5, Part I             272

## §1   EQUAL PAY

## Equal Pay Act 1970[1]
### (1970 c. 41)

**Sections, etc. printed**

| | | |
|---|---|---|
| 1 | Requirement of equal treatment for men and women in same employment | 136 |
| 2 | Disputes as to, and enforcement of, requirement of equal treatment | 139 |
| 2A | Procedure before tribunal in certain cases | 140 |
| 5 | Agricultural wages orders | 141 |
| 6 | Exclusion from ss 1 to 5 of pensions etc. | 142 |
| 7 | Service pay | 142 |
| 9 | Commencement | 143 |
| 11 | Short title, interpretation and extent | 143 |

## 1   Requirement of equal treatment for men and women in same employment

(1) If the terms of a contract under which a woman is employed at an establishment in Great Britain do not include (directly or by reference to a collective agreement or otherwise) an equality clause they shall be deemed to include one.

(2) An equality clause is a provision which relates to terms (whether concerned with pay or not) of a contract under which a woman is employed (the 'woman's contract'), and has the effect that–

(a) where the woman is employed on like work with a man in the same employment–

(i) if (apart from the equality clause) any term of the woman's contract is or becomes less favourable to the woman than a term of a similar kind in the contract under which that man is employed, that term of the woman's contract shall be treated as so modified as not to be less favourable, and

(ii) if (apart from the equality clause) at any time the woman's contract does not include a term corresponding to a term benefiting that man included in the contract under which he is

---

[1]   This Act is printed as amended by the Sex Discrimination Act 1975 and other legislation, including the Employment Protection Act 1975, the Employment Protection (Consolidation) Act 1978, the Armed Forces Act 1981, the Equal Pay (Amendment) Regulations 1983 (SI 1983 No 1794), the Sex Discrimination Act 1986 and the Social Security Act 1989. The Sex Discrimination Act 1975 repealed s. 8 of this Act, and the Sex Discrimination Act 1986 repealed ss 3 and 10. Section 4 was repealed by the Wages Act 1986.

employed, the woman's contract shall be treated as including such a term;

(b) where the woman is employed on work rated as equivalent with that of a man in the same employment–

    (i) if (apart from the equality clause) any term of the woman's contract determined by the rating of the work is or becomes less favourable to the woman than a term of a similar kind in the contract under which that man is employed, that term of the woman's contract shall be treated as so modified as not to be less favourable, and

    (ii) if (apart from the equality clause) at any time the woman's contract does not include a term corresponding to a term benefiting that man included in the contract under which he is employed and determined by the rating of the work, the woman's contract shall be treated as including such a term;

(c) where a woman is employed on work which, not being work in relation to which paragraph (a) or (b) above applies, is, in terms of the demands made on her (for instance under such headings as effort, skill and decision), of equal value to that of a man in the same employment–

    (i) if (apart from the equality clause) any term of the woman's contract is or becomes less favourable to the woman than a term of a similar kind in the contract under which that man is employed, that term of the woman's contract shall be treated as so modified as not to be less favourable, and

    (ii) if (apart from the equality clause) at any time the woman's contract does not include a term corresponding to a term benefiting that man included in the contract under which he is employed, the woman's contract shall be treated as including such a term.

(3) An equality clause shall not operate in relation to a variation between the woman's contract and the man's contract if the employer proves that the variation is genuinely due to a material factor which is not the difference of sex and that factor–

(a) in the case of an equality clause falling within subsection (2)(a) or (b) above, must be a material difference between the woman's case and the man's; and

(b) in the case of an equality clause falling within subsection (2)(c) above, may be such a material difference.

(4) A woman is to be regarded as employed on like work with men if, but only if, her work and theirs is of the same or a broadly similar nature, and the differences (if any) between the things she does and the things they do are not of practical importance in relation to terms and conditions of

employment; and accordingly in comparing her work with theirs regard shall be had to the frequency or otherwise with which any such differences occur in practice as well as to the nature and extent of the differences.

(5) A woman is to be regarded as employed on work rated as equivalent with that of any men if, but only if, her job and their job have been given an equal value, in terms of the demand made on a worker under various headings (for instance effort, skill, decision), on a study undertaken with a view to evaluating in those terms the jobs to be done by all or any of the employees in an undertaking or group of undertakings, or would have been given an equal value but for the evaluation being made on a system setting different values for men and women on the same demand under any heading.

(6) Subject to the following subsections, for purposes of this section–

(a) 'employed' means employed under a contract of service or of apprenticeship or a contract personally to execute any work or labour, and related expressions shall be construed accordingly;

(b) ...

(c) two employers are to be treated as associated if one is a company of which the other (directly or indirectly) has control or if both are companies of which a third person (directly or indirectly) has control,

and men shall be treated as in the same employment with a woman if they are men employed by her employer or any associated employer at the same establishment or at establishments in Great Britain which include that one and at which common terms and conditions of employment are observed either generally or for employees of the relevant classes.

(7) ...

(8) This section shall apply to–

(a) service for purposes of a Minister of the Crown or government department, other than service of a person holding a statutory office, or

(b) service on behalf of the Crown for purposes of a person holding a statutory office or purposes of a statutory body,

as it applies to employment by a private person, and shall so apply as if references to a contract of employment included references to the terms of service.

(9) Subsection (8) does not apply in relation to service in–

(a) the naval, military or air forces of the Crown,

(b) ...

(10) In this section 'statutory body' means a body set up by or in pursuance of an enactment, and 'statutory office' means an office so set up; and service 'for purposes of' a Minister of the Crown or government

department does not include service in any office in Schedule 2 (Ministerial offices) to the House of Commons Disqualification Act 1975 as for the time being in force.

(11) For the purposes of this Act it is immaterial whether the law which (apart from this subsection) is the proper law of a contract is the law of any part of the United Kingdom or not.

(12) In this Act 'Great Britain' includes such of the territorial waters of the United Kingdom as are adjacent to Great Britain.

(13) Provisions of this section and sections 2 and 2A below framed with reference to women and their treatment relative to men are to be read as applying equally in a converse case to men and their treatment relative to women.

## 2  Disputes as to, and enforcement of, requirement of equal treatment

(1)  Any claim in respect of the contravention of a term modified or included by virtue of an equality clause, including a claim for arrears of remuneration or damages in respect of the contravention, may be presented by way of a complaint to an industrial tribunal.

(1A) Where a dispute arises in relation to the effect of an equality clause the employer may apply to an industrial tribunal for an order declaring the rights of the employer and the employee in relation to the matter in question.

(2)  Where it appears to the Secretary of State that there may be a question whether the employer of any women is or has been contravening a term modified or included by virtue of their equality clauses, but that it is not reasonable to expect them to take steps to have the question determined, the question may be referred by him as respects all or any of them to an industrial tribunal and shall be dealt with as if the reference were of a claim by the women or woman against the employer.

(3)  Where it appears to the court in which any proceedings are pending that a claim or counter-claim in respect of the operation of an equality clause could more conveniently be disposed of separately by an industrial tribunal, the court may direct that the claim or counter-claim shall be struck out; and (without prejudice to the foregoing) where in proceedings before any court a question arises as to the operation of an equality clause, the court may on the application of any party to the proceedings or otherwise refer that question, or direct it to be referred by a party to the proceedings, to an industrial tribunal for determination by the tribunal, and may stay or sist the proceedings in the meantime.

(4)  No claim in respect of the operation of an equality clause relating to a woman's employment shall be referred to an industrial tribunal otherwise than by virtue of subsection (3) above, if she has not been employed in the employment within the six months preceding the date of the reference.

(5)   A woman shall not be entitled, in proceedings brought in respect of a failure to comply with an equality clause (including proceedings before an industrial tribunal), to be awarded any payment by way of arrears of remuneration or damages in respect of a time earlier than two years before the date on which the proceedings were instituted.

(6)   ...

(7)   ...

## 2A   Procedure before tribunal in certain cases

(1)   Where on a complaint or reference made to an industrial tribunal under section 2 above, a dispute arises as to whether any work is of equal value as mentioned in section 1(2)(c) above the tribunal shall not determine that question unless–

(a)   it is satisfied that there are not reasonable grounds for determining that the work is of equal value as so mentioned; or

(b)   it has required a member of the panel of independent experts to prepare a report with respect to that question and has received that report.

(2)   Without prejudice to the generality of paragraph (a) of subsection (1) above, there shall be taken, for the purposes of that paragraph, to be no reasonable grounds for determining that the work of a woman is of equal value as mentioned in section 1(2)(c) above if–

(a)   that work and the work of the man in question have been given different values on a study such as is mentioned in section 1(5) above; and

(b)   there are no reasonable grounds for determining that the evaluation contained in the study was (within the meaning of subsection (3) below) made on a system which discriminates on grounds of sex.

(3)   An evaluation contained in a study such as is mentioned in section 1(5) above is made on a system which discriminates on grounds of sex where a difference, or coincidence, between values set by that system on different demands under the same or different headings is not justifiable irrespective of the sex of the person on whom those demands are made.

(4)   In paragraph (b) of subsection (1) above the reference to a member of the panel of independent experts is a reference to a person who is for the time being designated by the Advisory, Conciliation and Arbitration Service for the purposes of that paragraph as such a member, being neither a member of the Council of that Service nor one of its officers or servants.

3   ...

4   ...

## 5  Agricultural wages orders

(1) Where an agricultural wages order made before or after the commencement of this Act contains any provision applying specifically to men only or to women only, the order may be referred by the Secretary of State to the Central Arbitration Committee to declare what amendments need to be made in the order, in accordance with the like rules as apply under section 3(4) above to the amendment under that section of a collective agreement, so as to remove that discrimination between men and women; and when the Central Arbitration Committee have declared the amendments needing to be so made, it shall be the duty of the Agricultural Wages Board, by a further agricultural wages order coming into operation not later than five months after the date of the Central Arbitration Committee's decision, either to make those amendments in the order referred to the Central Arbitration Committee or otherwise to replace or amend that order so as to remove the discrimination.

(2) Where the Agricultural Wages Board certify that the effect of an agricultural wages order is only to make such amendments of a previous order as have under this section been declared by the Central Arbitration Committee to be needed, or to make such amendments as aforesaid with minor modifications or modifications of limited application, or is only to revoke and reproduce with such amendments a previous order, then the Agricultural Wages Board may instead of complying with paragraphs 1 and 2 of Schedule 4, or in the case of Scotland paragraphs 1 and 2 of Schedule 3, to the Agricultural Wages Act give notice of the proposed order in such manner as appears to the Agricultural Wages Board expedient in the circumstances, and may make the order at any time after the expiration of seven days from the giving of the notice.

(3) An agricultural wages order shall be referred to the Central Arbitration Committee under this section if the Secretary of State is requested so to refer it either–

(a) by a body for the time entitled to nominate for membership of the Agricultural Wages Board persons representing employers (or, if provision is made for any of the persons representing employers to be elected instead of nominated, then by a member or members representing employers); or

(b) by a body for the time being entitled to nominate for membership of the Agricultural Wages Board persons representing workers (or, if provision is made for any of the persons representing workers to be elected instead of nominated, then by a member or members representing workers);

or if in any case it appears to the Secretary of State that the order may be amendable under this section.

(4) In this section 'the Agricultural Wages Board' means the Agricultural Wages Board for England and Wales or the Scottish

Agricultural Wages Board, 'the Agricultural Wages Act' means the Agricultural Wages Act 1948 or the Agricultural Wages (Scotland) Act 1949 and 'agricultural wages order' means an order of the Agricultural Wages Board under the Agricultural Wages Act.

## 6 Exclusion from ss 1 to 5 of pensions etc.

(1) An equality clause shall not operate in relation to terms–

(a) affected by compliance with the laws regulating the employment of women, or

(b) affording special treatment to women in connection with pregnancy or childbirth.

(1A) An equality clause–

(a) shall operate in relation to terms relating to membership of an occupational pension scheme (within the meaning of the Social Security Pensions Act 1975) which is also an employment-related benefit scheme, within the meaning of Schedule 5 to the Social Security Act 1989, so far as those terms relate to any matter in respect of which the scheme has to comply with the principle of equal treatment in accordance with that Schedule; but

(b) subject to this, shall not operate in relation to terms related to death or retirement, or to any provision made in connection with death or retirement other than a term or provision which, in relation to retirement, affords access to opportunities for promotion, transfer or training or provides for a woman's dismissal or demotion.

(2) Any reference in this section to retirement includes retirement, whether voluntary or not, on grounds of age, length of service or incapacity and the reference in subsection (1A) above to a woman's dismissal shall be construed in accordance with section 82(1A) of the Sex Discrimination Act 1975 as a reference to her dismissal from employment.

## 7 Service pay

(1) The Secretary of State or Defence Council shall not make, or recommend to Her Majesty the making of, any instrument relating to the terms and conditions of service of members of the naval, military or air forces of the Crown, if the instrument has the effect of making a distinction, as regards pay, allowances or leave, between men and women who are members of those forces, not being a distinction fairly attributable to differences between the obligations undertaken by men and those undertaken by women as such members as aforesaid.

(2) The Secretary of State or Defence Council may refer to the Central Arbitration Committee for their advice any question whether a provision made or proposed to be made by any such instrument as is referred to in

subsection (1) above ought to be regarded for purposes of this section as making a distinction not permitted by that subsection.

**8** ...

## 9 Commencement

(1) The foregoing provisions of this Act shall come into force on the 29 December 1975 and references in this Act to its commencement shall be construed as referring to the coming into force of those provisions on that date.

(2)-(5)   ...

**10** ...

## 11 Short title, interpretation and extent

(1)   This Act may be cited as the Equal Pay Act 1970.

(2)   In this Act the expressions 'man' and 'woman' shall be read as applying to persons of whatever age.

(3)   This Act shall not extend to Northern Ireland.[1]

---

1     The equivalent legislation is the Equal Pay Act (Northern Ireland) 1970 which is, in all material respects, the same.

## §2   EQUAL TREATMENT

# Sex Discrimination Act 1975[1]
## (1975 c. 65)

### Sections, etc. printed

PART I: DISCRIMINATION TO WHICH ACT APPLIES

| | | |
|---|---|---|
| 1 | Sex discrimination against women | 146 |
| 2 | Sex discrimination against men | 146 |
| 3 | Discrimination against married persons in employment field | 147 |
| 4 | Discrimination by way of victimisation | 147 |
| 5 | Interpretation | 148 |

PART II: DISCRIMINATION IN THE EMPLOYMENT FIELD

*Discrimination by employers*

| | | |
|---|---|---|
| 6 | Discrimination against applicants and employees | 148 |
| 7 | Exception where sex is a genuine occupational qualification | 150 |
| 8 | Equal Pay Act 1970 | 152 |
| 9 | Discrimination against contract workers | 152 |
| 10 | Meaning of employment at establishment in Great Britain | 153 |

*Discrimination by other bodies*

| | | |
|---|---|---|
| 11 | Partnerships | 154 |
| 12 | Trade unions etc. | 155 |
| 13 | Qualifying bodies | 156 |
| 14 | Persons concerned with provision of vocational training | 156 |
| 15 | Employment agencies | 157 |
| 16 | Manpower Services Commission | 157 |

*Special cases*

| | | |
|---|---|---|
| 17 | Police | 157 |
| 18 | Prison officers | 159 |
| 19 | Ministers of religion etc. | 159 |
| 20 | Midwives | 159 |
| 21 | Mineworkers | 160 |

PART IV: OTHER UNLAWFUL ACTS

| | | |
|---|---|---|
| 37 | Discriminatory practices | 160 |
| 38 | Discriminatory advertisements | 160 |
| 39 | Instructions to discriminate | 161 |

---

[1]   There are here printed, in amended form, the elements of this Act which relate to employment. Omissions include Part III: Discrimination in other fields (ss 22-36), the related Sch. 2, and other connected provisions; the provisions of s. 8 and Sch. 1, which amend the Equal Pay Act 1970 (see p. 136 above); and Sch. 5 and 6 (amendments and repeals). Amendments of which account has been taken derive from the Employment Protection Act 1975; the Race Relations Act 1976; the Employment Protection (Consolidation) Act 1978; the Education (Scotland) Act 1980; the Armed Forces Act 1981; the Employment & Training Act 1981; the Criminal Justice Act 1982; the Oil & Gas (Enterprise) Act 1982; the County Courts Act 1984; the Sex Discrimination Act 1986; the Legal Aid (Scotland) Act 1986; the Legal Aid Act 1988; the Employment Acts 1988 and 1989; and the Social Security Act 1989.

40   Pressure to discriminate                                     161
41   Liability of employers and principals                        161
42   Aiding unlawful acts                                         162

PART V: GENERAL EXCEPTIONS FROM PARTS II TO IV

43   Charities                                                    162
46   Communal accommodation                                       163
47   Discriminatory training by certain bodies                    164
48   Other discriminatory training etc.                           164
49   Trade unions etc.: elective bodies                           165
50   Indirect access to benefits etc.                             166
51   Acts done for purposes of protection of women                166
51A  Acts done under statutory authority to be exempt
        from certain provisions of Part III                       167
52   Acts safeguarding national security                          167
52A  Construction of references to vocational training            168

PART VI: EQUAL OPPORTUNITIES COMMISSION

53   Establishment and duties of Commission                       168
54   Research and education                                       168
55   Review of discriminatory provisions in
        health and safety legislation                             169
56   Annual reports                                               169

*Codes of practice*

56A  Codes of practice                                            169

*Investigations*

57   Power to conduct formal investigations                       171
58   Terms of reference                                           171
59   Power to obtain information                                  172
60   Recommendations and reports on formal investigations         173
61   Restriction on disclosure of information                     174

PART VII: ENFORCEMENT

*General*

62   Restriction of proceedings for breach of Act                 175

*Enforcement in employment field*

63   Jurisdiction of industrial tribunals                         175
64   Conciliation in employment cases                             176
65   Remedies on complaint under section 63                       176

*Enforcement of Part III*

66   Claims under Part III                                        177

*Non-discrimination notices*

67   Issue of non-discrimination notice                           177
68   Appeal against non-discrimination notice                     179
69   Investigation as to compliance with non-discrimination notice 179
70   Register of non-discrimination notices                       179

*Other enforcement by Commission*

71   Persistent discrimination                                    180
72   Enforcement of ss 38 to 40                                   180
73   Preliminary action in employment cases                       181

*Help for persons suffering discrimination*

74   Help for aggrieved persons in obtaining information etc.          182
75   Assistance by Commission                                         183

*Period within which proceedings to be brought*

76   Period within which proceedings to be brought                    184

PART VIII: SUPPLEMENTAL

77   Validity and revision of contracts                               185
80   Power to amend certain provisions of Act                         186
81   Orders                                                           186
82   General interpretation provisions                                187
83   Transitional and commencement provisions,
        amendments and repeals                                        189
84   Financial provisions                                             190
85   Application to Crown                                             190
86   Government appointments outside section 6                        192
87   Short title and extent                                           192

SCHEDULES

Schedule 3: Equal Opportunities Commission                            192
Schedule 4: Transitional provisions                                   196

# PART I

## DISCRIMINATION TO WHICH ACT APPLIES

### 1  Sex discrimination against women

(1)  A person discriminates against a woman in any circumstances relevant for the purposes of any provision of this Act if–

(a)  on the ground of her sex he treats her less favourably than he treats or would treat a man, or

(b)  he applies to her a requirement or condition which applies or would apply equally to a man but–

   (i)  which is such that the proportion of women who can comply with it is considerably smaller than the proportion of men who can comply with it, and

   (ii)  which he cannot show to be justifiable irrespective of the sex of the person to whom it is applied, and

   (iii) which is to her detriment because she cannot comply with it.

(2)  If a person treats or would treat a man differently according to the man's marital status, his treatment of a woman is for the purposes of subsection (1)(a) to be compared to his treatment of a man having the like marital status.

### 2  Sex discrimination against men

(1)  Section 1, and the provisions of Parts II and III relating to sex discrimination against women, are to be read as applying equally to the

treatment of men, and for that purpose shall have effect with such modifications as are requisite.

(2) In the application of subsection (1) no account shall be taken of special treatment afforded to women in connection with pregnancy or childbirth.

### 3  Discrimination against married persons in employment field

(1) A person discriminates against a married person of either sex in any circumstances relevant for the purposes of any provision of Part II if–

- (a) on the ground of his or her marital status he treats that person less favourably than he treats or would treat an unmarried person of the same sex, or
- (b) he applies to that person a requirement or condition which he applies or would apply equally to an unmarried person but–
    - (i) which is such that the proportion of married persons who can comply with it is considerably smaller than the proportion of unmarried persons of the same sex who can comply with it, and
    - (ii) which he cannot show to be justifiable irrespective of the marital status of the person to whom it is applied, and
    - (iii) which is to that person's detriment because he cannot comply with it.

(2) For the purposes of subsection (1), a provision of Part II framed with reference to discrimination against women shall be treated as applying equally to the treatment of men, and for that purpose shall have effect with such modifications as are requisite.

### 4  Discrimination by way of victimisation

(1) A person ('the discriminator') discriminates against another person ('the person victimised') in any circumstances relevant for the purposes of any provision of this Act if he treats the person victimised less favourably than in those circumstances he treats or would treat other persons, and does so by reason that the person victimised has–

- (a) brought proceedings against the discriminator or any other person under this Act or the Equal Pay 1970 or Part I of Schedule 5 to the Social Security Act 1989, or
- (b) given evidence or information in connection with proceedings brought by any person against the discriminator or any other person under this Act or the Equal Pay Act 1970 or Part I of Schedule 5 to the Social Security Act 1989, or
- (c) otherwise done anything under or by reference to this Act or the Equal Pay Act 1970 or Part I of Schedule 5 to the Social Security Act 1989 in relation to the discriminator or any other person, or

(d) alleged that the discriminator or any other person has committed an act which (whether or not the allegation so states) would amount to a contravention of this Act or give rise to a claim under the Equal Pay Act 1970 or proceedings under Part I of Schedule 5 to the Social Security Act 1989,

or by reason that the discriminator knows the person victimised intends to do any of those things, or suspects the person victimised has done, or intends to do, any of them.

(2) Subsection (1) does not apply to treatment of a person by reason of any allegation made by him if the allegation was false and not made in good faith.

(3) For the purposes of subsection (1), a provision of Part II or III framed with reference to discrimination against women shall be treated as applying equally to the treatment of men and for that purpose shall have effect with such modifications as are requisite.

## 5  Interpretation

(1) In this Act–

(a) references to discrimination refer to any discrimination falling within sections 1 to 4; and
(b) references to sex discrimination refer to any discrimination falling within section 1 or 2,

and related expressions shall be construed accordingly.

(2) In this Act–

'woman' includes a female of any age, and
'man' includes a male of any age.

(3) A comparison of the cases of persons of different sex or marital status under section 1(1) or 3(1) must be such that the relevant circumstances in the one case are the same, or not materially different, in the other.

## PART II

### DISCRIMINATION IN THE EMPLOYMENT FIELD

*Discrimination by employers*

## 6  Discrimination against applicants and employees

(1) It is unlawful for a person, in relation to employment by him at an establishment in Great Britain, to discriminate against a woman–

(a) in the arrangements he makes for the purpose of determining who should be offered that employment, or
(b) in the terms on which he offers her that employment, or
(c) by refusing or deliberately omitting to offer her that employment.

(2) It is unlawful for a person, in the case of a woman employed by him at an establishment in Great Britain, to discriminate against her–

(a) in the way he affords her access to opportunities for promotion, transfer or training, or to any other benefits, facilities or services, or by refusing or deliberately omitting to afford her access to them, or

(b) by dismissing her, or subjecting her to any other detriment.

(3) ...

(4) Subsections (1)(b) and (2) do not apply to provision in relation to death or retirement except as provided in subsections (4A) and (4B) below.

(4A) Subsection (4) does not prevent the application of subsections (1)(b) and (2) to provision in relation to retirement in so far as those subsections render it unlawful for a person to discriminate against a woman–

(a) in such of the terms on which he offers her employment as make provision in relation to the way he will afford her access to opportunities for promotion, transfer or training or as provide for her dismissal or demotion; or

(b) in the way he affords her access to opportunities for promotion, transfer or training or by refusing or deliberately omitting to afford her access to any such opportunities; or

(c) by dismissing her or subjecting her to any detriment which results in her dismissal or consists in or involves her demotion.

(4B) Subsection (4) does not prevent the application of subsections (1)(b) and (2) to provision in relation to death or retirement in so far as those subsections render it unlawful for a person to discriminate against a woman–

(a) in such of the terms on which he offers her employment as make provision in relation to the way in which he will afford her access to any benefits, facilities or services under an occupational pension scheme; or

(b) in the way he affords her access to any such benefits, facilities or services; or

(c) by refusing or deliberately omitting to afford her access to any such benefits, facilities or services; or

(d) by subjecting her to any detriment in connection with any such scheme;

but an act of discrimination is rendered unlawful by virtue of this subsection only to the extent that the act relates to a matter in respect of which an occupational pension scheme has to comply with the principle of equal treatment in accordance with Part I of Schedule 5 to the Social Security Act 1989.

(4C) In the application of subsection (4B) to discrimination against married persons of either sex, Part I of Schedule 5 to the Social Security Act 1989 shall be taken to apply to less favourable treatment of married persons on the basis of their marital status as it applies in relation to less favourable treatment of persons on the basis of sex, and references to persons of either sex shall be construed accordingly.

(5) Subject to section 8(3), subsection (1)(b) does not apply to any provision for the payment of money which, if the woman in question were given the employment, would be included (directly or otherwise) in the contract under which she was employed.

(6) Subsection (2) does not apply to benefits consisting of the payment of money when the provision of those benefits is regulated by the woman's contract of employment.

(7) Subsection (2) does not apply to benefits, facilities or services of any description if the employer is concerned with the provision (for payment or not) of benefits, facilities or services of that description to the public, or to a section of the public comprising the woman in question, unless–

(a) that provision differs in a material respect from the provision of the benefits, facilities or services by the employer to his employees, or
(b) that provision of the benefits, facilities or services to the woman in question is regulated by her contract of employment, or
(c) the benefits, facilities or services relate to training.

(8) In this section 'occupational pension scheme' means an occupational pension scheme, within the meaning of the Social Security Pensions Act 1975, which is also an employment-related benefit scheme, within the meaning of Schedule 5 to the Social Security Act 1989.

## 7 Exception where sex is a genuine occupational qualification

(1) In relation to sex discrimination–

(a) section 6(1)(a) or (c) does not apply to any employment where being a man is a genuine occupational qualification for the job, and
(b) section 6(2)(a) does not apply to opportunities for promotion or transfer to, or training for, such employment.

(2) Being a man is a genuine occupational qualification for a job only where–

(a) the essential nature of the job calls for a man for reasons of physiology (excluding physical strength or stamina) or, in a dramatic performance or other entertainment, for reasons of authenticity, so that the essential nature of the job would be materially different if carried out by a woman; or
(b) the job needs to be held by a man to preserve decency or privacy because–

(i) it is likely to involve physical contact with men in circumstances where they might reasonably object to its being carried out by a woman, or

(ii) the holder of the job is likely to do his work in circumstances where men might reasonably object to the presence of a woman because they are in a state of undress or are using sanitary facilities; or

(ba) the job is likely to involve the holder of the job doing his work, or living, in a private home and needs to be held by a man because objection might reasonably be taken to allowing to a woman–

(i) the degree of physical or social contact with a person living in the home, or

(ii) the knowledge of intimate details of such a person's life, which is likely, because of the nature or circumstances of the job or of the home, to be allowed to, or available to, the holder of the job; or

(c) the nature or location of the establishment makes it impracticable for the holder of the job to live elsewhere than in premises provided by the employer, and–

(i) the only such premises which are available for persons holding that kind of job are lived in, or normally lived in, by men and are not equipped with separate sleeping accommodation for women and sanitary facilities which could be used by women in privacy from men, and

(ii) it is not reasonable to expect the employer either to equip those premises with such accommodation and facilities or to provide other premises for women; or

(d) the nature of the establishment, or of the part of it within which the work is done, requires the job to be held by a man because–

(i) it is, or is part of, a hospital, prison or other establishment for persons requiring special care, supervision or attention, and

(ii) those persons are all men (disregarding any woman whose presence is exceptional), and

(iii) it is reasonable, having regard to the essential character of the establishment or that part, that the job should not be held by a woman; or

(e) the holder of the job provides individuals with personal services promoting their welfare or education, or similar personal services, and those services can most effectively be provided by a man, or

(f) ...

(g) the job needs to be held by a man because it is likely to involve the performance of duties outside the United Kingdom in a country whose laws or customs are such that the duties could not, or could not effectively, be performed by a woman, or

(h) the job is one of two to be held by a married couple.

(3) Subsection (2) applies where some only of the duties of the job fall within paragraphs (a) to (g) as well as where all of them do.

(4) Paragraph (a), (b), (c), (d), (e) or (g) of subsection (2) does not apply in relation to the filling of a vacancy at a time when the employer already has male employees–

(a) who are capable of carrying out the duties falling within that paragraph, and
(b) whom it would be reasonable to employ on those duties, and
(c) whose numbers are sufficient to meet the employer's likely requirements in respect of those duties without undue inconvenience.

## 8  Equal Pay Act 1970

(1) ...

(2) Section 1(1) of the Equal Pay Act 1970 ... does not apply in determining for the purposes of section 6(1)(b) of this Act the terms on which employment is offered.

(3) Where a person offers a woman employment on certain terms, and if she accepted the offer then, by virtue of an equality clause, any of those terms would fall to be modified, or any additional term would fall to be included, the offer shall be taken to contravene section 6(1)(b).

(4) Where a person offers a woman employment on certain terms, and subsection (3) would apply but for the fact that, on her acceptance of the offer, section 1(3) of the Equal Pay Act 1970 (as set out in subsection (1) above) would prevent the equality clause from operating, the offer shall be taken not to contravene section 6(1)(b).

(5) An act does not contravene section 6(2) if–

(a) it contravenes a term modified or included by virtue of an equality clause, or
(b) it would contravene such a term but for the fact that the equality clause is prevented from operating by section 1(3) of the Equal Pay Act 1970.

(6) ...

## 9  Discrimination against contract workers

(1) This section applies to any work for a person ('the principal') which is available for doing by individuals ('contract workers') who are employed not by the principal himself but by another person, who supplies them under a contract made with the principal.

(2) It is unlawful for the principal, in relation to work to which this section applies, to discriminate against a woman who is a contract worker–

(a)  in the terms on which he allows her to do that work, or

(b)  by not allowing her to do it or continue to do it, or

(c)  in the way he affords her access to any benefits, facilities or services or by refusing or deliberately omitting to afford her access to them, or

(d)  by subjecting her to any other detriment.

(3)  The principal does not contravene subsection (2)(b) by doing any act in relation to a woman at a time when if the work were to be done by a person taken into his employment being a man would be a genuine occupational qualification for the job.

(4)  Subsection (2)(c) does not apply to benefits, facilities or services of any description if the principal is concerned with the provision (for payment or not) of benefits, facilities or services of that description to the public, or to a section of the public to which the woman belongs, unless that provision differs in a material respect from the provision of the benefits, facilities or services by the principal to his contract workers.

## 10   Meaning of employment at establishment in Great Britain[1]

(1)  For the purposes of this Part and section 1 of the Equal Pay Act 1970 ('the relevant purposes'), employment is to be regarded as being at an establishment in Great Britain unless the employee does his work wholly or mainly outside Great Britain.

(2)  Subsection (1) does not apply to–

(a)  employment on board a ship registered at a port of registry in Great Britain, or

---

[1]   The Sex Discrimination & Equal Pay (Offshore Employment) Order 1987 (SI 1987 No 930) provides (in part):

2 (1) In relation to employment concerned with exploration of the sea bed or sub-soil or the exploitation of their natural resources, but subject to paragraph (2), subsections (1) and (2) of section 10 of the 1975 Act shall have effect as if the last reference to Great Britain in those subsections included–

(a) any area for the time being designated under section 1 (7) of the Continental Shelf Act 1964, except an area or part of an area in which the law of Northern Ireland applies; and

(b) in relation to employment concerned with the exploration or exploitation of the Frigg Gas Field, the part of the Norwegian sector of the Continental Shelf described in the Schedule to this Order.

(2) This Order shall have no application to employment which is concerned with the exploration or exploitation of the Frigg Gas Field unless the employer is:

(a) a company registered under the Companies Act 1985;

(b) an oversea company which has established a place of business within Great Britain from which it directs the offshore operations in question, or

(c) any other person who has a place of business within Great Britain from which he directs the offshore operations in question.

(b) employment on aircraft or hovercraft registered in the United Kingdom and operated by a person who has his principal place of business, or is ordinarily resident, in Great Britain,

but for the relevant purposes such employment is to be regarded as being at an establishment in Great Britain unless the employee does his work wholly outside Great Britain.

(3) In the case of employment on board a ship registered at a port of registry in Great Britain (except where the employee does his work wholly outside Great Britain, and outside any area added under subsection (5)) the ship shall for the relevant purposes be deemed to be the establishment.

(4) Where work is not done at an establishment it shall be treated for the relevant purposes as done at the establishment from which it is done or (where it is not done from any establishment) at the establishment with which it has the closest connection.

(5) In relation to employment concerned with any activity falling within section 23(2) of the Oil and Gas (Enterprise) Act 1982, Her Majesty may by Order in Council provide that subsections (1) and (2) shall each have effect as if the last reference to Great Britain included any area for the time being designated under section 1(7) of the Continental Shelf Act 1964 or specified under section 22(5) of the Oil and Gas (Enterprise) Act, except an area or part of an area in which the law of Northern Ireland applies.

(6) An Order in Council under subsection (5) may provide that, in relation to employment to which the Order applies, this Part and section 1 of the Equal Pay Act 1970 are to have effect with such modifications as are specified in the Order.

(7) An Order in Council under subsection (5) shall be of no effect unless a draft of the Order was laid before and approved by each House of Parliament.

*Discrimination by other bodies*

## 11   Partnerships

(1) It is unlawful for a firm, in relation to a position as partner in the firm, to discriminate against a woman–

(a) in the arrangements they make for the purpose of determining who should be offered that position, or
(b) in the terms on which they offer her that position, or
(c) by refusing or deliberately omitting to offer her that position, or
(d) in a case where the woman already holds that position–

(i) in the way they afford her access to any benefits, facilities or services, or by refusing or deliberately omitting to afford her access to them, or

(ii)  by expelling her from that position, or subjecting her to any other detriment.

(2)  Subsection (1) shall apply in relation to persons proposing to form themselves into a partnership as it applies in relation to a firm.

(3)  Subsection (1)(a) and (c) do not apply to a position as partner where, if it were employment, being a man would be a genuine occupational qualification for the job.

(4)  Subsection (1)(b) and (d) do not apply to provision made in relation to death or retirement except in so far as, in their application to provision made in relation to retirement, they render it unlawful for a firm to discriminate against a woman–

(a)  in such of the terms on which they offer her a position as partner as provide for her expulsion from that position; or

(b)  by expelling her from a position as partner or subjecting her to any detriment which results in her expulsion from such a position.

(5)  In the case of a limited partnership references in subsection (1) to a partner shall be construed as references to a general partner as defined in section 3 of the Limited Partnerships Act 1907.

## 12   Trade unions etc.

(1)  This section applies to an organisation of workers, an organisation of employers, or any other organisation whose members carry on a particular profession or trade for the purposes of which the organisation exists.

(2)  It is unlawful for an organisation to which this section applies, in the case of a woman who is not a member of the organisation, to discriminate against her–

(a)  in the terms on which it is prepared to admit her to membership, or

(b)  by refusing, or deliberately omitting to accept, her application for membership.

(3)  It is unlawful for an organisation to which this section applies, in the case of a woman who is a member of the organisation, to discriminate against her–

(a)  in the way it affords her access to any benefits, facilities or services, or by refusing or deliberately omitting to afford her access to them, or

(b)  by depriving her of membership, or varying the terms on which she is a member, or

(c)  by subjecting her to any other detriment.

(4)  This section does not apply to provision made in relation to the death or retirement from work of a member.

**13   Qualifying bodies**

(1) It is unlawful for an authority or body which can confer an authorisation or qualification which is needed for, or facilitates, engagement in a particular profession or trade to discriminate against a woman–

 (a) in the terms on which it is prepared to confer on her that authorisation or qualification, or
 (b) by refusing or deliberately omitting to grant her application for it, or
 (c) by withdrawing it from her or varying the terms on which she holds it.

(2)   Where an authority or body is required by law to satisfy itself as to his good character before conferring on a person an authorisation or qualification which is needed for, or facilitates, his engagement in any profession or trade then, without prejudice to any other duty to which it is subject, that requirement shall be taken to impose on the authority or body a duty to have regard to any evidence tending to show that he, or any of his employees, or agents (whether past or present), has practised unlawful discrimination in, or in connection with, the carrying on of any profession or trade.

(3)   In this section–

 (a) 'authorisation or qualification' includes recognition, registration, enrolment, approval and certification,
 (b) 'confer' includes renew or extend.

(4)   Subsection (1) does not apply to discrimination which is rendered unlawful by section 22 or 23.

**14   Persons concerned with provision of vocational training**

(1) It is unlawful, in the case of a woman seeking or undergoing training which would help fit her for any employment, for any person who provides, or makes arrangements for the provision of, facilities for such training to discriminate against her–

 (a) in the terms on which that person affords her access to any training course or other facilities concerned with such training, or
 (b) by refusing or deliberately omitting to afford her such access, or
 (c) by terminating her training, or
 (d) by subjecting her to any detriment during the course of her training.

(2)   Subsection (1) does not apply to–

 (a) discrimination which is rendered unlawful by section 6(1) or (2) or section 22 or 23, or
 (b) discrimination which would be rendered unlawful by any of those provisions but for the operation of any other provision of this Act.

## 15   Employment agencies

(1)   It is unlawful for an employment agency to discriminate against a woman–

(a)   in the terms on which the agency offers to provide any of its services, or

(b)   by refusing or deliberately omitting to provide any of its services, or

(c)   in the way it provides any of its services.

(2)   It is unlawful for a local education authority or an education authority to do any act in the performance of its functions under section 8 of the Employment and Training Act 1973 which constitutes discrimination.

(3)   References in subsection (1) to the services of an employment agency include guidance on careers and any other services related to employment.

(4)   This section does not apply if the discrimination only concerns employment which the employer could lawfully refuse to offer the woman.

(5)   An employment agency or local education authority or an education authority shall not be subject to any liability under this section if it proves–

(a)   that it acted in reliance on a statement made to it by the employer to the effect that, by reason of the operation of subsection (4), its action would not be unlawful, and

(b)   that it was reasonable for it to rely on the statement.

(6)   A person who knowingly or recklessly makes a statement such as is referred to in subsection (5)(a) which in a material respect is false or misleading commits an offence, and shall be liable on summary conviction to a fine not exceeding level 5 on the standard scale.

## 16   Manpower Services Commission

(1)   It is unlawful for the Secretary of State to discriminate in the provision of facilities or services under section 2 of the Employment and Training Act 1973.

(1A)   ...

(2)   This section does not apply in a case where–

(a)   section 14 applies, or

(b)   the Secretary of State is acting as an employment agency.

*Special cases*

## 17   Police

(1)   For the purposes of this Part, the holding of the office of constable shall be treated as employment–

(a)  by the chief officer of police as respects any act done by him in relation to a constable or that office;

(b)  by the police authority as respects any act done by them in relation to a constable or that office.

(2)  Regulations made under section 33, 34 or 35 of the Police Act 1964 shall not treat men and women differently except–

(a)  as to requirements relating to height, uniform or equipment, or allowances in lieu of uniform or equipment, or

(b)  so far as special treatment is accorded to women in connection with pregnancy or childbirth, or

(c)  in relation to pensions to or in respect of special constables or police cadets.

(3)  Nothing in this Part renders unlawful any discrimination between male and female constables as to matters such as are mentioned in subsection (2)(a).

(4)  There shall be paid out of the police fund–

(a)  any compensation, costs or expenses awarded against a chief officer of police in any proceedings brought against him under this Act, and any costs or expenses incurred by him in any such proceedings so far as not recovered by him in the proceedings; and

(b)  any sum required by a chief officer of police for the settlement of any claim made against him under this Act if the settlement is approved by the police authority.

(5)  Any proceedings under this Act which, by virtue of subsection (1), would lie against a chief officer of police shall be brought against the chief officer of police for the time being or, in the case of a vacancy in that office, against the person for the time being performing the functions of that office; and references in subsection (4) to the chief officer of police shall be construed accordingly.

(6)  Subsections (1) and (3) apply to a police cadet and appointment as a police cadet as they apply to a constable and the office of constable.

(7)  In this section–

'chief officer of police'–

(a)  in relation to a person appointed, or an appointment falling to be made, under a specified Act, has the same meaning as in the Police Act 1964,

(b)  in relation to any other person or appointment means the officer who has the direction and control of the body of constables or cadets in question;

'police authority'–

(a)  in relation to a person appointed, or an appointment falling to be made, under a specified Act, has the same meaning as in the Police Act 1964,

(b)  in relation to any other person or appointment, means the authority by whom the person in question is or on appointment would be paid;

'police cadet' means any person appointed to undergo training with a view to becoming a constable;

'police fund' in relation to a chief officer of police within paragraph (a) of the above definition of that term has the same meaning as in the Police Act 1964, and in any other case means money provided by the police authority;

'specified Act' means the Metropolitan Police Act 1829, the City of London Police Act 1839 or the Police Act 1964.

(8)  In the application of this section to Scotland, in subsection (7) for any reference to the Police Act 1964 there shall be substituted a reference to the Police (Scotland) Act 1967, and for the reference to sections 33, 34 and 35 of the former Act in subsection (2) there shall be substituted a reference to sections 26 and 27 of the latter Act.

## 18  Prison officers

(1)  Nothing in this Part renders unlawful any discrimination between male and female prison officers as to requirements relating to height.

(2)  In section 7(2) of the Prisons Act 1952, the words 'and if women only are received in a prison, the Governor shall be a woman' are repealed.

## 19  Ministers of religion etc.

(1)  Nothing in this Part applies to employment for purposes of an organised religion where the employment is limited to one sex so as to comply with the doctrines of the religion or avoid offending the religious susceptibilities of a significant number of its followers.

(2)  Nothing in section 13 applies to an authorisation or qualification (as defined in that section) for purposes of an organised religion where the authorisation or qualification is limited to one sex so as to comply with the doctrines of the religion or avoid offending the religious susceptibilities of a significant number of its followers.

## 20  Midwives

(1)  Until 1 September 1983 section 6(1) does not apply to employment as a midwife.

(2)  Until 1 September 1983 section 6(2)(a) does not apply to promotion, transfer or training as a midwife.

(3) Until 1 September 1983 section 14 does not apply to training as a midwife.

(4), (5) …

## 21 Mineworkers

(1) …

(2) Throughout the Coal Mines Regulations Act 1908, for 'workman' or 'man' there is substituted 'worker', and for 'workmen' or 'men' there is substituted 'workers'.

## PART III

### DISCRIMINATION IN OTHER FIELDS

**22-36** …

## PART IV

### OTHER UNLAWFUL ACTS

## 37 Discriminatory practices

(1) In this section 'discriminatory practice' means the application of a requirement or condition which results in an act of discrimination which is unlawful by virtue of any provision of Part II or III taken with section 1(1)(b) or 3(1)(b) or which would be likely to result in such an act of discrimination if the persons to whom it is applied were not all of one sex.

(2) A person acts in contravention of this section if and so long as–

(a) he applies a discriminatory practice, or

(b) he operates practices or other arrangements which in any circumstances would call for the application by him of a discriminatory practice.

(3) Proceedings in respect of a contravention of this section shall be brought only by the Commission in accordance with sections 67 to 71.

## 38 Discriminatory advertisements

(1) It is unlawful to publish or cause to be published an advertisement which indicates, or might reasonably be understood as indicating, an intention by a person to do any act which is or might be unlawful by virtue of Part II or III.

(2) Subsection (1) does not apply to an advertisement if the intended act would not in fact be unlawful.

(3) For the purposes of subsection (1), use of a job description with a sexual connotation (such as 'waiter', 'salesgirl', 'postman' or 'stewardess')

shall be taken to indicate an intention to discriminate, unless the advertisement contains an indication to the contrary.

(4) The publisher of an advertisement made unlawful by subsection (1) shall not be subject to any liability under that subsection in respect of the publication of the advertisement if he proves–

(a) that the advertisement was published in reliance on a statement made to him by the person who caused it to be published to the effect that, by reason of the operation of subsection (2), the publication would not be unlawful, and

(b) that it was reasonable for him to rely on the statement.

(5) A person who knowingly or recklessly makes a statement such as is referred to in subsection (4) which in a material respect is false or misleading commits an offence, and shall be liable on summary conviction to a fine not exceeding level 5 on the standard scale.

## 39   Instructions to discriminate

It is unlawful for a person–

(a) who has authority over another person, or

(b) in accordance with whose wishes that other person is accustomed to act,

to instruct him to do any act which is unlawful by virtue of Part II or III, or procure or attempt to procure the doing by him of any such act.

## 40   Pressure to discriminate

(1) It is unlawful to induce, or attempt to induce, a person to do any act which contravenes Part II or III by–

(a) providing or offering to provide him with any benefit, or

(b) subjecting or threatening to subject him to any detriment.

(2) An offer or threat is not prevented from falling within subsection (1) because it is not made directly to the person in question, if it is made in such a way that he is likely to hear of it.

## 41   Liability of employers and principals

(1) Anything done by a person in the course of his employment shall be treated for the purposes of this Act as done by his employer as well as by him, whether or not it was done with the employer's knowledge or approval.

(2) Anything done by a person as agent for another person with the authority (whether express or implied, and whether precedent or subsequent) of that other person shall be treated for the purposes of this Act as done by that other person as well as by him.

(3) In proceedings brought under this Act against any person in respect of an act alleged to have been done by an employee of his it shall be a

defence for that person to prove that he took such steps as were reasonably practicable to prevent the employee from doing that act, or from doing in the course of his employment acts of that description.

## 42   Aiding unlawful acts

(1)   A person who knowingly aids another person to do an act made unlawful by this Act shall be treated for the purpose of this Act as himself doing an unlawful act of the like description.

(2)   For the purposes of subsection (1) an employee or agent for whose act the employer or principal is liable under section 41 (or would be so liable but for section 41(3)) shall be deemed to aid the doing of the act by the employer or principal.

(3)   A person does not under this section knowingly aid another to do an unlawful act if–

(a)   he acts in reliance on a statement made to him by that other person that, by reason of any provision of this Act, the act which he aids would not be unlawful, and

(b)   it is reasonable for him to rely on the statement.

(4)   A person who knowingly or recklessly makes a statement such as is referred to in subsection (3)(a) which in a material respect is false or misleading commits an offence, and shall be liable on summary conviction to a fine not exceeding level 5 on the standard scale.

### PART V

### GENERAL EXCEPTIONS FROM PARTS II TO IV

## 43   Charities

(1)   Nothing in Parts II to IV shall–

(a)   be construed as affecting a provision to which this subsection applies, or

(b)   render unlawful an act which is done in order to give effect to such a provision.

(2)   Subsection (1) applies to a provision for conferring benefits on persons of one sex only (disregarding any benefits to persons of the opposite sex which are exceptional or are relatively insignificant), being a provision which is contained in a charitable instrument.

(3)   In this section 'charitable instrument' means an enactment or other instrument passed or made for charitable purposes, or an enactment or other instrument so far as it relates to charitable purposes, and in Scotland includes the governing instrument of an endowment or of an educational endowment as those expressions are defined in section 135(1) of the Education (Scotland) Act 1962.

In the application of this section to England and Wales, 'charitable purposes' means purposes which are exclusively charitable according to the law of England and Wales.

**44-45**   ...

## 46   Communal accommodation

(1) In this section 'communal accommodation' means residential accommodation which includes dormitories or other shared sleeping accommodation which for reasons of privacy or decency should be used by men only, or by women only (but which may include some shared sleeping accommodation for men, and some for women, or some ordinary sleeping accommodation).

(2) In this section 'communal accommodation' also includes residential accommodation all or part of which should be used by men only, or by women only, because of the nature of the sanitary facilities serving the accommodation.

(3) Nothing in Part II or III shall render unlawful sex discrimination in the admission of persons to communal accommodation if the accommodation is managed in a way which, given the exigencies of the situation, comes as near as may be to fair and equitable treatment of men and women.

(4) In applying subsection (3) account shall be taken of–

(a) whether and how far it is reasonable to expect that the accommodation should be altered or extended, or that further alternative accommodation should be provided; and

(b) the frequency of the demand or need for use of the accommodation by men as compared with women.

(5) Nothing in Part II or III shall render unlawful sex discrimination against a woman, or against a man, as respects the provision of any benefit, facility or service if–

(a) the benefit, facility or service cannot properly and effectively be provided except for those using communal accommodation, and

(b) in the relevant circumstances the woman or, as the case may be, the man could lawfully be refused the use of the accommodation by virtue of subsection (3).

(6) Neither subsection (3) nor subsection (5) is a defence to an act of sex discrimination under Part II unless such arrangements as are reasonably practicable are made to compensate for the detriment caused by the discrimination; but in considering under subsection (5)(b) whether the use of communal accommodation could lawfully be refused (in a case based on Part II), it shall be assumed that the requirements of this subsection have been complied with as respects subsection (3).

(7) Section 25 shall not apply to sex discrimination within subsection (3) or (5).

(8) This section is without prejudice to the generality of section 35(1)(c).

## 47   Discriminatory training by certain bodies

(1) Nothing in Parts II to IV shall render unlawful any act done in relation to particular work by any person in, or in connection with–

    (a) affording women only, or men only, access to facilities for training which would help to fit them for that work, or

    (b) encouraging women only, or men only, to take advantage of opportunities for doing that work,

where it reasonably appears to that person that at any time within the 12 months immediately preceding the doing of the act there were no persons of the sex in question doing that work in Great Britain, or the number of persons of that sex doing the work in Great Britain was comparatively small.

(2) Where in relation to particular work it reasonably appears to any person that although the condition for the operation of subsection (1) is not met for the whole of Great Britain it is met for an area within Great Britain, nothing in Parts II to IV shall render unlawful any act done by that person in, or in connection with–

    (a) affording persons who are of the sex in question, and who appear likely to take up that work in that area, access to facilities for training which would help to fit them for that work, or

    (b) encouraging persons of that sex to take advantage of opportunities in the area for doing that work.

(3) Nothing in Parts II to IV shall render unlawful any act done by any person in, or in connection with, affording persons access to facilities for training which would help to fit them for employment, where it reasonably appears to that person that those persons are in special need of training by reason of the period for which they have been discharging domestic or family responsibilities to the exclusion of regular full time employment.

The discrimination in relation to which this subsection applies may result from confining the training to persons who have been discharging domestic or family responsibilities, or from the way persons are selected for training, or both.

(4) The preceding provisions of this section shall not apply in relation to any discrimination which is rendered unlawful by section 6.

## 48   Other discriminatory training etc.

(1) Nothing in Parts II to IV shall render unlawful any act done by an employer in relation to particular work in his employment, being an act done in, or in connection with–

(a)  affording his female employees only, or his male employees only, access to facilities for training which would help to fit them for that work, or

(b)  encouraging women only, or men only, to take advantage of opportunities for doing that work,

where at any time within the twelve months immediately preceding the doing of the act there were no persons of the sex in question among those doing that work or the number of persons of that sex doing the work was comparatively small.

(2)  Nothing in section 12 shall render unlawful any act done by an organisation to which that section applies in, or in connection with–

(a)  affording female members of the organisation only, or male members of the organisation only, access to facilities for training which would help to fit them for holding a post of any kind in the organisation, or

(b)  encouraging female members only, or male members only, to take advantage of opportunities for holding such posts in the organisation,

where at any time within the twelve months immediately preceding the doing of the act there were no persons of the sex in question among persons holding such posts in the organisation or the number of persons of that sex holding such posts was comparatively small.

(3)  Nothing in Parts II to IV shall render unlawful any act done by an organisation to which section 12 applies in, or in connection with, encouraging women only, or men only, to become members of the organisation where at any time within the twelve months immediately preceding the doing of the act there were no persons of the sex in question among those members or the number of persons of that sex among the members was comparatively small.

### 49   Trade unions etc.: elective bodies

(1)  If an organisation to which section 12 applies comprises a body the membership of which is wholly or mainly elected, nothing in section 12 shall render unlawful provision which ensures that a minimum number of persons of one sex are members of the body–

(a)  by reserving seats on the body for persons of that sex, or

(b)  by making extra seats on the body available (by election or co-option or otherwise) for persons of that sex on occasions when the number of persons of that sex in the other seats is below the minimum,

where in the opinion of the organisation the provision is in the circumstances needed to secure a reasonable lower limit to the number of members of that sex serving on the body; and nothing in Parts II to IV shall render unlawful any act done in order to give effect to such a provision.

(2)   This section shall not be taken as making lawful–

(a)   discrimination in the arrangements for determining the persons entitled to vote in an election of members of the body, or otherwise to choose the persons to serve on the body, or

(b)   discrimination in any arrangements concerning membership of the organisation itself.

## 50   Indirect access to benefits etc.

(1)   References in this Act to the affording by any persons of access to benefits, facilities or services are not limited to benefits, facilities or services provided by that person himself, but include any means by which it is in that person's power to facilitate access to benefits, facilities or services provided by any other person (the 'actual provider').

(2)   Where by any provision of this Act the affording by any person of access to benefits, facilities or services in a discriminatory way is in certain circumstances prevented from being unlawful, the effect of the provision shall extend also to the liability under this Act of any actual provider.

## 51   Acts done for purposes of protection of women

(1)   Nothing in the following provisions, namely–

(a)   Part II,
(b)   Part III so far as it applies to vocational training, or
(c)   Part IV so far as it has effect in relation to the provisions mentioned in paragraphs (a) and (b),

shall render unlawful any act done by a person in relation to a woman if–

(i)    it was necessary for that person to do it in order to comply with a requirement of an existing statutory provision concerning the protection of women, or

(ii)   it was necessary for that person to do it in order to comply with a requirement of a relevant statutory provision (within the meaning of Part I of the Health and Safety at Work etc. Act 1974) and it was done by that person for the purpose of the protection of the woman in question (or any class of women that included that woman).

(2) In subsection (1)–

(a)   the reference in paragraph (i) of that subsection to an existing statutory provision concerning the protection of women is a reference to any such provision having effect for the purpose of protecting women as regards–

(i)    pregnancy or maternity, or

(ii)   other circumstances giving rise to risks specifically affecting women, whether the provision relates only to such protection or to the protection of any other class of persons as well; and

(b)   the reference in paragraph (ii) of that subsection to the protection of women is a reference to the protection of that woman or those women as regards any circumstances falling within paragraph (a)(i) or (ii) above.

(3) In this section 'existing statutory provision' means (subject to subsection (4)) any provision of–

(a)   an Act passed before this Act, or

(b)   an instrument approved or made by or under such an Act (including one approved or made after the passing of this Act).

(4) Where an Act passed after this Act re-enacts (with or without modification) a provision of an Act passed before this Act, that provision as re-enacted shall be treated for the purposes of subsection (3) as if it continued to be contained in an Act passed before this Act.

## 51A   Acts done under statutory authority to be exempt from certain provisions of Part III

(1) Nothing in–

(a)   the relevant provisions of Part III, or

(b)   Part IV so far as it has effect in relation to those provisions,

shall render unlawful any act done by a person if it was necessary for that person to do it in order to comply with a requirement of an existing statutory provision within the meaning of section 51.

(2) In subsection (1) 'the relevant provisions of Part III' means the provisions of that Part except so far as they apply to vocational training.

## 52   Acts safeguarding national security[1]

(1)   Nothing in Parts II to IV shall render unlawful an act done for the purpose of safeguarding national security.

(2)   A certificate purporting to be signed by or on behalf of a Minister of the Crown and certifying that an act specified in the certificate was done for the purpose of safeguarding national security shall be conclusive evidence that it was done for that purpose.

---

[1]   The Sex Discrimination (Amendment) Order 1988 (SI 1988 No 249) provides (in part):

2   Subsections (2) and (3) of section 52 of the Sex Discrimination Act 1975 (certificate that act done for purpose of safeguarding national security to be conclusive evidence of that fact) shall cease to have effect in relation to the determination of the question whether any act is rendered unlawful by Part II of that Act, by Part III of that Act, so far as it applies to vocational training, or by Part IV of that Act taken with Part II or with Part III so far as it so applies.

(3)  A document purporting to be a certificate such as is mentioned in subsection (2) shall be received in evidence and, unless the contrary is proved, shall be deemed to be such a certificate.

### 52A  Construction of references to vocational training

In the following provisions, namely–

(a)  sections 51 and 51A, and
(b)  the provisions of any Order in Council modifying the effect of section 52,

'vocational training' includes advanced vocational training and retraining; and any reference to vocational training in those provisions shall be construed as including a reference to vocational guidance.

PART VI

EQUAL OPPORTUNITIES COMMISSION

### 53  Establishment and duties of Commission

(1)  There shall be a body of Commissioners named the Equal Opportunities Commission, consisting of at least but not more than fifteen individuals each appointed by the Secretary of State on a full-time or part-time basis, which shall have the following duties–

(a)  to work towards the elimination of discrimination,
(b)  to promote equality of opportunity between men and women generally, and
(c)  to keep under review the working of this Act and the Equal Pay Act 1970 and, when they are so required by the Secretary of State or otherwise think it necessary, draw up and submit to the Secretary of State proposals for amending them.

(2)  The Secretary of State shall appoint–

(a)  one of the Commissioners to be chairman of the Commission, and
(b)  either one or two of the Commissioners (as the Secretary of State thinks fit) to be deputy chairman or deputy chairmen of the Commission.

(3)  The Secretary of State may by order amend subsection (1) so far as it regulates the number of Commissioners.

(4)  Schedule 3 shall have effect with respect to the Commission.

### 54  Research and education

(1)  The Commission may undertake or assist (financially or otherwise) the undertaking by other persons of any research, and any educational activities, which appear to the Commission necessary or expedient for the purposes of section 53(1).

(2) The Commission may make charges for educational or other facilities or services made available by them.

## 55 Review of discriminatory provisions in health and safety legislation

(1) Without prejudice to the generality of section 53(1), the Commission, in pursuance of the duties imposed by paragraphs (a) and (b) of that subsection–

    (a) shall keep under review the relevant statutory provisions in so far as they require men and women to be treated differently, and

    (b) if so required by the Secretary of State, make to him a report on any matter specified by him which is connected with those duties and concerns the relevant statutory provisions.

Any such report shall be made within the time specified by the Secretary of State, and the Secretary of State shall cause the report to be published.

(2) Whenever the Commission think it necessary, they shall draw up and submit to the Secretary of State proposals for amending the relevant statutory provisions.

(3) The Commission shall carry out their duties in relation to the relevant statutory provisions in consultation with the Health and Safety Commission.

(4) In this section 'the relevant statutory provisions' has the meaning given by section 53 of the Health and Safety at Work etc. Act 1974.

## 56 Annual reports

(1) As soon as practicable after the end of each calendar year the Commission shall make to the Secretary of State a report on their activities during the year (an 'annual report').

(2) Each annual report shall include a general survey of developments, during the period to which it relates, in respect of matters falling within the scope of the Commission's duties.

(3) The Secretary of State shall lay a copy of every annual report before each House of Parliament, and shall cause the report to be published.

### Codes of practice

## 56A Codes of practice

(1) The Commission may issue codes of practice containing such practical guidance as the Commission think fit for either or both of the following purposes, namely–

    (a) the elimination of discrimination in the field of employment;

(b)   the promotion of equality of opportunity in that field between men and women.

(2)   When the Commission propose to issue a code of practice, they shall prepare and publish a draft of that code, shall consider any representations made to them about the draft and may modify the draft accordingly.

(3)   In the course of preparing any draft code of practice for eventual publication under subsection (2) the Commission shall consult with–

(a)   such organisations or associations of organisations representative of employers or of workers; and
(b)   such other organisations, or bodies,
as appear to the Commission to be appropriate.

(4)   If the Commission determine to proceed with the draft, they shall transmit the draft to the Secretary of State who shall–

(a)   if he approves of it, lay it before both Houses of Parliament; and
(b)   if he does not approve of it, publish details of his reasons for withholding approval.

(5)   If, within the period of forty days beginning with the day on which a copy of a draft code of practice is laid before each House of Parliament, or, if such copies are laid on different days, with the later of the two days, either House so resolves, no further proceedings shall be taken thereon, but without prejudice to the laying before Parliament of a new draft.

(6)   In reckoning the period of forty days referred to in subsection (5), no account shall be taken of any period during which Parliament is dissolved or prorogued or during which both Houses are adjourned for more than four days.

(7)   If no such resolution is passed as is referred to in subsection (5), the Commission shall issue the code in the form of the draft and the code shall come into effect on such day as the Secretary of State may by order appoint.

(8)   Without prejudice to section 81(4), an order under subsection (7) may contain such transitional provisions or savings as appear to the Secretary of State to be necessary or expedient in connection with the code of practice thereby brought into operation.

(9)   The Commission may from time to time revise the whole or any part of a code of practice issued under this section and issue that revised code, and subsections (2) to (8) shall apply (with appropriate modifications) to such a revised code as they apply to the first issue of a code.

(10)  A failure on the part of any person to observe any provision of a code of practice shall not of itself render him liable to any proceedings; but in any proceedings under this Act before an industrial tribunal any code of practice issued under this section shall be admissible in evidence, and if any

provision of such a code appears to the tribunal to be relevant to any question arising in the proceedings it shall be taken into account in determining that question.

(11) Without prejudice to subsection (1), a code of practice issued under this section may include such practical guidance as the Commission think fit as to what steps it is reasonably practicable for employers to take for the purpose of preventing their employees from doing in the course of their employment acts made unlawful by this Act.

## Investigations

### 57  Power to conduct formal investigations

(1) Without prejudice to their general power to do anything requisite for the performance of their duties under section 53(1), the Commission may if they think fit, and shall if required by the Secretary of State, conduct a formal investigation for any purpose connected with the carrying out of those duties.

(2) The Commission may, with the approval of the Secretary of State, appoint, on a full-time or part-time basis, one or more individuals as additional Commissioners for the purposes of a formal investigation.

(3) The Commission may nominate one or more Commissioners, with or without one or more additional Commissioners, to conduct a formal investigation on their behalf, and may delegate any of their functions in relation to the investigation to the persons so nominated.

### 58  Terms of reference

(1) The Commission shall not embark on a formal investigation unless the requirements of this section have been complied with.

(2) Terms of reference for the investigation shall be drawn up by the Commission or, if the Commission were required by the Secretary of State to conduct the investigation, by the Secretary of State after consulting the Commission.

(3) It shall be the duty of the Commission to give general notice of the holding of the investigation unless the terms of reference confine it to activities of persons named in them, but in such a case the Commission shall in the prescribed manner give those persons notice of the holding of the investigation.

(3A)  Where the terms of reference of the investigation confine it to activities of persons named in them and the Commission in the course of it propose to investigate any act made unlawful by this Act which they believe that a person so named may have done, the Commission shall—

(a)  inform that person of their belief and of their proposal to investigate the act in question; and

(b)  offer him an opportunity of making oral or written representations with regard to it (or both oral and written representations if he thinks fit);

and a person so named who avails himself of an opportunity under this subsection of making oral representations may be represented–

(i)  by counsel or a solicitor; or

(ii)  by some other person of his choice, not being a person to whom the Commission object on the ground that he is unsuitable.

(4)  The Commission or, if the Commission were required by the Secretary of State to conduct the investigation, the Secretary of State after consulting the Commission may from time to time revise the terms of reference; and subsections (1), (3) and (3A) shall apply to the revised investigation and terms of reference as they applied to the original.

## 59  Power to obtain information

(1)  For the purposes of a formal investigation the Commission, by a notice in the prescribed form served on him in the prescribed manner–

(a)  may require any person to furnish such written information as may be described in the notice, and may specify the time at which, and the manner and form in which, the information is to be furnished;

(b)  may require any person to attend at such time and place as is specified in the notice and give oral information about, and produce all documents in his possession or control relating to, any matter specified in the notice.

(2)  Except as provided by section 69, a notice shall be served under subsection (1) only where–

(a)  service of the notice was authorised by an order made by or on behalf of the Secretary of State, or

(b)  the terms of reference of the investigation state that the Commission believe that a person named in them may have done or may be doing acts of all or any of the following descriptions–

(i)  unlawful discriminatory acts,

(ii)  contraventions of section 37,

(iii)  contraventions of sections 38, 39, or 40, and

(iv)  acts in breach of a term modified or included by virtue of an equality clause,

and confine the investigation to those acts.

(3)  A notice under subsection (1) shall not require a person–

(a) to give information, or produce any documents, which he could not be compelled to give in evidence, or produce, in civil proceedings before the High Court or the Court of Session, or

(b) to attend at any place unless the necessary expenses of his journey to and from that place are paid or tendered to him.

(4) If a person fails to comply with a notice served on him under subsection (1) or the Commission has reasonable cause to believe that he intends not to comply with it, the Commission may apply to a county court for an order requiring him to comply with it or with such directions for the like purpose as may be contained in the order; and section 55 (penalty for neglecting or refusing to give evidence) of the County Courts Act 1984 shall apply to failure without reasonable excuse to comply with any such order as it applies in the cases there provided.

(5) In the application of subsection (4) to Scotland–

(a) for the reference to a county court there shall be substituted a reference to a sheriff court, and

(b) for the words after 'order; and' to the end of the subsection there shall be substituted the words 'paragraph 73 of the First Schedule to the Sheriff Courts (Scotland) Act 1907 (power of sheriff to grant second diligence for compelling the attendances of witnesses or havers) shall apply to any such order as it applies in proceedings in the sheriff court'.

(6) A person commits an offence if he–

(a) wilfully alters, suppresses, conceals or destroys a document which he has been required by a notice or order under this section to produce, or

(b) in complying with such a notice or order, knowingly or recklessly makes any statement which is false in a material particular,

and shall be liable on summary conviction to a fine not exceeding level 5 on the standard scale.

(7) Proceedings for an offence under subsection (6) may (without prejudice to any jurisdiction exercisable apart from this subsection) be instituted–

(a) against any person at any place at which he has an office or other place of business;

(b) against an individual at any place where he resides, or at which he is for the time being.

## 60  Recommendations and reports on formal investigations

(1) If in the light of any of their findings in a formal investigation it appears to the Commission necessary or expedient, whether during the course of the investigation or after its conclusion–

(a) to make to any persons, with a view to promoting equality of opportunity between men and women who are affected by any of their activities, recommendations for changes in their policies or procedures, or as to any other matters, or

(b) to make to the Secretary of State any recommendations, whether for changes in the law or otherwise,

the Commission shall make those recommendations accordingly.

(2) The Commission shall prepare a report of their findings in any formal investigations conducted by them.

(3) If the formal investigation is one required by the Secretary of State–

(a) the Commission shall deliver the report to the Secretary of State, and

(b) the Secretary of State shall cause the report to be published,

and unless required by the Secretary of State the Commission shall not publish the report.

(4) If the formal investigation is not one required by the Secretary of State, the Commission shall either publish the report, or make it available for inspection in accordance with subsection (5).

(5) Where under subsection (4) a report is to be made available for inspection, any person shall be entitled, on payment of such fee (if any) as may be determined by the Commission–

(a) to inspect the report during ordinary office hours and take copies of all or any part of the report, or

(b) to obtain from the Commission a copy, certified by the Commission to be correct, of the report.

(6) The Commission may if they think fit determine that the right conferred by subsection (5)(a) shall be exercisable in relation to a copy of the report instead of, or in addition to, the original.

(7) The Commission shall give general notice of the place or places where, and the times when, reports may be inspected under subsection (5).

## 61　Restriction on disclosure of information

(1) No information given to the Commission by any person ('the informant') in connection with a formal investigation shall be disclosed by the Commission, or by any person who is or has been a Commissioner, additional Commissioner or employee of the Commission, except–

(a) on the order of any court, or

(b) with the informant's consent, or

(c) in the form of a summary or other general statement published by the Commission which does not identify the informant or any other person to whom the information relates, or

(d) in a report of the investigation published by the Commission or made available for inspection under section 60(5), or

(e) to the Commissioners, additional Commissioners or employees of the Commission, or, so far as may be necessary for the proper performance of the functions of the Commission, to other persons, or

(f) for the purpose of any civil proceedings under this Act to which the Commission are a party, or any criminal proceedings.

(2) Any person who discloses information in contravention of subsection (1) commits an offence and shall be liable on summary conviction to a fine not exceeding level 5 on the standard scale.

(3) In preparing any report for publication or for inspection the Commission shall exclude, so far as is consistent with their duties and the object of the report, any matter which relates to the private affairs of any individual or business interests of any person where the publication of that matter might, in the opinion of the Commission, prejudicially affect that individual or person.

## PART VII

### ENFORCEMENT

### *General*

### 62   Restriction of proceedings for breach of Act

(1) Except as provided by this Act no proceedings, whether civil or criminal, shall lie against any person in respect of an act by reason that the act is unlawful by virtue of a provision of this Act.

(2) Subsection (1) does not preclude the making of an order of certiorari, mandamus or prohibition.

(3) In Scotland, subsection (1) does not preclude the exercise of the jurisdiction of the Court of Session to entertain an application for reduction or suspension of any order or determination, or otherwise to consider the validity of any order or determination, or to require reasons for any order or determination to be stated.

### *Enforcement in employment field*

### 63   Jurisdiction of industrial tribunals

(1) A complaint by any person ('the complainant') that another person ('the respondent')—

(a) has committed an act of discrimination against the complainant which is unlawful by virtue of Part II, or

(b) is by virtue of section 41 or 42 to be treated as having committed such an act of discrimination against the complainant, may be presented to an industrial tribunal.

(2)  Subsection (1) does not apply to a complaint under section 13(1) of an act in respect of which an appeal, or proceedings in the nature of an appeal, may be brought under any enactment.

## 64   Conciliation in employment cases

(1)  Where a complaint has been presented to an industrial tribunal under section 63, or under section 2(1) of the Equal Pay Act 1970, and a copy of the complaint has been sent to a conciliation officer, it shall be the duty of the conciliation officer–

(a)   if he is requested to do so both by the complainant and the respondent, or

(b)   if, in the absence of requests by the complainant and the respondent, he considers that he could act under this subsection with a reasonable prospect of success,

to endeavour to promote a settlement of the complaint without its being determined by an industrial tribunal.

(2)  Where, before a complaint such as is mentioned in subsection (1) has been presented to an industrial tribunal, a request is made to a conciliation officer to make his services available in the matter by a person who, if the complaint were so presented, would be the complainant or respondent, subsection (1) shall apply as if the complaint had been so presented and a copy of it had been sent to the conciliation officer.

(3)  In proceeding under subsection (1) or (2), a conciliation officer shall where appropriate have regard to the desirability of encouraging the use of other procedures available for the settlement of grievances.

(4)  Anything communicated to a conciliation officer in connection with the performance of his functions under this section shall not be admissible in evidence in any proceedings before an industrial tribunal except with the consent of the person who communicated it to that officer.

## 65   Remedies on complaint under section 63

(1)  Where an industrial tribunal finds that a complaint presented to it under section 63 is well-founded the tribunal shall make such of the following as it considers just and equitable–

(a)   an order declaring the rights of the complainant and the respondent in relation to the act to which the complaint relates;

(b)   an order requiring the respondent to pay to the complainant compensation of an amount corresponding to any damages he could have been ordered by a county court or by a sheriff court to pay to the complainant if the complaint had fallen to be dealt with under section 66;

(c) a recommendation that the respondent take within a specified period action appearing to the tribunal to be practicable for the purpose of obviating or reducing the adverse effect on the complainant of any act of discrimination to which the complaint relates.

(2) The amount of compensation awarded to a person under subsection (1)(b) shall not exceed the limit for the time being imposed by section 75 of the Employment Protection (Consolidation) Act 1978.

(3) If without reasonable justification the respondent to a complaint fails to comply with a recommendation made by an industrial tribunal under subsection (1)(c), then, if they think it just and equitable to do so–

(a) the tribunal may (subject to the limit in subsection (2)) increase the amount of compensation required to be paid to the complainant in respect of the complaint by an order made under subsection (1)(b), or

(b) if an order under subsection (1)(b) could have been made but was not, the tribunal may make such an order.

*Enforcement of Part III*

## 66  Claims under Part III

(1), (2)  ...

(3) As respects an unlawful act of discrimination falling within section 1(1)(b) (or, where this section is applied by section 65(1)(b), section 3(1)(b)) no award of damages shall be made if the respondent proves that the requirement or condition in question was not applied with the intention of treating the claimant unfavourably on the ground of his sex or marital status as the case may be.

(4) For the avoidance of doubt it is hereby declared that damages in respect of an unlawful act of discrimination may include compensation for injury to feelings whether or not they include compensation under any other head.

(5)-(8)  ...

*Non-discrimination notices*

## 67  Issue of non-discrimination notice

(1) This section applies to–

(a) an unlawful discriminatory act, and
(b) a contravention of section 37, and
(c) a contravention of section 38, 39 or 40, and

(d)  an act in breach of a term modified or included by virtue of an
     equality clause,
and so applies whether or not proceedings have been brought in respect of
the act.

(2)  If in the course of a formal investigation the Commission become
satisfied that a person is committing, or has committed, any such acts, the
Commission may in the prescribed manner serve on him a notice in the
prescribed form ('a non-discrimination notice') requiring him–

(a)  not to commit any such acts, and
(b)  where compliance with paragraph (a) involves changes in any of
     his practices or other arrangements–

     (i)   to inform the Commission that he has effected those changes
           and what those changes are, and
     (ii)  to take such steps as may be reasonably required by the notice
           for the purpose of affording that information to other persons
           concerned.

(3)  A non-discrimination notice may also require the person on whom
it is served to furnish the Commission with such other information as may be
reasonably required by the notice in order to verify that the notice has been
complied with.

(4)  The notice may specify the time at which, and the manner and form
in which, any information is to be furnished to the Commission, but the time
at which any information is to be furnished in compliance with the notice
shall not be later than five years after the notice has become final.

(5)  The Commission shall not serve a non-discrimination notice in
respect of any person unless they have first–

(a)  given him notice that they are minded to issue a non-discrimination
     notice in this case, specifying the grounds on which they
     contemplate doing so, and
(b)  offered him an opportunity of making oral or written
     representations in the matter (or both oral and written
     representations if he thinks fit) within a period of not less than 28
     days specified in the notice, and
(c)  taken account of any representations so made by him.

(6)  Subsection (2) does not apply to any acts in respect of which the
Secretary of State could exercise the powers conferred on him by section
25(2) and (3); but if the Commission become aware of any such acts they
shall give notice of them to the Secretary of State.

(7)  Section 59(4) shall apply to requirements under subsection (2)(b),
(3) and (4) contained in a non-discrimination notice which has become final
as it applies to requirements in a notice served under section 59(1).

## 68  Appeal against non-discrimination notice

(1)  Not later than six weeks after a non-discrimination notice is served on any person he may appeal against any requirement of the notice–

(a)  to an industrial tribunal, so far as the requirement relates to acts which are within the jurisdiction of the tribunal;

(b)  to a county court or to a sheriff court so far as the requirement relates to acts which are within the jurisdiction of the court and are not within the jurisdiction of an industrial tribunal.

(2)  Where the court or tribunal considers a requirement in respect of which an appeal is brought under subsection (1) to be unreasonable because it is based on an incorrect finding of fact or for any other reason, the court or tribunal shall quash the requirement.

(3)  On quashing a requirement under subsection (2) the court or tribunal may direct that the non-discrimination notice shall be treated as if, in place of the requirement quashed, it had contained a requirement in terms specified in the direction.

(4)  Subsection (1) does not apply to a requirement treated as included in a non-discrimination notice by virtue of a direction under subsection (3).

## 69  Investigation as to compliance with non-discrimination notice

(1)  If–

(a)  the terms of reference of a formal investigation state that its purpose is to determine whether any requirements of a non-discrimination notice are being or have been carried out, but section 59(2)(b) does not apply, and

(b)  section 58(3) is complied with in relation to the investigation on a date ('the commencement date') not later than the expiration of the period of five years beginning when the non-discrimination notice became final,

the Commission may within the period referred to in subsection (2) serve notices under section 59(1) for the purposes of the investigation without needing to obtain the consent of the Secretary of State.

(2)  The said period begins on the commencement date and ends on the later of the following dates–

(a)  the date on which the period of five years mentioned in subsection (1) (b) expires;

(b)  the date two years after the commencement date.

## 70  Register of non-discrimination notices

(1)  The Commission shall establish and maintain a register ('the register') of non-discrimination notices which have become final.

(2)  Any person shall be entitled, on payment of such fee (if any) as may be determined by the Commission,–

(a)  to inspect the register during ordinary office hours and take copies of any entry, or
(b)  to obtain from the Commission a copy, certified by the Commission to be correct, of any entry in the register.

(3)  The Commission may, if they think fit, determine that the right conferred by subsection (2)(a) shall be exercisable in relation to a copy of the register instead of, or in addition to, the original.

(4)  The Commission shall give general notice of the place or places where, and the times when, the register or a copy of it may be inspected.

*Other enforcement by Commission*

## 71  Persistent discrimination

(1)  If, during the period of five years beginning on the date on which either of the following became final in the case of any person, namely–

(a)  a non-discrimination notice served on him,
(b)  a finding by a court or tribunal under section 63 or 66, or section 2 of the Equal Pay Act 1970, that he has done an unlawful discriminatory act or an act in breach of a term modified or included by virtue of an equality clause,

it appears to the Commission that unless restrained he is likely to do one or more acts falling within paragraph (b), or contravening section 37, the Commission may apply to a county court for an injunction, or to the sheriff court for an order, restraining him from doing so; and the court, if satisfied that the application is well-founded, may grant the injunction or order in the terms applied for or in more limited terms.

(2)  In proceedings under this section the Commission shall not allege that the person to whom the proceedings relate has done an act which is within the jurisdiction of an industrial tribunal unless a finding by an industrial tribunal that he did that act has become final.

## 72  Enforcement of ss 38 to 40

(1)  Proceedings in respect of a contravention of section 38, 39, or 40 shall be brought only by the Commission in accordance with the following provisions of this section.

(2)  The proceedings shall be–

(a)  an application for a decision whether the alleged contravention occurred, or
(b)  an application under subsection (4) below,

or both.

(3) An application under subsection (2)(a) shall be made–

(a) in a case based on any provision of Part II, to an industrial tribunal, and

(b) in any other case to a county court or sheriff court.

(4) If it appears to the Commission–

(a) that a person has done an act which by virtue of section 38, 39 or 40 was unlawful, and

(b) that unless restrained he is likely to do further acts which by virtue of that section are unlawful,

the Commission may apply to a county court for an injunction, or to a sheriff court for an order, restraining him from doing such acts; and the court, if satisfied that the application is well-founded, may grant the injunction or order in the terms applied for or more limited terms.

(5) In proceedings under subsection (4) the Commission shall not allege that the person to whom the proceedings relate has done an act which is unlawful under this Act and within the jurisdiction of an industrial tribunal unless a finding by an industrial tribunal that he did that act has become final.

## 73 Preliminary action in employment cases

(1) With a view to making an application under section 71(1) or 72(4) in relation to a person the Commission may present to an industrial tribunal a complaint that he has done an act within the jurisdiction of an industrial tribunal, and if the tribunal considers that the complaint is well-founded they shall make a finding to that effect and, if they think it just and equitable to do so in the case of an act contravening any provision of Part II may also (as if the complaint had been presented by the person discriminated against) make an order such as is referred to in section 65(1)(a), or a recommendation such as is referred to in section 65(1)(c), or both.

(2) Subsection (1) is without prejudice to the jurisdiction conferred by section 72(2).

(3) Any finding of an industrial tribunal under–

(a) this Act, or

(b) the Equal Pay Act 1970,

in respect of any act shall, if it has become final, be treated as conclusive–

(i) by the county court or sheriff court on an application under section 71(1) or 72(4) or in proceedings on an equality clause,

(ii) by an industrial tribunal on a complaint made by the person affected by the act under section 63 or in relation to an equality clause.

(4) In sections 71 and 72 and this section, the acts 'within the jurisdiction of an industrial tribunal' are those in respect of which such jurisdiction is conferred by sections 63 and 72 and by section 2 of the Equal Pay Act 1970.

*Help for persons suffering discrimination*

### 74   Help for aggrieved persons in obtaining information etc.

(1) With a view to helping a person ('the person aggrieved') who considers he may have been discriminated against in contravention of this Act to decide whether to institute proceedings and, if he does so, to formulate and present his case in the most effective manner, the Secretary of State shall by order prescribe–

(a) forms by which the person aggrieved may question the respondent on his reasons for doing any relevant act, or on any other matter which is or may be relevant;

(b) forms by which the respondent may if he so wishes reply to any questions.

(2) Where the person aggrieved questions the respondent (whether in accordance with an order under subsection (1) or not)–

(a) the question, and any reply by the respondent (whether in accordance with such an order or not) shall, subject to the following provisions of this section, be admissible as evidence in the proceedings;

(b) if it appears to the court or tribunal that the respondent deliberately, and without reasonable excuse, omitted to reply within a reasonable period or that his reply is evasive or equivocal, the court or tribunal may draw any inference from that fact that it considers it just and equitable to draw, including an inference that he committed an unlawful act.

(3) The Secretary of State may by order–

(a) prescribe the period within which questions must be duly served in order to be admissible under subsection (2)(a), and

(b) prescribe the manner in which a question, and any reply by the respondent, may be duly served.

(4) Rules may enable the court entertaining a claim under section 66 to determine, before the date fixed for the hearing of the claim, whether a question or reply is admissible under this section or not.

(5) This section is without prejudice to any other enactment or rule of law regulating interlocutory and preliminary matters in proceedings before a county court, sheriff court or industrial tribunal, and has effect subject to any enactment or rule of law regulating the admissibility of evidence in such proceedings.

(6)  In this section 'respondent' includes a prospective respondent and 'rules'–

(a)  in relation to county court proceedings, means county court rules;

(b)  in relation to sheriff court proceedings, means sheriff court rules.

## 75  Assistance by Commission

(1)  Where, in relation to proceedings or prospective proceedings either under this Act or in respect of an equality clause, an individual who is an actual or prospective complainant or claimant applies to the Commission for assistance under this section, the Commission shall consider the application and may grant it if they think fit to do so on the ground that–

(a)  the case raises a question of principle, or

(b)  it is unreasonable, having regard to the complexity of the case or the applicant's position in relation to the respondent or another person involved or any other matter, to expect the applicant to deal with the case unaided,

or by reason of any other special consideration.

(2)  Assistance by the Commission under this section may include–

(a)  giving advice;

(b)  procuring or attempting to procure the settlement of any matter in dispute;

(c)  arranging for the giving of advice or assistance by a solicitor or counsel;

(d)  arranging for representation by any person including all such assistance as is usually given by a solicitor or counsel in the steps preliminary or incidental to any proceedings, or in arriving at or giving effect to a compromise to avoid or bring to an end any proceedings,

(e)  any other form of assistance which the Commission may consider appropriate,

but paragraph (d) shall not affect the law and practice regulating the descriptions of persons who may appear in, conduct, defend and address the Court in, any proceedings.

(3)  In so far as expenses are incurred by the Commission in providing the applicant with assistance under this section the recovery of those expenses (as taxed or assessed in such manner as may be prescribed by rules or regulations) shall constitute a first charge for the benefit of the Commission–

(a)  on any costs or expenses which (whether by virtue of a judgment or order of a court or tribunal or an agreement or otherwise) are payable to the applicant by any other person in respect of the matter in connection with which the assistance is given, and

(b) so far as relates to any costs or expenses, on his rights under any compromise or settlement arrived at in connection with that matter to avoid or bring to an end any proceedings.

(4) The charge conferred by subsection (3) is subject to any charge under the Legal Aid Act 1988, or any charge or obligation for payment in priority to other debts under the Legal Aid (Scotland) Act 1986, and is subject to any provision in either of those Acts for payment of any sum to the Legal Aid Board or into the Scottish Legal Aid Fund.

(5) In this section 'respondent' includes a prospective respondent and 'rules or regulations'–

(a) in relation to county court proceedings, means county court rules;

(b) in relation to sheriff court proceedings, means sheriff court rules;

(c) in relation to industrial tribunal proceedings, means regulations made under paragraph 1 of Schedule 9 to the Employment Protection (Consolidation) Act 1978.

*Period within which proceedings to be brought*

## 76　Period within which proceedings to be brought

(1) An industrial tribunal shall not consider a complaint under section 63 unless it is presented to the tribunal before the end of the period of three months beginning when the act complained of was done.

(2) A county court or a sheriff court shall not consider a claim under section 66 unless proceedings in respect of the claim are instituted before the end of–

(a) the period of six months beginning when the act complained of was done; or

(b) in a case to which section 66(5) applies, the period of eight months so beginning.

(3) An industrial tribunal, county court or sheriff court shall not consider an application under section 72(2)(a) unless it is made before the end of the period of six months beginning when the act to which it relates was done; and a county court or sheriff court shall not consider an application under section 72(4) unless it is made before the end of the period of five years so beginning.

(4) An industrial tribunal shall not consider a complaint under section 73(1) unless it is presented to the tribunal before the end of the period of six months beginning when the act complained of was done.

(5) A court or tribunal may nevertheless consider any such complaint, claim or application which is out of time if, in all the circumstances of the case, it considers that it is just and equitable to do so.

(6)  For the purposes of this section–

(a)  where the inclusion of any term in a contract renders the making of the contract an unlawful act that act shall be treated as extending throughout the duration of the contract, and

(b)  any act extending over a period shall be treated as done at the end of that period, and

(c)  a deliberate omission shall be treated as done when the person in question decided upon it,

and in the absence of evidence establishing the contrary a person shall be taken for the purposes of this section to decide upon an omission when he does an act inconsistent with doing the omitted act or, if he has done no such inconsistent act, when the period expires within which he might reasonably have been expected to do the omitted act if it was to be done.

## PART VIII

### SUPPLEMENTAL

**77  Validity and revision of contracts**

(1)  A term of a contract is void where–

(a)  its inclusion renders the making of the contract unlawful by virtue of this Act, or

(b)  it is included in furtherance of an act rendered unlawful by this Act, or

(c)  it provides for the doing of an act which would be rendered unlawful by this Act.

(2)  Subsection (1) does not apply to a term the inclusion of which constitutes, or is in furtherance of, or provides for, unlawful discrimination against a party to the contract, but the term shall be unenforceable against that party.

(3)  A term in a contract which purports to exclude or limit any provision of this Act or the Equal Pay Act 1970 is unenforceable by any person in whose favour the term would operate apart from this subsection.

(4)  Subsection (3) does not apply–

(a)  to a contract settling a complaint to which section 63(1) of this Act or section 2 of the Equal Pay Act 1970 applies where the contract is made with the assistance of a conciliation officer;

(b)  to a contract settling a claim to which section 66 applies.

(5)  On the application of any person interested in a contract to which subsection (2) applies, a county court or sheriff court may make such order as it thinks just for removing or modifying any term made unenforceable by that subsection; but such an order shall not be made unless all persons affected have been given notice of the application (except where under rules

of court notice may be dispensed with) and have been afforded an opportunity to make representations to the court.

(6)  An order under subsection (5) may include provision as respects any period before the making of the order.

**78, 79**   ...

### 80   Power to amend certain provisions of Act

(1)  The Secretary of State may by an order the draft of which has been approved by each House of Parliament–

    (a)  amend any of the following provisions, namely, sections 6(3), 7, 19, 20(1), (2) and (3), 31(2), 32, 34, 35 and 43 to 48 (including any such provision as amended by a previous order under this subsection);

    (b)  amend or repeal any of the following provisions namely, sections 11(4), 12(4), 33 and 49 (including any such provision as amended by a previous order under this subsection);

    (c)  amend Part II, III or IV so as to render lawful an act which, apart from the amendment, would be unlawful by reason of section 6(1) or (2), 29(1), 30 or 31.

    (d)  ...

(2)  The Secretary of State shall not lay before Parliament the draft of an order under subsection (1) unless he has consulted the Commission about the contents of the draft.

(3)  An order under subsection (1)(c) may make such amendments to the list of provisions given in subsection (1)(a) as in the opinion of the Secretary of State are expedient having regard to the contents of the order.

### 81   Orders

(1)  Any power of the Secretary of State to make orders under the provisions of this Act (except sections 27 and 59(2)) shall be exercisable by statutory instrument.

(2)  An order made by the Secretary of State under the preceding provisions of this Act (except sections 27, 59(2) and 80(1)) shall be subject to annulment in pursuance of a resolution of either House of Parliament.

(3)  Subsections (1) and (2) do not apply to an order under section 78 or 79, but–

    (a)  an order under section 78 which modifies an enactment, and

    (b)  any order under section 79 other than one which relates to an endowment to which section 115 of the Education (Scotland) Act 1980 (small endowments) applies, shall be made by statutory instrument subject to annulment in pursuance of a resolution of either House of Parliament.

(4) An order under this Act may make different provision in relation to different cases or classes of case, may exclude certain cases or classes of case, and may contain transitional provisions and savings.

(5) Any power conferred by this Act to make orders includes power (exercisable in the like manner and subject to the like conditions) to vary or revoke any order so made.

## 82 General interpretation provisions

(1) In this Act, unless the context otherwise requires—

'access' shall be construed in accordance with section 50;

'act' includes a deliberate omission;

'advertisement' includes every form of advertisement, whether to the public or not, and whether in a newspaper or other publication, by television or radio, by display of notices, signs, labels, showcards or goods, by distribution of samples, circulars, catalogues, price lists or other material, by exhibition of pictures, models or films, or in any other way, and references to the publishing of advertisements shall be construed accordingly;

'associated employer' shall be construed in accordance with subsection (2);

'the Commission' means the Equal Opportunities Commission;

'Commissioner' means a member of the Commission;

'designate' shall be construed in accordance with subsection (3);

'discrimination' and related terms shall be construed in accordance with section 5(1);

'dispose', in relation to premises, includes granting a right to occupy the premises, and any reference to acquiring premises shall be construed accordingly;

'education' includes any form of training or instruction;

'education authority' and 'educational establishment' in relation to Scotland have the same meaning as they have respectively in section 135(1) of the Education (Scotland) Act 1980;

'employment' means employment under a contract of service or of apprenticeship or a contract personally to execute any work or labour, and related expressions shall be construed accordingly;

'employment agency' means a person who, for profit or not, provides services for the purpose of finding employment for workers or supplying employers with workers;

'equality clause' has the meaning given in section 1(2) of the Equal Pay Act 1970 (as set out in section 8(1) of this Act);

'estate agent' means a person who, by way of profession or trade, provides services for the purpose of finding premises for persons seeking to acquire them or assisting in the disposal of premises;

'final' shall be construed in accordance with subsection (4);

'firm' has the meaning given by section 4 of the Partnership Act 1890;

'formal investigation' means an investigation under section 57;

'further education' has the meaning given by section 41(a) of the Education Act 1944;

'general notice', in relation to any person, means a notice published by him at a time and in a manner appearing to him suitable for securing that the notice is seen within a reasonable time by persons likely to be affected by it;

'genuine occupational qualification' shall be construed in accordance with section 7(2);

'Great Britain' includes such of the territorial waters of the United Kingdom as are adjacent to Great Britain;

'independent school' has the meaning given by section 114(1) of the Education Act 1944;

'man' includes a male of any age;

'near relative' shall be construed in accordance with subsection (5);

'non-discrimination notice' means a notice under section 67;

'notice' means a notice in writing;

'prescribed' means prescribed by regulations made by the Secretary of State by statutory instrument;

'profession' includes any vocation or occupation;

'proprietor', in relation to any school, has the meaning given by section 114(1) of the Education Act 1944;

'pupil', in Scotland includes a student of any age;

'retirement' includes retirement (whether voluntary or not) on grounds of age, length of service or incapacity;

'school' has the meaning given by section 114(1) of the Education Act 1944;

'school education' has the same meaning given by section 135(1) of the Education (Scotland) Act 1980;

'trade' includes any business;

'training' includes any form of education or instruction;

'university' includes a university college and the college, school or hall of a university;

'upper limit of compulsory school age' means, subject to section 9 of the Education Act 1962, the age that is that limit by virtue of section 35 of the Education Act 1944 and the Order in Council made under that section;

'woman' includes a female of any age.

(1A) References in this Act to the dismissal of a person from employment or to the expulsion of a person from a position as partner include references-

(a)  to the termination of that person's employment or partnership by the expiration of any period (including a period expiring by reference to an event or circumstance), not being a termination immediately after which the employment or partnership is renewed on the same terms; and

(b) to the termination of that person's employment or partnership by any act of his (including the giving of notice) in circumstances such that he is entitled to terminate it without notice by reason of the conduct of the employer or, as the case may be, the conduct of the other partners.

(2) For the purposes of this Act two employers are to be treated as associated if one is a company of which the other (directly or indirectly) has control or if both are companies of which a third person (directly or indirectly) has control.

(3) Any power conferred by this Act to designate establishments or persons may be exercised either by naming them or by identifying them by reference to a class or other description.

(4) For the purposes of this Act a non-discrimination notice or a finding by a court or tribunal becomes final when an appeal against the notice or finding is dismissed, withdrawn or abandoned or when the time for appealing expires without an appeal having been brought; and for this purpose an appeal against a non-discrimination notice shall be taken to be dismissed if, notwithstanding that a requirement of the notice is quashed on appeal, a direction is given in respect of it under section 68(3).

(5) For the purposes of this Act a person is a near relative of another if that person is the wife or husband, a parent or child, a grandparent or grandchild, or a brother or sister of the other (whether of full blood or half-blood or by affinity), and 'child' includes an illegitimate child and the wife or husband of an illegitimate child.

(6) Except so far as the context otherwise requires, any reference in this Act to an enactment shall be construed as a reference to that enactment as amended by or under any other enactment including this Act.

(7) In this Act, except where otherwise indicated–

(a) a reference to a numbered Part, section or Schedule is a reference to the Part or section of, or the Schedule to, this Act so numbered, and

(b) a reference in a section to a numbered subsection is a reference to the subsection of that section so numbered, and

(c) a reference in a section, subsection or Schedule to a numbered paragraph is a reference to the paragraph of that section, subsection or Schedule so numbered, and

(d) a reference to any provision of an Act (including this Act) includes a Schedule incorporated in the Act by that provision.

## 83 Transitional and commencement provisions, amendments and repeals

(1) The provisions of Schedule 4 shall have effect for making transitional provision for the purposes of this Act.

(2) Parts II to VII shall come into operation on such day as the Secretary of State may by order appoint, and different days may be so appointed for different provisions and for different purposes.

(3) Subject to subsection (4)–

(a) the enactments specified in Schedule 5 shall have effect subject to the amendments specified in that Schedule (being minor amendments or amendments consequential on the preceding provisions of this Act), and

(b) the enactments specified in Schedule 6 are hereby repealed to the extent shown in column 3 of that Schedule.

(4) The Secretary of State shall by order provide for the coming into operation of the amendments contained in Schedule 5 and the repeals contained in Schedule 6, and those amendments and repeals shall have effect only as provided by an order so made.

(5) An order under this section may make such transitional provision as appears to the Secretary of State to be necessary or expedient in connection with the provisions thereby brought into operation, including such adaptations of those provisions, or of any provisions of this Act then in operation, as appear to the Secretary of State necessary or expedient in consequence of the partial operation of this Act.

## 84   Financial provisions

There shall be defrayed out of money provided by Parliament–

(a) sums required by the Secretary of State for making payments under paragraph 5 or 14 of Schedule 3, and for defraying any other expenditure falling to be made by him under or by virtue of this Act;

(b) ... ; and

(c) any increase attributable to the provisions of this Act in the sums payable out of money provided by Parliament under any other Act.

## 85   Application to Crown

(1) This Act applies–

(a) to an act done by or for purposes of a Minister of the Crown or government department, or

(b) to an act done on behalf of the Crown by a statutory body, or a person holding a statutory office,

as it applies to an act done by a private person.

(2) Parts II and IV apply to–

(a) service for purposes of a Minister of the Crown or government department, other than service of a person holding a statutory office, or

(b)   service on behalf of the Crown for purposes· of a person holding a statutory office or purposes of a statutory body,

as they apply to employment by a private person, and shall so apply as if references to a contract of employment included references to the terms of service.

(3)   Subsections (1) and (2) have effect subject to section 17.

(4)   Subsections (1) and (2) do not apply in relation to service in–

(a)   the naval, military or air forces of the Crown,

(b)   ...

(5)   Nothing in this Act shall render unlawful discrimination in admission to the Army Cadet Force, Air Training Corps, Sea Cadet Corps or Combined Cadet Force, or any other cadet training corps for the time being administered by the Ministry of Defence.

(6)   This Act (except section 8(1) and (6)) does not apply to employment in the case of which the employee may be required to serve in support of a force mentioned in subsection (4).

(7)   Subsection (2) of section 10 shall have effect in relation to any ship, aircraft or hovercraft belonging to or possessed by Her Majesty in right of the Government of the United Kingdom as it has effect in relation to a ship, aircraft or hovercraft mentioned in paragraph (a) or (b) of that subsection, and section 10(5) shall apply accordingly.

(8)   The provisions of Parts II to IV of the Crown Proceedings Act 1947 shall apply to proceedings against the Crown under this Act as they apply to proceedings in England and Wales which by virtue of section 23 of that Act are treated for the purposes of Part II of that Act as civil proceedings by or against the Crown, except that in their application to proceedings under this Act section 20 of that Act (removal of proceedings from county court to High Court) shall not apply.

(9)   The provisions of Part V of the Crown Proceedings Act 1947 shall apply to proceedings against the Crown under this Act as they apply to proceedings in Scotland which by virtue of the said Part are treated as civil proceedings by or against the Crown, except that in their application to proceedings under this Act the proviso to section 44 of that Act (removal of proceedings from the sheriff court to the Court of Session) shall not apply.

(10)   In this section 'statutory body' means a body set up by or in pursuance of an enactment, and 'statutory office' means an office so set up; and service 'for purposes of' a Minister of the Crown or government department does not include service in any office in Schedule 2 (Ministerial offices) to the House of Commons Disqualification Act 1975 as for the time being in force.

## 86    Government appointments outside section 6

(1)  This section applies to any appointment by a Minister of the Crown or government department to an office or post where section 6 does not apply in relation to the appointment.

(2)  In making the appointment, and in making the arrangements for determining who should be offered the office or post, the Minister of the Crown or government department shall not do an act which would be unlawful under section 6 if the Crown were the employer for the purposes of this Act.

## 87    Short title and extent

(1)  This Act may be cited as the Sex Discrimination Act 1975.

(2)  ...

SCHEDULES

SCHEDULE 1

...

SCHEDULE 2

...

SCHEDULE 3

EQUAL OPPORTUNITIES COMMISSION

*Incorporation and status*

1    On the appointment by the Secretary of State of the first Commissioners, the Commission shall come into existence as a body corporate with perpetual succession and a common seal.

2    (1)  The Commission is not an emanation of the Crown, and shall not act or be treated as the servant or agent of the Crown.

(2)  Accordingly–

(a)  neither the Commission nor a Commissioner or member of its staff as such is entitled to any status, immunity, privilege or exemption enjoyed by the Crown;

(b)  the Commissioners and members of the staff of the Commission as such are not civil servants; and

(c)  the Commission's property is not the property of, or held on behalf of, the Crown.

### Tenure of office of Commissioners

3    (1)  A Commissioner shall hold and vacate his office in accordance with the terms of his appointment.

(2)  A person shall not be appointed a Commissioner for more than five years.

(3)  With the consent of the Commissioner concerned, the Secretary of State may alter the terms of an appointment so as to make a full-time Commissioner into a part-time Commissioner or vice versa, or for any other purpose.

(4)  A Commissioner may resign by notice to the Secretary of State.

(5)  The Secretary of State may terminate the appointment of a Commissioner if satisfied that–

    (a)  without the consent of the Commission, he failed to attend the meetings of the Commission during a continuous period of six months beginning not earlier than nine months before the termination; or

    (b)  he is an undischarged bankrupt, or has made an arrangement with his creditors, or is insolvent within the meaning of paragraph 9(2) of Schedule 3 to the Conveyancing and Feudal Reform (Scotland) Act 1970; or

    (c)  he is by reason of physical or mental illness, or for any other reason, incapable of carrying out his duties.

(6)  Past service as a Commissioner is no bar to re-appointment.

### Tenure of office of chairman and deputy chairman

4    (1)  The chairman and each deputy chairman shall hold and vacate his office in accordance with the terms of his appointment, and may resign by notice to the Secretary of State.

(2)  The office of the chairman or a deputy chairman is vacated if he ceases to be a Commissioner.

(3)  Past service as chairman or a deputy chairman is no bar to re-appointment.

### Remuneration of Commissioners

5    The Secretary of State may pay, or make such payments towards the provision of, such remuneration, pensions, allowances or gratuities to or in respect of the Commissioners or any of them as, with the consent of the Minister for the Civil Service, he may determine.

6    Where a person ceases to be a Commissioner otherwise than on the expiry of his term of office, and it appears to the Secretary of State that there are special circumstances which make it right for that person to receive compensation, the Secretary of State may with the consent of the Minister for the Civil Service direct the Commission to make to that person a payment of such amount as, with the consent of that Minister, the Secretary of State may determine.

### Additional Commissioners

7    (1) Paragraphs 2(2), 3(1) and (6), and 6 shall apply to additional Commissioners appointed under section 57(2) as they apply to Commissioners.

(2) The Commission may pay, or make such payments towards the provision of such remuneration, pensions, allowances or gratuities to or in respect of an additional Commissioner as the Secretary of State, with the consent of the Minister for the Civil Service, may determine.

(3) With the approval of the Secretary of State and the consent of the additional Commissioners concerned, the Commission may alter the terms of an appointment of an additional Commissioner so as to make a full-time additional Commissioner into a part-time additional Commissioner or vice versa, or for any other purpose.

(4) An additional Commissioner may resign by notice to the Commission.

(5) The Secretary of State, or the Commission acting with the approval of the Secretary of State, may terminate the appointment of an additional Commissioner if satisfied that–

    (a)   without reasonable excuse he failed to carry out the duties for which he was appointed during a continuous period of three months beginning not earlier than six months before the termination; or

    (b)   he is a person such as is mentioned in paragraph 3(5)(b); or

    (c)   he is by reason of physical or mental illness, or for any other reason, incapable of carrying out his duties.

(6) The appointment of an additional Commissioner shall terminate at the conclusion of the investigation for which he was appointed, if not sooner.

### Staff

8    The Commission may, after consultation with the Secretary of State, appoint such officers and servants as they think fit, subject to the approval of the Minister for the Civil Service as to numbers and as to remuneration and other terms and conditions of service.

9  (1)  Employment with the Commission shall be included among the kinds of employment to which a superannuation scheme under section 1 of the Superannuation Act 1972 can apply, and accordingly in Schedule 1 to that Act (in which those kinds of employment are listed) the words 'Equal Opportunities Commission' shall be inserted at the appropriate place in alphabetical order.

(2)  Where a person who is employed by the Commission and is by reference to that employment a participant in a scheme under section 1 of the Superannuation Act 1972 becomes a Commissioner or an additional Commissioner, the Minister for the Civil Service may determine that his service as a Commissioner or additional Commissioner shall be treated for the purposes of the scheme as service as an employee of the Commission; and his rights under the scheme shall not be affected by paragraph 5 or 7(2).

10  The Employers' Liability (Compulsory Insurance) Act 1969 shall not require insurance to be effected by the Commission.

## Proceedings and business

11  (1)  Subject to the provisions of this Act, the Commission may make arrangements for the regulation of their proceedings and business, and may vary or revoke those arrangements.

(2)  The arrangements may, with the approval of the Secretary of State, provide for the discharge under the general direction of the Commission of any of the Commission's functions by a committee of the Commission, or by two or more Commissioners.

(3)  Anything done by or in relation to a committee, or Commissioners, in the discharge of the Commission's functions shall have the same effect as if done by or in relation to the Commission.

12  The validity of any proceedings of the Commission shall not be affected by any vacancy among the members of the Commission or by any defect in the appointment of any Commissioner or additional Commissioner.

13  The quorum for meetings of the Commission shall in the first instance be determined by a meeting of the Commission attended by not less than five Commissioners.

## Finance

14  The Secretary of State shall pay to the Commission expenses incurred or to be incurred by it under paragraphs 6, 7 and 8, and, with the consent of the Minister for the Civil Service and the Treasury, shall pay to the Commission

such sums as the Secretary of State thinks fit for enabling the Commission to meet other expenses.

15  (1)  The accounting year of the Commission shall be the twelve months ending on 31 March.

(2)  It shall be the duty of the Commission–

(a)  to keep proper accounts and proper records in relation to the accounts;

(b)  to prepare in respect of each accounting year a statement of account in such form as the Secretary of State may direct with the approval of the Treasury; and

(c)  to send copies of the statement to the Secretary of State and the Comptroller and Auditor General before the end of the month of November next following the accounting year to which the statement relates.

(3)  The Comptroller and Auditor General shall examine, certify and report on each statement received by him in pursuance of this Schedule and shall lay copies of each statement and of his report before each House of Parliament.

SCHEDULE 4

TRANSITIONAL PROVISIONS

1, 2 ...

3  (1)  Until a date specified by order made by the Secretary of State the courses of training to be undergone by men as a condition of registration as midwives under the Nurses, Midwives and Health Visitors Act 1979 must be courses approved in writing by or on behalf of the Secretary or State for the purposes of this paragraph.

(2), (3)  ...

(4)  An order under this paragraph shall be laid in draft before each House of Parliament, and section 6(1) of the Statutory Instruments Act 1946 (Parliamentary control by negative resolution of draft instruments) shall apply accordingly.

4  ...

5  (1)  Section 6 of the Equal Pay Act 1970 (as amended by paragraph 3 of Schedule 1 to this Act) shall apply as if the references to death or retirement in subsection (1A)(b) of the said section 6 included references to sums payable on marriage in pursuance of a contract of employment made

before the passing of this Act, or the commutation, at any time, of the right to such sums.

(2)   In relation to service within section 1(8) of the said Act of 1970 (service of the Crown) for the reference in this paragraph to a contract of employment made before the passing of this Act there shall be substituted a reference to terms of service entered into before the passing of this Act.

SCHEDULE 5

...

SCHEDULE 6

...

# Code of Practice
# for the Elimination of Discrimination on the Grounds of Sex and Marriage and the Promotion of Equality of Opportunity in Employment (1985)[1]

**Texts printed**

INTRODUCTION                                                199

Small Businesses                                            199
Employers' Responsibility                                   199
Individual Employee's Responsibility                        199
Trade Union Responsibility                                  200
Employment Agencies                                         200
Definitions                                                 200

PART 1:  THE ROLE OF GOOD EMPLOYMENT PRACTICES IN
         ELIMINATING SEX AND MARRIAGE DISCRIMINATION  200

Recruitment                                                 201
Genuine Occupational Qualifications                         201
Sources of Recruitment                                      202
    Advertising                                             202
    Careers Service/Schools                                 203
Selection Methods                                           203
    Tests                                                   203
    Applications and Interviewing                           203
Promotion, Transfer and Training                            204
Health and Safety Legislation                               205
Terms of Employment, Benefits, Facilities and Services      205
Grievances, Disciplinary Procedures and Victimisation       206
Dismissals, Redundancies and other unfavourable treatment
    of employees                                            206

PART 2:  THE ROLE OF GOOD EMPLOYMENT PRACTICES IN
         PROMOTING EQUALITY OF OPPORTUNITY                  207

Formulating an Equal Opportunities Policy                   207
Implementing the Policy                                     208
Monitoring                                                  208
Positive Action                                             208
    Recruitment, Training and Promotion                     208
    Other Working Arrangements                              209

---

[1]    This Code of Practice was issued by the Equal Opportunities Commission under
s. 56A of the Sex Discrimination Act 1975 and was brought into effect on 30 April
1985 by the Sex Discrimination Code of Practice Order 1985 (SI 1985 No 387). The
Legal Annex, which summarises the relevant provisions of the 1975 Act, is omitted.
For the legal effect of the Code see s. 56 A of the 1975 Act.
The text here printed preserves the principal typographical characteristics of the
original text.

# INTRODUCTION

1    The EOC issues this Code of Practice for the following purposes:
(a)  for the elimination of discrimination in employment
(b)  to give guidance as to what steps it is reasonably practicable for employers to take to ensure that their employees do not in the course of their employment act unlawfully contrary to the Sex Discrimination Act (SDA)
(c)  for the promotion of equality of opportunity between men and women in employment.

The SDA prohibits discrimination against men, as well as against women. It also requires that married people should not be treated less favourably than single people of the same sex.

It should be noted that the provisions of the SDA–and therefore of this Code–apply to the UK-based subsidiaries of foreign companies.

2    The Code gives guidance to employers, trade unions and employment agencies on measures which can be taken to achieve equality. The chances of success of any organisation will clearly be improved if it seeks to develop the abilities of all employees, and the Code shows the close link which exists between equal opportunity and good employment practice. In some cases, an initial cost may be involved, but this should be more than compensated for by better relationships and better use of human resources.

## SMALL BUSINESSES

3    The Code has to deal in general terms and it will be necessary for employers to adapt it in a way appropriate to the size and structure of their organisations. Small businesses, for example, will require much simpler procedures than organisations with complex structures and it may not always be reasonable for them to carry out all the Code's detailed recommendations. In adapting the Code's recommendations, small firms should, however, ensure that their practices comply with the Sex Discrimination Act.

## EMPLOYERS' RESPONSIBILITY

4    **The primary responsibility at law rests with each employer to ensure that there is no unlawful discrimination.** It is important, however, that measures to eliminate discrimination or promote equality of opportunity should be understood and supported by all employees. Employers are therefore recommended to involve their employees in equal opportunity policies.

## INDIVIDUAL EMPLOYEES' RESPONSIBILITY

5    While the main responsibility for eliminating discrimination and providing equal opportunity is that of the employer, individual employees at

all levels have responsibilities too. They must not discriminate or knowingly aid their employer to do so.

## TRADE UNION RESPONSIBILITY

6    The full commitment of trade unions is essential for the elimination of discrimination and for the successful operation of an equal opportunities policy. Much can be achieved by collective bargaining and throughout the Code it is assumed that all the normal procedures will be followed.

7    It is recommended that unions should co-operate in the introduction and implementation of equal opportunities policies where employers have decided to introduce them, and should urge that such policies be adopted where they have not yet been introduced.

8    Trade Unions have a responsibility to ensure that their representatives and members do not unlawfully discriminate on grounds of sex or marriage in the admission or treatment of members. The guidance in this Code also applies to trade unions in their role as employers.

## EMPLOYMENT AGENCIES

9    Employment agencies have a responsibility as suppliers of job applicants to avoid unlawful discrimination on the grounds of sex or marriage in providing services to clients. The guidance in this Code also applies to employment agencies in their role as employers.

## DEFINITIONS

10   For ease of reference, the main employment provisions of the Sex Discrimination Act, including definition of direct and indirect sex and marriage discrimination, are provided in a Legal Annex to this Code.

## PART 1

## THE ROLE OF GOOD EMPLOYMENT PRACTICES IN ELIMINATING SEX AND MARRIAGE DISCRIMINATION

11   This section of the Code describes those good employment practices which will help to eliminate unlawful discrimination. It recommends the establishment and use of consistent criteria for selection, training, promotion, redundancy and dismissal which are made known to all employees. Without this consistency, decisions can be subjective and leave the way open for unlawful discrimination to occur.

## RECRUITMENT

12   It is unlawful: UNLESS THE JOB IS COVERED BY AN EXCEPTION[1]:
TO DISCRIMINATE DIRECTLY OR INDIRECTLY ON THE GROUNDS OF SEX OR
MARRIAGE
- IN THE ARRANGEMENTS MADE FOR DECIDING WHO SHOULD BE
  OFFERED A JOB
- IN ANY TERMS OF EMPLOYMENT
- BY REFUSING OR OMITTING TO OFFER A PERSON EMPLOYMENT

[*Section 6(1)(a); 6(1)(b); 6(1)(c)*]

13   It is therefore recommended that:

(a)   each individual should be assessed according to his or her personal
      capability to carry out a given job. It should not be assumed that
      men only or women only will be able to perform certain kinds of
      work;
(b)   any qualifications or requirements applied to a job which
      effectively inhibit applications from one sex or from married
      people should be retained only if they are justifiable in terms of the
      job to be done;
      [*Section 6(1)(a); together with section 1(1)(b) or 3(1)(b)*]
(c)   any age limits should be retained only if they are necessary for the
      job. An unjustifiable age limit could constitute unlawful indirect
      discrimination, for example, against women who have taken time
      out of employment for child-rearing;
(d)   where trade unions uphold such qualifications or requirements as
      union policy, they should amend that policy in the light of any
      potentially unlawful effect.

### GENUINE OCCUPATIONAL QUALIFICATIONS (GOQs)

14   It is unlawful: EXCEPT FOR CERTAIN JOBS WHEN A PERSON'S SEX IS A
GENUINE OCCUPATIONAL QUALIFICATION (GOQ) FOR THAT JOB to select
candidates on the ground of sex.
[*Section 7(2), 7(3) and 7(4)*]

15   There are very few instances in which a job will qualify for a GOQ on
the ground of sex. However, exceptions may arise, for example, where
considerations of privacy and decency or authenticity are involved. The SDA
expressly states that the need of the job for strength and stamina does not
justify restricting it to men. When a GOQ exists for a job, it applies also to
promotion, transfer, or training for that job, but cannot be used to justify a
dismissal.

---

1     There are a number of exceptions to the requirements of the SDA that employers
      must not discriminate against their employees or against potential employees.

16   In some instances, the GOQ will apply to some of the duties only. A GOQ will not be valid, however, where members of the appropriate sex are already employed in sufficient numbers to meet the employer's likely requirements without undue inconvenience. For example, in a job where sales assistants may be required to undertake changing room duties, it might not be lawful to claim a GOQ in respect of *all* the assistants on the grounds that any of them might be required to undertake changing room duties from time to time.

17   It is therefore recommended that:

– A job for which a GOQ was used in the past should be re-examined if the post falls vacant to see whether the GOQ still applies. Circumstances may well have changed, rendering the GOQ inapplicable.

## SOURCES OF RECRUITMENT

18   It is unlawful: UNLESS THE JOB IS COVERED BY AN EXCEPTION:

– TO DISCRIMINATE ON GROUNDS OF SEX OR MARRIAGE IN THE ARRANGEMENTS MADE FOR DETERMINING WHO SHOULD BE OFFERED EMPLOYMENT WHETHER RECRUITING BY ADVERTISEMENTS, THROUGH EMPLOYMENT AGENCIES, JOBCENTRES, OR CAREER OFFICES.
– TO IMPLY THAT APPLICATIONS FROM ONE SEX OR FROM MARRIED PEOPLE WILL NOT BE CONSIDERED.
[*Section 6(1)(a)*]
– TO INSTRUCT OR PUT PRESSURE ON OTHERS TO OMIT TO REFER FOR EMPLOYMENT PEOPLE OF ONE SEX OR MARRIED PEOPLE UNLESS THE JOB IS COVERED BY AN EXCEPTION.
[Sections 39 and 40]

It is also unlawful WHEN ADVERTISING JOB VACANCIES,

– TO PUBLISH OR CAUSE TO BE PUBLISHED AN ADVERTISEMENT WHICH INDICATES OR MIGHT REASONABLY BE UNDERSTOOD AS INDICATING AN INTENTION TO DISCRIMINATE UNLAWFULLY ON GROUNDS OF SEX OR MARRIAGE.
[*Section 38*]

19   It is therefore recommended that:

### Advertising

(a)   job advertising should be carried out in such a way as to encourage applications from suitable candidates of both sexes. This can be achieved both by the wording of the advertisements and, for example, by placing advertisements in publications likely to reach both sexes. All advertising material and accompanying literature relating to employment or training issues should be reviewed to ensure that it avoids presenting men and women in stereotyped roles. Such stereotyping tends to perpetuate sex segregation in jobs and can also lead people of the opposite sex to believe that they would be unsuccessful in applying for particular jobs;

(b) where vacancies are filled by promotion or transfer, they should be published to all eligible employees in such a way that they do not restrict applications from either sex;

(c) recruitment solely or primarily by word of mouth may unnecessarily restrict the choice of applicants available. The method should be avoided in a workforce predominantly of one sex, if in practice it prevents members of the opposite sex from applying;

(d) where applicants are supplied through trade unions and members of one sex only come forward, this should be discussed with the unions and an alternative approach adopted.

## Careers Service/Schools

20   When notifying vacancies to the Careers Service, employers should specify that these are open to both boys and girls. This is especially important when a job has traditionally been done exclusively or mainly by one sex. If dealing with single sex schools, they should ensure, where possible, that both boys' and girls' schools are approached; it is also a good idea to remind mixed schools that jobs are open to boys and girls.

## SELECTION METHODS

### Tests

21   (a)   If selection tests are used, they should be specifically related to job and/or career requirements and should measure an individual's actual or inherent ability to do or train for the work or career.

(b)   Tests should be reviewed regularly to ensure that they remain relevant and free from any unjustifiable bias, either in content or in scoring mechanism.

### Applications and Interviewing

22   It is unlawful: UNLESS THE JOB IS COVERED BY AN EXCEPTION: TO DISCRIMINATE ON GROUNDS OF SEX OR MARRIAGE BY REFUSING OR DELIBERATELY OMITTING TO OFFER EMPLOYMENT.
[Section 6(1)(c)]

23   It is therefore recommended that:

(a)   employers should ensure that personnel staff, line managers and all other employees who may come into contact with job applicants, should be trained in the provisions of the SDA, including the fact that it is unlawful to instruct or put pressure on others to discriminate;

(b) applications from men and women should be processed in exactly the same way. For example, there should not be separate lists of male and female or married and single applicants. All those handling applications and conducting interviews should be trained in the avoidance of unlawful discrimination and records of interviews kept, where practicable, showing why applicants were or were not appointed;

(c) questions should relate to the requirements of the job. Where it is necessary to assess whether personal circumstances will affect performance of the job (for example, where it involves unsocial hours or extensive travel) this should be discussed objectively without detailed questions based on assumptions about marital status, children and domestic obligations. Questions about marriage plans or family intentions should not be asked, as they could be construed as showing bias against women. Information necessary for personnel records can be collected after a job offer has been made.

## PROMOTION, TRANSFER AND TRAINING

24   It is unlawful: UNLESS THE JOB IS COVERED BY AN EXCEPTION, FOR EMPLOYERS TO DISCRIMINATE DIRECTLY OR INDIRECTLY ON THE GROUNDS OF SEX OR MARRIAGE IN THE WAY THEY AFFORD ACCESS TO OPPORTUNITIES FOR PROMOTION, TRANSFER OR TRAINING.
[Section 6(2)(a)]

25   It is therefore recommended that:

(a) where an appraisal system is in operation, the assessment criteria should be examined to ensure that they are not unlawfully discriminatory and the scheme monitored to assess how it is working in practice;

(b) when a group of workers predominantly of one sex is excluded from an appraisal scheme, access to promotion, transfer and training and to other benefits should be reviewed, to ensure that there is no unlawful indirect discrimination;

(c) promotion and career development patterns are reviewed to ensure that the traditional qualifications are justifiable requirements for the job to be done. In some circumstances, for example, promotion on the basis of length of service could amount to unlawful indirect discrimination, as it may unjustifiably affect more women than men;

(d) when general ability and personal qualities are the main requirements for promotion to a post, care should be taken to consider favourably candidates of both sexes with differing career patterns and general experience;

(e) rules which restrict or preclude transfer between certain jobs should be questioned and changed if they are found to be unlawfully discriminatory. Employees of one sex may be concentrated in sections from which transfers are traditionally restricted without real justification;

(f) policies and practices regarding selection for training, day release and personal development should be examined for unlawful direct and indirect discrimination. Where there is found to be an imbalance in training as between sexes, the cause should be identified to ensure that it is not discriminatory;

(g) age limits for access to training and promotion should be questioned.

## HEALTH AND SAFETY LEGISLATION

26 Equal treatment of men and women may be limited by statutory provisions which require men and women to be treated differently. For example, the Factories Act 1961 places restrictions on the hours of work of female manual employees, although the Health and Safety Executive can exempt employers from these restrictions, subject to certain conditions. The Mines and Quarries Act 1954 imposes limitations on women's work and there are restrictions where there is special concern for the unborn child (e.g. lead and ionising radiation). However the broad duties placed on employers by the Health and Safety at Work, etc., Act 1974 makes no distinctions between men and women. Section 2(1) requires employers to ensure, so far as is reasonably practicable, the health and safety and welfare at work of *all* employees.

SPECIFIC HEALTH AND SAFETY REQUIREMENTS UNDER EARLIER LEGISLATION ARE UNAFFECTED BY THE ACT.

It is therefore recommended that

– company policy should be reviewed and serious consideration given to any significant differences in treatment between men and women, and there should be well-founded reasons if such differences are maintained or introduced.

## TERMS OF EMPLOYMENT, BENEFITS, FACILITIES AND SERVICES

27 It is unlawful: UNLESS THE JOB IS COVERED BY AN EXCEPTION: TO DISCRIMINATE ON THE GROUNDS OF SEX OR MARRIAGE, DIRECTLY OR INDIRECTLY, IN THE TERMS ON WHICH EMPLOYMENT IS OFFERED OR IN AFFORDING ACCESS TO ANY BENEFITS[1], FACILITIES OR SERVICES.
[*Section 6(1)(b), 6(2)(a), 29*]

---

1    Certain provisions relating to death and retirement are exempt from the Act.

28 It is therefore recommended that:

   (a) all terms of employment, benefits, facilities and services are reviewed to ensure that there is no unlawful discrimination on grounds of sex or marriage. For example, part-time work, domestic leave, company cars and benefits for dependants should be available to both male and female employees in the same or not materially different circumstances.

29 In an establishment where part-timers are solely or mainly women, unlawful indirect discrimination may arise if, as a group, they are treated less favourably than other employees without justification.

   It is therefore recommended that:

   (b) where part-time workers do not enjoy pro-rata pay or benefits with full-time workers, the arrangements should be reviewed to ensure that they are justified without regard to sex.

## GRIEVANCES, DISCIPLINARY PROCEDURES AND VICTIMISATION

30 It is unlawful: TO VICTIMISE AN INDIVIDUAL FOR A COMPLAINT MADE IN GOOD FAITH ABOUT SEX OR MARRIAGE DISCRIMINATION OR FOR GIVING EVIDENCE ABOUT SUCH A COMPLAINT.
[*Section 4(1), 4(2) and 4(3)*].

31 It is therefore recommended that:

   (a) particular care is taken to ensure that an employee who has in good faith taken action under the Sex Discrimination Act or the Equal Pay Act does not receive less favourable treatment than other employees, for example by being disciplined or dismissed;
   (b) employees should be advised to use the internal procedures, where appropriate, but this is without prejudice to the individual's right to apply to an industrial tribunal within the statutory time limit, i.e. before the end of the period of three months beginning when the act complained of was done. (There is no time limit if the victimisation is continuing);
   (c) particular care is taken to deal effectively with all complaints of discrimination, victimisation or harassment. It should not be assumed that they are made by those who are over-sensitive.

## DISMISSALS, REDUNDANCIES AND OTHER UNFAVOURABLE TREATMENT OF EMPLOYEES

32 It is unlawful: TO DISCRIMINATE DIRECTLY OR INDIRECTLY ON GROUNDS OF SEX OR MARRIAGE IN DISMISSALS OR BY TREATING AN EMPLOYEE UNFAVOURABLY IN ANY OTHER WAY.
[*Section 6(2)(b)*].

It is therefore recommended that:

(a) care is taken that members of one sex are not disciplined or dismissed for performance or behaviour which would be overlooked or condoned in the other sex;

(b) redundancy procedures affecting a group of employees predominantly of one sex should be reviewed, so as to remove any effects which could be disproportionate and unjustifiable;

(c) conditions of access to voluntary redundancy benefit[1] should be made available on equal terms to male and female employees in the same or not materially different circumstances;

(d) where there is down-grading or short-time working (for example, owing to a change in the nature or volume of an employer's business) the arrangements should not unlawfully discriminate on the ground of sex;

(e) all reasonably practical steps should be taken to ensure that a standard of conduct or behaviour is observed which prevents members of either sex from being intimidated, harassed or otherwise subjected to unfavourable treatment on the ground of their sex.

## PART II

### THE ROLE OF GOOD EMPLOYMENT PRACTICES IN PROMOTING EQUALITY OF OPPORTUNITY

33 This section of the Code describes those employment practices which help to promote equality of opportunity. It gives information about the formulation and implementation of equal opportunities policies. While such policies are not required by law, their value has been recognised by a number of employers who have voluntarily adopted them. Others may wish to follow this example.

#### FORMULATING AN EQUAL OPPORTUNITIES POLICY

34 An equal opportunities policy will ensure the effective use of human resources in the best interests of both the organisation and its employees. It is a commitment by an employer to the development and use of employment procedures and practices which do not discriminate on grounds of sex or marriage and which provide genuine equality of opportunity for all employees. The detail of the policy will vary according to size of the organisations.

---

1　Certain provisions relating to death and retirement are exempt from the Act.

## IMPLEMENTING THE POLICY

35   An equal opportunities policy must be seen to have the active support of management at the highest level. To ensure that the policy is fully effective, the following procedure is recommended:
- (a) the policy should be clearly stated and, where appropriate, included in a collective agreement;
- (b) overall responsibility for implementing the policy should rest with senior management;
- (c) the policy should be made known to all employees and, where reasonably practicable, to all job applicants.

36   Trade unions have a very important part to play in implementing genuine equality of opportunity and they will obviously be involved in the review of established procedures to ensure that these are consistent with the law.

## MONITORING

37   It is recommended that the policy is monitored regularly to ensure that it is working in practice. Consideration could be given to setting up a joint Management/Trade Union Review Committee.

38   In a small firm with a simple structure it may be quite adequate to assess the distribution and payment of employees from personal knowledge.

39   In a large and complex organisation a more formal analysis will be necessary, for example, by sex, grade and payment in each unit. This may need to be introduced by stages as resources permit. Any formal analysis should be regularly updated and available to Management and Trade Unions to enable any necessary action to be taken.

40   Sensible monitoring will show, for example, whether members of one sex:
- (a) do not apply for employment or promotion, or that fewer apply than might be expected;
- (b) are not recruited, promoted or selected for training and development or are appointed/selected in a significantly lower proportion than their rate of application;
- (c) are concentrated in certain jobs, sections or departments.

## POSITIVE ACTION

### Recruitment, Training and Promotion

41   Selection for recruitment or promotion must be on merit, irrespective of sex. However, the Sex Discrimination Act does allow certain steps to redress

the effects of previous unequal opportunities. Where there have been few or no members of one sex in particular work in their employment for the previous 12 months, the Act allows employers to give special encouragement to, and provide specific training for, the minority sex. Such measures are usually described as Positive Action.
[*Section 48*]

42   Employers may wish to consider positive measures such as:

(a)   training their own employees (male or female) for work which is traditionally the preserve of the other sex, for example, training women for skilled manual or technical work;

(b)   positive encouragement to women to apply for management posts – special courses may be needed;

(c)   advertisements which encourage application from the minority sex, but make it clear that selection will be on merit without reference to sex;

(d)   notifying job agencies, as part of a Positive Action Programme that they wish to encourage members of one sex to apply for vacancies, where few or no members of that sex are doing the work in question. In these circumstances, job agencies should tell both men and women about the posts and, in addition, let the under-represented sex know that applications from them are particularly welcome. Withholding information from one sex in an attempt to encourage applications from the opposite sex would be unlawful.

## Other Working Arrangements

43   There are other forms of action which could assist both employer and employee by helping to provide continuity of employment to working parents, many of whom will have valuable experience or skills.

Employers may wish to consider with their employees whether:

(a)   certain jobs can be carried out on a part-time or flexi-time basis;

(b)   personal leave arrangements are adequate and available to both sexes. It should not be assumed that men may not need to undertake domestic responsibilities on occasion, especially at the time of childbirth;

(c)   child-care facilities are available locally or whether it would be feasible to establish nursery facilities on the premises or combine with other employers to provide them;

(d)   residential training could be facilitated for employees with young children. For example, where this type of training is necessary, by informing staff who are selected well in advance to enable them to make childcare and other personal arrangements; employers with their own residential training centres could also consider whether childcare facilities might be provided;

(e)  the statutory maternity leave provisions could be enhanced, for
     example, by reducing the qualifying service period, extending the
     leave period, or giving access to part-time arrangements on return.

These arrangements, and others, are helpful to both sexes but are of
particular benefit to women in helping them to remain in gainful employment
during the years of child-rearing.

# Sex Discrimination Act 1986
## (1986 c. 59)[1]

### Sections, etc. printed

| | | |
|---|---|---|
| 3 | Age of retirement etc.: unfair dismissal | 211 |
| 5 | Discrimination required by public entertainment licences | 211 |
| 6 | Collective agreements and rules of undertakings | 212 |
| 8 | Repeal of Baking Industry (Hours of Work) Act 1954 | 213 |
| 9 | Consequential amendment, repeals and saving | 213 |
| 10 | Short title, commencement and extent | 214 |

**1, 2** ...

### 3 Age of retirement etc.: unfair dismissal

(1) ...

(2) In subsection (6) of section 73 of the said Act of 1978[2] (definitions for the purpose of the provision for reducing a basic award for unfair dismissal), for the words from 'the specified anniversary' to 'her birth' there shall be substituted the words 'the specified anniversary in relation to an employee means the sixty-fourth anniversary of the day of his birth'.

(3) Subsection (2) above shall not affect any award for the unfair dismissal of an employee in relation to whom the effective date of termination (within the meaning of Part V of the said Act of 1978) was before the coming into force of that subsection.

**4** ...

### 5 Discrimination required by public entertainment licences

(1) Without prejudice to the generality of section 1(1) of the Employment Act 1989, nothing in–

(a) any licence granted (whether before or after the coming into force of this section) under Schedule 1 to the Local Government (Miscellaneous Provisions) Act 1982 or Schedule 12 to the London Government Act 1963 (public entertainment licences); or

---

1   The Act came into force in stages: ss 4, 5, 9 (2) and 10 on 7 November 1986; ss 1, 6, 9(1) and (3) on 7 February 1987; ss 7 (for certain purposes) and 8 on 27 February 1987; ss 2 and 3 on 7 November 1987. The text is printed here as amended by the Employment Act 1989. It does not include provisions which amend other statutes printed in this book; the amendments are incorporated at the relevant point in the text of those statutes.

2   The Employment Protection (Consolidation) Act 1978.

(b) any regulations made for the purpose of prescribing the terms, conditions or restrictions on or subject to which any such licence is deemed to be granted,

shall have effect, at any time after the coming into force of this section, so as to require any person to do any act which is rendered unlawful by Part II of the 1975 Act (discrimination in relation to employment) or by so much of Part IV of the 1975 Act as related to acts rendered unlawful by the said Part II.

(2) In this section 'act' has the same meaning as in the 1975 Act.

## 6  Collective agreements and rules of undertakings

(1) Without prejudice to the generality of section 77 of the 1975 Act (which makes provision with respect to the validity and revision of contracts), that section shall apply, as it applies in relation to the term of a contract, to the following, namely–

(a) any term of a collective agreement, including an agreement which was not intended, or is presumed not to have been intended, to be a legally enforceable contract;

(b) any rule made by an employer for application to all or any of the persons who are employed by him or who apply to be, or are, considered by him for employment;

(c) any rule made by an organisation, authority or body to which subsection (2) below applies for application to all or any of its members or prospective members or to all or any of the persons on whom it has conferred authorisations or qualifications or who are seeking the authorisations or qualifications which it has power to confer;

and that section shall so apply whether the agreement was entered into, or the rule made, before or after the coming into force of this section.

(2) This subsection applies to–

(a) any organisation of workers;
(b) any organisation of employers;
(c) any organisation whose members carry on a particular profession or trade for the purposes of which the organisation exists;
(d) any authority or body which can confer an authorisation or qualification which is needed for, or facilitates, engagement in a particular profession or trade.

(3) For the purposes of the said section 77 a term or rule shall be deemed to provide for the doing of an act which would be rendered unlawful by the 1975 Act if–

(a) it provides for the inclusion in any contract of employment of any term which by virtue of an equality clause would fall either to be modified or to be supplemented by an additional term; and

(b)   that clause would not be prevented from operating in relation to that contract by section 1(3) of the Equal Pay Act 1970 (material factors justifying discrimination).

(4)   Nothing in the said section 77 shall affect the operation of any term or rule in so far as it provides for the doing of a particular act in the circumstances where the doing of that act would not be, or be deemed by virtue of subsection (3) above to be, rendered unlawful by the 1975 Act.

(5)   The avoidance by virtue of the said section 77 of any term or rule which provides for any person to be discriminated against shall be without prejudice to the following rights except in so far as they enable any person to require another person to be treated less favourably than himself, namely–

(a)   such of the rights of the person to be discriminated against; and
(b)   such of the rights of any person who will be treated more favourably in direct or indirect consequence of the discrimination,

as are conferred by or in respect of a contract made or modified wholly or partly in pursuance of, or by reference to, that term or rule.

(6)   In this section 'collective agreement' means any agreement relating to one or more of the matters mentioned in section 29(1) of the Trade Union and Labour Relations Act 1974 (meaning of trade dispute), being an agreement made by or on behalf of one or more employers or one or more organisations of employers or associations of such organisations with one or more organisations of workers or associations of such organisations.

(7)   Any expression used in this section and in the 1975 Act has the same meaning in this section as in that Act, and this section shall have effect as if the terms of any service to which Parts II and IV of that Act apply by virtue of subsection (2) of section 85 of that Act (Crown application) were terms of a contract of employment and, in relation to the terms of any such service, as if service for the purposes of any person mentioned in that subsection were employment by that person.

**7**   ...

## 8   Repeal of Baking Industry (Hours of Work) Act 1954

The Baking Industry (Hours of Work) Act 1954 (which imposes restrictions on the hours for which a bakery worker may do work in relation to which restrictions on the working hours of women are removed by virtue of section 7 above) shall cease to have effect.

## 9   Consequential amendment, repeals and saving

(1)   ...

(2)   The enactments mentioned in the Schedule to this Act (which include enactments that are no longer of practical effect) are hereby repealed to the extent specified in the third column of that Schedule.

(3)  Neither the repeal by this Act of section 3 of the Equal Pay Act 1970 (collective agreements and pay structures) nor the amendment made by subsection (1) above shall affect–

(a)  the continuing effect, after the coming into force of that repeal, of any declaration made under that section before the coming into force of that repeal; or

(b)  the operation, at any time after the coming into force of that repeal, of section 5(1) of that Act in so far as it refers to the rules which apply under subsection (4) of the said section 3.

## 10   Short title, commencement and extent

(1)  This Act may be cited as the Sex Discrimination Act 1986.

(2)  Sections 1, 6 and 9(1) and (3) above and Part II of the Schedule to this Act shall come into force at the end of the period of three months beginning with the day on which this Act is passed.

(3)  Subject to subsection (4) below, sections 2, 3 and 8 above and Part III of the Schedule to this Act shall come into force on such day as the Secretary of State may by order made by statutory instrument appoint, and different days may be so appointed for different provisions or for different purposes.

(4)  Except in so far as they come into force at an earlier time under subsection (3) above, sections 2 and 3 shall come into force at the end of the period of twelve months beginning with the day on which this Act is passed.

(5)  This Act does not extend to Northern Ireland.

# Employment Act 1989
## (1989 c. 38)

**Sections, etc. printed**

*Overriding of provisions requiring discrimination
as respects employment or training*

| | | |
|---|---|---|
| 1 | Overriding of statutory requirements which conflict with certain provisions of 1975 Act | 215 |
| 2 | Power of Secretary of State to repeal statutory provisions requiring discrimination as respects employment or training | 216 |

*Circumstances where discrimination as respects employment
or training is permissible*

| | | |
|---|---|---|
| 4 | Exemption for discrimination under certain provisions concerned with the protection of women at work | 217 |
| 5 | Exemption from discrimination in connection with certain educational appointments | 217 |
| 6 | Power of Secretary of State to exempt particular acts of discrimination required by or under statute | 218 |

*Discrimination as respects training*

| | | |
|---|---|---|
| 8 | Power to exempt discrimination in favour of lone parents in connection with training | 219 |

*Overriding of provisions requiring discrimination
as respects employment or training*

## 1 Overriding of statutory requirements which conflict with certain provisions of 1975 Act

(1) Any provision of—

(a) an Act passed before the Sex Discrimination Act 1975, or

(b) an instrument approved or made by or under such an Act (including one approved or made after the passing of the 1975 Act),

shall be of no effect in so far as it imposes a requirement to do an act which would be rendered unlawful by any of the provisions of that Act referred to in subsection (2).

(2) Those provisions are—

(a) Part II (discrimination as respects employment);

(b) Part III (discrimination as respects education etc.) so far as it applies to vocational training; and

(c) Part IV (other unlawful acts) so far as it has effect in relation to the provisions mentioned in paragraphs (a) and (b) above.

(3)   Where in any legal proceedings (of whatever nature) there falls to be determined the question whether subsection (1) operates to negative the effect of any provision in so far as it requires the application by any person of a requirement or condition falling within subsection (1)(b)(i) of section 1 or 3 of the 1975 Act (indirect discrimination on grounds of sex or marital status)–

(a)   it shall be for any party to the proceedings who claims that subsection (1) does not so operate in relation to that provision to show the requirement or condition in question to be justifiable as mentioned in subsection (1)(b)(ii) of that section; and

(b)   the said subsection (1)(b)(ii) shall accordingly have effect in relation to the requirement or condition as if the reference to the person applying it were a reference to any such party to the proceedings.

(4)   Where an Act passed after the 1975 Act, whether before or after the passage of this Act, re-enacts (with or without modification) a provision of an Act passed before the 1975 Act, that provision as re-enacted shall be treated for the purposes of subsection (1) as if it continued to be contained in an Act passed before the 1975 Act.

## 2  Power of Secretary of State to repeal statutory provisions requiring discrimination as respects employment or training

(1)   Where it appears to the Secretary of State that a relevant provision, namely any provision of–

(a)   an Act passed before this Act, or

(b)   an instrument approved or made by or under such an Act (including one approved or made after the passing of this Act),

requires the doing of an act which would (within the meaning of the 1975 Act) constitute an act of discrimination in circumstances relevant for the purposes of any of the provisions of that Act falling within section 1(2) above, he may by order make such provision (whether by amending, repealing or revoking the relevant provision or otherwise) as he considers appropriate for removing any such requirement.

(2)   Subsection (1) shall have effect in relation to a provision to which section 1(1) above applies as if the reference to a relevant provision requiring the doing of an act were a reference to its so requiring but for the operation of section 1(1).

(3)   Any order under this section which makes any amendment, repeal or revocation of a relevant provision within the meaning of subsection (1) may (without prejudice to the generality of section 28(5) below) amend or repeal any provision of this Act by virtue of which acts done in pursuance of the relevant provision are not to be unlawful for the purposes of provisions of the 1975 Act.

(4)  Where an Act passed after this Act re-enacts (with or without modification) a provision of an Act passed before this Act, that provision as re-enacted shall be treated for the purposes of subsection (1) as if it continued to be contained in an Act passed before this Act.

*Circumstances where discrimination as respects employment or training is permissible*

**3**  ...

### 4  Exemption for discrimination under certain provisions concerned with the protection of women at work

(1)  Without prejudice to the operation of section 51 of the 1975 Act (as substituted by section 3(3) above), nothing in–

    (a)  Part II of that Act,

    (b)  Part III of that Act so far as it applies to vocational training, or

    (c)  Part IV of that Act so far as it has effect in relation to the provisions mentioned in paragraphs (a) and (b) above,

shall render unlawful any act done by a person in relation to a woman if it was necessary for that person to do that act in order to comply with any requirement of any of the provisions specified in Schedule 1 to this Act (which are concerned with the protection of women at work).

(2)  Each of the last two entries in that Schedule shall be construed as including a reference to any provision or provisions for the time being having effect in place of the provision or provisions specified in that entry.

(3)  In this section 'woman' means a female person of any age.

### 5  Exemption for discrimination in connection with certain educational appointments

(1)  Nothing in Parts II to IV of the 1975 Act shall render unlawful any act done by a person in connection with the employment of another person as the head teacher or principal of any educational establishment if it was necessary for that person to do that act in order to comply with any requirement of any instrument relating to the establishment that its head teacher or principal should be a member of a particular religious order.

(2)  Nothing in–

    (a)  Part II of the 1975 Act, or

    (b)  Part IV of that Act so far as it has effect in relation to Part II,

shall render unlawful any act done by a person in connection with the employment of another person as a professor in any university if the professorship in question is, in accordance with any Act or instrument relating to the university, either a canon professorship or one to which a canonry is annexed.

(3) Nothing in the provisions of the 1975 Act referred to in subsection (2)(a) or (b) shall render unlawful any act done by a person in connection with the employment of another person as the head, a fellow or any other member of the academic staff of any college, or institution in the nature of a college, in a university if it was necessary for that person to do that act in order to comply with any requirement of any instrument relating to the college or institution that the holder of the position in question should be a woman.

(4) Subsection (3) shall not apply in relation to instruments taking effect after the commencement of that subsection; and section 6(b) of the Interpretation Act 1978 (words importing the feminine gender to include the masculine) shall not apply to that subsection.

(5) The Secretary of State may by order provide that any provision of subsections (1) to (3) shall not have effect in relation to—

(a) any educational establishment or university specified in the order; or

(b) any class or description of educational establishments so specified.

(6) In this section 'educational establishment' means—

(a) any school within the meaning of the Education Act 1944 or the Education (Scotland) Act 1980;

(b) any college, or institution in the nature of a college, in a university; or

(c) any institution to which section 156 of the Educational Reform Act 1988 applies (further and higher education institutions) or any constituent institution of an institution to which that section applies.

(7) Nothing in this section shall be construed as prejudicing the operation of section 19 of the 1975 Act (exemption for discrimination in relation to employment of ministers of religion).

## 6 Power of Secretary of State to exempt particular acts of discrimination required by or under statute

(1) The Secretary of State may by order make such provision as he considers appropriate—

(a) for disapplying subsection (1) of section 1 above in the case of any provision to which it appears to him that that subsection would otherwise apply;

(b) for rendering lawful under any of the provisions of the 1975 Act falling within section 1(2) above acts done in order to comply with any requirement—

(i) of a provision whose effect is preserved by virtue of paragraph (a) above, or

(ii) of an instrument approved or made by or under an Act passed after the 1975 Act but before this Act (including one approved or made after the passing of this Act).

(2) Where an Act passed after this Act re-enacts (with or without modification) a provision of an Act passed as mentioned in sub-paragraph (ii) of subsection (1)(b), that provision as re-enacted shall be treated for the purposes of that sub-paragraph as if it continued to be contained in an Act passed as mentioned in that sub-paragraph.

*Discrimination as respects training*

7 ...

## 8 Power to exempt discrimination in favour of lone parents in connection with training

(1) The Secretary of State may by order provide with respect to–

(a) any specified arrangements made under section 2 of the Employment and Training Act 1973 (functions of the Secretary of State as respects employment and training), or

(b) any specified class or description of training for employment provided otherwise than in pursuance of that section, or

(c) any specified scheme set up under section 1 of the Employment Subsidies Act 1978 (schemes for financing employment),

that this section shall apply to such special treatment afforded to or in respect of lone parents in connection with their participation in those arrangements, or in that training or scheme, as is specified or referred to in the order.

(2) Where this section applies to any treatment afforded to or in respect of lone parents, neither the treatment so afforded nor any act done in the implementation of any such treatment shall be regarded for the purposes of the 1975 Act as giving rise to any discrimination falling within section 3 of that Act (discrimination against married persons for purposes of Part II of that Act).

(3) An order under subsection (1) above may specify or refer to special treatment afforded as mentioned in that subsection–

(a) whether it is afforded by the making of any payment or by the fixing of special conditions for participation in the arrangements, training or scheme in question, or otherwise, and

(b) whether it is afforded by the Secretary of State or by some other person;

and without prejudice to the generality of paragraph (b) of that subsection, any class or description of training for employment specified in such an order by virtue of that paragraph may be framed by reference to the person, or the class or description of persons, by whom the training is provided.

(4)  In this section–

(a)  'employment' and 'training' have the same meaning as in the Employment and Training Act 1973; and

(b)  'lone parent' has the same meaning as it has for the purposes of any regulations made in pursuance of section 20(1)(a) of the Social Security Act 1986 (income support).

**9–30**      ...

## §3  EQUAL PAY AND EQUAL TREATMENT ENFORCEMENT: FURTHER PROVISIONS

## Sex Discrimination (Formal Investigations) Regulations 1975
(SI 1975 No 1993)[1]

### Regulations, etc. printed

| | | |
|---|---|---|
| 1 | Citation and operation | 221 |
| 2 | Interpretation | 221 |
| 3 | Service of notices | 222 |
| 4 | Notice of holding of formal investigation | 222 |
| 5 | Requirement to furnish or give information or produce documents | 222 |
| 6 | Non-discrimination notice | 222 |

#### SCHEDULES

| | |
|---|---|
| Schedule 1: Requirement to Furnish Written Information or Give Oral Evidence and Produce Documents | 222 |
| Schedule 2: Non-discrimination Notice | 223 |

## 1  Citation and operation

These Regulations may be cited as the Sex Discrimination (Formal Investigations) Regulations 1975 and shall come into operation on 29 December 1975.

## 2  Interpretation

(1)  In these Regulations any reference to the Act is a reference to the Sex Discrimination Act 1975.

(2)  Any reference to the Commission, in Regulations 4, 5 and 6 below, is a reference to the Equal Opportunities Commission except that, as respects any of the functions of the Commission in relation to a formal investigation which the Commission have delegated under section 57(3) of the Act, any such reference in Regulation 4 or 5 is a reference to the persons, being either Commissioners or Additional Commissioners, to whom those functions have been so delegated.

(3)  The Interpretation Act 1889 shall apply for the interpretation of these Regulations as it applies for the interpretation of an Act of Parliament.

---

[1]  Made on 3 December 1975 under the Sex Discrimination Act 1975, ss 58(3), 59(1), 67(2) and 82(1), and coming into operation on 29 December 1975. Printed as amended by the Sex Discrimination (Formal Investigations) (Amendment) Regulations 1977 (SI 1977 No 843) which replaced Sch. 2.

### 3  Service of notices

Any reference to a person being served with a notice, in Regulations 4, 5 and 6 below, is a reference to service of the notice on him being effected–

    (a)  by delivering it to him, or

    (b)  by sending it by post to him at his usual or last-known residence or place of business; or

    (c)  where the person is a body corporate or is a trade union or employers' association within the meaning of the Trade Union and Labour Relations Act 1974, by delivering it to the secretary or clerk of the body, union or association at its registered or principal office or by sending it by post to that secretary or clerk at that office; or

    (d)  where the person is acting by a solicitor by delivering it at, or by sending it by post to, the solicitor's address for service.

### 4  Notice of holding of formal investigation

(1)  Where, in pursuance of section 58 of the Act, notice of the holding of a formal investigation falls to be given by the Commission to a person named in the terms of reference for the investigation, that person shall be served with a notice setting out the terms of reference.

(2)  Where the terms of reference for a formal investigation are revised, paragraph (1) shall apply in relation to the revised investigation and terms of reference as it applied to the original.

### 5  Requirement to furnish or give information or produce documents

Where, in pursuance of section 59(1) of the Act, the Commission require a person to furnish written information, give oral information or produce documents, that person shall be served with a notice in the form set out in Schedule 1 to these Regulations or a form to the like effect, with such variations as the circumstances may require.

### 6  Non-discrimination notice

Where, in pursuance of section 67(2) of the Act, the Commission issue a non-discrimination notice, the person to whom it is directed shall be served with a notice in the form set out in Schedule 2 to these Regulations or a form to the like effect, with such variations as the circumstances may require.

SCHEDULES

SCHEDULE 1

REQUIREMENT TO FURNISH WRITTEN INFORMATION
OR GIVE ORAL EVIDENCE AND PRODUCE DOCUMENTS
*(Sex Discrimination Act 1975, s. 59(1))*

To A. B. of

For the purposes of the formal investigation being conducted by the Equal Opportunities Commission ('the Commission') the terms of reference of which [were given to you in a notice dated ...] [are set out in the Schedule hereto], you are hereby required, in pursuance of section 59(1) of the Sex Discrimination Act 1975 ('the Act') and subject to section 59(3) thereof, [to furnish such written information as is hereinafter described, namely, (*description of information*). The said information is to be furnished (*specify the time or times at which, and the manner and form in which, the information is to be furnished*)] [to attend at (*insert time*) on (*insert date*) at (*insert place*) and give oral information about (*or* give oral evidence about, and produce all documents in your possession or control relating to) such matters as are hereinafter specified namely (*specify matters*)].

Dated the ... day of ... 19...

This notice was issued by the [Commission] [Commissioners /Commissioners and Additional Commissioners to whom the Commission have, in pursuance of section 57(3) of the Act and in relation to the investigation, delegated their functions under section 59(1)(a) thereof].

[Service of this notice was authorised by an order made in pursuance of section 59(2)(a) of the Act and dated (*insert date*), a copy of which is attached.]

[Having regard to the terms of reference of the investigation and the provisions of section 59(2)(b)/section 69 of the Act, service of this notice does not require the consent of the Secretary of State.]

C.D.
[Commissioner.]
[Chief Officer (*or other appropriate officer*) of the Commission.]

[SCHEDULE
TERMS OF REFERENCE OF INVESTIGATION]


SCHEDULE 2

NON-DISCRIMINATION NOTICE
*(Sex Discrimination Act 1975, s. 67)*

To A. B. of

Whereas, in the course of a formal investigation, the Equal Opportunities Commission ('the Commission') have become satisfied that you were committing/had committed an act/acts to which section 67(2) of the Sex Discrimination Act 1975 ('the Act') applies, namely (*insert particulars of act or acts*) [and are of the opinion that further such acts are likely to be committed unless changes are made in your practices or other arrangements as respects (*insert particulars*)].

Now, therefore, without prejudice to your other duties under the Act or the Equal Pay Act 1970, you are hereby required, in pursuance of section 67(2) of the Act, not to commit any such act as aforesaid or any other act which is [an unlawful discriminatory act by virtue of (*insert reference to relevant Part or provision of the Act*)] [a contravention of section 37 of the Act] [an act which is a contravention of section 38/39/40 of the Act by reference to Part II/Part III thereof] [an act in breach of a term of a contract under which a person is employed, being a term modified or included by virtue of an equality clause within the meaning of the Equal Pay Act 1970].

In so far as compliance with the aforesaid requirement involves changes in any of your practices or other arrangements, you are further required, in pursuance of the said section 67(2), to inform the Commission [as hereinafter provided] that you have effected those changes and what those changes are [and to take the following steps for the purpose of affording that information to other persons concerned, namely (*specify steps to be taken*)].

[You are further required, in pursuance of section 67(3) of the Act, to furnish the Commission as hereinafter provided with the following information, to enable them to verify your compliance with this notice, namely (*insert description of information required*).]

[The information to be furnished by you to the Commission in pursuance of this notice shall be furnished as follows, namely (*specify the time or times at which, and the manner and form in which, the information, or information of a particular description, is to be furnished*).]

Dated the ... day of ... 19...

This notice was issued by the Commission, the provisions of section 67(5) of the Act having been complied with.

C.D.
[Commissioner.]
[Chief Officer (*or other appropriate officer*) of the Commission.]

# Sex Discrimination (Questions and Replies) Order 1975
## (SI 1975 No 2048)[1]

### Articles, etc. printed

| | | |
|---|---|---|
| 1 | Citation and operation | 225 |
| 2 | Interpretation | 225 |
| 3 | Forms for asking and answering questions | 225 |
| 4 | Period for service of questions—court cases | 226 |
| 5 | Period for service of questions—tribunal cases | 226 |
| 6 | Manner of service of questions and replies | 226 |

### SCHEDULES

Schedule 1: The Sex Discrimination Act 1975, s. 74(1)(a):
Questionnaire of person aggrieved          227
Schedule 2: The Sex Discrimination Act 1975, s. 74(1)(b):
Reply by respondent          227

## 1  Citation and operation

This Order may be cited as the Sex Discrimination (Questions and Replies) Order 1975 and shall come into operation on 29 December 1975.

## 2  Interpretation

(1)  In this Order 'the Act' means the Sex Discrimination Act 1975.

(2)  In this Order any reference to a court is a reference to a county court in England or Wales or a sheriff court in Scotland and any reference to a tribunal is a reference to an industrial tribunal.

(3)  The Interpretation Act 1889 shall apply to the interpretation of this Order as it applies to the interpretation of an Act of Parliament.

## 3  Forms for asking and answering questions

The forms respectively set out in Schedules 1 and 2 to this Order or forms to the like effect with such variation as the circumstances may require are, respectively, hereby prescribed as forms—

(a)  by which a person aggrieved may question a respondent as mentioned in subsection (1)(a) of section 74 of the Act;

(b)  by which a respondent may if he so wishes reply to such questions as mentioned in subsection (1)(b) of that section.

---

[1]  Made on 5 December 1975 under the Sex Discrimination Act 1975, ss 74 and 81(4), and coming into operation on 29 December 1975. Printed as amended by the Sex Discrimination (Questions and Replies) (Amendment) Order 1977 (SI 1977 No 844).

### 4  Period for service of questions–court cases

In proceedings before a court, a question shall only be admissible as evidence in pursuance of section 74(2)(a) of the Act–

(a)  where it was served before those proceedings had been instituted, if it was so served during–
    (i)  the period of six months beginning when the act complained of was done, or
    (ii)  in a case to which section 66(5) of the Act applies, the period of eight months so beginning;]

(b)  where it was served when those proceedings had been instituted, if it was served with the leave of, and within a period specified by, the court.

### 5  Period for service of questions–tribunal cases

In proceedings before a tribunal, a question shall only be admissible as evidence in pursuance of section 74(2)(a) of the Act–

(a)  where it was served before a complaint had been presented to a tribunal, if it was so served within the period of three months beginning when the act complained of was done;

(b)  where it was served when a complaint had been presented to a tribunal, either if it was so served within the period of twenty-one days beginning with the day on which the complaint was presented or if it was so served later with leave given, and within a period specified, by a direction of a tribunal.

### 6  Manner of service of questions and replies

A question and any reply thereto may be served on the respondent or, as the case may be, on the person aggrieved–

(a)  by delivering it to him; or

(b)  by sending it by post to him at his usual or last-known residence or place of business; or

(c)  where the person to be served is a body corporate or is a trade union or employers' association within the meaning of the Trade Union and Labour Relations Act 1974, by delivering it to the secretary or clerk of the body, union or association at its registered or principal office or by sending it by post to the secretary or clerk at that office; or

(d)  where the person to be served is acting by a solicitor, by delivering it at, or by sending it by post to, the solicitor's address for service; or

(e)  where the person to be served is the person aggrieved, by delivering the reply, or sending it by post, to him at his address for reply as stated by him in the document containing the questions.

## SCHEDULES

## SCHEDULE 1

### THE SEX DISCRIMINATION ACT 1975, s. 74 (1)(a)
### QUESTIONNAIRE OF PERSON AGGRIEVED

To ... (*name of person to be questioned*) of ... (*address*)

1.   (1)   I ... (*name of questioner*) of ... (*address*) consider that you may have discriminated against me contrary to the Sex Discrimination Act 1975.

(2)   (*Give date, approximate time and a factual description of the treatment received and of the circumstances leading up to the treatment.*)

(3)   I consider that this treatment may have been unlawful [because ... (*complete if you wish to give reasons, otherwise delete*)].

2.   Do you agree that the statement in paragraph 1(2) above is an accurate description of what happened? If not, in what respect do you disagree or what is your version of what happened?

3.   Do you accept that your treatment of me was unlawful discrimination by you against me?
     If not–
(a)   why not,
(b)   for what reason did I receive the treatment accorded to me, and
(c)   how far did my sex or marital status affect your treatment of me?

4.   (*Any other questions you wish to ask*)

5.   My address for any reply you may wish to give to the questions raised above is [that set out in paragraph 1(1) above] [the following address ...].
... (*signature of questioner*)
... (*date*)

> N.B.: By virtue of section 74 of the Act this questionnaire and any reply are (subject to the provisions of the section) admissible in proceedings under the Act and a court or tribunal may draw any such inference as is just and equitable from a failure without reasonable excuse to reply within a reasonable period, or from an evasive or equivocal reply, including an inference that the person questioned has discriminated unlawfully.

## SCHEDULE 2

### THE SEX DISCRIMINATION ACT 1975, s. 74 (1)(b)
### REPLY BY RESPONDENT

To ... (*name of questioner*) of ... (*address*)

1.    I ... (*name of person questioned*) of ... (*address*) hereby acknowledge receipt of the questionnaire signed by you and dated ... which was served on me on ... (*date*).

2.    [I agree that the statement in paragraph 1(2) of the questionnaire is an accurate description of what happened.]
      [I disagree with the statement in paragraph 1(2) of the questionnaire in that ... ..]

3.    I accept/dispute that my treatment of you was unlawful discrimination by me against you.
      [My reasons for so disputing are ... . The reason why you received the treatment accorded to you and the answers to the other questions in paragraph 3 of the questionnaire are ...].

4.    (*Replies to questions in paragraph 4 of the questionnaire*)

[5.    I have deleted (in whole or in part) the paragraph(s) numbered ... above, since I am unable/unwilling to reply to the relevant questions in the correspondingly numbered paragraph(s) of the questionnaire for the following reasons ... .]
... (*signature of person questioned*)
... (*date*)

# Industrial Tribunals (Non-discrimination Notices Appeals) Regulations 1977
## (SI 1977 No 1094)[1]

**Regulations, etc. printed**

| | | |
|---|---|---|
| 1 | Citation and commencement | 229 |
| 2 | Interpretation | 229 |
| 3 | Proceedings of tribunals | 231 |
| 4 | Proof of decision of tribunal | 231 |

SCHEDULE: RULES OF PROCEDURE

| | | |
|---|---|---|
| 1 | Notice of appeal | 231 |
| 2 | Action upon receipt of notice of appeal | 231 |
| 3 | Power to require attendance of witnesses and production of documents, etc. | 231 |
| 4 | Time and place of hearing | 232 |
| 5 | The hearing | 232 |
| 6 | Written representations | 233 |
| 7 | Right of appearance | 233 |
| 8 | Procedure at hearing | 233 |
| 9 | Decision of tribunal | 234 |
| 10 | Review of tribunal's decision | 234 |
| 11 | Costs | 235 |
| 12 | Miscellaneous powers of tribunal | 235 |
| 13 | Notices, etc. | 236 |

## 1 Citation and commencement

(1) These Regulations may be cited as the Industrial Tribunals (Non-discrimination Notices Appeals) Regulations 1977 and shall come into operation on 5 August 1977.

(2) The Industrial Tribunals (Non-discrimination Notices Appeals) Regulations 1975 shall cease to have effect except in relation to proceedings instituted before that date.

## 2. Interpretation

(1) The Interpretation Act 1889 shall apply to these Regulations as it applies to an Act of Parliament as if these Regulations and the Regulations hereby revoked were Acts of Parliament.

(2) In these Regulations, unless the context otherwise requires, the following expressions have the meaning hereby assigned to them respectively, that is to say—

'the 1974 Act' means the Trade Union and Labour Relations Act 1974 as amended by the Employment Protection Act 1975 and the Trade Union and Labour Relations (Amendment) Act 1976;

---

[1]   Made on 29 June 1977 under para. 21 of Pt III of Sch. 1 to the Trade Union & Labour Relations Act 1974, as amended, and coming into operation on 5 August 1977.

'the 1975 Act' means the Sex Discrimination Act 1975;

'the 1976 Act' means the Race Relations Act 1976;

'appellant' means a person who has appealed to a tribunal under section 68 of the 1975 Act or, as the case may be, under section 59 of the 1976 Act;

'the clerk to the tribunal' means the person appointed by the Secretary of the Tribunals or an Assistant Secretary to act in that capacity at one or more hearings;

'decision' in relation to a tribunal includes a direction under section 68(3) of the 1975 Act or, as the case may be, under section 59(3) of the 1976 Act and any other order which is not an interlocutory order;

'hearing' means a sitting of a tribunal duly constituted for the purpose of receiving evidence, hearing addresses and witnesses or doing anything lawfully requisite to enable the tribunal to reach a decision on any question;

'non-discrimination notice' means a notice under section 67 of the 1975 Act or, as the case may be, under section 58 of the 1976 Act;

'nominated chairman' means a member of the panel of chairmen for the time being nominated by the President;

'the Office of the Tribunals' means the Central Office of the Industrial Tribunals (England and Wales);

'the panel of chairmen' means the panel of persons, being barristers or solicitors of not less than seven years' standing, appointed by the Lord Chancellor in pursuance of Regulation 5(2) of the Industrial Tribunals (England and Wales) Regulations 1965, as amended;

'party' means the appellant and the respondent;

'the President' means the President of the Industrial Tribunals (England and Wales) or the person nominated by the Lord Chancellor to discharge for the time being the functions of the President;

'Regional Office of the Industrial Tribunals' means a regional office which has been established under the Office of the Tribunals for an area specified by the President;

'Register' means the Register kept in pursuance of the Industrial Tribunals (Labour Relations) Regulations 1974;

'respondent' means the Equal Opportunities Commission established under section 53 of the 1975 Act or, as the case may be, the Commission for Racial Equality established under section 43 of the 1976 Act;

'Rule' means a Rule of Procedure contained in the Schedule to these Regulations;

'the Secretary of the Tribunals' and 'an Assistant Secretary of the Tribunals' mean respectively the persons for the time being acting as the Secretary of the Office of the Tribunals and as the Assistant Secretary of a Regional Office of the Industrial Tribunals;

'tribunal' means an industrial tribunal (England and Wales) established in pursuance of the Industrial Tribunals (England and Wales)

Regulations 1965, as amended, and in relation to any proceedings means the tribunal to which the proceedings have been referred by the President or by a nominated chairman.

## 3  Proceedings of tribunals

The Rules of Procedure contained in the Schedule to these Regulations shall have effect in relation to appeals to a tribunal under section 68 of the 1975 Act and under section 59 of the 1976 Act against non-discrimination notices relating to matters arising in England and Wales.

## 4  Proof of decision of tribunals

The production in any proceedings in any court of a document purporting to be certified by the Secretary of the Tribunals to be a true copy of an entry of a decision in the Register shall, unless the contrary is proved, be sufficient evidence of the document and of the facts stated therein.

SCHEDULE

RULES OF PROCEDURE

## 1  Notice of appeal

An appeal shall be commenced not later than six weeks after service of the non-discrimination notice, as specified in section 68(1) of the 1975 Act and in section 59(1) of the 1976 Act, by the appellant sending to the Secretary of the Tribunals a notice of appeal which shall be in writing and shall set out:

   (a)  the name of the appellant and his address for the service of documents;
   (b)  the date of the non-discrimination notice appealed against;
   (c)  the name and address of the respondent;
   (d)  particulars of the requirements appealed against; and
   (e)  the grounds of the appeal.

## 2  Action upon receipt of notice of appeal

Upon receiving a notice of appeal the Secretary of the Tribunals shall enter particulars of it in the Register and shall forthwith send a copy of it to the respondent and inform the parties in writing of the case number of the appeal entered in the Register (which shall thereafter constitute the title of the proceedings) and of the address to which notices and other communications to the Secretary of the Tribunals shall be sent.

## 3  Power to require attendance of witnesses and production of documents, etc.

(1)  A tribunal may on the application of a party made either by notice to the Secretary of the Tribunals or at the hearing–

(a)  require a party to furnish in writing to another party further particulars of the grounds on which he relies and of any facts and contentions relevant thereto;

(b)  grant to a party such discovery or inspection of documents as might be granted by a county court; and

(c)  require the attendance of any person as a witness or require the production of any document relating to the matter to be determined,

and may appoint the time at or within which or the place at which any act required in pursuance of this Rule is to be done.

(2)  The tribunal shall not under paragraph (1) of this Rule require the production of any document certified by the Secretary of State as being a document of which the production would be against the interests of national security.

(3)  A person on whom a requirement has been made under paragraph (1) of this Rule may apply to the tribunal either by notice to the Secretary of the Tribunals or at the hearing to vary or set aside the requirement.

(4)  No such application to vary or set aside shall be entertained in a case where a time has been appointed under paragraph (1) of this Rule in relation to the requirement unless it is made before the time or, as the case may be, expiration of the time so appointed.

(5)  Every document containing a requirement under paragraph (1)(b) or (c) of this Rule shall contain a reference to the fact that under paragraph 21(6) of Part III of Schedule 1 to the 1974 Act any person who without reasonable excuse fails to comply with any such requirement shall be liable on summary conviction to a fine not exceeding £100.

## 4  Time and place of hearing

(1)  The President or a nominated chairman shall fix the date, time and place of the hearing of the appeal and the Secretary of the Tribunals shall not less than 14 days (or such shorter time as may be agreed by him with the parties) before the date so fixed send to each party a notice of hearing which shall include information and guidance as to attendance at the hearing, witnesses and the bringing of documents (if any), representation by another person and written representations.

(2)  Where the President or nominated chairman so directs, the Secretary of the Tribunals shall also send notice of the hearing to such persons as may be directed, but the requirements as to the period of notice contained in the foregoing paragraph of this rule shall not apply to any such notices.

## 5  The hearing

(1)  Any hearing of or in connection with an appeal shall take place in public unless the tribunal on the application of a party decides that a private

hearing is appropriate for the purpose of hearing evidence which relates to matters of such a nature that it would be against the interests of national security to allow the evidence to be given in public or hearing evidence from any person which in the opinion of the tribunal is likely to consist of information the disclosure of which would cause substantial injury to the undertaking of the appellant or of any undertaking in which he works for reasons other than its effect on negotiators with respect to any of the matters mentioned in section 29(1) of the 1974 Act.

(2)  In cases to which the foregoing provisions of this Rule apply, a member of the Council on Tribunals in his capacity as such shall be entitled to attend the hearing.

## 6  Written representations

If a party shall desire to submit representations in writing for consideration by a tribunal at the hearing of the appeal, that party shall send such representation to the Secretary of the Tribunals not less than 7 days before the hearing and shall at the same time send a copy thereof to the other party.

## 7  Right of appearance

At any hearing of or in connection with an appeal a party may appear before the tribunal in person or may be represented by counsel or by a solicitor or by any other person whom he desires to represent him, including in the case of the appellant a representative of a trade union or an employers' association.

## 8  Procedure at hearing

(1)  At any hearing of or in connection with an appeal a party shall be entitled to make an opening statement, to give evidence, to call witnesses, to cross-examine any witnesses called by the other party and to address the tribunal.

(2)  If a party shall fail to appear or to be represented at the time and place fixed for the hearing of an appeal, the tribunal may dispose of the appeal in the absence of that party or may adjourn the hearing to a later date: Provided that before disposing of an appeal in the absence of a party the tribunal shall consider any written representations submitted by that party in pursuance of Rule 6.

(3)  A tribunal may require any witness to give evidence on oath or affirmation and for that purpose there may be administered an oath or affirmation in due form.

## 9  Decision of tribunal

(1)  A decision of a tribunal may be taken by a majority thereof and, if the tribunal shall be constituted of two members only, the chairman shall have a second or casting vote.

(2)  The decision of a tribunal shall be recorded in a document signed by the chairman which shall contain the reasons for the decision.

(3)  The clerk to the tribunal shall transmit the document signed by the chairman to the Secretary of the Tribunals who shall as soon as may be enter it in the Register and shall send a copy of the entry to each of the parties.

(4)  The specification of the reasons for the decision shall be omitted from the Register in any case in which evidence has been heard in private and the tribunal so directs and in that event a specification of the reasons shall be sent to the parties and to any superior court in any proceedings relating to such decision together with the copy of the entry.

(5)  The Register shall be kept at the Office of the Tribunals and shall be open to the inspection of any person without charge at all reasonable hours.

(6)  The chairman of a tribunal shall have power by certificate under his hand to correct in documents recording the tribunal's decisions clerical mistakes or errors arising therein from any accidental slip or omission.

(7)  The clerk to the tribunal shall send a copy of any document so corrected and the certificate of the chairman to the Secretary of the Tribunals who shall as soon as may be make such corrections as may be necessary in the Register and shall send a copy of the corrected entry or of the corrected specification of the reasons, as the case may be, to each of the parties.

(8)  If any decision is–

(a)  corrected under paragraph (6) of this Rule; or
(b)  reviewed, revoked or varied under Rule 10; or
(c)  altered in any way by order of a superior court,

the Secretary of the Tribunals shall alter the entry in the Register to conform with any such certificate or order and shall send a copy of the new entry to each of the parties.

## 10  Review of tribunal's decision

(1)  A tribunal shall have power on the application of a party to review and to revoke or vary by certificate under the chairman's hand any of its decisions in a case in which a county court has power to order a new trial on the grounds that–

(a)  the decision was wrongly made as a result of an error on the part of the tribunal staff; or
(b)  a party did not receive notice of the proceedings leading to the decision; or

(c)  the decision was made in the absence of a party; or

(d)  new evidence has become available since the making of the decision provided that its existence could not have been reasonably known of or foreseen; or

(e)  the interests of justice require such a review.

(2)  An application for the purposes of paragraph (1) of this Rule may be made at the hearing. If the application is not made at the hearing, such application shall be made to the Secretary of the Tribunals at any time from the date of the hearing until 14 days after the date on which the decision was sent to the parties and must be in writing stating the grounds in full.

(3)  An application for the purposes of paragraph (1) of this Rule may be refused by the chairman of the tribunal which decided the case, by the President or by a nominated chairman if in his opinion it has no reasonable prospect of success and he shall state the reasons for his opinion.

(4)  If such an application is not refused under paragraph (3) of this Rule, it shall be heard by the tribunal and if it is granted the tribunal shall either vary its decision or revoke its decision and order a re-hearing.

(5)  The clerk to the tribunal shall send to the Secretary of the Tribunals the certificate of the chairman as to any revocation or variation of the tribunal's decision under this Rule. The Secretary of the Tribunals shall as soon as may be make such correction as may be necessary in the Register and shall send a copy of the entry to each of the parties.


## 11  Costs

(1)  A tribunal may make an order that a party shall pay to another party either a specified sum in respect of the costs of or in connection with an appeal incurred by that other party or, in default of agreement, the taxed amount of those costs.

(2)  Any costs required by an order under this Rule to be taxed may be taxed in the county court according to such of the scales prescribed by the county court rules for proceedings in the county court as shall be directed by the order.

## 12  Miscellaneous powers of tribunal

(1)  Subject to the provision of these Rules, a tribunal may regulate its own procedure.

(2)  A tribunal may, if it thinks fit–

(a)  postpone the day or time fixed for, or adjourn, any hearing;

(b)  before granting an application under Rule 3 or 10 require the party making the application to give notice thereof to the other party;

(c)  either on the application of any person or of its own motion, direct any other person to be joined as a party to the appeal (giving such consequential directions at it considers necessary), but may do so only after having given to the person proposed to be joined a reasonable opportunity of making written or oral objection;

(d) make any necessary amendments to the description of a party in the Register and in other documents relating to the appeal;

(e) if the appellant shall at any time give notice of the abandonment of his appeal, dismiss the appeal;

(f) if the parties agree in writing upon the terms of a decision to be made by the tribunal, decide accordingly.

(3) Any act, other than the hearing of an appeal or of an application for the purposes of Rule 10(1), required or authorised by these Rules to be done by a tribunal may be done by, or on the direction of, the President, the chairman of the tribunal or a nominated chairman.

(4) Rule 11 shall apply to an order dismissing proceedings under paragraph (2) of this Rule.

(5) Any functions of the Secretary of the Tribunals may be performed by an Assistant Secretary of the Tribunals.

**13 Notices, etc.**

(1) Any notice given under these Rules shall be in writing and all notices and documents required or authorised by these Rules to be sent or given to any person hereinafter mentioned may be sent by post (subject to paragraph (3) and (4) of this Rule) or delivered to or at–

(a) in a case of a document directed to the Secretary of the Tribunals, the Office of the Tribunals or such other office as may be notified by the Secretary of the Tribunals to the parties;

(b) in the case of a document directed to a party, his address for service specified in the notice of appeal or in a notice under paragraph (2) of this Rule or (if no address for service is so specified) his last known address or place of business in the United Kingdom or, if the party is a corporation, the corporation's registered or principal office;

(c) in the case of a document directed to any person (other than a person specified in the foregoing provisions of this paragraph), his address or place of business in the United Kingdom, or if such a person is a corporation, the corporation's registered or principal office;

and if sent or given to the authorised representative of a party shall be deemed to have been sent or given to that party.

(2) A party may at any time by notice to the Secretary of the Tribunals and to the other party change his address for service under these Rules.

(3) Where a notice of appeal is not delivered, it shall be sent by the recorded delivery service.

(4)   Where for any sufficient reason service of any document or notice cannot be effected in the manner prescribed under this Rule, the President or a nominated chairman may make an order for substituted service in such manner as he may deem fit and such service shall have the same effect as service in the manner prescribed under this Rule.

# Industrial Tribunals (Rules of Procedure) Regulations 1985
## (SI 1985 No 16)[1]

### Regulations, etc. printed

| | | |
|---|---|---|
| 1 | Citation, commencement and revocation | 238 |
| 2 | Interpretation | 239 |
| 3 | Proceedings of tribunals | 241 |
| 4 | Proof of decisions of tribunals | 241 |

SCHEDULE 1: RULES OF PROCEDURE

| | | |
|---|---|---|
| 1 | Originating application | 241 |
| 2 | Action upon receipt of originating application | 242 |
| 3 | Appearance by respondent | 242 |
| 4 | Power to require further particulars and attendance of witnesses and to grant discovery | 243 |
| 5 | Time and place of hearing and appointment of assessor | 244 |
| 6 | Pre-hearing assessment | 245 |
| 7 | The hearing | 245 |
| 8 | Procedure at hearing | 246 |
| 9 | Decision of tribunal | 247 |
| 10 | Review of tribunal's decision | 248 |
| 11 | Costs | 249 |
| 12 | Miscellaneous powers of tribunal | 251 |
| 13 | Extension of time and directions | 252 |
| 14 | Joinder and representative respondents | 252 |
| 15 | Consolidation of proceedings | 252 |
| 16 | Transfer of proceedings | 253 |
| 17 | Notices, etc. | 253 |

SCHEDULE 2: COMPLEMENTARY RULES OF PROCEDURE

*For use only in proceedings involving an equal value claim*

| | | |
|---|---|---|
| 4 | Power to require further particulars and attendance of witnesses and to grant discovery | 255 |
| 7A | Procedure relating to expert's report | 256 |
| 8 | Procedure at hearing | 258 |
| 9 | Decision of tribunal | 260 |
| 11 | Costs | 261 |
| 12 | Miscellaneous powers of tribunal | 262 |
| 17 | Notices, etc. | 264 |

## 1 Citation, commencement and revocation

(1) These Regulations may be cited as the Industrial Tribunals (Rules of Procedure) Regulations 1985 (and the Rules of Procedure contained in Schedules 1 and 2 of these Regulations may be referred to as the Industrial

---

[1] Made on 9 January 1985 under para. 1 of Sch. 9 of the Employment Protection (Consolidation) Act 1978, and coming into operation on 1 March 1985.

Tribunals Rules of Procedure 1985 and the Industrial Tribunals Complementary Rules of Procedure 1985 respectively). They shall come into operation on 1 March 1985.

(2) The Industrial Tribunals (Rules of Procedure) Regulations 1980 and the Industrial Tribunals (Rules of Procedure) (Equal Value Amendment) Regulations 1983 shall cease to have effect on 1 March 1985 except in relation to proceedings instituted before that date.

## 2 Interpretation

In these Regulations, unless the context otherwise requires, the following expressions have the meaning hereby assigned to them respectively, that is to say–

'the 1966 Act' means the Docks and Harbours Act 1966;

'the 1978 Act' means the Employment Protection (Consolidation) Act 1978;

'applicant' means a person who in pursuance of Rule 1 has presented an originating application to the Secretary of the Tribunal for a decision of a tribunal and includes:

(a) the Secretary of State, the Board or a licensing authority,

(b) a claimant or complainant,

(c) in the case of proceedings under section 51 of the 1966 Act, a person on whose behalf an originating application has been sent by a trade union, and

(d) in relation to interlocutory applications under these Rules, a person who seeks any relief;

'the Board' means the National Dock Labour Board as reconstituted under the Dock Work Regulation Act 1976;

'the clerk to the tribunal' means the person appointed by the Secretary of the Tribunals or an Assistant Secretary to act in that capacity at one or more hearings;

'court' means a magistrates' court or the Crown Court;

'decision' in relation to a tribunal includes a declaration, an order (other than an interlocutory order), a recommendation or an award of the tribunal but does not include an opinion given pursuant to a pre-hearing assessment held under Rule 6;

'the Equal Pay Act' means the Equal Pay Act 1970;

'equal value claim' means a claim by an applicant which rests upon entitlement to the benefit of an equality clause by virtue of the operation of section 1(2)(c) of the Equal Pay Act;

'expert' means a member of the panel of independent experts within the meaning of section 2A(4) of the Equal Pay Act;

'hearing' means a sitting of a tribunal duly constituted for the purpose of receiving evidence, hearing addresses and witnesses or doing anything lawfully requisite to enable the tribunal to reach a decision on any question;

'licensing authority' means a body having the function of issuing licences under the 1966 Act;

'the Office of the Tribunals' means the Central Office of the Industrial Tribunals (England and Wales);

'the panel of chairmen' means the panel of persons, being barristers or solicitors of not less than seven years' standing, appointed by the Lord Chancellor in pursuance of Regulation 5(2) of the Industrial Tribunals (England and Wales) Regulations 1965;

'party' in relation to proceedings under section 51 of the 1966 Act means the applicant and the Board or the licensing authority with which or (as the case may be) any person with whom it appears to the applicant that he is in dispute about a question to which that section applies and, in a case where such a question is referred to a tribunal by a court, any party to the proceedings before the court in which the question arose;

'person entitled to appear' in relation to proceedings under section 51 of the 1966 Act means a party and any person who, under subsection (5) of that section, is entitled to appear and be heard before a tribunal in such proceedings;

'the President' means the President of the Industrial Tribunals (England and Wales) or the person nominated by the Lord Chancellor to discharge for the time being the functions of the President;

'the Race Relations Act' means the Race Relations Act 1976;

'Regional Chairman' means the chairman appointed by the President to take charge of the due administration of justice by tribunals in an area specified by the President, or a person nominated either by the President or the Regional Chairman to discharge for the time being the functions of the Regional Chairman;

'Regional Office of the Industrial Tribunals' means a regional office which has been established under the Office of the Tribunals for an area specified by the President;

'Register' means the Register of Applications and Decisions kept in pursuance of these Regulations;

'report' means a report required by a tribunal to be prepared by an expert, pursuant to section 2A(1)(b) of the Equal Pay Act;

'respondent' means a party to the proceedings before a tribunal other than the applicant, and other than the Secretary of State in proceedings under Parts III and VI of the 1978 Act in which he is not cited as the person against whom relief is sought;

'Rule' means, in Schedule 1 to these Regulations, a Rule of Procedure contained in the Schedule, and, in Schedule 2 to these Regulations, a Rule of Procedure contained in Schedule 1 or Schedule 2 as appropriate;

'the Secretary of the Tribunals' and 'an Assistant Secretary of the Tribunals' mean respectively the persons for the time being acting as the Secretary of the Office of the Tribunals and as the Assistant Secretary of a Regional Office of the Industrial Tribunals;

'the Sex Discrimination Act' means the Sex Discrimination Act 1975;

'tribunal' means an industrial tribunal (England and Wales) established in pursuance of the Industrial Tribunals (England and Wales) Regulations 1965 and in relation to any proceedings means the tribunal to which the proceedings have been referred by the President or by a Regional Chairman.

## 3  Proceedings of tribunals

(1) Except where separate Rules of Procedure made under the provisions of any enactment are applicable and subject to paragraph (2) of this Regulation, the Rules of Procedure contained in Schedule 1 to these Regulations shall have effect in relation to all proceedings before a tribunal where–

(a) the respondent or one of the respondents resides or carries on business in England or Wales; or

(b) had the remedy been by way of action in the county court, the cause of action would have arisen wholly or in part in England or Wales; or

(c) the proceedings are to determine a question which has been referred to the tribunal by a court in England or Wales; or

(d) in proceedings under the 1966 Act they are in relation to a port in England or Wales.

(2) In any such proceedings before a tribunal involving an equal value claim the Rules of Procedure contained in Schedule 2 to these Regulations (including Rule 7 A) shall replace Rules 4, 8, 9, 11, 12 and 17 in Schedule 1.

## 4  Proof of decisions of tribunals

The production in any proceedings in any court of a document purporting to be certified by the Secretary of the Tribunals to be a true copy of an entry of a decision in the Register shall, unless the contrary is proved, be sufficient evidence of the document and of the facts stated therein.

SCHEDULE 1

RULES OF PROCEDURE

## 1  Originating application

(1) Proceedings for the determination of any matter by a tribunal shall be instituted by the applicant (or, where applicable, by a court) presenting to the Secretary of the Tribunals an originating application, which shall be in writing and shall set out:

(a) the name and address of the applicant; and

(b) the names and addresses of the person or persons against whom relief is sought or (where applicable) of the parties to the proceedings before the court; and

(c)   the grounds, with particulars thereof, on which relief is sought, or in proceedings under section 51 of the 1966 Act the question for determination and (except where the question is referred by a court) the grounds on which relief is sought.

(2)   Where the Secretary of the Tribunals is of the opinion that the originating application does not seek or on the facts stated therein cannot entitle the applicant to a relief which a tribunal has power to give, he may give notice to that effect to the applicant stating the reasons for his opinion and informing him that the application will not be registered unless he states in writing that he wishes to proceed with it.

(3)   An application as respects which a notice has been given in pursuance of the preceding paragraph shall not be treated as having been received for the purposes of Rule 2 unless the applicant intimates in writing to the Secretary of the Tribunals that he wishes to proceed with it; and upon receipt of such an intimation the Secretary of the Tribunals shall proceed in accordance with that Rule.

## 2   Action upon receipt of originating application

Upon receiving an originating application the Secretary of the Tribunal shall enter particulars of it in the Register and shall forthwith send a copy of it to the respondent and inform the parties in writing of the case number of the originating application entered in the Register (which shall thereafter constitute the title of the proceedings) and of the address to which notices and other communications to the Secretary of the Tribunals shall be sent. Every copy of the originating application sent by the Secretary of the Tribunals under this Rule shall be accompanied by a written notice which shall include information, as appropriate to the case, about the means and time for entering an appearance, the consequences of failure to do so, and the right to receive a copy of the decision. The Secretary of the Tribunals shall also notify the parties that in all cases under the provisions of any enactment providing for conciliation the services of a conciliation officer are available to them.

## 3   Appearance by respondent

(1)   A respondent shall within 14 days of receiving the copy originating application enter an appearance to the proceedings by presenting to the Secretary of the Tribunals a written notice of appearance setting out his full name and address and stating whether or not he intends to resist the application and, if so, setting out sufficient particulars to show on what grounds. Upon receipt of a notice of appearance the Secretary of the Tribunals shall forthwith send a copy of it to any other party.

(2)   A respondent who has not entered an appearance shall not be entitled to take any part in the proceedings except–

   (i)    to apply under Rule 13(1) for an extension of the time appointed by this Rule for entering an appearance;

   (ii)   to make an application under Rule 4(1)(i);

   (iii) to make an application under Rule 10(2) in respect of Rule 10(1)(b);

   (iv)  to be called as a witness by another person;

   (v)   to be sent a copy of a document or corrected entry in pursuance of Rule 9(6), 9(10) or 10(5).

(3)  A notice of appearance which is presented to the Secretary of the Tribunals after the time appointed by this Rule for entering appearances shall be deemed to include an application under Rule 13(1) (by the respondent who has presented the notice of appearance) for an extension of the time so appointed. Without prejudice to Rule 13(4), if the tribunal grants the application (which it may do notwithstanding that the grounds of the application are not stated) the Secretary of the Tribunals shall forthwith send a copy of the notice of appearance to any other party. The tribunal shall not refuse an extension of time under this Rule unless it has sent notice to the person wishing to enter an appearance giving him an opportunity to show cause why the extension should be granted.

## 4  Power to require further particulars and attendance of witnesses and to grant discovery

(1)  A tribunal may:

(a)  subject to Rule 3(2), on the application of a party to the proceedings made either by notice to the Secretary of the Tribunals or at the hearing of the originating application, or

(b)  in relation to sub-paragraph (i) of this paragraph, if it thinks fit, of its own motion:

   (i)    require a party to furnish in writing to the person specified by the tribunal further particulars of the grounds on which he or it relies and of any facts and contentions relevant thereto;

   (ii)   grant to the person making the application such discovery or inspection (including the taking of copies) of documents as might be granted by a county court; and

   (iii) require the attendance of any person (including a party to the proceedings) as a witness, wherever such person may be within Great Britain, and may, if it does so require the attendance of a person, require him to produce any document relating to the matter to be determined;

and may appoint the time at or within which or the place at which any act required in pursuance of this Rule is to be done.

(2)  A party on whom a requirement has been made under paragraph (1)(i) or (1)(ii) of this Rule on an *ex parte* application, or (in relation to a requirement under paragraph 1(i)) on the tribunal's own motion, and a person on whom a requirement has been made under paragraph (1)(iii) may apply to

the tribunal by notice to the Secretary of the Tribunals before the appointed time at or within which the requirement is to be complied with to vary or set aside the requirement. Notice of an application under this paragraph to vary or set aside a requirement shall be given to the parties (other than the party making the application) and, where appropriate, in proceedings which may involve payments out of the Redundancy Fund or Maternity Pay Fund, the Secretary of State if not a party.

(3)  Every document containing a requirement under paragraph (1)(ii) or (1)(iii) of this Rule shall contain a reference to the fact that, under paragraph 1(7) of Schedule 9 to the 1978 Act, any person who without reasonable excuse fails to comply with any such requirement shall be liable on summary conviction to a fine, and the document shall state the amount of the current maximum fine.

(4)  If the requirement under paragraph (1)(i) or (1)(ii) of this Rule is not complied with, a tribunal, before or at the hearing, may dismiss the whole or part of the originating application, or, as the case may be, strike out the whole or part of the notice of appearance, and, where appropriate, direct that a respondent shall be debarred from defending altogether: Provided that a tribunal shall not so dismiss or strike out or give such a direction unless it has sent notice to the party who has not complied with the requirement giving him an opportunity to show cause why such should not be done.

## 5  Time and place of hearing and appointment of assessor

(1)  The President or a Regional Chairman shall fix the date, time and place of the hearing of the originating application and the Secretary of the Tribunals shall (subject to Rule 3(2)) not less than 14 days (or such shorter time as may be agreed by him with the parties) before the date so fixed send to each party a notice of hearing which shall include information and guidance as to attendance at the hearing, witnesses and the bringing of documents (if any), representation by another person and written representations.

(2)  In any proceedings under the 1966 Act in which the President or a Regional Chairman so directs, the Secretary of the Tribunals shall also take such of the following steps as may be so directed, namely–

(a)  publish in one or more newspapers circulating in the locality in which the port in question is situated notice of the hearing;

(b)  send notice of the hearing to such persons as may be directed;

(c)  post notices of the hearing in a conspicuous place or conspicuous places in or near the port in question;

but the requirement as to the period of notice contained in paragraph (1) of this Rule shall not apply to any such notices.

(3)  Where in the case of any proceedings it is provided for one or more assessors to be appointed, the President or a Regional Chairman may, if he

thinks fit, appoint a person or persons having special knowledge or experience in relation to the subject matter of the originating application to sit with the tribunal as assessor or assessors.

## 6  Pre-hearing assessment

(1) A tribunal may at any time before the hearing (either, subject to Rule 3(2), on the application of a party to the proceedings made by notice to the Secretary of the Tribunals or of its own motion) consider, by way of a pre-hearing assessment, the contents of the originating application and entry of appearance, any representations in writing which have been submitted and any oral argument advanced by or on behalf of a party.

(2) If upon a pre-hearing assessment, the tribunal considers that the originating application or the contentions or any particular contention of a party appear or, as the case may be, appears to have no reasonable prospect of success, it may indicate that in its opinion, if the originating application shall not be withdrawn or the contentions or contention of the party shall be persisted in up to or at the hearing, the party in question may have an order for costs made against him at the hearing under the provisions of Rule 11. A pre-hearing assessment shall not take place unless the tribunal has sent notice to the parties to the proceedings giving them (and, where appropriate, in proceedings which may involve payments out of the Redundancy Fund or Maternity Pay Fund, the Secretary of State, if not a party) an opportunity to submit representations in writing and to advance oral argument at the pre-hearing assessment if they so wish.

(3) Any indication of opinion made in accordance with paragraph (2) of this Rule shall be recorded in a document signed by the chairman, a copy of which shall be sent to the parties to the proceedings and a copy of which shall be available to the tribunal at the hearing.

(4) Where a tribunal has indicated its opinion in accordance with paragraph (2) of this Rule no member thereof shall be a member of the tribunal at the hearing.

## 7  The hearing

(1) Any hearing of or in connection with an originating application shall take place in public unless in the opinion of the tribunal a private hearing is appropriate for the purpose of hearing evidence which relates to matters of such a nature that it would be against the interests of national security to allow the evidence to be given in public or hearing evidence from any person which in the opinion of the tribunal is likely to consist of–

    (a)  information which he could not disclose without contravening a prohibition imposed by or under any enactment; or

    (b)  any information which has been communicated to him in confidence, or which he has otherwise obtained in consequence of the confidence reposed in him by another person; or

(c) information the disclosure of which would cause substantial injury to any undertaking of his or any undertaking in which he works for reasons other than its effect on negotiations with respect to any of the matters mentioned in section 29(1) of the Trade Union and Labour Relations Act 1974.

(2) A member of the Council on Tribunals shall be entitled to attend any hearing taking place in private in his capacity as such member.

(3) Subject to Rule 3(2), if a party shall desire to submit representations in writing for consideration by a tribunal at the hearing of the originating application that party shall present such representations to the Secretary of the Tribunals not less than 7 days before the hearing and shall at the same time send a copy to the other party or parties.

(4) Where a party has failed to attend or be represented at the hearing (whether or not he has sent any representations in writing) the contents of his originating application or, as the case may be, of his entry of appearance may be treated by a tribunal as representations in writing.

(5) The Secretary of State if he so elects shall be entitled to apply under Rule 4(1), 13(1) and (2), 15 and 16(1) and to appear as if he were a party and be heard at any hearing of or in connection with an originating application in proceedings in which he is not a party which may involve payments out of the Redundancy Fund or Maternity Pay Fund.

(6) Subject to Rule 3(2), at any hearing of or in connection with an originating application a party and any person entitled to appear may appear before the tribunal and may be heard in person or be represented by counsel or by a solicitor or by a representative of a trade union or an employers' association or by any other person whom he desires to represent him.

## 8 Procedure at hearing

(1) The tribunal shall conduct the hearing in such manner as it considers most suitable to the clarification of the issues before it and generally to the just handling of the proceedings; it shall so far as appears to it appropriate seek to avoid formality in its proceedings and it shall not be bound by any enactment or rule of law relating to the admissibility of evidence in proceedings before the courts of law.

(2) Subject to paragraph (1) of this Rule, at the hearing of the originating application a party (unless disentitled by virtue of Rule 3(2)), the Secretary of State (if, not being a party, he elects to appear as provided in Rule 7(5)) and any other person entitled to appear shall be entitled to give evidence, to call witnesses, to question any witnesses and to address the tribunal.

(3) If a party shall fail to appear or to be represented at the time and place fixed for the hearing, the tribunal may, if that party is an applicant dismiss, or, in any case, dispose of the application in the absence of that

party or may adjourn the hearing to a later date: Provided that before deciding to dismiss or disposing of any application in the absence of a party the tribunal shall consider any representations submitted by that party in pursuance of Rule 7(3).

(4) A tribunal may require any witness to give evidence on oath or affirmation and for that purpose there may be administered an oath or affirmation in due form.

## 9 Decision of tribunal

(1) A decision of a tribunal may be taken by a majority thereof and, if the tribunal shall be constituted of two members only, the chairman shall have a second or casting vote.

(2) The decision of a tribunal, which may be given orally at the end of a hearing or reserved, shall be recorded in a document signed by the chairman.

(3) The tribunal shall give reasons, which may be in full or in summary form, for its decision.

(4) The reasons for the decision of the tribunal shall be recorded in a document signed by the chairman, which shall also contain a statement as to whether the reasons are in full or in summary form.

(5) Where:

(a) the proceedings before the tribunal involved the determination of an issue arising under or relating to section 51 of the 1966 Act, the Equal Pay Act, the Sex Discrimination Act, the Race Relations Act, sections 23, 58, 59(a) or 77 of the 1978 Act, or sections 4 or 5 of the Employment Act 1980; or

(b) the reasons have been given in summary form and it appears at any time to the tribunal that the reasons should be given in full; or

(c) a request that the reasons be given in full is made orally at the hearing by a party or by a person entitled to appear who did so appear; or

(d) such a request is made in writing within 21 days of the date on which the document recording the reasons in summary form was sent to the parties;

the reasons shall be recorded in full in a document signed by the chairman.

(6) The clerk to the tribunal shall transmit any document referred to in paragraphs (2), (4) and (5) of this Rule to the Secretary of the Tribunals who shall as soon as may be enter it in the Register and shall send a copy of the entry to each of the parties and to the persons entitled to appear who did so appear and, where the originating application was sent to a tribunal by a court, to that court.

(7) Any document referred to in paragraphs (4) and (5) of this Rule shall be omitted from the Register in any case in which evidence has been

heard in private and the tribunal so directs and in that event any such document shall be sent to the parties and to any superior court in any proceedings relating to such decision together with the copy of the entry.

(8) The Register shall be kept at the Office of the Tribunals and shall be open to the inspection of any person without charge at all reasonable hours.

(9) Clerical mistakes in any document referred to in paragraphs (2), (4) and (5) of this Rule, or errors arising in such a document from an accidental slip or omission, may at any time be corrected by the chairman by certificate under his hand.

(10) The clerk to the tribunal shall send a copy of any document so corrected and the certificate of the chairman to the Secretary of the Tribunals who shall as soon as may be make such correction as may be necessary in the Register and shall send a copy of the corrected entry or of any corrected document containing reasons for the tribunal's decision, as the case may be, to each of the parties and, in the case of a corrected entry, to the persons entitled to appear who did so appear and, where the originating application was sent to the tribunal by a court, to that court.

(11) If any decision is–

(a) corrected under paragraph (9) of this Rule,

(b) reviewed, revoked or varied under Rule 10, or

(c) altered in any way by order of a superior court,

the Secretary of the Tribunals shall alter the entry in the Register to conform with any such certificate or order and shall send a copy of the new entry to each of the parties and to the persons entitled to appear who did so appear and, where the originating application was sent to the tribunal by a court, to that court.

(12) Where by this Rule a document is required to be signed by the chairman but by reason of death or incapacity the chairman is unable to sign such document it shall be signed by the other members of the tribunal, who shall certify that the chairman is unable to sign.

## 10   Review of tribunal's decision

(1) A tribunal shall have power to review and to revoke or vary by certificate under the chairman's hand any decision on the grounds that–

(a) the decision was wrongly made as a result of an error on the part of the tribunal staff; or

(b) a party did not receive notice of the proceedings leading to the decision; or

(c) the decision was made in the absence of a party or person entitled to be heard; or

(d) new evidence has become available since the conclusion of the hearing to which the decision relates provided that its existence could not have been reasonably known of or foreseen; or

(e)   the interests of justice require such a review.

(2)   An application for the purposes of paragraph (1) of this Rule may be made at the hearing. If the application is not made at the hearing, such application shall be made to the Secretary of the Tribunals at any time from the date of the hearing until 14 days after the date on which the decision was sent to the parties and must be in writing stating the grounds in full.

(3)   An application for the purposes of paragraph (1) of this Rule may be refused by the President or by the chairman of the tribunal which decided the case or by a Regional Chairman if in his opinion it has no reasonable prospect of success.

(4)   If such an application is not refused under paragraph (3) of this Rule it shall be heard by the tribunal which decided the case or–

(a)   where it is not practicable for it to be heard by that tribunal, or
(b)   where the decision was made by a chairman acting alone under Rule 12(4),

by a tribunal appointed either by the President or a Regional Chairman, and if the application is granted the tribunal shall proceed to a review of the decision and, having reviewed it, may confirm, vary or revoke that decision, and if the tribunal revokes the decision it shall order a re-hearing before either the same or a differently constituted tribunal.

(5)   The clerk to the tribunal shall send to the Secretary of the Tribunals the certificate of the chairman as to any revocation or variation of the tribunal's decision under this Rule. The Secretary of the Tribunals shall as soon as may be make such correction as may be necessary in the Register and shall send a copy of the entry to each of the parties and to the persons entitled to appear who did so appear and where the originating application was sent to a tribunal by a court, to that court.

## 11   Costs

(1)   Subject to paragraphs (2), (3) and (4) of this Rule, a tribunal shall not normally make an award in respect of the costs or expenses incurred by a party to the proceedings but where in its opinion a party (and if he is a respondent whether or not he has entered an appearance) has in bringing or conducting the proceedings acted frivolously, vexatiously or otherwise unreasonably the tribunal may make–

(a)   an order that that party shall pay to another party (or to the Secretary of State if, not being a party, he has acted as provided in Rule 7(5)) either a specified sum in respect of the costs or expenses incurred by that other party (or, as the case may be, by the Secretary of State) or the whole or part of those costs or expenses as taxed (if not otherwise agreed);
(b)   an order that that party shall pay to the Secretary of State the whole, or any part, of any allowances (other than allowances paid

to members of tribunals or assessors) paid by the Secretary of State under paragraph 10 of Schedule 9 to the 1978 Act to any person for the purposes of, or in connection with, his attendance at the tribunal.

(2) Where the tribunal has on the application of a party to the proceedings postponed the day or time fixed for or adjourned the hearing, the tribunal may make orders against or, as the case may require, in favour of that party as at paragraph (1)(a) and (b) of this Rule as respects any costs or expenses incurred or any allowances paid as a result of the postponement or adjournment.

(3) Where, on a complaint of unfair dismissal in respect of which–

(i)   the applicant has expressed a wish to be reinstated or re-engaged which has been communicated to the respondent at least 7 days before the hearing of the complaint, or

(ii)  the proceedings arise out of the respondent's failure to permit the applicant to return to work after an absence due to pregnancy or confinement,

any postponement or adjournment of the hearing has been caused by the respondent's failure, without a special reason, to adduce reasonable evidence as to the availability of the job from which the applicant was dismissed, or as the case may be, which she held before her absence, or of comparable or suitable employment, the tribunal shall make orders against that respondent as at paragraph (1)(a) and (b) of this Rule as respects any costs or expenses incurred or any allowances paid as a result of the postponement or adjournment.

(4) In any proceedings under the 1966 Act a tribunal may make–

(a)   an order that a party, or any other person entitled to appear who did so appear, shall pay to another party or such person either a specified sum in respect of the costs or expenses incurred by that other party or person or the whole or part of those costs or expenses as taxed (if not otherwise agreed);

(b)   an order that a party, or any other person entitled to appear who did so appear, shall pay to the Secretary of State a specified sum in respect of the whole, or any part, of any allowances (other than allowances paid to members of tribunals) paid by the Secretary of State under paragraph 10 of Schedule 9 to the 1978 Act to any person for the purpose of, or in connection with, his attendance at the tribunal.

(5) Any costs required by an order under this Rule to be taxed may be taxed in the county court according to such of the scales prescribed by the county court rules for proceedings in the county court as shall be directed by the order.

## 12   Miscellaneous powers of tribunal

(1)   Subject to the provisions of these Rules, a tribunal may regulate its own procedure.

(2)   A tribunal may, if it thinks fit–

(a)   extend the time appointed by or under these Rules for doing any act notwithstanding that the time appointed may have expired;

(b)   postpone the day or time fixed for, or adjourn, any hearing (particularly as respects cases under the provisions of any enactment providing for conciliation for the purpose of giving an opportunity for the complaint to be settled by way of conciliation and withdrawn);

(c)   if the applicant shall at any time give notice of the withdrawal of his originating application, dismiss the proceedings;

(d)   except in proceedings under the 1966 Act, if both or all the parties (and the Secretary of State, if, not being a party, he has acted as provided in Rule 7(5)) agree in writing upon the terms of a decision to be made by the tribunal, decide accordingly;

(e)   subject to the Proviso below, at any stage of the proceedings order to be struck out or amended any originating application or notice of appearance or anything in such application or notice of appearance on the grounds that it is scandalous, frivolous or vexatious;

(f)   subject to the Proviso below, on the application of the respondent, or of its own motion, order to be struck out any originating application for want of prosecution;

Provided that before making any order under (e) or (f) above the tribunal shall send notice to the party against whom it is proposed that any such order should be made giving him an opportunity to show cause why such an order should not be made.

(3)   Subject to Rule 4(2), a tribunal may, if it thinks fit, before granting an application under Rule 4 or Rule 13 require the party (or, as the case may be, the Secretary of State) making the application to give notice of it to the other party or parties. The notice shall give particulars of the application and indicate the address to which and the time within which any objection to the application shall be made being an address and time specified for the purposes of the application by the tribunal.

(4)   Any act other than the holding of a pre-hearing assessment under Rule 6, the hearing of an originating application or the making of an order under Rule 10(1), required or authorised by these Rules to be done by a tribunal may be done by, or on the direction of, the President or the chairman of the tribunal, or any chairman being a member of the panel of chairmen.

(5)   Rule 11 shall apply to an order dismissing proceedings under paragraph (2)(c) of this Rule.

(6)   Any functions of the Secretary of the Tribunals other than that mentioned in Rule 1(2) may be performed by an Assistant Secretary of the Tribunals.

### 13   Extension of time and directions

(1)   An application to a tribunal for an extension of the time appointed by these Rules for doing any act may be made by a party either before or after the expiration of any time so appointed.

(2)   Subject to Rule 3(2), a party may at any time apply to a tribunal for directions on any matter arising in connection with the proceedings.

(3)   An application under the foregoing provisions of this Rule shall be made by presenting to the Secretary of the Tribunals a notice of application, which shall state the title of the proceedings and shall set out the grounds of the application.

(4)   The Secretary of the Tribunals shall give notice to both or all the parties (subject to Rule 3(2)) of any extension of time granted under Rule 12(2)(a) or any directions given in pursuance of this Rule.

### 14   Joinder and representative respondents

(1)   A tribunal may at any time either upon the application of any person or, where appropriate, of its own motion, direct any person against whom any relief is sought to be joined as a party to the proceedings, and give such consequential directions as it considers necessary.

(2)   A tribunal may likewise, either upon such application or of its own motion, order that any respondent named in the originating application or subsequently added, who shall appear to the tribunal not to have been, or to have ceased to be, directly interested in the subject of the originating application, be dismissed from the proceedings.

(3)   Where there are numerous persons having the same interest in an originating application, one or more of them may be cited as the person or persons against whom relief is sought, or may be authorised by the tribunal, before or at the hearing, to defend on behalf of all the persons so interested.

### 15   Consolidation of proceedings

Where there are pending before the industrial tribunals two or more originating applications, then, if at any time upon the application of a party or of its own motion it appears to a tribunal that–

(a)   some common question of law or fact arises in both or all the originating applications, or

(b)   the relief claimed therein is in respect of or arises out of the same set of facts, or

(c)   for some other reason it is desirable to make an order under this Rule,

the tribunal may order that some (as specified in the order) or all of the originating applications shall be considered together, and may give such consequential directions as may be necessary: Provided that the tribunal shall not make an order under this Rule without sending notice to all parties concerned giving them an opportunity to show cause why such an order should not be made.

## 16   Transfer of proceedings

(1) Where there is pending before the industrial tribunals an originating application in respect of which it appears to the President or a Regional Chairman that the proceedings could be determined in an industrial tribunal (Scotland) established in pursuance of the Industrial Tribunals (Scotland) Regulations 1965 and that the originating application would more conveniently be determined by such a tribunal, the President or a Regional Chairman may, at any time upon the application of a party or of his own motion, with the consent of the President of the Industrial Tribunals (Scotland), direct that the said proceedings be transferred to the Office of the Industrial Tribunals (Scotland): Provided that no such direction shall be made unless notice has been sent to all parties concerned giving them an opportunity to show cause why such a direction should not be made.

(2) Where proceedings have been transferred to the Office of the Industrial Tribunals (England and Wales) under Rule 16(1) of the Industrial Tribunals (Rules of Procedure) (Scotland) Regulations 1985 they shall be treated as if in all respects they had been commenced by an originating application pursuant to Rule 1.

## 17   Notices, etc.

(1) Any notice given under these Rules shall be in writing.

(2) All notices and documents required by these Rules to be presented to the Secretary of the Tribunals may be presented at the Office of the Tribunals or such other office as may be notified by the Secretary of the Tribunals to the parties.

(3) All notices and documents required or authorised by these Rules to be sent or given to any person hereinafter mentioned may be sent by post (subject to paragraph (5) of this Rule) or delivered to or at–

   (a) in the case of a notice or document directed to the Secretary of the State in proceedings to which he is not a party, the offices of the Department of Employment at Caxton House, Tothill Street, London SW1H 9NF, or such other office as may be notified by the Secretary of State;

   (b) in the case of a notice or document directed to the Board, the principal office of the Board;

   (c) in the case of a notice or document directed to a court, the office of the clerk of the court;

   (d) in the case of a notice or document directed to a party:—

    (i)   his address for service specified in the originating application or in a notice of appearance or in a notice under paragraph (4) of this Rule; or

   (ii)   if no address for service has been so specified, his last known address or place of business in the United Kingdom or, if the party is a corporation, the corporation's registered or principal office in the United Kingdom, or, in any case, such address or place outside the United Kingdom as the President or a Regional Chairman may allow;

(e)   in the case of a notice or document directed to any person (other than a person specified in the foregoing provisions of this paragraph), his address or place of business in the United Kingdom, or if such a person is a corporation, the corporation's registered or principal office in the United Kingdom;

and if sent or given to the authorised representative of a party shall be deemed to have been sent or given to that party.

(4) A party may at any time by notice to the Secretary of the Tribunals and to the other party or parties (and, where appropriate, to the appropriate conciliation officer) change his address for service under these Rules.

(5) The recorded delivery service shall be used instead of the ordinary post:—

(a)   when a second set of documents or notices is to be sent to a respondent who has not entered an appearance under Rule 3(1);

(b)   for service of an order made under Rule 4(1)(iii) requiring the attendance of a witness.

(6) Where for any sufficient reason service of any document or notice cannot be effected in the manner prescribed under this Rule, the President or a Regional Chairman may make an order for substituted service in such manner as he may deem fit and such service shall have the same effect as service in the manner prescribed under this Rule.

(7) In proceedings brought under the provisions of any enactment providing for conciliation the Secretary of the Tribunals shall send copies of all documents and notices to a conciliation officer who in the opinion of the Secretary is an appropriate officer to receive them.

(8) In proceedings which may involve payments out of the Redundancy Fund or Maternity Pay Fund, the Secretary of the Tribunals shall, where appropriate, send copies of all documents and notices to the Secretary of State notwithstanding the fact that he may not be a party to such proceedings.

(9) In proceedings under the Equal Pay Act, the Sex Discrimination Act or the Race Relations Act the Secretary of the Tribunals shall send to the Equal Opportunities Commission or, as the case may be, the Commission for Racial Equality copies of all documents sent to the parties under Rule 9(6), (10) and (11) and Rule 10(5).

## SCHEDULE 2

## COMPLEMENTARY RULES OF PROCEDURE

*For use only in proceedings involving an equal value claim*

**4  Power to require further particulars and attendance of witnesses and to grant discovery**

(1)  A tribunal may—

(a)  subject to Rule 3(2), on the application of a party to the proceedings made either by notice to the Secretary of the Tribunals or at the hearing of the originating application, or

(b)  in relation to sub-paragraph (i) of this paragraph, if it thinks fit, of its own motion–

    (i)  require a party to furnish in writing to the person specified by the tribunal further particulars of the grounds on which he or it relies and of the facts and contentions relevant thereto;

    (ii)  grant to the person making the application such discovery or inspection (including the taking of copies) of documents as might be granted by a county court; and

    (iii)  require the attendance of any person (including a party to the proceedings) as a witness, wherever such person may be within Great Britain, and may, if it does so require the attendance of a person, require him to produce any document relating to the matter to be determined;

and may appoint the time at or within which or the place at which any act required in pursuance of this Rule is to be done.

(1A)  Subject to paragraph (1B), a tribunal may, on the application of an expert who has been required by the tribunal to prepare a report,

(a)  require any person who the tribunal is satisfied may have information which may be relevant to the question or matter on which the expert is required to report to furnish, in writing, such information as the tribunal may require;

(b)  require any person to produce any documents which are in the possession, custody or power of that person and which the tribunal is satisfied may contain matter relevant to the question on which the expert is required to report;

and any information so required to be furnished or document so required to be produced shall be furnished or produced, at or within such time as the tribunal may appoint, to the Secretary of the Tribunals who shall send the information or document to the expert.

(1B)  A tribunal shall not make a requirement under paragraph (1A) of this Rule—

(a)  of a conciliation officer who has acted in connection with the complaint under section 64 of the Sex Discrimination Act, or

(b)  if it is satisfied that the person so required would have good grounds for refusing to comply with the requirement if it were a requirement made in connection with a hearing before the tribunal.

(2)  A party on whom a requirement has been made under paragraph (1)(i) or (1)(ii) of this Rule on an *ex parte* application, or (in relation to a requirement under paragraph (1)(i)) on the tribunal's own motion, and a person on whom a requirement has been made under paragraph (1)(iii) may apply to the tribunal by notice to the Secretary of the Tribunals before the appointed time at or within which the requirement is to be complied with to vary or set aside the requirement. Notice of an application under this paragraph to vary or set aside a requirement shall be given to the parties (other than the party making the application) and, where appropriate, in proceedings which may involve payments out of the Redundancy Fund or Maternity Pay Fund, the Secretary of State if not a party.

(2A)  A person, whether or not a party to the proceedings, upon whom a requirement has been made under paragraph (1A) of this Rule, may apply to the tribunal by notice to the Secretary of the Tribunals before the appointed time at or within which the application shall be given to the parties and to the expert upon whose application the requirement was made.

(3)  Every document containing a requirement under paragraph (1)(ii) or (1)(iii) or paragraph (1A) of this Rule shall contain a reference to the fact that, under paragraph 1(7) of Schedule 9 to the 1978 Act, any person who without reasonable excuse fails to comply with any such requirement shall be liable on summary conviction to a fine, and the document shall state the amount of the current maximum fine.

(4)  If the requirement under paragraph (1)(i) or (1)(ii) of this Rule is not complied with, a tribunal, before or at the hearing, may dismiss the whole or part of the originating application, or, as the case may be, strike out the whole or part of the notice of appearance, and, where appropriate, direct that a respondent shall be debarred from defending altogether: Provided that a tribunal shall not so dismiss or strike out or give such a direction unless it has sent notice to the party who has not complied with the requirement giving him an opportunity to show cause why such should not be done.

## 7A  Procedure relating to expert's report

(1)  In any case involving an equal value claim where a dispute arises as to whether any work is of equal value to other work in terms of the demands made on the person employed on the work (for instance under such headings as effort, skill and decision) (in this Rule hereinafter referred to as 'the question'), a tribunal shall, before considering the question, except in cases to which section 2A(1)(a) of the Equal Pay Act applies, require an expert to prepare a report with respect to the question and the requirement shall be made in accordance with paragraphs (2) and (3) of this Rule.

(2) The requirement shall be made in writing and shall set out—

(a) the name and address of each of the parties;

(b) the address of the establishment at which the applicant is (or, as the case may be, was) employed;

(c) the question; and

(d) the identity of the person with reference to whose work the question arises;

and a copy of the requirement shall be sent to each of the parties.

(3) The requirement shall stipulate that the expert shall—

(a) take account of all such information supplied and all such representations made to him as have a bearing on the question;

(b) before drawing up his report, produce and send to the parties a written summary of the said information and representations and invite the representations of the parties upon the material contained therein;

(c) make his report to the tribunal in a document which shall reproduce the summary and contain a brief account of any representations received from the parties upon it, any conclusion he may have reached upon the question and the reasons for that conclusion or, as the case may be, for his failure to reach such a conclusion;

(d) take no account of the difference of sex and at all times act fairly.

(4) Without prejudice to the generality of Rule 12(2)(b), where a tribunal requires an expert to prepare a report, it shall adjourn the hearing.

(5) If, on the application of one or more of the parties made not less than 42 days after a tribunal has notified an expert of the requirement to prepare a report, the tribunal forms the view that there has been or is likely to be undue delay in receiving that report, the tribunal may require the expert to provide in writing to the tribunal an explanation for the delay or information as to his progress and may, in consideration of any such explanation or information as may be provided and after seeking representations from the parties, revoke, by notice in writing to the expert, the requirement to prepare a report, and in such a case paragraph (1) of this Rule shall again apply.

(6) Where a tribunal has received the report of an expert, it shall forthwith send a copy of the report to each of the parties and shall fix a date for the hearing of the case to be resumed; provided that the date so fixed shall be at least 14 days after the date on which the report is sent to the parties.

(7) Upon the resuming of the hearing of the case in accordance with paragraph (6) of this Rule the report shall be admitted as evidence in the case unless the tribunal has exercised its power under paragraph (8) of this Rule not to admit the report.

(8) Where the tribunal, on application of one or more of the parties or otherwise, forms the view—

(a) that the expert has not complied with a stipulation in paragraph (3) of this Rule, or

(b) that the conclusion contained in the report is one which, taking due account of the information supplied and representations made to the expert, could not reasonably have been reached, or

(c) that for some other material reason (other than disagreement with the conclusion that the applicant's work is or is not of equal value or with the reasoning leading to the conclusion) the report is unsatisfactory,

the tribunal may, if it thinks fit, determine not to admit the report, and in such a case paragraph (1) of this Rule shall again apply.

(9) In forming its view on the matters contained in paragraph (8)(a), (b) and (c) of this Rule, the tribunal shall take account of any representations of the parties thereon and may in that connection, subject to Rule 8(2A) and (2B), permit any party to give evidence upon, to call witnesses and to question any witness upon any matter relevant thereto.

(10) The tribunal may, at any time after it has received the report of an expert, require that expert (or, if that is impracticable, another expert) to explain any matter contained in his report or, having regard to such matters as may be set out in the requirement, to give further consideration to the question.

(11) The requirement in paragraph (10) of this Rule shall comply with paragraph (2) of this Rule and shall stipulate that the expert shall make his reply in writing to the tribunal, giving his explanation or, as the case may be, setting down any conclusion which may result from his further consideration and his reasons for that conclusion.

(12) Where the tribunal has received a reply from the expert under paragraph (11) of this Rule, it shall forthwith send a copy of the reply to each of the parties and shall allow the parties to make representations thereon, and the reply shall be treated as information furnished to the tribunal and be given such weight as the tribunal thinks fit.

(13) Where a tribunal has determined not to admit a report under paragraph (8), that report shall be treated for all purposes (other than the award of costs or expenses under Rule 11) connected with the proceedings as if it had not been received by the tribunal and no further account shall be taken of it, and the requirement on the expert to prepare a report shall lapse.

## 8  Procedure at hearing

(1) Subject to paragraphs (2A), (2B), (2C), (2D) and (2E) of this Rule the tribunal shall conduct the hearing in such manner as it considers most suitable to the clarification of the issues before it and generally to the just handling of the proceedings; it shall so far as appears to it appropriate seek to avoid formality in its proceedings and it shall not be bound by any enactment

or rule of law relating to the admissibility of evidence in proceedings before the courts of law.

(2)   Subject to paragraphs (1), (2A), (2B), (2C) and (2D) of this Rule, at the hearing of the originating application a party (unless disentitled by virtue of Rule 3(2)), the Secretary of State (if, not being a party, he elects to appear as provided in Rule 7(5)) and any other person entitled to appear shall be entitled to give evidence, to call witnesses, to question any witnesses and to address the tribunal.

(2A) The tribunal may, and shall upon the application of a party, require the attendance of an expert who has prepared a report in connection with an equal value claim in any hearing relating to that claim. Where an expert attends in compliance with such requirement any party may, subject to paragraph (1) of this Rule, cross-examine the expert on his report and on any other matter pertaining to the question on which the expert was required to report.

(2B) At any time after the tribunal has received the report of the expert, any party may, on giving reasonable notice of his intention to do so to the tribunal and to any other party to the claim, call one witness to give expert evidence on the question on which the tribunal has required the expert to prepare a report; and where such evidence is given, any other party may cross-examine the person giving that evidence upon it.

(2C) Except as provided in rule 7A(9) or by paragraph (2D) of this Rule, no party may give evidence upon, or question any witness upon, any matter of fact upon which a conclusion in the report of the expert is based.

(2D) Subject to paragraph (2A) and (2B) of this Rule, a tribunal may, notwithstanding paragraph (2C) of this Rule, permit a party to give evidence upon, to call witnesses and to question any witness upon any such matters of fact as are referred to in that paragraph if either—

(a)   the matter of fact is relevant to and is raised in connection with the issue contained in subsection (3) of section 1 of the Equal Pay Act (defence of genuine material factor) upon which the determination of the tribunal is being sought; or

(b)   the report of the expert contains no conclusion on the question of whether the applicant's work and the work of the person identified in the requirement of the tribunal under Rule 7A(2) are of equal value and the tribunal is satisfied that the absence of that conclusion is wholly or mainly due to the refusal or deliberate omission of a person required by the tribunal under Rule 4(1A) to furnish information or to produce documents to comply with that requirement.

(2E) A tribunal may, on the application of a party, if in the circumstances of the case, having regard to the considerations expressed in paragraph (1) of this Rule, it considers that it is appropriate so to proceed, hear evidence upon and permit the parties to address it upon the issue contained in subsection (3) of section 1 of the Equal Pay Act (defence of genuine material factor) before it requires an expert to prepare a report under Rule 7A. Where the tribunal so proceeds, it shall be without prejudice to further consideration of that issue after the tribunal has received the report.

(3)  If a party shall fail to appear or to be represented at the time and place fixed for the hearing, the tribunal may, if that party is an applicant, dismiss or, in any case, dispose of the application in the absence of that party or may adjourn the hearing to a later date: Provided that before deciding to dismiss or disposing of any application in the absence of a party the tribunal shall consider any representations submitted by that party in pursuance of Rule 7(3).

(4)  A tribunal may require any witness to give evidence on oath or affirmation and for that purpose there may be administered an oath or affirmation in due form.

## 9  Decision of tribunal

(1)  A decision of a tribunal may be taken by a majority thereof and, if the tribunal shall be constituted of two members only, the chairman shall have a second or casting vote.

(2)  The decision of a tribunal, which may be given orally at the end of a hearing or reserved, shall be recorded in a document signed by the chairman.

(3)  A tribunal shall give reasons for its decision.

(4)  The reasons for the decision of the tribunal shall be recorded in full form in a document signed by the chairman.

(4A)  There shall be appended to the document referred to in paragraph (4) of this Rule a copy of the report (if any) of an expert received by the tribunal in the course of the proceedings.

[paragraph (5) is omitted because it has no relevance in proceedings involving an equal value claim]

(6)  The clerk to the tribunal shall transmit any document referred to in paragraphs (2), (4) and (4A) of this Rule to the Secretary of the Tribunals who shall as soon as may be enter it in the Register and shall send a copy of the entry to each of the parties and to the persons entitled to appear who did so appear and, where the originating application was sent to a tribunal by a court, to that court.

(7)  Any document referred to in paragraph (4) and (4A) of this Rule shall be omitted from the Register in any case in which evidence has been heard in private and the tribunal so directs and in that event any such document shall be sent to the parties and to any superior court in any proceedings relating to such decision together with the copy of the entry.

(8) The Register shall be kept at the Office of the Tribunals and shall be open to the inspection of any person without charge at all reasonable hours.

(9) Clerical mistakes in any document referred to in paragraphs (2) and (4) of this Rule, or errors arising in such a document from an accidental slip or omission, may at any time be corrected by the chairman by certificate under his hand.

(10) The clerk to the tribunal shall send a copy of any document so corrected and the certificate of the chairman to the Secretary of the Tribunals who shall as soon as may be make such correction as may be necessary in the Register and shall send a copy of any corrected entry or of any corrected document containing reasons for the tribunal's decision, as the case may be, to each of the parties and, in the case of a corrected entry, to the persons entitled to appear who did so appear and, where the originating application was sent to the tribunal by a court, to that court.

(11) If any decision is—

(a) corrected under paragraph (9) of this Rule,
(b) reviewed, revoked or varied under Rule 10, or
(c) altered in any way by order of a superior court,

the Secretary of the Tribunals shall alter the entry in the Register to conform with any such certificate or order and shall send a copy of the new entry to each of the parties and to the persons entitled to appear who did so appear and, where the originating application was sent to the tribunal by a court, to that court.

(12) Where by this Rule a document is required to be signed by the chairman but by reason of death or incapacity the chairman is unable to sign such document it shall be signed by the other members of the tribunal, who shall certify that the chairman is unable to sign.

## 11 Costs

(1) Subject to paragraphs (2) and (3) of this Rule, a tribunal shall not normally make an award in respect of the costs or expenses incurred by a party to the proceedings but where in its opinion a party (and if he is a respondent whether or not he has entered an appearance) has in bringing or conducting the proceedings acted frivolously, vexatiously or otherwise unreasonably the tribunal may make—

(a) an order that that party shall pay to another party (or to the Secretary of State, if, not being a party, he has acted as provided in Rule 7(5)) either a specified sum in respect of the costs or expenses incurred by that other party (or, as the case may be, by the Secretary of State) or the whole or part of those costs or expenses as taxed (if not otherwise agreed);

(b) an order that that party shall pay to the Secretary of State the whole, or any part, of any allowances (other than allowances paid to members of tribunals, experts or assessors) paid by the Secretary of State under paragraph 10 of Schedule 9 to the 1978 Act to any person for the purposes of, or in connection with, his attendance at the tribunal.

(1A) For the purposes of paragraph (1)(a) of this Rule, the costs or expenses in respect of which a tribunal may make an order include costs or expenses incurred by the party in whose favour the order is to be made in or in connection with the investigations carried out by the expert in preparing his report.

(2) Where the tribunal has on the application of a party to the proceedings postponed the day or time fixed for or adjourned the hearing, the tribunal may make orders against or, as the case may require, in favour of that party as at paragraph (1)(a) and (b) of this Rule as respects any costs or expenses incurred or any allowances paid as a result of the postponement or adjournment.

(3) Where, on a complaint of unfair dismissal in respect of which—

(i) the applicant has expressed a wish to be reinstated or re-engaged which has been communicated to the respondent at least 7 days before the hearing of the complaint, or

(ii) the proceedings arise out of the respondent's failure to permit the applicant to return to work after an absence due to pregnancy or confinement,

any postponement or adjournment of the hearing has been caused by the respondent's failure, without a special reason, to adduce reasonable evidence as to the availability of the job from which the applicant was dismissed, or, as the case may be, which she held before her absence, or of comparable or suitable employment, the tribunal shall make orders against that respondent as at paragraph (1)(a) and (b) of this Rule as respects any costs or expenses incurred or any allowances paid as a result of the postponement or adjournment.

[paragraph (4) is omitted because it has no relevance in proceedings involving an equal value claim]

(5) Any costs required by an order under this Rule to be taxed may be taxed in the county court according to such of the scales prescribed by the county court rules for proceedings in the county court as shall be directed by the order.

## 12   Miscellaneous powers of tribunal

(1) Subject to the provisions of these Rules, a tribunal may regulate its own procedure.

(2)   A tribunal may, if it thinks fit—

(a)   extend the time appointed by or under those Rules for doing any act notwithstanding that the time appointed may have expired;

(b)   postpone the day or time fixed for, or adjourn, any hearing (particularly as respects cases under the provisions of any enactment providing for conciliation for the purpose of giving an opportunity for the complaint to be settled by way of conciliation and withdrawn);

(c)   if the applicant shall at any time give notice of the withdrawal of his originating application, dismiss the proceedings;

(d)   except in proceedings under the 1966 Act, if both or all the parties (and the Secretary of State, if, not being a party, he has acted as provided in Rule 7(5)) agree in writing upon the terms of a decision to be made by the tribunal, decide accordingly;

(e)   subject to the Proviso below, at any stage of the proceedings order to be struck out or amended any originating application or notice of appearance or anything in such application or notice of appearance on the grounds that it is scandalous, frivolous or vexatious;

(f)   subject to the Proviso below, on the application of the respondent, or of its own motion, order to be struck out any originating application for want of prosecution;

Provided that before making any order under (e) or (f) above the tribunal shall send notice to the party against whom it is proposed that any such order should be made giving him an opportunity to show cause why such an order should not be made.

(2A) Without prejudice to the generality of paragraph (2)(b) of this Rule, the tribunal shall, before proceeding to hear the parties on an equal value claim, invite them to apply for an adjournment for the purpose of seeking to reach a settlement of the claim and shall, if both or all the parties agree to such a course, grant an adjournment for that purpose.

(2B) If, after the tribunal has adjourned the hearing under Rule 7A(4) but before the tribunal has received the report of the expert, the applicant gives notice under paragraph (2)(c) of this Rule, the tribunal shall forthwith notify the expert that the requirement to prepare a report has ceased. The notice shall be without prejudice to the operation of Rule 11(1A).

(3)   Subject to Rule 4(2), and (2A), a tribunal may, if it thinks fit, before granting an application under Rule 4 or Rule 13 require the party (or, as the case may be, the Secretary of State or, in the case of an application under Rule 4(1A), the expert) making the application to give notice of it to the other party or parties (or, in the case of an application by an expert, the parties and any other person in respect of whom the tribunal is asked, in the application, to impose a requirement). The notice shall give particulars of the application and indicate the address to which and the time within which any objection to the application shall be made being an address and time specified for the purposes of the application by the tribunal.

(4) Any act other than the holding of a pre-hearing assessment under Rule 6, the hearing of an originating application, or the making of an order under Rule 10(1), required or authorised by these Rules to be done by a tribunal may be done by, or on the direction of, the President or the chairman of the tribunal, or any chairman being a member of the panel of chairmen.

(5) Rule 11 shall apply to an order dismissing proceedings under paragraph (2)(c) of this Rule.

(6) Any functions of the Secretary of the Tribunals other than that mentioned in Rule 1(2) may be performed by an Assistant Secretary of the Tribunals.

### 17   Notices, etc.

(1) Any notice given under these Rules shall be in writing.

(2) All notices and documents required by these Rules to be presented to the Secretary of the Tribunals may be presented at the Office of the Tribunals or such other office as may be notified by the Secretary of the Tribunals to the parties.

(3) All notices and documents required or authorised by these Rules to be sent or given to any person hereinafter mentioned may be sent by post (subject to paragraph (5) of this Rule) or delivered to or at—

   (a)   in the case of a notice or document directed to the Secretary of State in proceedings to which he is not a party, the offices of the Department of Employment at Caxton House, Tothill Street, London SW1H 9NF, or such other office as may be notified by the Secretary of State;
   [sub-paragraph (b) is omitted because it has no relevance in proceedings involving an equal value claim];
   (c)   in the case of a notice or document directed to a court, the office of the clerk of the court;
   (d)   in the case of a notice or document directed to a party:

      (i)   his address for service specified in the originating application or in a notice of appearance or in a notice under paragraph (4) of this Rule; or
      (ii)  if no address for service has been so specified, his last known address or place of business in the United Kingdom or, if the party is a corporation, the corporation's registered or principal office in the United Kingdom or, in any case, such address or place outside the United Kingdom as the President or a Regional Chairman may allow;

   (e)   in the case of a notice or document directed to any person (other than a person specified in the foregoing provisions of this paragraph), his address or place of business in the United Kingdom, or if such a person is a corporation, the corporation's registered or principal office in the United Kingdom;

and if sent or given to the authorised representative of a party shall be deemed to have been sent or given to that party.

(4)  A party may at any time by notice to the Secretary of the Tribunals and to the other party or parties (and, where appropriate, to the appropriate conciliation officer and the appropriate expert) change his address for service under these Rules.

(5)  The recorded delivery service shall be used instead of the ordinary post:—

(a)  when a second set of documents or notices is to be sent to a respondent who has not entered an appearance under Rule 3(1);

(b)  for service of an order made under Rule 4(1)(iii) or (1A).

(6)  Where for any sufficient reason service of any document or notice cannot be effected in the manner prescribed under this Rule, the President or a Regional Chairman may make an order for substituted service in such manner as he may deem fit and such service shall have the same effect as service in the manner prescribed under this Rule.

(7)  In proceedings brought under the provisions of any enactment providing for conciliation the Secretary of the Tribunals shall send copies of all documents and notices to a conciliation officer who in the opinion of the Secretary is an appropriate officer to receive them.

(8)  In proceedings which may involve payments out of the Redundancy Fund or Maternity Pay Fund, the Secretary of the Tribunals shall, where appropriate, send copies of all documents and notices to the Secretary of State notwithstanding the fact that he may not be a party to such proceedings.

(9)  In proceedings under the Equal Pay Act, the Sex Discrimination Act or the Race Relations Act the Secretary of the Tribunals shall send to the Equal Opportunities Commission or, as the case may be, the Commission for Racial Equality copies of all documents sent to the parties under Rule 9(6), (10) and (11) and Rule 10(5).

## §4  EQUALITY IN SOCIAL SECURITY

## Social Security Act 1980[1]
### (1980 c. 30)

SCHEDULE 1[2]

AMENDMENTS OF SOCIAL SECURITY ACT 1975

PART I

AMENDMENTS RELATING TO SIMILAR TREATMENT
FOR MEN AND WOMEN

1  (1)  Subsection (6) of section 41 and subsection (4) of section 65 (under which a married woman residing with her husband is not entitled to an increase in benefit in respect of dependent children by virtue of that section unless her husband is incapable of self-support) shall be amended as follows—

(a)  in the said subsection (6) for the words 'incapable of self-support' there shall be substituted the words 'not engaged in any one or more employments from which his weekly earnings exceed the amount specified in relation to the benefit or beneficiary in question in Schedule 4, Part IV, column (3)';

(b)  in the said subsection (4) for the words 'not incapable of self-support' there shall be substituted the words 'engaged in any one or more employments from which his weekly earnings exceed the amount specified in relation to the pension in Schedule 4, Part V, paragraph 12'.

(2)  The said subsections (6) and (4) as amended by the preceding sub-paragraph shall cease to have effect on the coming into force of this sub-paragraph.

2  ...

3  Paragraph (b) of section 44(3), paragraph (b) of section 47(1) and paragraph (c) of section 66(1) (by virtue of which certain benefits are

---

[1]  As amended.

[2]  Part I of this Schedule (paras 1-7) is designed to implement Directive 79/7/EEC of 19 December 1978 on the equal treatment of men and women in matters of social security. The Directive was intended to ensure equality of treatment by 21 December 1984. This part of the Schedule provides for the removal of discrimination in two stages, the first relating to claims for increase of benefit for children by women by reference to the husband's earnings, the second regardless of those earnings.

increased for any period during which the beneficiary has living with him and is maintaining such a relative as is there mentioned) shall cease to have effect; but a person who, immediately before the date when this paragraph comes into force, was entitled to an increase by virtue of any those paragraphs, shall continue to be entitled to it for any period not exceeding two years beginning with that date, during which, if the paragraph in question and any regulations having effect by virtue of the paragraph immediately before that date were still in force, he would have been, and would not have ceased to be, entitled to the increase by virtue of that paragraph.

4    Sections 44(3)(c), 46(2) and 66(1)(d) (which relate to increases of benefit by reference to a female person, not a child, who has the care of a child or children in respect of whom the beneficiary is entitled to child benefit) shall be amended by substituting for the words 'female person (not a child)'—

(a)  in sections 44(3)(c) and 66(1)(d) the words 'person who is neither the spouse of the beneficiary nor a child';
(b)  in section 46(2) the words 'person who is neither the spouse of the pensioner nor a child';

and in sections 46(4) and 66(6)(b) (which refer to the female person mentioned in sections 46(2) and 66(1)(d) respectively) for the words from 'female person' to 'residing' there shall be substituted the words 'person there referred to is a female residing'.

5    (1) Subsection (5) of section 44 and subsection (2) of section 47 (which provide that, in the case of unemployment or sickness benefit or invalidity pensions payable to certain persons over pensionable age, the benefit or pensions shall not be increased under provisions providing for increases in respect of certain periods and shall only be increased by the amounts of the increases which would be made in relevant retirement pensions where the rates of those pensions would be calculated under provisions relating to the partial satisfaction of contribution conditions) shall cease to have effect; and after section 47 there shall be inserted the following section—

**47A    Rate of increase where associated retirement pension is attributable to reduced contributions**

Where a person is entitled to unemployment or sickness benefit by virtue of section 14(2)(b) or (c) or to an invalidity pension by virtue of section 15(2) of this Act and would have been entitled only by virtue of section 33 to the retirement pension by reference to which the rate of the said benefit or invalidity pension is determined, the amount of any increase of the said benefit or invalidity pension attributable to sections 44 to 47 of this Act shall not be determined in accordance with those sections but shall be determined in accordance with regulations.

(2) Accordingly in section 44 (1) for the words 'subject to the provisions of this section' there shall be substituted the words 'Subject to section 47A', in section 44(2) for the words 'Subject to the following subsections' there shall be substituted the words 'Subject to subsection (4) below and section 47A' and in section 47(1) for the words 'Subject to subsection (2) below' there shall be substituted the words 'Subject to section 47A'.

6    In section 66(1)(a) (which provides for increases in certain cases of disablement pension for periods during which the pensioner's wife is residing with him or he is contributing to the maintenance of his wife at a specified rate), for the word 'wife' in both places there shall be substituted the word 'spouse'.

7    In Schedule 20 (which contains a glossary of expressions) the entry relating to the expression 'Incapable of self-support' (including both paragraphs in the second column of the entry) shall be omitted, and after the entry relating to the expression 'Pensionable age' there shall be inserted the following—

| | |
|---|---|
| 'Permanently incapable of self-support'   ...    ... | A person is 'permanently incapable of self-support' if (but only if) he is incapable of supporting himself by reason of physical or mental infirmity and is likely to remain so incapable for the remainder of his life. |

# Health and Social Security Act 1984
## (1984 c. 48)

### 11¹  Severe disablement allowance

(1)  The following section shall be substituted for section 36 of the Social Security Act 1975—

#### 36  Severe disablement allowance

(1)  Subject to the provisions of this section, a person shall be entitled to a severe disablement allowance for any day ('the relevant day') if he satisfies—

(a)  the conditions specified in subsection (2) below; or
(b)  the conditions specified in subsection (3) below.

(2)  The conditions mentioned in subsection (1)(a) above are that—

(a)  on the relevant day he is incapable of work; and
(b)  he has been incapable of work for a period of not less than 196 consecutive days—

    (i)  beginning not later than the day on which he attained the age of 20; and
    (ii)  ending immediately before the relevant day.

(3)  The conditions mentioned in subsection (1)(b) above are that—

(a)  on the relevant day he is both incapable of work and disabled; and
(b)  he has been both incapable of work and disabled for a period of not less than 196 consecutive days ending immediately before the relevant day.

(4)  A person shall not be entitled to a severe disablement allowance if—

(a)  he is under the age of 16; or
(b)  he is receiving full-time education; or
(c)  he does not satisfy the prescribed conditions—

    (i)  as to residence in Great Britain; or
    (ii)  as to presence there; or

(d)  he has attained pensionable age and was not entitled to a severe disablement allowance immediately before he attained it and is not treated by regulations as having been so entitled immediately before he attained it.

(5)  A person is disabled for the purposes of this section if he suffers from loss of physical or mental faculty such that the assessed extent of the resulting disablement amounts to not less than 80 per cent.

(6)  A severe disablement allowance shall be paid at the weekly rate specified in relation thereto in Schedule 4, Part III, paragraph 2.

(7)  Regulations—

---

1   The note to this section in *Current Law Statutes Annotated 1984* comments as follows:

This section replaces the non-contributory invalidity pension (NCIP), and the house-wives' non-contributory invalidity pension (HNCIP), with a new severe disablement allowance. The HNCIP had, in particular, been strongly criticised, for being blatantly sexist in that it provided special tests of competence in 'household duties' for married or cohabiting women.

(a) may direct that persons who—

    (i) have attained retiring age; and

    (ii) were entitled to a severe disablement allowance immediately before they attained it, shall continue to be so entitled notwithstanding that they do not satisfy the conditions specified in subsection (2) or (3) above;

(b) may direct—

    (i) that persons who have previously been entitled to a severe disablement allowance shall be entitled to such an allowance notwithstanding that they do not satisfy the conditions specified in subsection (2)(b) or (3)(b) above;

    (ii) that those paragraphs shall have effect in relation to such persons subject to such modifications as may be specified in the regulations;

(c) may prescribe the circumstances in which a person is or is not to be treated—

    (i) as incapable of work; or

    (ii) as receiving full-time education; and

(d) may provide for disqualifying a person from receiving a severe disablement allowance for such period not exceeding 6 weeks as may be determined in accordance with sections 97 to 104 below if—

    (i) he has become incapable of work through his own misconduct; or

    (ii) he fails without good cause to attend for, or to submit himself to, such medical or other examination or treatment as may be required in accordance with the regulations, or to observe any prescribed rules of behaviour.

(8) In this section—

'assessed' means assessed in accordance with Schedule 8 to this Act; and
'retiring age' means, in the case of a man, 70 and, in the case of a woman, 65.'


(2) Schedule 4 to this Act, which makes amendments to other enactments consequential on subsection (1) above, shall have effect.

# Social Security Act 1986
## (1986 c. 50)

### 37[1] Invalid care allowance for women

(1) Section 37(3) of the Social Security Act 1975 shall have effect, and shall be treated as having had effect from 22 December 1984, as if the words from 'and a woman' to the end were omitted.

(2) The Social Security Benefit (Dependency) Regulations 1977 shall have effect, and shall be treated as having had effect from 22 December 1984, as if the following sub-paragraphs were substituted for sub-paragraphs (a) and (b) of paragraph 7 of Schedule 2 (increases of invalid care allowance)—

(a) a spouse who is not engaged in any one or more employments from which the spouse's weekly earnings exceed that amount; or

(b) some person (not being a child) who—

(i) has the care of a child or children in respect of whom the beneficiary is entitled to child benefit, being a child or children in respect of whom the beneficiary is entitled to an increase of an invalid care allowance or would be so entitled but for the provisions of any regulations for the time being in force under the Act relating to overlapping benefits;

(ii) is not undergoing imprisonment or detention in legal custody;

(iii) is not engaged in any one or more employments (other than employment by the beneficiary in caring for a child or children in respect of whom the beneficiary is entitled to child benefit) from which the person's weekly earnings exceed that amount;

(iv) is not absent from Great Britain, except for any period during which the person is residing with the beneficiary outside Great Britain and for which the beneficiary is entitled to an invalid care allowance.

---

1　The note to this section in *Current Law Statutes Annotated 1986* comments as follows:

This section was introduced at the Report stage in the House of Lords, implementing a commitment which had been given by the Government on 23 June [1986]. The commitment was in turn made in anticipation of the decision of the ECJ in *Drake* v. *Chief Adjudication Officer,* Case 150/85, [1986] ECR 1995, [1987] QB 166, [1986] 3 All ER 65.

Under s. 37 of the Social Security Act 1975 invalid care allowance is payable to a person who is engaged in caring for a severely disabled person provided that the carer is not in gainful employment. The statute is, however, sexist in the sense that by s. 37(3) a woman was not entitled if, for example, she was married and living with her husband. The effect of s. 37 is to extend invalid care allowance to married women, and those living with a man as his wife, on equal terms with men and single women.

# Social Security Act 1989
## (1989 c. 24)

## SCHEDULE 5

### EMPLOYMENT-RELATED SCHEMES FOR PENSIONS OR OTHER BENEFITS: EQUAL TREATMENT FOR MEN AND WOMEN

### *Part I–Compliance by Schemes*

### 1  Schemes to comply with the principle of equal treatment

Every employment-related benefit scheme shall comply with the principle of equal treatment.

### 2  The principle

(1)  The principle of equal treatment is that persons of the one sex shall not, on the basis of sex, be treated less favourably than persons of the other sex in any respect relating to an employment-related scheme.

(2)  Sub-paragraphs (3) to (6) below have effect, where applicable, for the purpose of determining whether a scheme complies with the principle of equal treatment.

(3)  Where any provision of the scheme imposes on both male and female members a requirement or condition–

(a)  which is such that the proportion of persons of the one sex ('the sex affected') who can comply with it is considerably smaller than the proportion of persons of the other sex who can do so, and

(b)  which is not justifiable irrespective of the sex of the members,

the imposition of that requirement or condition shall be regarded as less favourable treatment of persons of the sex affected.

(4)  No account shall be taken of–

(a)  any difference, on the basis of the sex of members, in the levels of contributions–

  (i)  which members are required to make, to the extent that the difference is justifiable on actuarial grounds, or

  (ii)  which the employer makes, to the extent that the difference is for the purpose of removing or limiting differences, as between men and women, in the amount of value of money purchase benefits;

(b)  any difference, on the basis of sex, in the amount or value of money purchase benefits, to the extent that the difference is justifiable on actuarial grounds;

(c)  any special treatment for the benefit of women in connection with pregnancy or childbirth;

(d) any permitted age-related differences;

(e) any difference of treatment in relation to benefits for a deceased member's surviving husband, wife or other dependants;

(f) any difference of treatment in relation to any optional provisions available; or

(g) any provisions of a scheme to the extent that they have been specially arranged for the benefit of one particular member of the scheme;

but where the scheme includes any unfair maternity provisions, it shall to that extent be regarded as according less favourable treatment to women on the basis of sex.

(5) Where the scheme treats persons of the one sex differently according to their marital or family status, that treatment is to be compared with the scheme's treatment of persons of the other sex who have the same status.

(6) The principle of equal treatment applies in relation to members' dependants as it applies in relation to members.

(7) If any question arises whether a condition or requirement falling within sub-paragraph (3)(a) above is or is not justifiable irrespective of the sex of the members, it shall be for those who assert that it is so justifiable to prove that fact.

(8) In this paragraph–

'money purchase benefits' has the meaning given by section 84(1) of the 1986 Act, but with the substitution for references to a personal or occupational pension scheme of references to an employment-related scheme;

'optional provisions available' means those provisions of a scheme–

(a) which apply only in the case of members who elect for them to do so; and

(b) whose purpose is to secure for those members–

(i) benefits in addition to those otherwise provided under the scheme; or

(ii) a choice with respect to the date on which benefits under the scheme are to commence; or

(iii) a choice between any two or more benefits;

'permitted age-related difference' means any difference, on the basis of sex, in the age–

(a) at which a service-related benefit in respect of old age or retirement commences; or

(b) at which, in consequence of the commencement of such a benefit, any other service-related benefit either ceases to be payable or becomes payable at a reduced rate calculated by reference to the amount of the benefit so commencing.

(9)  For the purposes of this paragraph–

(a)  any reference to a person's family status is a reference to his having an unmarried partner or any dependants; and

(b)  a person 'has an unmarried partner' if that person and some other person to whom he is not married live together as husband and wife.

### 3  Non-compliance: compulsory levelling up

(1)  To the extent that any provision of an employment-related benefit scheme does not comply with the principle of equal treatment, it shall be overridden by this Schedule and the more favourable treatment accorded to persons of the one sex shall also be accorded to persons of the other sex.

(2)  Where more favourable treatment is accorded to any persons by virtue of sub-paragraph (1) above, that sub-paragraph requires them, in accordance with the principle of equal treatment–

(a)  to pay contributions at a level appropriate to the treatment so accorded; and

(b)  to bear any other burden which is an incident of that treatment;
but persons of either sex may instead elect to receive the less favourable treatment and, in accordance with the principle of equal treatment, pay contributions at the level appropriate to that treatment and bear the other burdens incidental to it.

(3)  Where any provision of a scheme is overridden by sub-paragraph (1) above, nothing in this Schedule shall affect any rights accrued or obligations incurred during the period before the date on which that provision is so overridden.

(4)  Sub-paragraph (1) above is without prejudice to the exercise, in compliance with the principle of equal treatment, of any power to amend the scheme.

### 4  Modification of schemes by the Occupational Pensions Board

(1)  On an application made to them in respect of an employment-related benefit scheme, other than a public service scheme, by persons competent to make such an application, the Occupational Pensions Board (the 'Board') may make an order modifying, or authorising the modification of, the scheme, for the purpose–

(a)  of making provision implementing the principle of equal treatment otherwise than as provided by sub-paragraph (1) of paragraph 3 above; or

(b)  of reflecting in the rules of the scheme any changes consequential upon the operation of that sub-paragraph.

(2)  In relation to any employment-related benefit scheme, the persons competent to make an application to the Board under this paragraph are–

(a)  the trustees or managers of the scheme;

(b)  any person other than the trustees or managers who has power to alter the rules of the scheme;

(c)  any person who is an employer of persons in service in an employment to which the scheme applies; and

(d)  such other persons as regulations may specify, in relation to any category of schemes into which the scheme falls, as being proper persons to make an application for the purposes of this paragraph in respect of a scheme of that category.

(3)  The Board shall not entertain an application for an order by them under this paragraph unless they are satisfied that the modification of the scheme in question–

(a)  cannot be achieved otherwise than by means of such an order; or

(b)  can only be achieved in accordance with a procedure which is liable to be unduly complex or protracted, or involves the obtaining of consents which cannot be obtained, or can only be obtained with undue delay or difficulty.

(4)  Subject to sub-paragraph (3) above, the Board may on an application under this paragraph make (with the consent of the applicants) an order under sub-paragraph (1) above and may exercise their powers under this paragraph from time to time; and the extent of their powers under this paragraph is not limited, in relation to any purposes for which they are exercisable, to the minimum necessary to achieve those purposes.

(5)  An order of the Board under sub-paragraph (1) above authorising the modification of a scheme shall be framed so as to confer the power of modification on such persons as the Board think proper (including persons who were not parties to the application made to the Board) and shall include such directions as the Board think appropriate indicating the modifications which they consider to be desirable.

## 5  Unfair maternity provisions

(1)  In this Schedule 'unfair maternity provisions', in relation to an employment-related benefit scheme, means any provision–

(a)  which relates to continuing membership of, or the accrual of rights under, the scheme during any period of paid maternity absence in the case of any woman who is (or who, immediately before the commencement of such period, was) an employed earner and which treats such a woman otherwise than in accordance with the normal employment requirement; or

(b)  which requires the amount of any benefit payable under the scheme to or in respect of any such woman, to the extent that it falls to be determined by reference to her earnings during a period which included a period of paid maternity absence, to be determined otherwise than in accordance with the normal employment requirement.

(2)  In the case of any unfair maternity provision–

(a)  the more favourable treatment required by paragraph 3(1) above is treatment no less favourable than would be accorded to the women members in accordance with the normal employment requirement;

(b)  paragraph 3(2) above does not authorise the making of any such election as is there mentioned; and

(c)  paragraph 4(1) above does not authorise the making of any modification which does not satisfy the requirements of paragraph (a) above;

but, in respect of a period of paid maternity absence, a woman shall only be required to pay contributions on the amount of contractual remuneration or statutory maternity pay actually paid to or for her in respect of that period.

(3)  In this paragraph–

(a)  'period of paid maternity absence' means any period–

(i)  throughout which a woman is absent from work due to pregnancy or confinement; and

(ii)  for which her employer (or, if she is no longer in his employment, her former employer) pays her any contractual remuneration or statutory maternity pay;

(b)  'the normal employment requirement' is the requirement that any period of paid maternity absence shall be treated as if it were a period throughout which the woman in question works normally and receives the remuneration likely to be paid for doing so.

## 6  Unfair family leave provisions

(1)  Where an employment-related benefit scheme includes any unfair family leave provisions (irrespective of any differences on the basis of sex in the treatment accorded to members under those provisions), then–

(a)  the scheme shall be regarded to that extent as not complying with the principle of equal treatment; and

(b)  subject to sub-paragraph (3) below, this Schedule shall apply accordingly.

(2)  In this Schedule 'unfair family leave provisions' means any provision–

(a)  which relates to continuing membership of, or the accrual of rights under, the scheme during any period of paid family leave in the case of any member who is an employed earner and which treats such a member otherwise than in accordance with the normal leave requirement; or

(b) which requires the amount of any benefit payable under the scheme to or in respect of any such member to the extent that it falls to be determined by reference to earnings during a period which included a period of paid family leave, to be determined otherwise than in accordance with the normal family leave requirement.

(3) In the case of any unfair family leave provision–

(a) the more favourable treatment required by paragraph 3(1) above is treatment no less favourable than would be accorded to the members in accordance with the normal leave requirement;

(b) paragraph 3(2) above does not authorise the making of any such election as is there mentioned; and

(c) paragraph 4(1)(a) above does not authorise the making of any modification which does not satisfy the requirements of paragraph (a) above;

but in respect of a period of paid family leave, a member shall only be required to pay contributions on the amount of contractual remuneration actually paid to or for him in respect of that period.

(4) In this paragraph–

(a) 'period of paid family leave' means any period–

(i) throughout which a member is absent from work for family reasons; and

(ii) for which the employer pays him any contractual remuneration;

(b) 'the normal leave requirement' is the requirement that any period of paid family leave shall be treated as if it were a period throughout which the members in question works normally but only receives the remuneration in fact paid to him for that period.

## 7 Meaning of 'employment-related benefit scheme' etc.

In this Schedule–

(a) 'employment-related benefit scheme' means any scheme or arrangement which is comprised in one or more instruments or agreements and which has, or is capable of having, effect in relation to one or more descriptions or categories of employments so as to provide service-related benefits to or in respect of employed or self-employed earners–

(i) who have qualifying service in an employment of any such description or category, or

(ii) who have made arrangements with the trustees or managers of the scheme to enable them to become members of the scheme, but does not include a limited scheme;

(b) 'limited scheme' means–

    (i) any personal scheme for employed earners to which the employer does not contribute;

    (ii) any scheme which has only one member, other than a personal scheme for an employed earner to which his employer contributes;

    (iii) any contract of insurance which is made for the benefit of employed earners only and to which the employer is not a party;

(c) 'personal scheme' means any scheme or arrangement which falls within paragraph (a) above by virtue of sub-paragraph (ii) of that paragraph (or which would so fall apart from paragraph (b) above);

(d) 'public service scheme' has the meaning given by section 51(3)(b) of the 1973 Act;

(e) 'service-related benefits' means benefits, in the form of pensions or otherwise, payable in money or money's worth in respect of–

    (i) termination of service;

    (ii) retirement, old age or death;

    (iii) interruptions of service by reason of sickness or invalidity;

    (iv) accidents, injuries or diseases connected with employment;

    (v) unemployment; or

    (vi) expenses incurred in connection with children or other dependants;

and includes, in the case of a member who is an employed earner, any other benefit so payable to or in respect of the member in consequence of his employment.

## 8  Extension of ban on compulsory membership

Section 15(1) of the 1986 Act (which renders void any provision making membership of a pension scheme compulsory for an employed earner) shall apply in relation to a self-employed earner as it applies in relation to an employed earner, but with the substitution for references to a personal pension scheme of references to an employment-related benefit scheme which would be such a pension scheme if self-employed earners were regarded as employed earners.

## 9  Jurisdiction

(1) The Court, on the application of any person interested, shall have jurisdiction to determine any question arising as to–

(a) whether any provision of an employment-related benefit scheme does or does not comply with the principle of equal treatment; or

(b) whether, and with what effect, any such provision is overridden by paragraph 3 above.

(2)   In sub-paragraph (1) above 'the court' means–

(a)   in England and Wales, the High Court or a county court; and

(b)   in Scotland, the Court of Session or the sheriff court.

(3)   An application under sub-paragraph (1) above may be commenced in a county court notwithstanding–

(a)   any financial limit otherwise imposed on the jurisdiction of such a court; or

(b)   that the only relief claimed is a declaration or an injunction.

## 10   Interpretation

Expressions other than 'benefit' which are used in this Part of this Schedule and in the principal Act have the same meaning in this Part of this Schedule as they have in that Act.

## 11   ...

## 12   Future repeal of actuarial provisions

The Secretary of State may by order repeal paragraph 2(4)(a)(i) above; and if and to the extent that he has not done so before 30 July 1999 it shall cease to have effect on that date.

# SECTION II

# CASES

## Contents

**§1    Equal Pay**

A    House of Lords

Hayward v. Cammell Laird Shipbuilders Ltd (No 2)          282
Leverton v. Clwyd County Council                          293
Pickstone v. Freemans plc                                 306
Rainey v. Greater Glasgow Health Authority                318

B    Court of Appeal

Bromley v. H. & J. Quick                                  326

C    Lower Court or Tribunal

Jenkins v. Kingsgate (Clothing Productions) Ltd (No 2)    338

**§2    Equal Treatment**

A    House of Lords

Duke v. GEC Reliance                                      347
James v. Eastleigh Borough Council                        356

B    Court of Appeal

Baker v. Cornwall County Council                          379
Briggs v. NE Education & Library Board                    388
Hampson v. Department of Education & Science              407
Meer v. London Borough of Tower Hamlets                   411
Skyrail Oceanic Ltd v. Coleman                            420
Strathclyde Regional Council v. Porcelli                  425
Wallace v. SE Education & Library Board                   436
West Midlands PTE v. Singh                                439

C    Lower Court or Tribunal

Balgobin & Francis v. London Borough of Tower Hamlets     447
Clarke & Powell v. Eley (IMI) Kynoch Ltd                  454
Home Office v. Holmes                                      464
Horsey v. Dyfed County Council                            470
Page v. Freight Hire (Tank Haulage) Ltd                   476
Price v. Civil Service Commission                         483
Snowball v. Gardner Merchant Ltd                          488
Webb v. Emo Air Cargo (UK) Ltd                            491

**§3    Equality in Social Security**

Court of Appeal

Secretary of State for Social Security v. Thomas          500

## §1   EQUAL PAY

### A   HOUSE OF LORDS

## Hayward *v*. Cammell Laird Shipbuilders Ltd (No 2)[1]

LORD MACKAY OF CLASHFERN: My Lords, This is an appeal by Julie Ann Hayward, whom I shall refer to as the appellant, who is employed by Cammell Laird Shipbuilders Ltd, to whom I shall refer as the respondents, as a cook.

In February 1984 the appellant issued an originating application against the respondents in the Industrial Tribunal alleging that she did work of equal value to that of three men also employed by the respondents, a painter, a joiner and a thermal insulation engineer, and claiming equal pay to the men. This was the first equal value claim to be brought in the United Kingdom. The Industrial Tribunal ([1984] IRLR 463) held that the appellant did work of equal value to that of the three men and that the respondents could not rely on s. 1(3) of the Equal Pay Act 1970 because they had made it clear that they were not relying on that defence. The Industrial Tribunal stated that in the event of the parties being unable to agree on relief either party could apply for a further Order. There was no appeal against this decision of the Industrial Tribunal.

The parties being unable to agree on relief, a further hearing took place before the Industrial Tribunal. At that hearing it was agreed that the appellant received less favourable basic pay than the men and that she received less favourable overtime rates than the men. However, the respondents argued that, looking at her contract and the men's contracts as a whole - including provisions for sickness benefit and meal breaks - the appellant was as favourably treated as the men. The Industrial Tribunal held (by a majority of two to one) that, as a matter of law, the appellant was not entitled to relief in respect of specific terms of her contract if her contract, considered as a whole, was as favourable as the contracts of the men. The Industrial Tribunal did not make any finding on whether in fact the appellant's contract, considered as a whole, was as favourable as the contracts of the men. The appellant appealed to the Employment Appeal Tribunal ([1986] IRLR 287), who dismissed the appeal. The Court of Appeal ([1987] IRLR 186) dismissed a further appeal and this appeal from that decision of the Court of Appeal is brought with leave of this House.

...

---

1    [1988] AC 894, [1988] 2 WLR 1134, [1988] 2 All ER 257, [1988] ICR 464, [1988] IRLR 257, HL (E).

I deal first with the issue between the parties arising on the United Kingdom legislation to which I have referred. The issue is whether in terms of the Equal Pay Act as amended the woman who can point to a term of her contract which is less favourable than a term of a similar kind in the man's contract is entitled to have that term made not less favourable irrespective of whether she is as favourably treated as the man when the whole of her contract and the whole of his contract are considered, as the appellant submits, or whether although she shows that a particular term of her contract is less favourable to her than a term of a similar kind in the man's contract, her claim can nevertheless be defeated if it is shown that the terms of her contract considered as a whole are not less favourable to her than the terms of the man's contract considered as a whole, as the respondents submit.

No authority dealing with this question was referred to in the argument before your Lordships. There is no definition of the word 'term' in the legislation. In that situation I am of opinion that the natural meaning of the word 'term' in this context is a distinct provision or part of the contract which has sufficient content to make it possible to compare it from the point of view of the benefits it confers with similar provision or part in another contract. For example, Miss Hayward was employed on her accepting terms set out in a letter to her from the respondents which includes the following:

> We can offer you a position on our staff as a cook at a salary of £5,165 per annum. The base rate on which overtime is based is £4,741 ... .

There is a provision in the letter setting out the normal hours of work, providing that the overtime payment shall be plain time rate plus a third (two-thirds on Saturday and Sunday).

The corresponding provision with regard to basic pay in the men's contracts is less specific and refers to a national agreement from which the rate of wages to be paid weekly in arrears is to be determined. Overtime payments are to be determined also in accordance with the national agreement.

It appears to me that it would be natural to compare the appellant's basic salary as set out in her contract with the basic salary determined under the men's contract. I think it would be natural to treat the provision relating to basic pay as a term in each of the contracts.

However, one has to take account of the hours to be worked in order to earn this money and I think this consideration points to the importance of the provision in question being one which is capable of being compared from the point of view of the benefit it confers with a corresponding provision in another contract to see whether or nor it is more beneficial than that provision. Accordingly, I am of opinion that the natural application of the word 'term' to this contract is that it applies, for example, to the basic pay, and that the appropriate comparison is with the hourly rate of basic pay.

But the respondents say that this is not correct. They say that the use of the expression in s. 1(2) defining an equality clause as a provision which 'relates to terms (whether concerned with pay or not) of a contract' shows that Parliament had in mind that all provisions relating to pay were to be considered as a single term and that accordingly, it is only by taking account of all the contractual provisions relating to pay that you can make the comparison which is envisaged. They go on to say that if this is not correct, many difficulties are likely to arise. For example, they say where a woman employee engaged on work of equal value with a man is paid a basic salary of say, £7,500 per annum and she also has the use of a car valued at say, £3,500 per annum, whereas the man is paid £11,000 per annum, it would be wrong to say that she is entitled to have the term dealing with basic pay of £7,500 put up to £11,000 and the man on applying under the same legislation would be able to say that there was no term in his contract giving him the use of a car and therefore he was entitled to one and thus got the value of another £3,500. The result would be, say the respondents, that by application of this legislation both man and woman would receive an enhancement of their remuneration in a way quite unnecessary in order to produce equality. The respondents submit strongly that the only way out this difficulty is to consider together as one term all matters relating to pay, however expressed, in order to produce a result that the woman is put up to equality with the man and no further, and the man put up to equality with the woman and no further, so that there is no general enhancement of their total remuneration.

It was the difficulties involved in this and similar examples that weighed with the Court of Appeal and the Employment Appeal Tribunal in deciding the respondents' favour.

While one can envisage difficult examples, in the ordinary case such as the present no such difficulty arises and in my opinion it would be wrong to depart from the natural reading of the words Parliament has used because of the difficulty in their application to particular examples, especially when those examples do not arise in actual cases.

The difficulty of reconciling the respondents' construction with the words used in the Act is emphasised when one considers the provisions of part (ii) in each of the subclauses (a), (b) and (c) of s. 1(2) as was pointed out by my noble and learned friend, Lord Bridge of Harwich, in the course of the hearing before your Lordships.

It is, I think, impossible to believe that Parliament envisaged a contract with no provision for pay at all and therefore if the respondents' construction is adopted, part (ii) in each of the subsections could apply only to other benefits. This seems a most unlikely construction when one notices that the introductory words of subs. (2), which apply to parts (i) and (ii), speak of terms (whether concerned with pay or not).

Reference was made in the course of the argument before your Lordships to s. 3(4) of the Equal Pay Act 1970. Although that section has now been repealed by the Sex Discrimination Act 1986, in considering the construction of the Act the provisions it originally contained are relevant. Section 3(4) originally provided:

> Subject to s. 6 below, the amendments to be made in a collective agreement under this section shall be such as are needed—
> (a) to extend to both men and women any provision applying specifically to men only or to women only; and
> (b) to eliminate any resulting duplication in the provisions of the agreement in such a way as not to make the terms and conditions agreed for men, or those agreed for women, less favourable in any respect than they would have been without the amendments;
> but the amendments shall not extend the operation of the collective agreement to men or to women not previously falling within it, and where accordingly a provision applying specifically to men only or to women only continues to be required for a category of men or of women (there being no provision in the agreement for women or, as the case may be, for men of that category), then the provision shall be limited to men or women of that category but there shall be made to it such amendments, if any, as are needed to secure that the terms and conditions of the men or women of that category are not in any respect less favourable than those of all persons of the other sex to whom the agreement applies.

This provision seems strongly to support the argument for the appellant. Counsel for the respondents countered by suggesting that where a collective agreement deliberately and expressly differentiated between men and women there might be room for a stronger corrective as a matter of policy than where without deliberate and express differentiation between men and women inevitably resulted. In my opinion, however, the terms of s. 3(4) as originally enacted, which I have quoted to support the view that the policy of the Act is more consistent with what in any event I had taken to be the natural meaning of the words in question in s. 1(2), than with the meaning put forward by the respondents, which would require a sharp difference in policy between s. 1(2) and s. 3(4) of the Act.

For these reasons, in my opinion, the appellant's construction of s. 1(2) of the Act of 1970 is to be preferred to that offered by the respondents and this case should be remitted to the Industrial Tribunal for determination in accordance with this opinion.

On this view of the matter it is not strictly necessary to consider the question of Community law. Generally speaking primary legislation in the United Kingdom could confer a greater benefit on the appellant than she would be entitled to under the Community legislation. The present case is special since the particular provisions on which the appellant relies for her case were inserted by regulations made under the European Communities Act 1972 and accordingly it might be questioned whether, if higher rights than those conferred under Community law were provided in this way in domestic law, the making of the regulations was a proper exercise of the statutory power conferred by the European Communities Act. In the present case the matter has not been argued on this basis by the respondents and it would be particularly difficult to do so since the provisions of s. 1 of the Act of 1970 which apply to like work and work rated as equivalent are contained in primary legislation in respect of which an argument precisely the same as that advanced by the respondents could have been raised.

I have already referred to the relevant Community provisions. In *Jenkins* v. *Kingsgate (Clothing Productions) Ltd* ([1981] IRLR 228), the Court of Justice of the European Communities said (p. 234, para. 79):

> The provisions of art. 1 of that Directive are confined, in the first paragraph, to restating the principle of equal pay set out in art. 119 of the Treaty and specify, in the second paragraph, the conditions for applying that principle where a job classification system is used for determining pay.
>
> It follows, therefore, that art. 1 of the Council Directive (75/117/EEC), which is principally designed to facilitate the practical application of the principle of equal pay outlined in art. 119 of the Treaty, in no way alters the content or scope of that principle as defined in the Treaty.

In my opinion the terms of art. 1 are consistent with the appellant's submission. When elimination of all discrimination on grounds of sex is to be applied to all aspects and conditions of remuneration I consider this requires each of these aspects to be considered and discrimination existing in any aspect to be eliminated irrespective of the other aspects. It does not appear to me to be a natural reading of art. 1 to say that if the remuneration as a whole provides the same result for a man and a woman it does not matter that some aspects of the remuneration discriminate in favour of the woman so long as there are corresponding discriminations in other aspects in favour of the man.

I therefore conclude that there is nothing in the European legislation which detracts from the force of the appellant's argument on the domestic legislation and that if it were necessary to come to an opinion upon the matter I would reach the same result on the European legislation only.

As I said earlier, s. 1(3) of the Equal Pay Act has not at any stage been relied on by the respondents. In the course of the argument reference was sometimes made to s. 1(3) by counsel for the appellant to suggest that difficult examples might be dealt with by reference to that section. Since in the nature of the dispute between the parties s. 1(3) has never been in issue in this case I prefer to express no concluded opinion about its construction but I am presently of the view that s. 1(3) would not provide a defence to an employer against whom it was shown that a term in the woman's contract was less favourable to her than a corresponding term in the man's contract on the basis that there was another term in the woman's contract which was more favourable to her than the corresponding term in the man's contract. At the very least for s. 1(3) to operate it would have to be shown that the unfavourable character of the term in the woman's contract was in fact due to the difference in the opposite sense in the other term and that the difference was not due to the reason of sex. I consider that counsel for the appellant succeeds on the natural reading of the words of s. 1(2) which are in issue and that your Lordships do not require to reach any final conclusion in this case on the meaning and effect of s. 1(3).

...

LORD GOFF OF CHIEVELEY: My Lords, this appeal raises a question of construction of s. 1 of the Equal Pay Act 1970. ... The problem arises upon the construction of s. 1(2), when read together with s. 1(3). The contention of the appellant has been that s. 1(2) refers to the specific term or terms of which complaint is made, and that she is entitled to redress in respect of those specific terms, irrespective of any other terms of her contract or of the male comparator's contract which may have an impact on the overall comparison of their respective contractual positions. This contention has been rejected by a majority of the Industrial Tribunal ([1984] IRLR 463), by a unanimous Employment Appeal Tribunal ([1986] IRLR 287) and by a unanimous Court of Appeal, as leading to such absurd consequences that it cannot be right. Focusing upon the provisions of s. 1(2)(a)(i), (b)(i) and (c)(i), Nicholls LJ (who delivered the judgment of the Court of Appeal) had this to say ([1987] IRLR 186 at p. 189, para. 27):

> The Act requires the 'term' of the woman's contract to be compared with a 'term of a similar kind'. Terms in contracts of employment are of many 'kinds'; concerning the nature of the work, working conditions, hours of work, pay, and so forth. Where the complaint relates to pay, the provisions which have to be compared are the terms concerning pay. The 'term' in the woman's contract concerning pay must not be less favourable than the 'term' concerning pay in the man's contract. This involves looking, in the case of the woman and of the man, at the whole of the relevant term, viz. the term concerning pay. This will be so even if the complainant seeks to isolate one item of her remuneration and compare that alone with a corresponding item in the man's remuneration. The complainant cannot, by limiting her claim in such a way, elevate to the status of a term what is, in the context of the statutory comparison, only part of the relevant term.

Nicholls LJ then proceeded to consider a number of examples with reference to his preferred construction of the Act, in a manner which shows that he would, for this purpose, construe 'pay' in a very wide sense, as including, for example, cash bonuses, benefits in kind, sickness benefits and length of paid holidays. Of sickness benefits he said (at p. 190, para. 30):

They form part of the employees' remuneration; they are part of their 'pay', giving that word the wide meaning which, in step with art. 119 and the equal pay directive, it must surely bear in the context of the Equal Pay Act 1970, as amended.

Now I have to confess that, faced with such strength of opinion in the courts below, and by a unanimity of view in both the Employment Appeal Tribunal and the Court of Appeal, I am very reluctant to depart from that view - especially as, in both courts, the approach favoured by the appellant was stigmatised as leading to absurd and unreal consequences. This feeling was reinforced by the powerful argument of Lord Irvine QC for the respondents, who, too, criticised the appellant's approach in very strong terms. Yet, in the end, I have to consider the point as one of construction of the Act, and in particular of s. 1(2); and to the construction of that subsection I now turn.

Section 1(2) is subdivided into three subsubsections - the first, (a) being concerned with like work, the second, (b) with work rated as equivalent, and the third, (c) with work of equal value. Each of these subsubsections makes provision for two alternative situations - (i) where any term of the woman's contract is (or becomes) less favourable to her than a term of a similar kind in the male comparator's contract, and (ii) where the woman's contract does not include a term corresponding to a term benefiting the male comparator included in his contract. I will call the first situation the case of the less favourable term, and the second situation the case of the absent term.

In considering the question of construction, it is plain that we have to consider it in relation both to the case of the less favourable term, and the case of the absent term, for the same policy considerations must underlie each. Furthermore, I find it easier to approach the problem by considering first the case of the absent term, because the provisions of subsubs. (ii) of each subsection are in simpler terms than those of subsubs. (i), and are therefore easier to construe.

What does subsubs. (ii) in each case provide? It provides that if the woman's contract does not include a term corresponding to a term benefiting the male comparator included in his contract, her contract shall be treated as including such a term. Next, what does such a provision mean? If I look at the words used, and give them their natural and ordinary meaning, they mean quite simply that one looks at the man's contract and at the woman's contract, and if one finds in the man's contract a term benefiting him which is not included in the woman's contract, then that term is treated as included in hers. On this simple and literal approach, the words 'benefiting that man' mean precisely what they say - that the term must be one which is beneficial to him, as opposed to being burdensome. So if, for example, the man's contract contains a term that he is to be provided with the use of a car, and the woman's contract does not include such a term, then her contract is to be treated as including such a term.

It is obvious that this approach cannot be reconciled with the approach favoured by the Court of Appeal, because it does not require, or indeed permit, the court to look at the overall contractual position of each party, or even to look at their overall position as regards one particular matter, for example, 'pay' in the wide sense adopted by the Court of Appeal. To achieve that result, it would be necessary, in subsubs. (ii), to construe the word 'term' as referring to the totality of the relevant contractual provisions relating to a particular subject matter, for example 'pay' or alternatively to construe the words 'benefiting that man' as importing the necessity of a comparison in relation to the totality of the relevant contractual provisions concerning a particular subject matter and then for a conclusion to be reached that, on balance, the man has thereby benefited. The latter construction I find impossible to derive from the words of the statute; and, to be fair, I do not think that there is any evidence that it would have found favour with the Court of Appeal. But what of the former, which is consistent with the judgment of the Court of Appeal? Again, I find myself unable to accept it. First, it would mean that the situation of the absent term must be confined only to those cases where there was *no* provision relating, for example, to pay - or, I suppose, to overtime, or to some other wholly distinct topic. I cannot think that that was the intention of the legislature. In common-sense terms, it means that subsubs. (ii) would hardly ever be relevant at all; certainly, since every contract of employment makes some provision for 'pay' in the broad sense adopted by the Court of Appeal, subsubs. (ii) would never be relevant in relation to pay or any other form of remuneration in cash or in kind or in the form of other benefits. I find this proposition to be startling. Second, it imposes upon the word 'term' a meaning which I myself do not regard as its natural or ordinary meaning. If a contract contains provisions relating to (1) basic pay, (2) benefits in kind such as the use of a car, (3) cash bonuses, and (4) sickness benefits, it would never occur to me to lump all these together as one 'term' of the contract, simply because they can all together be considered as providing for the total 'remuneration' for the services to be performed under the contract. It truth, these would include a number of different terms, and in my opinion it does unacceptable violence to the words of the statute to construe the word 'term' in subsubs. (ii) as embracing collectively all these different terms.

It is against the background of this reasoning in relation to the case of the absent term, that I turn to subsubs. (i) and the case of the less favourable term. Here the Court of Appeal was able to build their construction upon the basis of a reference, in the subsubsection, to 'a term of a similar kind' in the male comparator's contract. They considered that these words referred necessarily to a term relating to the same overall subject matter, in particular pay; and that the question whether the relevant term in the woman's contract was less favourable than that in the man's contract could only sensibly be considered by comparing all the provisions relating to this subject matter in the contracts of each. From this they derived the broad meaning of the word 'term' which I have described.

For my part, I cannot accept this reasoning. Suppose that there is a term in a woman's contract which provides that she is to be paid £x per hour, and that there is a term in the male comparator's contract that he is to be paid £y per hour, y being greater than x. On the natural and ordinary meaning of the words in the statute, there is, in my opinion, in such a case, a term of the woman's contract which is less favourable to her than a term of a similar kind in the male comparator's contract; and that would be so even if there was some other provision in her contract which conferred upon her a benefit (which fell within her overall 'remuneration') which the man was not entitled to receive under his contract, such as, for example, the use of a car. I do not consider that the words 'a term of a similar kind' are capable of constituting a basis for building the construction of the word 'term' favoured by the Court of Appeal. Again, in my opinion, the words mean precisely what they say. You look at the two contracts: you ask yourself the common-sense question - is there in each contract a term of a similar kind, i.e. a term making a comparable provision for the same subject matter; if there is, then you compare the two, and if, on that comparison, the term of the woman's contract proves to be less favourable than the term of the man's contract, then the term in the woman's contract is to be treated as modified so as to make it not less favourable. I am, of course, much fortified in this approach in that it appears to me to be consistent with the only construction of subsubs. (ii), concerned with the case of the absent term, which I find to be acceptable. But, in addition, I feel that the Court of Appeal's attempt to introduce the element of overall comparison placed them firmly, or rather infirmly, upon a slippery slope; because, once they departed from the natural and ordinary meaning of the word 'term', they in reality found it impossible to control the ambit of the comparison which they considered to be required. For almost any, indeed perhaps any, benefit will fall within 'pay' in the very wide sense favoured by them, in which event it is difficult to segregate any sensible meaning of the word 'term.'

Now I fully appreciate that this construction of s. 1(2) will always lead, where the section is held to apply, to enhancement of the relevant term in the woman's contract. Likewise, it will in the converse case lead to enhancement of the relevant term in the man's contract. This appears to me to be the effect of the philosophy underlying the subsection. I also appreciate that this may, in some cases, lead to what has been called mutual enhancement or leapfrogging, as terms of the woman's contract and the man's contract are both, so to speak, upgraded to bring them into line with each other. It is this effect which was found to be so offensive by both the Employment Appeal Tribunal and the Court of Appeal. They viewed with dismay the possibility of equality being achieved only by mutual enhancement, and not by an overall consideration of the respective contractual terms of both the man and the woman, at least in relation to a particular subject matter, such as overall remuneration, considering that mutual enhancement transcended the underlying philosophy of the Equal Pay Act and that it could have a profoundly inflationary effect.

To these fears there are, I consider, two different answers on two different levels. The first answer is that given by Mr Lester QC, for the appellant, which is that the employer must, where he can, have recourse to s. 1(3). I, for my part, see great force in this argument. I am, however, a little troubled about embarking upon any deep discussion of the meaning and effect of the subsection in the present case. First, we were told that no reliance was placed upon the subsection in this case, so that its effect has no direct bearing upon your Lordships decision in this appeal. Second, and for the same reason, we have before us no concrete facts upon which to consider the application of the subsection in the context of the present case. Third, it appears that the construction of the subsection has caused, and indeed is causing, very considerable difficulty: to substantiate this, I need only refer to the helpful discussion in *Pannick on Sex Discrimination Law* (1985) at pp. 105-114. Even so, I do not think that it would be right in the present case to ignore the possible impact of s. 1(3). I propose, however, only to make these observations. First, it must be right, when construing the subsection to have regard both to the statutory context, and in particular to the effect of the neighbouring subs. 1(2); and it must also be right to have regard to the philosophy underlying the whole legislation. If regard is to be had to these, then, as Mr Lester suggests, s. 1(3) could indeed have the effect, in appropriate cases, of preventing the mutual enhancement which was so much feared by the Court of Appeal in the present case. An example may be derived from the recent decision of the Employment Appeal Tribunal in *Reed Packaging Ltd* v. *Boozer* [1988] ICR 391 (EAT), decided after the argument before your Lordships' House in the present case. In that case the Tribunal held that different pay structures for the woman and her male comparator, wholly devoid of discrimination on the ground of sex, could constitute a material fact which is not the difference of sex, within s. 1(3). I must not be taken as stating that the particular case was correctly decided, since its correctness is not in issue before your Lordships' House in the present case: I use it only for the purpose of illustration. Of course s. 1(3) must not be used so as to promote either direct or indirect discrimination (cf. *Clay Cross (Quarry Services) Ltd* v. *Fletcher* [1978] IRLR 361). So where, for example, there is direct or indirect discrimination embedded in the two relevant pay structures of the woman and her male comparator, it would appear that s. 1(3) cannot be invoked by the employer. In such a case, it may be that the effect of the statute, as I would construe it, is that it is capable of leading to mutual enhancement of the contractual terms of the man and the woman; though I entertain some doubt whether some of the examples considered in the course of argument are likely to arise in practice.

This brings me to my second answer, which is that, if the construction of s. 1(2) which I prefer does not accord with the true intention of

Parliament, then the appropriate course for Parliament is to amend the legislation to bring it into line with its true intention. In the meanwhile, however, the decision of your Lordships' House may have the salutary effect of drawing to the attention of employers and trade unions the absolute need for ensuring that the pay structures for various groups of employees do not contain any element of sex discrimination, direct or indirect, because otherwise s. 1(3) will not be available to mitigate the effects which s. 1(2), in this present form, is capable of producing on its own.

For these reasons, I would allow the appeal.

# Leverton v. Clwyd County Council[1]

LORD BRIDGE OF HARWICH: My Lords, the appellant is employed as a qualified nursery nurse by the respondents at the Golftyn Infants' School, Connah's Quay, Clwyd. On 4 September 1984 she applied to an Industrial Tribunal claiming under s. 1(2)(c) of the Equal Pay Act 1970, as amended by the Equal Pay (Amendment) Regulations 1983, that she was employed on work of equal value to that of male employees of the respondent. The initial application was clearly defective in that it failed to name the comparators. However, after obtaining on discovery particulars of the terms and conditions of employment of some 200 men employed, as she is, in the administrative, professional, technical and clerical ('APT & C') services of the respondents, she nominated 11 male comparators by reference to whom the application proceeded. At the time of the hearing by the Industrial Tribunal in June 1985 the appellant was in receipt of an annual salary of £5,058. The annual salaries of the comparators ranged from £6,081 to £8,532.

By virtue of the equality clause deemed to be included in her contract of employment under s. 1(1) of the Act of 1970, the appellant, if she could establish that she was employed on work of equal value to that of 'a man in the same employment', would *prima facie* be entitled under s. 1(2)(c) to have the terms of her contract treated as modified as provided by the section to bring them into line with the terms of his contract. The far-reaching scope of that modification appears from your Lordships' decision in *Hayward* v. *Cammell Laird Shipbuilders Ltd* [1988] IRLR 257.

The respondents resisted the appellant's claim, *inter alia*, on the grounds (1) that none of the comparators was 'a man in the same employment' with the appellant, and (2) that the variation between the appellant's contract and the contracts of the comparators was 'genuinely due to a material factor which is not the difference of sex.' These two grounds relied on by the respondents, each, if well founded, sufficient to defeat the appellant's claim, give rise to the two issues for decision in the present appeal. They depend on subss (6) and (3) respectively of s. 1. ....

It will be necessary to examine some aspects of the facts in detail later, but it is convenient at this point to summarise the facts which are of central importance. None of the comparators works at the same establishment as the appellant. The appellant and all the comparators, however, are employed on terms and conditions derived from the same collective agreement known as the 'purple book', being a scheme agreed by the National Joint Council for Local Authorities' APT & C Services. Under the terms of that agreement the appellant's salary is on scale 1; the salaries of the comparators are at different points on scales 3 and 4. The appellant's basic working week including paid

---

1    [1989] AC 706, [1989] 2 WLR 47, [1989] 1 All ER 78, [1989] ICR 33, [1989] IRLR 28, HL (E).

lunch breaks is 32 1/2 hours. Her holidays are coterminous with the school holidays. The comparators' basic working week is 37 hours (in one case 39 hours). Their annual holiday entitlement is 20 days plus eight statutory and three local holidays with increments after five years' service. The effect of these differences is that each of the comparators works many more hours in the year to earn his annual salary than the appellant works to earn hers. As one measure of the extent of this difference the respondents put forward for comparison at the hearing a *pro rata* calculation of notional hourly income yielding figures of £4.42 for the appellant and £4.40 for the comparator who works 37 hours a week and earns the maximum salary under scale 4. Although rejecting this method of comparison as inappropriate, the Industrial Tribunal appear to have accepted the accuracy of the arithmetical calculation.

The majority of the Industrial Tribunal held both that the appellant was not 'in the same employment' with the comparators as that phrase is defined by s. 1(6) and that the respondents had established what it will be convenient to call 'the material factor defence' under s. 1(3) in that the variation between the appellant's contract and the comparator's contracts was genuinely due to a material factor which was not the difference in sex, *viz.* the difference in working hours and length of holidays, being a material difference between her case and theirs. They accordingly dismissed the application. The minority member dissented on both grounds. The Employment Appeal Tribunal ([1987] 1 WLR 65) affirmed the decision of the Industrial Tribunal on the ground that the appellant and the comparators were not in the same employment. They held, however, that the Industrial Tribunal had erred in law in upholding the material factor defence on the ground that there was no evidence capable of supporting a finding that the variation between the appellant's contract and the comparators' contract was 'genuinely due' to a material factor which was not the difference of sex. The Court of Appeal (May, Balcombe and Stocker LJJ) affirmed by a majority (May LJ dissenting) the conclusion of both Tribunals that the appellant and the comparators were not in the same employment and held by a majority (Balcombe LJ dissenting) that there was evidence to support the finding by the majority of the Industrial Tribunal that the respondents had established the material factor defence and that there was accordingly no ground upon which the Employment Appeal Tribunal could reverse this finding as erroneous in law. The appellant now appeals to your Lordships' House by leave of the Court of Appeal.

On the question of whether the appellant was in the same employment as the comparators working at different establishments, the view which prevailed with the majority of the Industrial Tribunal, the Employment Appeal Tribunal, and the majority of the Court of Appeal was that the comparison called for by s. 1(6) was between the terms and conditions of employment of the appellant on the one hand and of the comparators on the other and that it was only if this comparison showed their terms and conditions of employment to be 'broadly similar' that the test applied by the phrase 'common terms and conditions of employment' in s. 1(6) was satisfied. The majority of the Industrial Tribunal affirmed by the Employment Appeal Tribunal and the majority of the Court of Appeal, held that the difference in this case in working hours and holidays was a radical difference in the 'core terms' of the respective contracts of employment which prevented the comparison from satisfying the statutory test. The contrary view embraced by the dissenting member of the Industrial Tribunal and by May LJ in the Court of Appeal was that the comparison called for was much broader, *viz.* a comparison between the terms and conditions of employment observed at two or more establishments, embracing both the establishment at which the woman is employed and the establishment at which the men are employed, and applicable either generally, i.e. to all the employees at the relevant establishments, or to a particular class or classes of employees to which both the woman and the men belong. Basing himself implicitly on this view, the dissenting member of the Industrial Tribunal expressed his conclusion in the matter tersely. Having referred to the purple book, he said:

> 3.    Within that agreement there are nine sections and numerous clauses. They do not apply, with few exceptions, to any particular grade. It is clearly a general agreement and not specific to any particular group or class of employee.
> 4.    It is, in my opinion, beyond doubt that the applicant and the comparators are employed on common terms and conditions, i.e. the APT & C agreement, and clearly it is within the provisions of s. 1(6).

My Lords, this is an important difference in principle which depends on the true construction of s. 1(6). I have no hesitation in preferring the minority to the majority view expressed in the courts below. It seems to me, first, that the language of the subsection is clear and unambiguous. It poses the question whether the terms and conditions of employment 'observed' at two or more establishments (at which the relevant woman and the relevant men are employed) are 'common', being terms and conditions of employment observed 'either generally or for employees of the relevant classes.' The concept of common terms and conditions of employment observed generally at different establishments necessarily contemplates terms and conditions applicable to a wide range of employees whose individual terms will vary greatly *inter se*. On the construction of the subsection adopted by the majority below the phrase 'observed either generally or for employees of the relevant classes' is given no content. Terms and conditions of employment governed by the same collective agreement seem to me to represent the paradigm, though not necessarily the only example, of the common terms and conditions of employment contemplated by the subsection.

But if, contrary to my view, there is any such ambiguity in the language of s. 1(6) as to permit the question whether a woman and men employed by the same employer in different establishments are in the same employment to depend on a direct comparison establishing a 'broad similarity' between the woman's terms and conditions of employment and those of her claimed comparators, I should reject a construction of the subsection in this sense on the ground that it frustrates rather than serves the manifest purpose of the legislation. That purpose is to enable a woman to eliminate discriminatory differences between the terms of her contract and those of any male fellow employee doing like work, work rated as equivalent or work of equal value, whether he works in the same establishment as her or in another establishment where terms and conditions of employment common to both establishments are observed. With all respect to the majority view which prevailed below, it cannot, in my opinion, possibly have been the intention of Parliament to require a woman claiming equality with a man in another establishment to prove an undefined substratum of similarity between the particular terms of her contract and his as the basis of her entitlement to eliminate any discriminatory differences between those terms.

On the construction of s. 1(6) which I would adopt there is a sensible and rational explanation for the limitation of equality claims as between men and women employed at different establishments to establishments at which common terms and conditions of employment are observed. There may be perfectly good geographical or historical reasons why a single employer should operate essentially different employment regimes at different establishments. In such cases the limitation imposed by s. 1(6) will operate to defeat claims under s. 1 as between men and women at the different establishments. I take two examples by way of illustration. A single employer has two establishments, one in London and one in Newcastle. The rate of pay earned by persons of both sexes for the same work are substantially higher in London than in Newcastle. Looking at either the London establishment or the Newcastle establishment in isolation there is no sex discrimination. If the women in Newcastle could invoke s. 1 of the Act of 1970 to achieve equality with the men in London this would eliminate a differential in earnings which is due not to sex but to geography. Section 1(6) prevents them from doing so. An employer operates factory A where he has a long standing collective agreement with the ABC union. The same employer takes over a company operating factory X and becomes an 'associated employer' of the persons working there. The previous owner of factory X had a long standing collective agreement with the XYZ union which the new employer continues to operate. The two collective agreements have produced quite different structures governing pay and other terms and conditions of employment at the two factories. Here again s. 1(6) will operate to prevent women in factory A claiming equality with men in factory X and *vice versa*. These examples are not, of course, intended to be exhaustive. So long as Industrial Tribunals direct themselves correctly in law to make the appropriate broad comparison, it will always be a question of fact for them, in any particular case, to decide whether, as between two different establishments, 'common terms and conditions of employment are observed either generally or for employees of the relevant classes.' Here the majority of the Industrial Tribunal misdirected themselves in law and their conclusion on this point cannot be supported.

Before turning to the issue which arises directly for decision in relation to the material factor defence, it is appropriate to refer to certain wider considerations to which your Lordships' attention was drawn in the course of the argument. When considering an equal pay claim made by a woman under s. 1(2)(c) of the Act of 1970 with respect to any man who is in the same employment with her, subject to any material factor defence, which the Industrial Tribunal has a discretion to entertain at the preliminary stage, the Industrial Tribunal is obliged to refer the claim to an expert under s. 2A(1) unless 'satisfied that there are no reasonable grounds for determining that the work is of equal value.' In this case the Industrial Tribunal was not so satisfied. Accordingly the next step, if the material factor defence did not succeed at this stage, would be to refer the claim to an expert who would be required to carry out a job evaluation to determine, as between the applicant and each comparator, whether their work was of equal value. 'Job evaluation', a phrase derived from the language of s. 1(5), is a term of art describing the highly sophisticated technique adopted by the English legislation to give effect to Community law by measuring what, apart from 'like work' as defined by s. 1(4), is to qualify as 'equal work' under art. 119 of the EEC Treaty (Cmnd 5179-11) or 'work to which equal value is attributed' under art. 1 of Council Directive EEC 75/117. A general job evaluation study is a study undertaken of the jobs of all the employees, or of any group of employees, in an undertaking or group of undertakings which, as described in s. 1(5), evaluates their jobs 'in terms of the demand made on a worker under various headings (for instance effort, skill, decision).' Such a study may operate in two ways. If a woman's and a man's jobs are rated as equal by the study, she may claim the benefits of an equality clause in relation to him under s. 1(2)(b). If a woman's and a man's jobs are rated as unequal by the study, the employer may rely on the study to defeat the woman's equal value claim under s. 1(2)(c) *in limine* under s. 2A(1) provided there are no reasonable grounds for determining that the study itself discriminated on grounds of sex. Just how complex and sophisticated the process of job evaluation is required to be to satisfy the statutory criteria embodied in s. 1(5) and s. 2A(3) for eliminating sex discrimination will be appreciated by anyone who reads the judgments of the Court of Appeal in *Bromley* v. *H & J Quick Ltd* [1988] IRLR 249. Where, as here, there has been no relevant general job evaluation study, the expert, if the matter were referred to him, would have to apply the same technique of evaluation, as required by the language of s. 1(2)(c) 'work which ... is, in terms of the demands made on her (for instance under such headings as effort, skill and decision), of equal value etc.', in carrying out what would be, in effect, an *ad hoc* job evaluation study as between the appellant and her comparators.

In the course of their very thorough examination of every aspect of this case, the Industrial Tribunal considered whether the differences in hours of work and holidays between the appellant and the comparators might be a matter for assessment by the expert when considering the 'demands' made upon them by their respective jobs. They concluded as follows:

> We are unanimously agreed that such an assessment would not fall within his expertise and experience of job evaluation studies and that the Tribunal must address itself to this fundamental difference.

Your Lordships were assured by counsel appearing in the appeal, whose collective experience in this somewhat esoteric field of law must be unrivalled, that in job evaluation studies the demands made by different jobs have in practice always been assessed under whatever headings are adopted on a qualitative, not a quantitative, basis. That this is the correct basis, if English law is to conform to Community law, seems to be amply borne out by the judgment of the European Court of Justice in *Macarthys Ltd* v. *Smith* (Case 129/79) [1980] IRLR 210; see also *National Coal Board* v. *Sherwin* [1978] IRLR 122. I have no doubt that demand in terms of hours worked is not only beyond the expertise of the job evaluator but is, on the true construction of s. 1(2)(c) and (5), a factor which is outside the scope of job evaluation.

It was suggested by counsel for the appellant, instructed not only by the appellant's union but also by the Equal Opportunities Commission, that in relation to the material factor defence the present appeal raised some great issue of principle which called for a general pronouncement by your Lordships' House in order to clarify the law as to the nature and scope of the burden which an employer must discharge when seeking to justify a pay practice which has the effect, whether directly or indirectly, of differentiating between men and women. Since the decision of the Industrial Tribunal in the instant case there have been two judgments of first importance relevant to the consideration of a material factor defence: the judgment of the European Court of Justice in *Bilka-Kaufhaus GmbH* v. *Weber von Hartz* (Case 170/84) [1987] IRLR 317, and the judgment of this House in *Rainey* v. *Greater Glasgow Health Board* [1987] IRLR 26. Although the Industrial Tribunal did not have the advantage of the guidance afforded by those cases, they did consider and apply the principles which had been expressed in the judgment of Browne-Wilkinson J in *Jenkins* v. *Kingsgate (Clothing Productions) Ltd* [1981] IRLR 228, to which the House in *Rainey* gave its full approval. In the circumstances it does not appear to me that any new problem of law arises here for resolution. The speech of my noble and learned friend Lord Keith of Kinkel in *Rainey* expressing the unanimous opinion of the House, expounds the applicable principles, if I may say so, with admirable lucidity and it seems to me quite unnecessary for your Lordships in the instant case to traverse the same ground. The question which arises here is not what principles are applicable, but whether the applicable principles were correctly applied or, more accurately, whether there is any indication that the majority of the Industrial Tribunal erred in principle or, to apply the well known test in *Edwards* v. *Bairstow* [1956] AC 14 at p. 36, *per* Lord Radcliffe whether their determination contradicted the 'true and only reasonable conclusion' to which the evidence before them led.

I must now turn to examine in more detail the facts on which the material factor defence depends. I have already referred to the notional calculation put forward by the respondents to compare the appellant's salary with that of the comparators on an hourly rate basis. It is not wholly clear whether the respondents were advancing this in support of a defence that the terms of the appellant's contract were not less favourable than those of any of the comparators. If so, the Industrial Tribunal rightly rejected it as misconceived, anticipating the decision of your Lordships' House in *Hayward* v. *Cammell Laird Shipbuilders Ltd (No 2)* [1988] IRLR 257. But the decision records that, if the method of approach involved in this comparison were proper, the Industrial Tribunal would regard the respondents' point as 'well made.' It adds later that the comparison is viewed by the majority as 'casting interesting light on the broader merits of the case.' The majority must have had this comparison in mind, as they were entitled to, when considering the material factor defence.

Between the date of the appellant's application to the Industrial Tribunal and the hearing a difference between the staff side and the employers' side of the National Joint Council on rates of pay for the APT & C services of local authorities had been referred to arbitration by the Central Arbitration Committee ('CAC') under s. 3 of the Employment Protection Act 1975. The arbitration resulted in an award which enhanced the pay of all grades concerned, but also enhanced the pay of nursery nurses and nursing assistants relative to other grades. The report of the CAC promulgating the award shows that the relative remuneration of nursery nurses and nursing assistants, taking account of the difference in hours worked and holidays, was fully examined in the course of the arbitration and the CAC report and award were naturally much relied on by the respondents before the Industrial Tribunal. It is common ground, however, than an arbitration under s. 3 of the Act of 1975 is not directly concerned with questions of sexual discrimination.

At the time of the hearing before the Industrial Tribunal a general job evaluation study has been undertaken but not completed in relation to all the respondents' employees in the APT & C services except nursery nurses and nursing assistants. These latter had been excluded from the job evaluation study by agreement between the respondents and the unions concerned on behalf of the nurses.

When the appellant appealed to the Employment Appeal Tribunal her case was taken up by the Equal Opportunities Commission. One of the grounds of appeal relied on was that:

The Industrial Tribunal failed to decide whether or not the pay difference was due to, that is caused by, the different working hours and holidays for the appellants and the male comparables.

Since it was to be argued that there was no evidence to establish the necessary causal link, the Equal Opportunities Commission wrote to the Employment Appeal Tribunal seeking the chairman's notes of evidence and the request was passed on to the Industrial Tribunal. A reply was written on behalf of the chairman dated 5 December 1988 enclosing certain notes of evidence. The covering letter reads, so far as material:

> Further to your letter dated 26 November 1985, the chairman directs me to say that his notes of submissions and evidence cover 105 sides. He has refreshed his memory by going through the notes. The question of causality raised at paragraph 3(ii)(d) of the notice of appeal was not raised at the tribunal and not dealt with specifically in evidence. Any causal link can only be inferred from the evidence. The chairman has extracted those passages that seem to him relevant ... .

Although I have expressed my disagreement with the conclusion reached by the majority of the Industrial Tribunal on the issue which arose under s. 1(6), I must express my admiration for the care, lucidity and thoroughness with which the majority examined every issue in the case and explained the reasoning which led to their conclusions. In particular, they considered the implications of the differences in hours of work and holidays between the appellant and the comparators in great detail. They concluded that, though the appellant might in certain circumstances be required to work outside school hours, such work was of 'very limited significance.' Likewise hours worked outside the school term were 'extremely limited.'

In examining the effect of the CAC arbitration report and award, the majority directed themselves in the following terms:

> It is clear from the judgment of Browne-Wilkinson J in *Jenkins* v. *Kingsgate (Clothing Productions) Ltd (No 2)* [1981] IRLR 388 at paragraph 35, that some parallel exists between the concept of material factor or material difference and the concept of justifiability of indirect sexual discrimination under the Sex Discrimination Act. It is for the respondents to show that the factor upon which they rely was reasonably necessary to achieve some objective other than an objective related to the sex of the worker.

They concluded, in effect, that they could not safely rely on the CAC report and award *per se* and in advance of an expert job evaluation as necessarily having eliminated any element of unintentional sex discrimination between the almost exclusively female nursery nurses and the male comparators employed in other APT & C services. It was suggested that there was some inconsistency between this conclusion and the conclusion that the difference in hours of work and holidays established the material factor defence. I see no such inconsistency. On the contrary the way in which the majority of the Industrial Tribunal dealt with the argument for the respondents based on the CAC report and award leaves me in no doubt that they had the appropriate criteria of reasonable necessity and objective justifiability clearly in mind when they addressed the question whether, in their own judgment, the difference in hours of work and holidays as between the appellant and any comparator in receipt of the maximum salary on scale 4 established a material factor defence. In reciting the respondents' argument they clearly directed themselves to the question whether 'the variation in pay is genuinely due to these different terms', sc. the difference in hours of work and holidays, 'which constitute a material factor which is not the difference of sex.' They set out their conclusion in the following terms:

> The majority of the Tribunal is satisfied at this stage on the evidence that we have heard that the differing contractual terms on hours and holidays are a genuine material factor which make it reasonably necessary for the respondent to impose pay differentials between the applicant and the relevant comparators. We at this stage would dismiss the application upon the additional basis that the respondents have fully established that material factor defence.

Looking no further, I should conclude that this was a finding of fact which was amply justified by the evidence as a whole, but perhaps particularly by the comparison between the rates of pay and hours worked. Where a woman's and man's regular annual working hours, unaffected by any significant additional hours of work, can be translated into a notional hourly rate which yields no significant difference, it is surely a legitimate, if not a necessary, inference that the difference in their annual salaries is both due to and justified by the difference in the hours they work in the course of a year and has nothing to do with the difference in sex.

I cannot help thinking that the rejection of the material factor defence by the Employment Appeal Tribunal and by Balcombe LJ in his dissent on this point was due to the circumstance that they concentrated attention on the letter written on behalf of the chairman of the Industrial Tribunal six months after the hearing rather than on the decision itself. It was this, I believe, which led them into error. I doubt if it was legitimate to attach any significance to the chairman's letter at all. But it certainly did not afford a ground for impugning the decision if the decision itself was otherwise unassailable. Equally, the enclosure with the letter of three pages of evidence which the chairman presumably considered of immediate relevance could not justify confining attention to that evidence alone, to the exclusion of all the other material summarised and examined in the course of the decision, as the basis of any inference which the majority had drawn.

For these reasons I would dismiss the appeal.

I cannot leave this case without adding a word about the procedure involved in equal value claims under s. 1(2)(c) of the Act of 1970. If such a clam is referred to an expert under s. 2A, the expert's job evaluation and the subsequent procedural steps which follow the presentation of his report under the special rules of procedure governing equal value claims in Schedule 2 to the Industrial Tribunals (Rules of Procedure) Regulations 1985 will involve a lengthy, elaborate and, I apprehend, expensive process. The larger the number of comparators whose jobs have to be evaluated, the more elaborate and expensive the process is likely to be. Here, as already mentioned, the appellant spread her net very widely by claiming equality with eleven comparators. But by the time the case reached the House, your Lordships were told that, if her appeal succeeded, she would only seek a reference to an expert in relation to four of the original comparators. This only goes to show what a lot of time and money would have been wasted if the matter had proceeded on a reference to an expert with respect to all the 11 comparators. I do not in any way criticise the Industrial Tribunal in this case for deciding under s. 2A(1)(a) that they could not be satisfied that there were no reasonable grounds for determining her work to be of equal value with any one of the comparators. But I think that Industrial Tribunals should, so far as possible, be alert to prevent abuse of the equal value claims procedure by applicants who cast their net over too wide a spread of comparators. To take an extreme case, an applicant who claimed equality with A who earns £X and also with B who earns £2X could hardly complain if an Industrial Tribunal concluded that her claim of equality with A itself demonstrated that there were no reasonable grounds for her claim of equality with B. That said, however, it is right to point out that an employer's most effective safeguard against oppressive equal value claims is to initiate his own comprehensive job evaluation study under s. 1(5) which, if properly carried out, will afford him complete protection.

LORD TEMPLEMAN: My Lords, art. 119 of the EEC Treaty requires and the Equal Pay Directive (75/117/EEC) reiterates that Member States shall secure the elimination of all discrimination on grounds of sex in conformity with the principle of equal pay for the same work or for work of equal value. The United Kingdom complied with its Community obligations by the Equal Pay Act 1970 which was enacted, as its title indicates:

... to prevent discrimination, as regards terms and conditions of employment, between men and women.

By s. 1(2) of the Act of 1970 (as amended):

(c)   where a woman is employed on work which ... is, in terms of the demands made on her (for instance under such headings as effort, skill and decision), of equal value to that of a man in the same employment– ... if ... any term of the woman's contract is ... less favourable to the woman than a term of a similar kind in the contract under which that man is employed, that term of the woman's contract shall be treated as so modified as not to be less favourable ... .

In the present case the appellant, Mrs Leverton, claims under the Act of 1970 salary equality with men named by her and employed, like her, by the respondent Clwyd County Council. Mrs Leverton alleges that the men are paid more than Mrs Leverton although her work is equal in value to the work of the men. The council resists Mrs Leverton's claim on the grounds, *inter alia*, that even if the work of Mrs Leverton is equal in value to the work of the men, the difference in salary is not due to sex discrimination but is due to the fact that Mrs Leverton enjoys a shorter working week and longer holidays than the men.

Mrs Leverton is employed as a nursery nurse at an infants school. Nursery nurses and the men with whom she claims salary equality are employed by the council in the administrative, professional, technical and clerical services of the council. The salary scales for men and women employed in such services are determined in default of agreement by the Central Arbitration Committee appointed under s. 10 of the Employment Protection Act 1975 to resolve trade disputes by arbitration. The Central Arbitration Committee last made a relevant award in 1985 when special improvements were made to salaries of nursery nurses. The council employ 400 nursery nurses of whom all but one are women; they are paid salaries in accordance with scale 1 as determined and adjusted by the Central Arbitration Committee in 1985. Other staff employed by the council include 205 paid on scale 3; of these 148 are women. Other staff include 79 paid on scale 4; of these 42 are women. The difference between scale 1 and scale 3 salaries is roughly £1,000 per annum; the difference between scale 1 and scale 4 is roughly £1,500.

After initiating these present proceedings by making a general complaint that nursery nurses were unfairly paid, Mrs Leverton obtained discovery concerning over 200 employees of the council on scale 3 and scale 4. Mrs Leverton then complained of 11 employees. The Industrial Tribunal found that of these 11, numbers 6, 7, and 9 were the most obviously appropriate comparators. Number 6 is a library assistant employed in the library department of the council on scale 3. Number 7 is a driver/assistant employed in the library department on scale 3. Number 9 is a caretaker/supervisor employed in the administrative and legal department on scale 4. Mrs Leverton works 32 1/2 hours a week against 37 hours worked by the men with whom she claims salary equality, apart from one employee who works for 39 hours. Mrs Leverton enjoys 70 days' holiday; the men are entitled to 20 days' holiday plus increments after five years' service. It has not been decided whether the work performed by Mrs Leverton is in fact equal in value to the work of one or more of the scale 3 and scale 4 men with whom she seeks salary equality. But even if work of equal value were established, Mrs Leverton is not entitled to equality of salary unless the difference in salary is attributable to sex discrimination, conscious or unconscious. Article 119 and the Equal Pay Directive and the Act of 1970 are directed to the elimination of sex discrimination and not to the elimination of wage differences. Accordingly, s. 1 of the Act of 1970 (as amended) provides that:

(3)    An equality clause shall not operate in relation to a variation between the woman's contract and the man's contract if the employer proves that the variation is genuinely due to a material factor which is not the difference of sex ... .

The Industrial Tribunal found by a majority that the difference between the salary paid to Mrs Leverton and the salaries to the men she chose for comparison was not due to a difference of sex but to the difference between the hours worked and holidays enjoyed by Mrs Leverton, on the one hand, and her chosen comparators on the other hand. The Industrial Tribunal decided that the difference in hours and holidays was a 'material factor' within the meaning of s. 1(3) of the Act of 1970 and that the difference in salaries was 'genuinely due' to that material factor. On behalf of Mrs Leverton it was said that there was no evidence that the difference in hours of work and holidays was a 'material factor.' But the difference between the hours and holidays of Mrs Leverton, on the one hand, and of the comparators on the other hand, is sufficiently striking to constitute *prima facie* evidence of a material factor without calling any witness to say so. It was then said that there was no evidence that the difference between salaries corresponded exactly to the difference between hours and holidays. Exact correspondence is impossible to evaluate and unnecessary; s. 1(3) only requires that the difference in salaries be 'genuinely due' to the difference in hours and holidays which constitutes the relevant 'material factor.' The division of annual salary by hours worked attributed £4.42 for every hour worked by Mrs Leverton and £4.40 for every hour worked by the highest paid comparator. The Industrial Tribunal rightly rejected the argument that this hourly calculation proved that Mrs Leverton was paid as much as or more than the comparators. Nevertheless the calculation supported the council's contention that the difference in hours and holidays was a material factor which genuinely accounted for the difference in annual salary. Mrs Leverton did not produce any evidence to the contrary and did not produce any evidence which might have raised the suspicion that the difference in salary was due to sex discrimination. In the course of this appeal it was said on behalf of Mrs Leverton that for historical or other reasons the work of the Central Arbitration Committee might be tainted, consciously or unconsciously, by sex discrimination in favour of men and against women. The Central Arbitration Committee considered a submission that nursery nurses were underpaid and were informed on behalf of local authorities that nursery nurses only worked a 32 1/2 hour week. The Central Arbitration Committee made its award in 1985 in the light of these and other submissions and must have been fully cognisant of and desirous of giving effect to the principle of equal pay which formed part of Community law when the United Kingdom joined the Community in 1972 and which is embodied in the Act of 1970 (as amended). The Industrial Tribunal by a majority decided, on the evidence adduced, that the difference in hours and holidays was a material factor which genuinely accounted for the difference in salary. The soundness of that decision is illuminated by a consideration of the results which might have followed a finding in favour of Mrs Leverton. If she were entitled to an increase of £1,500 in her annual salary, all scales 1, 3 and 4 employees could claim to be paid the same salary and all scales 1, 3 and 4 employees could claim a 32 1/2 hour working week and the enjoyment of 70 days of holiday. Nursery nurses are not indispensable, and such a result could have fatal consequences to the profession of nursery nurses and serious consequences for local authorities and all employees of local authorities. The elimination of sex discrimination may produce results which are painful to employers and surprising to some employees. But the Industrial Tribunal was not bound to assume sex discrimination against the evidence or to tear up the Central Arbitration Committee award in order to account for the difference between the salary paid to nursing nurses and the salary paid to scale 3 and 4 employees, male and female. The evidence entitled the Industrial Tribunal to conclude that the difference in salaries was genuinely due to the material factor that there was a substantial difference in hours worked and holidays enjoyed.

For these reasons and for the reasons given by my noble and learned friend, Lord Bridge of Harwich, with whose speech I am in complete agreement, I would dismiss the appeal.

## Pickstone v. Freemans plc[1]

LORD KEITH OF KINKEL: ... In the present case the respondent, Mrs Pickstone, who is employed by the appellant employers as a 'warehouse operative', claims that her work as such is of equal value with that of a man, Mr Phillips, who is employed in the same establishment as a 'checker ware house operative', and who is paid £4.22 per week more than she is paid. However, it happens to be the fact that one man is employed in the establishment as a warehouse operative doing the same work as Mrs Pickstone. The employers maintain that the existence of this fact precludes Mrs Pickstone from claiming equal pay with Mr Phillips under s. 1(2)(c) of the Act of 1970 as amended, notwithstanding that she may be performing work of equal value with his and notwithstanding that the difference in pay may be the result of discrimination on grounds of sex.

This argument is based on the words in para. (c) 'not being work in relation to which para. (a) or (b) above applies.' The employers say that the work on which Mrs Pickstone is employed is work to which para. (a) applies because it is like work with a man in the same employment, namely the one male warehouse operative. So Mrs Pickstone's work does not qualify under para. (c).

The question is whether the exclusionary words in para. (c) are intended to have effect whenever the employers are able to point to some man who is employed by them on like work with the woman claimant within the meaning of para. (a) or work rated as equivalent with hers within the meaning of para. (b) or whether they are intended to have effect only where the particular man with whom she seeks comparison is employed on such work. In my opinion the latter is the correct answer. The opposite result would leave a large gap in the equal work provision enabling an employer to evade it by employing one token man on the same work as a group of potential women claimants who were deliberately paid less than a group of men employed on work of equal value with that of the women. This would mean that the United Kingdom had failed yet again fully to implement its obligations under art. 119 of the Treaty and the Equal Pay Directive, and had not given full effect to the decision of the European Court in *Commission* v. *United Kingdom* [1982] IRLR 333. It is plain that Parliament cannot possibly have intended such a failure. The draft Regulations of 1983 were presented to Parliament as giving full effect to the decision in question. The draft Regulations were not subject to the Parliamentary process of consideration and amendment in Committee, as a Bill would have been. In these circumstances and in the context of s. 2 of the European Communities Act 1972 I consider it to be entirely legitimate for the purpose of ascertaining the intention of Parliament to take into account the terms in which the draft was

---

[1]    [1989] AC 66, [1988] 3 WLR 265, [1988] 2 All ER 803, [1988] ICR 697, [1988] IRLR 357, HL(E)

presented by the responsible Minister and which formed the basis of its acceptance. The terms in which it was presented to the House of Commons are set out in the speech of my noble and learned friend, Lord Templeman. Much the same was said before the House of Lords. There was no suggestion that the exclusionary words in para. (c) were intended to apply in any other situation than where the man selected by a woman complainant for comparison was one in relation to whose work para. (a) or para. (b) applied. It may be that, in order to confine the words in question to that situation, some necessary implication falls to be made into their literal meaning. The precise terms of that implication do not seem to me to matter. It is sufficient to say that the words must be construed purposively in order to give effect to the manifest broad intention of the maker of the Regulations and of Parliament. I would therefore reject the appellant's argument.

In the circumstances it is unnecessary to consider the ground upon which the Court of Appeal found in favour of the respondents, namely that art. 119 was directly enforceable in such a way as to enable their claim to be supported irrespective of the true construction of the Regulations of 1983.

My Lords, for these reasons and those given by my noble and learned friends, Lord Templeman and Lord Oliver of Aylmerton, I would dismiss the appeal.

...

LORD TEMPLEMAN: My Lords, the appellants, Freemans plc ('the employers') conduct a mail order business. The respondents are five women who work for the employers as 'warehouse operatives'; their basic weekly wage is £77.66. Mr Phillips is a man who works for the employers as a 'checker warehouse operative'; his basic weekly wage is £81.88. The respondents assert that the work carried out by the respondents is equal in value to the work of Mr Phillips in terms of the demands, effort, skill and decision-making involved. The respondents say that the difference of £4.22 between the respondents' pay and the pay of Mr Phillips is due to the difference of sex; the respondents are paid less because they are women. The respondents complained to an Industrial Tribunal that they were the victims of sex discrimination, contrary to the provisions of the Equal Pay Act 1970 and contrary to Community law. When the complaints of the respondents came before the Tribunal, investigation might have shown that there was no discrimination, that the work of Mr Phillips was of greater value than the work of the respondents or that for some other reason the difference between the pay of Mr Phillips and the pay of the respondents was not due to the difference of sex. By agreement between the parties, however, the Industrial Tribunal was asked to decide a preliminary point of law which is the subject of this appeal on assumed facts. The assumptions are that the respondents are factually correct in their complaint; that the work of the respondents is equal in value to the work of Mr Phillips; that the respondents are paid £4.22 less on the grounds of difference of sex and for no other reason; that, in short, the respondents are the victims of discrimination. It is unlawful under British law and under Community law for an employer to discriminate against a woman by paying her less than a man if the work of the woman is the same as or is equal in value to the work of the man. Nevertheless, the employers contend that under British law and under Community law, the respondents have no right to or, alternatively, no remedy for the discrimination, which on the assumed facts, is practised by the employer against the respondents and in favour of Mr Phillips. The employers' argument is based on the fact that it so happens that one of the employers' warehouse operatives is a man, doing the same work as the respondents. According to the employers this fact makes all the difference. The respondents are entitled to complain if they are discriminated against by reason of the fact that they are not paid the same as the man who does the same work. Therefore, it is argued, the respondents are not entitled to complain if they are discriminated against by reason of the fact that they are not paid the same as Mr Phillips, who does work of equal value. The employers admit that if there were 15 warehouse operators and all the warehouse operators were women, paid £77.66, for work equal in value to the work of 10 checker warehouse operatives, all men, paid £81.88 and the difference was due to difference in sex, the respondents would be entitled to an increase in pay of £4.22. But the employers claim that if there were 14 women warehouse operatives, one male warehouse operative, and 10 checker warehouse operatives the respondents would be obliged to rest content with £77.66 and would have no remedy for the admitted discrimination based on difference in sex. The Industrial Tribunal and the Employment Appeal Tribunal accepted the argument of the employers. The Court of Appeal (Purchas and Nicholls LJJ and Sir Roualeyn Cumming-Bruce) decided that under Community law the respondents had an enforceable right on the assumed facts to equal pay with Mr Phillips for work of equal value. The employers appeal to this House.

...

According to the employers in the present appeal, the Regulations of 1983 had the additional effect of depriving some women of the right to pursue their claims by judicial process or otherwise although they considered themselves wronged by failure to apply the principle of equal pay. The respondents may have a valid complaint in that they are not receiving equal pay with Mr Phillips for work of equal value. But if the respondents seek to remedy that discrimination under s. 1(2)(c) of the Act of 1970 as amended by the Regulations, they will be debarred because they are employed on 'work in relation to which para. (a) or (b) above applies.' It is said that para. (a) operates, not because the respondents are employed on like work with Mr Phillips but because the respondents are employed on like work with some other man. Since para. (c) is expressed to apply only when a woman is employed on work which is not 'work in relation to which para. (a) or (b) above applies', it follows, so it is said, that where a woman is employed on like work with any man or where a woman is employed on work rated as equivalent with any man, no claim can be made under para. (c) in respect of some other man who is engaged on work of equal value. In my opinion para. (a) or (b) only debars a claim under para. (c) where para. (a) or (b) applies to the man who is the subject of the complaint made by the woman. If the Tribunal decide that the respondents are engaged 'on like work' with Mr Phillips then para. (a) applies and the respondents are not entitled to proceed under para. (c) and to obtain the report of an ACAS expert. If there is a job evaluation study which covers the work of the respondents and the work of Mr Phillips then the respondents are debarred from proceeding under para. (c) unless the job evaluation study itself was discriminatory.

Whenever there is a claim for equal pay, the complainant, or the complainant's trade union representative supporting the claimant, may wish to obtain a report from an ACAS expert under para. (c) to use for the purpose of general pay bargaining and in the hope of finding ammunition which will lead to a general increase in wage levels irrespective of discrimination. For this purpose the more ACAS reports there are the better. It may be significant that in the present case a claim is made under para. (c) and not under para. (a) as well, or, in the alternative, although it is obvious that work of equal value in terms of the demands made on a woman under such headings as effort, skill and decision which may amount to discrimination under para. (c) may also be work of a broadly similar nature with differences of no practical importance which found a complaint under para. (a). If there is discrimination in pay the Industrial Tribunal must be able to grant a remedy. But the remedy available under para. (c) is not to be applied if the complainant has a remedy in respect of the male employee with whom she demands parity under para. (a) or if para. (b) applies to the woman and to that male employee. To prevent exploitation of para. (c) the Tribunal must decide in the first instance whether the complainant and the man with whom she seeks parity are engaged on 'like work' under para. (a). If para. (a) applies, no ACAS report is required. If para. (a) does not apply, then the Tribunal considers whether para. (b) applies to the complainant and the man with whom she seeks parity; if so, the Tribunal can only proceed under para. (c) if the job evaluation study obtained for the purposes of para. (b) is itself discriminatory. If para. (b) applies then, again, no ACAS report is necessary. If paras (a) and (b) do not apply, the Tribunal must next consider whether there are reasonable grounds for determining that the work of the complainant and the work of the man with whom she seeks parity is of equal value. If the Tribunal are not so satisfied, then no ACAS report is required. The words in para. (c) on which the employers rely were not intended to create a new form of permitted discrimination. Para. (c) enables a claim to equal pay as against a specified man to be made without injustice to an employer. When a woman claims equal pay for work of equal value, she specifies the man with whom she demands parity. If the work of the woman is work in relation to which para. (a) or (b) applies in relation to that man, then the woman cannot proceed under para. (c) and cannot obtain a report from an ACAS expert. In my opinion there must be implied in para. (c) after the word 'applies' the words 'as between the woman and the man with whom she claims equality.' This construction is consistent with Community law. The employers' construction is inconsistent with Community law and creates a permitted form of discrimination without rhyme or reason.

Under Community law, a woman is entitled to equal pay for work of equal value to that of a man in the same employment. That right is not dependent on there being no man who is employed on the same work as the woman. Under British law, namely the Equal Pay Act 1970 as amended in 1975, a woman was entitled to equal pay for work rated as equivalent with that of a man in the same employment. That right was not dependent on there being no man who was employed on the same work as the woman. Under the ruling of the European Court of Justice in *Commission of the European Communities* v. *United Kingdom* [1982] IRLR 333, the Equal Pay Act as amended in 1975 was held to be defective because the Act did not entitle every woman to claim before a competent authority that her work had the same value as other work, but only allowed a claim by a woman who succeeded in persuading her employer to consent to a job evaluation scheme. The Regulations of 1983 were intended to give full effect to Community law and to the ruling of the European Court of Justice which directed the United Kingdom Government to introduce legislation entitling any woman to equal pay with any man for work of equal value if the difference in pay is due to the difference in sex and is therefore discriminatory. I am of the opinion that the Regulations of 1983, upon their true construction, achieve the required result of affording a remedy to any woman who is not in receipt of equal pay for work equal in value to the work of a man in the same employment.

In *Mary Murphy* v. *Bord Telecom Eireann* [1988] IRLR 267, 29 women were employed as factory workers engaged in such tasks as dismantling, cleaning, oiling and reassembling telephones and other equipment; they claimed the right to be paid at the same rate as a specified male worker employed in the same factory as a stores labourer engaged in cleaning, collecting and delivering equipment and components and in lending general assistance as required. The European Court of Justice in their judgment at p. 269, para. 35 said that the principle of equal pay for men and women:

> forbids workers of one sex engaged in work of equal value to that of workers of the opposite sex to be paid a lower wage than the latter on grounds of sex; it *a fortiori* prohibits such a difference in pay where the lower-paid category of workers is engaged in work of higher value.

I cannot think that in Community law or in British law the result would be any different if instead of there being 29 women working on telephone maintenance and one male stores labourer, there were 28 women and one man working on telephone maintenance and one male stores labourer.

The draft of the Regulations of 1983 was not subject to any process of amendment by Parliament. In these circumstances the explanations of the Government and the criticisms voiced by Members of Parliament in the debates which led to approval of the draft Regulations provide some indications of the intentions of Parliament. The debate on the draft Regulations in the House of Commons which led to their approval by Resolution was initiated by the Under Secretary of State for Employment who, in the reports of the House of Commons for 20 July 1983 at column 479 *et seq.* said this:

> The Equal Pay Act allows a woman to claim equal pay with a man ... if she is doing the same or broadly similar work, or if her job and his have been rated equal through job evaluation in effort, skill and decision. However, if a woman is doing different work from a comparable man, or if the jobs are not covered by a job evaluation study, the woman has at present no right to make a claim for equal pay. This is the gap, identified by the European Court which we are closing ... .

In the course of his speech at column 485, the Minister outlined the procedure which will apply if a claim is made under para. (c) in the following words:

> Under the amending Regulations which are the subject of this debate, an employee will be able to bring a claim for equal pay with an employee of the opposite sex working in the same employment on the ground that the work is of equal value. When this happens, conciliation will first be attempted as in all equal pay claims. If conciliation is unsuccessful, the Industrial Tribunal will take the following steps. First, it will check that the work is not in fact so similar that the case can be heard under the current Act. Secondly, it will consider whether the jobs have already been covered by a job evaluation scheme and judged not to be of equal value. If this is the case, the claim may proceed only if the original job evaluation scheme is shown to have been sexually discriminatory. Having decided that the case should proceed, the Tribunal will first invite the parties to see if they can settle the claim voluntarily. If not, the Tribunal will consider whether to commission an independent expert to report on the value of the jobs. It will not commission an expert's report if it feels that it is unreasonable to determine the question of value - for example, if the two jobs are quite obviously of unequal value. Nor ... will it commission an expert's report if the employer shows as this stage that inequality in pay is due to material factors other than sex discrimination ... .

Thus it is clear that the construction which I have placed upon the Regulations corresponds to the intentions of the Government in introducing the Regulations. In the course of the debate in the House of Commons, and in the corresponding debate in the House of Lords, no one suggested that a claim for equal pay for equal work might be defeated under the Regulations by an employer who proved that a man who was not the subject of the complaint was employed on the same or on similar work with the complaint. The Minister took the view, and Parliament accepted the view, that para. (c) will only apply if paras. (a) and (b) are first held by the

Tribunal not to apply in respect of the work of the woman and the work of the man with whom she seeks parity of pay. This is also the only view consistent with Community law.

In *von Colson & Kamann* v. *Land Nordrhein-Westfalen* (Case 14/83) [1984] ECR 1891, 1910, 1911, the European Court of Justice advised that in dealing with national legislation designed to give effect to a Directive:

> 3 ... It is for the national court to interpret and apply the legislation adopted for the implementation of the Directive in conformity with the requirements of Community law, insofar as it is given discretion to do so under national law.

In *Duke* v. *GEC Reliance Systems Ltd* [1988] IRLR 118, at p. 124 this House declined to distort the construction of an Act of Parliament which was not drafted to give effect to a Directive and which was not capable of complying with the Directive as subsequently construed by the European Court of Justice. In the present case I can see no difficulty in construing the Regulations of 1983 in a way which gives effect to the declared intention of the Government of the United Kingdom responsible for drafting the Regulations and is consistent with the objects of the European Community Treaty, the provisions of the Equal Pay Directive and the rulings of the European Court of justice. I would dismiss the appeal.

LORD OLIVER OF AYLMERTON: My Lords, the respondents to this appeal are assumed to be engaged upon work which is, for all practical purposes, identical with work upon which at least one man employed in the same establishment is engaged and they are employed upon the same terms as he is. They claim, however, that there are other men employed in the same establishment whose work, though not the same as theirs, is of equal value to theirs and who are remunerated at a higher rate and they claim that the difference is due to discrimination against them on the grounds of their sex. The appellants have resisted the claim for parity with this latter group, from whom the respondents selected a Mr Phillips as the comparator, on the preliminary point that, even assuming the discrimination claimed by the respondents to be established, they have no remedy. There are, they contend, three reasons for this. First, the claim is precluded by the terms of the Equal Pay Act 1970 (as amended) so that the Industrial Tribunal has no jurisdiction to entertain the claim. Secondly, it is said that even on the construction of art. 119 of the Treaty of Rome and the Equal Pay Directive (75/117/EEC) which clarified it, assuming the article and Directive to be directly applicable as a matter of domestic law, a claim to parity for work of equal value cannot be made by a woman who is employed on the same work as another man. Thirdly, it is said that even could such a claim subsist as a matter of the construction of art. 119, the article is not directly enforceable in such a case in domestic law. Your Lordships were therefore invited by the appellants to submit both the question of construction of the article and the question of direct enforceability to the European Court of Justice under the provisions of art. 177 of the Treaty. The Court of Appeal, whilst upholding the appellants' contentions as regards the construction of the Act, entertained no doubts that the discrimination claimed, if proved, contravened the terms of the Treaty and the Directive, and referred the matter back to the Industrial Tribunal to deal with the claim on the footing that the respondents' rights were directly enforceable as a matter of domestic law.

My Lords, whilst, like the Court of Appeal, I entertain no doubt that the discrimination claimed falls squarely within the general principle of equal pay for equal work (or work of equal value) which is enshrined in art. 119, I confess to some doubt whether, if the appellants' construction of the Act of 1970 is correct, the article is directly enforceable in the circumstances of the instant case and before reading the draft of the speech of my noble and learned friend, Lord Templeman, I should, for my part, have been minded to accede to the appellants' request that that question at least be submitted to the European Court of Justice. Broadly, my doubts arise from this, that the cases in the European Court to which your Lordships have been referred clearly establish that there is an area within which the article is not directly applicable. The bounds of that area are far from clear to me, however, but the cases appear to indicate that the article may not be directly applicable in an 'equal value' claim, at any rate where there is no machinery in the domestic law by which the criterion of what is work of equal value can be readily ascertained. The difficulty in this case arises from the fact that the Industrial Tribunal is a statutory Tribunal whose jurisdiction and procedure is circumscribed by statutory instrument, so that although machinery is provided for the ascertainment of what is 'work of equal value', that machinery is confined by definition to a claim falling within s. 1(2)(c) of the Act of 1970 (see Industrial Tribunals (Rules of Procedure) Regulations 1985 (SI 1985 No 16), regulation 3(2) and the definition of 'equal value claim' in Schedule 2 to the Regulations). If therefore, the Act does, as the appellants claim, restrict the entertainment of claims by the Tribunal to cases in which there is no man performing the same work as the claimant, the Tribunal's machinery for establishing the criterion of what is work of equal value is equally restricted.

The critical question, therefore, is whether the Court of Appeal, in common with the Industrial Tribunal and the Employment Appeal Tribunal, were right in concluding that the respondents' claim was not one which could be made under the provisions of the Act of 1970. I have to confess to sympathising with that conclusion which coincided with the very definite opinion which I myself had formed at the conclusion of the hearing. Indeed, it is only the persuasive speech delivered by my noble and learned friend, Lord Templeman, which has enabled me to change the opinion which I had formed. It is beyond dispute that the Act in its amended form in 1975 was intended to give effect to the United Kingdom's obligations under art. 119 and the Equal Pay Directive and that the amendment introduced in 1983, following the ruling of the European Court of Justice in *Commission of the European Communities* v. *United Kingdom* [1982] IRLR 333, was intended to fill the gap to which that case had drawn attention and to complete what was quite obviously intended to be a comprehensive code for dealing with sex discrimination in the area of pay and conditions at work. What has to be said, if the appellants are right, is that Parliament simply failed in its purpose and that is a conclusion the court must strive to avoid - particularly having regard to the provisions of s. 2(4) of the European Communities Act 1972 - unless it is compulsively driven to it. It has, I think, to be said that if the section falls to be construed in isolation apart from the evident purpose of the Act, there is very little scope for a construction other than that to which the Court of Appeal felt itself driven. In contrast to the way in which, for instance, the Belgian legislature complied with the Treaty obligation by simply reproducing the terms of the article as part of the domestic legislation, the way in which the United Kingdom Act seeks to accomplish its object is by reading into every woman's contract of employment a deemed contractual term, described as 'an equality clause.' The terms of the clause are not spelled out but the effect of it - broadly that the terms of a woman's contract are to be brought into line with those of a comparable man - is stated and is related to three, and only three, prescribed situations, viz.: (a) where the woman is employed on like work with a man in the same employment; (b) where the woman is employed on work rated as equivalent with that of a man in the same employment; and (c) where a woman is employed on work which, not being work in relation to which para. (a) or (b) above applies, is ... of equal value to that of a man in the same employment. Now, on the face of it, where a man is employed on the same work as a woman, para. (a) applies to that work and the equality clause in the woman's contract has the effect specified in that paragraph. If she then makes a claim for equal pay with someone whose work she claims to be of equal value with hers but which is not the same, she does not change the nature of her work. It remains work which has the effect specified in para. (a) and to which, therefore, that paragraph 'applies.' If, therefore, the section is to be read literally and in accordance with its terms, para. (c) cannot apply to that work so long as para. (a) applies to it. It can be made to apply in only one of two ways. Either there has to be given to the word 'applies' an artificial meaning which will enable it to be read in the sense of 'is applied by the claimant as part of her claim' or there has to be read into the Act some qualifying words which will restrict the word 'applies' to a particular comparator selected by the claimant. Either way, a construction which permits the section to operate as a proper fulfilment of the United Kingdom's obligation under the Treaty involves not so much doing violence to the language of the section as filling a gap by an implication which arises, not from the words used, but from the manifest purpose of the Act and the mischief it was intended to remedy. The question is whether that can be justified by the necessity - indeed the obligation - to apply a purposive construction which will implement the United Kingdom's obligations under the Treaty.

For the reasons given by my noble and learned friend, Lord Templeman, I am now persuaded that it can and that para. (c) is to be construed as if modified in the manner suggested by my noble and learned friend or as if it included a parenthetic phrase and read (c) 'where a woman is employed on work which, not being work in relation to which (in respect of the man hereinafter mentioned) para. (a) or (b) above applied, is ... etc.' It must, I think, be recognised that so to construe a provision which, on its face, is unambiguous involves a departure from a number of well-established rules of construction. The intention of Parliament has, it is said, to be ascertained from the words which it has used and those words are to be construed according to their plain and ordinary meaning. The fact that a statute is passed to give effect to an international Treaty does not, of itself, enable the Treaty to be referred to in order to construe the words used in other than in their plain and unambiguous sense. Moreover, even in the case of ambiguity, what is said in Parliament in the course of the passage of the Bill, cannot ordinarily be referred to to assist in construction. I think, however, that it has also to be recognised that a statute which is passed in order to give effect to the United Kingdom's obligations under the Treaty of Rome falls into a special category and it does so because, unlike other treaty obligations, those obligations have, in effect, been incorporated into English law by the European Communities Act 1972. Section 2(1) of that Act provides that:

> all such ... obligations ... from time to time created by the Treaties ... as in accordance with the Treaties are without further enactment to be given legal effect or used in the United Kingdom shall be recognised and available in law, and be enforced, allowed and followed accordingly ... .

Although, at any rate on one construction, this may be said to apply only to rights which are clearly directly applicable, subs. (2) goes on to provide for a designated Minister to make provision by regulation for the purpose of implementing any Community obligations of the United Kingdom and 'for the purpose of dealing with matters arising out of or related to any such obligations.' Subsection (4) provides that a provision made under subs. (2) includes such provision as might be made by Acts of Parliament, and that 'any enactment passed or to be passed ... shall be construed and have effect subject to the foregoing provisions of this section.' One is thus thrown back to the provisions of subs. (1). Subsection 1(2)(c) of the Equal Pay Act 1970 was inserted into the Act under this power by the Equal Pay (Amendment) Regulations 1983, which recited that the Secretary of State was the designated Minister 'in relation to measures to prevent discrimination between men and women as regards terms and conditions of employment.' The history of the legislation up to that point has been fully recited in the speech of my noble and learned friend, Lord Templeman, and it is perfectly plain that the amendments to the Act were inserted for the purpose of completing the compliance by the United Kingdom with its Treaty obligations under art. 119 and the Equal Pay Directive by remedying what was then perceived as the only remaining lacuna, namely that a woman was excluded from making an equal value claim unless she could persuade her employer to initiate a work evaluation study. It is worth noting that the explanatory note (which is not, of course, part of the Regulations but is of use in identifying the mischief which the Regulations were attempting to remedy) states that:

> Regulation 2 amends s. 1 of the Equal Pay Act 1970 to enable a woman to take advantage of an equality clause where she is employed on work of equal value to that of a man in the same employment.

Those Regulations having been passed with the manifest and express purpose of producing a full compliance with the United Kingdom's obligation, they fall to be construed accordingly and that which I have suggested as falling to be implied into s. 1(2)(c) is necessary to achieve that purpose. In *Garland* v. *British Rail* [1982] IRLR 257 at p. 259, para. 7, Lord Diplock observed:

> My Lords, even if the obligation to observe the provisions of art. 119 were an obligation assumed by the United Kingdom under an ordinary international Treaty or convention and there were no question of the Treaty obligation being directly applicable as part of the law to be applied by the courts in this country without need for any further enactment, it is a principle of construction of United Kingdom statutes, now too well established to call for citation of authority, that the words of the statute passed after the Treaty has been signed and dealing with the subject matter of the international obligation of the United Kingdom, are to be construed, if they are reasonably capable of bearing such a meaning, as intended to carry out the obligation, and not to be inconsistent with it. *A fortiori* is this the case where the Treaty obligation arises under one of the Community Treaties to which s. 2 of the European Communities Act 1972 applies.
>
> The instant appeal does not present an appropriate occasion to consider whether, having regard to the express direction as to the construction of enactments 'to be passed' which is contained in s. 2(4), anything short of an express positive statement in an Act of Parliament passed after 1 January 1973, that a particular provision is intended to be made in breach of an obligation assumed by the United Kingdom under a Community Treaty, would justify an English court in construing that provision in a manner inconsistent with a Community Treaty obligation of the United Kingdom, however wide a departure from the *prima facie* meaning of the language of the provision might be needed in order to achieve consistency ... .

In the instant case, the strict and literal construction of the section does indeed involve the conclusion that the Regulations, although purporting to give full effect to the United Kingdom's obligations under art. 119, were in fact in breach of those obligations. The question, following Lord Diplock's formulation of principle, is whether they are reasonably capable of bearing a meaning which does in fact comply with the obligations imposed by the Treaty. I was, initially, in some doubt whether, if the section is to be construed in the way for which the respondents contend, any sensible purpose could be given to the exclusionary words 'not being work in relation in para. (a) or (b) above applies.'

However, the Regulations which introduced para. (c) into the Act introduced at the same time the procedural provisions in s. 2A and the

significance of the exclusionary words in the context of the Industrial
Tribunals procedure and of the definition of 'like work' which is contained in
s. 1(4) is demonstrated in the analysis of my noble and learned friend, Lord
Templeman. That doubt removed, I am satisfied that the words of s. 1(2)(c),
whilst on the face of them unequivocal, are reasonably capable of bearing a
meaning which will not put the United Kingdom in breach of its Treaty
obligations. This conclusion is justified, in my judgment, by the manifest
purpose of the legislation, by its history, and by the compulsive provision of
s. 2(4) of the Act of 1972. It is comforting indeed to find, from the statement
made by the Minister to which my noble and learned friend has referred, that
this construction does in fact conform not only with what clearly was the
parliamentary intention but also with what was stated to be the parliamentary
intention. I do not, however, think that it is necessary to rely upon this, since
the conclusion is, in my judgment, amply justified and by the other factors
which I have mentioned. For these reasons and for those given by my noble
and learned friend, Lord Templeman, I agree that the appeal should be
dismissed.

...

## Rainey v. Greater Glasgow Health Authority[1]

LORD KEITH OF KINKEL: ... . The appellant, a woman, has since 1 October 1980 been employed by the respondent board at the Belvidere Hospital Glasgow, as a prosthetist. A prosthetist is one who is concerned with the fitting of artificial limbs. Before 1980 no prosthetist was directly employed by any health authority in Scotland. The requisite services were provided by private contractors themselves employing qualified prosthetists who worked in a number of hospitals, including Belvidere Hospital. One of these was a Mr Alan Crumlin. In 1979 the Secretary of State for Scotland decided to establish a prosthetic fitting service within the National Health Service in Scotland, and to discontinue the arrangement under which the service was provided by private contractors. To achieve this object it was necessary that a sufficient number of qualified prosthetists should be recruited to the National Health Service *en bloc*. The only prosthetists then available were those employed by the private contractors. The remuneration of employees of the National Health Service is determined by negotiation and agreement in the Whitley Councils for the Health Services. It was decided by the Scottish Home and Health Department that, in general, the remuneration of employees in the new prosthetic service should be related to the Whitley Council scale, and that the appropriate scale for them would be that for medical physics technicians. Since, however, it was appreciated this might not be attractive to the prosthetists in the employment of private contractors, whom it was desired to recruit *en bloc*, it was decided to offer them an option. That option, as set out in a letter from the Department of Mr Crumlin dated 1 January 1980 was either to come into the National Health Service on National Health Service rates of pay and conditions of service or to remain on the rates of pay and conditions of service which he presently received, subject to future changes as negotiated by his trade union, ASTMS, for the prosthetists employed by contractors. It is to be observed that in England prosthetic services were to continue to be provided through private contractors. Mr Crumlin and all the other prosthetists who received the offer (about 20 in number who all happened to be men) opted for the second alternative. This meant that they retained their existing salaries and that future increases were to be negotiated with ASTMS and not the Whitley Council. Mr Crumlin commenced employment with the National Health Service at Belvidere Hospital in July 1980 at the salary of £6,680 p.a., the same as he had been receiving from his former employer. At the time of the hearing before the industrial tribunal, on 23 March 1983, it had increased to £10,085 p.a.

The appellant entered the employment of the National Health Service as a prosthetist working at Belvidere Hospital on 1 October 1980. She did so directly, not having been previously employed by a private contractor. Her

---

[1]    [1987] AC 224, [1986] 3 WLR 1017, [1987] 1 All ER 65, [1987] ICR 129, [1987] IRLR 26, HL (Sc.)

qualifications and experience were broadly similar to those of Mr Crumlin. The rates of pay and conditions of service offered to and accepted by her corresponded to those of a medical physics technician at the appropriate point on the Whitley Council scale. Her starting salary was £4,773, and at the time of the hearing before the industrial tribunal it had increased to £7,295. A male prosthetist, Mr Davey, was engaged at the same time and on the same conditions. He has since left his employment.

No prosthetists have since 1980 transferred from private employment to National Health Service employment, and no such transfers on special terms will be permitted in the future. Any prosthetists engaged by the respondents in the future, whether male or female, will do so on the National Health Service scale of remuneration. No arrangements have been made for phasing out the disparity between the prosthetists who transferred from the private sector in 1980, such as Mr Crumlin, and those who entered the National Health Service employment directly, such as the appellant.

In these circumstances, the appellant applied to an industrial tribunal, under the 1970 Act, for a declaration that she was entitled to the same pay as Mr Crumlin.

...

The board did not dispute that the appellant was employed on like work with Mr Crumlin, nor that the term of her contract as regards remuneration was less favourable than the corresponding term of Mr Crumlin's contract. They founded on s. 1(3) of the Act and undertook the burden of satisfying its provisions, which at the material time were in these terms:

> An equality clause shall not operate in relation to a variation between the woman's contract and the man's contract if the employer proves that the variation is genuinely due to a material difference (other than the difference of sex) between her case and his.

The industrial tribunal dismissed the appellant's application. Having narrated the facts of the case as found by them and the contentions of the parties they stated:

> Having considered the evidence the Tribunal is satisfied that what has caused the difference in the salary scale of the applicant and Mr Crumlin is not market forces but is the fact that Mr Crumlin is paid on a scale negotiated and agreed between his trade union and the Scottish Home and Health Department whereas the applicant is paid according to a different scale. The scale upon which the applicant is paid is an *ad hoc* scale and not one which has been negotiated between her trade union and the Scottish Home and Health Department. There was clear evidence that any male employees recruited at the same time as or after the recruitment of the applicant would be paid the same rate as the applicant was and subject to the same scale. We had no doubt on the evidence that had any of the prosthetists employed by the

private contractors been female they would have been paid the same higher rate of pay as the male prosthetists transferred from the private contractor. The Tribunal were therefore forced to the conclusion that the difference had nothing to do with the fact that the applicant was female. We were satisfied that the reason for the difference was because of the different method of entry and had nothing to do with sex. The application must therefore be dismissed.

The appellant appealed to the Employment Appeal Tribunal which, by a majority, dismissed the appeal. A further appeal to the Court of Session was also dismissed by the First Division of the Inner House (Lord President Emslie and Lord Cameron, Lord Grieve dissenting).

The facts found by the industrial tribunal make it clear that the Secretary of State for Scotland decided, as a matter of general policy, that the Whitley Council scale of remuneration and negotiating machinery, which applied throughout the National Health Service in Scotland, was appropriate for employees in the prosthetic service. It was also decided that the appropriate part of the scale for such employees was that applicable to medical physics technicians, presumably because the nature of their work was considered comparable to that of the prosthetists. So all direct entrants to the service, whether male or female, were to be placed on that part of the scale and made subject to Whitley Council negotiations. But it was apparent that the new service would not get off the ground unless a sufficient number of the prosthetists in the employment of the private contractors could be attracted into it. So the further policy decision was taken to offer these prosthetists the option of entering the service at their existing salaries and subject to the ASTMS negotiating machinery. As it happened, all the prosthetists privately employed were male. In the result, Mr Crumlin had the benefit of the offer and so emerged with a higher salary and better prospects for an increase than did the appellant, who did not have that benefit.

The main question at issue in the appeal is whether those circumstances are capable in law of constituting, within the meaning of s. 1(3) of the 1970 Act, 'a material difference (other than the difference of sex) between her case and his.'

Counsel for the appellant argued that nothing can constitute such a difference which is not related to the personal circumstances of the two employees, such as their respective skills, experience or training. Reliance was placed upon the decision of the Court of Appeal in *Fletcher* v. *Clay Cross (Quarry Services) Ltd* [1978] IRLR 361. In that case a woman sales clerk was employed at a lower wage than a male sales clerk who had been engaged at a later date. The employers relied, as being the material difference between her case and his, on the circumstance that the male clerk had been the only suitable applicant for the post and that he had refused to accept it unless he was paid the same wage as he had received in his previous job. The Employment Appeal Tribunal had accepted this as discharging the onus on the employers under s. 1(3) of the 1970 Act, but their decision was reversed by the Court of Appeal. Lord Denning MR said, at p. 363:

> The issue depends on whether there is a material difference (other than sex) between her case and his. Take heed to the words 'between her case and his'. They show that the tribunal is to have regard to *her* and to *him* - to the personal equation of the woman as compared to that of the man - irrespective of any extrinsic forces which led to the variation in pay. As I said in *Shields* v. *E. Coomes (Holdings) Ltd* [1978] IRLR 263 at p. 266, the subsection applies when 'the personal equation of the man is such that he deserves to be paid at a higher rate than the woman.' Thus the personal equation of the man may warrant a wage differential if he has much longer length of service, or has superior skill or qualifications; or gives bigger output or productivity; or has been placed, owing to downgrading, in a protected pay category, vividly described as 'red-circled', or to other circumstances personal to him in doing his job.
>
> But the tribunal is not to have regard to any extrinsic forces which have led to the man being paid more. An employer cannot avoid his obligations under the Act by saying: 'I paid him more because he asked for more'; or 'I paid her less because she was willing to come for less.' If any such excuse were permitted, the Act would be a dead letter. Those are the very reasons why there was unequal pay before the statute. They are the very circumstances in which the statute was intended to operate.
>
> Nor can the employer avoid his obligations by giving the reasons why he submitted to the extrinsic forces. As for instance by saying: 'He asked for that sum because it was what he was getting in his previous job', or 'He was the only applicant for the job, so I had no option.' In such cases the employer may beat his breast, and say: 'I did not pay him more because he was a man, I paid it because he was the only suitable person who applied for the job. Man or woman made no difference to me.' Those are reasons personal to the employer. If any such reasons were permitted as an excuse, the door would be wide open. Every employer who wished to avoid the statute would walk straight through it.

Lawton LJ said, at p. 364:

> What does s. 1(3) in its context in both the Equal Pay Act 1970 and the Sex Discrimination Act 1975 mean? The context is important. The overall object of both Acts is to ensure that women are treated no less favourably than men. If a woman is treated less favourably than a man there is a presumption of discrimination which can only be rebutted in the sphere of employment if the employer brings himself within s. 1(3). He cannot do so merely by proving that he did not intend to discriminate. There are more ways of discriminating against women than by deliberately setting out to do so: see s. 1(1)(b) of the Sex Discrimination Act 1975. If lack of intention had provided a lawful excuse for variation, s. 1(3) would surely have been worded differently. The variation must have been genuinely due to (that is, caused by) a material difference (that is, one which was relevant and real) between - and now come the important words - her case and his. What is her case? And what is his? In my judgment, her case embraces what appertains to her *in* her job, such as the qualifications she brought to it, the length of time she has been in it, the skill she has acquired, the responsibilities she has undertaken and where and under what conditions she has to do it. It is on this kind of basis that her case is to be

compared with that of a man's. What does not appertain to her job or to his are the circumstances in which they came to be employed. These are collateral to the jobs as such.

In my opinion these statements are unduly restrictive of the proper interpretation of s. 1(3). The difference must be 'material', which I would construe as meaning 'significant and relevant', and it must be between 'her case and his.' Consideration of a person's case must necessarily involve consideration of all the circumstances of that case. These may well go beyond what is not very happily described as 'the personal equation', i.e. the personal qualities by way of skill, experience or training which the individual brings to the job. Some circumstances may on examination prove to be not significant or not relevant, but others may do so, though not relating to the personal qualities of the employer. In particular, where there is no question of intentional sex discrimination whether direct or indirect (and there is none here) a difference which is connected with economic factors affecting the efficient carrying on of the employer's business or other activity may well be relevant.

This view is supported by two decisions of the European Court of Justice upon the interpretation of art. 119 of the Treaty of Rome, requiring the application 'of the principle that men and women should receive equal pay for equal work', and to the implementation of which the Equal Pay Act 1970 is directed. The first of these decisions is *Jenkins* v. *Kingsgate (Clothing Productions) Ltd* (Case No 96/80) [1981] IRLR 228, which originated in the Employment Appeal Tribunal in England. A company employed full-time and part-time workers on like work, but paid the latter, almost all of whom were female, less than the former, who were predominantly male. The company claimed that it did so in order to encourage full-time work and hence achieve fuller utilisation of machinery, and this was accepted by an industrial tribunal as discharging the onus under s. 1(3). The Employment Appeal Tribunal referred to the European Court questions directed to ascertaining whether the employer's policy constituted a contravention of art. 119.

...

When the case was again before the Employment Appeal Tribunal, Browne-Wilkinson J, delivering judgment, accepted ([1981] IRLR 388) that the ruling of the European Court established that a differential in pay between part-time workers, who are predominantly women, and full-time male workers can be justified as being a material difference by showing that the pay differential does in fact achieve economic advantages for the employer. He found difficulty, however, in elucidating whether the judgment and ruling of the European Court meant that it was sufficient for the employer to show that he had no intention of discriminating because his pay practice was directed to some legitimate economic objective, or that he must show that the practice was in fact reasonably necessary in order to achieve that objective. In the result, he took the view that if art. 119 as construed by the European Court was satisfied if the employer met the less demanding criterion, nevertheless s. 1(3) of the 1970 Act went further than that and required the employer to meet the more demanding one.

...

In the result, the case was remitted to the industrial tribunal to find whether the lower rate of pay for part-time workers was in fact reasonably necessary in order to enable the employers to reduce absenteeism and to obtain the maximum utilisation of their plant.

The European Court had occasion to consider the question afresh in *Bilka-Kaufhaus GmbH* v. *Weber von Hartz* (Case No 170/84) [1987] IRLR 317. A German department store operated an occupational pension scheme for its employees, under which part-time employees were eligible for pensions only if they had worked full time for at least 15 years over a total period of 20 years. That provision affected disproportionately more women than men. A female part-time employee claimed that the provision contravened art. 119 of the Treaty. The employers contended that it was based upon objectively justified economic grounds, in that it encouraged full-time work which resulted in lower ancillary costs and the utilisation of staff throughout opening hours. The European Court by its decision made it clear it was not sufficient for the employers merely to show absence of any intention to discriminate.

...

It therefore appears that the European Court has resolved the doubts expressed by Browne-Wilkinson J in *Jenkins* v. *Kingsgate (Clothing Productions) Ltd* [1981] IRLR 388 and established that the true meaning and effect of art. 119 in this particular context is the same as that there attributed to s. 1(3) of the 1970 Act by the Employment Appeal Tribunal. Although the European Court at one point refers to 'economic' grounds objectively justified, whereas Browne-Wilkinson J speaks of 'economic or other reasons', I consider that read as a whole the ruling of the European Court would not exclude objectively justified grounds which are other than economic, such as administrative efficiency in a concern not engaged in commerce or business.

The decision of the European Court on art. 119 must be accepted as authoritative and the judgment of the Employment Appeal Tribunal on s. 1(3) of the 1970 Act which in my opinion is correct, is in harmony with it. There is now no reason to construe s. 1(3) as conferring greater rights on a worker in this context than does art. 119 of the Treaty. It follows that a relevant difference for purposes of s. 1(3) may relate to circumstances other than the personal qualifications or merits of the male and female workers who are the subject of comparison.

In the present case the difference between the case of the appellant and that of Mr Crumlin is that the former is a person who entered the National Health Service at Belvidere Hospital directly while the latter is a person who entered it from employment with a private contractor. The fact that one is a woman and the other a man is an accident. The findings of the industrial tribunal make it clear that the new prosthetic service could never have been established within a reasonable time if Mr Crumlin and others like him had not been offered a scale of remuneration no less favourable than that which they were then enjoying. That was undoubtedly a good and objectively justified ground for offering him that scale of remuneration. But it was argued for the appellant that it did not constitute a good and objectively justified reason for paying the appellant and other direct entrants a lower scale of remuneration. This aspect does not appear to have been specifically considered by either of the tribunals or by their Lordships of the First Division, apart from Lord Grieve who said ([1985] IRLR 414 at p. 425):

> I accept that the facts which provided the evidence before both tribunals were sufficient to explain why Mr Crumlin (and his colleagues) were paid on a scale equivalent to that which they had been receiving while employed in the private sector, but in my opinion that evidence is not sufficient to explain why, when the National [Health] Service door was opened to the appellant (and other prosthetists not previously employed in the private sector) the appellant (and her fellow prosthetists) were paid on a lower scale. In the absence of a reasonable explanation as to why the appellant was paid on a lower scale than Mr Crumlin I am of opinion that the respondents have not discharged the onus placed upon them by s. 1(3) of the 1970 Act, and that the majority of the Employment Appeal Tribunal were not entitled on the facts before them to conclude that they had.

The position in 1980 was that all National Health Service employees were paid on the Whitley Council scale, and that the Whitley Council negotiating machinery applied to them. The prosthetic service was intended to be a branch of the National Health Service. It is therefore easy to see that from the administrative point of view it would have been highly anomalous and inconvenient if prosthetists alone, over the whole tract of future time for which the prosthetic service would endure, were to have been subject to a different salary scale and different negotiating machinery. It is significant that a large part of the difference which has opened up between the appellant's salary and Mr Crumlin's is due to the different negotiating machinery. Accordingly, there were sound objectively justified administrative reasons, in my view, for placing prosthetists in general, men and women alike, on the Whitley Council scale and subjecting them to its negotiating machinery. There is no suggestion that it was unreasonable to place them on the particular point of the Whitley Council scale which was in fact selected, ascertained by reference to the position of medical physics technicians and entirely regardless of sex. It is in any event the fact that the general scale of remuneration for prosthetists was laid down accordingly by the Secretary of State. It was not a question of the appellant being paid less than the norm but of Mr Crumlin being paid more. He was paid more because of the necessity to attract him and other privately employed prosthetists into forming the nucleus of the new service.

I am therefore of the opinion that the grounds founded on by the board as constituting the material difference between the appellant's case and that of Mr Crumlin were capable in law of constituting a relevant difference for purposes of s. 1(3) of the 1970 Act, and that on the facts found by the industrial tribunal they were objectively justified.

Counsel for the appellant put forward an argument based on s. 1(1)(b) of the Sex Discrimination Act 1975.

...

This provision has the effect of prohibiting indirect discrimination between women and men. In my opinion it does not, for present purposes, add anything to s. 1(3) of the 1970 Act, since, upon the view which I have taken as to the proper construction of the latter, a difference which demonstrated unjustified indirect discrimination would not discharge the onus placed on the employer. Further, there would not appear to be any material distinction in principle between the need to demonstrate objectively justified grounds of difference for purposes of s. 1(3) and the need to justify a requirement or condition under s. 1(1)(b)(ii) of the 1975 Act. It is therefore unnecessary to consider the argument further.

...

*(Appeal dismissed).*

**B    COURT OF APPEAL**

# Bromley v. H. & J. Quick[1]

LORD JUSTICE DILLON: This is an appeal by 11 ladies who are employees of the respondent company, H. & J. Quick Ltd, against a decision of the Employment Appeal Tribunal under the chairmanship of Sir Ralph Kilner-Brown which, by a majority, dismissed an appeal by the appellants against a unanimous decision of an Industrial Tribunal.

The issues on the appeal are concerned with the true construction and application of provisions in the Equal Pay Act 1970, as amended to give effect to the requirements of European Community law after the decision of the European Court in the case of *Commission of the European Communities* v. *United Kingdom* [1982] IRLR 333. The amendments were enacted to extend the scope of the Act, which had initially been concerned with equal pay for equal work, to cover also the concept under European law of equal pay for work of equal value, and to make certain other alterations to give effect to art. 119 of the EEC Treaty and Council Directive No 75/117 of the EEC. This appeal is particularly concerned with the provisions of the amended Act which relate to job evaluation studies.

...

It may be noted that s. 1(5) serves two different functions under the Act. One the one hand, if a woman wants to claim that she is within subheading (b) of s. 1(2) as a woman employed on work rated as equivalent with that of a man she has to point to a job evaluation study such as is mentioned in s. 1(5) which has so rated the work of her job. On the other hand, if an application is made by the woman employee to an Industrial Tribunal and the employer wishes to avoid a reference to a member of the panel of independent experts for report, it is for the employer to show if he can, under s. 2A(2),

(a) that the work of the woman and the work of the man in question have been given different values on a job evaluation study such as is mentioned in s. 1(5), and
(b) that there are no reasonable grounds for determining that the evaluation contained in that study was, within the meaning of s. 2A(3), made on a system which discriminated on grounds of sex.

It is in this latter context that the questions have arisen in the present case, since the respondent company sought to have the appellants' claims dismissed by the Industrial Tribunal under s. 2A(1) because of the job

---

1     [1988] ICR 623, [1988] IRLR 249 (CA).

evaluation study that there had been. The onus was therefore initially, in my judgment, on the respondent company to show, to put it briefly,

(a) that there had been a job evaluation study which satisfied the requirements of s. 1(5) and thus was 'a study such as is mentioned in s. 1(5)', and

(b) that there are no reasonable grounds for determining that the evaluation contained in that study was tainted by sex discrimination.

In this court, the position as to onus is considerably different for two reasons. In the first place, it is not open to the appellants to take for the first time in this court a point which was not taken before the Industrial Tribunal and to which, had it been taken, evidence might have been directed by the respondent company. This is important because before the Industrial Tribunal the attack on the job evaluation study was directed at the procedures and machinery used as matters of procedure and machinery and not at any alleged direct or indirect discrimination in the choice of benchmark jobs or in the relative values put on the factors on which the study was said to be based. This is very much a case which turns on the question whether the procedures followed satisfy the requirements of the Act. In the second place, the Industrial Tribunal is the Tribunal charged with finding the facts; this court is limited to hearing appeals on points of law and has to keep *Edwards* v. *Bairstow* [1956] AC 14 considerations in mind - *O'Kelly* v. *Trusthouse Forte* [1983] IRLR 369.

As to the facts, the respondent company carries on business as a main agent for Ford motor vehicles. That involves car sales, car hire and car servicing and repair work, with, I apprehend, various ancillary activities. It has several sites in Cheshire and Lancashire. It decided to carry out a job evaluation study for its staff, other than management and sales staff, and to that end retained a firm of independent management consultants called Inbucon. It is not in doubt that the management of the respondent company and the representatives of Inbucon were well aware that there are dangers of indirect sexual discrimination, and were concerned to avoid, if they could, all dangers of direct or indirect discrimination. The majority in the Employment Appeal Tribunal seem to have attached great importance to this, but in truth the good intentions of the parties are of relatively minor importance when the question is whether the procedures followed in a job evaluation study matched up to the requirements of the Act as amended.

The employees whom the study was intended to cover were divided into two categories. The first consisted of shop floor and manual workers, who were in fact all men; these were referred to as 'NJC workers' because their pay and conditions of work are in general governed by the National Joint Council for the Motor Retail and Repair industries. The second consisted of clerical and administrative workers referred to as 'staff workers' many of whom - 23% - were women. Two panels were then set up, one an NJC panel consisting of 15 NJC workers and two senior management representatives and the other a staff panel consisting of 17 staff workers and the same senior management representatives. Each panel was then charged with producing a list of 37 representative NJC or staff jobs, as the case might be, from which a smaller number of benchmark jobs would be selected (in fact in the staff list only 36 jobs were selected with one dummy, but nothing has turned on that).

Under the guidance of Inbucon, five - initially six - factors were selected for consideration in the study, *viz.* skill/training/experience, mental demand, responsibility, physical environment and external contacts. 'Physical environment' was a combination of two factors, physical demand and working conditions, one of which was apparently found to be of low significance on its own in the context of the respondent company. Nothing turns in this case on the choice of factors; the number of factors chosen might of course have been greater than six. How the factors were used I shall come to in due course; that is of the greatest importance.

With the co-operation of the holders of the 74 (or 73) representative jobs thus selected and their superiors, a four-page job description was prepared by a freelance management consultant for each of the 74 jobs. This set out the main purpose of the job and the main tasks, and general comments were then added, under the separate headings of each of the chosen six factors, with reference to that factor. Each panel was supplied with the job descriptions of the 37 selected jobs with which it was concerned and armed with these the panel proceeded to put the 37 jobs in order of value. This was done by paired comparisons comparing each of the 37 jobs with each of the other 36. In considering each pair of jobs, the panel asked whether one was more important or less important than the other or whether they were equal; if they were equal, each was given one point, but otherwise the more important was given two points and the less important none. For safety and consistency, the process was gone through three times over. The ranking of the 37 jobs was done on an assessment of each of the jobs as a whole - i.e. what Mr Lester QC for the appellants has called a 'whole job' basis - and not by a comparison of each job with all the others under a separate heading for each of the factors, but the panel members had of course before them the details under the headings of the factors, given in the job descriptions of the jobs.

A joint panel was then formed consisting of 13 members of whom three were from management, five were NJC workers who had been members of the NJC panel and five (of whom four were women) were staff workers (who had been members of the staff panel). The joint panel then selected from the 74 jobs 23 - 11 NJC jobs and 12 staff jobs - to be the representative benchmark jobs in the study. The joint panel then had to rank the 23 jobs in a single order. This they did by paired comparisons, again on a whole job basis, going through the whole operation twice as a cross-check. They also separately ranked the 23 jobs in order by paired comparisons under each of the six factor headings. These rankings under the factor headings were used, by a mathematical process carried out by computer, to calculate the weightings or factor values to be given to each of the factors, which had, by the combination I have mentioned, now become five. The resultant factor values were as follows:

| | |
|---|---|
| Skill/training experience | 43% |
| Mental demand | 37% |
| Responsibility | 10% |
| Physical environment | 7% |
| External contacts | 3% |

These represent the weightings to be applied to the rankings under the separate factor headings to achieve, substantially, the rankings on a whole job basis which had been previously calculated by the paired comparisons. The purpose of thus calculating these weightings was so that they were available to be applied to other jobs in order to fit those other jobs into a single rank order with the 23 benchmark jobs. However (as will appear), in the event they were not so applied, save on appeals. The joint panel (or its management members with tacit acceptance by the others) made certain alterations to the rankings achieved by the paired comparison method, in order to correct on a 'felt fair' basis what were perceived to be obvious anomalies. The making of these alterations has been criticised on behalf of the appellants and I must return to it later.

It is not expected that small differences in the values of jobs would each inevitably be reflected in small differences in the pay for the jobs. It is accepted that it is permissible for an employer to adopt, as the respondent company did, a system of grading under which all jobs are classified according to a number of grades, and all jobs within the same grade carry the same basic rate of pay whether held by men or women. In the present case there were five grades, A to E, A being the lowest paid. The grade boundaries were set by the management at the points in the scale which seemed to them to be the natural breaks for grade changes and the management, as they were entitled to, set the rate of pay for jobs in each grade. In fact a pay bracket was set for each grade to cover pay factors personal to the job holder (such as long service) as opposed to the factors relevant to the nature of the job which were supposed to have been covered by the fixing of the basic pay for the job by the job evaluation study.

It was finally necessary to slot all other jobs into order of ranking of the 23 benchmark jobs, so that the other jobs would find their appropriate grades. This is the object of having benchmark jobs. The remainder of the 74 jobs originally selected and for which job descriptions had been prepared were slotted in first. Then the rest of the jobs, which included the jobs of the 11 appellants and of the three or four male comparators they have since selected for the purposes of these proceedings were slotted in; no written job descriptions for these jobs were produced. The slotting in was done by management representatives on an assessment of the whole job in each case, without regard to the six or five factors.

There was provision for an appeal to an appeals panel if any employee was not satisfied with the grading, under the foregoing procedure, of his or her job. Two of the appellants, Mrs Bromley and Mrs Owen, did appeal. The appeals panel consisted of the two senior management representatives who had been members both of the NJC panel and of the staff panel, two (male) members of the NJC panel and two (female) members of the staff panel. A short job description was prepared in respect of each appellant to the appeals panel and this was discussed with the appellant at an oral hearing of the appeal; the job description did not, however, contain any special details under the six, or five, factor headings. At the end of the oral hearing, the appeals panel considered the appellant's job under each of the factor headings to find which of the benchmark jobs the appellant's job was nearest to in the ranking under that factor heading. The number, in the ranking under each factor heading, of the nearest equivalent benchmark job was then multiplied by the factor value (taken from the table of factor values as set out above) of that factor, and by the addition of the resultant figures under all the factor headings a figure was arrived at which represented the job value of the appellant's job, on the basis of which it was slotted in among the job values of the 23 benchmark jobs. Mrs Bromley's appeal in fact resulted in her promotion from grade A to grade B.

The form of the applications by the appellants to the Industrial Tribunal was that each appellant claimed that her work was of equal value to the work of a named male comparator employed by the respondent company. This was the first linking of the appellants' names with those of the males who are now the comparators. Previously, while the Inbucon job evaluation study was being undertaken, there had been no special occasion for considering the appellants' jobs specifically in relation to those of the comparators, rather than in relation to the benchmark jobs or to other jobs in general. Each appellant's job and the job of the man in question were in fact given different values on the job evaluation study. Accordingly, the next point for consideration is whether that study satisfies the description of having been a study 'such as is mentioned in s. 1(5).'

It is clear from the decision of the European Court in *Rummler* v. *Dato-Druck GmbH* [1987] IRLR 32 that the consideration of any job, and of the qualities required to perform that job, under a job evaluation study must be objective.

...

The approach of English law to the construction of s. 1(5) appears to be in line with the European law approach: see *Eaton Ltd* v. *Nuttall* [1977] IRLR 71 at p. 74, para. 13, where Phillips J said:

It seems to us that subs. (5) can only apply to what may be called a valid evaluation study. By that, we mean a study satisfying the test of being thorough in analysis and capable of impartial application ... . One which does not satisfy that test, and requires the management to make a subjective argument concerning the nature of the work before the employee can be fitted into the appropriate place in the appropriate salary grade, would seem to us not to be a valid study for the purpose or subs. (5).

The same judge made observations to the same effect in *England* v. *Bromley London Borough Council* [1978] ICR 1 at p. 5 E-F. One has to be a little careful, however, in considering what is meant by 'objective' since, so far as the evidence, in the present case goes, there are no universally accepted external criteria available for measuring how much of a factor or quality is involved in a particular job or for measuring what relative weights ought to be attached to different factors or qualities involved, to differing extents, in various jobs. Every attempt at job evaluation will, as the expert witnesses seem to have agreed, inevitably at some stages involve value judgments, which are inherently to some extent subjective or 'felt fair.' Thus in the present case it seems to me that the paired comparisons between jobs carried out first by the NJC panel and the staff panel on a whole job basis and then by the joint panel on a whole job basis and also on a factor basis are to be regarded as having been objective, even though each involved a value judgment as between the two jobs being compared. Again, though in the present case the relative factor values of the five factors were computed mathematically by applying the ranking of the 23 benchmark jobs by paired comparison on a factor basis to the ranking of the same jobs by paired comparison on a whole job basis, it is recognised in the Equal Opportunities Commission booklet, 'Job evaluation schemes free of sex bias', at p. 10 that deciding what weights should be applied to the factor scores to reflect the relative importance of the various factors may be a highly subjective process.

It must follow that, within measure, there may be subjective elements in an objective process. Where there are such subjective elements, care has to be taken to see that discrimination is not, inadvertently, let in. But such a possibility of discrimination falls to be considered, in the present case, in considering s. 2A(2)(b) of the Act ('whether there are no reasonable grounds for determining that the evaluation contained in the study was made on a system which discriminates on grounds of sex') and not in considering whether the study was 'such a study as is mentioned in s. 1(5).'

Much the same considerations apply, in my judgment, to the complaint that alterations to the rankings were made to correct what were perceived to be anomalies. If there are no universally accepted external criteria for measuring the factors involved in assessing jobs, and the relative values of such factors, it seems to me to be only sense, at the end of a calculation, to take an overall look at the result to see if it looks right (as in the assessment of damages in some cases) and to make any necessary adjustments.

Particular care would have to be taken to see that the adjustments are not the result of ingrained attitudes of discrimination, but that is again a matter for consideration under s. 2A(2)(b), and the making of such adjustments, which are an ancillary part of the study, do not, in my judgment, automatically make the study not one 'such as is mentioned in s. 1(5).'

What s. 1(5) does require is, however, a study undertaken with a view to evaluating jobs in terms of the demand made on a worker under various headings (for instance effort, skill, decision). To apply that to s. 2A(2)(a) it is necessary, in my judgment, that both the work of the woman who has made application to the Industrial Tribunal and the work of the man who is her chosen comparator should have been valued in such terms of demand made on the worker under various headings. Mr Lester submitted that the method used on undertaking a study within s. 1(5) must necessarily be 'analytical', a word he used in the sense of describing the process of dividing a physical or abstract whole into its constituent parts to determine their relationship or value. Sir Ralph Kilner-Brown criticised the use of the word 'analytical' as a gloss on the section. In my judgment, the word is not a gloss, but indicates conveniently the general nature of what is required by the section, *viz.* that the jobs of each worker covered by the study must have been valued in terms of the demand made on the worker under various headings. The original application of s. 1(5) to women within subheading (b) in s. 1(2) of the Act (women employed on work rated equivalent to that of a man) necessarily required that the woman's work and the man's should each have been valued in terms of the demand made on the worker under appropriate headings; the wording of s. 2A(2)(a), read with that of s. 1(5), necessarily shows that the same applies to the present appellants who claim to be within subheading (c), and their male comparators. It is not enough, in my judgment, that the 23 benchmark jobs were valued - if indeed they were (and on this I do not go so far as Woolf LJ and I do not find it necessary to do so) - on the factor demand basis required by s. 1(5), if the jobs of the appellants and their comparators were not.

But on the facts it is clear that none of the comparators' jobs and none of the appellants' jobs, save those of Mrs Bromley and Mrs Owen at the appeal stage, were ever valued according to the demands made on the worker under the five or six selected headings. The relative weightings of the selected factors had indeed been worked out by reference to the 23 benchmark jobs as I have indicated. But short of the appeal stage those weightings were not used in evaluating any of the other jobs, nor were those other jobs, including those of the appellants and their comparators, broken down under the factor headings. What happened at the appeal stage in relation to Mrs Bromley and Mrs Owen makes no difference to the outcome in their cases, since there was never any appeal by their comparator.

Mr Pannick submits that it is enough that every worker covered by the study had a right of appeal which, if exercised, would have led to the sort of analysis accorded to the jobs of Mrs Bromley and Mrs Owen on their appeals. I reject this. The words used in s. 2A(2)(a) are 'have been given' not 'would have been given if they had chosen to ask for it.'

Accordingly *quoad* the appellants and their comparators there never has been such a study as is mentioned in s. 1(5). This point does not seem to have been specifically dealt with in the decisions of the Industrial Tribunal and of the majority of the Employment Appeal Tribunal, possibly because the majority directed themselves too exclusively to the separate question whether any actual discrimination in the job evaluation study was made out. The point is, however, entirely a point of law as to the construction of the Act against facts which are not in dispute, and it is one of the points taken by the dissenting member of the Employment Appeal Tribunal. It is a point open to the appellants on this appeal and it follows that the appeal must succeed.

I turn to consider the requirements of s. 2A(2)(b).

Mr Lester submitted at one stage of his opening of this appeal that there were reasonable grounds for determining that the study was made on a system which discriminated on grounds of sex because, he submitted, it appeared that in the grading of the various benchmark jobs certain staff jobs which had scored higher factor scores than certain NJC jobs were placed in lower grades than the NJC jobs. Had the point been open to him, Mr Lester would, in my judgment, have been right in saying that such a point afforded reasonable grounds for determining that the study had been made on a discriminatory system. On objection by Mr Pannick, however, Mr Lester accepted that the point had never been suggested before the Industrial Tribunal. Since it is a point which depends on the facts and to which evidence could have been directed it cannot be open to him to take it for the first time in this Court.

It is to be noted that the procedure which the respondent company has invoked under s. 2A is a procedure which if successfully invoked would put, as the Industrial Tribunal held it did, a summary end to the appellants' applications without the otherwise mandatory reference of the questions raised by those applications to an independent expert under s. 2A(1)(b). Section 2A(2)(b) puts the onus on the employer to show that there are no reasonable grounds for determining that the evaluation contained in a job evaluation study such as is mentioned in s. 1(5) was made on a system which discriminates on grounds of sex. If in the view of the Industrial Tribunal there are reasonable grounds for so determining, the Industrial Tribunal cannot summarily dismiss an application, but must refer the relevant question to an independent expert for report.

It must follow that it is for the employer to explain how any job evaluation study worked and what was taken into account at each stage.

Mr Lester referred to this as a question of 'transparency', i.e. it must be possible to see through to what actually happened. In my judgment this is a matter of evidence, rather than a question of an inherent ingredient in the study. If the Industrial Tribunal is not satisfied on the evidence that there are no reasonable grounds for determining that the valuation contained in a study was made on a system which discriminated on grounds of sex, it will direct reference to an independent expert. It may not be satisfied on the evidence in a particular case if the evidence offers no explanation of the basis on which some apparently wholly subjective decision was made. But if the Tribunal is satisfied on the evidence that there are no reasonable grounds, the Tribunal's decision could only be challenged on *Edwards* v. *Bairstow* grounds of appeal.

There has been discussion at various stages in the lower courts as to how far the Industrial Tribunal is required to investigate matters which are alleged to constitute reasonable grounds for determining that the evaluation contained in a study was made on a system which discriminated on grounds of sex. I find it unnecessary to go far into this subject in the context of this appeal. In practice, where there has been a job evaluation study and there is evidence from the employer as to how that study was carried out, the applicant is likely to point to particular matters as indicating, or possibly indicating, that the system involved direct or indirect sex discrimination. Natural justice will then require that the employer be given an opportunity of explaining these matters. In some cases it may be easy for an employer to show that some point taken is based on a misunderstanding of what happened or of how some figures were worked out. In other cases the point taken may be more difficult or impossible for the employer to surmount. It will be for the Industrial Tribunal to decide at the end of the hearing, whether or not they are satisfied that there are no reasonable grounds for determining that the evaluation made in the study was made on a system which discriminated on grounds of sex.

I should mention one further point taken by Mr Lester. In support of his argument on the need for 'transparency', he referred to the decision of the European Court in the case of *Johnston* v. *Chief Constable of the Royal Ulster Constabulary* [1986] IRLR 263. What was in issue there was the effect of a certificate of the Secretary of State for Northern Ireland, which had by a statutory instrument been declared to be conclusive evidence of its contents, *viz.* that the applicant had been refused employment on a particular ground. It was held by the European Court that the provisions of the statutory instrument making the certificate conclusive evidence purported to enable the Secretary of State to prevent an individual from asserting his or her right before a court, and accordingly contravened the right to effective judicial process provided by an EEC Council directive. Mr Lester argued that for the decisions taken in carrying out a job evaluation study to have been subjective and not fully explained, and *a fortiori* if any decisions in the operation of such a study were taken by the management of the employer and not by an independent body, was similarly objectionable in preventing the appellants asserting their rights before a court. For my part, however, I do not see any relevant similarity. There is a court, the Industrial Tribunal, to consider the appellants' claims, and it is not suggested that the summary procedure for disposing of claims where there are, or are deemed to be, no reasonable grounds for determining that the work in question is of equal value, is *per se* objectionable to European law. There is nothing in the present case like the certificate of the Secretary of State which purported to remove issues from the consideration of the Court. The court was left in the present case with complete freedom to weigh the evidence, such as it was, and contentions put before it, and to decide whether, taken as a whole, the evidence was or was not sufficient to lead to a certain conclusion.

However, for the reasons given earlier in this judgment, I would allow this appeal, and set aside the Orders of the Industrial Tribunal and the Employment Appeal Tribunal. Instead I would remit the appellants' claims to the Industrial Tribunal with a direction that they be referred to a member of the panel of independent experts for report under s. 2A(1)(b) of the Act.

LORD JUSTICE NEILL: ... It is clear that many, if not most, job evaluation schemes involve the selection of benchmark jobs which are used as a standard against which other jobs can be assessed. I shall therefore assume, without deciding, that in broad outline the Inbucon scheme was a satisfactory scheme and that the selection of the benchmark jobs is not open to criticism.

The crucial question for decision, however, is whether, in the case of each of the individual appellants, her work and the work of her male comparator were given different values 'on a study such as is mentioned in s. 1(5)' of the 1970 Act. It is therefore necessary to consider whether her job and the job of her male comparator have been evaluated 'in terms of the demand made on a worker under various headings (for instance effort, skill, decision).'

In the main the facts are not in dispute. Once the ranking of the 23 benchmark jobs had been completed the remainder of the original 74 jobs which had been selected, and for which job descriptions had been prepared, were slotted in. Finally, the rest of the jobs, including the jobs of the 11 appellants and of their male comparators, were slotted in by management representatives. This final process was carried out on a 'whole job' basis in each case and without regard to the five factors for which weightings had been calculated. It is also apparent that, save in the case of the two appellants who made use of the internal appeal procedure and for whom more detailed job descriptions were prepared, the job descriptions which were used did not contain sufficient information to enable the individual factors to be assessed. It also seems to be plain that no detailed job descriptions were prepared in respect of any of the three or four male comparators.

It is submitted on behalf of the appellants that for the purpose of a valid s. 1(5) study it is always necessary to have a detailed *written* job description for each of the individuals concerned. Clearly if such a job description is prepared it will be must easier to give the selected factors their proper weighting in relation to each individual.

I am not satisfied, however, that it is necessary to have a written description in every case provided the comparison between the individual woman and her male comparator is made by reference to 'the demand made on (each of them) under (the selected) headings.'

In the present case the 'slotting in' was done on a 'whole job' basis and no comparison was made by reference to the selected factors between the demands made on the individual appellant and her male comparator.

Accordingly I would decide this matter on the short point that the employers have not proved that in relation to any of the appellants a valid s. 1(5) study was made between her and her male comparator.

I therefore agree that the appeals should be allowed and I concur in the Order which has been proposed by Dillon LJ.

LORD JUSTICE WOOLF: I agree that this appeal should be allowed. The facts are set out in the judgment of Dillon LJ and I agree with the order which he proposes. In these circumstances I can confine this judgment to the following comments which indicate my approach to the problems created by this appeal:

(a)  The reason this appeal succeeds is that with the exception of Ms Bromley and Ms Owen it is not established that any of the appellants' jobs and any of their respective comparators' (including the comparators of Ms Bromley and Ms Owen) were ever evaluated under various headings as required by s. 1(5). However, subject to this critical defect in my view the employers' study complied with s. 1(5). If both an appellant's job and her comparator's job had been the same job as any of the 23 benchmark jobs or 73 representative jobs the study in relation to that appellant and comparator would have fulfilled the requirements of s. 1(5).

(b)  In order to comply with s. 1(5) it was not necessary for employers to have arranged for every single job performed by their employees to be subject to the same exhaustive process as took place and is described by Dillon LJ in relation to 73 and 23 jobs. Such a requirement would make a benchmark study wholly useless and place an immense burden on many employers. The employers can identify a group of jobs which when evaluated under the headings have no material difference. Then one of that group of jobs can be evaluated under headings and slotted into the rank in the appropriate position having taken into account the factor value and that job can then represent the other jobs within the group. It is possible (as the 73 were chosen as typical) that this is what in fact happened in the case of the appellants and their comparators but if it did there was no evidence of this and as the onus is on the employers to satisfy s. 1(5) the absence of evidence is fatal to their case.

(c)  If, however, a system of choosing a representative job for a group of jobs is adopted then in relation to a job which has not been evaluated under headings it will be open to an employee to contend that his or her job is materially different from the alleged representative job and if this is the case the study will not comply with s. 1(5).

(d)  Although the appeal provision in this case did not assist the employers, if on the appeals which did take place both the appellant's and the comparator's job had been evaluated under headings, which could be by reference to the benchmark study, this could, depending on the circumstances on the appeal, have complied with s. 1(5).

(e)  While the requirements of s. 2A(2) and s. 1(5) are highly technical it is to be remembered that s. 2A(2) is 'without prejudice to the generality' of s. 2A(1)(a) and a defective study could still, at least in theory, assist in establishing that there are no reasonable grounds for determining that the work is of equal value.

...

## C    LOWER COURT OR TRIBUNAL

## Jenkins *v*. Kingsgate (Clothing Productions) Ltd (No 2)[1]

MR JUSTICE BROWNE-WILKINSON: In this case, the appellant, Mrs Jenkins, a part-time worker, is claiming that she ought to be paid the same hourly rate as that paid to full-time male employees of Kingsgate (Clothing Productions) Ltd, the employers. Her claim was originally brought solely under the Equal Pay Act 1970, but, as will appear, she now also relies on art. 119 of the EEC Treaty.

Her claim was dismissed by an industrial tribunal sitting in London. The industrial tribunal give their reasons very shortly. However, this case was referred by the appeal tribunal to the European Court of Justice for their ruling and the order making that reference sets out many more facts than are contained in the findings of the industrial tribunal. We understand that the statement of facts set out in the order was agreed by the parties. They must therefore now be taken to be established facts. They are as follows.

The employers are manufacturers of ladies' clothing at a factory in Harlow, Essex, where they employ 90 workers. Prior to 1975 the employers paid their male and female workers at different rates but there was no difference in the hourly rate of pay of full-time and part-time workers, whether male or female. By November 1975, the full-time rate of pay, that is the rate for those working 40 hours per week, was equalised for male and female workers. However, part-time workers, that is, those working for fewer than 40 hours per week, were paid ten per cent less than the full-time rate. The difference between the full-time and the part-time rates was introduced as a result of negotiations between representatives of the employers and representatives of the relevant trade union whereby it was further agreed that the lower hourly rate would also be applicable to any full-time worker who persistently failed to work 40 hours per week.

The employers maintained the difference in pay rates as between full-time and part-time workers to discourage absenteeism in their factory and to try to ensure that all their expensive machinery was being used for as many hours every day as was possible.

The applicant, who was regarded by the employers as expert at her job, was engaged on like work with Mr Bannan as a special machinist (grade 2). She worked either a little more or a little less than 30 hours per week. In the section where she worked there were 17 machines and five machinists. None of the machines was regarded as being the applicant's own particular machine. Some of the machines were used more often than others, according

---

[1]    [1981] 1 WLR 1485, [1981] ICR 715, [1981] IRLR 388 (EAT).

to the work requirements, and when the work in hand did not require the use of a particular machine that machine would stand idle. Some of the machines were duplicated to cope with extra work. The applicant operated several machines, including the bluffing, basting and buttonholing machine. She might use four different machines in the course of two hours depending on the type of work to be done.

Overtime was available to full-time workers who worked more than nine hours a day, their normal working week of 40 hours being divided into five days. Saturday morning overtime was available to both full-time and part-time workers and the applicant sometimes worked on Saturday mornings when she received her basic rate of pay plus a supplement of 37 1/2 per cent of her basic rate.

At the date of her application to the industrial tribunal the part-time workers were all women. At the date of the hearing before the industrial tribunal there was a male part-time worker who had recently retired and had unusually been allowed to stay on beyond normal retiring age. His was regarded as an exceptional case and he had worked 16 hours per week since 2 January 1979, retaining his staff status and not clocking in but being paid at ten per cent less than the hourly rate he had received before retirement. He was a skilled craftsman capable of doing almost all jobs in the factory. It was a mutually convenient arrangement between him and the employers but was subject to a six to eight week trial period.

...

Counsel for the applicant submitted that the equal pay provisions of art. 119 of the EEC Treaty and art. 1 of Council Directive 75/117/EEC affected the case and that there were questions of interpretation which ought to be immediately referred to the European Court of Justice. The employers did not oppose this course and the preliminary ruling of the European Court of Justice was accordingly requested.

...

As appears from the decision of the European Court of Justice, in the UK 93 per cent of all part-time workers are women. Therefore, not only in relation to these particular employers but in general, the impact of lower pay for part-time workers bears much more heavily on women than on men.

Two points should be noted at this stage. First, the agreed facts we have stated negate any intention by the employers to discriminate against women. Secondly, there is no finding by the industrial tribunal or agreement between the parties that the pay differential was in fact effective or required to reduce absenteeism or to increase the utilisation of the employers' machinery: the only finding or agreement is that it was for those purposes and with that intention that the employers maintained the pay differential. The importance of those points will emerge in due course.

The opinion of Mr Advocate-General Warner was delivered on 28 January 1981, and the judgment of the full court of the European Court of Justice was delivered on 31 March 1981: see [1981] ICR 592.

...

The case now comes back before us to apply those rulings in the present case.

...

The questions which arise in this case as a result of the judgment of the European Court of Justice are as follows.

(1) Is the fact that the woman is a part-time worker and the comparable man a full-time worker by itself, and without more, a 'material difference' within s. 1(3) of the Act of 1970 such as to prevent the equality clause from operating?

(2) Is the fact that the woman is a part-time worker and the comparable man a full-time worker an irrelevant factor in considering whether there is a material difference for the purposes of s. 1(3)?

(3) Is the fact (if it be a fact) that the differential in pay between part-time workers and full-time workers encourages greater utilisation of the employers' plant and discourages absenteeism a relevant or sufficient material difference for the purposes of s. 1(3)?

(4) Is it sufficient for the purposes of s. 1(3) of the Act of 1970 and art. 119 for the employers to show that they had no intention of discriminating or must they also show that the differential in pay is objectively justified for some other reason?

Before considering these questions we must say a word about the effect of art. 119 on the internal UK law. It is now established that art. 119 applies directly in the UK at least for the purposes of this case: see ruling 2 of the European Court of Justice. Therefore under s. 2(1) of the European Communities Act 1972, art. 119 is to be:

> recognised and available in law, and be enforced, allowed and followed accordingly.

Under s. 2(4) of the Act:

> any enactment passed or to be passed ... shall be construed and have effect subject to the foregoing provisions of this section.

Although difficult questions may arise in cases where the clear construction of the internal UK statute conflicts with art. 119, where there is any ambiguity as to the ambit or meaning of an internal UK statute it ought to be construed so as to accord with art. 119: see *Macarthys Ltd* v. *Smith* (Case No 129/79) [1980] ICR 672, at p. 694. In our view, there is an ambiguity as to the exact meaning of the words in s. 1(3) of the 1970 Act:

> genuinely due to a material difference (other than the difference of sex) between her case and his.

Therefore, to the extent that the judgment of the European Court of Justice indicates the effect of art. 119, s. 1(3) of the Act of 1970 should be construed so far as possible as having the same effect. However, as we understand the matter, although the UK statutes are to be construed as far as possible so as to confer rights at least as great as those conferred by art. 119, there is in law no reason why the UK statutes should not confer greater rights than those conferred by art. 119.

We turn then to the four questions mentioned above.

(1) *Is the difference between part-time and full-time work by itself a material difference?*

The decision of the appeal tribunal in *Kearns* v. *Trust House Forte Catering Ltd*, is in our judgment a clear decision that the difference between part-time and full-time work is by itself 'a material difference' for the purposes of s. 1(3). In *Handley* v. *H. Mono Ltd* [1979] ICR 147, there are passages in the judgment which indicate the same view, although the *Kearns* case was not apparently cited: Slynn J at p. 155, referred to a part-time job being 'basically a different kind of job in the quantitative sense.' But in that case there were other material points which the appeal tribunal took into account in holding that, on the facts of that case, there was a 'material difference', as Slynn J pointed out on the first hearing of this case before the appeal tribunal. Slynn J also pointed out that there were material points (apart from the simple fact that the woman was a part-time worker) which arose for consideration in *Durrant* v. *North Yorkshire Area Health Authority* [1979] IRLR 401.

In our judgment the decision of the European Court of Justice clearly establishes that a differential in pay cannot be justified simply by showing that the women are part-time workers. The ruling we have already quoted demonstrates that something more has to be shown. What that 'something more' is, we will consider in dealing with question 4 below.

Therefore, in our judgment, where the circumstances are such that part-time workers are wholly or mainly women, an employer cannot justify paying less for like work to a part-time woman than to a full-time man by simply relying on the fact that the woman is a part-time employee. *Kearns* v. *Trust Houses Forte Catering Ltd* can no longer be regarded as good law.

(2) *Is the difference between full-time and part-time work an irrelevant factor in considering whether there is a 'material difference'?*

We are not sure whether Mr Lester, for the applicant, ever put his case as high as to submit that the difference between part-time and full-time work was wholly irrelevant when considering the question whether there was a 'material difference' for the purposes of s. 1(3). The judgment of the

European Court of Justice certainly establishes that this is a relevant consideration which can in some circumstances justify a differential in pay. What those circumstances are we will again consider when dealing with question 4 below.

(3) *Is the fact that a differential in pay between part-time and full-time workers achieves greater utilisation of plant or reduces absenteeism a 'material difference'?*

We must emphasise that this question arises only if employers prove that the differential in pay in fact produces these results; it does not deal with the case where an employer intends to produce these results without showing that the results are in fact produced.

Mr Lester submitted, in reliance on the decision of the Court of Appeal in *Fletcher* v. *Clay Cross (Quarry Services) Ltd* [1979] ICR 1 that the attainment by the employers of other objectives which relate solely to the profitability of their business were extrinsic factors and could not be regarded as relevant 'material differences.' In the *Clay Cross* case, the employer relied on the fact that the man who was receiving higher pay had been the sole applicant for the job and had demanded higher pay. The employer submitted that this constituted 'a material difference.' The Court of Appeal rejected this submission, saying that to constitute a material difference one had to look at the personal equations of the woman and the man (i.e. matters personal to them and to their work) and that reasons 'personal to the employer' or 'economic factors' were irrelevant. By analogy, Mr Lester argued that considerations such as increasing the utilisation of plant were economic factors personal to the employers which could not constitute a 'material difference.'

The first question put to the European Court of Justice was directed to this submission. Before us, Mr Lester accepted that the decision of the European Court of Justice really concluded the point against him. Paragraph 12 of the judgment ([1981] ICR 592 at p. 613) gives as an example of a case where a pay differential may be justified where:

> the employer is endeavouring, on economic grounds which may be objectively justified, to encourage full-time work irrespective of the sex of the worker.

Therefore, in our judgment a differential in pay between part-time workers, who are predominantly women, and full-time male workers can be justified as being due to a material difference by showing that the pay differential does in fact achieve economic advantages for the employer.

(4) *Is it sufficient for the purposes of s. 1(3) of the Act of 1970 and art. 119 for the employer to show only that he had no intention of discriminating or must he also show that the differential in pay is objectively justified for some other reason?*

This is the question which has caused us the greatest difficulty. It is highlighted in this case because of the findings of fact of the industrial tribunal and the facts agreed by the parties. No one has yet apparently considered whether the payment of a lower rate of pay to part-time workers in this case is in fact an effective or necessary way to reduce absenteeism and increase utilisation of the employers' machinery. All that has been found is that the pay differential was introduced with that intention thereby negating an intention to discriminate against women. Therefore, in order to decide this appeal, we have to answer this question: unfortunately it is not one on which the judgment of the European Court of Justice gives us clear guidance.

It is desirable first to state the sense in which we are using certain terminology. We use the phrase 'direct discrimination' to mean cases where a distinction is drawn between the rights of men and the rights of women overtly on the ground of their sex. 'Indirect discrimination' covers cases where, because a class of persons consist wholly or mainly of women, a difference drawn between that class and other persons operates in fact in a manner which is discriminatory against women, e.g. the present case. Indirect discrimination may itself be either intentional or unintentional. It is intentional if the employer (although not overtly discriminating) treats the class differently because he intends to differentiate on grounds of sex, i.e. he is dissimulating his real intentions. Indirect discrimination is unintentional where the employer has no intention of discriminating against women on the ground of sex but intends to achieve some different purpose, such as the greater utilisation of his machinery.

The fact that indirect discrimination is unintentional does not necessarily mean that it is lawful. Thus, under the Sex Discrimination Act 1975, indirect discrimination is rendered unlawful by s. 1(1)(b) even if it is unintentional. To escape acting unlawfully, the alleged discriminator has to show that the requirement which operates in a discriminatory fashion is justifiable because, viewed objectively, the requirement is reasonably necessary to achieve some other purpose. The same is true in relation to racial discrimination under the Race Relations Act 1976, and under the law of the United States of America: see *Griggs* v. *Duke Power Co.* (1971) 401 US 424. The question we have to decide is whether the same principle applies to s. 1(3) of the Act of 1970, or whether for the purposes of s. 1(3) it is enough to show that the employer had no actual covert intention of discriminating against women.

Were it not for the judgment of the European Court of Justice, we would have held that s. 1(3) requires an employer to do more than disprove an intention to discriminate. The equality clause implied by s. 1(2) of the Act of 1970 operates to counteract all discrimination whether direct or indirect and whether intentional or unintentional; it looks at the effect of the contractual terms, not at whether they are expressed in overtly discriminatory words or with any particular intention. Section 1(3) then operates by taking out of subs. (2) those cases where the variation in the terms between man and woman is:

> genuinely due to a material difference (other than the difference of sex) between her case and his.

The word 'genuinely' and 'other than the difference of sex' plainly prevent an employer who is intentionally discriminating (whether directly or indirectly) from escaping the effect of the equality clause. In our view, for the variation in pay to be 'due to' a material difference it would have to be shown that there was some other matter which in fact justified the variation. It would not be enough simply to show that the employer had an intention to achieve some other legitimate objective (although this might disprove any intention to discriminate): the employer would have to show that the pay differential actually achieved that different objective.

This view is supported by authority. In *Shields* v. *E. Coomes (Holdings) Ltd* [1978] ICR 1159, the Court of Appeal held that so far as possible the Sex Discrimination Act 1975 and the Equal Pay Act 1970 should be construed together so as to produce a harmonious result. Bridge LJ said, at p. 1178:

> In the sphere of employment the provisions of the Sex Discrimination Act and the Equal Pay Act aimed at eliminating discrimination on grounds of sex are closely interlocking and provide in effect a single comprehensive code. The particular provisions designed to prevent overlapping between the two statutes are complex, and it may often be difficult to determine whether a particular matter of complaint falls to be redressed under one Act or the other. But what is abundantly clear is that both Acts should be construed and applied as a harmonious whole and in such a way that the broad principles which underlie the whole scheme of legislation are not frustrated by a narrow interpretation or restrictive application or particular provisions.

To make s. 1(3) of the Act of 1970 accord harmoniously with s. 1(1)(b) of the Sex Discrimination Act 1975 requires that it should be construed as imposing on the employer the onus of proving that the variation in pay is in fact reasonably required to achieve some other objective.

Moreover, in the *Clay Cross* case, Lord Denning MR treated the principles laid down in the *Griggs* case as applicable to s. 1(3) of the Act of 1970. The principle of the *Griggs* case is that requirements which operate in an indirectly discriminatory fashion have to be objectively justified as being required for some purpose other than a purpose linked to the sex of the person on whom the requirement is imposed. This again indicates that s. 1(3) is not satisfied merely by the employer showing that he had no intention to discriminate.

However, when one turns to the judgment of the European Court of Justice one is left in considerable doubt as to the effect of art. 119 in relation to unintentional indirect discrimination. There are passages in the judgment which support the view that it is not enough for the employer simply to show that he had no intention of discriminating. Thus in para. 11 ([1981] ICR 592 at p. 613) the judgment states that in cases where both male and female part-time workers are paid less than full-time workers:

> the fact that work paid at time rates is remunerated at an hourly rate which varies according to the number of hours worked per week does not offend against the principle of equal pay laid down in art. 119 of the Treaty in so far as the difference in pay between part-time work and full-time work is attributable to factors which are objectively justified and are in no way related to any discrimination based on sex.

This approach is again reflected in para. 12 of the judgment and echoes the opinion of the advocate-general. He adopted the approach of the United State Supreme Court in the *Griggs* case and plainly required that indirect discrimination must be objectively justified irrespective of the employer's intention.

On the other hand the formal ruling of the full court seems to approach the matter on the basis that if, by showing some other intention, the employer negates any covert intention to discriminate there will be no infringement of art. 119; this same approach is reflected in para. 14 and 15 of the judgment.

We will assume, without deciding, that art. 119 as construed by the European Court of Justice does not apply to cases of unintentional indirect discrimination. How then are we to construe the UK statute? Although we must construe the UK legislation so as not to conflict with art. 119 and so far as possible to make it accord with art. 119, it does not necessarily follow that the UK legislation must in all respects have the same effect as art. 119. It would not contravene s. 2 of the *European Communities Act 1972* if the UK statutes conferred on employees greater rights than they enjoy under art. 119. Since the Act of 1970 is an integral part of one code against sex discrimination and the rest of the code plainly renders unlawful indirect discrimination even if unintentional, it seems to us right that we should construe the Equal Pay Act 1970 as requiring any difference in pay to be objectively justified even if this confers on employees greater rights than they would enjoy under art. 119 of the EEC Treaty. We therefore hold that in order to show a 'material difference' within s. 1(3) of the Act of 1970 an employer must show that the lower pay for part-time workers is in fact reasonably necessary in order to achieve some objective other than an objective related to the sex of the part-time worker.

To sum up, an industrial tribunal in considering cases of part-time workers under the Act of 1970 will have to consider the following points.

(1) Do the part-time workers consist mainly of women?
(2) Do the part-time workers do 'like work' to full-time male employees of the same employer?

(3)  If the answers to (1) and (2) are 'yes', the equality clause will apply unless the employer can justify the differential in pay by showing a material difference for the purposes of s. 1(3).

(4)  If the industrial tribunal finds that the employer intended to discriminate against women by paying part-time workers less, the employer cannot succeed under s. 1(3).

(5)  Even if the employers had no such intention, for s. 1(3) to apply the employer must show that the difference in pay between full-time and part-time workers is reasonably necessary in order to obtain some result (other than cheap female labour) which the employer desires for economic or other reasons.

Applying these principles to the present case, the industrial tribunal decided in favour of the employers on the short ground that the fact that the applicant was a part-time worker whereas the comparable man was a full-time worker was, by itself, a material difference for the purposes of s. 1(3). That is not a correct approach in law. We must therefore allow the appeal. We will remit the case to the industrial tribunal to find whether the lower rate of pay for part-time workers paid by the employers in this case was in fact reasonably necessary in order to enable the employers to reduce absenteeism and to obtain the maximum utilisation of their plant.

We are conscious that our decision may have far-reaching consequences. In particular it is likely to involve many industrial and other employers in increased labour costs at a time when they and the country can ill afford it. This in turn may lead to a decrease in the total number of women employed. But it is not our function to weigh these factors, even if we were capable of assessing them, against the merits of the social policy reflected in the Acts of 1970 and 1975. Our function is simply to seek to apply the law as it now is. It is unfortunate that in a case of such importance we have not had the advantage of legal argument on behalf of the employers and we would welcome an early consideration of the matter by a higher court.

Finally we remit this case with considerable reluctance. The employers are not a large company and, without having any evil discriminatory intentions, have been caught up in a long test case raising questions of fundamental importance to the Equal Opportunities Commission and to women employees in general but of small importance to the employers. Not surprisingly, they have felt unable to go on incurring legal costs in these proceedings. We suggest that before the Equal Opportunities Commission and the applicant put this small company to even more expense and trouble by a further hearing before the industrial tribunal, consideration might be given to whether it is not possible to reach agreement as to whether, in this particular case, the employers can or cannot satisfy the requirements we have sought to summarise above.

*(Appeal allowed. Case remitted to industrial tribunal).*

## §2 EQUAL TREATMENT

### A HOUSE OF LORDS

## Duke v. GEC Reliance[1]

LORD TEMPLEMAN: My Lords, this appeal raises a question of construction of an Act of the Parliament of the United Kingdom in the light of laws passed by the European Economic Community. The appellant, Mrs Duke, was employed by the respondent, GEC Reliance Systems Ltd. The policy of the respondent was to enforce the retirement of employees when they reached the pensionable age of 60 in the case of women and 65 in the case of men. In conformity with this policy the respondent ceased to employ the appellant after she attained the age of 60 and before she attained the age of 65; if she had been a man her employment would not have discontinued on account of her age before the age of 65. The appellant claims that she was the victim of discrimination on the grounds of sex and that she is entitled to damages under the Sex Discrimination Act 1975 because the discriminatory retirement enforced on her was rendered unlawful by s. 6(2) of the Act which prohibits discrimination against a woman by dismissing her. The respondent admits that the appellant was discriminated against by dismissal but denies that the discriminatory dismissal was unlawful because, by s. 6(4) of the Act, s. 6(2) does not 'apply to provision in relation to death or retirement.' The appellant argues that s. 6(4) only applies to discriminatory benefits provided after retirement and does not authorise discriminatory retirement ages. Alternatively, the appellant submits, s. 6(4) must be construed in a sense favourable to the appellant in order to harmonise the Sex Discrimination Act 1975 with Community law. The respondent argues that the practice of dismissing men at 65 and women at 60 was 'provision in relation to' retirement and that a British court which accepts that construction is bound to give effect to it. If the dismissal of the appellant was an unlawful act of discrimination, the appellant was entitled by ss 63-66 of the Act of 1975 to complain to an industrial court and to be awarded damages on the basis that the unlawful act of discrimination must be treated as a tort. The appellant complained to an Industrial Tribunal but her complaint was dismissed on the ground that s. 6(4) preserved the right of an employer to operate discriminatory ages of retirement. The decision of the Industrial Tribunal was upheld by the Employment Appeal Tribunal and by the Court of Appeal which were bound by earlier Court of Appeal authorities. The appellant now appeals to this House.

...

In *Roberts* v. *Cleveland Area Health Authority* [1977] IRLR 401, the plaintiff, Mrs Roberts, was dismissed by the health authority pursuant to 'the

---

1    [1988] AC 618, [1988] 1 All ER 626, [1988] ICR 339, [1988] IRLR 118, HL (E).

policy of the area health authority under which the normal retirement age for female employees was 60 whereas the normal retirement age for male employees was 65'; *per* Phillips J in the judgment of the Employment Appeal Tribunal at p. 401. Mrs Roberts claimed damages under the Sex Discrimination Act 1975 for her discriminatory dismissal. The health authority successfully pleaded that the dismissal of Mrs Roberts was lawful under s. 6(4) of the Act. The only argument of substance put before the Tribunal and repeated in the course of the present appeal on behalf of the appellant was that in s. 6(4) provision 'in relation to death' must mean provision 'consequent upon a death' and therefore provision 'in relation to retirement' must be limited to provision 'consequent upon retirement.' Phillips J rejected this argument. He said at p. 402 that the word 'provision' in s. 6(4) is an expression intentionally wide and covers all the employer's arrangements relating to retirement including matters of policy, including the fixing of the date of retirement. He thought it likely that the draftsman

> recognised that death and retirement are in different categories in this matter, in that one cannot fix a date of death but one can fix a date of retirement; and that he had to use a form of words, in the one subsection, which was apt to cover both.

My Lords, s. 6(4) makes lawful a dismissal which would otherwise be unlawful under s. 6(2). The discriminatory dismissal made lawful by s. 6(4) is confined to a dismissal for which provision is made in relation to retirement. If an employer dismisses a woman in order to replace her by a man, the dismissal will infringe s. 6(2) and will not be saved by s. 6(4). But if an employer dismisses a woman because the employer has made provision for men and women alike to retire when they reach their retirement ages, then if there are differential retirement ages, the dismissal is saved from being unlawful by s. 6(4) because the dismissal is pursuant to provision relating to retirement. The respondent made provision for men and women to be dismissed when they reached the retirement age of 60 in the case of women and 65 in the case of men. If an employer does not discriminate against a woman by dismissing her but provides that her retirement benefits are to be less favourable than the benefits accorded to a man, then the employer will not be dismissing her within s. 6(2) but he will be subjecting her to another detriment within s. 6(2). This discriminatory detriment is also saved by s. 6(4). Section 11(1) of the Sex Discrimination Act 1975 is to the like effect. That section renders it unlawful for partners in relation to a position as partner in the firm to discriminate against a woman -

...

(b)  in the terms on which they offer her that position, or

...

(d)  in a case where the woman already holds that position -
　　(i)   in the way they afford her access to any benefits, facilities or services or by refusing or deliberately omitting to afford her access to them, or
　　(ii)  by expelling her from that position, or subjecting her to any other detriment.

But s. 11(4) provides that subss (1)(b) and (d) do not apply to provision made in relation to death or retirement.

Thus partners may lawfully offer a partnership to a woman on the terms that she will retire at 60 with power to expel her if she does not. Or if there is a partnership position which is terminable on notice, with no provision for retirement, the firm may give notice enforcing the retirement of the woman at 60 notwithstanding that men are only obliged to retire at 65. So too in the Equal Pay Act 1970 which deals with contractual obligation s. 6(1A)(b) enables an employer to contract with men and women for retirement at different ages without incurring the penalty of an equality clause. There can be no logical distinction between s. 6(1A)(b) of the Equal Pay Act 1970, s. 6(4) of the Sex Discrimination Act 1975 and s. 11(4) of the latter Act; in my opinion all three subsections make lawful discriminatory retirement ages.

On 19 December 1978 the Council of Ministers adopted a Social Security Directive (79/7/EEC) (*Official Journal* No L6 of 1979, p. 24) which had been foreshadowed and reserved by the Equal Treatment Directive. The Social Security Directive obliged Member States to put into effect equal treatment for social security within six years but by art. 7:

7.1  This Directive shall be without prejudice to the right of Member States to exclude from its scope:
(a)  The determination of pensionable age for the purposes of granting old age and retirement pensions and the possible consequences thereof for other benefits.

Thus Community law did not require the abrogation of British statutory retirement pension schemes whereby the pensionable age of women is 60 and the pensionable age of men is 65.

In *Roberts* v. *Cleveland Area Health Authority* [1979] IRLR 244, the Court of Appeal upheld the decision of the Employment Appeal Tribunal that s. 6(4) of the Sex Discrimination Act 1975 allowed discriminatory retirement ages. Lawton LJ. said at p. 246:

My first impression was that the words 'provision in relation to death or retirement' meant 'provision about retirement'. Nothing has been said in the arguments which has made me change that first impression ... . To fix a retirement age is to make a provision in relation to retirement.

Finally, so far as English law is concerned it is material to consider the circumstances in which the Equal Pay Act 1970 and the Sex Discrimination Act 1975 were enacted. In *Roberts* v. *Cleveland Area Health Authority* [1977] IRLR 401 Phillips J said this:

It is common knowledge that outside the public service, at all events, large parts of industry and commerce are organised on the basis that men and women do retire at different ages. The matter is highly controversial. There are different political and sociological views held about it; different economic views, and so on. But in 1975 it was an established fact that this was what frequently happened in practice. Furthermore, it reflects the long-standing course of social legislation going back ... 37 years to 1940, to the Old Age and Widows' Pension Act of that year. For very many years indeed, employers have made all their arrangements upon this basis. Pension funds are so organised, recruitment is so organised; and everything is organised on that basis. Obviously, in the Sex Discrimination Act 1975 there is no reason why Parliament should not, had it wished to do so, have brought all that to an end; but it seems to us largely improbable that Parliament would have brought it to an end, or would have intended to bring it to an end, at a clean sweep. The Equal Pay Act 1970 itself was given five years to be brought into operation; and when one considers the practical consequences of a reform of that character, the arrangements that would have to be made, the consultation that would be needed, the mind boggles at the thought that it should happen overnight, between the end of one night and the beginning of the following day ... . Furthermore it is not without relevance that other Acts such as the Equal Pay Act 1970 and the Trade Union and Labour Relations Act 1974 are in part in conformity with the view that we have indicated.

Similarly in *Roberts* v. *Tate & Lyle Food & Distribution Ltd* [1983] IRLR 240 Browne-Wilkinson J delivering the judgment of the Employment Appeal Tribunal said at p. 243:

We consider that the purpose of s. 6(4) is fairly apparent. Parliament, in enacting the Act of 1975, was seeking to eliminate all discrimination between men and women. However, it was faced by a widespread and inherently discriminatory practice deeply embedded in the social organisation of the country, namely, the differential in retirement ages between men and women. This differential treatment was blatantly discriminatory. However, the effect of such discriminatory practice percolated throughout society. State pensions reflected the differential; the vast majority of occupational pension schemes reflected the differential; normal ages of retirement maintained the differential. Accordingly, unless all this was to be swept away, the Act had to exclude claims arising out of this inherently discriminatory practice. For this reason s. 6(4) appeared in the Act.

My Lords, I agree with the views expressed by Phillips J and Browne-Wilkinson J and would add this. If the Government had intended to sweep away the widespread practice of differential retirement ages, the 1974 White Paper would not have given a contrary assurance and if Parliament had intended to outlaw differential retirement ages s. 6(4) of the Sex Discrimination Act would have been very differently worded in order to make clear the profound change which Parliament contemplated. For the reasons I have given and for the reasons advanced by the Employment Appeal Tribunal and the Court of Appeal in the judgments I have cited, I am of the opinion that the legality of discrimination between men and women with regard to retirement ages was preserved, whether as a matter of contract to which the Equal Pay Act was directed or as a matter of practice to which the Sex Discrimination Act applied.

The United Kingdom Government considered that the Equal Treatment Directive (76/207) did not prohibit discriminatory ages of retirement. The argument of the Government put forward in *Marshall* v. *Southampton & SW Hampshire Area Health Authority* [1986] IRLR 140 was that art. 7(1) of the Social Security Directive allowed discrimination in the determination of pension age; retirement provisions were conditioned by pension age. Women retired at 60 when they qualified for a pension. Men retired at 65 because they did not reach pensionable age until then. The discrimination under Community law permitted in pensionable ages must extend to discrimination in retirement ages; pensionable ages and retirement ages ran in harness. This argument was rejected by the European Court of Justice in *Marshall's* case. The court in its decision as reported in [1986] IRLR 140 at p. 148 decided that:

> 38 ... Article 5(1) of Council Directive (76/207/EEC) must be interpreted as meaning that a general policy concerning dismissal involving the dismissal of a woman solely because she has attained the qualifying age for a State pension, which age is different under national legislation for men and for women, constitutes discrimination on grounds of sex, contrary to that Directive.

The United Kingdom, pursuant to its obligations under the Treaty of Rome to give effect to Community legislation as construed by the European Court of Justice and following the decision in *Marshall's* case, enacted the Sex Discrimination Act 1986 passed on 7 November 1986 and, *inter alia*, amended s. 6(1A) of the Equal Pay Act 1970 and s. 6(4) of the Sex Discrimination Act 1975 so as to render unlawful discriminatory retirement ages as between men and women. The Act of 1986 was not retrospective and does not avail the appellant.

*Marshall's* case decided that the Equal Treatment Directive required Member States to prohibit discrimination with regard to retirement or dismissal in accordance with an employer's policy. In the present case therefore, the appellant can show that her forcible retirement before reaching the age of 65 years was discrimination contrary to the requirements of the Equal Treatment Directive. But *Marshall's* case also decided that the Equal Treatment Directive did not possess direct effect as between individuals, so that the appellant cannot claim damages against the respondent simply for breach of the Directive. In their decision [1986] IRLR 140 at p. 149 the European Court of Justice said that:

> 48 ... according to art. 189 of the EEC Treaty the binding nature of a Directive, which constitutes the basis for the possibility of relying on the directive before a national court, exists only in relation to 'each Member State to which it is addressed'. It follows that a Directive may not of itself impose obligations on a individual and that a provision of a Directive may not be relied upon as such against such a person ... .

Nevertheless, it is now submitted that the appellant is entitled to damages from the respondent because Community law requires the Equal Pay Act enacted on 29 May 1970 and the Sex Discrimination Act enacted on 12 November 1975 to be construed in a manner which gives effect to the Equal Treatment Directive dated 9 February 1976 as construed by the European Court of Justice in *Marshall's* case published on 20 February 1986. Of course a British court will always be willing and anxious to conclude that United Kingdom law is consistent with Community law. Where an Act is passed for the purpose of giving effect to an obligation imposed by a Directive or other instrument a British court will seldom encounter difficulty in concluding that the language of the Act is effective for the intended purpose. But the construction of a British Act of Parliament is a matter of judgment to be determined by British Courts and to be derived from the language of the legislation considered in the light of the circumstances prevailing at the date of enactment. The circumstances in which the Equal Pay Act 1970 and the Sex Discrimination Act 1975 were enacted are set forth in the 1974 White Paper, in the judgment of Phillips J in *Roberts* v. *Cleveland Area Health Authority* [1977] IRLR 401, in the judgment of Browne-Wilkinson J in *Roberts* v. *Tate & Lyle* [1983] IRLR 240 and in the submission of the United Kingdom Government in *Marshall's* case [1986] IRLR 140. The Acts were not passed to give effect to the Equal Treatment Directive and were intended to preserve discriminatory retirement ages. Proposals for the Equal Treatment Directive dated 9 February 1976 were in circulation when the Bill for the Sex Discrimination Act 1975 was under discussion but it does not appear that these proposals were understood by the British Government or the Parliament of the United Kingdom to involve the prohibition of differential retirement ages linked to differential pensionable ages.

The appellant relied on the speech of Lord Diplock in *Garland* v. *British Rail Engineering Ltd* [1982] IRLR 257. Lord Diplock expressed the view that s. 6(4) of the Sex Discrimination Act 1975 could and should be construed in the manner consistent with art. 119 of the Treaty of Rome, the Equal Pay Directive and the Equal Treatment Directive. In *Garland's* case, following a reference to the European Court of Justice, it was established that there had been discrimination contrary to art. 119 which has direct effect between individuals. It was thus unnecessary to consider the effect of the Equal Treatment Directive. Lord Diplock observed at p. 259 that:

> even if the obligation to observe the provisions of art. 119 were an obligation assumed by the United Kingdom under an ordinary international treaty or convention and there was no question of the Treaty obligation being directly applicable as part of the law to be applied by the courts in this country without need for any further enactment, it is a principle of construction of United Kingdom statutes, now too well established to call for citation of authority, that the words of a statute passed after the Treaty has been signed and dealing with the subject matter of the international obligation of the United Kingdom, are to be construed, if they are reasonably capable of bearing such a meaning, as intended to carry out the

obligation, and not to be inconsistent with it ... . The instant appeal does not present an appropriate occasion to consider whether, having regard to the express direction as to the construction of enactments 'to be passed' which is contained in s. 2(4) anything short of an expressed positive statement in an Act of Parliament passed after 1 January 1973, that a particular provision is intended to be made in breach of an obligation assumed by the United Kingdom under a Community treaty, would justify an English court in construing that provision in a manner inconsistent with a Community treaty obligation of the United Kingdom, however wide a departure from the *prima facie* meaning of the language of the provision might be needed in order to achieve consistency.

On the hearing of this appeal, your Lordships have had the advantage, not available to Lord Diplock, of full argument which has satisfied me that the Sex Discrimination Act 1975 was not intended to give effect to the Equal Treatment Directive as subsequently construed in the *Marshall* case and that the words of s. 6(4) are not reasonably capable of being limited to the meaning ascribed to them by the appellant. Section 2(4) of the European Communities Act 1972 does not in my opinion enable or constrain a British court to distort the meaning of a British Statute in order to enforce against an individual a Community Directive which has no direct effect between individuals. Section 2(4) applies and only applies where Community provisions are directly applicable.

...

The submission that the Sex Discrimination Act 1975 must be construed in a manner which gives effect to the Equal Treatment Directive as construed by the European Court of Justice in *Marshall's* case is said to be derived from the decision of the European Court of Justice in *von Colson and Kamann* v. *Land Nordrhein-Westfalen* (Case 14/83) [1984] ECR 1891, delivered on 10 April 1984. In the *von Colson* case the European Court of Justice ruled that the provisions of the Equal Treatment Directive which require equal treatment for men and women in access to employment do not require a Member State to legislate so as to compel an employer to conclude a contract of employment with a woman who has been refused employment on the grounds of sex. The Directive does not specify the nature of the remedies which the Member States must afford to a victim of discrimination. But the court also ruled at p. 1910:

3. Although Directive 76/207/EEC [The Equal Treatment Directive] for the purpose of imposing a sanction for the breach of discrimination, leaves the Member State free to choose between the different solutions suitable for achieving its object, it nevertheless requires that if a Member State chooses to penalise breaches of that prohibition by the award of compensation, then in order to ensure that it is effective and that it has a deterrent effect, that compensation must in any event be adequate in relation to the damage sustained and must therefore amount to more than purely nominal compensation such as, for example, the reimbursement only of the expenses incurred in connection with the application. It is for the national court to

interpret and apply the legislation adopted for the implementation of the Directive in conformity with the requirements of Community law, insofar as it is given discretion to do so under national law.

In the *von Colson* case the German court which submitted the case for a ruling asked whether it was acceptable that a woman who applied for a job and was refused because she was a woman, contrary to the intent of the Equal Treatment Directive, was only entitled under the German domestic law prohibiting such discrimination to the recovery of her expenses (if any) of her application. The German Government in making representations to the European Court expressed the view that under German law compensation for discrimination could include general damages for the loss of the job or of the opportunity to take up the job. The ruling of the European Court of Justice did not constrain the national court to construe German law in accordance with Community law but ruled that if under German law the German court possessed the power to award damages which were adequate and which fulfilled the objective of the Equal Treatment Directive then it was the duty of the German Court to act accordingly.

The *von Colson* case is no authority for the proposition that the German court was bound to invent a German law of adequate compensation if no such law existed and so authority for the proposition that a court of a Member State must distort the meaning of a domestic Statute so as to conform with Community law which is not directly applicable. If, following the *von Colson* case, the German court adhered to the view that under German law it possessed no discretion to award adequate compensation, it would have been the duty of the German Government in fulfilment of its obligations under the Treaty of Rome to introduce legislation or evolve some other method which would enable adequate compensation to be obtained, just as the United Kingdom Government became bound to introduce legislation to amend the Equal Pay Act and the Sex Discrimination Act in the light of *Marshall's* case. Mrs Advocate-General Rozes in her opinion, delivered on 31 January 1984 in the *von Colson* case, said at p. 1919 that:

> In proceedings under art. 177 it is not for me to express a view on questions which fall exclusively within the jurisdiction of the national courts inasmuch as they concern the application of national law.

The Treaty of Rome does not interfere and the European Court of Justice in the *von Colson* case did not assert power to interfere with the method or result of the interpretation of national legislation by national courts.

It would be most unfair to the respondent to distort the construction of the 1975 Sex Discrimination Act in order to accommodate the 1976 Equal Treatment Directive as construed by the European Court of Justice in the 1986 *Marshall* case. As between the appellant and the respondent the Equal

Treatment Directive did not have direct effect and the respondent could not reasonably be expected to reduce to precision the opaque language which constitutes both the strength and the difficulty of some Community legislation. The respondent could not reasonably be expected to appreciate the logic of Community legislators in permitting differential retirement pension ages but prohibiting differential retirement ages. The respondent is not liable to the appellant under Community law. I decline to hold that liability under British law attaches to the respondent or any other private employer to pay damages based on wages which women over 60 and under 65 did not earn before the amending Sex Discrimination Act 1986 for the first time and without retrospective effect introduced the statutory tort of operating differential retirement ages. I would dismiss this appeal.

...

# James *v*. Eastleigh Borough Council[1]

LORD BRIDGE OF HARWICH: My Lords, in November 1985 the plaintiff and his wife were both aged 61. They went one day in that month to the Fleming Park Leisure centre where there is a public swimming pool operated by the respondent Council. Being of pensionable age the plaintiff's wife was admitted free. Not being of pensionable age the plaintiff had to pay 75p for admission. The plaintiff brought proceedings against the Council claiming that they had unlawfully discriminated against him on the ground of his sex contrary to s. 1(1)(a) and s. 29 of the Sex Discrimination Act 1975. The claim was heard by Judge Tucker QC in the Southampton County Court who dismissed it. An appeal against his judgment was dismissed by the Court of Appeal (Sir Nicolas Browne-Wilkinson VC, Parker and Nourse LJJ: [1989] IRLR 318). The plaintiff now appeals by leave of your Lordships' House.

At first glance this may seem to be a very trivial matter. But the truth is to the contrary. It is an important test case brought with the backing of the Equal Opportunities Commission in performance of their statutory functions under the Act. The phrase 'pensionable age' is a term of art derived from the definition in s. 27(1) of the Social Security Act 1975 where it means: '(a) in the case of a man, the age of 65 ; and (b) in the case of a woman, the age of 60.' In this sense it not only governs the age at which persons can first qualify for their state pensions, but is also used as the basis on which men and women qualify for a variety of concessions to the elderly such as free or reduced travel and free prescriptions under the National Health Service. The Commission's purpose in this litigation is to establish the principle for which they contend that in any sphere of activity in which discrimination on the ground of sex is prohibited by the Sex Discrimination Act 1975 the practice of denying to men between the ages of 60 and 65 benefits which are offered to women between those ages is unlawful unless it is authorized by other express statutory provisions.

...

The case for the plaintiff is that the Council were refusing to provide him with facilities, *viz.* admission to the swimming pool, on the like terms as were normal in relation to female members of the public of the same age as himself. This, it is said, was a clear contravention of s. 29(1) and s. 1(1)(a) because in the same relevant circumstances the Council were treating the plaintiff on the ground of his sex less favourably than they would treat a woman. If he had been a woman aged 61, he would have been admitted free. Because he was a man aged 61 he was charged 75p for admission.

---

1    [1990] 2 AC 751, [1990] 3 WLR 55, [1990] 2 All ER 607, [1990] ICR 554, [1990] IRLR 288, HL (E)

The main ground on which the Council sought to contest the claim in the County Court and the ground on which they succeeded there was that the relevant 'section of the public' which fell for consideration under s. 29(1) was the section of the public comprising persons of statutory pensionable age. This ground was rejected by the Court of Appeal. Sir Nicolas Browne-Wilkinson VC, delivering a judgment with which Parker and Nourse LJJ agreed, said, at p. 320:

> ... it is not permissible for a defendant in such a case to seek to define the section of the public to which it offers services in terms which are themselves discriminatory in terms of gender. If this were not so it would be lawful, for example, to provide free travel for men but not for women on the ground that the facility of free travel is only being provided for a section of the public comprising men. Whatever else may be meant by a 'section of the public', in my judgment it cannot mean a class defined by reference to sex or, under the Race Relations Act 1976, by reference to race ... .

This is clearly right and this ground was not pursued by the Council before your Lordships.

In the Court of Appeal the case took an entirely new turn and the Court found in favour of the Council on a ground first raised in argument by the Court themselves. It had been common ground in the County Court that the concession offered by the Council to persons of pensionable age was discriminatory in favour of women and against men under s. 1 of the Sex Discrimination Act 1975. But the Court of Appeal held that the Council's less favourable treatment of a man than a woman was not 'on the ground of his sex' and that there had accordingly been no direct discrimination contrary to s. 1(1)(a). The condition which the local authority applied to persons resorting to their swimming pool that in order to qualify for free admission they should be of pensionable age was, as the Court held, a condition applied equally to men and women. The condition, therefore, would only amount to unlawful discrimination under s. 1(1)(b) if the appellant could show '(i) ... that the proportion of men who can comply with it is considerably smaller than the proportion of women who can comply with it' and if the local authority failed to show the condition '(ii) ... to be justifiable irrespective of the sex of the person to whom it is applied.' The case for the appellant had not been pleaded or presented on this basis in the County Court. The Court of Appeal, therefore, declined to remit the case to the County Court and left it to the appellant and the Equal Opportunities Commission to bring fresh proceedings based on a fresh visit to the swimming pool if so advised.

In reaching these conclusions the judgment of Sir Nicolas Browne-Wilkinson VC first sets the scene in the following terms, at p. 321:

> There is no suggestion that the reason for the Council adopting its policy was a desire to discriminate against men. The Council's reason for giving free swimming to those of pensionable age was to give benefits to those whose resources would be likely to have been reduced by retirement. The aim was to aid the needy, whether

male or female, not to give preference to one sex over the other. Moreover the
condition which had to be satisfied in order to qualify for free swimming did not
refer expressly to sex at all. The condition was simply that the applicant had to be of
pensionable age. The undoubtedly discriminatory effect of that condition only
emerges when one gets to the next question, i.e. at what age do men and women
become pensionable? The question is whether the Council's policy amounts to direct
discrimination 'on the ground of his sex' within s. 1(1)(a) or indirect discrimination
within s. 1(1)(b) by reason of the Council having imposed a condition on men and
women alike with which a considerably smaller proportion of men than women can
comply.

The Vice-Chancellor summarised Mr Lester's submissions for the
appellant as follows, at p. 321:

> Mr Lester, for the plaintiff, forcefully submitted that there is direct discrimination in
> this case. He submitted that discrimination is 'on the ground of' sex within s. 1(1)(a)
> if the sex of the plaintiff is a substantial cause of the less favourable treatment. In
> this context, he says, the correct question is 'what would the position have been but
> for the sex of the plaintiff ?' If the position would be different if the plaintiff's sex
> were different, that is direct discrimination.

I do hope I do justice to the judgment if I recite only what seem to me to
be the two essential passages, at pp. 321 and 322, rejecting these submissions
as follows:

> In my judgment s. 1(1)(a) is looking to the case where, subjectively, the defendant
> has treated the plaintiff less favourably because of his or her sex. What is relevant is
> the defendant's reason for doing an act, not the causative effect of the act done by
> the defendant ... .
> There is a further objection to Mr Lester's construction of the section. If there is
> direct discrimination in every case where there is a substantial causative link
> between the defendant's treatment and the detriment suffered by the plaintiff as a
> result of his sex I can see no room for the operation of subsection (1)(b). In every
> case in which a sexually neutral condition in fact operates differently and
> detrimentally to one sex as opposed to the other, the imposition of such condition
> would be a substantial cause of detriment to the plaintiff by reason of his or her sex,
> i.e. it would fall within Mr Lester's causation test and therefore constitute direct
> discrimination under subsection (1)(a). This plainly was not the intention of
> Parliament which was drawing a clear distinction between, on the one hand, those
> cases where the defendant expressly or covertly acts by reference to sex of the
> plaintiff and, on the other, those cases where the defendant acted on the grounds not
> expressly or covertly related to sex but his actions have caused a disparate impact as
> between the sexes.

The fallacy, with all respect, which underlies and vitiates this reasoning
is a failure to recognise that the statutory pensionable age, being fixed at 60
for women and 65 for men, is itself a criterion which directly discriminates
between men and women in that it treats women more favourably than men
'on the ground of their sex.' This was readily conceded by Mr Beloff and is
indeed self-evident. It follows inevitably that any other differential treatment
of men and women which adopts the same criterion must equally involve

discrimination 'on the ground of sex.' As Mr Beloff was again constrained to concede, the Council would certainly have discriminated directly in favour of women and against men on the ground of their sex if they had *expressly* made their concession of free entry to the swimming pool available to women aged 60 and to men aged 65. He submits that the availability of the statutory concept of pensionable age in the Social Security Act 1975 to denote the criterion on which the concession is based and the fact that pensionable age, although now discriminatory, will not necessarily remain so, enables the Council to escape the charge of direct discrimination 'on the ground of sex.' But his simply will not do. The expression 'pensionable age' is no more than a convenient shorthand expression which refers to the age of 60 in a woman and to the age of 65 in a man. In considering whether there has been discrimination against a man 'on the ground of his sex' it cannot possibly make any difference whether the alleged discriminator uses the shorthand expression or spells out its full meaning.

The Court of Appeal's attempt to escape from these conclusions lies in construing the phrase 'on the ground of her sex' in s. 1(1)(a) as referring subjectively to the alleged discriminator's 'reason' for doing the act complained of. As already noted, the judgment had earlier identified the Council's reason as 'to give benefits to those whose resources would be likely to have been reduced by retirement' and 'to aid the needy, whether male or female.' But to construe the phase, 'on the ground of her sex' as referring to the alleged discriminator's reason in this sense is directly contrary to a long line of authority confirmed by your Lordships' House in *R. v. Birmingham City Council*, ex parte *Equal Opportunities Commission* [1989] IRLR 173. In that case the Council, as local education authority, was held to have discriminated against girls under s. 1(1)(a). At the Council's independent, single-sex grammar schools there were more places available for boys than girls. Consequently the Council were obliged to set a higher pass mark for girls than boys in the grammar school entrance examination. In his speech, expressing the unanimous opinion of the House, Lord Goff of Chieveley said, at p. 175:

The first argument advanced by the Council before your Lordships' House was that there had not been in the present case, less favourable treatment of the girls on the grounds of sex. Here two points were taken. It was submitted ... (2) that, if that burden had been discharged, it still had to be shown that there was less favourable treatment on grounds of sex, and that involved establishing an intention or motive on the part of the Council to discriminate against the girls. In my opinion, neither of these submissions is well-founded ...

As to the second point, it is, in my opinion, contrary to the terms of the statute. There is discrimination under the statute if there is less favourable treatment on the ground of sex in other words if the relevant girl or girls would have received the same treatment as the boys but for their sex. The intention or motive of the defendant to discriminate, though it may be relevant so far as remedies are concerned ... is not a necessary condition of liability; it is perfectly possible to envisage cases where the defendant had no such motive, and yet did in fact discriminate on the ground of sex. Indeed, as Mr Lester pointed out in the course of his argument, if the Council's submission were correct it would be a good defence for an employer to show that he discriminated against women not because he intended to do so but (for example) because of customer preference, or to save money, or even to avoid controversy. In the present case, whatever may have been the intention or motive of the Council, nevertheless it is because of their sex that the girls in question receive less favourable treatment that the boys, and so are the subject of discrimination under the Act of 1975. This is well established in a long line of authority: see, in particular, *Jenkins* v. *Kingsgate (Clothing Productions) Ltd* [1981] IRLR 388, pp. 393, 394 *per* Browne-Wilkinson J and *R.* v. *Secretary of State for Education & Science,* ex parte *Keating* (1985) 84 LGR 469, per Taylor J, at p. 475; see also *Ministry of Defence* v. *Jeremiah* [1979] IRLR 437 per Lord Denning MR. I can see no reason to depart from this established view.

Lord Goff's test, it will be observed, is not subjective, but objective. Adopting it here the question becomes: 'Would the plaintiff, a man of 61, have received the same treatment as his wife but for his sex?' An affirmative answer is inescapable.

The judgment of the House in the *R.* v. *Birmingham City Council,* ex parte *Equal Opportunities Commission* was delivered after the instant case had been argued in the Court of Appeal but before they delivered their judgment. They did not, therefore, have the advantage of argument as to the effect of the decision. They sought to distinguish it. But it is, in my opinion, quite indistinguishable. It would not have availed the Birmingham City Council to say that the condition for grammar school entry was to have passed the entrance examination because the pass mark was set at different levels for boys and girls and discriminated against girls on the ground of their sex. By precise parity of reasoning it does not avail the Council in this case to say that the condition for free admission to the swimming pool is to have attained pensionable age because pensionable age is set at different levels for men and women and discriminates against men on the ground of their sex. Similarly the subjective reason for the differential treatment in both cases is quite irrelevant. The Birmingham City Council had the best of motives for discriminating as they did. They could not otherwise have matched the entry of boys and girls into the grammar school places available. The Council in this case had the best of motives for discriminating as they did. They wished to benefit 'those whose resources were likely to have been reduced by retirement' and 'to aid the needy, whether male or female.' The criterion of pensionable age was a convenient one to apply because it was readily verified by possession of a pension book or a bus pass. But the purity of the discriminator's subjective motive, intention or reason for discriminating cannot save the criterion applied from the objective taint of discrimination on the ground of sex.

The question of indirect discrimination under s. 1(1)(b) arises only where the 'requirement or condition' applied by the alleged discriminator to a person of one sex is applied by him equally to a person of the other sex. Pensionable age cannot be regarded as a requirement or condition which is applied equally to persons of either sex precisely because it is itself discriminatory between the sexes. Whether or not the proportion of men of pensionable age resorting to the Council's swimming pool was smaller than the proportion of women of pensionable age was quite irrelevant. Women were being treated more favourably than men because they attained the age to qualify for free admission five years earlier than men.

The Court of Appeal detected and properly criticised the error made by the trial judge in the application of s. 29 in that he sought to define the 'section of the public' to whom services were provided by the Council 'in terms which are themselves discriminatory in terms of gender.' But they fell into the same error themselves in making the comparisons necessary under s. 1. Section 5(3) requires that in comparing the cases of persons of different sex under s. 1(1) the relevant circumstances must be the same. Because pensionable age is itself discriminatory it cannot be treated as a relevant circumstance in making a comparison for the purpose of s. 1 any more than it can be used to define a 'section of the public' under s. 29. It is only by wrongly treating pensionable age as a relevant circumstance under s. 5(3) that it is possible to arrive at the conclusion that the provisions of facilities on favourable terms to persons of pensionable age does not involve direct discrimination under s. 1(1)(b). On a proper application of s. 5(3) the relevant circumstance which was the same here for the purpose of comparing the treatment of the plaintiff and his wife was that they were both aged 61.

Statutory pensionable age is still used in some other statutory contexts, besides the Social Security Act 1975, as the basis of entitlement to enjoy certain other benefits or concessions. Thus, under travel concession schemes established by local authorities pursuant to s. 93 of the Transport Act 1985 men over 65 and women over 60 are eligible to receive concessions: s. 93(7)(a). Similarly by regulation 7 of the National Health Service (Charges for Drugs and Appliances) Regulations 1980 (SI 1980 No 1503) men over 65 and women over 60 are exempt from the charges imposed by the Regulations. But it is impossible to infer from these or any other specific statutory provisions requiring or authorising discrimination in defined circumstances the existence of a general exception to the prohibition of sex discrimination in the provision of goods, facilities and services imposed by s. 29 of the Sex Discrimination Act 1975 such that discrimination in favour of women and against men between the ages of 60 and 65 is always permitted. In the absence of express statutory authority derived from some other enactment, such discrimination is prohibited.

I would accordingly allow the appeal, set aside the Order of the courts below and declare the Council discriminated against the plaintiff on the ground of his sex contrary to ss 1(1)(a) and 29 of the Sex Discrimination Act 1975 by refusing to provide him with swimming facilities on the terms as were normal in the case of women, in that men aged 60 to 65 (including the plaintiff) were charged for entry, whereas women aged 60 to 65 were admitted free. I would propose that there should be no order for the payment of costs.

LORD GRIFFITHS: My Lords, I am unable to agree with the majority of your Lordships that this appeal should be allowed. When the Eastleigh Borough Council decided to allow free swimming facilities to persons of pensionable age they did not do so because they wished women over 60 to swim free because they were women or to deny that privilege to men until they were 65 because they were men. The Council were following the very widespread and, in my view, wholly admirable practice of treating old age pensioners with generosity. The Council were giving free swimming to people because they were pensioners, not because they were either men or women.

When people are living on a pension they are almost always less well off than when in employment and less able to afford leisure and travel facilities although they may have more time in which to enjoy them. When the Sex Discrimination Act 1975 was before Parliament every member of both Houses must have known that it was an attractive feature of our national life that those who provided entertainment and travel facilities gave generous treatment to old age pensioners by providing them free or at concessionary rates. I cannot believe that it was the intention of Parliament that this benevolent practice should be declared to be unlawful - but such is the result of your Lordships' decision.

I appreciate of course that adopting pensionable age as the criterion to judge whether a person is living on a pension is to adopt a broad brush approach. But given that it is the intention to give the concession to those who are living on a pension and thus of reduced means, it appears to me to be the only practical criterion to adopt. It would be quite impossible to interrogate every person as to whether they were or were not living on a pension or to apply some other form of means test before admitting them to the swimming pool. I believe that against the pattern of employment in this country, and in particular the pattern as it was in 1975, pensionable age is a fair test to apply to establish those who are likely to be living on reduced incomes, and that it is a fair assumption that those of pensionable age are living on pensions. Where I entirely part company from your Lordships is in the view that the Council used the words 'pensionable age' as 'no more than a convenient shorthand expression which refers to the age of 60 in a woman and to the age of 65 in a man.' In my view the reference to 'pensionable age' carries with it the unmistakable intention of the Council to give the free swimming facilities to people because they are pensioners and not because they are men or women.

Suppose the Council had resolved to allow free swimming to everyone living on a pension. That would surely not be discriminating on the 'grounds of sex' under s. 1(1)(a). Suppose that the Council had added that it would accept proof of pensionable age as sufficient proof of living on a pension - would that have converted their decision to one on the 'grounds of sex'? Again, I would have thought the answer was manifestly not, assuming of course that such an assumption was reasonable.

Whether a person treats another less favourably 'on the grounds of sex' is a question that does not permit of much refinement. It means did they do what they did because she was a woman (or a man). It is a question of fact which has to be answered by applying common sense to the facts of the particular case. I agree that the motive behind the action is not determinative although it may cast light on the question - see in particular the discussion of the question in the judgment of Woolf J in *R.* v. *Commission for Racial Equality*, ex parte *Westminster City Council* [1985] IRLR 426.

I was a party to the decision in *R.* v. *Birmingham City Council* ex parte *Equal Opportunity Commission*, and agreed with the speech of Lord Goff of Chieveley. But in that speech I had read Lord Goff as using intention and motive interchangeably and had obviously failed to appreciate the full significance that would be attached to a 'but for' test. In the *Birmingham* case no one could doubt that it was because of their sex that it was more difficult for girls to get a place in a grammar school than boys: there were more places for boys than there were for girls and that was the end of it. So a 'but for' test in that case led to the result that girls were being discriminated against, and the fact that the Council were very unhappy about the situation and did not wish to discriminate did not alter the fact that they were discriminating. That case establishes that the subjective motive is not determinative in a case of sex discrimination under s. 1(1)(a). But on reflection I do not think that a 'but for' test will in all cases answer the question - was the favourable treatment 'on the grounds of sex.'

Obviously imposing a retirement age of 60 on women and 65 on men is discriminatory on the grounds of sex. It will result in women being less well off than men at 60. But what I do not accept is that an attempt to redress the result of that unfair act of discrimination by offering free facilities to those disadvantaged by the earlier act of discrimination is, itself, necessarily discriminatory, 'on the grounds of sex.' The question in this case is did the Council refuse to give free swimming to the plaintiff because he was a man, to which I would answer, no, they refused because he was not an old age pensioner and therefore could presumably afford to pay 75p to swim.

The result of your Lordships' decision will be that either free facilities must be withdrawn from those who can ill afford to pay for them or, alternatively, given free to those who can well afford to pay for them. I consider both alternatives regrettable. I cannot believe that Parliament intended such a result and I do not believe that the words 'on the grounds of sex' compel such a result.

Since writing this short speech I have had the advantage of reading the much fuller discussion of the problem contained in the speech of Lord Lowry. I agree entirely with his reasoning and conclusion.

I would dismiss the appeal.

LORD ACKNER: My Lords, I so entirely agree with the views expressed by my noble and leaned friends Lord Bridge of Harwich and Lord Goff of Chieveley in their speeches that I had not intended to provide yet another speech. However, in case it may be thought that your Lordships' decision involves such complex reasoning as not to be readily comprehensible to the senior citizens of Eastleigh, two of whom have generated this litigation, I add this short contribution.

It is clear from the evidence given in the County Court by the assistant manager of the Fleming Park Leisure Centre, the only witness called on behalf of the respondent Council, that Mr and Mrs James, on seeking free admission to the swimming pool, would have been asked to provide proof of their ages. Having done so Mrs James would have been let in free but her husband would have been required to pay the full price of 75p, although they were each aged 61. If Mr James, as he may well have done, had asked why he was thus being treated differently, i.e. being discriminated against, he would have been told that it was the Council's policy to allow free swimming to women over the age of 60 but in the case of men, that facility was only available after they had reached the age of 65.

The essential question raised by this appeal is whether this less favourable treatment received by Mr James was, to quote the important words of s. 1(1)(a) of the Sex Discrimination Act 1975, 'on the ground of his sex' and therefore unlawful being contrary to the subsection and s. 29 of the Act.

The answer, in my respectful submission, is clearly in the affirmative. It was common ground in the courts below, and indeed it was so accepted by Mr Beloff QC before your Lordships, that the Council's policy was discriminatory. The Council was applying a gender determinative formula for entitlement to free swimming. You had to be a person 'who had reached pensionable age' (60 for women and 65 for men). Such a formula was inherently discriminatory. In the County Court no evidence was given as to why the Council had decided on this policy. This omission was in my view fully justified because such evidence would have been irrelevant. The policy itself was crystal clear - if you were a male you had, vis-à-vis a female, a five-year handicap. You had to achieve the age of 65 before you were allowed to swim free of payment, but if you were a female you qualified for free swimming five years earlier. The reason why this policy was adopted can in no way affect or alter the fact that the Council had decided to implement and had implemented a policy by virtue of which men were to be treated less favourably than women, and were to be so treated on the ground of, i.e. because of, their sex.

There might have been many reasons which had persuaded the Council to adopt this policy. The Court of Appeal have inferred that 'the Council's reason for giving free swimming to those of pensionable age was to give benefits to those whose resources would be likely to have been reduced by retirement' (*per* Sir Nicolas Browne-Wilkinson VC [1989] IRLR 318). I am quite prepared to make a similar assumption, but the Council's motive for this discrimination is nothing to the point (see the decision of this House in *R.* v. *Birmingham City Council,* ex parte *Equal Opportunities Commission* [1989] IRLR 173).

My Lords, I am not troubled by the suggested consequences of your Lordships' decision. In the light of the changed and changing work practices between the sexes there is much to be said for linking benefits to actual age rather than to state pensionable age.

I, too, would allow this appeal.

LORD GOFF OF CHIEVELEY: My Lords, for the reasons given by my noble and learned friend Lord Bridge of Harwich, I too would allow the appeal. However, since a passage in the speech which I delivered in *R.* v. *Birmingham City Council,* ex parte *Equal Opportunities Commission* [1989] IRLR 173 at p. 175, has been referred to, I think it right to add a few words of my own.

In the Court of Appeal in the present case, Sir Nicolas Browne-Wilkinson VC approached the matter as follows. Referring to s. 1(1)(a) of the Sex Discrimination Act 1975, which is usually said to be concerned with cases of 'direct' discrimination, he said [1989] IRLR 318 at p. 321:

> In the case of direct discrimination 'a person discriminates against a [man] ... if on the ground of [his] sex he treats [him] less favourably ... '. Those words indicate that one is looking, not to the causative link between the defendant's behaviour and the detriment to the plaintiff, but to the reason why the defendant treated the plaintiff less favourably. The relevant question is 'did the defendant act on the ground of sex?' not 'did the less favourable treatment result from the defendant's action?' Thus, if the overt basis for affording less favourable treatment was sex (e.g. an employer saying 'no women employees') that is direct discrimination. If the overt reason does not in terms relate to sex (e.g. in selection for redundancy, part-time employees are the first to go) that is not on the face of it direct discrimination since sex does not come into the overt reason given for the action. If, but only if, it is shown that the overt reason is not the true reason but there is a covert reason why the employer adopted those criteria (i.e. to get rid of his female employees) will it be direct discrimination. In such a case the true reason for the policy is the desire to treat women less favourably than men: the employer is therefore acting on that ground.

On this approach, a defendant will only have committed an action of direct discrimination if either his overt or his covert *reason* for his action is the sex of the complainant. So the question whether or not there has been direct discrimination can only be answered by asking *why* the defendant acted as he did. The Vice-Chancellor however went on to state that the defendant's intention or motive may be relevant for the purpose of ascertaining the defendant's reason for his behaviour. I will return to the use of these three words - intention, motive and reason - at a later stage.

In reaching this conclusion, the Vice-Chancellor was influenced primarily by the wording of the subsection. He considered that the words 'on the ground of sex' referred, in this context, not to the causative link between the defendant's behaviour and detriment to the complainant, but to the reason why the defendant treated the complainant less favourably. But he was also influenced by his understanding that, to read those words in the subsection as referring to a causative link, would so widen the ambit of s. 1(1)(a) as effectively to emasculate s. 1(1)(b). He said, at pp. 321, 322:

> There is a further objection to Mr Lester's construction of the section. If there is a direct discrimination in every case where there is a substantial causative link between the defendant's treatment and the detriment suffered by the plaintiff as a result of his sex I can see no room for the operation of subs. (1)(b). In every case in which a sexually neutral condition in fact operates differentially and detrimentally to one sex as opposed to the other, the imposition of such condition would be a substantial cause of detriment to the plaintiff by reason of his or her sex, i.e. it would fall within Mr Lester's causation test and therefore constitute direct discrimination under subs. (1)(a). This plainly was not the intention of Parliament which was drawing a clear distinction between, on the one hand, those cases where the defendant expressly or covertly acts by reference to the sex of the plaintiff and, on the other, those cases where the defendant acted on grounds not expressly or covertly related to sex but his actions have caused a disparate impact as between the sexes.

I wish to state at once that I find this latter part of the Vice-Chancellor's reasoning unpersuasive. We are concerned in the present case with the application of a requirement or condition - pensionable age - which is itself gender-based, since a person's pensionable age differs, depending upon his or her sex. Now I have difficulty in seeing how s. 1(1)(b) can sensibly apply in the case of such a requirement or condition. This is because two of the conditions for the application of s. 1(1)(b) are that the requirement or condition in question is 'such that the proportion of women who can comply with it is considerably smaller than the proportion of men who can comply with it', and that it is to her detriment because she cannot comply with it. These conditions appear to be irrelevant in the case of a requirement or condition which is itself gender-based. They presuppose rather a requirement or condition which is of itself gender-neutral (such as the physical height of persons in the relevant group, or the nature of their employment), in which case it would be relevant to enquire about the proportion of men and women affected by it. It follows, in my opinion, that where the requirement or condition in question is gender-based, the question is whether or not there has been direct discrimination under s. 1(1)(a). I wish however to point out that the fact that such cases fall for consideration under s. 1(1)(a), rather than s. 1(1)(b), does not have the effect of emasculating the latter subsection, under which it may be appropriate to consider cases concerned with gender-neutral requirements or conditions, to which the conditions specified in the subsection can sensibly be applied.

I turn to that part of the Vice-Chancellor's reasoning which is based upon the wording of s. 1(1)(a). The problem in the present case can be reduced to the simple question - did the defendant Council, on the ground of sex, treat the plaintiff less favourably than it treated or would treat a woman? As a matter of impression, it seems to me that, without doing any violence to the words used in the subsection, it can properly be said that, by applying to the plaintiff a gender-based criterion, unfavourable to men, which it has adopted as the basis for a concession of free entry to its swimming pool, it did on the ground of sex treat him less favourably than it treated women of the same age, and in particular Mrs James. In other words, I do not read the words 'on the ground of sex' as necessarily referring only to the reason why the defendant acted as he did, but as embracing cases in which a gender-based criterion is the basis upon which the complainant has been selected for the relevant treatment. Of course, there may be cases where the defendant's reason for his action may bring the case within the subsection, as when the defendant is motivated by an animus against persons of the complainant's sex, or otherwise selects the complainant for the relevant treatment because of his or her sex. But it does not follow that the words 'on the ground of sex' refer only to cases where the defendant's reason for his action is the sex of the complainant; and, in my opinion, the application by the defendant to the complainant of a gender-based criterion which favours the opposite sex is just as much a case of unfavourable treatment on the ground of sex. Such a conclusion seems to me to be consistent with the policy of the Act, which is the active promotion of equal treatment of men and women. Indeed, the present case is no different from one in which the defendant adopts a criterion which favours widows as against widowers, on the basis that the former are likely to be less well off; or indeed, as my noble and learned friend, Lord Bridge of Harwich has pointed out, a criterion which favours women between the ages of 60 and 65, as against men between the same ages, on the same basis. It is plain to me that, in those cases, a man in either category who was so treated could properly say that he was treated less favourably on the ground of sex, and that the fact that the defendant had so treated him for a benign motive (to help women in the same category, because they are likely to be less well off ) was irrelevant.

I fully appreciate that this conclusion means that some people, seeking to do practical good for the best of motives, may be inhibited in the sense that they will be precluded from using gender-based criteria to achieve their purpose. This is the position in which the Council finds itself in the present case. It is, I understand, anxious to assist, by means of a free concession, elderly persons who are retired and so are likely to be less well off than those who are still at work. For this purpose, it has for practical reasons adopted the criterion of pensionable age. Of course, it by no means follows that, because a person is of pensionable age, he will no longer be working, especially nowadays when he can draw his full pension when he is still in employment; but no doubt pensionable age is easily established by the production of a document, and, as a rough and ready test of retirement, it is reasonably acceptable. But the simple fact is that, under s. 1(1)(a) of the Act of 1975, which is concerned actively to promote equality of treatment of the two sexes, the adoption for this purpose of a gender-based criterion is unlawful; and the task of the Council is to find some other reasonably practical criterion, which does not contravene the Act of 1975, by which it can achieve its laudable purpose.

Finally, I wish briefly to refer to the use, in the present context, of such words as intention, motive, reason and purpose. In the course of argument and in the judgment of the Vice-Chancellor, attention was focused upon the use of those words. Indeed it has been suggested that, for the purpose of identifying the meaning of those words in the present context, recourse might usefully be had to the law of murder, and in particular to the speech of my noble and learned friend, Lord Bridge of Harwich, in *R.* v. *Moloney* [1985] AC 905 at p. 914. I must confess, however, to being very dubious about the validity of this comparison. In the law of murder, which at present requires either an intention to kill or an intention to cause grievous bodily harm, the intention is related to a specific consequence flowing from the act of the accused; so that, in the great majority of cases, it is not difficult to focus upon the relevant intention in the sense of the immediate purpose of the accused, by asking the questions: did he mean to kill the victim, or did he mean to cause him really serious bodily harm? In this way, intention can be distinguished from motive because, although motive is also concerned with purpose (e.g. the accused killed his victim in order to get his money), it is concerned with an ulterior purpose, i.e. the reason why he decided to kill. The law of murder is, I suppose, useful in the sense that it assists to show how, in a certain context, intention and motive can be distinguished, although the concept of purpose may be regarded as relevant to both. But the fact that the concept of purpose may be relevant to both demonstrates how easily they can be confused, and how, without a precise definition of the specific question under consideration and of the context in which it is being asked, it may be possible to use the terms interchangeably, at least in ordinary speech, without abuse of language. For it may be said of a man who kills another for his money either that he intended to get the money or that getting the money was his motive for killing. It follows that, in a legal context, if words such as intention or motive are to be used as a basis for decision, they require the most careful handling, and it also follows that their use in one context may not be a safe guide to their use in another context.

For these reasons, I am reluctant to have to conclude that those who are concerned with the day to day administration of legislation such a the Sex Discrimination Act 1975, who are mainly those who sit on industrial tribunals, should have to grapple with such elusive concepts as these. However, taking the case of direct discrimination under s. 1(1)(a) of the Act, I incline to the opinion that, if it were necessary to identify the requisite intention of the defendant, that intention is simply an intention to perform the relevant act of less favourable treatment. Whether or not the treatment is less favourable in the relevant sense, i.e. on the ground of sex, may derive either from the application of a gender-based criterion to the complainant, or from selection by the defendant of the complainant because of his or her sex; but, in either event, it is not saved from constituting unlawful discrimination by the fact that the defendant acted from a benign motive. However, in a majority of cases, I doubt if it is necessary to focus upon the intention or motive of the defendant in this way. This is because, as I see it, cases of direct discrimination under s. 1(1)(a) can be considered by asking the simple question: would the complainant have received the same treatment from the defendant but for his or her sex? This simple test possesses the double virtue that, on the one hand, it embraces both the case where the treatment derives from the application of a gender-based criterion, and the case where it derives from the selection of the complainant because of his or her sex; and on the other hand it avoids, in most cases at least, complicated questions relating to concepts such as intention, motive, reason or purpose, and the danger of confusion arising from the misuse of those elusive terms. I have to stress, however, that the 'but for' test is not appropriate for cases of indirect discrimination against persons of one sex under that subsection, although a (proportionately smaller) group of persons of the opposite sex is adversely affected in the same way.

I trust that the foregoing will explain why I expressed myself as I did, I fear too tersely, in R. v. *Birmingham City Council* ex parte *Equal Opportunities Commission* at p. 175. I wish to express my gratitude to counsel for the assistance which they have given to your Lordships in the present case, which has encouraged me to ponder again and more deeply upon the problem of construction of s. 1(1) of the Act of 1975, and to express more fully the reasons for the solution of that problem which I myself favour.

LORD LOWRY: My Lords, the facts of this appeal are simple, but I confess to having had some difficulty in deciding it. I can discern in your Lordship's speeches, which I have had the advantage of reading in draft, two logical and persuasive trains of thought which lead to opposite conclusions, and the question is how to choose between them.

The case has been presented by the plaintiff as an example of direct discrimination, an apt and by now customary description of a breach of

s. 1(1)(a) of the Sex Discrimination Act 1975 which, as applied to men, provides:

> A person discriminates against a [man] in any circumstances relevant for the purpose of any provision of this Act if − (a) on the ground of [his] sex he treats [him] less favourably than the treats or would treat a [woman].

There are two questions for decision: (1) What, on its true construction, does this provision mean? (2) When the provision, properly construed, is applied to the facts, did the Council discriminate against the appellant contrary to s. 1(1)(a)?

With a view to construction, the crucial words are 'on the ground of his sex.' Mr Lester for the appellant, submits that this phrase means 'due to his sex' and does not involve any consideration of the reason which has led the alleged discriminator to treat the man less favourably than he treats or would treat a woman. I shall call this the causative construction and will presently advert to it. Mr Beloff, for the Council, contends for what I shall call the subjective construction, which involves considering the reason why the discriminator has treated the man unfavourably. He submits that this construction accords with the plain meaning of the words and the grammatical structure of the sentence in which they occur. I accept Mr Beloff's construction and I proceed to explain why I do so.

On reading s. 1(1)(a), it can be seen that the discriminator does something to the victim, that is, he treats him in a certain fashion, to wit, less favourably than he treats or would treat a woman. And he treats him in that fashion on a certain *ground*, namely, *on the ground of his sex*. These words, it is scarcely necessary for me to point out, constitute an adverbial phrase modifying the transitive verb 'treats' in a clause of which the discriminator is the subject and the victim is the object. While anxious not to weary your Lordships with a grammatical excursus, the point I wish to make is that the *ground* on which the alleged discriminator treats the victim less favourably is inescapably linked to the subject and the verb; it is the reason which has caused him to act. The meaning of the vital words, in the sentence where they occur, cannot be expressed by saying that the victim receives treatment which on the ground of (his) sex is less favourable to him than to a person of the opposite sex. The structure of that sentence makes the words 'on the ground of his sex' easily capable of meaning 'due to his sex' if the context so requires or permits.

Mr Beloff gave your Lordships a definition of 'ground' from the *Oxford English Dictionary* 2nd ed., Vol VI, p. 876:

> ... a circumstance on which an opinion, inference, argument, statement or claim is founded, or which has given rise to an action, procedure or mental feeling; a reason, motive. Often with additional implication: a valid reason, justifying motive, or what is alleged as such.

Mr Lester conceded that in ordinary speech to ask on what grounds a particular decision is taken invites consideration of the mental processes of the decision-maker. And your Lordships are only too familiar with the use in a legal context of the word 'ground' as synonymous with reasons. It is also interesting to note one dictionary definition of 'discriminate' as 'to make a distinction, especially unjustly, on the grounds of race or colour or sex.' As Mr Beloff put it, s. 1(1)(a) refers to the activities of the discriminator: the words 'on the ground of his sex' provide the link between the alleged discriminator and his less favourable treatment of another. They introduce a subjective element into the analysis and pose here the question: 'Was the sex of the appellant a consideration in the Council's decision?' Putting it another way, a 'ground' is a reason, in ordinary speech, for which a person takes a certain course. He knows what he is doing and why he has decided to do it. In the context of s. 1(1)(a) the discriminator knows that he is treating the victim less favourably and he also knows the ground on which he is doing so. In no case are the discriminator's thought processes immaterial.

In the Court of Appeal Sir Nicolas Browne-Wilkinson VC said ([1989] IRLR 318 at p. 320):

> As the facts of this case demonstrate, there is no doubt that the Council's policy has a discriminatory impact as between men and women who are over the age of 60 but under ... 65. Women of that age enjoy the concession: men of the same age do not. But not all conduct having a discriminatory effect is unlawful: discriminatory behaviour has to fall within the statutory definition of discrimination and to have occurred in a context (e.g. in relation to employment or the provision of facilities) in which the Act renders such discrimination unlawful.

Then (I am simply dealing with the construction point) he said, at p. 321:

> Mr Lester, for the plaintiff, forcefully submitted that there is direct discrimination in this case. He submitted that discrimination is 'on the ground of' sex within s. 1(1)(a) if the sex of the plaintiff is a substantial cause of the less favourable treatment. In this context, he says, the correct question is: 'What would the position have been but for the sex of the plaintiff?' If the position would be different if the plaintiff's sex were different, that is direct discrimination.
> I do not accept that construction of s. 1. In my judgment s. 1(1)(a) is looking to the case where, subjectively, the defendant has treated the plaintiff less favourably because of his or her sex. What is relevant is the defendant's reason for doing an act, not the causative effect of the act done by the defendant. As Mr Towler for the Council pointed out, s. 1(1) is referring throughout to the activities of the alleged discriminator. In the case of direct discrimination 'a person discriminates against a [man] ... if on the ground of [his] sex he treats [him] less favourably ...'. Those words indicate that one is looking, not to the causative link between the defendant's behaviour and the detriment of the plaintiff, but to the reason why the defendant treated the plaintiff less favourably. The relevant question is 'did the defendant act on the ground of sex?' not 'did the less favourable treatment result from the defendant's actions?'

I agree with and adopt those observations of the Vice-Chancellor, which I consider to be entirely consistent with the decision reached by your Lordships' House in *R. v. Birmingham City Council*, ex parte *Equal Opportunities Commission*, on which Mr Lester has so strongly relied and to which I must soon give my attention.

While still on the construction point, I might mention *Armagh District Council* v. *Fair Employment Agency* [1984] IRLR 234, which was a decision of the Court of Appeal in Northern Ireland on the Fair Employment (Northern Ireland) Act 1976. Section 16(2) of the Act provided:

> For the purposes of this Act a person discriminates against another person on the ground of religious belief or political opinion if, on either of those grounds, he treats that other person less favourably in any circumstances than he treats or would treat any other person in those circumstances ... .

The facts were concerned with the appointment of a wages clerk by a district council and do not assist in the resolution of this appeal, but perhaps I may be permitted to refer to a passage in my judgment where I said, at p. 238:

> It must not be forgotten that when the Act uses the word 'discrimination' or 'discriminate' it is referring to an employer who makes a choice between one candidate and another *on the ground* of religious belief or political opinion; it is not speaking of an incidental disadvantage which is due to a difference between the religion of the employer and of the candidate but of a deliberate, intentional action on the part of the appointing body or individual.
>
> Here I must dispose of a misleading argument which was raised before the learned County Court judge but not seriously pursued in this Court. An action may be deliberate without being malicious. Most acts of discrimination are both, but the only *essential* quality is deliberation. If a Protestant employer does not engage a Roman Catholic applicant because he genuinely believes that the applicant will not be able to get on with Protestant fellow workmen, he is discriminating against the applicant on the ground of his religious belief, although that employer's motives may be above reproach. If women are allowed to stop work five minutes early in order to avoid being endangered when the day's work ends, it has been decided that the men in the workforce are discriminated against on the ground that they are men. The employer's decision to keep the men at work longer, though reached in good faith, was deliberately based on the fact that they were men.
>
> Accordingly, it can be stated that, although malice (while often present) is not essential, deliberate intention to differentiate on the ground of religion, politics, sex, colour or nationality (whatever is aimed at by the legislation) is an indispensable element in the concept of discrimination. The distinction is sometimes expressed as one between motive and intention. In *Peake* v. *Automotive Products Ltd* [1977] IRLR 105, the case about releasing women early from their work, Phillips J states: 'it seems to us that [counsel] is confusing the motive or the purpose of the act complained of with the factual nature of the act itself. Section 1(1)(a) requires one to look to see what in fact is done amounting to less favourable treatment and whether it is done to the man or the woman because he, is, a man or a woman. If so,

it is of no relevance that it is done with no discriminatory motive.' This idea runs though all the cases.

The *Peake* decision was reversed on appeal [1977] IRLR 365, but has subsequently been recognised as correct: *Ministry of Defence* v. *Jeremiah* [1979] IRLR 436.

Section 66 of the Act deals with the enforcement of claims under Part III, which includes the relevant s. 29. Subsection (3) provides:

As respects an unlawful act of discrimination falling within s. 1(1)(b) (or, where this section is applied by s. 65(1)(b), s. 3(1)(b)) no award of damages shall be made if the respondent proves that the requirement or condition in question was not applied with the intention of treating the claimant unfavourably on the ground of his sex or marital status as the case may be.

Damages may be awarded in respect of all acts of direct discrimination and therefore, as Mr Beloff persuasively contends, the subjective construction of s. 1(1)(a) would be consistent with the principle of making damages available only in cases where the discrimination has been intentional.

As I have said, and as the Vice-Chancellor stated in the Court of Appeal, Mr Lester espoused the causative construction of the vital words which, as he submitted, has the virtue of simplicity; it eliminates consideration of the discriminator's mental processes and of such protean and slippery concepts as intention, purpose, motive, desire, animus, prejudice, malice and reason. The basic difficulty of this approach, I consider, is that one has to disregard or distort the phrase - 'on the ground of his sex' in order to make it work. Counsel argued that the subjective construction 'artificially confines the meaning of "ground".' I must disagree: the subjective construction uses 'ground' in its natural meaning. The phrase 'on the ground of' does not mean 'by reason of'; moreover, 'ground' must certainly not be confused with 'intention.'

Mr Lester rightly submits that the policy of the Act is to discourage discrimination and promote equality. But the Act pursues that policy by means of the words which Parliament has used. Some inequality may be justified (see s. 1(1)(b)(ii)) and some is accepted (see ss 6(4) and 51 (now 51A as amended by s. 3 of the Employment Act 1989)). The phrase 'on the ground of his sex' does not, as alleged, constitute an exception to the policy and therefore does not fall to be narrowly construed. The words in question constitute an ingredient of unlawful discrimination contrary to s. 1(1)(a).

As I have said, the appellant relies strongly on the *Birmingham* case. The relevant extracts from the speech of my noble and learned friend, Lord Goff of Chieveley, have already been cited by him and by my noble and learned friend, Lord Bridge of Harwich. Your Lordships will recall that Lord Goff of Chieveley said at p. 175:

There is discrimination under the statute if there is less favourable treatment on the ground of sex, in other words if the relevant girl or girls would have received the same treatment as the boys but for their sex. The intention or motive of the defendant to discriminate, though it may be relevant so far as remedies are concerned (see s. 66(3) of the Act of 1975), is not a necessary condition of liability; it is perfectly possible to envisage cases where the defendant had no such motive, and yet did in fact discriminate on the ground of sex. Indeed, as Mr Lester pointed out in the course of his argument, if the Council's submission were correct it would be a good defence for an employer to show that he discriminated against women not because he intended to do so but (for example) because of customer preference, or to save money, or even to avoid controversy. In the present case, whatever may have been the intention or motive of the Council, nevertheless it is because of their sex that girls in question receive less favourable treatment than the boys, and so are the subject of discrimination under the Act of 1975. This is well established in a long line of authority: see, in particular, *Jenkins* v. *Kingsgate (Clothing Productions) Ltd* [1981] IRLR 388, pp. 393, 394, *per* Browne-Wilkinson J, and *R.* v. *Secretary of State for Education & Science*, ex parte *Keating* (1985) 84 LGR 469, *per* Taylor J, at p. 475; see also *Ministry of Defence* v. *Jeremiah* [1979] IRLR 436, *per* Lord Denning MR. I can see no reason to depart from this established view.

My Lords, as my noble and learned friend said, the Birmingham City Council did discriminate on the ground of sex. I have no difficulty in applying to the facts the subjective construction of s. 1(1)(a) and in appreciating on the basis of that construction that the Council treated the girls less favourably on the ground of their sex. At the qualifying stage many more places in the Birmingham grammar schools were available for boys of the appropriate age than for girls. The pupils concerned took a test and their performance was assessed in order to see which pupils had qualified. Because there were fewer places available for girls, they had to achieve higher marks than the boys and accordingly the Council, when considering the performance of a girl in the test, was obliged to demand from her a higher mark than if she had been a boy. In so doing the Council treated that girl less favourably than it treated a boy and did so on the ground of her sex. Your Lordships followed a well-trodden path in holding that the mere fact that the Council had no prejudice against girls and did not intend or desire to place them at a disadvantage and acted as it did from necessity (the defence put up by the Council) was of no avail against the established fact that the Council deliberately discriminated against the girls in the way I have described.

The appellant in this case, however, has relied, in favour of the causative construction, on my noble and learned friend's statement that there is discrimination if the girls 'would have received the same treatment as the boys but for their sex' and, to a lesser extent, on his further statement that 'it is because of their sex that the girls in question receive less favourable treatment than the boys.'

I feel that I would have no difficulty in dealing with this argument, but for the fact that it has commended itself to the majority of your Lordships, including the author of the passage in question. It is therefore with even more than the usual measure of respect that I make the observations which follow. In their context both of the statements which I have extracted are perfectly correct statements of fact, but that does not mean that they are a guide to the proper construction of s. 1(1)(a), which I have considered above. The defence was not that the less favourable treatment was a purely undesigned and adventitious consequence of the Council's policy. It would have to be admitted that the Council, however regretfully, knew it was treating the girls less favourably than the boys and that owing to the shortage of school places it had deliberately decided so to treat them because they were girls. The defence, based on absence of intention and motive, was rightly rejected and no other defence was made or could have been made. Whichever construction of s. 1(1)(a) had been applied, the Council would have lost, and no rival constructions of that provision were discussed. It is, I consider, worth noting that the examples and the cases which my noble and learned friend mentions are consistent with the subjective construction. If a men's hairdresser dismisses the only woman on his staff because the customers prefer to have their hair cut by a man, he may regret losing her but he treats her less favourably because she is a woman, that is, on the ground of her sex, having made a deliberate decision to do so. If the foreman dismisses an efficient and co-operative black road sweeper in order to avoid industrial action by the remaining (white) members of the squad, he treats him less favourably on racial grounds. If a decision is taken for reasons which may seem in other respects valid and sensible, not to employ a girl in a group otherwise consisting entirely of men, the employer has treated that girl less favourably than he would treat a man and he has done so consciously on the ground (which *he considers* to be proper ground) that she is a woman. In none of these cases is a defence provided by an excusable or even by a worthy motive.

It can thus be seen that the causative construction not only gets rid of unessential and often irrelevant mental ingredients, such as malice, prejudice, desire and motive, but also dispenses with an essential ingredient, namely, the ground on which the discriminator acts. The appellant's construction relieves the complainant of the need to prove anything except that A has done an act which results in less favourable treatment for B by reason of B's sex, which reduces to insignificance the words 'on the ground of.' Thus the causative test is too wide and is grammatically unsound, because it necessarily disregards the fact that the less favourable treatment is meted out to the victim *on the ground of* the victim's sex.

I now turn to an aspect of the case which has caused me greater difficulty, and that is the question whether, by adopting a gender based discriminatory criterion as a test of free admission to their swimming pool the Council have inevitably put themselves in a position of treating men between 60 and 64 'less favourably on the ground of their sex.' Without doubt the Council have treated men of that age group less favourably than they have treated women of the same age group. But have they done so on the ground of the men's sex? There is a strong body of opinion in favour of an affirmative answer. Three of your Lordships have adopted it and a number of academic writers on the subject, who know what they are talking about, have taken the same view.

This view is variously expressed. One way of putting it is that the expression 'persons who have reached state pension age' is just a shorthand expression which denotes the age of 60 in a woman and the age of 65 in a man. I hope it is not a mere quibble to point out that shorthand is normally a substitute for the original expression and not the original expression itself. Another approach, mooted during argument, is that the Council might as well have put up a notice: 'Admission 75p. Children under 3, women over 60 and men over 65 admitted free.' The wording of the second part of such a notice would be openly discriminatory, but another way of describing that wording would be to call it a spelling out of the Council's policy of granting free admission to all persons who had reached pension age. The same might be said of age-related provisions about concessionary rail and bus fares and free medical prescriptions. Yet another, and also a logical theory, is that, if the Council are bound to foresee that the test which they have adopted inevitably leads to the result that men of the 60-64 age group will receive from the Council less favourable treatment than women of the same age group, the Council, without the need of further proof, are incontrovertibly shown to have deliberately and knowingly treated those men unfavourably *on the ground of their sex*.

I can see the force of this point. Indeed, when the hearing concluded, it seemed to me likely to be decisive. But I have come away from that view because, in my opinion, the foreseeability, even the inevitability, of the result as viewed or viewable by an alleged discriminator does not provide the touchstone of liability: that is supplied by the *ground on which* he has acted and the foreseeability test, adopted by analogy with the criminal law as an indication of the intention of the accused, is not the appropriate test for deciding on what ground, that is, for what reason the person acted and, accordingly, whether there has been direct discrimination contrary to s. 1(1)(a).

Here I adopt the convincing argument of my noble and learned friend, Lord Griffiths. The Council were providing free swimming for a certain group of people because they were of pensionable age and not because they were men and women of specific but different ages. Therefore the Council did not use the expression 'persons who have reached the state pension age' as a convenient way of describing women over 60 and men over 65. The Council refused to provide free swimming for the appellant, not because he was a man under 65, but because he had not reached the state pensionable age and therefore could fairly be expected to pay the normal charge of 75p. The distinction drawn by the Council depended on the presence or absence of pensionable status and not sex. Apposite is Mr Beloff's suggestion that the Council's policy would not change, even if the state pension age were altered for either sex or for both sexes.

There is no suggestion that the Council here were guilty of bad faith in the shape of covert discrimination. They were, it seems, adopting a time-honoured and rough and ready, if most imperfect, means test which, right up to the present, has continued to commend itself to the Government and to Parliament, as the many statutory examples produced by learned counsel to your Lordships have shown. In saying this, I do not indulge in a vain attempt to defend the Council by reference to its worthy motives. I am simply concerned to point out that when primary legislation permits, and subordinate legislation employs, the age differential of 60 for women and 65 for men, that legislation should not be taken as indicating an intention by Parliament to place men at a disadvantage on the ground that they are men.

The conclusion I have come to provides an explanation for the reluctance of the appellant's very able and experienced leading counsel to accept the subjective interpretation of the words 'on the ground of his sex' and for his unswerving adherence to the causative 'but for' test. If the subjective interpretation is correct, the fact that a discriminatory result is foreseeable does not offer the appellant a satisfactory solution of his problem, because the foreseeable *result* does not show *on what ground* the alleged discriminator acted. That involves a question of fact the answer to which will depend on what is proved or admitted and on what may be inferred from the evidence.

My Lords, there is just one other point which I would mention. The appellant's argument seemed to infer that the Council's action, since it was not indirect discrimination under s. 1(1)(b), must be caught by s. 1(1)(a) because it involves less favourable treatment of men and ought not to escape entirely from the purview of the Act. This suggested conclusion, however, cannot prevail over the meaning of s. 1(1)(a) if that meaning is clear. Furthermore, I would not, in the absence of argument on both sides, be prepared to accept that the Vice-Chancellor was wrong to contemplate the possibility of a claim of indirect discrimination on the present facts. The key words in s. 1(1)(b) are '[if] he applies to her a requirement or condition *which he applies* ... equally to a man', and not '... *which applies* equally to a man.' A prospective employer may *apply equally* to men and women alike a height or strength requirement which is sexually neutral, but the overall result of applying the requirement will be predictable. It seems to me, so far as the point has any relevance, that it can be argued that the Council have *applied equally* to men and women the requirement of their having reached state pension age, although the requirement itself was discriminatory. By parity of reasoning, I would also need to be convinced that the Vice-Chancellor acted inconsistently when he rejected the test of the judge in the County Court and yet held s. 1(1)(b) to be relevant if relied upon. Your Lordships will already have noted that the appellant, whose cause was promoted throughout by the Equal Opportunities Commission, expressly relied on s. 1(1)(a) of the Act to the exclusion of s. 1(1)(b).

For the reasons contained in the speech of my noble and learned friend, Lord Griffiths and also for those which I have given, I would dismiss the appeal.

**B    COURT OF APPEAL**

# Baker v. Cornwall County Council[1]

LORD JUSTICE NEILL: This is an appeal by Mrs Jacqueline Anne Baker from the Order of the Employment Appeal Tribunal dated 26 February 1988 dismissing her appeal from the decision dated 29 July 1987 of an Industrial Tribunal sitting at St Austell in Cornwall.

By their decision the Industrial Tribunal rejected the appellant's complaint that she had been discriminated against unlawfully in the course of her employment by the Cornwall County Council on the grounds of her sex. The appeal is brought by leave of a single Lord Justice.

Mrs Baker is a married woman. After leaving school she attended the Plymouth College of Further Education, where she took a course in construction. Subsequently she worked as a site technician for a large firm of construction engineers and for several other employers. In April 1985 she joined the Highways Department of the Cornwall County Court as a technical clerk. She was interested in the technical aspect of highway construction but she found that her job as a technical clerk meant that she spent a considerable amount of her time in the office and that she had few opportunities to work outside in the field.

In April 1986 a vacancy became available for a work checker/site surveyor at Bodmin. The advertisement for the post stated that the duties would involve 'on site measurements of highway construction and maintenance work, including preparation of estimates, work on the income and management information systems associated with highway and civil engineering construction, together with the calculation of bonus payments for county roadmen and to be of general assistance in the section.'

Mrs Baker applied for the job and was interviewed in May, but her application was unsuccessful.

Though the May 1986 interview was not the subject of any specific complaint to the Industrial Tribunal, Mrs Baker gave evidence about it in support of her general case that she had been the victim of discrimination. The Industrial Tribunal referred to her account of this interview in these terms:

> She described in detail the interview. She was questioned about her previous work experience, what she had done on site, asked about her present post and a crash barrier survey which she was involved in. She was asked about her studies.

---

1    [1990] ICR 452, [1990] IRLR 194 (CA).

The conversation then turned to the children, ages, schools, and she volunteered the information without it being asked of her that she had arrangements for minding the children in the event of illness. She said that on previous interviews she had been asked that type of question, and she introduced it herself to allay any fears.

She told us that she was sickened by this attitude, it was so predictable and very annoying. She was then asked about her car, and any problems concerning transport. She said that she was interviewed by Mr Davis, the work study officer of the County Council, and she specifically said that he told her that she was allowed 10-15 minutes, whereas the others had half an hour. She saw that as discrimination.

The Industrial Tribunal did not accept Mrs Baker's contention that she had been allocated a shorter time for her interview.

In November 1986 a further advertisement was published. On this occasion the advertisement was for three posts of site surveyor/work checkers at Scorrier, Bodmin and Tolpetherwin. It was stated that two of the posts were initially at either the Bodmin Group Centre or the Tolpetherwin Group Centre and the third post was at the Scorrier Group Centre near Redruth. The advertisement continued:

The duties connected with these posts will include on-site measurements of highway construction and maintenance and preparation of management information for highway and civil engineering construction. These include the calculation of bonus payments for county roadmen and other work associated with estimates and final measurements.

Recent school leavers with good 'O' levels or with National or Higher National Certificate in construction or allied subjects or persons with relevant experience will be considered. However, further opportunities for training will be given to suitable successful applicants.

Applicants must hold a current driving licence and a casual users' car allowance on the Council's scale will be paid to the postholders using their cars in connection with these duties. Commencing salary will be related to experience and qualifications.

Scorrier was some distance from Mrs Baker's home and this post was not of interest to her. She applied, however, for one of the posts at Tolpetherwin or Bodmin. In her letter of application dated 22 November 1986 to the county surveyor she gave some details of her qualifications, of an examination in highway technology which she had recently taken and of a course which she was just about to start in highway legislation and administration.

Her letter concluded:

By April I will have worked in local government for five years, two of those years having been spent in the Highways Department. I would therefore like to think that the knowledge I have acquired in administration and the routine, together with my previous site experience, would allow me to become a suitable candidate for this post.

There were 17 applicants for these two posts, though Mrs Baker was the only woman.

One of the posts was filled by Mr Tape, who was already carrying out the work satisfactorily on a temporary basis. The Scorrier post was filled by Mr Penhaligon. The Industrial Tribunal concluded that there could be no criticism of the selection of either Mr Tape or Mr Penhaligon.

In their reasons the Industrial Tribunal reviewed the position as it was at the beginning of 1987:

> 25.   That left one vacancy in the Bodmin/Tolpetherwin area. The Council concluded that Mrs Baker was the only applicant who might be acceptable, but they were not entirely satisfied that she was the appropriate person. They clearly had some reservations but there was no evidence to suggest that was simply because she was a woman. It occurred to Mr Davis, the work study officer, that they had actually advertised in the wrong newspaper. The paper which had produced the 17 applicants circulated to North Cornwall, rather than in the catchment area of Caradon.

On 16 January 1987 an advertisement was published in the Cornish Times for a post of site surveyor/work checker in the work study section based at Tolpetherwin Group Centre. The advertisement was in similar terms to those which had appeared earlier. The post was also advertised internally. On this occasion there were again 17 applicants, 15 being men and two (including Mrs Baker) being women. Of these applicants four were chosen for short-listing though one of them later withdrew. The three remaining candidates on the shortlist were Mrs Baker, Mr Rice and a third person. The County Council decided after interviewing these candidates that the order of merit was Mr Rice, Mrs Baker and then the third person. As a result Mr Rice was appointed to the post.

Mrs Baker was very dissatisfied with the way in which her interview, which took place on 20 February 1987, had been conducted and she considered that she had been the victim of sex discrimination.

On 28 March 1987 she sent a questionnaire to the county surveyor setting out a number of questions which she required answering. This questionnaire was sent in accordance with s. 74(1)(a) of the Sex Discrimination Act 1975. In this questionnaire Mrs Baker summarised her complaint as follows:

> On Friday 20 February 1987, time 11.20 am at EGC Tolpetherwin I was interviewed for site surveyor/work checker post.
> *Events.* In November 1986 a work study post (to which the above refers) was vacated and it was decided to advertise two posts, one being the vacated post and the other to sort out the anomaly of a roadman performing work study duties. The posts were advertised (along with another for the Scorrier region) at the end of November (internally and externally). I put in my application. I heard no more until after Christmas when, without an interview for either the vacated post or to compete for the post relating to the 'anomaly', I was told indirectly (via a member of the staff in the work study section at Tolpetherwin) that the roadman had accepted his post to officially join the staff; and that the other post was to be readvertised.

At this stage, I contacted the senior steward of NALGO, who then contacted Mr Davis on my behalf. Later the same morning NALGO 'phoned me to say I would be getting an interview. The post was finally readvertised 16 January 1987 (internally and externally). I was then interviewed by Mr Deacon and Mr Davis for approx. 10 minutes on 20 February 1987 and was asked irrelevant questions to the post such as how old are your children; what school do they go to, etc.
Later that day, I received a 'phone call at approx. 1.50 pm from Mr Davis to inform me that a roadman (only recently promoted to chargehand) was awarded the post. There was no explanation as to why I was turned down, and no advice given on what was necessary of me before I could be given serious consideration.

On the same day, 28 March 1987, Mrs Baker applied to the Industrial Tribunal for a finding of sex discrimination. In her application form Mrs Baker set out the history of the matter including her application for the vacancy which occurred in the spring of 1986. She concluded as follows:

I feel that the reason behind all this is sex discrimination because:
(1)   Some posts can be advertised internally only (as a subsequent post at County Hall) whereas the one I applied for appeared to remain open until such time someone suitable, other than myself, being female, could be found.
(2)   It is also my view that I can do no more to prove my aptitude, ability and interest in respect of this post. If I was given the opportunity to compete on equal terms I would abide by my employers' decisions. To date, however, my employers have not been able to say exactly why I have been turned down or what it is I have to achieve before being considered. This is why I wish to bring further action.

The hearing before the Industrial Tribunal took place on 16 and 17 July 1987. In their reserved decision, which was sent to the parties on 29 July 1987, the Tribunal unanimously rejected Mrs Baker's complaint. In the final paragraph of their reasons they said:

We are unable to fault the choice by Cornwall County Council, and we are similarly unable to find that in the interview which led to that choice there was any discrimination against Mrs Baker on the grounds of her sex. She is an ambitious and enthusiastic employee who was simply disappointed that she was not offered the job which she sought. Accordingly, the application is dismissed.

Mrs Baker then appealed to the Employment Appeal Tribunal. The hearing of the appeal took place on 3 February 1988. In their reserved decision the Employment Appeal Tribunal dismissed the appeal.

In the judgment of the Employment Appeal Tribunal Popplewell J set out in some detail the submissions which had been made in support of the appeal. At p. 2G he said:

The main thrust of Mr Allen's argument before us has been that the Industrial Tribunal wholly failed to understand what the applicant's case was. He says that what the Industrial Tribunal have done is to concentrate on the questions that were asked at the interview for the Bodmin post which they found were not sexist and find that that was the only claim that the applicant was in fact making and therefore to dismiss her case. He says they have wholly failed to apply their mind to the appointment of Mr Tape direct, to the failure to appoint Mrs Baker to the second Bodmin post without readvertising and to look at the whole of the interview when it took place in relation to the Bodmin post, not simply to the questions alone.

The Employment Appeal Tribunal in their judgment then examined the three matters of which complaint was made.

### (1) *The appointment of Mr Tape*
At p. 4D of the judgment Popplewell J set out the conclusions of the Employment Appeal Tribunal on this aspect of the case:

> It is self-evident that in appointing Mr Tape without interview and in not giving Mrs Baker or indeed any of the other candidates an interview, they and Mrs Baker were being treated less favourably. It is not necessary for an industrial tribunal to say 'we have to ask that question and the answer is "yes"' because that is self-evident. What they then had to consider and in our judgment what they have considered is whether the less favourable treatment of Mrs Baker was due to her sex. The Tribunal say:
>
>> Mr Tape was put into one of the positions. This was because in practical terms he was already carrying out the work satisfactorily, having replaced the established person as a temporary measure. He was the obvious candidate, and there can be no criticism of the Council's choice of Mr Tape.
>
> That was a finding that Mr Tape was appointed because he was already in post and was the obviously suitable candidate. That was a finding of fact. It does not support an allegation that Mrs Baker was not considered because she was a woman.

### (2) *The readvertisement of the second Bodmin/Tolpetherwin post*
In the judgment of the Employment Appeal Tribunal Popplewell J set out a passage from the reasons of the Industrial Tribunal and the argument of Mr Allen on this part of the case. At p. 5F Popplewell J continued:

> Little, if any, cross-examination seems to have been devoted to this issue and so far as the 'reservations' were concerned all the Tribunal seem to be saying was that the employers did not think that the applicant was such an outstanding candidate to be offered the post without it being properly advertised. The Tribunal saw nothing wrong with that or anything to suggest that that was done (if it was a matter which could be described as treating her less favourably than somebody else) as being due to sex.

### (3) *The interview on 20 February 1987*
The Employment Appeal Tribunal dealt with this aspect of the matter at some length at pp. 6 to 9 of the judgment. They referred to the criticisms which Mr Allen had made to them of the findings made by the Industrial Tribunal. At p. 8 Popplewell J stated the conclusion of the Employment Appeal Tribunal that the Industrial Tribunal had found that the interview had been carried out with the 'express purpose of finding the best person for the

job' and that the questions which were put to Mrs Baker 'neither sought to treat her less favourably nor did they in fact treat her less favourably.'

Popplewell J then dealt with a number of subsidiary arguments raised by Mr Allen. At the end of the judgment he stated that the Employment Appeal Tribunal had not been persuaded that the conclusions of the Industrial Tribunal could be upset. The appeal was therefore dismissed.

In this Court we have had the advantage not only of hearing the full and careful arguments by Mr Stephen Sedley QC but also of having before us the detailed written submissions which have been prepared on behalf of the appellant.

The Court was reminded of the guidance given by the Employment Appeal Tribunal in *Khanna* v. *Ministry of Defence* [1981] IRLR 331. In that case Browne-Wilkinson J emphasised at p. 333 that 'direct evidence of discrimination is seldom going to be available and that, accordingly, in these cases the affirmative evidence of the discrimination will normally consist of inferences to be drawn from the primary facts.' He continued:

> If the primary facts indicate that there has been discrimination of some kind, the employer is called on to give an explanation and, failing clear and specific explanation being given by the employer to the satisfaction of the Industrial Tribunal, an inference of unlawful discrimination from the primary facts will mean the complaint succeeds.

We were also referred to the guidance to the same effect given by the Employment Appeal Tribunal in *Chattopadhyay* v. *Headmaster of Holloway School* [1981] IRLR 487, where Browne-Wilkinson J said at p. 490:

> As has been pointed out many times, a person complaining that he has been unlawfully discriminated against faces great difficulties. There is normally not available to him any evidence of overtly racial discriminatory words or actions used by the respondent. All that the applicant can do is to point to certain facts which, if unexplained, are consistent with his having been treated less favourably than others on racial grounds. In the majority of cases it is only the respondents and their witnesses who are able to say whether in fact the allegedly discriminatory act was motivated by racial discrimination or by other, perfectly innocent, motivations. It is for this reason that the law has been established that if an applicant shows that he has been treated less favourably than others in circumstances which are consistent with that treatment being based on racial grounds, the industrial tribunal should draw an inference that such treatment was on racial grounds, unless the respondent can satisfy the industrial tribunal that there is an innocent explanation.

In the present case, submitted Mr Sedley, the correct approach was to examine the primary facts to see what inferences could be properly drawn from them. Any instructed examination would lead inevitably to the conclusion that Mrs Baker had been discriminated against. It was then necessary to consider whether the Council had produced any acceptable explanation for this discrimination. It was submitted that no satisfactory explanation had been put forward and that the Industrial Tribunal had failed to address the essential issue in this case because they had concerned themselves too much with the detail.

Mr Sedley drew our attention to a number of facts from which the inferences of discrimination were to be drawn, including in particular the following:

(a) Mrs Baker was a woman of undoubted ability and commitment who had obtained for herself the appropriate qualifications.
(b) The post was in an entirely male section of the work-force, indeed few women were employed on outdoor work anywhere in the Highways Department.
(c) The wording used in the notice of appearance was significant where it was said:

> ... it was felt that he (Mr Rice) would be more suited to fitting into the organisation as a work checker/site surveyor where a high degree of tact and maturity is required.

It was submitted that a requirement to 'fit in' was a very productive source of unintended acts of discrimination because it tended to perpetuate historic patterns of employment and to ensure that existing segregated groups remained unaltered. Fully qualified candidates from outside and of a different sex would not 'fit in' in the same way.
(d) It was accepted by the Council and indeed was apparent from the advertisement that the job could be done by a school-leaver with appropriate training.
(e) The fact that the number of male applicants greatly exceeded the female applicants clearly suggested that the post was perceived as 'a man's work.'
(f) It was significant that the Recruitment and Selection Guide issued by the Personnel Unit of the Council contained no reference either to the Sex Discrimination Act 1975 or to the Code of Practice issued by the Equal Opportunities Commission.

Looking at the facts and at the absence of any adequate explanation it was the inevitable inference, said counsel, that Mrs Baker had been the victim of unlawful discrimination within the meaning of s. 6 of the Sex Discrimination Act 1975. The Council had contravened either s. 6(1)(c), by 'refusing or deliberately omitting to offer' Mrs Baker the employment, or s. 6(2)(a), in the way that they had afforded Mrs Baker access to opportunities for promotion or transfer.

For my part I would strongly endorse the guidance given by Browne-Wilkinson J in the passages which I have cited as to the approach to be adopted in cases of alleged unlawful discrimination. This guidance is of general application to both cases of alleged sex discrimination and alleged racial discrimination. Thus it is important to recognise:

(a) that a person who complains that he or she has been the victim of unlawful discrimination will almost always face great difficulties in proving the case because the alleged discriminator is most unlikely to admit the discrimination; and
(b) that discrimination can often result from a wish to preserve an existing pattern of employment in, for example, a particular workshop or department which has worked well and harmoniously in the past rather than from any deliberate wish to exclude the complainant as an individual. An excuse such as 'we wanted someone who would fit in' is often a danger signal that the choice was influenced not by the qualifications of the successful candidate but by the sex or race of that candidate.

Accordingly if discrimination takes place in circumstances which are consistent with the treatment being based on grounds of sex or race the industrial tribunal should be prepared to draw the inference that the discrimination was on such grounds unless the alleged discriminator can satisfy the tribunal that there was some other innocent explanation.

I turn therefore to the facts of the present case.

I have found this a difficult matter. I see force in the argument that the case should properly be regarded as a case of unconscious discrimination where the Council, faced with an existing workforce which was largely male, chose Mr Rice in preference to Mrs Baker because he would fit in better and could cope more easily with subordinate staff. Indeed, had the complaint succeeded I would have found it impossible to say that there was not ample evidence to support a finding of discrimination. But in this Court, as in the Employment Appeal Tribunal, the appeal is on questions of law alone.

Counsel for the appellant submitted that the Industrial Tribunal had indeed erred in law because they did not approach the case in the right way and had failed to appreciate that the primary facts led inevitably to an inference of unlawful discrimination.

I have taken time to consider and look again at all the evidence in this case and at the findings of the Industrial Tribunal. In the end I have come to the conclusion that Mr Pannick, who appeared for the Council, was right in his contention that it would be wrong for this Court to interfere with the decision. As he pointed out, the Industrial Tribunal heard oral evidence. The witnesses for the Council testified that they had treated the appellant's candidature on its merits. It follows therefore that on the evidence before them, which included a substantial amount of evidence about the interview on 20 February 1987, the Industrial Tribunal were satisfied with the explanations given to them. It cannot be said that there was no evidence to justify their findings nor can it be said that the successful candidate was unqualified for the post.

Accordingly I would dismiss this appeal.

I would only add one further comment. It may well be that the Council will wish to look again at their system of appointments to make sure that by the adoption of careful procedures the risk of a charge of unlawful discrimination in some future case is eliminated as far as possible.

...

## Briggs *v*. NE Education & Library Board[1]

LORD CHIEF JUSTICE HUTTON: The judgment which I am about to deliver is the judgment of the Court.

This is an appeal by case stated by the North Eastern Education and Library Board from a decision of an Industrial Tribunal that a teacher, Mrs Margaret Briggs, the respondent, is entitled to remedies against the Board as her employer, in respect of breach of the Sex Discrimination (Northern Ireland) Order 1976.

The facts in summary form are that Mrs Briggs, who has been a teacher for 20 years, took up a post in 1975 at Coleraine Girls' High School as an assistant science teacher. For some time she assisted in coaching badminton on a voluntary basis in the afternoon after school hours.

In 1982 she was promoted to a scale 2 post and the promotion was conditional upon her agreement to carry out certain additional duties. These additional duties were contained in a subsidiary agreement entitled 'Teachers Agreement - Subsidiary Agreement' signed by the respondent. The terms of the subsidiary agreement were as follows:

> School Coleraine Girls' Secondary. Post Scale 2. The duties referred to in clause 1 of the main agreement with The North Eastern Education and Library Board (hereinafter called 'the employing authority') appointing you to a post in the above-named school shall include the following duties as a condition of your appointment to a scale 2 post. To be responsible for co-ordinating and developing health education across the subject boundaries and to ensure that a pupil whatever her ability, has the opportunity to obtain at least a core of knowledge to help her achieve good mental and physical health. To assist with extra-curricular school games.
> Should you voluntarily relinquish these duties you will, if the employing authority so determines, cease to be remunerated on the scale appropriate to the above appointment.
> In the event of these duties not being performed to the satisfaction of the employing authority the matter will be dealt with in accordance with any disciplinary procedure agreed by the General Committee of the Teachers' Salaries and Conditions of Service Negotiating Machinery and the disciplinary action may include removal from the scale appropriate to the above appointment.

After signing the subsidiary agreement Mrs Briggs continued to carry on badminton coaching in the afternoon after school, but she did so in pursuance of her duty under the agreement to assist with extra-curricular school games and not on a voluntary basis as she had previously done. We think it is clear that at the time when Mrs Briggs signed the subsidiary agreement both she and the school authorities understood that badminton would be the extra-curricular game with which she would assist.

---

1    [1990] IRLR 181 (NICA).

In February 1984 Mrs Briggs and her husband adopted a daughter and Mrs Briggs was on leave from school until September 1984. When she returned to school she discontinued coaching badminton in the afternoon after school and began to coach at lunch time.

On 25 September 1984 the headmistress, Miss Carson, spoke to Mrs Briggs about the coaching of badminton and Miss Carson wrote to Mrs Briggs on 1 October 1984 asking her to confirm how she intended to change her practice with regard to the carrying out of her duties attaching to her graded post. Mrs Briggs replied in writing to say that she was taking first-year pupils for badminton on Thursdays at lunch time from 1.00 pm to 1.20 pm.

Miss Carson then wrote to the chief officer of the North Eastern Education and Library Board and told him that Mrs Briggs had advised her that she would not be available for after-school duties until her 18-month old daughter had reached school age. Miss Carson told the chief officer that the lunch time arrangement for coaching badminton was unsatisfactory.

The headmistress and Mrs Briggs met on a number of occasions to discuss the issue without reaching agreement and Miss Carson attended a lunch time coaching session to observe it. On 17 December 1984 Miss Carson wrote to Mrs Briggs as follows:

> I appreciate and sympathise with the fact that you have had difficulties reorganising your life after the adoption of your daughter, but I am also anxious that the service and opportunity I had expected to provide for our pupils by the introduction of this post is not so mutilated that it ceases to have any real significance in the life of the school. For the benefit of all our young people I must ask you again to reintroduce badminton after school for a reasonable length of time on a day which is mutually agreed by you and the head of the PEd Department.

After receiving this letter Mrs Briggs increased the coaching to twice a week at lunch time. Miss Carson wrote to her again asking her what she intended to do about coaching badminton. Mrs Briggs suggested taking badminton after school on Thursdays and eventually it was arranged that she would coach on Wednesday afternoons after school from 3.30 pm to 4.30 pm. About the time this arrangement came into operation the head of physical education at the school raised with Mrs Briggs the question of her taking the badminton classes from September 1985 at the local leisure centre two miles from the school rather than at the school. Mrs Briggs was unwilling to do this and so the matter was referred to the North Eastern Education and Library Board as Mrs Briggs' employer by the headmistress, Miss Carson.

Mrs Briggs continued to coach badminton at the school on Wednesday afternoons after normal school hours until the end of the season in March 1985.

In April 1985 Miss Briggs was invited to attend a disciplinary meeting to be held on 1 May 1985. She was told 'at this meeting you will be required to account for the fact that you persistently failed to fulfil to the satisfaction of the head teacher, the duties attaching to your graded post and detailed in your subsidiary agreement.'

At the disciplinary meeting Mrs Briggs confirmed that because of the adoption of her daughter she could not make a regular after-school commitment in terms of badminton practice sessions for the future. She stated that she was prepared to take the badminton practice at lunch time and the under-14 local league matches after school.

The members of the disciplinary meeting consulted the headmistress to see if the proposal was acceptable and they were told that it was not. Then they consulted the Board's physical education adviser and he expressed the view that lunch time sessions could only be seen as supplement to after-school practices and that the use of leisure centre facilities was important to the development of badminton within schools.

The disciplinary authority informed Mrs Briggs by letter dated 15 May 1985 that the Board was of the opinion that:

> ... you have unilaterally changed the basis upon which you were awarded the above scale post to such a degree that your involvement in both activities, i.e. the co-ordination and development of health education and your assistance with extra-curricular school games, is unsatisfactory to the principal. In these circumstances we have no option but to assume that you are no longer in a position to continue to undertake the duties and fulfil the contractual obligations of your subsidiary agreement. As such it is the decision of the disciplinary authority that your above scale/post, attaching to that agreement, should be removed and you should revert to being remunerated on scale 1 with effect from 1 June 1985.

Mrs Briggs exercised her right of appeal to the chief officer of the Board and he delegated the matter to a Mr McCune. Mrs Briggs attended a meeting conducted by Mr McCune on 26 June 1985 with her representative. Following the appeal hearing Mr McCune came to the conclusion 'that the disciplinary action by the disciplinary authority, taken after careful consideration and detailed review, is reasonable and correct. I further conclude that I have no reason not to uphold their decision.'

Following this Mrs Briggs was advised by the Department of Education that the change in her salary with effect from 1 September 1985 would be reduction from £9,597 to £9,201.

Mrs Briggs then brought an original application dated 26 February 1988 before an Industrial Tribunal. Her application sought decisions on the following questions:

1.   Disciplinary proceedings should be struck from the record.
2.   Failure to renegotiate subsidiary contract was unlawful. Sex Discrimination (Northern Ireland) Order 1986.

The Tribunal exercised their jurisdiction under art. 76(5) of the Sex Discrimination (Northern Ireland) Order 1976 to hear the application which was out of time, as they considered that it was just and equitable to do so in all the circumstances of the case.

Having decided this preliminary issue the Tribunal then proceeded to hear the application on 5 and 11 March 1987 and 9 April and 7 December 1987. It was submitted on behalf of Mrs Briggs that the board had discriminated against her both directly and indirectly. The Tribunal made no finding in respect of the claim of direct discrimination. The case stated sets out the findings of the Tribunal in respect of the claim of indirect discrimination as follows:

6.   The majority of the Tribunal concluded that the complainant/respondent had raised a *prima facie* case of indirect discrimination arising out of the requirement or condition applied by the respondent/appellant whereby the respondent/appellant had insisted that the complainant/respondent should hold badminton practice after school.
   The Tribunal further found that, because the complainant/respondent could not comply with the said requirement or condition, she had suffered a detriment.
7.   In order to proceed to the next stage of the case, the Tribunal announced its findings on these points to the parties and their representatives on 26 January 1988. The Tribunal also indicated that its written findings in that respect would be incorporated in the final decision to be issued by the Tribunal when all matters pertinent to the case had been dealt with.
8.   The Tribunal then proceeded to consider whether the above-mentioned requirement or condition was justifiable irrespective of the sex or marital status of the complainant. The majority of the Tribunal found that the respondent/appellant had not satisfied the requirement of showing justifiability and that the complainant/respondent's claim was well founded.

The majority view of the Tribunal was that compensation should be awarded to Mrs Briggs made up as follows:

(a) Loss from 1 September 1985 to 30 September 1987 - £921.95
(b) The Tribunal directed that the complainant should, with immediate effect, be placed on the point of the scale at 1 October 1987 which she would have been put on had she not been demoted and that she should receive compensation from the date of that placing back to 1 October 1987.
(c) A payment of £75 in respect of the cost of arranging child-minding.
(d) £100 in respect of injury to feelings.

...

The provisions of s. 1(1), s. 3(1), s. 5(3) and s. 6(2) of the Sex Discrimination Act 1975 in England are identical to art. 3(1), art. 5(1), art. 7 and art. 8(2) of the 1976 Order.

In the present appeal five questions arise, all of which the Tribunal, or a majority of the Tribunal, answered in favour of the respondent. In their decision the Tribunal did not draw a distinction between art. 3 and art. 5 and decided that there had been discrimination against the respondent as a woman under art. 3 and also against the respondent as a married person under art. 5. No submissions were advanced to this Court in relation to the distinction between art. 3 and art. 5 in the context of this case but we consider that it is more appropriate to consider the case under art. 3.

*The first question*

The first question is whether in requiring the respondent to supervise badminton after the end of afternoon classes the appellant was, within the meaning of art. 3(1)(b), 'applying' to her 'a requirement or condition.' Waite J in *Home Office* v. *Holmes* [1984] IRLR 299 and Wood J in *Clymo* v. *Wandsworth London Borough Council* [1989] IRLR 241 expressed differing opinions in relation to this question. In *Home Office* v. *Holmes* the applicant's terms of engagement required her to work full time, and in her grade within her department there were no part-time workers. After the birth of two children the appellant requested the Home Office that she be permitted to return to work on a part-time basis, but this request was refused. The Industrial Tribunal held that the refusal constituted indirect discrimination and this decision was upheld by Waite J delivering the judgment of the Employment Appeal Tribunal. Counsel for the Home Office submitted that because the appellant was employed to do a full-time job it followed that the employer did not apply 'a requirement or condition' to her in holding her to a fundamental obligation of her contract. At p. 301 Waite J stated:

> In support of his first submission, counsel for the Home Office urges that full-time service is not a matter which sounds in condition or requirement at all. It is the whole job. It is not a term of the job. It is *the* job. Part-time service, he says, is not a variant of full-time service. It is a different job. 'Requirement' or 'condition' are terms which, properly regarded in their statutory context, denote some hurdle, qualification or obstacle placed in the way of the employee. They are not apt, he says, to describe anything so fundamental as the duty of service in general or the duty of full-time service in particular.
>
> We have not felt able to accept that argument. It appears to us that words like 'requirement' and 'condition' are plain, clear words of wide import fully capable of including any obligation of service whether for full or for part time, and we see no basis for giving them a restrictive interpretation in the light of the policy underlying the [1975] Act, or in the light of public policy as reflected in a later submission of counsel for the Home Office to which we shall be referring shortly.

In *Clymo* v. *Wandsworth London Borough Council* the Employment Appeal Tribunal took a different view and the relevant part of the headnote is as follows:

The Industrial Tribunal had correctly held in the alternative that the respondent employers had not indirectly discriminated against the appellant contrary to s. 1(1)(b) of the Sex Discrimination Act.

The Industrial Tribunal were entitled to find that the employers had not 'applied' a requirement or condition of full-time working in that full-time working was a requirement or condition of the terms of the employment the appellant was offered and accepted, but was not something which the employers had positively 'applied' to her other than when they had offered her employment. In any event, on the facts of the present case, 'full-time' working was part of the nature of the job itself rather than a requirement or condition applied by the employers. In any working structure, there will be a grade or position where the job or appointment by its very nature requires full-time attendance. If a cleaner is required to work full-time it would clearly be a requirement or condition, whereas in the case of a managing director it would be part of the nature of the appointment. It is for the employer, acting reasonably, to decide what is required for the purposes of running his business or establishment. If the decision of the EAT in *Home Office* v. *Holmes* was to be read as indicating that it was for the Tribunal to decide whether or not a job of itself required full-time work, it would be disagreed with. The decision is one for management, provided that the decision is reasonable - made upon adequate grounds - and responsible - bearing in mind the need to avoid discrimination based upon sex and balancing that against other needs and responsibilities.

In delivering judgment Wood J states at p. 247, para. 39:

> In order to succeed the applicant had to prove to the satisfaction of the Tribunal that the local authority had applied a term and condition to which each of the sub sub-paragraphs of s. 1(1)(b) applied. Those subsubparagraphs are conjunctive. In para. 23 of the judgment the Tribunal says this:
>
> > 23. The Tribunal agree that 'full time' is 'a requirement or condition' of the terms of the employment she was offered and accepted. But the Tribunal did not consider that this was something which the respondents had 'applied' to her other than when they had offered her employment. Thereafter the respondents took no further positive act in that respect.
>
> Mr Allen submits that the Tribunal was wrong in that the word 'applies' only means that the applicant was required to work full time. But we see no grounds for criticising the approach taken by the Tribunal. However, Mr Lynch criticises the Tribunal for finding that 'full-time working' is a term or condition. He submits that the phrase 'requirement or condition' refers to that upon which the alleged discriminator has insisted such as height or educational qualifications. He submits that for the local authority to tell their current employees that a job continues to be 'full time' is not applying anything and that on the facts of the present case 'full time' is part of the nature of the job itself.
>
> We were referred to *Francis and others* v. *British Airways Engineering Overhaul Ltd* [1982] IRLR 10. In that case Mrs Francis and 13 other women employed as aircraft component workers complained that they had been unlawfully discriminated on grounds of sex. The ACWs were Schedule VI of the employer's grading structure for lower grade employees. There were no women employees in Schedules I to V inclusive. Those employees are divided into at least two grades.

There is only one grade in Schedule VI; as a result anyone who was not in Schedule VI had opportunities for promotion within the Schedule in which he was employed, but those in Schedule VI had no way of being promoted within their Schedule. Those employed in Schedule VI were predominantly composed of women and it was the lack of promotion opportunity which was the substance of the complaint. The applicants made complaint under s. 1(1)(b) and s. 6(2) of the Sex Discrimination Act and contended 'The implicit requirement that the applicants move to other grades of employment in order to seek promotion and by not setting up a careers structure in the applicants' grade to enable the applicants to progress' were breaches of that subsection. The Industrial Tribunal rejected the application and found that the lack of opportunity or promotion was part and parcel of the job of an aircraft component worker. At para. 15 of the judgment Sir Nicholas Browne-Wilkinson says this:

> As formulated, the question is simply whether any 'requirement or condition' is applied to Schedule VI employees looked at in isolation. We agree with the Industrial Tribunal that we can detect no such requirement or condition. A lack of any opportunity for promotion within that Schedule is the consequence of the structure of the job of an ACW; it is a job which does not provide opportunities for promotion. There is no obligation on an employer to provide opportunities for promotion in any job. Since there is no opportunity for promotion within the Schedule for any ACW, there cannot be a requirement or condition restricting access to such opportunities. Therefore on the only point before the Industrial Tribunal we think its decision is correct.

We were also referred to *Home Office* v. *Holmes* [1984] IRLR 299 in which full-time working was held to be a requirement or condition by this court under the presidency of Waite J. He did, however, envisage that there might well be cases where such a requirement was part and parcel of the job itself. *Francis* was not cited in that case, nor in the present case, and it occurs to us that if it had been it may very well be that the Tribunal would have taken a different view, because it seems clear that in many working structures whether in industry or public bodies, local government or elsewhere, there will be a grade or position where the job or appointment by its very nature requires full-time attendance. At one end of the scale if a cleaner was required to work full time it would clearly be a requirement or condition. Whereas in the case of a managing director it would be part of the nature of the appointment. In between there will be many gradations but it will be for an employer, acting reasonably, to decide - a managerial decision - what is required for the purposes of running his business or his establishment. In the present case it must not be forgotten there is an obligation upon the local authority to maintain and manage a library system. The judgment in *Holmes* was not reserved and if the passage at p. 300 is to be read to indicate that in testing whether or not the decision that a job of itself required full-time work was a decision for the Tribunal, then we would respectfully disagree. Provided that the decision made by the respondent is reasonable - made upon adequate grounds - and responsible - bearing in mind the need to avoid discrimination based upon sex and balancing that against other needs and responsibilities - then the decision is one for management.

We consider that the construction placed upon s. 1(1)(b) of the 1975 Act by Waite J is correct and we would not, with respect, follow the reasoning of Wood J. The essence of his reasoning was that there are many jobs where the requirement to work full time is part and parcel of the job, and accordingly after a person has accepted appointment to such a job it cannot be said that in requiring the employee to work full time the employer was positively 'applying' to her a 'requirement.' This is a possible interpretation of the words of s. 1(1)(b), but it is a restrictive interpretation. We would not adopt that interpretation and we think it right to adopt the less narrow construction adopted by Waite J (expressly in relation to the word 'requirement' and impliedly in relation to the word 'applies' for the reasons stated by him and also by Browne-Wilkinson J (as he then was). Waite J stated:

> ... words like 'requirement' and 'condition' are plain, clear words of wide import fully capable of including any obligation of service whether for full or for part time, and we see no basis for giving them a restrictive interpretation in the light of the policy underlying the 1975 Act.

In *Clarke* v. *Eley (IMI) Kynoch Ltd* [1982] IRLR 482 Browne-Wilkinson J stated with reference to the words 'requirement or condition' at p. 485, para. 12:

> In our view it is not right to give these words a narrow construction. The purpose of the legislature in introducing the concept of indirect discrimination into the 1975 Act and the Race Relations Act 1976 was to seek to eliminate those practices which had a disproportionate impact on women or ethnic minorities and were not justifiable for other reasons. The concept was derived from that developed in the law of the United States which held to be unlawful practices which had a disproportionate impact on black workers as opposed to white workers: see *Griggs* v. *Duke Power Co.* (1971) 401 US 424. If the elimination of such practices is the policy lying behind the Act, although such policy cannot be used to give the words any wider meaning than they naturally bear it is in our view a powerful argument against giving the words a narrower meaning thereby excluding cases which fall within the mischief which the act was meant to deal with.

Accordingly we are of opinion that the consideration that the nature of the job requires full-time attendance does not prevent there being a 'requirement' within the meaning of s. 1(1)(b) and art. 3(1)(b). We are further of opinion that the fact that the employer requires the employee to carry out the job she is employed to do does not mean that the employer does not 'apply' a requirement to her.

If the employer wishes to advance the defence that there is no unlawful discrimination if he employs a woman to do a full-time job and then requires her to work full time, we consider that the defence should be advanced under art. 3(1)(b)(ii) which permits him to argue that the requirement which he applies to her is justifiable irrespective of the sex of the person to whom it is applied.

Therefore we consider that the Tribunal were correct in answering the first question in favour of the respondent.

## The second question

The second question relates to the comparison between women and men and is whether, within the meaning of art. 3(1)(b)(i), the requirement applied to the respondent was a requirement which was such that the proportion of women who could comply with it was considerably smaller than the proportion of men who could comply with it. The majority of the Tribunal stated their approach to this question and their answer to it as follows in paras 48, 49 and 53 of their decision:

48.    With regard to the ... question posed (above), the complainant's contention is that the respondent's insistence that she should conduct the badminton practice after school is a requirement or condition that a considerably smaller proportion of women than men (or married persons than unmarried persons of the same sex) can comply with by reason of the fact that more (women) than (men) and more married than single women have responsibility for looking after children.

Further, that whilst there is no statistical evidence to establish the point about 'considerably smaller proportion', the Tribunal should decide that this is the case from within its own knowledge.

The complainant also contended that 'can comply' should be interpreted in the terms set out by Phillips J in *Price v. The Civil Service Commission* [1977] IRLR 291 at p. 293 as follows:

... the requirement or condition ... in the present case seems to be that candidates for the post of executive officer must not be over 28 years of age ... In one sense it can be said that any female applicant can comply with the condition. She is not obliged to marry, or to have children, or to mind children; she may find somebody to look after them, and as a last resort she may put them into care. In this sense ... any female applicant can comply with the condition. Such a construction appears to be wholly out of sympathy with the spirit and intent of the [1975] Act ... 'Can' is defined (Shorter Oxford Dictionary) as 'to be able: to have the power or capacity'. It is a word with many shades of meaning and we are satisfied that it should not be too narrowly, or too broadly, construed in its context. ... It should not be said that a person 'can' do something merely because it is theoretically possible for him to do so: it is necessary to see whether he can do so in practice. Applying this approach to the circumstances of the case, it is relevant in determining whether women can comply with the condition to take into account the current usual behaviour of women in this respect, as observed in practice, putting on one side behaviour and responses which are unusual or extreme.

49.    The complainant's contention is that simply because someone does comply with a condition or requirement does not mean that they 'can comply'. Even looking at a 'pool' smaller than that of women in general, the Tribunal concluded that, using the pool of women teachers and applying the test of 'can comply' (above), the requirement of 'disproportionate effect' would be satisfied.

...

53.    The majority of the Tribunal accepts the contentions of the complainant and finds that, of its own knowledge and experience, a 'considerably smaller proportion' of women than men or married persons than unmarried persons of the same sex could comply with this requirement because of the fact that women and married females have the main responsibility for looking after children.

As Waite J noted in the case of *Home Office* v. *Holmes* (above) at p. 300:

> ... despite the changes in the role of women in modern society, it is still a fact that the raising of children tends to place a greater burden on them than it does upon men.

The Tribunal also noted that the Employment Appeal Tribunal in the *Price* case (above) took account of knowledge and experience in arriving at its decision.

By paying additional money and suffering disruption to her family life, it was theoretically possible for the complainant to comply with this condition or requirement but the majority concluded that this did not satisfy the test of 'can comply' set out in the *Price* case (above). Both parties and the Tribunal accepted the principle that a tribunal may find that of its own knowledge and experience a 'considerably smaller' proportion of women than men or married persons than unmarried persons of the same sex could comply with such a requirement.

Mr Lyttle, for the appellant, submitted that the approach of the Tribunal to this second question and their conclusion in respect of it was wrong in law for two reasons. First, because the Tribunal had compared women with men generally, rather than female married teachers with male married teachers. Secondly, because the Tribunal had had no evidence before them to support their finding that the proportion of female married teachers who could comply with the requirement was considerably smaller than the proportion of male married teachers or unmarried female teachers who could comply with it.

We do not accept Mr Lyttle's submissions in relation to the Tribunal's finding in respect of the second question. It is clear from para. 49 of their decision that the Tribunal did look at a 'pool' smaller than that of women in general and looked at the 'pool' of women teachers. We further consider that Mr Lyttle cannot sustain his second submission in view of the last sentence in para. 53 of the Tribunal's decision which is set out above.

It is unnecessary for us to express a concluded opinion on whether a tribunal, in the absence of agreement by the parties, can make a decision in relation to art. 3(1)(b)(i) by relying on their own knowledge and experience without any evidence being adduced before them on that point. But we are in agreement with the approach taken in the English cases that a tribunal are not debarred from taking account of their own knowledge and experience (see *Price* v. *Civil Service Commission* [1977] IRLR 291 and *Clymo* v. *Wandsworth London Borough Council* at p. 247, para. 43 to p. 248, para. 44, and that it is most undesirable that, in all cases of alleged indirect discrimination, elaborate statistical evidence should be required before the case can be found proved: *per* Browne-Wilkinson J in *Perera* v. *Civil Service Commission* [1982] IRLR 147 at p. 151, para. 29.

*The third question*
The third question also related to art. 3(1)(b)(i) and it relates to the words 'can comply' in that subparagraph.

In *Price* v. *Civil Service Commission* [1977] IRLR 291 at p. 293, para. 8 Phillips J stated:

> We do not accept the submission of counsel for the Commission that the words 'can comply' must be construed narrowly, and we think that the Industrial Tribunal were wrong to accept this submission. In one sense it can be said that any female applicant can comply with the condition. She is not obliged to marry, or to have children, or to mind children; she may find somebody to look after them and, as a last resort she may put them into care. In this sense no doubt counsel for the Commission is right in saying that any female applicant can comply with the condition. Such a construction appears to us to be wholly out of sympathy with the spirit and intent of the 1975 Act. Further, it should be repeated that compliance with sub-para. (i) is only a preliminary step, which does not lead to a finding that an act is one of discrimination unless the person acting fails to show that it is justifiable. 'Can' is defined (Shorter Oxford English Dictionary) as 'to be able: to have the power or capacity'. It is a word with many shades of meaning, and we are satisfied that it should not be said that a person 'can' do something merely because it is theoretically possible for him to do so: it is necessary to see whether he can do so in practice. Applying this approach to the circumstances of this case, it is relevant in determining whether women can comply with the condition to take into account the current usual behaviour of women in this respect, as observed in practice, putting on one side behaviour and responses which are unusual or extreme.

In *Mandla* v. *Dowell Lee* [1983] IRLR 209 at p. 213, para. 20 Lord Fraser approved of this construction of the word 'can.'

We regard the finding of the majority of the Tribunal that the respondent had established that the requirement applied to her by the appellant was one with which a smaller proportion of women than men or married persons than unmarried persons 'could comply' was somewhat surprising, because the requirement only meant that a married woman teacher would have to remain away from home for an hour immediately after school on only one afternoon in the week. However this Court can only set aside the finding of the Tribunal on this point if the finding was one to which no reasonable tribunal properly directing themselves on the law could have come, and whilst we think that the finding was very favourable to the respondent, we do not consider that we are entitled to hold that it was so unreasonable that this Court should set it aside.

### The fourth question

The fourth question is whether within the meaning of art. 3(1)(b)(iii) the requirement applied to the respondent is a requirement which is to her detriment because she cannot comply with it. We consider that the verb 'can' in the term 'cannot comply with' in art. 3(1)(b)(iii) must be given the same interpretation as the verb 'can' in the term 'can comply with' in art. 3(1)(b)(i) and that the two subsubparagraphs are reverse sides of the same test in so far as they refer to being able to comply.

In *Clymo's* case in considering the word 'detriment' in the term 'subjecting her to any other detriment' in s. 6(2)(b) Wood J stated at p. 246, para. 35:

Lastly, under s. 6(2)(b) it is necessary to consider the word 'detriment'. The Tribunal dealt with it as follows:

22. The amended further and better particulars alleging that 'the refusal to permit the applicant to job share her job of branch librarian has the effect of applying to her a requirement or condition that she work full time if she wishes to continue employment as a branch librarian' with its ensuing result that she suffered the detriment of losing her job, had no appeal whatever to the Tribunal. Although it is undeniably true that in s. 6(1) the words 'to discriminate against a woman' come at the beginning, the Tribunal were of the view that as a matter of common sense and ordered thinking there was a necessity first to identify the offending conduct of the employer. The facts reveal that the conduct of this employer was a refusal to allow the applicant to change her term of employment. The Tribunal did not consider that that conduct could possibly be described as 'subjecting her to a detriment'. Quite to the contrary, the respondents had fully complied with all the maternity provisions and the applicant's right to return to work in her previous job as required by the Employment Protection (Consolidation) Act 1978. They had offered to assist her by arranging child-minding for her. They had allowed her to take quite unusual leave for a period of nearly five months after her return to work, despite her expressed intention that she would return to work full time.

Mr Allen criticises this finding and suggests that the Tribunal were finding that because there was no breach of contract there was no detriment. We do not take the same view.

First, it seems to us that the word 'detriment' as used in this subsection must occur during and arising out of the applicant's employment by the local authority - it must be some unpleasantness or burden or less favourable treatment arising out of or in the course of that employment. It cannot amount to a failure to provide some advantage so long as such an advantage is not offered to others in the same grade of employment, i.e. to other branch librarians. Thus for instance it would not be a detriment to the applicant if the local authority failed to offer her the perk of a company car or the right to work overtime which it had not offered to others in the same grade.

In the present case job sharing was not an option for branch librarians and thus the applicant was no worse off than other branch librarians. She resigned - left of her own accord - and this does not seem to us to be a 'detriment' caused by anyone but herself. We were referred to *Ministry of Defence* v. *Jeremiah* [1979] IRLR 436; and *De Souza* v. *Automobile Association* [1986] IRLR 103 but we see no necessity to refer to those cases in reaching our conclusion on this aspect of this case.

We consider that this interpretation of the word 'detriment' by the Industrial Tribunal and upheld by the Employment Appeal Tribunal, *viz.* that when an employer refused to allow an employee to change 'her term of employment' this could not be described as subjecting her to detriment, was influenced by the opinion of the Employment Appeal Tribunal that no 'requirement' was 'applied' if the nature of the employment was full time and the employer required the employee to work full time, which is an interpretation from which we have already respectfully expressed our dissent. Moreover the Employment Appeal Tribunal in *Clymo's* case appears to have been influenced by the consideration that in that case the appellant resigned - which the Employment Appeal Tribunal considered was not a detriment caused by anyone but herself.

In the present case the majority of the Tribunal found that the respondent had suffered detriment and stated in para. 54 of their decision:

> Finally the majority concluded that the complainant had suffered detriment in the terms outlined by her (see para. 50 above).

Paragraph 50 was as follows:

> Finally, the complainant contended that the requirement or condition could not only not be complied with by her because of her responsibilities to her adopted child but also that it was to her detriment.
>
> The complainant established that she suffered anxiety as a result of the situation, there was disruption to her family life, that her husband suffered loss of holidays when he had to take time off to look after the child, that by having to spend more time with her child after returning late from school, her housework routine was disrupted and she suffered loss of sleep. Further that she had to pay an addition £5 per week to have the child minded when she was taking the badminton practice after school.

Again, we consider that the finding that the respondent had proved that the requirement relating to one hour in one afternoon in the week was to her detriment because she could not comply with it, was a finding very favourable to her, but we consider that we cannot set the finding aside as being so unreasonable that no tribunal properly directing themselves on the law could have come to it.

### *The fifth question*

The fifth question is whether the appellant can show, under art. 3(1)(b)(ii), that the requirement which it applied to the respondent that her obligation under her contract to assist with extra-curricular school games should be performed during an afternoon after school, rather that in the lunch time break, was justifiable irrespective of her sex.

In *Hampson* v. *Department of Education and Science* [1989] IRLR 69, ICR 179, the Court of Appeal in England considered whether the imposition of a condition was 'justifiable' within the meaning of s. 1(1)(b)(ii) of the Race Relations Act 1976. The first part of the ICR headnote reads:

> ... when considering whether the imposition of a condition was 'justifiable' within the meaning of s. 1(1)(b)(ii) of the Race Relations Act 1976 industrial tribunals, applying an objective test, had to balance the discriminatory effect of the condition against the reasonable needs of the person who applied the condition; that only if the discriminatory effect could be objectively justified by those needs would the

condition be 'justifiable'; that in reaching their decision on that issue, the Tribunal had to give full reasons sufficient to explain to the parties why they had either lost or won; that as the Tribunal had failed to identify the standards by which they were testing the Secretary of State's justification of the condition or to make any findings comparing the applicant's courses with the domestic one, their reasons were deficient; and that, accordingly, their decision on the conditions applied by the Secretary of State could not be upheld.

In his judgment at IRLR p. 75 Balcombe LJ referred to the judgments of the Court of Appeal in *Ojutiku* v. *Manpower Services Commission* [1982] IRLR 418 concerning the meaning of 'justifiable' where it appears in s. 1(1)(b)(ii) of the Act of 1976. He said:

> With all due respect to [Eveleigh and Kerr LJJ], I derive little help from these judgments. 'Justifiable' and 'justify' are the words which connote a value judgment, as is evident from the dictionary definition cited by Eveleigh LJ - 'to produce *adequate* grounds for', but neither Lord Justice indicates what tests should be applied. Kerr LJ says it applies a lower standard than 'necessary', but does not indicate how much lower. It was, however, accepted by Mr Carlisle, and rightly so, that whatever test is to be applied it is an objective one: it is not sufficient for the employer to establish that he considered his reasons adequate. However I do derive considerable assistance from the judgment of Stephenson LJ. At p. 423, he referred to:
>
> > ... the comments, which I regard as sound, made by Lord McDonald, giving the judgment of the Employment Appeal Tribunal in Scotland in *Singh* v. *Rowntree Mackintosh Ltd* [1979] IRLR 199 on the judgment of the Appeal Tribunal given by Phillips J in *Steel* v. *Union of Post Office Workers* [1977] IRLR 288, to which [Eveleigh and Kerr LJJ] have referred. What Phillips J there said is valuable as rejecting justification by convenience and requiring the party applying the discriminatory condition to prove it to be justifiable in all the circumstances on balancing its discriminatory effect against the discriminator's need for it. But that need is what is reasonably needed by the party who applied the condition ... .
>
> In my judgment 'justifiable' requires an objective balance between the discriminatory effect of the condition and the reasonable needs of the party who applies the condition. This construction is supported by the recent decision of the House of Lords in *Rainey* v. *Greater Glasgow Health Board* [1987] IRLR 26, a case under the Equal Pay Act 1970, and turning on the provisions of s. 1(3) of that Act which at the material time was in the following terms:
>
> > An equality clause shall not operate in relation to a variation between a woman's contract and the man's contract if the employer proves that the variation is genuinely due to material difference (other than the difference of sex) between her case and his.
>
> The House of Lords held, applying the decision of the European Court in *Bilka-Kaufhaus GmbH* v. *Weber von Hartz* [1986] IRLR 317, that to justify a material difference under s. 1(3) of the Equal Pay Act 1970, the employer had to show a real need on the part of the undertaking, objectively justified, although that need was not

confined to economic grounds; it might, for instance, include administrative efficiency in a concern not engaged in commerce or business. Clearly it may, as in the present case, be possible to justify by reference to grounds other than economic or administrative efficiency. At p. 31 Lord Keith of Kinkel, who gave the leading speech, with which all the other Law Lords agreed, said, in reference to an argument based on s. 1(1)(b)(ii) of the Sex Discrimination Act 1975, which is identical, *mutatis mutandis*, to s. 1(1)(b)(ii) of the Act of 1976:

> This provision has the effect of prohibiting indirect discrimination between women and men. In my opinion it does not, for present purposes, add anything to s. 1(3) of the Act of 1970, since, upon the view which I have taken as the proper construction of the latter, a difference which demonstrated unjustified indirect discrimination would not discharge the onus placed on the employer. Further, there would not appear to be any material distinction in principle between the need to demonstrate objectively justified grounds of difference for purposes of s. 1(3) and the need to justify a requirement or condition under s. 1(1)(b)(ii) of the Act of 1975.

At p. 77 Nourse LJ agreed with Balcombe LJ that the best interpretation which can be put on the authorities is:

> That the correct test is one which requires an objective balance to be struck between the discriminatory effect of the requirement or condition and the reasonable needs of the person who applies it. If, and only if, its discriminatory effect can be objectively justified by those needs will the requirement or condition be 'justifiable' within s. 1(1)(b)(ii) of the Race Relations Act 1976.

Parker LJ at p. 82 said:

> With regard to the meaning of justifiable and the adequacy of the Industrial Tribunal's reasons I agree with Balcombe LJ and have nothing to add.

The majority of the Tribunal held that the appellant had not proved that the requirement was justifiable under art. 3(1)(b)(ii). Therefore, in deciding whether the decision of the Tribunal was one to which a reasonable tribunal properly directing themselves on the law could have come, we must have regard to the test laid down by the Court of Appeal in *Hampson* v. *Department of Education*, which is that the Tribunal, applying an objective test, must balance the discriminatory effect of the requirement against the reasonable needs of the employer, and that only if the discriminatory effect could be objectively justified by those needs would the requirement be justifiable.

In para. 62 of their decision the Tribunal stated that the reasons put forward by the appellant for the requirement were these:

> Turning to the facts of the present case, the respondent's evidence was that it was not acceptable for the girls to have badminton practice at lunch time since that did not allow sufficient time for proper practice sessions to be undertaken. The respondent's view was that the only effective way of developing badminton within the school was to provide for badminton practice after school. In addition, as noted

above, the school had decided that an appropriate way of developing badminton within the school was to provide badminton practice at the local leisure centre where there were more courts than at the school and thus greater opportunities for all the girls to have longer periods of practice at each session.

We can see nothing in any other part of the decision or the case stated or in the documents annexed to the case stated to suggest that the Tribunal thought that any of the reasons advanced by the appellant and summarised in para. 62 were invalid.

In our opinion the reality was that the respondent had been saying to the appellant: 'I wish to perform my contractual obligation of extra-curricular coaching for badminton in the lunch break.' The Court was informed that the lunch break was between 12.35 pm and 1.20 pm, with the buzzer going at 1.15 pm for the children to go into the classrooms to be ready to start lessons at 1.20 pm. This meant that if there was coaching of badminton in the lunch break the girls would have to have lunch after 12.35 pm when the last morning class ended, after lunch they would have to change, then take part in the badminton, then change back into their normal school clothes, and be ready to resume class work at 1.20 pm. In response to the respondent's request that she should be allowed to coach during the lunch break the appellant, having considered the matter, replied that the proper coaching of badminton necessitated coaching in the afternoon after school and that coaching in the lunch break would be unsatisfactory.

It appears to us that the response of the appellant to the respondent's suggestion was entirely understandable and reasonable. The question therefore arises why did the majority of the Tribunal take a different view. The answer appears in para. 63 of the decision which states:

> It is perhaps not a matter for the Tribunal to adjudge what is the best way of conducting badminton practice in the interests of the school. What the Tribunal must look at, however, are the circumstances in which the school applied the requirement or condition to the complainant of conducting badminton practice after school.

(The underlining is ours.)

The first sentence of this paragraph is a clear misdirection in law. The respondent was employed to coach badminton for the benefit of the girls. The dispute which had arisen between the parties related to whether coaching at lunch time was satisfactory. The school authorities decided that it was not, and for this reason terminated the respondent's subsidiary contract because she was only prepared to coach during lunch break. The issue for the Tribunal under art. 3(1)(b)(ii) was whether the requirement applied by the school authorities was justifiable. The question as to what was the best way of conducting badminton practice in the interests of the school, which was why the respondent was employed to coach the girls in that game, lay at the very heart of the case. Therefore, as we have stated, for the Tribunal to decide not to consider this question (and the use of the word 'perhaps' in para. 63 does not alter the fact that they did not consider it) constituted a serious misdirection to themselves in law. Instead, as the second sentence in para. 63 makes clear, the Tribunal looked at the circumstances in which the school authorities applied the requirement to the respondent of conducting extra-curricular badminton practice. Paragraphs 64 to 71 of the decision are as follows:

64.    The complainant had been able to provide badminton practice after school prior to the adoption of her baby. After she returned from adoption leave, she found that she could only provide badminton practice after school with some difficulty (as outlined above in para. 50).

She sought to make other arrangements by holding practices at lunch time but these were not acceptable to the school. The complainant explained to Miss Carson her difficulties in this respect. As noted above, correspondence took place between the complainant and Miss Carson, the upshot of which was that Miss Carson insisted that badminton practice should be held after school. The complainant, as noted above, reluctantly agreed to this. At the point, however, where she continued to take the badminton practice after school an additional requirement or condition was applied by Miss Carson to the effect that the badminton practices should be taken at the local leisure centre from September 1985.

65.    As noted above, the complainant, during the course of her discussions with Miss Carson, asked for her contract to be renegotiated with her union. Also, as noted above, Miss Carson referred the matter to the Board. This took place by the letter dated 15 February 1985 referred to in para. 29 above.

66.    The Tribunal is satisfied that the complainant's understanding was that the matter was being referred to the Board for the purposes of considering renegotiation of the contract with her union and she at no time, at this stage, considered or was aware that disciplinary proceedings might be instituted against her. Indeed, the matter of disciplinary proceedings was not raised with her until she received the letter dated 1 April 1985 from Mrs Fryers (referred to in para. 30 above).

67.    As also noted above, Mr Corr asked at the meeting held on 1 May 1985 for the complainant's contract to be renegotiated (see para. 32 above).

68.    The Board ignored requests for renegotiation and, as outlined above, proceeded to advise the complainant that the taking of badminton at lunch time was not acceptable and, on foot of its conclusions on this and on the related matters of the carrying out of her health education duties, proceeded to remove her from her scale 2 post.

Bearing in mind the fact that the health education duties were not put in issue before the Tribunal, the Tribunal has concentrated solely on the badminton issue. As noted earlier, in para. 43 above, the Tribunal concluded that the complainant's main responsibility under the scale 2 post subsidiary contract was that relating to health education; the extra-curricular games duties being a minor part of that contract. Further, that the latter duties were not clearly defined.

69.    Even applying the less strict test as to justifiability set out in the *Ojutiku* case (above), i.e. has the respondent produced reasons for applying the requirement or condition relating to the badminton which would be acceptable to right-thinking

persons as sound and tolerable reasons for so doing, or, as indicated in the *Panesar* case, was it right and proper in the circumstances to adopt the requirement, the majority of the Tribunal was unable to say that the respondent in this case has satisfied that test of justifiability.

Certainly, applying the stricter test in the *Steel* case (above) the respondent would not have satisfied the test of justifiability.

70.  In particular, the majority of the Tribunal noted that neither Miss Carson nor the Board had, throughout the course of the events in question and up to the date of the complainant's removal from her scale 2 post, considered the possibility of reorganising the duties of the applicant's post or providing for some other method which would be acceptable of fulfilling the requirements relating to badminton. This was in spite of evidence that the duties of other scale posts had previously been changed in individual cases.

71.  In the circumstances of this particular case, outlined above, and given the unclear nature of the complainant's duties under her subsidiary agreement relating to extra-curricular games duties, the majority of the Tribunal did not accept that the Board had sound and tolerable reasons for insisting that the complainant must either carry out the after-school badminton duties or lose her scale 2 post.

Therefore, having stated in para. 63 that it was not a matter for the Tribunal to decide what was the best way of conducting badminton practice in the interests of the school, the Tribunal concentrated on how the school authorities negotiated with the respondent without, it appears, paying regard to the most important question, which was whether badminton coaching in the lunch hour would or would not be for the advantage of the girls whom it was intended to benefit. Furthermore, we consider that the points made by the majority of the Tribunal in para. 68 of the decision that the coaching duties were a minor part of the contract and that the duties were not clearly defined do not support their conclusion that the attitude of the appellant was unjustifiable. Coaching games, even if a minor part of the contract, is a not unimportant function in a school and it was at no time suggested by the respondent that badminton coaching did not constitute part of her duties. Moreover we consider that the term 'extra-curricular school games' means that games may be played after school hours. Indeed it is quite clear that at the time the respondent entered into the contract with the school authorities they both did so on the basis that her duties would be to take badminton practice and that both understood that she would continue to take the practice in the afternoon after school hours as she had done in the past.

Accordingly we consider, applying the test stated by the Court of Appeal in *Hampson's* case, that the reasonable needs of the appellant that badminton practice should be conducted in the interest of the school and for the benefit of the girls clearly necessitated that the badminton practice should not be carried out in the lunch break but should be carried out in the afternoon after school, and that the discriminatory effect of the requirement applied to the respondent was clearly objectively justified by those needs. We further consider that in deciding to the contrary the majority of the

Tribunal came to a decision to which no reasonable tribunal, properly directing themselves as to the law, could have come.

*Hampson's* case was not reported until after the Tribunal had given their decision but we would observe that the test in relation to justifiability stated in *Hampson's* case is not more favourable to the person against whom discrimination is alleged than the tests discussed in the judgments in *Ojutiku* v. *Manpower Services Commission* [1982] IRLR 418 which were considered by the Tribunal in their decision.

We consider, for the reasons which we have stated and which apply to art. 5 as well as to art. 3, that the decision of the majority of the Tribunal was erroneous in relation to art. 3(1)(b)(ii) and art. 5(1)(b)(ii) and accordingly we quash the decision and the award.

Paragraph 5 of the case states:

It was submitted on behalf of the complainant/respondent that she had been directly discriminated against by the respondent/appellant but the Tribunal made no finding on this issue.

We consider it to be clear that there is no direct discrimination against the respondent, and therefore it is unnecessary to remit the matter to the Tribunal in respect of this claim.

...

# Hampson v. Department of Education & Science[1]

LORD JUSTICE BALCOMBE: ... The appellant, Mrs Theresa Lee Ping Li Hampson, who is a Hong Kong Chinese woman, was born in 1950. Between 1968 and 1970 she took a two years' initial teacher training course at Grantham College of Education in Hong Kong. She was therefore qualified to teach in Hong Kong; this she did for a period of eight years. In 1978/79 she took a third year full-time general teaching course, specialising in English, at the Northcote College also in Hong Kong. In July 1980 she was appointed assistant inspector of the Education Department of Hong Kong which post she held until August 1984. It was shortly thereafter that she came to England.

Qualified teacher status is a necessary qualification to teach in state schools in England. Mrs Hampson applied to the Secretary of State for qualified teacher status. He refused her application.

Thereafter there was some correspondence between her and the Department but it was not until 22 October 1985 that it was fully made clear to Mrs Hampson the reason why the Department rejected her application. In their letter they wrote:

> As explained in previous correspondence Mrs Hampson's initial course of training is not comparable to our training because it was only two years in length. We cannot regard her subsequent one-year course completed eight years later, as an integral part of the initial training. When assessing overseas teacher training we also look at the content and standard of the course and we find that, apart from the length of the initial course, the content of the courses Mrs Hampson completed in Hong Kong does not meet our requirement either.

At the hearing before the Industrial Tribunal Mrs Hampson complained of racial discrimination. The complaint was two-fold. First, that there had been direct discrimination and, secondly, that there was indirect discrimination because the Department applied to Mrs Hampson a requirement or condition which it did not apply or would not apply to persons who were not Hong Kong Chinese and that it was a requirement or condition which satisfied the conditions set out in s. 1(1)(b) of the Race Relations Act 1976.

The Tribunal, after hearing evidence, rejected the allegation of direct discrimination, although they found Mrs Hampson's belief that there had been direct discrimination unsurprising, in view of the inept way in which the Department had dealt with her application. Against that finding there was no appeal.

---

1    [1989] ICR 179, [1989] IRLR 72 (CA).

The Industrial Tribunal also rejected Mrs Hampson's claim of indirect discrimination. It was against that decision that she appealed to the Employment Appeal Tribunal and now to this court.

...

Indirect discrimination is defined by s. 1(1)(b) of the 1976 Act as follows:

A person discriminates against another in any circumstances relevant for the purposes of any provision of this Act if:

(a)    ...

(b)    he applies to that other a requirement or condition which he applies or would apply equally to persons not of the same racial group as that other but -

    (i)    which is such that the proportions of persons of the same racial group as that other who can comply with it is considerably smaller than the proportion of persons not of that racial group who can comply with it; and

    (ii)    which he cannot show to be justifiable irrespective of the colour, race, nationality or ethnic or national origins of the person to whom it is applied; and

    (iii)    which is to the detriment of that other because he cannot comply with it.

...

### The test of justifiability

In *Ojutiku* v. *Manpower Services* this court was concerned with the meaning of 'justifiable' where it appears in s. 1(1)(b)(ii) of the 1976 Act and of course that decision is binding on us insofar as it decides that meaning. (See In re *Norway's Application (No 2)* [1988] 3 WLR 603). However, I regret that I do not find, in two of the judgments in *Ojutiku*, any clear decision as to that meaning.

...

With all due respect to Eveleigh LJ. and Kerr LJ., I derive little help from these judgments. 'Justifiable' and 'justify' are words which connote a value judgment, as is evident from the dictionary definition cited by Eveleigh LJ: 'to produce *adequate* grounds for', but neither lord justice indicates what test should be applied. Kerr LJ says it applies a lower standard than 'necessary', but does not indicate how much lower. It was, however, accepted by Mr Carlisle, and rightly so, that whatever test is to be applied it is an objective one: it is not sufficient for the employer to establish that he considered his reasons adequate.

However, I do derive considerable assistance from the judgment of Stephenson LJ. At p. 423 he referred to:

... the comments, which I regard as sound, made by Lord McDonald, giving the judgment of the Employment Appeal Tribunal in Scotland in the cases of *Singh* v. *Rowntree Mackintosh Ltd* [1979] IRLR 199, on the judgment of the Appeal Tribunal given by Phillips J in *Steel* v. *Union of Post Office Workers* to which my Lords have referred.

What Phillips J there said is valuable as rejecting justification by convenience and requiring the party applying the discriminatory condition to prove it to be justifiable in all the circumstances on balancing its discriminatory effect against the discriminator's need for it. But that need is what is reasonably needed by the party who applies the condition ... .

In my judgment 'justifiable' requires an objective balance between the discriminatory effect of the condition and the reasonable needs of the party who applies the condition.

This construction is supported by the recent decision of the House of Lords in *Rainey* v. *Greater Glasgow Health Board* [1987] IRLR 26, a case under the Equal Pay Act 1970, and turning on the provisions of s. 1(3) of that Act which at the material time was in the following terms:

An equality clause shall not operate in relation to a variation between the woman's contract and the man's contract if the employer proves that the variation is genuinely due to a material difference (other than the difference of sex) between her case and his.

The House of Lords held, applying the decision of the European Court in *Bilka-Kaufhaus GmbH* v. *Weber von Hartz* [1986] IRLR 317, that to justify a material difference under s. 1(3) of the 1970 Act, the employer had to show a real need on the part of the undertaking, objectively justified, although that need was not confined to economic grounds; it might, for instance, include administrative efficiency in a concern not engaged in commerce or business. Clearly it may, as in the present case, be possible to justify by reference to grounds other than economic or administrative efficiency.

At p. 31, Lord Keith of Kinkel (who gave the leading speech, with which all the other law lords agreed) said, in reference to an argument based on s. 1(1)(b)(ii) of the Sex Discrimination Act 1975, which is identical, *mutatis mutandis*, to s. 1(1)(b)(ii) of the 1976 Act:

This provision has the effect of prohibiting indirect discrimination between women and men. In my opinion it does not, for present purposes, add anything to s. 1(3) of the Act of 1970, since, upon the view which I have taken as to the proper construction of the latter, a difference which demonstrated unjustified indirect discrimination would not discharge the onus placed on the employer. Further, there would not appear to be any material distinction in principle between the need to demonstrate objectively justified grounds of difference for purposes of s. 1(3) and the need to justify a requirement or condition under s. 1(1)(b)(ii) of the Act of 1975.

Mr Sedley constructed an elaborate argument designed to show that *Ojutiku* had been overruled by *Rainey*. (This argument will be found set out in detail in the judgment of the EAT in [1988] IRLR at pp. 93-96. However, I do not find it necessary to consider this argument further here). For my part

I can find no significant difference between the test adopted by Stephenson LJ in *Ojutiku* and that adopted by the House of Lords in *Rainey*. Since neither Eveleigh nor Kerr LJJ in *Ojutiku* indicated what they considered the test to be - although Kerr LJ said what it was not - I am content to adopt Stephenson LJ's test as I have expressed it above, which I consider to be consistent with *Rainey*. It is obviously desirable that the tests of justifiability applied in all these closely related fields should be consistent with each other.

The Employment Appeal Tribunal, in their consideration of the construction of 'justifiable' in s. 1(1)(b)(ii) of the 1976 Act, sought to rely on what happened in relation to this clause when the Bill was passing through Parliament. That was clearly impermissible - see *Hadmor Productions Ltd* v. *Hamilton* [1982] IRLR 102 - and Mr Carlisle did not seek to justify it before us.

...

# Meer *v*. London Borough of Tower Hamlets[1]

LORD JUSTICE BALCOMBE: This is an appeal with the leave of Neill LJ from a decision of the Employment Appeal Tribunal presided over by French J given on 15 May 1987. By that decision the Employment Appeal Tribunal dismissed the appellant's appeal against the decision of the Industrial Tribunal given on 21 April 1986 which had in turn dismissed his complaint that he had been discriminated against by the respondents, the London Borough of Tower Hamlets, contrary to the Race Relations Act 1976. The appellant, Mr Meer, is of Indian origin. He is an admitted solicitor. He has local government experience in legal posts going back to 1967. At the time with which the case was concerned he had been a principal solicitor to the London Borough of Brent since 12 January 1976. Early in 1985, the London Borough of Tower Hamlets had a vacancy for the head of its legal department and in February of 1985 it advertised that vacancy. The form of that advertisement is given at p. 76 of our bundle and I will refer to its more important points. It is headed 'London Borough of Tower Hamlets, Solicitor to the Council.' There is a salary range mentioned and the reason for the vacancy. It continues: 'The successful applicant will have had extensive experience as a local government solicitor … '. It makes certain other general requirements as to experience. 'Applicants are considered on the basis of their suitability for the post regardless of sex, racial origin, marital status, disablement or age.' It then contains information as to where application forms can be obtained and appears to have been inserted both in the Law Society Gazette, the Local Government Chronicle and in two magazines which circulate amongst the ethnic population. The appellant saw the advertisement in the Local Government Chronicle and he applied for the post.

We now know that there were 23 applicants for the post, four of whom had had previous experience with the London Borough of Tower Hamlets. The reason for my stating that will shortly become apparent. Of those 23, 12 were selected for a long list by the use of certain criteria which appear in a letter which was subsequently written to Mr Meer and appears at p. 170 of our bundle. The letter states:

> The criteria for long-listing were based on an informal system arising from the following factors:
> 1.  Age
> 2.  Date of admission as solicitor …
> 3.  Present post
> 4.  Current salary
> 5.  Local government experience
> 6.  London government experience
> 7.  Inner London government experience

---

[1]    [1988] IRLR 399 (CA).

8.    Senior management experience
9.    Length in present post
10.   Tower Hamlets' experience.

The 12 people on the long list included all four of those who had Tower Hamlets' experience and they were interviewed. Of those 12, five were shortlisted, including two with Tower Hamlets' experience. From those five one was eventually appointed - again a person who had Tower Hamlets' experience. The appellant was not long-listed, although we were told at the beginning of this appeal - and I would like to record the fact to indicate that there was no personal objection to him - that he has since obtained a post as head of the legal department of another London borough.

The appellant applied to the Industrial Tribunal alleging discrimination. The claim before the Industrial Tribunal was based on direct discrimination under s. 1(1)(a) of the 1976 Act. That head of claim was dismissed and from it there has been no appeal. In the alternative the applicant claimed that there had been indirect discrimination under s. 1(1)(b) and it is that claim which the appellant has pursued before the Employment Appeal Tribunal and now before this court.

...

The first and major point of this appeal is whether the criterion of Tower Hamlets' experience, which I have quoted from the letter of 29 August 1985, was a condition or requirement of the arrangements made for the purpose of determining who should be offered the job at the head of the Tower Hamlets legal department. It is clear that it was not a condition of the same class as that the applicant had to be an admitted solicitor.

Mr Sedley, in an attractive argument, has put his case in this way. He submitted, first, that the condition or requirement was that to maximise his chance of selection the candidate must have had Tower Hamlets' experience, and secondly, the effect of this was to discriminate against the appellant's racial group who were unlikely to be able to fulfil the condition. As a matter of fact the Industrial Tribunal said that 'the evidence was slender and vague as to how many 'blacks' had ever been employed as solicitors in Tower Hamlets and there was no evidence about Indians in particular' and they inferred as a finding of fact that it was 'appropriate to draw the inference that no Indian solicitors at all were likely to be able to fulfil this condition.'

I go back to the question of the meaning of 'condition or requirement.' On this we were referred to a number of cases which suggest that the policy of the 1976 Act is to construe the words 'requirement or condition' generously. I refer in particular to a decision of the Employment Appeal Tribunal, with Browne-Wilkinson J presiding, in *Clarke* v. *Eley (IMI) Kynoch Ltd* [1982] IRLR 482 and to a passage at paras. 9 to 12. I need say no more about it because, although the passage undoubtedly says that 'requirement or condition' shall be given a liberal construction, it was in a context wholly different from that which we have to consider in this case.

However, in this case the Employment Appeal Tribunal held that the point had been concluded by a decision of this court in *Perera* v. *Civil Service Commission and another (No 2)* [1983] IRLR 166, also reported in [1983] ICR 428. If they are right we are equally bound, so I turn to *Perera*. I start with the headnote:

> The complainant, aged 42, was a qualified advocate in Sri Lanka when he came to England in 1973. He became an executive officer in the Civil Service and a member of the English Bar. In 1977, he applied for the position of legal assistant in the Civil Service and he was interviewed and assessed as unsuitable for the post by an interview board. He complained to an industrial tribunal, *inter alia*, that the board discriminated against him, contrary to s. 1(1)(a) and (b) of the Race Relations Act 1976, by taking into account factors relating to experience in the United Kingdom, command of English, British nationality and age. The industrial tribunal, having found that the board took those and other factors into account but, also, that the decision was based on the complainant's personal qualities, dismissed the complaint. The Employment Appeal Tribunal upheld the industrial tribunal's decision.

On the complainant's appeal:
(The first part of the headnote deals with 'direct discrimination' under s. 1(1)(a), which was not in issue in this case by the time it reached the Employment Appeal Tribunal)

> (2)   That a person claiming, by virtue of s. 1(1)(b) of the Act, that he had been discriminated against must prove that a requirement or condition had been applied to him with which he had been unable to comply and with which a substantially smaller proportion of qualified persons of his racial group would be able to comply than the proportion of similarly qualified persons of a different racial group; that the board in taking a number of factors into account in assessing the personal qualities of the applicant were not thereby applying a condition or requirement and, accordingly, the complaint under s. 1(1)(b) also failed.

It is to be noted that the complainant in *Perera's* case appeared in person. He was, of course, a member of the Bar.

I take the facts of that case, so far as they are relevant, from the judgment of Stephenson LJ at [1983] IRLR 167 para. 7:

> According to the Appeal Tribunal, it was clear from the evidence before the Industrial Tribunal that in making their selection the board took four factors into account among others: whether the complainant had experience in the United Kingdom, whether he had a good command of the English language, whether he had British nationality or intended to apply for it, and his age. His interview with the board lasted for about half an hour. He was asked a number of questions and he was graded under four letters, A to D. C meant only fair and D meant poor.

## I turn to para. 19:

Indirect discrimination is always more difficult to consider and decide. The Appeal Tribunal considered it with care. They pointed out that the complainant's case on indirect discrimination arose in an unfortunate way. In giving the judgment of the Appeal Tribunal Browne-Wilkinson J said [what now follows is a quotation from the judgment of Browne-Wilkinson in the Employment Appeal Tribunal]:

... the complainant's case based on indirect discrimination arose in an unfortunate way. The case based on indirect discrimination was not opened and the respondents were not aware that any such case was being put until counsel made his closing speech on behalf of Mr Perera. Counsel for the respondents protested, but the Industrial Tribunal did not rule on the point. It follows that all the evidence was taken and the submissions for the respondents were made in ignorance that a case of indirect discrimination was being made under this head. As a result, no evidence was led on whether any requirement imposed by the employers could be justified for the purposes of s. 1(1)(b)(ii) of the Act.

Before us, the complainant has submitted that, although there was no 'requirement or condition' expressly applied to him or communicated to him, the way in which the interview was conducted showed that the lack of a number of factors taken into account by the interviewing board in fact constituted the application of a condition or requirement. Thus, he says, although lack of, say, British nationality by itself might not have been a bar to selection, a candidate who was neither a British national, nor had United Kingdom experience, nor whose command of English was very good, nor was young, stood no chance of selection. Therefore, says Mr Perera, the interviewing body in fact applied a requirement that candidates of whatever racial origin should have these qualities. That this happened in this case, says the complainant, is shown by the evidence and by the chairman's remark that he was 'clearly short of minimum recruitment standard'.

## Stephenson LJ continues:

The Appeal Tribunal went on to criticise the way in which the Industrial Tribunal had dealt with the case of indirect discrimination ... . The Appeal Tribunal pointed out that the Industrial Tribunal did not expressly deal with that argument of the complainant, saying ... :

We do not find their reasoning in dismissing the claim based on indirect discrimination very satisfactory. It seems to us that, quite possibly due to the late stage at which the point was taken, the Industrial Tribunal have not really appreciated that there can be indirect discrimination without the employers having displayed or intended any racial prejudice of any kind. Where indirect discrimination is alleged, the issues are entirely objective: was there a requirement or condition? Was it more difficult for those of the complainant's ethnic group to meet such requirements? The relevant question is not whether any requirement or condition was imposed for the purpose of making it more difficult for those of the complainant's ethnic group to qualify.

## A little later Stephenson LJ continued:

They went on to uphold [the submission of Miss Caws] that there was no evidence to support indirect discrimination in the case. They pointed out that if the lack of a combination of features - a number of factors - was held to constitute an absolute bar to selection, that might constitute the application of a requirement or condition; but they said that there was no attempt made, either in examination or cross-examination, to establish that the combination of the several factors admittedly taken into account by the board as plus or minus factors together produced a requirement or condition; that was necessary, and only if the evidence had established that the combined lack of a number of those factors constituted an absolute bar to selection would it have been demonstrated that a condition or requirement had been applied. They found that the evidence did not go anywhere near that far, and accordingly they held that the complainant had not established his case on the basis of indirect discrimination.

## At para. 25 he continued:

The matters which have to be established by an applicant who claims that he has been discriminated against indirectly are, first of all, that there has been a requirement or condition, as the complainant put it, a 'must': something which has to be complied with. Here there was a requirement or condition for candidates for the post of legal assistant in the Civil Service: it was that the candidate should be either a qualified member of the English Bar or a qualified solicitor of the Supreme Court of this country - an admitted man or a barrister; and those conditions or requirements - those 'musts' - were fulfilled by the complainant. But as he admitted in his argument before the Appeal Tribunal and before this court, there is no other express requirement or condition, and he has to find a requirement or condition in the general combination of factors which he says the interview board took into account. He cannot formulate, as in my judgment he has to, what the particular requirement or condition is which he says has been applied to him and to his attempt to obtain a post of legal assistant. That is the hurdle which, as it seems to me, he is unable to get over. If he were able to prove a particular requirement or condition, he would then have to prove that it had been applied by the board. Then he would have to prove one further thing, namely, that a substantially smaller proportion of persons of his racial group would be able to comply with that requirement than the proportion of similarly qualified persons in a different racial group - similarly qualified because, as Miss Caws has pointed out, like must be compared with like.

## Then at para. 29:

I do not find that the Industrial Tribunal singled out the four factors which are singled out by the Appeal Tribunal and on which Mr Perera so strongly relies. But in my opinion none of those factors could possibly be regarded as a requirement or a condition in the sense that the lack of it, whether of British nationality or even of the ability to communicate well in English, would be an absolute bar. The whole of the evidence indicates that a brilliant man whose personal qualities made him suitable as a legal assistant might well have been sent forward on a short list by the interview board in spite of being, perhaps, below standard on his knowledge of English and his ability to communicate in that language.

That is only an illustration, but once it appears clear from the evidence that the Industrial Tribunal were entitled to conclude that it was personal qualities for which the interviewing board were mainly looking, and it was personal qualities, as stated in the chairman's report and as was made clear by the markings of all the members of the board, which, in the opinion of the board, Mr Perera lacked, and that that was the reason for not sending him forward on the short list, the case of indirect discrimination which the complainant seeks to make, in my opinion, falls to the ground.

As I have said, I think the Appeal Tribunal correctly stated the law as to indirect discrimination. I agree with them that there was no application here of any requirement or condition, and no evidence of it. In my judgment the complainant has failed to prove what he has to prove in order to show a case of indirect discrimination.

I would have been content to express my agreement with the Appeal Tribunal on both direct and indirect discrimination, but because I feel considerable sympathy with the complainant, highly qualified in many respects as he is, and having his application to go forward for consideration for the post of legal assistant turned down, I have thought it right to go into more detail in the case which he has made before us before dismissing, as I feel bound to do, his appeal.

## O'Connor LJ., at para. 37, said:

Mr Perera has submitted that because the Civil Service Commission asked the interview board for their opinion on certain attributes of the candidates, those amounted to requirements or conditions.

For my part, I cannot accept that. It is only necessary to look at the request made by the commission to the interview board. In making their assessment, they were asked to give their opinion, individually, of the personal qualities of the applicant, his ability to communicate, his intellectual capacity and his potential; and in order to help the members of the board to form an opinion, the four categories were further particularised. For example, in considering their opinion on personal qualities they were asked to apply their minds to maturity, common sense and ability to get on with people; and, in expressing their opinion, limiting it to whether it was very good, good, fair or poor.

In my judgment it is quite impossible to say that that exercise was imposing any condition or requirement on the board in making up their mind or in giving their opinion. The evidence before the Industrial Tribunal from the two members of the interview board who gave evidence, as reflected in the judgment of the Appeal Tribunal, shows that in their general look at the applicants, and perhaps particularly at those applicants from overseas, they directed themselves that they should ask themselves whether the applicant had a good command of the English language, whether the applicant had British nationality or intended to apply for it, and the age of the applicant. Once again, it seems to me that none of those is a condition or a requirement; they are merely further examples of the means by which the individual members of the interview board were forming their opinion of an applicant. The fact that some applicants had opinions expressed about them which led to their not going forward on the short list is one of the facts of life; it is the whole purpose of an interview board and it is not the application of any condition or requirement within the meaning of s. 1(1)(b) of the Act of 1976.

Sir George Baker agreed with both judgments.

I will finally refer to a brief passage from the judgment of Browne-Wilkinson J in that case in the Employment Appeal Tribunal, which is reported in [1982] IRLR 147. The passage to which I refer is at para. 19 and it is summarised, although not quoted verbatim, in the decision of the Court of Appeal. Browne-Wilkinson J in a reserved judgment said this:

> In order to establish indirect discrimination in this way it is not enough to show that the board took into account one or more factors which candidates of the complainant's racial group were less likely to possess, since the lack of any one of those factors *by itself* could be offset by a plus factor. Only if the evidence has established that the combined lack of a number of those factors constituted an absolute bar to selection would it have been demonstrated the condition or requirement had been applied. As we have said, we do not think the evidence goes anywhere near this far and accordingly hold that Mr Perera has not established his case on the basis of indirect discrimination.

I have read from the judgment in *Perera* at rather greater length than I would have wished because of the way in which Mr Sedley has put his arguments to us. That case seems to me clear authority that a requirement or condition under s. 1(1)(b) of the 1976 Act is a must - something which has to be complied with. That case is therefore conclusive, unless it is not binding or is otherwise distinguishable.

...

Mr Sedley sought to distinguish *Perera* on the ground that whether a condition or requirement is a 'must' depends on what it is needed for. He submits that Tower Hamlets' experience was not a 'must' for getting on the long list, but it was a 'must' for having the maximum chance of selection. But applying the analogy, so was the knowledge of English language, for example, in the *Perera* case, although that was not spelt out in so many words. If we were to distinguish *Perera* on this ground, it would be making a distinction of the kind which in my judgment tends to bring the law into disrepute.

Had the case before us not been decided by *Perera*, as I believe it is, I accept that there are strong arguments for Mr Sedley's submission that the absolute bar construction of 'condition or requirement' may not be consistent with the object of the Act. But *Perera* is binding upon us. We have been referred to a recent article in the Equal Opportunities Review in which the author categorically states that '*Perera* was one of the worst decisions ever under discrimination law and many hoped it would quietly disappear'. That indicates to me a certain lack of understanding of the basis upon which the courts of this country operate. Decisions of the Court of Appeal are binding and, unless they can properly be distinguished, do not disappear. I accept that there are arguments - and we have been referred to two papers from the

Equal Opportunities Commission - which suggest that the law as stated by *Perera*, might need reform. But that is not a matter for this court to speculate upon; it may be for Parliament.

In the circumstances I have not thought it necessary to deal with the many other points that were argued before us and other authorities that were cited. That would burden an already long judgment. I would therefore dismiss this appeal.

LORD JUSTICE STAUGHTON: I agree that this appeal must be dismissed because we ought to follow the decision of this court in *Perera* v. *Civil Service Commission* [1983] IRLR 166. If I had not held that we ought to follow that decision, I am by no means sure that I would have reached a different conclusion from that established by *Perera*. That is because s. 1(1)(b) of the Race Relations Act 1976 would have such an extraordinarily wide and capricious effect if the appellant's submissions were correct. Once an employer takes into account any factor whatsoever, which is not justifiable in terms of s. 1(1)(b)(ii), he may be exposed to a charge of racial discrimination. That is so whether or not he had the slightest intention to discriminate on racial grounds and whether or not racial grounds had any effect whatever on his decision. I say that because it must almost always be possible to find a racial group with a smaller proportion of persons able to pray in aid that factor than the proportion of persons not in that group who can pray it in aid, and there will be a risk that someone in that racial group may have applied for a job and not been awarded it.

To illustrate the point I take an extreme example. Suppose an employer takes into account, amongst other things, whether an applicant's surname begins with the letter 'A'. If it does, that is a factor to be taken into account in his favour. Suppose also, and this is not difficult, that the letter 'A' has no relevance to the job on offer and the requirement or factor is not justified - it is just adopted at the whim of the employer. I do not doubt that a racial group could be found somewhere in which the proportion of persons whose surname begins with a letter 'A' is considerably smaller than the proportion of persons not in that group whose surnames begin with the letter 'A'. There will be a risk that a person from that racial group whose surname does not begin with a letter 'A' will have applied for the job and not been awarded it. The employer would be guilty of racial discrimination. The applicant will be able to say that he suffered a detriment in the shape of inability to take advantage of a factor which would have told in his favour. That is an extreme example in order to make the point clear.

As the law stands at present, if it were a mandatory requirement that a surname should begin with the letter 'A', that would be racial discrimination. If the law is to be changed so that a factor merely taken into account and not mandatory can amount to indirect discrimination on such slender grounds, I would expect detailed consideration and inquiry as to whether the change is justified by the extent of racial discrimination presently taking place and not caught by the Act.

LORD JUSTICE DILLON: I agree that this appeal must be dismissed. The case of *Perera* decided that there can only be a requirement or condition within s. 1(1)(b) of the Race Relations Act 1976 if the requirement or condition, or whatever other word may be used to describe it, is mandatory and an absolute bar to selection. That appears from the passages which my Lord has cited from the judgment at first instance in *Perera* of Browne-Wilkinson J, which was specifically approved in this court and from the judgment of Stephenson LJ with which both other members of this court agreed. It cannot be said that the inclusion of Tower Hamlets' experience as a factor for consideration, which was only satisfied by four out of the 23 applicants, four out of the 11 on the long list and two out of the five on the short list, was a mandatory requirement and its absence an absolute bar to selection: therefore this appeal must fail.

I do not find it necessary to express any view one way or the other on what conclusion I might have reached had we not been bound by *Perera*. It may well be that if *Perera* reflects the true state of the law there are reasons for altering the law, but that is not a matter for this court; still less is it for this court to draft an appropriate amendment.

...

# Skyrail Oceanic Ltd *v*. Coleman[1]

LORD JUSTICE LAWTON: This is an appeal by Mrs Rosalind Coleman, who is a young married woman now aged 21, against that part of the judgment of the Employment Appeal Tribunal that set aside a finding of an industrial tribunal that she had been unlawfully discriminated against under the Sex Discrimination Act 1975. Her appeal has been supported by the Equal Opportunities Commission, who, so her counsel, Mr Anthony Lester, told us, regard the case as one of importance because the respondents, her employers, when deciding to dismiss her, assumed that her husband was the breadwinner. Mr Lester submitted that assumptions of that kind about women, which are not based on evidence, amounted to unlawful discrimination against them on the ground of their sex, contrary to ss 1(1)(a) and 6(2)(b) of the Act of 1975.

The facts out of which the appeal arises are unusual. On 1 August 1977, the appellant, who was then a spinster aged 17, began work as a booking clerk with the respondents, who trade as Goodmos Tours. They are travel agents, specialising in chartering aircraft for tourist flights to Israel. They have been engaged in this kind of business for some years. The appellant in the course of her work was bound to get to know of business information that would be of value to rival firms, some of whom engaged in trade espionage. In March 1978, when she was 18, she became engaged to the man whom she married on 5 September 1978. He worked for a rival firm of travel agents, Travel the World Ltd, who wanted to undertake charter flights to Israel. She announced her engagement. News of it disturbed the respondents, managing director, a Mr Mozes. He appreciated the possibility that she might divulge information about the respondents' business to her fiancé. He had a talk with her, stressing the need for confidentiality, and said that if she did divulge information he would sack her. She promised not to do so. She continued in her employment.

There were two leakages of information from the respondents in July 1978. One was to Travel the World Ltd. The appellant was not accused at the time of being the source of the leaks, nor was any suggestion to that effect made before the industrial tribunal. There was some evidence that, when her engagement became known, some senior members of the respondents' staff told Mr Mozes that he ought to dismiss her because of the danger of leaks. About that time, Mr Mozes's son had a talk with a director of Travel the World Ltd, a Mr Levinson. Neither were called as witnesses, but Mr Mozes said this about the talk:

> ... he [that is, Mr Levinson] told my son of the engagement of the applicant and her present husband. He said it would not be fair to carry on as we were as we would be accusing one another of leakages.

---

1    [1981] ICR 864, [1981] IRLR 398 (CA)

Mr Mozes attended the wedding on 5 September 1978. The next day, he dismissed the appellant by letter, giving her two weeks' pay in lieu of notice. The explanation that he gave for dismissing her was as follows:

> Regretfully I have to come to the conclusion that it would not be fair to your husband in his position to keep you employed in a similar capacity competing in the same business and dealing with the same clientele. Neither would it be fair to yourself nor to the respective companies.

He added a postscript:

> For your information Mr Levinson of Travel the World has spoken to us about the same problem and is of the same opinion.

On 4 December 1978, the appellant made an application to an industrial tribunal alleging unfair dismissal. On the facts then known to her that was the only claim that she could make. The respondents appeared and gave notice on 18 December 1978, that they admitted dismissing the appellant but alleged that they had a valid reason for doing so. They set out their version of the facts and concluded with what they described as relevant points. One, lettered (b), was as follows:

> The husband's employers inquired as to what we proposed to do after the marriage, as with them both occupied in similar fields they too were worried about leakages. We did say that we would probably dismiss her and they agreed that this was the only course open to us. As the husband presumably was the breadwinner we thought it fairer to handle it amicably from our end.

At some date, which I infer was after the filing of the respondents' answer, the appellant amended her claim to include applications under s. 1(1)(a) and 3(1)(a) of the Sex Discrimination Act 1975. The latter is the section that makes discrimination against married persons of either sex unlawful.

The industrial tribunal heard the application on 3 and 4 October 1979, and decided that the respondents had discriminated against the appellant unlawfully within the meaning of the Act of 1975 and that she had been unfairly dismissed. They awarded her £1,666 compensation, of which £1,000 was for injury to feelings. They found that she had been dismissed because she was a woman instead of being a man, which was discrimination within s. 1(1)(a) of the Act of 1975. That finding was based on what the respondents had put in their answer and what Mr Mozes had said when giving evidence. The industrial tribunal also decided that the respondents had discriminated against the appellant because she was a married woman. We have not had to concern ourselves with that finding because Mr Lester accepted that on the facts of this case the discrimination, if there had been any, had been because the appellant was a woman. The respondents have not challenged before us either the industrial tribunal's finding or the Employment Appeal Tribunal's confirmation of that finding, that the appellant was unfairly dismissed. Before the Employment Appeal Tribunal, they successfully challenged the award to £666 for unfair dismissal, but before us they accepted that, if the appellant has been unlawfully discriminated against under the Act of 1975, they could not challenge the sum of £666 as calculated by the industrial tribunal for pecuniary loss arising from the s. 1(1)(a) discrimination but they did challenge the award of £1,000 for injury to feelings. They were probably encouraged to do so by the industrial tribunal's statement that they would welcome guidance from a higher tribunal about the assessment of compensation under this head. Mr Lester informed us that nearly all assessments of compensation for injury to feelings have in the past been for small sums.

The Employment Appeal Tribunal adjudged that there had been no discrimination under s. 1(1)(a) of the Act of 1975. They decided as they did on the ground that there had been no material on which the industrial tribunal could have concluded that the respondents had treated the appellant less favourably than they treated, or would have treated, a man employed by them in the same situation. They also adjudged that in any event an award of £1,000 for injury to feelings was too high and that £250 would have been more appropriate.

The foundation of Mr Lester's submission that there had been unlawful discrimination against the appellant because of her sex was the evidence provided by the respondents' answer in the relevant point (b), to which I have already referred, and Mr Mozes's evidence when he had said:

We came to that decision [that is, to dismiss the appellant] on the assumption that the husband was the breadwinner.

The respondents made no inquiries about the financial position of the husband. Had they done so, they would have discovered that he was earning a modest wage of £46 per week net, which in 1978 would have provided a poor standard of living for himself and his wife if she did not make any contribution to the family income. General assumptions of that kind, said Mr Lester, did discriminate against women because they took no account of individual circumstances and all too often were without any factual basis. That was so with regard to the assumption that Mr Mozes had made. The statistics set out in the Fifth Annual Report of the Equal Opportunities Commission (1980) shows that in 56.2 per cent of all households married women contribute to the income. The courts, both in the UK and in the US, have adjudged that general assumptions, or, as they are called in the US 'stereotyped assumptions', do amount to discrimination against women. That this has been accepted by the Supreme Court of the United States seems clear: see *Weinberger* v. *Wiesenfeld* (1975) 95 SC 1225 and *City of Los Angeles Department of Water and Power* v. *Manhart* (1978) 98 SC 1370.

The authorities in this country are not so clear. In *Noble* v. *David Gold & Son (Holdings) Ltd* [1980] ICR 543, which was concerned with the reasons why a number of women had been made redundant, discrimination on grounds of sex being alleged on their behalf, this court found for the employers, but the reason that Lord Denning MR, gave was different from that which I gave. Ackner LJ agreed with both of us. The reason I gave, at p. 551, was:

> ... employers when offering jobs must not assume that women are less capable of doing them than men, and *vice versa* ... . Much will depend upon the applicant's personal attributes.

I adjudged that, on the evidence in that case, the employers had regard to personal qualities. In deciding as I did I thought that I was following the decision of this court in *Shields* v. *E. Coomes (Holdings) Ltd* [1978] ICR 1159. Mr Lester submitted that I had been right to decide as I had, and Mr Burke-Gaffney on behalf of the respondents did not submit otherwise. Having considered this matter again, I am satisfied that the dismissal of a woman based on an assumption that men are more likely than women to be the primary supporters of their spouses and children can amount to discrimination under the Act of 1975.

The problem that Mr Lester had to overcome in this case was that the respondents had a reason for dismissing the appellant that had nothing to do with her sex. What mattered to them was the fact that she was on intimate terms with an employee of a rival firm. Mr Lester submitted, however, that what had triggered off their decision to dismiss the appellant was their assumption that her husband would be the breadwinner after their marriage. It was that that had led them to treat her less favourably than they would have treated a man in their employment who happened to have a wife working for a rival firm.

Mr Burke-Gaffney met that argument with a concise and clear submission based on s. 5(3) of the Act of 1975, which provides:

> A comparison of the cases of persons of different sex or marital status under s. 1(1) or 3 (1) must be such that the relevant circumstances in the one case are the same, or not materially different, in the other.

Mr Burke-Gaffney said that, in order to find out whether the respondents would have treated the appellant less favourably than a man, the court had to envisage a situation in which a rival firm employed a wife whom they were reluctant to dismiss. In that situation, on the evidence the respondents would have dismissed the husband, and such dismissal would have had nothing to do with sex. What is wrong with that argument, as Mr Lester pointed out in his reply, is that there is no evidence that the rival firm were reluctant to dismiss Mr Coleman. All that the industrial tribunal decided was that Mr Coleman was employed by the rival firm. There was evidence that the respondents and Mr Levinson of the rival firm had discussed the problem arising from the fact that they were employing a married couple. Following that discussion, the appellant had been dismissed because of the assumption that was made. The evidence is not clear as to who made the assumption. It seems to me likely that it was made by both the respondents and Mr Levinson in the course of their discussion, and, even if it was not, it was made by the respondents. Mr Burke-Gaffney's analysis and comparison ignored the evidence about the assumption, as did the judgment of Slynn J, when this case was before the Employment Appeal Tribunal. In my judgment, it cannot be ignored.

Mr Burke-Gaffney also submitted that the evidence did not establish that the respondents had discriminated against the appellant on the ground of her sex. The assumption that they had made had had no sexual connotation because a breadwinner could be of either sex. That is so, but, in the circumstances of this case, the assumption was that husbands were breadwinners and wives were not. Such an assumption is, in my judgment, based on sex. On the issue of liability, I would allow the appeal.

. . .

# Strathclyde Regional Council v. Porcelli[1]

THE LORD PRESIDENT: The respondent, Mrs Porcelli, is a science laboratory technician employed by the appellants. Between August 1980 and 19 September 1983 she was employed by them in that capacity at Bellahouston Academy. On the latter date she was, at her own request, transferred to St Roch's Secondary School. On 2 December 1983 she complained to an Industrial Tribunal that in contravention of s. 6(2)(b) of the Sex Discrimination Act 1975, her employers had discriminated against her to her detriment. ...

I do not trouble to rehearse the details of Mrs Porcelli's complaint as they were eventually set out in her application to the Industrial Tribunal. Suffice it to say that her complaint included allegations that two of her fellow employees, both males, subjected her to a course of vindictive and unpleasant treatment, which took various forms, which achieved her tormentors' objective, that is to say, compelling her to seek a transfer to another school. Her case was that this course of treatment, or at least certain aspects of it, amounted to discrimination against her within the meaning of the statute, and that her employers were responsible for the actings of two men.

From the findings of the Industrial Tribunal it appears that in August 1980 there were three laboratory technicians on the staff at Bellahouston Academy, including Mrs Porcelli. Her two colleagues were female. By December 1982 these two ladies had left the school and their places were taken by two men, Coles and Reid, who were of the same status as Mrs Porcelli although they did not have as many years of experience. The Industrial Tribunal had no doubt that from the moment when they arrived in the school Coles and Reid pursued a policy of vindictive unpleasantness towards Mrs Porcelli for the deliberate purpose of making her apply for a transfer to another school, and they went on to say that they had no doubt that they treated Mrs Porcelli quite shamefully and that it must have been a singularly unpleasant and distressing period of time for her when she had to work alongside them.

For a complete account of the unpleasant and vindictive actings of Coles and Reid towards Mrs Porcelli, which were established, we are content to refer to the reasons of the Industrial Tribunal, as amplified in the opinion of the Employment Appeal Tribunal. In summary, however, it is found that Coles made a practice of deliberately concealing from Mrs Porcelli information and instructions for all three laboratory technicians emanating from the principal teacher of chemistry. It is found that Coles also asserted that he did not require to tell Mrs Porcelli about the considerable changes which he was making in the operation of the technicians' service, with the

---

1    [1986] ICR 564, [1986] IRLR 134 (Ct of Sess.).

consent of that principal teacher. On one occasion an unpleasant incident took place in the technicians' base room which is described by the Industrial Tribunal thus:

> It seems that on one particular day the applicant returned to the technicians' base room and found Mr Coles and Mr Reid in the act of clearing out a drawer and throwing into a black plastic bag a number of personal belongings of the applicant which had been in that drawer. The applicant complained that she was subjected to considerable personal abuse and obscene language when she complained about what was happening and that she had difficulty in retrieving her personal belongings from the sack. There was no one else present in the room during that incident but the applicant, Mr Coles and Mr Reid and according to the evidence of Mr Coles and Mr Reid there was no unpleasantness. Both said that the drawer which was cleaned out was a drawer used in common and that what was thrown out was genuinely rubbish and not any personal belongings of the applicant. On this point, the Tribunal preferred the evidence of the applicant to the evidence of Mr Coles and Mr Reid and we did believe that the action of throwing out personal belongings of the applicant was undertaken by Mr Coles and Mr Reid and was undertaken deliberately with a view to upsetting the applicant as much as possible.

It was also established that as part of their deliberate policy of making life as difficult as possible for Mrs Porcelli, Coles and Reid stored heavy apparatus and large storage jars in a cupboard at such a height that a ladder was required to enable Mrs Porcelli to gain access to them. In addition, however, to subjecting Mrs Porcelli to the various kinds of treatment which I have just mentioned it is found that Coles subjected her to treatment which can be described, in popular language, as 'sexual harassment'. Mrs Porcelli's evidence about this treatment was accepted by the Industrial Tribunal who found that they could not, on any matter, place any reliance upon the evidence of Coles and Reid. Since it is agreed that the evidence given by Mrs Porcelli was in accordance with the particulars averred in support of her application it will be convenient to quote them in full:

> Shortly after the incident of my personal belongings being thrown out by Mr Coles and Mr Reid, Mr Coles began subjecting me to sexual harassment. During morning and afternoon tea breaks in the technicians' room I became aware of him deliberately staring at me and following me with his eyes when I moved about the room. He also began to make suggestive remarks. He would, for example, pick up a screw nail and ask me if I would like a screw. Another example was when he picked up a glass rod holder - which is shaped like a penis - and asked if I had any use for it. On several occasions he opened the Daily Record at page 3 and commented on my physical appearance in comparison with that of the nude female depicted in the newspaper. The atmosphere in the technicians' room became so unpleasant for me that I stopped using it during break times when Mr Coles and Mr Reid were there. After I had stopped using the technicians' room Mr Coles began to harass me in the preparation room. It was his practice to come behind me and take me unawares so that when I turned round he would brush against me. In addition to sexually harassing me Mr Coles began to behave in an intimidating way towards me. On several occasions he deliberately allowed swing doors to slam back in my face when I was carrying apparatus and could not protect myself.

In spite of these findings in fact, however, the Industrial Tribunal decided, with regret, to dismiss the application by Mrs Porcelli. Their reasons for this decision were expressed as follows:

We have no doubt that the course of conduct to which the applicant was subjected by Mr Reid and Mr Coles was to her detriment. It follows from that that if the Tribunal were satisfied that the reason for the discrimination was on her sex the applicant would have established her claim and be entitled to the remedy which she seeks. Section 1(1)(a) of the Sex Discrimination Act 1975 says that a person discriminates against a woman in any circumstances relevant for the purposes of any provision of this Act if on the ground of her sex he treats her less favourably than he treats or would treat a man. The Tribunal therefore had to consider whether the treatment which Mr Coles and Mr Reid meted out to the applicant was less favourable than they would have meted out to a man. It is clear that some of the treatment was different from what they would have directed towards a man in that there was certainly a degree of sexual harassment. Having considered the matter carefully however the Tribunal did not find itself able to say that they treated her less favourably on the ground of her sex than they would have treated a man. We were satisfied, with some regret, that had the applicant been a man whom Mr Coles and Mr Reid obviously disliked as much as they disliked the applicant, they would have treated him just as unfavourably as they treated the applicant. The specific nature of the unpleasantness might well have been different but would have been in our view no less unpleasant.

Against this decision of the Industrial Tribunal Mrs Porcelli appealed successfully to the Employment Appeal Tribunal which, as we understand and interpret a somewhat telegraphically expressed opinion, found itself entitled to interfere with the decision of the Industrial Tribunal on the ground that in reaching it that Tribunal had misdirected themselves in law. Although they were satisfied that Coles and Reid would have treated a male colleague whom they disliked as much as they disliked Mrs Porcelli just as unpleasantly, they appear to have accepted that the campaign against Mrs Porcelli included the treatment which I have labelled 'sexual harassment' - a weapon which would not have been employed in a comparable campaign against such a man. Such treatment was treatment of Mrs Porcelli because she was a woman, regardless of the motive behind it, and the Tribunal's error was in failing to appreciate that Mrs Porcelli, being exposed to that treatment, was to that extent being treated on the ground of her sex less favourably than an equally disliked male colleague would have been. At all events whether or not I am being unduly generous in my interpretation of the opinion of the Employment Appeal Tribunal there is no dispute between the parties in this appeal by Strathclyde Regional Council that the question for us is whether the decision of the Industrial Tribunal proceeded upon a failure correctly to understand, or to apply to the facts which they found, the provisions of s. 1(1)(a) of the Act.

Although it is necessary for a woman seeking to found a claim upon s. 6(2)(b) of the Act to establish that her employer had discriminated against her by dismissing her or subjecting her to some other detriment it is accepted by the appellants for the purposes of this appeal, that if Mrs Porcelli who was not dismissed, was discriminated against within the meaning of s. 1(1)(a) she was subjected to a detriment within the meaning of s. 6(2)(b). The appellants, in my opinion, were well advised to make that concession on the facts of this case for, as was pointed out by Brightman LJ (as he then was) in *Ministry of Defence* v. *Jeremiah* [1979] IRLR 436, 'detriment' simply means 'disadvantage' in its statutory context. I have to say also that for the purposes of this appeal the appellants did not seek to maintain that if Mrs Porcelli was discriminated against by Coles and Reid within the meaning of s. 1(1)(a) they would not be responsible for their actings. In the result, accordingly, the critical issues in the appeal required attention to be concentrated upon the decision of the Industrial Tribunal in so far as it bore to deal with the matter of discrimination within the meaning of s. 1(1)(a). Upon these issues no assistance whatever is to be found in any decided case in the United Kingdom or elsewhere and I am happy to record that we at least begin our task with the advantage that the parties to the appeal were at one in submitting, correctly in my opinion, that, as it applies to the facts of this case, s. 1(1)(a) gives rise to two questions: (first) was Mrs Porcelli subjected by Coles and Reid to treatment on the ground of her sex (i.e. because she was a woman) and (second) if so, was she treated less favourably than the man with whom she falls to be compared would have been treated by these men.

For the appellants the submission was that in the proved circumstances of this case the Industrial Tribunal was clearly of opinion that the episodes of 'sexual harassment' of Mrs Porcelli by Coles were merely part of a single campaign against her founded upon dislike for her as a colleague. Such treatment of Mrs Porcelli was not, accordingly, to be seen as having been meted out to her because she was a woman but because she was heartily disliked by Coles and Reid as a person and as a colleague. In any event, said counsel for the appellants, the Industrial Tribunal correctly understood and applied s. 1(1)(a) in that they went on to decide upon the evidence that Coles and Reid would have treated an equally disliked male colleague just as unfavourably as they had treated Mrs Porcelli. In these circumstances the Employment Appeal Tribunal was not entitled to interfere with their decision to dismiss Mrs Porcelli's application because it cannot be seen to be flawed by any error of approach in law.

After some initial hesitation which I freely confess, I have come to be of opinion that for the reasons advanced by the learned Dean of Faculty for the respondent the submissions for the appellants fall to be rejected. Section 1(1)(a) is concerned with 'treatment' and not with the motive or objective of the person responsible for it. Although in some cases it will be obvious that there is a sex related purpose in the mind of a person who indulges in unwanted and objectionable sexual overtures to a woman or exposes her to offensive sexual jokes or observations that is not this case. But it does not follow that because the campaign pursued against Mrs Porcelli as a whole had no sex related motive or objective, the treatment of Mrs Porcelli by Coles, which was of the nature of 'sexual harassment', is not to be regarded as having been 'on the ground of her sex' within the meaning of s. 1(1)(a). In my opinion this particular part of the campaign was plainly adopted against Mrs Porcelli because she was a woman. It was a particular kind of weapon, based upon the sex of the victim, which, as the Industrial Tribunal recognised would not have been used against an equally disliked man. Indeed, I do not understand from the reasons of the Industrial Tribunal that they were not entirely satisfied upon that matter, and they were in my opinion well entitled to be so satisfied upon a proper interpretation of s. 1(1)(a). As I read their reasons the decision against Mrs Porcelli, which they reached with evident regret, proceeded only upon their view that Coles and Reid would have treated an equally disliked male colleague just as unfavourably as they had treated Mrs Porcelli. It is at this point, in my opinion, that their decision is vulnerable.

The Industrial Tribunal reached their decision by finding that Coles' and Reid's treatment of an equally disliked male colleague would have been just as unpleasant. Where they went wrong, however, was in failing to notice that a material part of the campaign against Mrs Porcelli consisted of 'sexual harassment', a particularly degrading and unacceptable form of treatment which it must be taken to have been the intention of Parliament to restrain. From their reasons it is to be understood that they were satisfied that this form of treatment - sexual harassment in any form - would not have figured in a campaign by Coles and Reid directed against a man. In this situation the treatment of Mrs Porcelli fell to be seen as very different in a material respect from that which would have been inflicted on a male colleague, regardless of equality of overall unpleasantness, and that being so it appears to me that upon a proper application of s. 1(1)(a) the Industrial Tribunal ought to have asked themselves whether in that respect Mrs Porcelli had been treated by Coles (on the ground of her sex) 'less favourably' than he would have treated a man with whom her position fell to be compared. Had they asked themselves that question it is impossible to believe that they would not have answered it in the affirmative. In the result it has not been shown that the Employment Appeal Tribunal were not entitled to substitute their own decision in Mrs Porcelli's favour for that of the Industrial Tribunal and I am of opinion that the appeal by Strathclyde Regional Council should be refused.

...

LORD GRIEVE: This is an appeal by the Strathclyde Regional Council, against a decision of the Employment Appeal Tribunal, which held that the respondent, Mrs Jean Porcelli, had been discriminated against within the terms of s. 1(1)(a) of the Sex Discrimination Act 1975 thereinafter referred to as 'the 1975 Act' in the course of her employment with the appellants as a laboratory technician. The Appeal Tribunal also held that the discrimination was to the respondent's detriment, as required by s. 6(2)(b) of the said Act. In the debate before us it was accepted by the appellants that the treatment which the Industrial Tribunal held had been meted out to the respondent had been to the respondent's detriment. Accordingly, this Court was only concerned with the question as to whether, on the facts which were found to have been established by the Industrial Tribunal, that Tribunal was entitled to conclude, as it did, that the treatment meted out to the respondents in course of her employment with the appellants as a laboratory technician, was not struck at by the provisions of s. 1(1)(a) of the 1975 Act.

...

In the claim which the respondent submitted to the Industrial Tribunal she maintained that, while employed as a laboratory technician at Bellahouston Academy, she had been treated less favourably than a man in her position would have been treated, because she was a woman, and thus discriminated against in terms of the 1975 Act. The treatment of which she mainly founded as being discriminatory, was that accorded to her by a Miss Caldwell, the teacher in charge of the Chemistry Department, and also, and more specifically, the treatment accorded to her by her fellow laboratory technicians, a Mr Coles and a Mr Reid. The appellants accepted that they were vicariously liable for the actings of Miss Caldwell and Messrs Coles and Reid.

It is unnecessary to rehearse the Industrial Tribunal's careful survey of the evidence relative to the respondent's specific complaints. It is only necessary to look at that survey in order to discover which of the complaints the Industrial Tribunal held were established. These are not in dispute, and can be summarised for present purposes as follows:

(1)  That while the respondent, Mr Coles and Mr Reid were all of equal status, Mr Coles concealed information and instructions from the respondent which all three technicians required to know. Such information and instructions emanated from Miss Caldwell.
(2)  That Mr Coles had told the respondent that he did not require to tell her of the considerable changes which he, with the consent of Miss Caldwell, was making in the operation of the technician service.
(3)  That Mr Coles and Mr Reid had thrown out some of the respondent's personal belongings, which had been in a drawer, and that this had been done with the purpose of upsetting the respondent.
(4)  That when the respondent complained, on the grounds of safety, of heavy apparatus and large storage jars being stored at a height which could only be reached with the use of a ladder, Mr Reid commented 'If you can't climb a ladder you shouldn't be in the fucking job.' The Industrial Tribunal found this was part of a deliberate policy adopted by Messrs Coles and Reid towards the respondent. The respondent claimed that Mr Reid's remark was made because she was a woman.

(5) That she had been subjected to sexual harassment by Mr Reid and Mr Coles in several ways as part of their campaign to pressure the respondent into leaving Bellahouston Academy. In reaching their conclusion on this particular complaint the Industrial Tribunal did not give details of the nature of the sexual harassment, but the respondent did give particulars of this to the Appeal Tribunal, which they understood coincided with the evidence which she had given before the Industrial Tribunal. The particulars are set out in the judgment of the Appeal Tribunal, and it is reasonable to assume that, in finding that the respondent had been subjected to sexual harassment, the Industrial Tribunal had accepted the evidence of the respondent in regard to that particular complaint. What is significant about that evidence is that the specific behaviour referred to is given only as an 'example' of the conduct complained of. It is therefore reasonable to assume that other 'examples' could have been given by the respondent. The appellants' counsel did not at any stage submit that we should not accept the particulars set out by the Appeal Tribunal as an accurate summary of the respondent's evidence, on this particular matter. On my reading of the judgment of the Industrial Tribunal it was on these findings that they proceeded to reach a conclusion. They did so in the following way. They concluded that the evidence was not sufficiently clear for them to accept that there was any general belief that Bellahouston Academy was biased against female science laboratory technicians. They then said 'It seemed to the Tribunal that the real crux of the case was the complaint of the applicant about the conduct of Mr Coles and Mr Reid.' They proceeded to review the evidence relative to that conduct and, having done so, said 'The Tribunal had no doubt that from the moment when they arrived in the school Mr Coles and Mr Reid pursued a policy of vindictive unpleasantness towards the applicant for the deliberate purpose of making the applicant apply for a transfer from the school ... we had no doubt that they treated the applicant quite shamefully and that it must have been a singularly unpleasant and distressing period of time for the applicant when she had to work alongside them.'

The Industrial Tribunal's decision is contained in the following passage in their judgment.

It followed from what we have said in this decision that the applicant was discriminated against by Mr Coles and Mr Reid and that the respondents have to be responsible for that discrimination. We have no doubt that the course of conduct to which the applicant was subjected by Mr Reid and Mr Coles was to her detriment. It follows from that that if the Tribunal were satisfied that the reason for the discrimination was on her sex the applicant would have established her claim and be entitled to the remedy which she seeks. Section 1(1)(a) of the Sex Discrimination Act 1975 says that a person discriminates against a woman in any circumstances relevant for the purpose of any provision of this Act if on the ground of her sex they treat her less favourably than a man. The Tribunal therefore had to consider whether the treatment which Mr Coles and Mr Reid meted out to the applicant was less favourable than they would have meted out to a man. It is clear that some of the treatment was different from that which would have been directed towards a man in that there was certainly a degree of sexual harassment. Having considered the matter carefully however the Tribunal did not find itself able to say that they treated her less favourably on the ground of her sex than they would have treated a man. We were satisfied, with some regret, that, had the applicant been a man whom Mr Coles and Mr Reid obviously disliked as much as they disliked the applicant, they would have treated him just as unfavourably as they treated the applicant. The specific nature of the unpleasantness might well have been different but would have been in our view no less unpleasant.

It is clear from the context that in the opening sentence of that passage the Industrial Tribunal are not using the word 'discrimination' as it is statutorily defined in s. 1 of the 1975 Act. The word is being used in the sense of 'a course of conduct.'

The question for this Court is whether, in that passage, the Industrial Tribunal asked themselves the right questions in the right order having regard to the statutory provisions in the 1975 Act.

Counsel on both sides of the Bar submitted, in my opinion correctly, that the first question which had to be asked and answered in a case such as this, was 'What was the nature of the treatment which was meted out to the complainer?' The next question in a case such as this, where there is no man in a similar position to the complainer against whose treatment by the employer that accorded to the complainer can be compared, is 'was the treatment meted out to the complainer less favourable than would have been meted out to a man in a similar position to her?' If that question is answered in the affirmative the final question is: 'Was the treatment, or any material part of it, meted out to the complainer less favourable on the ground of her sex?' I quote the words of the section, but in what I have to say I propose to use the phrase 'because she was a woman.'

While the general approach of counsel was to the same effect I rather think, as will appear from the consideration of the submissions made on behalf of the appellants, that they would have omitted the words 'or any material part of it' from the final question.

The submissions made by counsel for the appellants were brief, but succinct. In adopting the approach outlined above counsel submitted that it was erroneous to select, and consider in isolation, the complaints with a sexual connotation which the Industrial Tribunal had held to have been established. To do so would be to ignore the findings in fact to the effect that the treatment meted out to the respondent, while different in kind to that which would have been meted out to a man in a similar position, would have been no less favourable. The treatment found proved had to be looked at as a whole, and by doing so, if the Industrial Tribunal had to proceed to the final question, i.e. 'Was the respondent treated the way she was because she was a woman?', the answer to that question would be in the negative. It was clear from the conclusion of the Industrial Tribunal that the treatment accorded to the respondent by Messrs Coles and Reid was accorded to her because they disliked her as a person, and not because she was a woman. The appeal should be allowed.

At the start of his submissions the Dean of Faculty emphasised, and with respect, I think quite rightly, that the most important thing to identify in cases of this kind was the nature of the treatment complained of. It is the treatment of men and women in employment which the statute is trying to regulate and control. Some forms of treatment can be clearly identified as being meted out on the ground of a person's sex, others cannot. The treatment accorded to a person can be identified and considered in its context, unlike the reasons for the dislike of one person by another. If some aspects of the treatment of a woman have sexual connotations, and other aspects have not, you should not consider the former is isolation. In this case the treatment accorded to the respondent included a variety of things, some sexually related, some not. What is clear from the findings of the Industrial Tribunal, so the submission continued, is that while the treatment which the Tribunal considered would have been accorded to the notional man in the respondent's position would have been no less unpleasant than that accorded to the respondent, it would not have included any sexual harassment. That is a fair inference from the sentence quoted above to the effect: 'The specific nature of the unpleasantness might well have been different but would have been in our view no less unpleasant.' The nature of the treatment, in so far as its harshness or unpleasantness was concerned, was not the criterion. In making a comparison between the treatment accorded to a woman, and that which would have been accorded to a notional man as regards favourability, a conclusion could be reached that one was no less favourable than the other, but that was not necessarily an end of the matter. In order to decide whether there had been a breach of s. 1(1)(a) consideration still had to be given - to use the learned Dean of Faculty's words - to the weapons used against the complainer. If any could be identified as what I called 'a sexual sword', and it was clear that the wound it inflicted was more than a mere scratch, the conclusion must be that the sword had been unsheathed and used because the victim was a woman. In such a circumstance there would have been a breach of s. 1(1)(a). That it was submitted is the case here. The Industrial Tribunal had concentrated on the unpleasantness of the treatment meted out to the respondent and compared it with the unpleasantness of the treatment which they considered would have been meted out to a man whom his colleagues had disliked as much as her colleagues disliked the respondent. That was a question of fact: but the question which had to be asked after that conclusion had been reached was 'Was the treatment, or any part of it, which was meted out to the respondent less favourable, than that which would have been meted out to the notional man because the respondent was a woman?' The answer in this case, having regard to the two findings listed above as (4) and

(5), must be in the affirmative. The Tribunal had applied the wrong test in relation to favourableness.

I have come to the conclusion that the submissions made on behalf of the respondent are to be preferred to those made on behalf of the appellant. A very reasonable inference, in my opinion, which can be taken from complaint (4) as held established by the Industrial Tribunal, is that the offensive observation was directed at the respondent because she was a woman. No doubt the same observation could have been made to a man who had complained about the place where the jars had been stored on the grounds of safety, but I very much doubt that it would have been.

The detailed 'example' given by the respondent, and accepted by both Tribunals under head (5) of the respondent's complaint would clearly have been quite pointless if made to a man in the respondent's position. They were observations which could only have been offensive to a woman, and the only reasonable inference is that they were made to the respondent because she was a woman. Even if the observation about the ladder were regarded as being only marginally related to the respondent's sex, the 'examples' given under (5) were clearly directed at the sex of the respondent, and would have had no relevance if directed at a man. In my opinion these offensive remarks were examples of the use by Messrs Coles and Reid of 'a sexual sword', and were of a sufficiently material nature to be to the respondent's detriment.

It follows that the decision of the Employment Appeal Tribunal must be upheld and the case remitted back to the Industrial Tribunal to proceed as accords. In so saying however I am not to be taken as agreeing with the reasoning of the Appeal Tribunal. They concentrated, in my respectful opinion, wrongly, on a consideration of what they called 'sexual harassment', a phrase which finds no place in the 1975 Act.

In approaching the construction of ss 1(1)(a), 5(3) and 6(2)(b), it is imperative to keep in mind one of the main purposes of the 1975 Act, which is to prevent persons in employment being discriminated against on the ground of their sex, that is to say being treated less favourably than they would have been had it not been for their sex. The treatment must first be identified and, if necessary, analysed, if it is not clear that it, or any part of it, is sexually orientated. In making the comparison between the treatment accorded to a woman and that accorded to a man in a similar position as required by s. 5(3) in a case where such a direct comparison is possible, if it appears that that accorded to the man is infinitely more cruel than that accorded to the woman (assuming her to be the complainer) that does not answer the question which the provisions of s. 1(1)(a) require to be answered. The reason for that is that while the treatment accorded to the woman may be less cruel than that accorded to the man, it may still have been meted out to her on the ground of her sex, and therefore be 'less favourable' in terms of s. 1(1)(a).

In my opinion the Industrial Tribunal concentrated on the motive behind the actings of Messrs Coles and Reid towards the respondent, rather than on the nature of the means employed by them to achieve their objective. In so doing the Industrial Tribunal misdirected themselves. The Appeal Tribunal were right, albeit for reasons which are open to criticism, to conclude the Industrial Tribunal had misdirected themselves, and accordingly, this appeal must fail.

# Wallace *v*. SE Education & Library Board[1]

LORD CHIEF JUSTICE LOWRY: ... The appellant, who was born on 5 March 1944, commenced employment with the respondent in November 1974 as a part-time Audio Visual Aids Technician. She was to work 23 hours a week and was obliged to spend half her time at Bangor and half at Newtownards. In practice the greater part of her time was, for good operational reasons, spent at Bangor. She spent four or five hours each week at Newtownards and occasionally worked at other centres. She lived in Bangor and received a travelling allowance in respect of her visits to Newtownards and other centres.

About November 1978 Mr Jardine, the Principal of the North Down Technical Area, was informed that he could appoint more technicians. It was decided to appoint a full-time audio visual technician, with a part-time technician at Newtownards. Mr Jardine called the appellant to his office and told her of the decision and gave her to understand that she would be appointed to the new post. She inquired whether the rank would be that of Senior Technician. Mr Jardine found out that it would be and advised the appellant that the appointment would have to be 'trawled', that is advertised within the Northern Ireland Education Boards. This was done and an Appointment Board was constituted. It consisted of Mr Jardine, Mr Brown (the Vice-Principal), Mr Baird (the Head of Engineering) and Mr Cairnduff (the Registrar) and interviewed the appellant, Mr Parr (the successful candidate) and two other men on 28 December 1978. A code for the conduct of Boards had been prepared which recommended that candidates' referees should be consulted before appointments were made, but the code had not been finally adopted by the respondent. In fact this step was not taken.

Mr Parr was appointed to the new full-time post with the appellant in second place in case he did not accept. The appellant was informed on 29 December that she had been unsuccessful and by notice dated 15 March 1979 she applied to the Industrial Tribunal for a decision under the Sex Discrimination (Northern Ireland) Order 1976 ('the Order') to the effect that the respondent had unfairly discriminated against her on grounds of sex by failing to make proper arrangements to determine who should be offered the employment and by failing to offer the appellant promotion.

...

The appellant's argument was, and continues to be, that, since her qualifications and experience were superior to those of Mr Parr and, may I add, since her commitment to the job and past performance could not be faulted, discrimination had occurred and that it was for the respondent to show that the discrimination was not on the ground of her sex.

---

1     [1980] IRLR 193 (NICA).

Mr Maxwell appeared for the appellant in this Court and referred to arts 3(1)(a), 8(1)(c) and 8(2)(a) of the Order. He also submitted that it was significant that, when about to prefer the less qualified candidate, the Appointment Board did not, even at that stage, think it necessary to consult either the referees of the candidates or their annual reports. He further submitted that the findings of the Tribunal showed that the appointment of the less qualified candidate indicated discrimination, which placed on the respondents the evidential burden of showing that the discrimination had not been on the ground of the appellant's sex.

Counsel relied on *Moberly* v. *Commonwealth Hall (University of London)* [1977] IRLR 176 and *Brunt* v. *NIES* ([1979] NI Judgments Bulletin No 2), to which I shall refer, and also on *Grieg* v. *Community Industry* [1979] IRLR 158.

The respondents' argument at the Tribunal hearing (para. 5(p)) was that Mr Parr had been appointed because he was superior on grounds of qualifications, experience and commitment. This submission is so directly contradicted by the Tribunal's findings and so manifestly at variance with the facts recorded by the Tribunal that one immediately looks for another, but unexpressed, reason for Mr Parr's preferment.

Mr Ferriss, for the respondent in this Court, adopted *Edwards* v. *Bairstow* [1956] AC 14 ('a two-edged sword', as Jones LJ aptly remarked) as a test of the Court's duty in reviewing the findings of the Tribunal and argued that, even though there was some *prima facie* evidence which would support a finding of discrimination, one could not assail the Tribunal's decision that the appellant had not discharged the overall burden of showing that she had been discriminated against on the ground of her sex. It could not, he said, be assumed that the decision of the Appointment Board had been reached in bad faith: it was open to them to prefer the apparently less well qualified candidate if they genuinely thought him better fitted for the post. He also pointed out that the appellant had been placed second out of four candidates, the other three being men.

Only rarely in cases under the Order will direct evidence be available of discrimination on the grounds of sex; one is more often left to infer discrimination from the circumstances. If this could not be done, the object of the legislation would be largely defeated, so long as the authority alleged to be guilty of discrimination made no expressly discriminatory statements and did not attempt to justify its actions by evidence.

This court is not entitled to substitute its own view for a finding of the Tribunal (particularly a negative finding) which has evidence to support it, but, once the evidential burden has shifted, as it clearly did in this case, the question then is whether there is any evidence to justify the conclusion that the evidential burden has been discharged by the respondent.

I respectfully agree with the observation of Kilner Brown J in *Moberly's* case at p. 178:

> We would take the view that where there has been established an act of discrimination, and where it has been established that one party to the act of discrimination is male and the other party is female, *prima facie* that raises a case which calls for an answer.

and perhaps I may be permitted to refer to my own judgment in *Brunt* v. *NIES* where, in a case under the Equal Pay Act (Northern Ireland) 1970, I said (at p. 11):

> The standard of proof (and here I again respectfully adopt what has been said in England) is simply on the balance of probabilities, but nebulous phrases are not a substitute for evidence at any level of proof and, without trying to introduce a higher standard of proof by the side door, I consider that, where the object of the legislation is to prevent discrimination and the sense of grievance which it causes, it is most important for employers to explain clearly the basis of inequality and for Tribunals to be specific as to their reasons, if and when they accept the employer's contention.

One of the significant points here is that neither the respondent before the Tribunal nor the Tribunal in its case stated, although each had an interest to justify its own decision, advanced *any* reason, in the one case, for appointing Mr Parr in preference to the better qualified Mrs Wallace or, in the other, for deciding that there was no evidence of discrimination on the ground of sex.

Lest any doubt be entertained on the point, the fact that the appellant was the runner-up for the post (instead of being placed behind all her male rivals) may reflect the degree of discrimination practised, but in this case does nothing to indicate that there was *no* discrimination on the ground of sex.

...

# West Midlands PTE v. Singh[1]

LORD JUSTICE BALCOMBE: This is the judgment of the court.

This is an appeal, with the leave of the Employment Appeal Tribunal, from an order of that Tribunal dated 17 June 1987. By that order the Employment Appeal Tribunal dismissed an appeal by the appellants from an order of an Industrial Tribunal sitting at Birmingham on 1 September 1986, when they made an order for discovery in the respondent's favour. As the Employment Appeal Tribunal said at the start of their judgment:

> This appeal raises a question of deceptive simplicity. The issues involved are of fundamental importance.

The relevant facts can be shortly stated. The respondent, who is coloured, was employed by the appellants at first as a bus driver, and since 1977 as an inspector. In September 1983 the appellants adopted an equal opportunity policy statement and in October 1984 they commenced ethnic monitoring of applications for, and appointments to, non-manual posts. At the end of September 1985 the appellants invited applications from existing inspectors for 13 senior inspector posts. The post of senior inspector is a manual post and at this time the appellants commenced ethnic monitoring for manual posts. On 1 October 1985 the respondent applied for promotion to a senior inspector post. There were 55 applicants of whom 26, including the respondent, were short-listed. Four of those short-listed were coloured. The respondent was interviewed on 13 December 1985. On 16 December 1985 the appellants decided to appoint nine senior inspectors and the respondent was not among those appointed (in fact none of the appointees was coloured). The respondent was notified of his lack of success on 16 December.

On 4 March 1986 the respondent filed an originating application to the Industrial Tribunal alleging racial discrimination in respect of the December 1985 decision and two days later served on the appellants a questionnaire under the Race Relations Act. In both their answers to the questionnaire and in their notice of appearance the appellants denied the alleged racial discrimination and referred specifically to their equal opportunities policy statement of 1983.

Correspondence between the Commission for Racial Equality and the appellants led to voluntary discovery by the appellants of certain classes of documents including:

(a)  a schedule showing the ethnic origins, qualifications and experience of all 55 applicants for the posts of senior inspector; and

---

1    [1988] 1 WLR 730, [1988] 2 All ER 873, [1988] ICR 614, [1988] IRLR 186 (CA).

(b)  application forms, interim report forms, managers' reports and decision letters in respect of each of the 25 short-listed candidates, edited to prevent identification of individuals.

However, the appellants resisted the respondent's application for further discovery, and in particular for details of the ethnic origins of applicants for, and appointees to, posts within a band of grades broadly comparable to that for which the respondent applied in December 1985, for the period since the adoption of the appellants' equal opportunities policy in 1983. On 1 September 1986 the Industrial Tribunal made an order for discovery of these details. The appellants appealed to the Employment Appeal Tribunal, and it was then agreed between the parties that, because of the inability of the appellants to give details in the particular form ordered, the order if upheld should take effect as an order for discovery of a schedule showing the number of white and non-white persons applying for, and appointed to, the post of traffic supervisor during the period from October 1984 until 17 December 1985. The order was upheld by the Employment Appeal Tribunal and the appellants now appeal to this Court.

The issue is whether evidence that a particular employer has or has not appointed any or many coloured applicants in the past is material to the question whether he has discriminated on racial grounds against a particular complainant; and whether discovery devoted to ascertaining the percentage of successful coloured applicants with successful white applicants should be ordered. Or as the Employment Appeal Tribunal put it in their judgment:

> Assuming for the purpose of argument that no single coloured applicant who has applied over the last 18 months for a succession of these jobs has succeeded in obtaining them, is that fact in any way logically probative that in the instant application by the applicant there may be race discrimination. Put another way, is it open to an Industrial Tribunal to draw an inference from a long history of unsuccessful applications by coloured applicants that an employer has adopted a discriminatory policy and has exercised it in the particular instant case?

Discovery in an Industrial Tribunal is governed by r. 4(1)(b)(ii) of the Industrial Tribunals Rules of Procedure 1985 (contained in Schedule 1 to the Industrial Tribunals (Rules of Procedure) Regulations 1985 (SI 1985 No 16)):

> A Tribunal may ... on the application of a party to the proceedings ... grant to the person making the application such discovery ... of documents as might be granted by a county court.

Order 14, r. 8(1) of the County Court Rules 1981 provides that:

> On hearing of an application [for discovery or disclosure of particular documents] the court ... shall in any case refuse to make an order if and so far it is of opinion that discovery [or] disclosure .. as the case may be, is not necessary either for disposing fairly of the action or matter or for saving costs.

We should also mention r. 8(1) of the Industrial Tribunals Rules of Procedure 1985, which gives an Industrial Tribunal a general power to conduct hearings as it thinks fit and specifically provides that the Tribunal:

... shall not be bound by an enactment or rule of law relating to the admissibility of evidence in proceedings before the courts of law.

The main argument before us was whether the discovery ordered by the Employment Appeal Tribunal is 'necessary for disposing fairly of the matter.' However, as the Employment Appeal Tribunal pointed out in their judgment, if the material which the respondent seeks to elicit is properly admissible in evidence, then a witness for the appellants might be asked at the hearing questions about the number of white and non-white persons applying for, and appointed to, the post of traffic supervisor between October 1984 and December 1985. If he were to reply that the information was available in documents, but that he did not have those documents with him, then the matter would have to be adjourned for the documents to be obtained. Thus if the material is relevant to the issues on the respondent's application, it is both necessary for disposing fairly of the matter and for saving costs.

In order to see what are the issues raised by the respondent's application, it is necessary to consider the relevant provisions of the Race Relations Act 1976. Section 4(2)(b) of that Act provides that it is unlawful for a person, in the case of a person employed by him at an establishment in Great Britain, to discriminate against that employee in the way he affords him access to opportunities for promotion, or by refusing or deliberately omitting to afford him access to them. Section 1(1)(a) provides that a person discriminates against another in any circumstances relevant for the purposes of any provision of the Act if on racial grounds he treats that other person less favourably than he treats or would treat other persons. 'Racial grounds' are defined by s. 3(1) and include colour, race and ethnic origins. Thus in the present case the respondent will have to establish that the appellants' decision of December 1985 to refuse his application for promotion to the post of senior inspector was on account of his race or colour, i.e. on racial grounds.

In considering the relevance of the material sought to be adduced, it is pertinent to note that cases based on racial (or sexual) discrimination have a number of special features.

(1) ... a person complaining that he has been unlawfully discriminated against faces great difficulties. There is normally not available to him any evidence of overtly racial discriminatory words or actions used by the respondent. All that the applicant can do is to point to certain facts which, if unexplained, are consistent with his having been treated less favourably than others on racial grounds. In the majority of cases it is only the respondents and their witnesses who are able to say whether in fact the allegedly discriminatory act was motivated by racial

discrimination or by other, perfectly innocent, motivations. It is for this reason that the law has been established that if an applicant shows that he has been treated less favourably than others in circumstances which are consistent with that treatment being based on racial grounds, the Industrial Tribunal should draw an inference that such treatment was on racial grounds, unless the respondent can satisfy the Industrial Tribunal that there is an innocent explanation: see, e.g. *Oxford* v. *Department of Health & Social Security* [1977] IRLR 225; *Wallace* v. *South Eastern Education & Library Board* [1980] IRLR 193 and *Khanna* v. *Ministry of Defence* [1981] IRLR 331;

*per* Browne-Wilkinson J, giving the judgment of the EAT in *Chattopadhyay* v. *Headmaster of Holloway School* [1981] IRLR 487 p. 490, para. 18.

(2)   The evidence adduced in a discrimination case need not decisively prove that the respondent acted on racial grounds:

... the question is not whether the evidence, if admitted, would be decisive but whether it may tend to prove the case. If the applicant could establish (a) that a relevant person had behaved in a hostile way and (b) that such hostility was racialist, this would have a probative value in establishing that that person had racialist motives on 12 March 1979. Both '(a)' and '(b)' are relevant facts in making the case sought to be made. It is not in our judgment legitimate to exclude fact '(a)', if it is a fact of a kind which calls for an explanation, in the absence of proof of fact '(b)', racialist intent, if fact '(a)' is such that from it the intent could be inferred.

- *Chattopadhyay* (*supra*) at p. 490, para. 22.

(3)   Direct discrimination involves that an individual is not treated on his merits but receives unfavourable treatment because he is a member of a group. Statistical evidence may establish a discernible pattern in the treatment of a particular group: if that pattern demonstrates a regular failure of members of the group to obtain promotion to particular jobs and to under-representation in such jobs, it may give rise to an inference of discrimination against the group. That is the reason why the Race Relations Code of Practice which came into effect on 1 April 1984 - see the Race Relations Code of Practice Order 1983 (SI 1983 No 1801) - recommends ethnic monitoring of the workforce and of applications for promotion and recruitment, a practice adopted by the appellants in their own organisation. Statistics obtained through monitoring are not conclusive in themselves, but if they show racial or ethnic imbalance or disparities, then they may indicate areas of racial discrimination.

(4)   If a practice is being operated against a group then, in the absence of a satisfactory explanation in a particular case, it is reasonable to infer that the complainant, as a member of the group, has himself been treated less favourably on grounds of race. Indeed, evidence of discriminatory treatment against the group in relation to promotion may be more persuasive of discrimination in the particular case than previous treatment of the applicant,

which may be indicative of personal factors peculiar to the applicant and not necessarily racially motivated.

> (5) It has been a regular feature of the cases conducted before Industrial Tribunals in race discrimination cases for employers to give evidence that persons holding responsible positions include both white and non-white as demonstrating that they have a policy of non-discrimination and as providing evidence from which an Industrial Tribunal could decide in an instant case that the particular applicant had not been discriminated against.

- Judgment of the Employment Tribunal, transcript, p. 17.

The validity of this practice, and its probative effect, have been approved by this court in *Owen and Briggs* v. *James* [1982] IRLR 502, 503-5, approving a similar approach by the EAT in that case: [1981] IRLR 133, 134-7. If evidence of a non-discriminatory attitude on the part of an employer is accepted as having probative force, as being likely to have governed his behaviour in the particular case, then evidence of a discriminatory attitude on his part may also have probative effect.

(6) The suitability of candidates can rarely be measured objectively; often subjective judgments will be made. If there is evidence of a high percentage rate of failure to achieve promotion at particular levels by members of a particular racial group, this may indicate that the real reason for refusal is a conscious or unconscious racial attitude which involves stereotyped assumptions about members of that group.

Mr Beloff QC, for the appellants, submitted that the statistical material ordered by the Employment Appeal Tribunal was not relevant, because it was not logically probative of the question in issue, namely whether the appellants discriminated against the respondent on racial grounds when they denied him promotion in December 1985. The fact that the statistical evidence might show that the appellants had between October 1984 and December 1985 rejected all coloured applicants for the post of traffic supervisor would not of itself prove racial discrimination; in every case there may have been good, non-racial, reasons for the rejection of the particular applicant. And even if there had been racial discrimination by the appellants on other occasions, it would not of itself prove racial discrimination against the respondent on this particular occasion. As a matter of strict logic both these propositions are true. Nevertheless, the courts do not apply so stringent a test in deciding on the relevance of material to be used as evidence:

> ... relevant (i.e. logically probative or disprobative) evidence is evidence which makes the matter which requires proof more or less probable.

- *per* Lord Simon of Glaisdale in *R.* v. *Kilbourne* [1973] AC 729 at p. 756, cited with approval by Lord Hailsham of St Marylebone in *R.* v. *Boardman* [1975] AC 421 at p. 449. See also Lord Wilberforce in *R.* v. *Boardman* (*supra*) at p. 444:

... in judging whether one fact is probative of another, experience plays as large a place as logic.

A number of cases on 'similar fact' evidence, in both the criminal and the civil field, were cited to us. We did not find these of assistance in answering the question with which we are faced. We are satisfied, for the reasons set out above, that the statistical material ordered is relevant to the issues in this case, in that:

(i)   it may assist the respondent in establishing a positive case that treatment of coloured employees was on racial grounds, which was an effective cause for their, and his, failure to obtain promotion;

(ii)  it may assist the respondent to rebut the appellants' contention that it operated in practice an equal opportunities policy which was applied in this case.

However, although relevance is a necessary ingredient for discovery, it is not an automatic test - see *Science Research Council* v. *Nassé* [1979] IRLR 465. The ultimate test is whether discovery is necessary for *fairly* (our emphasis) disposing of the proceedings. Thus, as the Employment Appeal Tribunal observed:

> We add one note of caution. Discovery as we have indicated above is governed by the County Court Rules. There may be objections to giving discovery on the ground that it (is) fishing. The Tribunal may decide that the particular request is oppressive and even where it is relevant it shall not be ordered if the court is of the opinion that it is not necessary either for disposing fairly (of) the proceedings or for saving costs.

Discovery may be oppressive in two respects. (1) It may require the provision of material not readily to hand, which can only be made available with difficulty and at great expense. It was not suggested that the order made by the EAT is oppressive in this manner. (2) It is also possible that the effect of discovery may be to require the party ordered to make discovery to embark on a course which will add unreasonably to the length and cost of the hearing. Mr Beloff submitted that the possible effect of requiring the appellants to produce the statistical material might be that they would have to prove, in every case thrown up by the statistics, that they had good, non-racial, grounds for the action they had taken. They put in no evidence to this effect and, although we accept that, if there were such evidence, that might be a ground for the Industrial Tribunal refusing to exercise its discretion to order discovery in a particular case, there is no ground to challenge the manner in which the Industrial Tribunal exercised its discretion in this case.

Thus far we have considered this case as a matter of principle. However, there is one authority directly in point: *Jalota* v. *Imperial Metal Industry (Kynoch) Ltd* [1979] IRLR 313. In that case the appellant, who appeared in person, alleged that he had been discriminated against on the grounds of his colour or race when his application for transfer to a position of shift production analyst was turned down by the respondent employers.

He asked first for details to be given of the number of coloured employees as on a specified date, both on the staff and payroll employees, in the rolled metal division and strip mill of the respondents. The ground on which he required that information, and such documents as had that information contained in them, was that it would establish a company policy not to employ coloured persons - see [1979] IRLR at p. 315, para. 5. The Employment Appeal Tribunal refused that application on two grounds:

(i) that it was irrelevant, going only to credit. We can see that there may be some force in the suggestion that, even if an employer discriminates against coloured persons in offering them employment, that does not lead to any inference that he will discriminate against existing coloured employees when it comes to the question of promotion;
(ii) that in the particular circumstances of the respondents in that case, the request was unreasonable.

The appellant then asked for details of (*inter alia*) the race, colour and ethnic origin of the successful candidates for those posts with the respondents for which he has previously applied unsuccessfully. Again, the Employment Appeal Tribunal rejected this request, again on two grounds:

(i) that again his application went only to the respondents' credit, since he was only endeavouring to show that the respondents had acted discreditably in the past by discriminating against him, and that this was not probative of the act of discrimination of which he then complained - see [1979] IRLR at p. 315, paras 17 and 18;
(ii) that they had no ground for interfering with the exercise of its discretion by the Industrial Tribunal.

It may well be that the decision of the Employment Appeal Tribunal in that case was correct, on the second ground on both applications and (possibly) on the first ground on the first application. But, if and insofar as the case purported to lay down any general principles as to the probative effect of statistical evidence in racial discrimination cases, then it is inconsistent with the principles we have endeavoured to state above and should no longer be followed. In particular, the passage in the judgment - [1979] IRLR at p. 315, para. 13 - that it is unreasonable to expect employers to maintain records of the colour or ethnic origins of their employees, is inconsistent with the provisions as to monitoring contained in the Race Relations Code of Practice to which we have already referred and which has statutory effect under s. 47 of the Race Relations Act 1976.

The Employment Appeal Tribunal ended their judgment in the instant case with the following words:

Proceedings before an Industrial Tribunal are intended to be informal and the full panoply of inquiry open to litigants for instance in the commercial court was never intended to be part of the Industrial Tribunal structure. Industrial Tribunal chairmen are fully aware of this. However, the fact that it is of an informal nature does not mean that a litigant should be deprived of a proper weapon in the armoury provided by Parliament in seeking to establish facts known to the other side but unknown to him in order to advance his case. Industrial Tribunal chairmen have enormous experience in the hearing of these applications and on the few occasions when the matter comes before us it appears generally that they have approached the applications with common sense and we have rarely interfered. This leads us to the conclusion that the result of today's hearing will not lead to any undue increase in the length of interlocutory proceedings or in the length of trials or add an unreasonable additional burden to the parties.

We agree. We dismiss this appeal.

...

## C    LOWER COURT OR TRIBUNAL

## Balgobin & Francis v. London Borough of Tower Hamlets[1]

MR JUSTICE POPPLEWELL: ... The relevant facts can be shortly stated. The applicants were employed as cleaners and general assistants in the canteen area in a hostel run by the respondents for down-and-outs known as Tower House Hostel, Fieldgate Street, London E1. It provided accommodation for between 400 and 500 men. A Mr Clarke began working at Tower House Hostel in February 1985 as a probationary cook and in early June 1985 he was appointed cook.

The applicants complained to the Industrial Tribunal in January 1986 that between June 1985 and October 1985 they had been subjected to what is known as sexual harassment by Mr Clarke. The word sexual harassment is not a phrase which occurs in the Sex Discrimination Act 1975 and is shorthand for a type of activity which is well recognised. In October 1985 for the first time allegations were made by the applicants to management. Mr Clarke was suspended. An enquiry was held. The result of the enquiry was that the respondents were unable to determine the truth of the matter, thereafter the applicants and Mr Clarke continued to work in the same area in what were described by the Industrial Tribunal as intolerable conditions. The applicants made complaint to an Industrial Tribunal.

The Industrial Tribunal heard evidence and concluded that there had been acts of sexual harassment by Mr Clarke against the applicants in the period between June and October 1985. There is no appeal against that decision. They found that there were no acts of sexual harassment thereafter. That conclusion is not challenged either.

By s. 41 of the Sex Discrimination Act 1975:

(1)    Anything done by a person in the course of his employment shall be treated for the purposes of this Act as done by his employer as well as by him, whether or not it was done with the employer's knowledge or approval ...

(3)    In proceedings brought under this Act against any person in respect of an act alleged to have been done by an employee of his it shall be a defence for that person to prove that he took such steps as were reasonably practicable to prevent the employee from doing that act ... .

The Tribunal decided that what Mr Clarke had done was done by him in the course of his employment. That finding also is not challenged. They further found that the defence under s. 41(3) had been made out by the

---

1    [1987] ICR 829, [1987] IRLR 401 (EAT).

respondents and accordingly the respondents were not liable for the acts of sexual harassment which occurred between June and October 1985.

That finding is challenged and is the first ground of appeal before us.

The Tribunal found that there were no acts of sexual harassment between October and January and as to that there is no challenge. They also held that subjecting the applicants to what were found to be the intolerable conditions of having to work with Mr Clarke for the period from November until January was not an act of discrimination within s. 1(1)(a) of the Sex Discrimination Act 1975. That finding is challenged and is the second ground of appeal.

We are much indebted to both counsel for the succinctness and clarity of their arguments. So far as the defence under s. 41(3) is concerned the Industrial Tribunal made this finding:

> 18.    We now consider whether the respondents have established a defence under s. 41(3) of the Act. We are satisfied that no one in authority knew what was going on prior to 24 October 1985. Prior to that time the respondents were running the hostel with proper and adequate supervision insofar as the staff were concerned. They had made known their policy of equal opportunities. We do not think that there were any other practicable steps which they could have taken to foresee or prevent the acts complained of. We think that the defence is proved in respect of acts occurring prior to 24 October … .

It is not entirely clear from the material before us what the management structure was. The Tribunal found:

> 3.    At all relevant times the immediate management consisted of Mr Webb, the respondent's hostel manager, in general charge of Tower House and two or three other institutions. Next in line was the senior warden of Tower House, Mr Cavanna. There were then two assistant wardens, Miss Sheila Pentland and Miss Grace Sacki. There were three cooks, working on a rota system … .

There was, however, a Mr David Farmer who gave evidence, who described himself as an assistant warden supervising kitchens and general assistants.

Miss Gay has criticised the Industrial Tribunal's finding and says that the burden was on the respondents under the Act to prove that they took such steps as was reasonably practicable. She says that they gave no evidence or no worthwhile evidence about the steps they took; that such evidence as was given could only lead a properly directed Tribunal to the conclusion that so far as supervision and instruction generally the respondents were very lax indeed. She says that so far as the equal opportunity policy is concerned that although reference was made to it at the Industrial Tribunal there was no evidence given at the Tribunal that any of the employees were given any instruction or guidance as to its operation; those who like Mr Clarke were working with women were given no sort of indication that sexual harassment was an offence under the Act. There was no evidence from Mr Webb or Mr Cavanna about their knowledge of the Act or that any steps were taken by the employers to bring to the attention of their employees the provisions of the Act. Miss Gay pointed out that there was evidence that one of the assistant wardens, Miss Pentland, had been the object of Mr Clarke's attention but nothing thereafter had happened. Although there were complaints made by the applicants and indeed by Mr Clarke about other matters not involving sexual harassment, nothing was done about it; that indicated a lack of attention to supervision. She further pointed out that there was a certain amount of horse-play which seems to have been accepted by the respondents.

She then observed that a number of these ladies had substantial periods of time off work because of sickness and that no enquiry or no useful enquiry was made by the employers as to the reason for the absences. If a proper enquiry had been made and the employers had been exercising proper supervisory control, it is said that the activities of Mr Clarke would have been revealed at a much earlier time. Next, says Miss Gay, the passage of 11 days between the complaint by the ladies and the suspension of Mr Clarke indicates a lack of response at supervisory level which is indicative of the general lax approach to control. Finally, she said that after the enquiry Mr Webb and Mr Cavanna said that they were not responsible for the ladies working with Mr Clarke or for the intolerable conditions. That, says Miss Gay, shows that either there was no real line of communication in the hierarchy or that Mr Webb or Mr Cavanna were simply washing their hands of the whole affair.

She says that it is not for her to set out what practicable steps could have been taken by the employers and that while of course it may have been difficult to stop Mr Clarke's behaviour totally the duty on the employers was to minimise or reduce the danger to their employees from the activities of Mr Clarke. In essence it is a general complaint about lack of supervision and an allegation that the Tribunal's conclusion is not supported by evidence. What the Tribunal have done, she says, is really to accept the negative approach of the employers that they did not know about it; that they had no means of knowing about it and there was nothing they could have done before knowing about it to have prevented it.

Those no doubt were all arguments which were put forward on behalf of the applicants, at the Industrial Tribunal. The Tribunal clearly rejected them as a matter of fact as either not being reasonable or not being reasonably practicable. It is clear that the acts which were perpetrated on these ladies were perpetrated on each of them without the knowledge of the other over a period of three or four months. That fact itself may have led the Tribunal to the conclusion that no amount of extra supervision was likely to have been of any practicable effect. There was some evidence about the equal opportunities policy. Clearly there was some supervision both by the assistant wardens and by Mr Cavanna and Mr Webb. The extent of that is almost impossible to determine from the notes of evidence. It may well be as Miss Gay says that the supervision could have been improved. That is true of almost every situation where something has gone wrong.

Before we can interfere with what is essentially a finding of fact by the Industrial Tribunal we have to be satisfied in the words of May LJ in *Neale* v. *Hereford & Worcester County Council* [1985] IRLR 281, 'my goodness that was certainly wrong.' The majority find it very difficult to see what steps in practical terms the employers could reasonably have taken to prevent that which occurred from occurring. The majority would ourselves have come to the same conclusion as the Industrial Tribunal notwithstanding the cogent arguments of Miss Gay simply on reading the papers. The Industrial Tribunal had, however, the great advantage of hearing and seeing the witnesses which we did not and the majority have to say that we are unable to say that there is no evidence to support their finding or that their finding was perverse.

The minority member accepts the arguments put forward by Miss Gay. He does not think the employers have proved a defence under the Act and would find in favour of the applicant. However, the view of the majority must prevail.

We turn therefore to the second ground of appeal which is raised which is this. There is no doubt that after the enquiry when Mr Clarke and the applicants were working together again there was an intolerable situation. The respondents have been criticised for allowing that situation to arise. It is no part of our function to express our views about that. What we have to consider is whether by causing or permitting Mr Clarke to work together with these ladies or these ladies with Mr Clarke, it matters not which, they were treating them on the ground of their sex less favourably than they treated or would treat a man.

Miss Gay puts her argument in this way. The treatment of which complaint was made was of exposing the applicants to the anticipated risk of sexual harassment by Mr Clarke. That treatment was less favourable than would have been given to a man because Mr Clarke would not have sexually harassed a man. He might have been unpleasant but it is unlikely that he would have sexually harassed any man. There was therefore no sexual fear in a man comparable to that felt by these women. If the comparator were simply a victim who had been bullied he might have been exposed to the same intolerable atmosphere if he had had to work with Mr Clarke but it would not have been an intolerable position which was sexual and it would not therefore be contrary to the Sex Discrimination Act 1975.

Miss Gay says that the phrase 'on the ground of her sex' has to be looked at by reference back. Mr Clarke had sexually harassed these ladies because they were women; because they had been sexually harassed, putting them back with Mr Clarke was intolerable and therefore less favourable and that was due to the fact that they were women. The consequence of the treatment was that they suffered a detriment. They suffered that detriment on account of their sex because the risk of sexual harassment was due to the fact they were women. Accordingly they were less favourably treated than a man would have been treated.

The contrary argument which was put forward by Mr Rose was this. Accepting that allowing them to work together was treatment, the purpose of the Sex Discrimination Act 1975 is to prevent discrimination, i.e. to prevent a woman being placed in a less favourable position because she is a woman. It is therefore necessary to look at the treatment and not at the consequences of the treatment. Thus the treatment is the causing or permitting Mr Clarke and the ladies to work together: the consequences of the treatment is an intolerable situation. The treatment, i.e. causing and permitting them to work together, was not on the ground of the ladies' sex, it was because they were employees. It was the consequences, i.e. the risk of sexual harassment, which was on account of their sex.

Mr Rose says that having conducted the enquiry and having been unable to reach a conclusion because of the conflict of evidence, the reason that both parties went back to work together was because that was their employment. As both Mr Clarke and the ladies returned to work, there was no discrimination there.

Additionally, says Mr Rose, it has to be established that they have been treated less favourably than a man. There is no evidence as to how the employers would, for instance, have treated a situation where the victim was a man and homosexual advances were made. It was, however, accepted in argument that that would have been dealt with in the same way. Mr Rose says that if there is no evidence to show that the man would have been treated more favourably, alternatively, that the woman were treated less favourably, then there is no breach of the Sex Discrimination Act 1975.

The Tribunal found:

19    ... Mr Blundy relied on the intolerable working conditions. This, however, does not in our view come within the ambit of sex discrimination, whether it might or might not give rise to some other remedy.

Our attention was drawn to the decision of the Court of Session in *Strathclyde Regional Council* v. *Porcelli* [1986] IRLR 134. The facts of that case were that Mrs Porcelli was subjected to a campaign of sexual harassment by two employees. The Industrial Tribunal accepted that as a fact but reasoned that had Mrs Porcelli been a man whom the two employees equally disliked they would have treated him just as unfavourably and although the specific nature of the unpleasantness might have been different the provisions of s. 1(1)(a) were not satisfied. The Employment Appeal Tribunal overruled that decision and their decision was upheld by the Court of Session. The Court of Session criticised the Employment Appeal Tribunal who had asked the question, 'Was there sexual harassment and if so was it to the detriment of the employee?', and observed that sexual harassment was not a phrase found in the statute and the question which should have been asked was the question under s. 1(1)(a). The headnote reads:

> Held: ... In the present case, the treatment of the respondent which was of the nature of sexual harassment was adopted because she was a woman. The weapon used was based upon the sex of the victim. Since this form of treatment would not have been used against an equally disliked man, the treatment of the respondent was different in a material respect from that which would have been inflicted on a male colleague. That treatment which would have been accorded to an equally disliked man would have been equally unpleasant or even more cruel did not answer the question posed by s. 1(1)(a). Upon a proper application of s. 1(1)(a), it was impossible to say other than that the respondent has been treated less favourably on the ground of her sex than a man with whom her position fell to be compared would have been treated.

That finding plainly entitled the applicants in the instant case to bring a claim in relation to the period June to October had the respondents not established their defence under s. 41(3). The ratio has no particular bearing on the question as to the position between November and January but there are certain passages in the decision which are helpful in deciding between the respective arguments.

At para. 7, the Lord President (Lord Emslie) said:

> ... s. 1(1)(a) gives rise to two questions: (first) was Mrs Porcelli subjected by Coles and Reid to treatment on the ground of her sex (i.e. because she was a woman) and (second) if so, was she treated less favourably than the man with whom she falls to be compared would have been treated by these men?

At para. 30, Lord Grieve says:

> ... the question which had to be asked ... was 'Was the treatment, or any part of it, which was meted out to the respondent any less favourable than that which would have been meted out to the notional man because the respondent was a woman?' ... A very reasonable inference, in my opinion, which can be taken from complaint (4) as held established by the Industrial Tribunal, is that the offensive observation was directed at the respondent because she was a woman ... these offensive remarks were examples of the use by Messrs Coles and Reid of a 'sexual sword', and were of a sufficiently material nature to be to the respondent's detriment.

Further at para. 34, he said:

> In making a comparison between the treatment accorded to a woman, and that which would have been accorded to a notional man as regards favourability, a conclusion could be reached that one was no less favourable than the other, but that was not necessarily the end of the matter. In order to decide whether there had been

a breach of s. 1(1)(a) consideration still had to be given - to use the learned Dean of Faculty's words - to the weapons used against the complainer. If any could be identified as what I called 'a sexual sword', and it was clear that the wound it inflicted was more than a mere scratch, the conclusion must be that the sword had been unsheathed and used because the victim was a woman. In such circumstances there would have been a breach of s. 1(1)(a).

We have all come to the conclusion that the argument presented by Mr Rose as to the construction is accurate. There is no doubt but that the intolerable situation to which these ladies were exposed had a sexual context but the reason that they were exposed to that intolerable situation which affected them because they were women was not on account of their being women; the consequence of working with Mr Clarke was no doubt a detriment to them as women; but they were not required to work with Mr Clarke because they were women. Thus so far as the phrase 'on the grounds of her sex he treats her' we have to say that the employers did not require these applicants to work with Mr Clarke because of their sex. We would also, if necessary, have said that the employers were not treating them less favourably than they would a man, the comparator for this purpose, being a man to whom homosexual advances were made.

Accordingly the appeal is dismissed.

## Clarke & Powell *v*. Eley (IMI) Kynoch Ltd[1]

MR JUSTICE BROWNE-WILKINSON: These appeals raise the important question whether a redundancy agreement which provides that part-time workers shall be selected for redundancy before full-time workers unlawfully discriminates against women and, if so, whether it is unfair to dismiss women part-time workers pursuant to such an agreement. The facts are very fully and clearly set out in the decision of the industrial tribunal which is now reported at [1982] IRLR 131. For our purposes the facts can be summarised as follows.

Eley (IMI) Kynoch Ltd ('the Company') carry on business at Wilton, Birmingham. They employ a large labour force consisting of both men and women. In January 1981 there were 340 full-time women, 140 full-time men and 130 part-time women in the department with which this case is concerned. By October 1981 the number of part-time women had fallen to 60. During 1981 the Company got into a redundancy situation. On 27 July 1981 redundancy notices were served terminating the employment of all 60 part-time women, 20 full-time men and 26 full-time women. The two applicants, Mrs Clarke and Miss Powell, were both part-time workers and both were dismissed.

The industrial tribunal found that it was a long-standing practice of the company that where redundancies were necessary the criterion 'last in-first out' was applied save that part-time workers were first dismissed. That practice, with the tacit knowledge and agreement of the union, had continued since the 1960s. On 16 January 1981 the company signed an agreement with the Transport and General Workers' Union relating to this point. Item 5 of that agreement provides 'part-timers in the unit with redundancies to go before full-timers.' Item 6 specifies 'last in unit first out.' Before the agreement was signed, the union held a mass meeting of the workers to which the redundancy proposals were put. A large majority was in favour of the proposals. The tribunal accepted evidence that the overwhelming majority of full-time women workers voted for the proposal and the overwhelming majority of part-time workers voted against it. The industrial tribunal find that the reason for the dismissal of Mrs Clarke and Miss Powell was purely the implementation of that agreed procedure for redundancy selection. The tribunal were satisfied that neither the union nor the company intended or would have wished to have included any unlawful or discriminatory provision in the agreement and that they could and would readily renegotiate such terms of the agreement as might be held to be unlawful and discriminatory.

The circumstances of the two applicants are different. Miss Powell started work in 1975. She had a child in 1978. The industrial tribunal found

---

1    [1983] ICR 165, [1982] IRLR 482 (EAT).

that at no time did her domestic circumstances permit her to be a full-time worker. Mrs Clarke, on the other hand, started work in 1967. She has two adult children who had left school by 1975 or 1976. The industrial tribunal found that once both her children had left school there was thereafter no domestic reason why she should not have worked full time. The importance of the distinction between the domestic circumstances of the two ladies is that down to early 1980 there was nothing to prevent a part-time worker transferring so as to become a full-time worker. However, as from the middle of 1980 such transfer was not possible.

The only question arising under the Sex Discrimination Act 1975 is whether the employers, by selecting part-timers who were all women in preference to full-timers, have indirectly discriminated against women. Section 1 of the 1975 Act defines what constitutes discrimination for the purposes of the Act. Section 1(1)(a) deals with direct discrimination, i.e. where a woman is treated less favourably on the grounds of her sex: direct discrimination does not arise in this case. Section 1(1)(b) includes in the definition of discrimination acts which, although not done on the grounds of sex or with any intention to discriminate, have an unequal impact on women.

...

The industrial tribunal held first that the employers had applied a 'requirement or condition' viz. that in order to qualify for selection on the basis last in-first out the applicants (and other women) had to be employed full-time. Next, the tribunal found on the evidence that the proportion of women who could comply with that requirement or condition was considerably smaller than the proportion of men who could do so. They then turned to consider para (iii) and reached different conclusions in relation to Miss Powell and Mrs Clarke. Since Miss Powell's domestic circumstances have never permitted her to take employment as a full-time worker, the tribunal held that she could not comply with the requirement or condition and therefore (subject to the question of justification) her claim succeeded. So far as Mrs Clarke was concerned, they held that since she was at all times aware of the basis on which the company selected for redundancy and down to the middle of 1980 could have transferred to become a full-time worker, her case did not fall within para. (iii) and her claim under the 1975 Act failed. Next, the industrial tribunal considered whether the company could 'justify' the condition for the purposes of para. (ii). In reaching their decision on this issue they applied the test of justifiability as stated by this appeal tribunal in *Panesar* v. *The Nestlé Co. Ltd* [1980] IRLR 60, i.e. was it right and proper in the circumstances that the company should have adopted the discriminatory condition? The tribunal did not apply the test as stated in *Steel* v. *Union of Post Office Workers* [1978] ICR 181, which suggests that the test is one of 'overriding need.' Applying the less stringent *Panesar* test, the tribunal even so found that the company had not discharged the burden imposed by para. (ii).

The industrial tribunal therefore held that Mrs Clarke's claim under the 1975 Act failed but Miss Powell's succeeded. The industrial tribunal held that it could not award Miss Powell damages since the discrimination was not intentional (see s. 66(3) of the 1975 Act) and stood over the question whether they should make any declaration or recommendation under s. 65 of the 1975 Act.

...

Each of these decisions has given rise to complicated appeals and cross-appeals. Counsel very helpfully summarised the issues raised as follows ... :

(1) Did the implementation of the 'part-time workers first' clause apply a requirement or condition to either applicant within s. 1(1)(b)?
(2) Do the words 'can comply' in para. (i) and 'cannot comply' in para. (iii) include past opportunities to comply with the relevant requirement or condition?
(3) If so, was the industrial tribunal entitled to find that the proportion of women in the redundancy pool who could comply with the relevant requirement or condition was considerably smaller than the proportion of men who could have complied with it?
(4) If sex discrimination is found, what is the standard of justification needed to establish a defence to it?
(5) Has the industrial tribunal erred in law in finding justification not established?

...

We will deal with these issues is turn.

*I.    Was there a 'requirement or condition'?*

The industrial tribunal accepted that the company had applied the following requirement or condition in this case:

> The requirement or condition that, to rank in selection for redundancy by virtue of service in unit and the principle of last in first out, the applicant had to be employed full-time.

Both before the industrial tribunal and before us, Mr George for the company urged that Parliament must have used the two words 'requirement' and 'condition' in different senses. He submitted, on the basis of dictionary definitions, that a 'requirement' is something which calls for or demands something of the person to whom it is applied. Although he accepted that the word 'requirement' can be used in the sense of a qualification, he submitted that in the 1975 Act it should not be given that meaning. As to the word 'condition', it was submitted to the industrial tribunal that this referred only to a contractual stipulation: before us, it was accepted that it had a wider meaning in the 1975 Act and included a qualification for holding a position but not a qualification for immunity from a disadvantage.

On this aspect of the case we entirely agree with the conclusions and reasoning of the industrial tribunal. We can see no reason why the words 'requirement' and 'condition' should have wholly separate meanings. In our view, although not fully synonymous there is a large degree of overlap between the two words. Even taking Mr George's narrow formulation of the meaning of 'requirement' if a contract of employment should stipulate that within six months of starting work the employee should pass a particular exam, that could equally well be described as either a requirement or a condition of continued employment. The dictionary quotations relied on by Mr George show this overlap in meaning. Thus, 'requirement' is defined in terms referring to something which is a pre-requisite. Given that there is an overlap in the ordinary meaning of the two words, the purpose of the draftsmen in using both words must have been to extend the ambit of what is covered so as to include anything which fairly falls within the ordinary meaning of either word. As to Mr George's contention that the word 'condition' covers a qualification for holding a position but not a disqualification for continuing to hold such a position, we can see no logical or semantic reason for such a distinction.

In our view it is not right to give these words a narrow construction. The purpose of the legislature in introducing the concept of indirect discrimination in the 1975 Act and the Race Relations Act 1976 was to seek to eliminate those practices which had a disproportionate impact on women or ethnic minorities and were not justifiable for other reasons. The concept was derived from that developed in the law of the United States which held to be unlawful practices which had a disproportionate impact on black workers as opposed to white workers: see *Griggs* v. *Duke Power Co.* (1977) 401 US 424. If the elimination of such practices is the policy lying behind the Act, although such policy cannot be used to give the words any wider meaning than they naturally bear it is in our view a powerful argument against giving the words a narrower meaning thereby excluding cases which fall within the mischief which the Act was meant to deal with.

2.   *Do the words 'can comply' in para. (i) and 'cannot comply' in para. (iii) include past opportunities to comply?*

The question is whether the applicant's inability to comply with a requirement or condition has to be judged as at the date of selection for redundancy or dismissal or as at some earlier date. The point has a dual importance in this case. First, if it is legitimate to have regard to the ability of part-time workers to become full-time workers before 1980, then for the purposes of para. (i) the proportion of women who 'can comply' at that earlier date will be different from the proportion who 'can comply' in 1981 when transfer from part-time to full-time workers had become impossible. Secondly, the industrial tribunal held that Mrs Clarke failed to satisfy the requirement of para. (iii) because at some earlier date she could have transferred to full-time work and if she had done so she would not have suffered the detriment.

On this issue we are unable to agree with the industrial tribunal. Counsel are agreed that the relevant point in time at which the ability to comply has to be assessed must be the same under both para. (i) and para. (iii). We will consider the case under para. (iii) first. The industrial tribunal, although accepting that both ladies had suffered a detriment, said that they had to show that they could not comply as individuals with the requirement to be full-time workers. No doubt this was a paraphrase of the statutory words, but we think that the paraphrase may have led the industrial tribunal astray. Paragraph (iii) does not in terms impose on the complainant the burden of showing that she cannot comply with the requirement, she has to show that the requirement 'is to her detriment *because* she cannot comply with it.' The paragraph imposes the burden of showing detriment to the individual applicant by reason of inability to comply. If one asked the question 'At what date is the detriment to be demonstrated?' there can only be one answer: namely, at the date the discriminatory conduct has operated so as to create the alleged detriment. In this case the detriment relied upon is the dismissal for redundancy. Therefore the relevant question under para. (iii) is 'did the applicant suffer the detriment of dismissal for redundancy because she could not comply with the requirement to be a full-time worker'? So analysed, it seems to us that under para. (iii) the only material question is whether *at the date of the detriment* she can or cannot comply with the requirement. If she can, para. (iii) is not satisfied; if she cannot, it is satisfied. The use of the present tense - 'is' to her detriment because she 'cannot' comply - shows that only one point in time is being looked at.

Therefore in our view Mrs Clarke has discharged the burden imposed on her by para. (iii) since she has shown that she personally suffered the detriment of dismissal, the reason being that at the time she was dismissed she could not comply with the requirement that she should be a full-time worker. It is irrelevant that she could at some earlier date have avoided that detriment by becoming a full-time worker.

If we are right in thinking that the date of detriment is the only relevant date under para. (iii), we think that counsel are right in conceding that the same date is the only relevant date under para. (i). If that is not the relevant date for the purposes of para. (i) what other date is to be taken? The proportion of men and women who can comply with any given requirement may well vary from time to time. In this case for example the company is arguing that the requirements of para. (i) have not been satisfied because there was no evidence before the industrial tribunal as to what proportion of women part-time workers could, like Mrs Clarke, in the past have become full-time workers. If that line of enquiry is open, then the proportion of part-time workers whose domestic circumstances permitted them to take full-time work will vary from time to time. At what point in time is the comparison between women and men to be made?

For these reasons we think that for all the purposes of s. 1(1)(b) the relevant point of time at which the ability or inability to comply has to be shown is the date on which the applicant alleges she has suffered detriment. This is in fact the same point in time as 'that at which the requirement or condition has to be fulfilled': see *Steel* v. *Union of Post Office Workers.*

In the light of our decision on issue 2, issue 3 does not arise.

### 4.  *The standard of justification under para. (ii).*

Once the applicants have shown that there has been applied to them a 'requirement or condition' within para. (i) and a detriment within para. (iii), the discrimination will be unlawful unless the employer shows that the requirement is 'justifiable' within para. (ii). Parliament has given no guidance either in the 1975 Act or in the Race Relations Act 1976 as to the circumstances in which other factors are to be held to justify an otherwise discriminatory practice.

The decisions of the Court of Appeal and of this appeal tribunal disclose a steady decline in the strictness of the requirements which an employer has to satisfy in order to show that a discriminatory condition is 'justified.' In *Steel* v. *Union of Post Office Workers* , this appeal tribunal, following the approach of the US Supreme Court in *Griggs* v. *Duke Power Co.,* indicated that a requirement could not be justified unless it was 'necessary' for some other purpose of the employer. This test of necessity was slightly eroded in *Singh* v. *Rowntree Mackintosh Ltd* [1979] IRLR 199 which, while stating that the test was 'necessity' indicated that that test had to be applied 'reasonably and with common sense.'

Then in the *Panesar* case, Slynn J, in giving the judgment of this appeal tribunal, said this (at para. 12):

We entirely accept that, as this Tribunal has said in the past, it is important for industrial tribunals to be satisfied that the requirement is genuinely introduced for the reason which is put forward. It is certainly right to take into account all the circumstances and to balance the discriminatory effect of the requirement against the reasons adduced by the employer for introducing the requirement. It is right to take account of the effect which this will have - the retention or removal of the requirement both upon the man and the Company and, indeed, in a case like the present, upon the consumer in whose interest the requirement is introduced. We entirely accept that it is *prima facie* not enough merely for an employer to show that a requirement is introduced as a matter of convenience. Tribunals must, as this Tribunal clearly set out to do, look at all the circumstances of the case; but what they must ask is whether it has been shown, regardless of the colour or race of the person concerned, that it is justifiable in the sense of right and proper in the circumstances, that it should be adopted by the Company. We do not read what was said by this Tribunal in the earlier case as laying down a rule that the employer must show that it is necessary in the sense for which [counsel] has contended.

The Court of Appeal ([1980] IRLR 64) refused leave to appeal against this decision and upheld the approach set out by the appeal tribunal. This decision seems to leave the question whether any particular practice is justifiable to a large extent within the discretion of the industrial tribunal or court of first instance which has to make up its mind what is 'right and proper.'

Finally, since the conclusion of the argument in this case we have received the transcript of the judgments of the Court of Appeal in *Ojutiku* v. *Manpower Services Commission* ([1982] ICR 661). In that case the question arose whether the Manpower Services Commission could justify a requirement that those who they accepted for certain management courses should have previous managerial experience. It was accepted that such requirement indirectly discriminated against coloured immigrants. The Court of Appeal upheld the decision of the industrial tribunal and the Employment Appeal Tribunal that such requirement was justified. All the members of the Court of Appeal rejected the test of necessity laid down in the *Steel* case. Eveleigh LJ, though reluctant to lay down any interpretation of the word 'justifiable', said (at p. 668):

> ... it seems to me that if a person produces reasons for doing something, which would be acceptable to right-thinking people as sound and tolerable reasons for so doing, then he has justified his conduct.

Kerr LJ also declined to put any gloss on the word 'justifiable' but said that it clearly applied a lower standard than the word 'necessary.' Stephenson LJ took a rather more stringent approach. He adopted the approach in the *Singh* case and said this (at p. 674) of the decision in the *Steel* case:

> What Phillips J there said is valuable as rejecting justification by convenience and requiring the party applying the discriminatory condition to prove it to be justifiable in all the circumstances on balancing its discriminatory effect against the discriminator's need for it. But that need is what is reasonably needed by the party who applies the condition ... .

The *Panesar* case was not mentioned in the judgments of the Court of Appeal.

On the hearing of this appeal we heard an interesting argument as to the right test to apply in deciding whether a requirement was 'justified.' However, in view of the unanimous decision of the Court of Appeal in the *Ojutiku* case, it is not open to us to do anything other than to see whether the decision of the industrial tribunal in this case follows the principles set out by the Court of Appeal in the *Ojutiku* case. As it seems to us, the Court of Appeal has now unanimously laid down what is the correct approach in law. Although the *Panesar* case was not considered by the Court of Appeal in the *Ojutiku* case, in our view the Court of Appeal seems to be adopting the same approach as was adopted in the *Panesar* case. In the *Ojutiku* case a requirement was said to be justified (p. 668):

> ... if a person produces reasons for doing something, which would be acceptable to right-thinking people as sound and tolerable reasons for so doing.

This is much the same as the approach in the *Panesar* case: was it right and proper in the circumstances to adopt the requirement? In the present case the industrial tribunal, in deciding that the requirement was not justified, applied the test as laid down in the *Panesar* case. This test is the same as that subsequently adopted by the Court of Appeal and is the most favourable to the employers. Therefore there is no error in law in the approach of the industrial tribunal in deciding this aspect of the case.

In case this or some other matter goes to the House of Lords, we would express some apprehension as to the direction in which the decision of the courts are going on this issue. To decide whether some action is 'justifiable' requires a value judgment to be made. On emotive matters such as racial or sex discrimination there is no generally accepted view as to the comparative importance of eliminating discriminatory practices on the one hand as against, for example, the profitability of a business on the other. In these circumstances, to leave the matter effectively within the unfettered decision of the many industrial tribunals throughout the country, each reflecting their own approach to the relative importance of these matters, seems to us likely to lead to widely differing decisions being reached. In our view, the law should lay down the degree of importance to be attached to eliminating indirect discrimination (which will very often be unintentional) so that industrial tribunals will know how to strike the balance between the discriminatory effect of a requirement on the one hand and the reasons urged as justification for imposing it on the other.

In the course of argument Mr George emphasised the difficulties with which the company and other employers were faced. He said that, following the industrial tribunal's decision, the company had been considering whether they could for the future lawfully adopt even the time-hallowed formula of 'last in - first out' in making selection for redundancy. The fear is that it might be said that, by reason of child-bearing and other domestic commitments, fewer women than men might have long service and therefore the criterion of 'last in - first out' might be unlawfully discriminatory.

It is most undesirable in present circumstances where redundancies are, unhappily, an everyday event that there should be a doubt as to the question whether or not the formula 'last in - first out' is lawful. Therefore, although we cannot ourselves decide the point, it is right that we should indicate our view so as to give as much reassurance as possible. In our view, bearing in mind that Parliament has encouraged the making of redundancy agreements between employers and unions and that 'last in - first out' has for very many years been far the most commonly agreed criterion for selection, it would be right for an industrial tribunal to hold that the adoption of 'last in - first out' was a necessary means (viewed in a reasonable and common-sense way) of achieving a necessary objective, i.e., an agreed criterion for selection. Accordingly such 'need' outweighs the limited discriminatory effect of adopting the criterion 'last in - first out', if any. In our view, to select on the basis 'last in - first out' is quite different from selecting on the basis 'part-time workers first.' Although 'last in - first out' may have a limited discriminatory effect, taking part-time workers first is grossly discriminatory. In the present case, 100 per cent of part-time workers were women: nationally over 80 per cent of part-time workers are women. Therefore, in balancing the need for an agreed criterion for selection for redundancy against the discriminatory effect of the criterion adopted, the scales are quite differently loaded in the two cases.

5. *Has the industrial tribunal erred in law in finding justification not established?*

Having directed themselves in accordance with the test laid down in the *Panesar* case the industrial tribunal considered in great detail all the various factors relevant to this case. They took into account the fact that there was a need for a clearly defined redundancy selection policy; that the agreement was supported by the majority of the workers; that, because women full-time workers outnumbered the men full-time workers, the discrimination in fact was to the advantage of women rather than of men; that it was convenient to get rid of the part-time workers since that facilitated the closing of the evening shift; that for part-time workers to go first made it easier to arrange hours of availability for the machines to be used. Having considered all these matters they reached the conclusion that, although the company had acted honourably and although they had sympathy for them in the predicament in which they found themselves, they were unanimously of the view that the company had not discharged the burden placed on it under para. (ii).

On the approach adopted by the Court of Appeal in the *Panesar* case and the *Ojutiku* case, those findings are findings of fact, the tribunal having directed itself correctly in law. Mr George has taken us carefully through the tribunal's consideration of the factors which they bore in mind, criticising a number of them in terms of the weight which the industrial tribunal attached to them. But he has not suggested that anything was taken into account by the industrial tribunal which should not have been or had been left out of account which should have been considered by them. He suggests that we should hold their finding that there was no justification to be perverse.

Bearing in mind that this was an agreement for selection which was patently discriminatory against women and that the union were prepared to change such agreement at any time if it was said to be unlawful, it is impossible for us to say that the decision of the industrial tribunal was perverse. Indeed, we agree with the industrial tribunal's conclusion and reasoning which on this aspect of the case, like all others, is both detailed and cogent.

...

# Home Office v. Holmes[1]

MR JUSTICE WAITE: This appeal challenges the finding by an industrial tribunal that the requirement in a woman civil servant's contract of employment that she should work full-time for her department was potentially, and in the particular circumstances actually, discriminatory against her on the ground of her sex.

She was one of a group of executive officers of mixed sexes, all of whose contracts of employment required them to serve full-time. That this requirement of full-time service within their grade in that particular department was an absolute and inflexible one became plain when the department rejected her application, on family grounds, for a change from full-time to part-time status. The department said that the decision not to allow part-timers working within her grade was a departmental policy decision from which no departure would be allowed.

The employee's response to that was to complain to an industrial tribunal that this policy represented a discriminatory requirement in her contract of employment of a kind rendered unlawful by the Sex Discrimination Act 1975. The industrial tribunal upheld her claim, and the employing department now appeals to our appeal tribunal from that decision contending that the industrial tribunal have misconstrued the legislation.

The employee in question, Ms Holmes, is 40 years of age. In 1968 she joined the Post Office National Giro as a clerical officer but was soon promoted, upon her transfer the following year to the Home Office as an executive officer. She was still occupying that grade in 1973 when the Home Office placed her in their Immigration and Nationality Department at Croydon (normally abbreviated to 'INI'). The duties of INI are concerned, among other things, with the applications of people who have come here from abroad and wish to extend their residence permits.

Ms Holmes was one of 250 executive officers (men and women) engaged on the relevant case work. They were all required by the terms of their engagement to work full-time, i.e. in their grade within that department there were no part-time workers permitted at all. That did not provide the least source of difficulty to Ms Holmes until the autumn of 1975 when she became a mother. She now has two children and hers is a single parent family. She took maternity leave for the birth of her first child in November 1975, and arranged to return to work after her confinement, but she found in practice that her duties as a mother made it difficult and almost impossible for her to fulfil the hours required. In the period of some two years and eight months between November 1975 and June 1978 she was forced to take no less than two years and two months unpaid leave. But then she seems to have

---

1    [1985] 1 WLR 71, [1984] 3 All ER 549, [1984] ICR 678, [1984] IRLR 299 (EAT).

been able to resume her normal working, though only for a short time because in September 1981 her second child was born. She availed herself of her right to take leave of absence for that birth under the 1978 Act.[1]

On 6 January 1982 she notified the Home Office that she was proposing to return to work in mid-April. But she coupled that notification with a request. She asked that when she returned to work she should be allowed to come back on a part-time basis. We do not suppose she needed to elaborate upon the reasons for that: past experience must have made it plain. Her request was considered by the appropriate authorities, and the Establishments Division of the Home Office replied to her on 8 February 1982, telling her that her application to change her job from full-time to part-time was refused. The letter stated that within her grade in that department there were no part-time posts available and that she only had the right to return under the same contractual terms as before, i.e. to full-time employment.

In fact Ms Holmes came back to work rather earlier than she had anticipated. She was back again by 19 March 1982, but her return to full-time employment was obviously under both difficulty and protest, for very soon afterwards on 29 March she presented her originating application to the industrial tribunal complaining that the Home Office had unlawfully discriminated against her under ss 1 and 6 of the 1975 Act by keeping her to the requirement that she should serve them full-time. In fact, the following May she was forced to leave work for a substantial period of sick leave not returning until 8 November 1982.

In that same month (November) the first day of the industrial tribunal hearing took place, but that had to be adjourned to enable the Home Office witnesses to take instructions about certain material that Ms Holmes, then appearing in person, wished to lay before the tribunal in the form of reports and similar documentation dealing with opportunities for part-time employment within the civil service. At the resumed hearings of the tribunal in September and December 1983 both sides were represented by counsel, and the evidential background, including the material just mentioned, was very fully investigated.

In applying the law to the facts presented to them the industrial tribunal directed themselves by reference to ss 1 and 6 of the 1975 Act which they interpreted as posing a number of questions which it was their duty to answer consecutively. That seems to us to be an entirely proper approach and is not one that has been criticised as an approach by Mr Goldsmith representing the Home Office, although he has powerful criticisms to make of the result.

The first question the tribunal members asked themselves was this: did the requirement of full-time service in Ms Holmes's contract of employment

---

[1]    The Employment Protection (Consolidation) Act 1978.

amount to a requirement or condition? There was no dispute that if it did, it was one which applied or was applicable within her grade and her department equally to a man. The tribunal took the view, in answer to that question, that her obligation to serve full-time was, indeed, a condition or requirement within the terms of s. 1(1)(b) of the Act. They said it was an essential term of her engagement because unless she went on working full-time she would not be allowed to continue in her job.

The second question they asked themselves was whether this requirement or condition (i.e. the requirement of full-time service) was such that the proportion of women who could comply with it is considerably smaller than the proportion of men who could comply with it. They reached the answer to that one unhesitatingly. It was yes; and the reason was that despite the changes in the role of women in modern society, it is still a fact that the raising of children tends to place a greater burden upon them than it does upon men.

Next, they posed for themselves the question whether the Home Office had been able to show the requirement or condition to be justifiable irrespective of the sex of the person to whom it was applied. This question brought them into that area of detailed evidence which we have already mentioned. They very carefully considered departmental reports and other relevant data and statistics including the recommendations emanating from a joint review group established by the Civil Service National Whitley Council. They heard on this same issue, too, the oral evidence on the Home Office side of two senior representatives; and on Ms Holmes's side the evidence of her union representative and herself. Their finding was that, in all the circumstances, they had no hesitation in preferring the evidence on those issues put forward on behalf of Ms Holmes, and they therefore found that the Home Office had been unable to show the requirement or condition of full-time service to be a justifiable one.

Then the industrial tribunal turned to the last of the questions demanded of them by s. 1 of the Act. They asked themselves whether the requirement or condition of full-time service was to her detriment because she could not comply with it. That was an issue on which very little evidence was required, and they expressed their finding briefly. They took the view that the requirement was to her detriment and that she could not comply with it; adding the comment that her parental responsibilities prevented her carrying out a normal full-time week's work, and that in trying to fulfil all of these at the same time she had had to suffer excessive demands on her time and energy.

But that did not exhaust the line of self-interrogation imposed upon the tribunal by the Act, for having been satisfied as to the matters raised by s. 1, they were then required to turn to s. 6 of the Act which contains the definition of unlawful discrimination within an employment context.

Subsection (2) of that section renders it unlawful for a person, in the case of a woman employee, to discriminate against her in a number of ways which, it is common ground, are not applicable to this case, but then goes on to say 'by dismissing her, or subjecting her to any other detriment.'

Ms Holmes, of course, was never dismissed. So the tribunal had to ask whether the Home Office had, within the terms of the section, subjected her to any other detriment. Again without hesitation, they answered that question by saying that she had been so subjected. They said it was all one and the same detriment. She was being compelled to do a duty with which she could not, in the circumstances, comply.

Having thus arrived at an affirmative answer to all the questions they posed themselves down the line of self-enquiry, the industrial tribunal came to the conclusion that a case of unlawful discrimination on the ground of Ms Holmes's sex was made out. They did not deal in their reserved decision, announced on 12 January 1984, with the issue of remedy. That, should the appeal be unsuccessful, will have to be dealt with at a further hearing unless it can be settled.

Mr Goldsmith attacks the basis of the industrial tribunal's reasoning by charging them in two respects with having misconstrued the statute. First, he contends that it is quite wrong to describe anything so fundamental as a servant's duty of full-time service as a requirement or condition of the kind contemplated by the 1975 Act; and second, he asserts that the tribunal had become hopelessly confused by the two concepts of detriment involved by the use of that term in s. 1 and 6 respectively.

In support of his first submission, Mr Goldsmith urges that full-time service is not a matter which sounds in condition or requirement at all. It is the whole job. It is not a term of the job. It is *the* job. Part-time service, he says, is not a variant of full-time service. It is a different job. 'Requirement' or 'condition' are terms which, properly regarded in their statutory context, denote some hurdle, qualification or obstacle placed in the way of the employee. They are not apt, he says, to describe anything so fundamental as the duty of service in general or the duty of full-time service in particular.

We have not felt able to accept that argument. It appears to us that words like 'requirement' and 'condition' are plain, clear words of wide import fully capable of including any obligation of service whether for full or for part time, and we see no basis for giving them a restrictive interpretation in the light of the policy underlying the Act, or in the light of public policy as reflected in a later submission of Mr Goldsmith's to which we shall be referring shortly.

In support of his second criticism of the industrial tribunal's self-direction, Mr Goldsmith points to the different contexts in which 'detriment' is mentioned in s. 1(1)(b)(iii) on the one hand, and in s. 6(2)(b) on the other. In the first case, the detriment is of a restricted kind. The 'requirement' under attack will only be detrimental if it can be shown that the woman employee cannot, in the circumstances, comply with it. Contrast that, says Mr Goldsmith, with the reference to detriment in s. 6(2)(b) where it is referred to in the widest terms as 'any other detriment.' Parliament, he argues, cannot have intended a double detriment. If a detriment of the restricted kind has to be shown under s. 1(1)(b)(iii), if the sting of discrimination is to bite at all, then surely, as a matter of common sense as well as logical statutory interpretation, the detriment referred to in s. 6(2)(b) must be a detriment of some different kind. One cannot, he says, have a double detriment composed of one and the same disadvantage.

That, again, is an argument which, for all its sophistication and ingenuity, we have found ourselves unable to accept. We regard it as entirely consistent with the scheme and language of the Act that the same disadvantage to a woman employee may be relied on to found the detriment of incapacity under s. 1 as to qualify under the broader head of detriment under s. 6. That is not to say that there may not be cases in which, upon the facts, the head of detriment may turn out to be different in the one case from the other. We say only that there appears to us to be no basis for criticising a tribunal which has decided that the detriment is the same in both instances.

In addition to those major arguments, Mr Goldsmith had two points which he pressed less strenuously. The first was that this is a case of a mother returning to work after the birth of her second child. That, he says, is a situation for which a complete legislative code has been laid down by the 1978 Act, and accordingly it would be wrong in principle to construe the 1975 Act as enlarging upon a mother's rights under that code.

We find that argument, with respect, artificial. Had Ms Holmes waited until after she had returned to work to make her application for a change to part-time status instead of making that application before she returned, the position would not, in our view, be materially different. The substance of the matter has to be looked at under the 1975 Act without regard to the limited and special rights afforded to mothers over the period of confinement, and shortly thereafter, by the Act of 1978.

Finally, Mr Goldsmith raised a point which was not introduced in the notice of appeal but Mr Hendy, for Ms Holmes, had not sought to stand in the way of its being argued. Without wishing in any way to reopen the complex evidence that was heard by the industrial tribunal on the issue of justification, Mr Goldsmith roundly submits that the tribunal's conclusion that the requirement or condition of full-time service in Ms Holmes's contract of employment had not been shown to be justifiable for the purposes of s. 1(1)(b)(ii) was a perverse conclusion. His ground for urging that is the following: the bulk of industry in this country and, in very large measure, the national and local government service is still organised upon the basis of full-time employment. The requirement in a particular case that a woman employee should serve her master full-time is therefore, he contends, self-evidently a justified requirement which needs no assistance from evidence to support it.

We applaud the courage of that submission, but cannot accept its correctness. It seems to us that the issue whether in a particular case a requirement as to length of service was justified or no is precisely the line of enquiry that Parliament intended to entrust to the industrial tribunals by the schemes and language of the 1975 Act.

Those were the grounds urged in support of the appeal. They have not, in our estimation, succeeded and it follows that the appeal will be dismissed. But before parting from the case, there is one comment we feel we should add in response to a final submission of general import that was addressed to us by Mr Goldsmith.

The scheme of the anti-discrimination legislation involves casting a wide net throwing upon employers the onus of justifying the relevant requirement or condition in particular instances. One must be careful, however, not to fall into the error of assuming that because the net is wide, the catch will necessarily be large. Mr Goldsmith eloquently invited us to envisage the shock to British industry and to our national and local government administration which, he submitted, would be bound to be suffered if, in addition to all their other problems, they now had to face a shoal of claims by women full-time workers alleging that it would be discriminatory to refuse them part-time status. In answer to that we emphasise, as did the industrial tribunal in the last sentence of their decision, that this one case of Ms Holmes and her particular difficulties within her particular grade in her particular department stands very much upon its own. It is easy to imagine other instances, not strikingly different where the result would not be the same. There will be cases where the requirement for full-time staff can be shown to be sufficiently flexible as arguably not to amount to a requirement or condition at all. There will be cases where a policy favouring full-time staff exclusively within a particular grade or department is found to be justified. There will be cases where no actual or no sufficient detriment can be proved by the employee. All such cases will turn upon their own particular facts. We only decide today that in this case the industrial tribunal were right, in our view, in saying that a case of unlawful discrimination had been made out.

# Horsey v. Dyfed County Council[1]

MR JUSTICE BROWNE-WILKINSON: Mrs Horsey claims that she has been unlawfully discriminated against by her employers, Dyfed County Council ('the County Council') on the grounds either of her sex or of her marital status. She brought a complaint before the industrial tribunal under the Sex Discrimination Act 1975. The industrial tribunal dismissed her complaint. She appeals to this appeal tribunal.

Mrs Horsey was brought up in Wales. In 1972 she went to Aberystwyth College of the University of Wales where she graduated in 1975. Whilst at that college she met her husband, Mr Christopher Horsey. After she graduated, she held various posts with local authorities in Wales until September 1977. In 1976, Mr Horsey took a job with British Rail at Cardiff. They married in March 1977.

In September 1977, she started a two-year social work course at Stirling University. Her husband then obtained a transfer to work with British Rail at Stirling. In March 1978, he gave up that job and started to train as a librarian in Stirling.

In September 1978, Mrs Horsey applied for a job with the county council as a trainee social worker. She and her husband were both keen to return to Dyfed. The appointment required that she should first work as a social worker but within one year should apply for and subsequently attend a social service course at a university or polytechnic. The course was to be paid for by the county council who would also pay her wages. She had to undertake that on completing her training she would return to work for the county council for a period of at least two years. Before accepting Mrs Horsey, the county council closely questioned her about her intention to return to the county council at the conclusion of her training.

Mrs Horsey took up the job with the county council in October 1979. She signed a contract which included her undertaking to return. At about the same time, her husband started a one-year post-graduate librarian course at Aberystwyth College. Mr and Mrs Horsey set up their home at Aberystwyth. In pursuance of her contractual obligation, in January 1980 Mrs Horsey started to apply for social service courses. On 18 June 1980 she received an offer of a two-year course at Hull. In mid-June 1980, her husband was appointed to a permanent post as librarian at the House of Commons in London. On 2 July 1980, Mrs Horsey received a further offer for a two-year course at Maidstone. She wished to accept the offer from Maidstone as this would enable her to live with her husband in the London area. She therefore applied to the county council for secondment to the course at Maidstone.

---

1    [1982] ICR 755, [1982] IRLR 395 (EAT).

Her case was considered by certain officers of the county council who satisfied themselves that, at the end of the course, Mrs Horsey would honour her obligation to return to work for the county council for two years. However, she had an interview with Mr Dewi Evans, the deputy director of social services, who informed her that he could not recommend her secondment to the course at least in that year. The industrial tribunal find that 'his expressed reason' for this decision 'was that he thought in view of the fact that her husband had obtained full-time permanent employment in the House of Commons that she would probably not return to serve two years with the Council at the termination of the course.' Prior to the hearing before the industrial tribunal, the solicitors for the parties had reached an agreement that at the hearing the county council would admit 'that the principal factor in the question in the decision by your Council to refuse secondment to [Mrs Horsey] was because [Mrs Horsey's] husband had been appointed to a post in the library of the House of Commons and that subsequently [Mrs Horsey] was unlikely to return to work for the Council upon completion of her course.'

The county council accordingly did not second Mrs Horsey to the course at Maidstone. She therefore resigned her post with effect from 15 September 1980 and took employment as a social worker in London.

Mrs Horsey complains that the refusal to second her to the Maidstone course unlawfully discriminated against her on the grounds of her sex or alternatively on the grounds of her marital status.

...

The industrial tribunal held that there was no evidence to suggest that Mrs Horsey had been discriminated against on the grounds of sex. They relied on statistics which showed that the majority of those seconded to training courses in the year 1980 were women. They further held that the reason for Mr Evans's refusing secondment was simply his doubt whether Mrs Horsey would return, not her married status. They say this:

> In our opinion the reason for Mr Evans's decision was not that Mrs Horsey was married but because, with good reason, he felt she would not return, because quite understandably, at the end of her course, she would decide to remain in the London area. He was not concerned with the reasons why she might come to such a decision. Such reasons could have been manifold. The one of which he was aware was that she would probably want to remain with someone in London. Her status, whether married or single, had nothing to do with the matter.

On the appeal, Mr Price (for Mrs Horsey) submitted that in dealing with the claim based on sex discrimination the industrial tribunal had not applied their minds to the right question. He submitted that by reason of s. 5(3)[1] the industrial tribunal should have compared the treatment of Mrs Horsey as a

---

1    Sex Discrimination Act 1975, s. 5(3).

married woman with that of a married man, since the fact that she was married was one of the 'relevant circumstances' to be taken into account. Then, he submitted that Mr Evans would not have applied to a married man the same assumption that he applied to Mrs Horsey, i.e. he would not return to Dyfed but stay with his wife at the place of her work. On the issue of discrimination on the grounds of marital status, Mr Price submitted that the finding of the industrial tribunal and the concession made by the county council which we have read show that the reason for doubting Mrs Horsey's intention to return was that she was married to Mr Horsey whose work was elsewhere, not that there was 'someone with whom she wanted to remain.' It was the fact of the marriage, not any other tie, which held Mr Evans to the view that she would stay in London.

Mr Griffiths (for the county council), in a conspicuously able argument, submitted that on the claim of sex discrimination there was no evidence that Mr Evans would have treated a married man any differently from the way he treated Mrs Horsey. He submitted that, in claims under s. 1, the married status of the complainant was not one of the 'relevant circumstances' to be taken into account under s. 5(3): he submitted that marital status is dealt with exclusively and separately by s. 1(2) and s. 3 of the Act. Although Mr Griffiths admitted that Mr Evans reached his conclusion because he assumed that, as a married woman, Mrs Horsey would live with her husband, he submitted that that was not the relevant point. In order to show that an act is done 'on the ground' of sex or marital status it is not enough to show that the sex of the complainant or the fact of marriage was part of the story: it has to be shown that her sex or marital status was the activating cause of Mr Evans's decision, the *causa sine qua non*. He relied on the decision in *Seide* v. *Gillette Industries Ltd* [1980] IRLR 427. In this case, said Mr Griffiths, the activating cause of Mr Evans's decision was not Mrs Horsey's sex or marital status but Mr Evans's doubt whether Mrs Horsey would return. He submitted that two matters showed that Mrs Horsey's sex or married status were not the decisive factors. If Mrs Horsey had been married to a man whose job was at Aberystwyth, there would have been no trouble. Contrariwise, if Mrs Horsey had not been married to Mr Horsey but simply living with him as man and wife on a permanent basis, Mr Evans's decision would have been just the same as if they were married. All this, said Mr Griffiths, showed that the activating cause of the decision was not Mrs Horsey's sex or married status: they were the context not the cause of the decision.

We have not found this an easy case to decide. Before dealing with these specific submissions made by the parties, there are certain general considerations which apply to discrimination under either s. 1 or s. 3 of the Act. Under both s. 1 and 3 of the Act (and also the corresponding provisions of s. 1 of the Race Relations Act 1976) unlawful discrimination consists in treating someone less favourably 'on the ground of' sex, marital status or race. Do those words cover only cases where the sex, marital status or race of the complainant in isolation is the reason for the decision, or do they extend to cover cases where the alleged discriminator acts on the basis of generalised assumptions as to the characteristics of women or married or coloured persons? In our view it is now established by authority that those words do not only cover cases where the sole factor influencing the decision of the alleged discriminator is the sex, marital status or race of the complainant. The words 'on the ground of' also cover cases where the reason for the discrimination was a generalised assumption that people of a particular sex, marital status or race possess or lack certain characteristics, e.g. 'I like women but I will not employ them because they are unreliable', 'I will not lend money to married women because they are not wage earners', or 'I will not employ coloured men because they are lazy.' Most discrimination flows from generalised assumptions of this kind and not from a simple prejudice dependent solely on the sex or colour of the complainant. The purpose of the legislation is to secure equal opportunity for individuals regardless of their sex, married status or race. This result would not be achieved if it were sufficient to escape liability to show that the reason for the discriminatory treatment was simply an assumption that women or coloured persons possessed or lacked particular characteristics and not that they were just women or coloured persons. The decision of the Court of Appeal in *Skyrail Oceanic Ltd* v. *Coleman* [1981] ICR 864 established that generalised assumptions of this kind constitute discrimination under the Acts: see also *Hurley* v. *Mustoe* [1981] ICR 490.

We turn to consider the particular submissions of the parties. In our view it is necessary to analyse the factors which led Mr Evans to refuse Mrs Horsey's secondment. They are as follows:
(a)  the fact that she was married;
(b)  the fact that her husband had a permanent job in London;
(c)  the assumption that married persons will want to live together;
(d)  the assumption that, in order to be able to live together, the husband would not move and seek a different job in Wales but the wife would follow her husband's job and live in London.
Therefore:
(e)  Mrs Horsey would not honour her undertaking.

If that analysis is correct, it seems to us that Mr Evans's decision was at least in part based on the generalised assumption that married women follow their husbands' jobs. In our view, s. 5(3) does require that, when considering the claim under s. 1, the tribunal has to compare the treatment of Mrs Horsey with the treatment which would have been afforded to a married man. We reject the submission that the presence of s. 1(2) and s. 3 in the Act forces one to exclude marriage as a relevant circumstance in considering cases under s. 1(1). In our view, s. 1(2) was inserted to make it clear that in the case specifically dealt with (i.e. different treatment of the comparable man according to his marital status) marital status is to be taken into account. The existence of that provision does not cut down the effect of the general words in s. 5(3) and on any reasonable interpretation of those words the question whether the woman is married must be a relevant circumstance.

As to the submission that there was no evidence that Mr Evans would have treated a married man differently from the way he treated Mrs Horsey, it is true that there was no direct evidence to that effect. However, in our view it is an inescapable inference from his approach to Mrs Horsey's case. Mrs Horsey had a permanent job with the county council in Wales; her husband had a permanent job at the House of Commons in London. Mr Evans assumed that Mr Horsey would not give up his job to join his wife, but that Mrs Horsey would give up her job to join her husband, i.e. he had made a general assumption on the basis of her sex that she would follow her husband's job and not *vice versa*. If Mr Evans had looked at the facts of this particular case instead of making that assumption he would have discovered a different pattern, namely that on two occasions Mr Horsey had followed his wife, i.e. he left Cardiff to join her at Stirling and left Stirling to join her at Aberystwyth.

In our view, therefore, the position is as follows. Under s. 1(1) one has to see whether on the ground of sex Mr Evans treated Mrs Horsey differently from the way he would have treated a comparable man. Mrs Horsey being married, under s. 5(3) the comparable man must also be taken to be a married man. Having assumed that Mrs Horsey would give up her permanent job to join her husband and that a married man (e.g. Mr Horsey) would not give up his permanent job to join his wife, Mr Evans has made a different assumption dependent upon the sex of the person under consideration. Therefore he has discriminated against Mrs Horsey on the grounds of her sex.

As to Mr Griffith's argument that this discriminatory assumption was not the activating cause of Mr Evans's decision, it is true that Mr Evans reached his decision because of his belief that Mrs Horsey would not return to Wales. But the assumption that she would follow her husband's job (and not *vice versa*) was an essential part of the reasoning which led Mr Evans to the belief that she would not return. In our view, a decision to treat a complainant in a particular way for reasons which, as an essential ingredient, contain a generalised assumption about a woman's behaviour is a decision made 'on the ground of' her sex. This case is not the same as that which was considered in *Seide* v. *Gillette*. In that case, Mr Seide alleged unlawful racialist conduct towards him by employee A. The employers therefore moved Mr Seide to work with employee B. Employee B was not himself guilty of any racialist conduct towards Mr Seide but was unhappy because he was involved in the continuing dispute between employee A and Mr Seide. Employee B therefore asked to be moved and the employers decided to move him. This tribunal held that the racialist conduct of employee A was not the activating cause of the decision to move Mr Seide for a second time away from employee B. The past act of unlawful discrimination by employee A had led to a state of affairs which required a further decision to be taken, which further decision was taken on grounds free of any discriminatory element. In such a case it is legitimate to consider the earlier act of discrimination as not being an activating cause of the second decision: it was part of the history but not a reason for the decision. The present case is quite different. There is only one decision under consideration. In reaching that decision an unlawful discriminatory assumption was a necessary part of Mr Evans's reasoning. It is impossible in such a case to say that such assumption was not an activating cause.

We consider that this case is indistinguishable from the principle applied by the Court of Appeal in the *Skyrail* case. In that case, the complainant was married to a man employed in a business which competed with that of the complainant's employer. The employer and competitor were both anxious lest by reason of the marriage there might be a leakage of confidential information and agreed that either the complainant or the husband would have to be dismissed. The employer dismissed the complainant 'as the husband was presumably the breadwinner.' The majority of the Court of Appeal held that she had been discriminated against on the grounds of her sex since the employer had assumed that the husband and not she was the breadwinner. Apart from the fact that the general assumption made by the employer in that case was different from the general assumption made by Mr Evans in this case, the two cases are indistinguishable. The direct reason for the decision in the *Skyrail* case was, not the sex of the complainant, but the fear of the leakage of confidential information: yet because the decision to dismiss her was reached on the basis of a discriminatory assumption, the decision was unlawful. So in this case, the direct reason for Mr Evans's decision to refuse Mrs Horsey secondment was, not Mrs Horsey's sex, but the opinion that she would not return: yet, because the decision to refuse Mrs Horsey's secondment was reached on the basis of an unlawful assumption as to a married woman's conduct, the decision was unlawful.

For these reasons, in our view Mrs Horsey was unlawfully discriminated against on the grounds of her sex and the decision of the industrial tribunal was wrong. In the circumstances it is unnecessary for us to consider whether she was discriminated against on the ground of her marriage status. We will allow the appeal.

To avoid doubt as to the effect of this decision, we are not deciding that an employer can never act on the basis that a wife will give up her job to join her husband. Current social attitudes demonstrate that frequently (but not invariably) a married couple will decide that the wife will give up her job in such circumstances. All that we are deciding in this case is that an employer cannot lawfully *assume* that a married woman will make that decision: the employer must look at the particular circumstances of each case and form his view as to the probabilities on the circumstances of that case and not on the basis of any general assumption.

## Page *v*. Freight Hire (Tank Haulage) Ltd[1]

MR JUSTICE SLYNN: Mrs Page was employed by Freight Hire (Tank Haulage) Ltd as a heavy goods vehicle driver. She is approximately 23 years of age. When she began to work for the employers it appears that she concentrated mainly on the driving of vehicles for relatively short routes. She worked on a regular basis from approximately June 1979 until September 1979, when, because of a shortage of work, her contract of employment was terminated.

Subsequently, she was asked to work on a casual daily basis, to drive when there was a need for her services. On 5 October 1979, she was told that one of the drivers employed on a regular basis had broken his leg, and she was asked to come on a casual daily basis but more frequently than she had in the past. One of the jobs that she was asked to do involved hauling chemicals between chemical plants in the Cleveland area; one of those was a chemical called dimethylformamide ('DMF') which is made by ICI Ltd.

On 17 October 1979, Mrs Page took a load of DMF from one of the ICI petrochemical works. Two days later, a senior manager from the Petrochemicals Division of ICI Ltd telephoned Mrs Lewis, the wife of the managing director of the employers, to say that because of the danger to women of child-bearing age Mrs Page must not be used on the haulage of that product again. Accordingly, the employers decided that they would not let her drive the vehicle which was carrying DMF.

She apparently said initially that she had been dismissed. She brought a claim alleging that there had been discrimination against her contrary to s. 1 of the Sex Discrimination Act 1975. The industrial tribunal which heard the case decided that she had not been dismissed but that she had been told that she would not be allowed to carry this particular chemical and, as a result, she had decided that she no longer wished to be employed by the employers. The tribunal found that in an interview with Mr Lewis she had made her position very clear: she had said that she knew of the dangers of DMF but that she was prepared both to accept them and to provide the employers with some form of indemnity.

The industrial tribunal concluded that there had been discrimination against her on the ground of her sex. They found that she was refused the opportunity of delivering this chemical because she was a woman, and that a male employee would have been allowed to continue carrying DMF. However, they took the view, on the basis of what was said in *Automotive Products Ltd* v. *Peake* [1978] QB 233, that it was an answer for an employer to show that what had been done was done in the interests of safety or in the interests of good administration. They decided that what the Court of Appeal

---

1    [1981] 1 All ER 394, [1981] ICR 299 (EAT).

had held there was not affected by the decision of the Court of Appeal in *Ministry of Defence* v. *Jeremiah* [1980] QB 87, and they were satisfied that what had been done here was in the interests of safety and that, accordingly, although there was discrimination there was here no breach of the statute.

The danger which was referred to with regard to this particular chemical was the subject matter of a certain amount of evidence before the tribunal. A document had been issued by ICI, headed with the name of the chemical, which referred to a number of precautions which ought to be taken by those concerned in the handling of the material. In addition, there was another document which bore the same title and referred to a number of hazards to personnel which were possible health risks. Some of those could have affected both men and women, i.e. loss of appetite, intestinal disorders, the possible effect on the liver, the stomach and the kidneys. The document also contained this statement:

> Recent publications have suggested that there may be an embryotoxic effect at levels of exposure greater than the Threshold Limit Value.

That was said to be ten parts per million in this particular product. It went on:

> Precautionary measures must therefore be rigorously applied when women of child-bearing age are likely to be exposed to the material. Regular monitoring of the atmosphere is essential.

Mrs Page admitted that she did know of the dangers before she began to carry this material in the middle of October 1979. It was her view, on what she had been told, about this product, that it was potentially harmful to women of child-bearing age. It appears, from the evidence which she gave, that she may have thought that this was capable of producing sterility in a woman. Evidence was given by a Mr Wilkinson as to what he understood the position to be. He had been a driver but was employed as a fitter. He said that he knew that if the vapour of this chemical was absorbed it could make one sterile. He thought that it affected men and women, that both were at risk of sterility.

Quite clearly the only evidence which was before the tribunal on which they could place any reliance was that contained in the second document to which we have referred. That indicates, not so much that there was a danger of sterility, but that there may be an effect on the foetus of a pregnant woman, that the dangerous effects of this particular chemical do not affect men.

But the issue arose because of the telephone call from the manager of ICI to which we have referred. On the evidence of Mrs Lewis it is quite clear that she said that he had told her that, because of the danger to women of child-bearing age, Mrs Page must not be used in the haulage of the product again. Mr Lewis's own evidence was, perhaps, not quite so specific. He said, from the notes of evidence taken by the chairman, that he was told that ICI did not allow women to come into contact with DMF. The note taken by the solicitor for Mrs Page in this case, which we have been invited to look at with the consent of both parties, is that Mr Lewis was not told by his wife specifically that ICI were banning women from driving. It is, however, quite clear that Mrs Lewis was saying that she had been told that they must not use Mrs Page to drive the vehicles which carried this particular chemical.

On this appeal, counsel for Mrs Page has submitted that the tribunal were quite wrong in deciding that considerations of safety were an answer to the allegations of discrimination, that, once the tribunal had found that there was discrimination, that really was the end of the case. He submits that the tribunal were wrong to say that the statements of the Court of Appeal in *Automotive Products Ltd* v. *Peake* still stood; they have been affected by the decision in *Ministry of Defence* v. *Jeremiah*.

If one turns to the decision in *Automotive Products Ltd* v. *Peake*, it is plain that Lord Denning MR (with whom, as we understand it, both the other judges, but particularly Goff LJ, agreed) was saying that arrangements which are made in the interests of safety or of good administration are not infringements of the law, even though they may be more favourable to women than to men, or conversely, more favourable to men than to women. When one comes to the decision in *Ministry of Defence* v. *Jeremiah* Lord Denning MR in his judgment, referred to the fact that good administrative arrangements and safety had been put forward as a justification for what was otherwise discrimination on the grounds of sex.

Brandon LJ did not express any views either way about the matter. Accordingly he is not to be taken as agreeing with Lord Denning MR.

Brightman LJ did not expressly refer to the decision in the *Peake* case, or to what effect the decision in the *Jeremiah* case was intended to have on what had been said there. He did say this ([1980] QB 87 at p. 103):

The question is whether the employer's solicitude towards females workers is unlawful under the Sex Discrimination Act 1975. I think it is.

He then went on to deal with the section. Reading his judgment as a whole, it seems to us that he was in substance intending to agree with Lord Denning MR in regarding the two reasons which were put forward in the *Peake* case as being a sufficient answer.

It seems to us that in this legislation, as has been said on an earlier occasion by Bridge LJ in *Shields* v. *E. Coomes (Holdings) Ltd* [1978] 1 WLR. 1408 (which is referred to in *Greig* v. *Community Industry* [1979] ICR 356 at p. 360, that the exceptions to the provisions which define what is a breach of the Sex Discrimination Act 1975 are to be found only in the sections of the Act itself, in particular, s. 7. It would seem to us, therefore, that this tribunal did err in regarding the interests of safety in itself as an answer to the case once they had found that there was discrimination.

But that is not the end of the case. Section 51(1) of the 1975 Act provides as follows:

> Nothing in Parts II to IV shall render unlawful any act done by a person if it was necessary for him to do it in order to comply with a requirement -
> a)    of an Act passed before this Act ....

The rest of the subsection is not relevant for present purposes.

The one Act which was in existence before the 1975 Act was passed was the Health and Safety at Work etc. Act 1974 which provides, in s. 2:

> (1)    It shall be the duty of every employer to ensure, so far as is reasonably practicable, the health, safety and welfare at work of all his employees.
> (2)    Without prejudice to the generality of an employer's duty under the preceding subsection, the matters to which that duty extends include in particular ...
> (b)    arrangements ensuring, so far as is reasonably practicable, safety and absence of risks to health in connection with the use, handling, storage and transport of articles and substances ... .

In this case it is submitted on behalf of Mrs Page that there was insufficient evidence here of the sort of hazard which could possibly justify the barring of her from driving a vehicle which carried this particular chemical. That view is supported by counsel who has appeared on behalf of the Equal Opportunities Commission and whom, with the consent of both parties, we invited to make submissions to us following a practice which had previously (we are told) been followed in the Court of Appeal when the Equal Opportunities Commission desired to put submissions before the court on a question arising under the 1975 Act. We felt it was right to accede to the application of the Equal Opportunities Commission that they should make submissions today, in particular because of the provisions of s. 55 of the 1975 Act which impose on the Commission statutory duties dealing with health and safety.

Counsel for the Equal Opportunities Commission and, indeed, counsel for Mrs Page have submitted that the proper approach here is to ask oneself: was it necessary for the employer to do what he did in order to comply with the requirements of the Health and Safety at Work etc. Act 1974? Counsel for the Commission submits that, as a matter of principle, it has to be shown that there is no other way of protecting a woman (or a man, in a case where a man is involved) other than by debarring her (or him) from taking up a job. He says that, when the matter is considered as a whole, the conclusion must inexorably lead to a need to debar the individual from doing the job, otherwise it cannot be said that it is necessary for the purposes of satisfying the requirements of the 1974 Act.

It seems to us that it is clearly right that it is not an answer, under s. 51(1) of the 1975 Act, for an employer to say:

> There was a risk and, accordingly, I am not going to allow you, a woman (or, in the appropriate case, you, a man), to do this particular job because you, a woman (or, if there is such a case, you, a man) are particularly vulnerable to risk because of your sex.

It is important to consider all the circumstances of the case, to consider the risk involved and the measures which it can be said are reasonably necessary to eliminate the risk. It may well be that the wishes of the person whom it is desired to protect give a factor. Here it was said that Mrs Page did not want to have a child and did not anticipate becoming pregnant, as she was divorced. We accept that the individual's wishes may be a factor to be looked at, although, in our judgment, where the risk is to the woman, of sterility, or to the foetus, whether actually in existence or likely to come into existence in the future, these wishes cannot be a conclusive factor.

We feel that the counsel for the Commission has put the matter too high. It does not seem to us that an employer, in order to satisfy the test of s. 51 of the 1975 Act (read with s. 2 of the 1974 Act) has to show that inexorably this was the only method available to him. It is to be remembered that the duty is to ensure, so far as is reasonably practicable, the health, safety and welfare at work of employees. It seems to us that there may well be cases where one course (which is suggested as being sufficient) may leave open some doubt whether it is going to achieve the desired level of protection. In such a case it may well be that an employer is complying with the requirements of the legislation if, in all the circumstances, he thinks it right not to allow an employee, for his (or her) own protection or safety, to do the particular job at all.

It is said here that the matter was not gone into in the kind of detail which was called for on the part of the employer, or alternatively that the tribunal itself should have gone into the matter in much greater detail. It is, as we have said on many occasions, for the tribunal to probe into the facts and material before them to see whether there is discrimination or not. But it does not seem to us that, once discrimination is established, it really is for the tribunal itself (as has been suggested here) to ensure that all the scientific information which might be relevant is brought before the tribunal. The tribunal has to decide the matter on the evidence which is there.

The question in this case is whether we can be satisfied, first, that the attitude of this tribunal would have been on the facts which they found had s. 51 of the 1975 Act been specifically in mind, and, secondly, whether those facts are sufficient, on the material before the tribunal, to justify the reliance of the employers on s. 51. If one looked simply at the second document to which we have referred, it might be that the employers would not satisfy that burden, because there it is said:

> Precautionary measures must be rigorously applied when women of child-bearing age are likely to be exposed to the material.

But that was not the whole of the material before the tribunal. The employers gave evidence of this very clear warning, indeed, direction, from ICI, the manufacturers of the substance, that a woman of child-bearing age could not with safety be concerned with the transport of this particular chemical. It seems to us that, on that direction from the manufacturers, and with that warning, the employers *prima facie* were entitled to say:

> Well, the only way in which we can ensure, so far as is reasonably practicable, the safety of this woman is not to allow her to drive a vehicle which is carrying this particular chemical, even if she is going to drive other vehicles.

If there had been material which suggested that this was an act of excessive caution on the part of the employers, that it really was being used as a device to prevent Mrs Page from being employed, then the situation would be very different. But it would appear here that, on the material, this tribunal was very concerned with the question of safety: its members attached great importance to what they described as 'the arrangement dictated by ICI'. Although they put it on the basis of the *Peake* case, it seems quite plain that, had they had their attentions drawn to s. 51 of the 1975 Act and to the provisions in detail of the Health and Safety at Work etc. Act 1974, they would have concluded that what was done was necessary in order for the company to comply with a requirement of the 1974 Act on the information which the company had before them at that particular time. Since there was no evidence to suggest that any other course was a sufficient form of protection for Mrs Page (who was clearly still potentially of child-bearing age, despite the fact that she was, at the time, divorced) it seems to us that the tribunal must have come to that particular conclusion.

It is said by counsel, on behalf of the employers, that in any event there is no finding by the tribunal that Mrs Page had suffered a detriment. Accordingly, he says that, if we be wrong on the view to which we have come on the first two points, in any event Mrs Page must fail. He says that all the tribunal decided was that there had been discrimination contrary to s. 1 of the 1975 Act in that she was treated less favourably than a man would have been treated. But he says that that is not enough: it is essential, for a claim of this kind to succeed, that one of the paragraphs of s. 6 of the 1975 Act should be satisfied. The only one that was relevant here was s. 6(2)(b), namely, the subjecting of Mrs Page to 'any other detriment'. He says that in the absence of a finding of a detriment the matter is concluded against her.

Even assuming that what has to be done, in a case of this kind, is a balancing of the detriment against the advantages which flow from it, it seems to us that (although the matter is not expressly dealt with) this tribunal was quite clearly intending to decide here that there had been a subjecting to a detriment, that, when they read ss 1 and 6 of the Act together and then said that they were satisfied that there had been a discrimination on the ground of sex, they were intending to include the finding of a detriment, as well as a finding under s. 1 of the 1975 Act. Accordingly, we do not accept the submissions put forward on behalf of the company on that second point. We consider that the tribunal came to the right conclusion, albeit on a different basis from that at which we have arrived.

It is important to bear in mind that we are here dealing with a case where the only evidence on which reliance can be placed was that there was a danger of embryotoxic effects at certain levels of exposure. This is not a case (despite the evidence given by Mr Wilkinson) where the tribunal had to decide what would happen if both men and women were subjected to the same kind of risk and the employers had decided that it was more desirable to protect the woman than to protect the man; wholly different considerations would arise in that kind of case. Here we are not concerned with a situation where a man's ability to procreate is involved; and it does not seem to us to be material in any way that both men and woman were liable to be affected by this chemical in other ways, i.e. in relation to their digestive organs, their liver and so on. That is a very different matter, and the only relevant aspect of the case is that with which we have been concerned.

Accordingly, in all the circumstances, it seems to us that this is not a case which we need to remit to an industrial tribunal. The evidence was such that this tribunal would have come to the same conclusion, for the reasons the industrial tribunal gave, but on the basis of s. 51 of the 1975 Act rather that of what was said in *Automotive Products Ltd* v. *Peake*.

The appeal is, accordingly, dismissed.

# Price v. Civil Service Commission[1]

MR JUSTICE PHILLIPS: Miss Price complains that the Civil Service Commission have unlawfully discriminated against her, within the Sex Discrimination Act 1975, by imposing a discriminatory condition for eligibility for appointment as an executive officer in the Civil Service. An industrial tribunal sitting in London on 28 October and 4 November 1976, by a decision entered on 24 November 1976, dismissed her complaint. From that decision she has appealed. Since the decision of the industrial tribunal, the Society of Civil and Public Servants have been added as respondents by order of the Registrar as having an interest in the outcome of the appeal.

Miss Price was born on 26 August 1940. She joined the Civil Service as a clerical officer when she was 17, and served for two years. At the age of 20 she married, and has since had two children and has done various work, mostly part-time. Towards the end of 1975 Miss Price saw an advertisement in the *Guardian* inviting applications for appointment in the Civil Service as executive officer. No mention was made there of any age limits. In response to her application she received a booklet setting out in detail the conditions of the appointment, and learnt that candidates 'should be at least 17 1/2 and under 28 years of age on 31 December 1976', a condition with which she could not comply. It is this age range which she contends to be discriminatory. She complains that women have greater difficulty in complying with it - particularly the upper age limit of 28 - than do men. Many women in their 20s are having children, or looking after children, or both and are thus prevented from applying. By the time they feel able to do so, say in the mid-30s, it is too late because of the 28-year bar.

Part I of the Sex Discrimination Act 1975 defines 'discrimination to which the Act applies'. The following parts render unlawful the specified acts of discrimination in particular fields; thus Part II relates to 'discrimination in the employment field'. There seems to be no doubt that if the Civil Service Commission have discriminated against Mrs Price, as defined in Part I, the act is unlawful under s. 6. The question is whether they have discriminated within Part I. Her case is put under s. 1(1)(b).

...

Section 1(1)(b) deals with indirect discrimination. The scheme is to define in subpara. (i) in fairly wide terms activities which are *prima facie* discriminatory, and in effect to provide that they are to constitute discrimination unless the person acting can within subpara. (ii) show that they are justifiable irrespective of the sex of the person discriminated against. Thus subpara. (i) proscribes a wide range of activity but permits the party acting to justify it. The test is whether the condition is such that the

---

1    [1978] ICR 27, {1977] IRLR 291 (EAT).

proportion of women who can comply with it is considerably smaller than the proportion of men who can comply with it. Examples usually given are of physical attributes such as height or strength or weight. But the subparagraph goes much further than that, and would extend to educational or professional qualifications, if they are of a kind which few women but many men possess. Thus an advertisement which required as a condition for appointment to a post of a degree in engineering, or the status of a barrister-at-law, would seem to be *prima facie* discriminatory in that the proportion of women who can comply with the condition is considerably smaller than the proportion of men who can comply with it. No doubt in those and other similar cases the advertiser would have no difficulty in showing the condition to be justifiable. Accordingly such cases are not brought in practice because it is known that though they might pass the test of subpara. (i) they will fail at that of subpara. (ii). Thus it by no means follows that because a claimant can satisfy subpara. (i) he or she will eventually be able to establish an act of discrimination. Miss Price failed to persuade the industrial tribunal that she could satisfy subpara. (ii). Thus the case has not yet been determined upon the merits, and we have not had the benefit of hearing the evidence and arguments relevant to the question whether the conditions can be shown to be justifiable. The case has not got beyond the preliminary point.

The industrial tribunal's main ground of decision is narrowly based. They accepted a submission at the end of Miss Price's case that the Civil Service Commission had no case to answer. It had been submitted on behalf of the Civil Service Commission that the words 'can comply' should be strictly construed and that it must be said of a woman that she can comply with a condition if it is physically possible for her to do so. The industrial tribunal accepted this submission. The argument went further, and was that since the number of women and the number of men in the population is not widely different it was impossible to say that the proportion of women who can comply with the age condition was considerably smaller than the proportion of men, because all men and all women had equal opportunity to comply with it. In para. 11 of the decision the industrial tribunal put it like this:

> We have unanimously decided that Mr Howard's submission on behalf of the respondent must be upheld on both grounds. We are of the view that the only requirement or condition was that applicants should be between the specified age groups. Since the applicant conceded that the proportion of women within these groups was not considerably smaller than the proportion of men, we are of the view that this concession is fatal to her case. In so far as the statistics are concerned, as Mr Howard submitted, no one can really say whether these women with children really wanted a job or chose to stay at home. If one takes the up to date statistics provided by the respondent we find that indeed more women than men applied for posts of Executive Officer posts than men. If they could apply for those posts then it follows that they could have applied for any other kind of job. It is also worth-while recording that during 1976 53.7% of women were accepted against 46.3% of men.

The appeal tribunal are not in agreement. Mr Alderton accepts this conclusion, and would dismiss the appeal. The majority take a different view, which is set out in the remainder of this judgment and which is theirs alone.

The industrial tribunal further decided that the statistics produced in evidence did not establish to their satisfaction why it was that fewer women applied for posts than men, and whether it was not that they chose not to do so, rather than that they were prevented from doing so. They were also impressed by the fact that during 1976 according to statistics produced of applications for executive officers, of those accepted 53.7 percent were women as against 46.3 per cent who were men. We do not regard this last point as significant, since the complaint is not that over the whole range of appointment between 17 1/2 and 28 years fewer women were successful than men, but that the age bar at 28 was more disadvantageous to women than to men.

Experience shows that when considering s. 1(1)(b) it is necessary to define with some precision the requirement or condition which is called in question. Even when the facts are not in dispute it is possible to formulate the requirements or condition, usually at all events, in more than one way: the precise formulation is important when considering subparas (i), (ii) and (iii). A fair way of putting it in the present case seems to be that candidates for the post of executive officer must not be over 28 years of age. We do not accept the submission of counsel for the Civil Service Commission that the words 'can comply' must be construed narrowly, and we think that the industrial tribunal were wrong to accept this submission. In one sense it can be said that any female applicant can comply with the condition. She is not obliged to marry, or to have children, or to mind children; she may find somebody to look after them, and as a last resort she may put them into care. In this sense no doubt counsel for the Civil Service Commission is right in saying that any female applicant can comply with the condition. Such a construction appears to us to be wholly out of sympathy with the spirit and intent of the Act. Further, it should be repeated that compliance with subpara. (i) is only a preliminary step, which does not lead to a finding that an act is one of discrimination unless the person acting fails to show that it is justifiable. 'Can' is defined (*Shorter Oxford English Dictionary*) 'to be able: to have the power or capacity'. It is a word with many shades of meaning, and we are satisfied that it should not be too narrowly - nor too broadly - construed in its context in s. 1(1)(b)(i). It should not be said that a person 'can' do something merely because it is theoretically possible for him to do so: it is necessary to see whether he can do so in practice. Applying this approach to the circumstances of this case, it is relevant in determining whether women can comply with the condition to take into account the current usual behaviour of women in this respect, as observed in practice, putting on one side behaviour and responses which are unusual or extreme.

Knowledge and experience suggest that a considerable number of women between the mid-20s and the mid-30s are engaged in bearing children and in minding children, and that while many find it possible to take up employment many others, while desiring to do so, find it impossible, and that many of the latter as their children get older find that they can follow their wish and seek employment. This knowledge and experience is confirmed by some of the statistical evidence produced to the industrial tribunal (and by certain additional statistical evidence put in by consent of the parties on the hearing of the appeal). This demonstrates clearly that the economic activity of women with at least one 'A'-level falls off markedly about the age of 23, reaching a bottom at about age 33 when it climbs gradually to a plateau at about 45.

Basing ourselves on this and other evidence, we should have no hesitation in concluding that our own knowledge and experience is confirmed, and that it is safe to say that the condition is one which it is in practice harder for women to comply with than it is for men. We should be inclined to go further and say that there are undoubtedly women of whom it may be properly said in the terms of s. 1(1)(b)(i) that they 'cannot' comply with the condition, because they are women; that is to say because of their involvement with their children. But this is not enough to enable Miss Price to satisfy the requirements of subpara. (i). The difficulty we have is in saying whether the proportion of women who can comply with the condition is *considerably smaller* than the proportion of men who can comply with it. It follows from what we have said earlier that we do not agree with the approach of the industrial tribunal to this question, and it follows that there has never been a finding of fact based upon the evidence correctly approached and interpreted.

...

Accordingly we propose to allow the appeal and to remit the case to be heard afresh, bearing in mind the terms of this judgment and such guidance as we have been able to give. It may perhaps be helpful to mention one other matter. The industrial tribunal in para. 12 rightly point out that when considering s. 1(1)(b)(i) and considering the proportion of women and the proportion of men, it may be proper to consider as the 'pool' of women or men available for the purpose something less than total female and male population. We agree with that, though, as we have pointed out, the industrial tribunal itself in the present case proceeded on the footing that it was appropriate to take into account the whole population, male and female respectively. We doubt whether that was the right approach, though we do not wish to lay down a proposition binding upon the industrial tribunal which will hear the remitted case. It seems to us, as at present advised, there would be a good deal in the present case for saying that the appropriate 'pool' is that of qualified men and qualified women as the case may be.

In this connection it is worth remarking, as indicating how widely s. 1(1)(b)(i) may operate, that if Miss Price's case had been limited to the proposition that there was *prima facie* discrimination in that an educational qualification was demanded of two 'A'-levels, it would be likely to succeed in as much as the proportion of women with two 'A'-levels to all women is considerably smaller than the proportion of men with two 'A'-levels to all men. Such a way of putting the case would have achieved nothing because the Civil Service Commission would have had little difficulty, if the attack had been limited in that way, in establishing that the condition was justifiable within subpara. (ii).

We think that it is desirable that the case should be remitted to be heard by a differently constituted industrial tribunal, not because there is any criticism of the tribunal which heard the present case, but because on the whole it is probably desirable that it should be approached afresh.

The order is the appeal be allowed, the decision of the industrial tribunal be set aside, and the case be remitted to be reheard by a differently constituted industrial tribunal. Leave to appeal given.

## Snowball *v.* Gardner Merchant Ltd[1]

SIR RALPH KILNER-BROWN : This case came before us by way of an appeal against a ruling by the majority of an Industrial Tribunal held at London (South) on 5 December 86 with reference to the cross-examination of the applicant and the admissibility of material for that purpose. After a full hearing extending for two days we expressed our decision in the form of an order of this court and reserved the publication of the reasons for our decision. It is an important case in that as far as we are aware it is the first time that the question of a woman's character and attitude to matters of sexual behaviour has been the subject of a ruling on admissibility of evidence in the context of an application to an Industrial Tribunal alleging discrimination on the ground of sex.

...

There is no dispute between the parties that for discrimination to succeed there must be shown to be a detriment. Detriment is any situation in which the employee would or might feel at a disadvantage, see *De Souza* v. *AA* [1986] IRLR 103. Sexual harassment may be a detriment and the motive behind it is irrelevant, see *Porcelli* v. *Strathclyde Council* [1984] IRLR 467. Compensation must relate to the degree of detriment and in that context there has to be an assessment of injury to the woman's feelings, which must be looked at not only subjectively with reference to her as an individual, but objectively with reference to what any ordinary reasonable female employee would feel.

...

The matter which led to argument between counsel and to the ruling which is the subject of this appeal arose during the cross-examination of the applicant as to her complaint of sexual harassment. Without going into the details which might titillate the salacious minded, the general tenor of the questioning was to the effect that she had not suffered any injury to her feelings because she talked freely to her fellow employees about 'a play-pen', black satin sheets and her attitude to sexual matters. The applicant denied the various suggestions. If the matter had been left there, there would have been no problem for the Industrial Tribunal to resolve. However, counsel for the applicant became aware of his opponent's intentions to call witnesses to establish the truth of the allegations which had been put in cross-examination and gave notice to the Tribunal that he would object if counsel tried to do that. His objection would be that the cross-examination was final. The Chairman of the Industrial Tribunal at first tried sensibly to avoid any immediate ruling and suggested that Mr Popplewell got on with his case by calling the gentleman who was accused of the sexual harassment. Mr Popplewell, perhaps overlooking the wide procedural powers vested in an

---

1    [1987] ICR 719, [1987] IRLR 397 (EAT).

Industrial Tribunal, objected that he did not want to be told how to direct the case. In our opinion the Chairman would have been well within his rights if he had insisted upon Mr Popplewell calling the accused gentleman first. However he did not do so and understandably thought that the whole question would be passed to the Employment Appeal Tribunal. That is why we have been privileged to listen for two whole days to counsel of great experience expatiating on the law of evidence and referring us to cases which go back in time to the year 1811 and in space from England to California and Florida.

We hope that neither counsel will in any way be discomfited if we deal with the argument on each side quite shortly. Mr Hendy for the appellant properly submitted that cases where a woman alleges sexual harassment involve a sensitive subject and require an Industrial Tribunal to exercise a tight control over the area of investigation. So far Mr Tabachnik was in agreement, but he advanced the well-known proposition that in sexual matters it is easy to accuse and difficult to refute and that there is no burden on a person accused to establish innocence. Therefore an Industrial Tribunal ought not overly to protect a complainant but give to the person accused a fair opportunity to test the truth of the allegations. On the other hand, Mr Hendy made the equally obvious point that in the process of so doing the complainant must not be subject to an attack by the calling of evidence as to her general character and her attitude to sexual matters. Up to this point these are generalities of which any reasonable Industrial Tribunal would be aware. We have every confidence that Industrial Tribunals always have been and always will be very careful in their conduct of cases involving allegations of sexual harassment.

In order to persuade us to prohibit the calling of the proffered evidence Mr Hendy has to establish that, either on strict grounds of admissibility or on grounds of public policy, no Industrial Tribunal should exercise its discretion to permit the calling of the sort of evidence which is proposed in this case. He sought to do so primarily on the ground that the proposed evidence did not concern the gentleman accused of sexual harassment and therefore was not relevant and consequently was inadmissible. The argument that the evidence would contradict her denials in cross-examination and therefore went to credibility was, he submitted, fallacious, because the credibility or otherwise of her denials in cross-examination had nothing to do with her claim. This submission led naturally to the further point that talking about sexual matters was a collateral issue and therefore answers given in cross-examination must be regarded as final; positive evidence to negative those answers should not be admitted. In this case, he submitted, the response on behalf of the respondent was not that she suffered no detriment, but that all her allegations were untrue. It follows therefore that evidence about her opinions on sexual behaviour do not affect the truth or otherwise of her allegations one way or the other. In consequence, whichever way it is tested the proffered evidence is irrelevant or concerns a collateral issue and no positive evidence should be admitted. On the aspect of public policy Mr Hendy repeated his general observations and said that it was not the function of an Industrial Tribunal to investigate the morals of an applicant alleging sexual harassment which is something which either had occurred or had not. There is no room in this sort of enquiry for an attack on the complainant's character. It is unfair and prejudicial, even if true, to inhibit an applicant from bringing a genuine case, if afraid of public criticism for a somewhat permissive attitude in conversation about sexual matters. A complainant attacked in this way is even less able to defend herself than a man may be who is alleged to have directed acts of sexual harassment at her.

On behalf of the respondent Mr Tabachnik reminded us that r. 8(1)[1] specifically provides for a free and unfettered discretion as to the admission of evidence. The only basis for interfering with the exercise of discretion would be if it could be shown that no reasonable Tribunal would admit evidence of this nature. In any event the evidence is doubly relevant and therefore admissible. Firstly, in order to challenge the alleged detriment and hurt to feelings, it is pertinent to enquire whether the complainant is either unduly sensitive, or as in this case, if the proposed evidence is right, is unlikely to be very upset by a degree of familiarity with a sexual connotation. This approach is a perfectly proper introduction to a testing of credibility in relation to her denials in cross-examination. Credibility, it is said, is an issue which lies at the heart of the case. The complainant's allegations are either true or false and there is no room for possible misunderstanding. He added that under the regulation an Industrial Tribunal has power to admit evidence which in strict law is inadmissible. In support of this contention reference was made to the case of *Rosedale Mouldings Ltd* v. *Sibley* [1980] IRLR 387. We have doubts about the validity of this proposition, because as we have said earlier in this judgment, our opinion is that the power extends in some cases to the exclusion of evidence which strictly may be admissible. In *Rosedale Mouldings* the wrongly excluded evidence was highly probative and there was no room for balancing prejudice against probative value. However we do not need to resolve this possible difficulty because we accept the main argument put forward by Mr Tabachnik. There is one final matter which we should mention which flows from our view of the double-ended power. It may well be that some of the details of the proffered evidence may seem to the Industrial Tribunal to have little or no relevance but merely create an atmosphere of prejudice. We have in mind, for example, the suggested attractiveness of black satin sheets. It would be open to the Industrial Tribunal to pay no attention to this whatsoever and perhaps for the Chairman to do some editing of his own before his colleagues were troubled with some of the matters.

...

---

1     Industrial Tribunals Rules of Procedure 1985, r. 8(1).

# Webb v. Emo Air Cargo (UK) Ltd[1]

MR JUSTICE WOOD (PRESIDENT): The facts in this case could not be simpler, but the issue raised will be thought by those involved in the field of discrimination law to be of fundamental importance. Different divisions of this Court have taken different views and for this reason we have sat as a five-member Court.

The respondent company is a small concern employing only some 16 (both male and female). It is involved in the import and export of goods and materials. The import department consists of some four employees including a Mrs Valerie Stuart who was an import operations clerk. There is no suggestion that the respondent company was not a considerate employer which gave due weight to issues of discrimination and maternity.

In June 1987 it was known that Mrs Stuart was pregnant and would be leaving at the end of that year to have her baby, which was due on 16 February 1988. She intended to return to work after maternity leave. The applicant was engaged late in that June as an import operations clerk subject to a three-month probationary period. It was recognised that she would need about six months' training from Mrs Stuart and that she would then be able to replace her from the beginning of 1988. However, the eventual return of Mrs Stuart would not mean that the applicant would have to leave.

The applicant started work on 1 July 1987.

About two weeks later the applicant thought that she herself might be pregnant and told Mrs Stuart. The applicant had no such suspicion at the start of her employment. This matter came to the hearing of Mr Fullicks, the managing director, who called the applicant to his office on the following day. The applicant told him that she thought she was pregnant but was not certain. Mr Fullicks told her that he had no alternative but to dismiss her. However, she could choose whether to leave that very day or at the end of the month. Having chosen the latter the applicant received a letter of 30 July stating:

> You will recall that at your interview some four weeks ago you were told that the job for which you applied and were given had become available because of one of our employees becoming pregnant. Since you have only now told me that you are also pregnant I have no alternative other than to terminate your employment with our company.

The applicant's employment thereupon terminated. Her pregnancy was in fact confirmed about a week after her meeting with Mr Fullicks. She did not tell him of that confirmation, but the Tribunal considered that nothing

---

1    [1990] ICR 442, [1990] IRLR 124 (EAT).

turned upon that. The applicant's own confinement was expected on 8 March 1988.

The Tribunal found specifically that if at the initial interview the applicant had said that she might be pregnant, she would not have been offered the post.

Before the Tribunal the applicant was represented by counsel and the respondent company by his managing director, Mr Fullicks, whose evidence was accepted. He did not seek to argue the issues of law. He has also appeared before us, but has really taken no part in the submissions made. In the circumstances we have thought it right to seek the assistance of an *amicus curiae* and we are grateful to Mr Pannick.

In February 1988 before an Industrial Tribunal under the chairmanship of Mr D S Laughton sitting in London (North), Mr Shrimpton for the applicant put his case in three ways. He argued for direct discrimination, indirect discrimination and under the provisions of EEC law. The Tribunal decided against his client on all three grounds. The applicant appealed by notice of 29 April 1988. The only basis for appeal taken by Mr Melville-Williams QC for the appellant is the argument based on direct discrimination - s. 1(1)(a) of the Sex Discrimination Act 1975. He abandons the other points. ...

There are two conflicting decisions of this Court. They are *Turley* v. *Allders Department Stores Ltd* [1980] IRLR 4, and *Hayes* v. *Malleable Working Men's Club & Institute* [1985] IRLR 367.

The case of *Turley* arose in unfortunate and inappropriate circumstances in that the Industrial Tribunal assumed for the purposes of the hearing that the applicant had been dismissed because she was pregnant and tried the preliminary issue of law, whether a dismissal on the ground of pregnancy could amount to discrimination within the meaning of s. 1(1)(a) of the Act. The Tribunal found that since a man could not become pregnant it was not possible to compare like with like as required by s. 5(3) and dismissed the complaint. By a majority the appeal was dismissed.

The minority view was that of Ms Pat Smith who expressed her judgment as follows:

> I do not accept the conclusion that a woman dismissed from her employment on the ground of pregnancy has no protection under the Sex Discrimination Act 1975. Such a bald assertion seems to me to contradict both the spirit and the letter of the statute.
>
> The provisions of the Sex Discrimination Act can be applied in a quite straightforward manner to this situation with simpler and fairer consequences than trying to interpret s. 1(1) as an impossible comparison between women who are

pregnant and men who cannot be pregnant. Mr Irvin's distinction between a woman and a pregnant woman and the fact that a woman has a choice about pregnancy seems to me to be irrelevant. So is the case of an employer choosing between three applicants, one a woman, one a pregnant woman, and one a man. In my view it may or may not be unlawful under the Sex Discrimination Act to dismiss a woman on the ground of pregnancy.

The case under the direct discrimination provision - s. 1(1)(a) - is a simple one. Pregnancy is a medical condition. It is a condition which applies only to women. It is a condition which will lead to a request for time off from work for the confinement. A man is in similar circumstances who is employed by the same employer and who in the course of the year will require time off for a hernia operation, to have his tonsils removed, or for other medical reasons. The employer must not discriminate by applying different and less favourable criteria to the pregnant woman than to the man requiring time off. That is the 'like for like' comparison, and not one between women who are pregnant and men who cannot become pregnant.

This argument does not conflict with the Employment Protection Act 1975. The right not to be dismissed on the ground of pregnancy and the maternity rights under the Employment Protection Act are, following a period of continuous employment, automatic unless s. 60(1)(a) or (b) apply. The Sex Discrimination Act would not give an automatic right; it would give a much more limited right, resting on a comparison with other employees; a right not to be singled out for dismissal for pregnancy - a female condition - as distinct from other medical conditions.

In the *Hayes* case there were in fact two appeals to this Court and in each of them the Industrial Tribunal had found that the reason for the dismissal was pregnancy but that they were bound by the previous decision in *Turley*; as there could be no masculine equivalent and no comparison, pregnancy was incapable as a matter of law of amounting to discrimination under the Act. This division of this Court took a different view of the law from the Court in *Turley* and indicated that the correct approach was to ask whether they were closely enough matched to enable a fair comparison to be made between the treatment accorded to a woman in the one situation and the man in the other and that accordingly the cases would be remitted to different Tribunals.

The applicants were supported by the Equal Opportunities Commission and it was not argued in *Hayes* case that there was any automatic discrimination because at the time of dismissal the two applicants were pregnant.

This Court sought to distinguish *Turley's* case but added this:

If we are wrong in so distinguishing *Turley's* case and it is an authority of principle, then with respect (and with sympathy for the views of the majority in the predicament presented to them by the need to determine a hypothetical question) we would feel bound to decline to follow it; and to prefer the views of Ms Smith - for which powerful support is provided, in our judgment, by the crucial requirement in s. 5(3) of the Act that for all purposes of comparison (whether direct or indirect discrimination is involved) the two cases must be the same 'or not materially different'. Like Ms Smith, we have not found any difficulty in visualising cases - for example that a sick male employee and a pregnant woman employee, where the circumstances, although they could never in strictness be called the same, could nevertheless be properly regarded as lacking any material difference.

The present Industrial Tribunal, having considered both *Turley* and *Hayes*, declined to follow *Turley*. It expressed its views in two paragraphs of the decision which read as follows:

11.    The question remains whether s. 1(1)(a) has, without reference to Community law, the meaning for which Mr Shrimpton contends. On the one hand we do not think (as we explain in para. 8 above) that dismissal for pregnancy cannot constitute discrimination. On the other hand, we do not think that dismissal for pregnancy can be *ipso facto* discrimination by virtue of s. 6(2)(b) and s. 1(1)(a) of the 1975 Act, except perhaps in rare cases such as moral objection to the pregnancy being taken by the employer. We think that our task under s. 1(1)(a) is to identify what is the real and significant reason for the dismissal and to assess the extent to which the employer by adopting this reason treats the employee less favourably than he treats or would treat an employee of the opposite sex. Section 5(3) indicates that a comparison is to be made between the sexes in the context of the degree of similarity or difference in the relevant circumstances. We do not think that such comparison is limited to the similarity of employment as suggested by Mr Shrimpton. We conclude that the dismissal of the applicant for pregnancy should not be considered *ipso facto* as discrimination within s. 1(1)(a) of the 1975 Act.

12.    As an alternative submission on direct discrimination, Mr Shrimpton asks us to make a comparison between the treatment of the applicant and the treatment of a man requiring time off for an operation. We find that there was no man in the employment of the respondents who could be used for an actual comparison. The words 'or would treat a man' in s. 1(1)(a) indicate that a comparison can and should, if possible, be made with a hypothetical man. We think that we should make a comparison based partly upon the facts of the previous practice of the respondents, partly upon the answers about hypothetical examples given in evidence by Mr Fullicks and partly upon inferences from these matters viewed in the light of the surrounding circumstances. Our analysis needs to consider not only whether the applicant was treated less favourably than a man but also whether such treatment was on the ground of her sex. Both elements must be present to constitute direct discrimination. To reach a conclusion on both we must determine the real and significant reason for the dismissal. It is clear from the evidence that the applicant was recruited for the specific purpose of covering the absence of Valerie Stuart, when she took her maternity leave; and that six months' training was needed for this purpose. Valerie Stuart was not dismissed when she became pregnant. The general practice was to grant substantial paid sick leave both to men and women. Ordinarily a woman going to the hospital to have a baby would be treated in the same way, i.e. given leave of absence rather than being dismissed, but the situation of the applicant was different because she was recruited specifically to cover the job of Valerie Stuart. We think that it is a reasonable and proper inference to draw from these facts (although there is no specific evidence to this effect) that if a man had been recruited instead of the applicant and that man had told Mr Fullicks that he would have to be absent for a comparable period to that expected of the applicant, the man

would have been dismissed in like manner. Our conclusion is that the real and significant reason for the dismissal of the applicant was her anticipated inability to carry out the primary task for which she was recruited. Her pregnancy was the particular physical reason for giving rise to the anticipation, but it was in this context no different to any other physical reason, whether relating to a woman or a man. Therefore the treatment of the applicant was not on the ground of her sex or of any matter related to her sex. Further the respondents did not treat her less favourably than they would have treated a man. It follows that the respondents did not directly discriminate against the applicant under s. 1(1)(a) by dismissing her.

Mr John Melville-Williams contends that there are three possible views of the true meaning of s. 1(1)(a) where a woman has been dismissed who at that time is pregnant:

(a)   First, that because a man cannot become pregnant no comparison can be made and therefore no direct discrimination can arise; the *Turley* solution.
(b)   Second, that direct discrimination can occur, but for it to be proved the woman must show less favourable treatment in comparison with a man whose medical condition has a similar effect to her pregnancy on the employer's business; the *Hayes* solution.

He submits that neither of those approaches is appropriate. His third contention is that although a comparison should be made between a woman applicant and a notional man, it is only possible to reach a result which accords with the intention of the Act if in considering the phrase 'relevant circumstances' in s. 5(3) of the Act you proceed, in the first place, to ignore the factor of sex and having then found those circumstances to be the same, but the result of the treatment to be different solely by reason of the physiological function of a woman in her pregnancy, which is unique and which is incapable of comparison with a male condition, then it must follow that the act of dismissal because of pregnancy must be direct discrimination. In his submission it would be wrong in this unique situation to make a comparison between an incapacity to work because of sickness or an operation which could be a factor common to both sexes and the reason for the operation is immaterial. For instance if it were a prostectomy or hysterectomy they would be peculiar to a man or a woman respectively.

It would seem to us that, in other words, he is submitting that the presence of the uniquely feminine factor automatically makes a dismissal direct discrimination.

He supports his argument in two main ways. First, he submits that it would be contrary to the purpose of the act if the phrase 'relevant circumstances' in s. 5(3) included circumstances which arose in the case of a woman exclusively from a characteristic unique to her sex; that there is no binding authority in support of the proposition that such characteristics are part of the comparative equation and it is wholly artificial so to treat them; it follows that the relevant circumstances are circumstances other than circumstances arising from the applicant's sex and that therefore the search for a man whose condition is equivalent to the condition of a pregnant woman is unnecessary and distorts the provisions of the Act. It seems to us that this latter part of his argument comes very close to the *Turley* view.

The second main plank in his argument relates to s. 2 of the 1975 Act which reads:

...

He submits that the purpose of s. 2(2) is to obviate the possibility of a man bringing proceedings alleging discrimination because special consideration has been given to a woman in connection with pregnancy or childbirth, and that therefore that such treatment of women is 'on the ground of sex.' No such exclusion applies in reverse and therefore to treat a woman differently than a man because she is pregnant must fall within s. 1(1)(a).

In examining these submissions let us turn at once to s. 2(2). We agree with the purpose suggested by Mr Melville-Williams. Without its existence it seems right to assume that the draftsman of the Act envisaged that a man could allege direct discrimination in those circumstances, but more importantly as Mr Pannick pointed out that the draftsman envisaged the possibility of a man comparing himself with a pregnant woman for the purpose of deciding the issue of less favourable treatment. Unless such a concept is accepted there is no need for s. 2(2).

The effect of the submission of Mr Melville-Williams is to argue for positive discrimination and s. 2(2) does not, in our judgment, point in that direction. It is an enabling provision which empowers an employer to discriminate in favour of women in connection with pregnancy or childbirth, but it does not require the employer to grant any such treatment.

In a sustained and impressive argument Mr David Pannick has persuaded us that the approach of the Industrial Tribunal was entirely correct. In the first place he points out that the appellant's present submissions really argue for automatic discrimination where pregnancy is involved. He emphasises that this point was not taken by Mr Anthony Lester QC appearing for the appellants in *Hayes* when it might very well have formed part of his argument.

He makes a number of points:

1.    Section 1(1)(a) defines direct discrimination by reference to a comparison between the treatment of the complainant and the treatment which a man does or would receive. Unless the applicant can point to a man who would be more favourably treated, there is no question of direct discrimination.

2.    To rely upon the fact that a man cannot become pregnant is to return to the *Turley* approach. It cannot be correct first, because of the existence of s. 2(2) to which we have referred above, and also to the provisions of s. 5(3)

...

This wording envisages that the circumstances of the complainant and the comparable man do not need to be identical. The 'materiality' is likely to be the impact upon the business and that impact is unlikely to be different according to whether an absence from work is due to pregnancy or a medical condition in a man. Thus, such conditions would not seem to be 'materially different' and therefore comparable.

3.    There is an important question of principle. In relation to direct discrimination the question for consideration is always whether the appellant was adversely treated because of her sex or because of a neutral factor. She may say she was dismissed because of her sex but an employer may say it was because of the inconvenience to the business if he continued to employ a person who was going to be absent for three to six months over a vital period. The issue of which explanation is correct has to be answered by the application of a test involving a principle. That test, whether the dismissal was on the ground of sex or some other neutral ground is whether she has been less favourably treated than a man was or would have been treated in comparable circumstances where those relevant circumstances are not materially different. If in comparable circumstances a man would have been treated in the same way the dismissal was not on the grounds of sex and there is no direct discrimination, it was because of business needs. The applicant will have failed to establish her case.

4.    If the appellant's submissions are correct, it would automatically be direct discrimination not to offer a woman employment because she is pregnant. The true reason might be that she was incapable of performing the necessary duties, or, the job needed to be carried out over the next few months and she would be away as also would be a man about the enter hospital. Thus, unless a court carries out a comparison of the treatment of the claimant with that which was or would have been accorded to a comparable man, there is no principal test by reference to which it can be decided whether the adverse treatment was on the ground of sex or some other ground.

We are unanimously of the view that the arguments of Mr Pannick should prevail. However there are further grounds for our accepting that the approach of the Industrial Tribunal was correct.

First, the wording of s. 1(1)(a) requires a comparison to be made if necessary with a hypothetical man. It can really not be understood in some other way.

Secondly, it is of interest to note that s. 60 of the Employment Protection (Consolidation) Act 1978 deals with dismissals on grounds of pregnancy. It originates from s. 34 of the Employment Protection Act 1975, which Act was passed at the same time as the Sex Discrimination Act of that year. The qualifying period under the 1975 Act was shorter than it is today.

The wording of s. 60 is not in absolute terms and we cannot think that jurisdiction under the Sex Discrimination Act 1975 and the Employment Protection Act 1975 were intended to be fundamentally different.

Thirdly, since this decision was given, the Court of Appeal has pronounced upon the true meaning of subs. 1(1)(a) in *James* v. *Eastleigh Borough Council* [1989] IRLR 381. Without citing at length from the judgment of the learned Vice-Chancellor, it seems to us that the approach of this Industrial Tribunal was in accordance with that decision. If s. 1(1)(a) is to be understood to be of automatic effect without regard to 'a reason', then the words 'on the grounds of her sex' are pure surplusage, because without them it is clear that the comparison is between a woman and a man. Thus, if she is less favourably treated discrimination would be established.

Our attention is also drawn to the recent decision of the House of Lords in *R.* v. *Birmingham City Council* ex parte *EOC* [1989] IRLR 173. On the facts of that case girls were clearly treated less favourably that boys in that the Council provided substantially fewer places for girls than boys in single-sex secondary schools. No other reason was offered for such treatment than that the female students, who would have been in the position of the applicants before an Industrial Tribunal, were girls, thus 'on the grounds of sex.' The sole submission being made in that case on the provisions of s. 1(1)(a) was that even if less favourable treatment was established '... it still had to be shown that there was less favourable treatment on grounds of sex, and that involved establishing an intention or motive on the part of the Council to discriminate against the girls' - *per* speech of Lord Goff of Chieveley at p. 175. This submission was rejected. Motive and intention are irrelevant.

However, unlike the *Birmingham* case where the sole issue of relevance to us at present was whether intention or motive was a necessary element in direct discrimination, this present case is not one where the less favourable treatment can exist only by reason of the sex element. If it is suggested that there were other reasons then it is for an Industrial Tribunal to decide whether the less favourable treatment was on the grounds of sex or for some other neutral reason.

The four industrial members unanimously take the view that discrimination is just one aspect of unfairness. They feel that sound industrial relations usually depend more on the maintenance of a balance rather than the rigid application of absolutes and the wording of s. 60 of the 1978 Act seems to be in accord with this approach.

It follows therefore for the reasons which we have given that this appeal must be dismissed.

## §3   EQUALITY IN SOCIAL SECURITY

See also *Duke* v. *GEC Reliance* (*supra*)

**COURT OF APPEAL**

**Secretary of State for Social Security *v.* Thomas**
**Secretary of State for Social Security *v.* Cooze**
**Secretary of State for Social Security *v.* Beard**
**Secretary of State for Social Security *v.* Murphy**
**Morley *v.* Secretary of State for Social Security[1]**

LORD JUSTICE SLADE: There are before the Court five appeals which raise important questions of law concerning the entitlement of women to severe disablement allowance ('SDA') or invalid care allowance ('ICA'). In four of them, the Secretary of State for Social Security is the appellant, and the respective respondents are Mrs Thomas, Mrs Cooze, Mrs Beard and Mrs Murphy (in addition to the Adjudication Officer who has not been represented). I will refer to these appeals respectively as 'the *Thomas* appeal', 'the *Cooze* appeal', 'the *Beard* appeal' and 'the *Murphy* appeal.' In the fifth ('the *Morley* appeal') Mrs Morley is the appellant and the Secretary of State is the respondent. In summary, the principal question in the *Thomas* and *Morley* appeals is whether, by reason of the European Communities Council Directive 79/7 of 19 December 1978 on the Progressive Implementation of the Principle of Equal Treatment for Men and Women in Matters of Social Security (OJ L6/1979, p. 24), Mrs Thomas and Mrs Morley, as the case may be, is entitled to SDA notwithstanding s. 36(4)(d) of the Social Security Act 1975 ('the 1975 Act'). In summary, the principal question in the *Cooze, Beard,* and *Murphy* appeals is whether, by reason of the last-mentioned Directive ('Directive 79/7'), the respondent is entitled to ICA, notwithstanding s. 37(5) of the 1975 Act. The answer to these two questions will in every case depend on whether art. 7(1)(a) of Directive 79/7 excludes s. 36(4)(d) or s. 37(5), as the case may be, from the ambit of Directive 79/7.

In all five appeals, the Secretary of State appears by Mr Plender QC and Mr Pannick. Mr Rowland appears for Mrs Cooze, Mrs Beard and Mrs Morley. Pursuant to leave granted by the Court of Appeal on 6 April 1989, the Equal Opportunities Commission ('the Commission') appears by Mr Lester QC, and Miss Beale to resist the appeal of the Secretary of State in the *Thomas* case. On 5 July 1990 this Court, without opposition, made an order on Mr Lester's application, pursuant to RSC Order 15 r.6, joining the Commission as a party to the *Thomas* proceedings. Mrs Murphy is not represented before this Court.

---

1    [1990] IRLR 436 (CA).

*Relevant UK statutory provisions*

It will be convenient to begin by setting out some of the relevant statutory provisions of this country. Section 36 of the 1975 Act, as substituted for an earlier s. 36 by the Health and Social Security Act 1984, introduced with effect from 29 November SDA as a new benefit. In relation to Mrs Thomas and Mrs Morley, the conditions for an award of the allowance were that on the relevant day she should be incapable of work and 'disabled' in terms of the section and have been so incapable and so disabled for a period of not less than 196 consecutive days ending immediately before the relevant day. Section 36(4)(d) provides:

A person shall not be entitled to a severe disablement allowance if ...

(d) he has attained pensionable age and was not entitled to a severe disablement allowance immediately before he attained it and is not treated by regulations as having been so entitled immediately before he attained it.

Section 27 of the 1975 Act defines 'pensionable age' as meaning:

(a) in the case of a man, the age of 65; and
(b) in the case of a woman the age of 60.

Section 36(7) of the 1975 Act provides for the making of regulations. Regulation 4 of the Social Security (Severe Disablement Allowance) Regulations 1984 (SI 1984 No 1303) ('the SDA regulations') provides:

A person who has attained pensionable age shall for the purposes of s. 36(4)(d) of the Act be treated as having been entitled to a severe disablement allowance immediately before attaining that age if immediately before attaining it -
(a) he would have satisfied the conditions for entitlement to that allowance or to a non-contributory invalidity pension but for the provisions of the Social Security (Overlapping Benefits) Regulations 1979, or
(b) he was entitled to a non-contributory invalidity pension.

Section 37 of the 1975 Act (as amended) deals with ICA. Subsection (1) provides:

Subject to the provisions of this section, a person shall be entitled to an invalid care allowance for any day on which he is engaged in caring for a severely disabled person if -
(a) he is regularly and substantially engaged in caring for that person; and
(b) he is not gainfully employed; and
(c) the severely disabled person is either such relative of his as may be prescribed or a person of any such other description as may be prescribed.

Section 37(2) defines 'severely disabled person.'

Sections 37(5) and 37(6) provide:

(5)   Subject to subsection (6) below, a person who has attained pensionable age shall not be entitled to an allowance under this section unless he was so entitled (or

is treated by regulations as having been so entitled) immediately before attaining that age.

(6)   Regulations may make provision whereby a person who has attained retiring age (meaning 70 in the case of a man and 65 in the case of a woman), and was entitled to an allowance under this section immediately before attaining that age, continues to be so entitled notwithstanding that he is not caring for a severely disabled person or no longer satisfies the requirements of subsection (1)(a) or (b) above.

Regulation 10 of the Social Security (Invalid Care Allowance) Regulations 1976, as amended ('the ICA Regulations') defines the circumstances in which a person over pensionable age is to be treated as having been entitled to ICA immediately before attaining that age. It provides:

10.   A person who has attained pensionable age shall for the purposes of section 37(5) of the Act be treated as having been entitled to invalid care allowance immediately before attaining that age if immediately before attaining it he would have satisfied the conditions for entitlement to that allowance but for the provisions of the Social Security (Overlapping Benefits) Regulations 1975, as amended.

*Relevant Provisions of Directive 79/7*

...

*The Thomas Appeal*

The claimant attained the age of 60 years on 8 July 1983. Having been employed in the Court Service for many years down to 16 November 1984, she then became finally incapable of work due to disablement. She made a claim for SDA on 26 May 1986. However, as a civil servant she was covered by the 'estains' (establishment and insurance) option down to 4 May 1985, and the real issue was whether she could be awarded SDA from 6 May 1985. At that date her husband was in receipt of an increase of invalidity benefit for her. The effect of the Social Security (Overlapping Benefits) Regulations 1979 (SI 1979 No 597) ('the Overlapping Benefits Regulations') was that she and her husband between them could not receive more than the higher of SDA and increase of disablement benefit for her. In fact, SDA was at a rate in excess of the increase for a wife down to November 1985, but has thereafter run at the same rate. An adjudication officer, by a decision issued on 3 October 1986, decided:

The claimant is not entitled to severe disablement allowance from 6 May 1985 to 27 November 1986 (both dates included) because she has attained pensionable age and she was not entitled and cannot be treated as so entitled to such an allowance immediately before attaining that age (Social Security Act 1975, s. 36(4) and the Social Security (Severe Disablement Allowance) Regulations, reg. 4).

His decision was upheld by the social security appeal tribunal. The claimant then appealed from that decision. Her appeal was heard by Mr

Commissioner Monroe. As he said in his decision of 30 March 1988, it was clear that she had not been entitled to SDA immediately before her 60th birthday because she did not then satisfy the medical conditions, and indeed SDA was not then in existence. However, he decided that:

> by reason of the provisions of [Directive 79/7] the claim is not precluded by s. 36(4)(d) of [the 1975 Act] from having title to [SDA] as from 23 December 1984 or any subsequent date and that the disablement questions referred to in s. 108(1)(b) of that Act be referred for determination accordingly.

The Secretary of State appeals from that decision. The Commissioner, unlike the adjudicating officer and the social security appeal tribunal, did not in terms confine his decision to the period 6 May 1985 to 27 November 1986. If and so far as this may be relevant, the Secretary of State contends that the Commissioner's decision would on any footing assist the claimant only in respect of the latter period.

## The Cooze appeal

The claimant attained the age of 60 on 23 February 1985. On 30 November 1986, she claimed ICA for a period beginning on 1 January 1986 on the grounds that she was looking after Mrs Yorke, a severely disabled person. Mrs Yorke had been awarded attendance allowance for the first time as from 5 May 1986. The claimant, in the event, ceased to look after her on 20 August 1987 when she went into an old persons' home. Her claim was rejected by an adjudicating officer by a decision issued on 6 April 1987 in the following terms:

> The claimant is not entitled to invalid care allowance because she has attained pensionable age and was not entitled and cannot be treated as having been entitled to invalid care allowance immediately before attaining that age (Social Security Act 1975, s. 37(5) and the Social Security (Invalid Care Allowance) Regulations, reg. 10).

She then appealed from this rejection to a social security appeal tribunal which, by a decision dated 3 August 1987, dismissed her appeal. By a decision of 6 April 1989, Mr Commissioner Hallett allowed her appeal from that dismissal. For reasons given by him in that decision, he held in substance that s. 37(5) of the 1975 Act, read with s. 27 and reg. 10 of the ICA regulations, had a discriminatory effect contrary to Directive 79/7 and that that effect was not preserved by art. 7(1)(a) of the Directive. His decision was that

(1) the decision of the tribunal dated 3 August 1987 was erroneous in law;
(2) it was expedient to make fresh and further findings of fact and give the appropriate decision;
(3) ICA was payable to the claimant:

(a) from 1 October 1986 to 20 August 1987, and

(b) subject to showing good cause for the delay in claiming, from 5 May 1986 to 30 September 1986;

(4)   failing agreement as to whether good cause had been shown there was to be liberty to apply for determination of that question.

The Secretary of State appeals from that decision.

## The Beard appeal

The claimant attained the age of 60 on 4 April 1986. She worked until 25 July 1986, but then gave up her employment to look after her mother who had been awarded attendance allowance from 1 July 1986. She claimed ICA with effect from 28 July 1986. Her claim was rejected by an adjudicating officer by a decision issued on 11 September 1986 in the same terms as those in which Mrs Cooze's application was subsequently rejected. She then appealed from this rejection to a social security appeal tribunal which, by a decision dated 1 October 1987, dismissed her appeal. By a decision of 6 April 1989, Mr Commissioner Hallett allowed her appeal from that dismissal for the reasons set out in his decision in the *Cooze* case. The Commissioner's decision was that

(1)   the decision of the tribunal dated 1 October 1987 was erroneous in law;

(2)   it was expedient that he should make fresh and further findings of fact and give the appropriate decision in the light of them;

(3)   the claimant was entitled to ICA from 28 July 1986.

The Secretary of State appeals from that decision.

## The Murphy appeal

The claimant attained the age of 60 on 2 March 1984. On 13 November 1986, she claimed ICA in respect of her husband, for whom attendance allowance had been payable from 20 June 1986. He died on 6 September 1986. He had had to retire on medical grounds and she had given up work at the age of 54 to look after him. Her claim was rejected by an adjudicating officer in a decision of 29 January 1987 for the same reasons as the adjudicating officer had rejected the claims on the *Cooze* and *Beard* cases. She then appealed to the social security appeal tribunal which, by a decision dated 1 October 1987, dismissed her appeal. By a decision of 6 April 1989, Mr Commissioner Hallett allowed her appeal from that decision for the reasons set out in his decision in the *Cooze* case. The Commissioner's decision was

(1)   the decision of the tribunal dated 6 August 1987 was erroneous in law;

(2)   it was further expedient that he should make fresh and further findings of fact and give the appropriate decision in the light of them;

(3) the claimant was entitled to ICA from 20 June 1986 to 6 September 1986.

## The Morley appeal

The claimant attained the age of 60 years on 30 September 1983. After some preceding periods of incapacity, it appears that she finally gave up employment at some time between May and July 1984. On 11 April 1985, she claimed SDA with effect from 29 November 1984. By a decision issued on 31 July 1985, an adjudicating officer, in reliance on s. 36(4) of the 1975 Act and reg. 4 of the 1984 Regulations, rejected her claim on the grounds that she had attained pensionable age and was not entitled, and could not be treated as entitled, to SDA immediately before attaining that age. She appealed from this rejection to a social security appeal tribunal which, by a decision dated 12 June 1986, confirmed the decision of the adjudicating officer. Mr Commissioner Morcom, by a decision of 3 May 1989, dismissed her appeal on the same grounds as those relied on by the adjudicating officer and the social security appeal tribunal. It would appear that before giving his decision, his attention was not directed to Directive 79/7 or to the decisions of Mr Commissioner Monroe and Mr Commissioner Hallett referred to earlier in this judgment, since he did not refer to any of them in his decision. On 2 July 1990 this Court, without opposition from the Secretary of State, granted Mrs Morley leave to appeal from that decision out of time. It is common ground that if the Secretary of State's four appeals are dismissed by this Court, Mrs Morley's appeal must be allowed, and that the appropriate course for this Court then to take will be to remit the matter to the Commissioner to make fresh and further findings of fact and to give the appropriate decision.

## Common ground

In the context of Directive 79/7 a number of points are in my judgment clear and indeed, I think, have been common ground on this appeal:

(1) All five ladies in this case gave up work either because they had themselves become incapable of work or because they were caring for a severely disabled person. All of them are therefore within the scope of Directive 79/7 by virtue of art. 2. The definition of 'working population' in that article is based on the idea that a person whose work has been interrupted by one of the risks referred to in art. 3 belongs to the working population: *Drake* v. *Chief Adjudication Officer* [1987] QB 166 at p. 176, para. 22.

(2) The provisions of the 1975 Act relating to SDA and ICA constitute statutory schemes providing protection against 'invalidity' within the meaning of art. 3 so that Directive 79/7 applies to them: see *Drake* v. *Chief Adjudication Officer* (*supra*). Accordingly, the principle of equal treatment applies under art. 4, subject to the operation of art. 7.

(3)   The statutory pensionable age being fixed at 60 for women and 65 for men is a criterion which directly discriminates between men and women within the meaning of the Sex Discrimination Act 1975 in that it treats women more favourably than men on the ground of their sex (though not falling foul of Directive 79/7 because of the first limb of art. 7(1)(a)): *James* v. *Eastleigh Borough Council* [1990] 3 WLR 55 at p. 60 *per* Lord Bridge of Harwich.

(4)   The effect of sections 36(4)(d) and 37(5) of the Social Security Act 1975, which involve differential treatment of men and women by adopting the same criterion, must equally involve discrimination on the ground of their sex: see *ibid.*. A submission to the contrary, advanced as ground 6 of the amended notice of appeal in the *Thomas* case based on the Court of Appeal decision in *James* v. *Eastleigh Borough Council* [1990] 1 QB 61, has not been pursued in this Court.

(5)   By failing to repeal or amend sections 36(4)(d) and 37(5) so as to remove the last-mentioned discrimination, the United Kingdom must be in breach of its obligations under arts 5 and 8(1) of Directive 79/7 unless the discrimination which those two subsections involved is permitted by art. 7(1)(a). (The 6 year period referred to in art. 8(1) expired on 23 December 1984.)

(6)   If the United Kingdom is in breach of those obligations in these respects, the five ladies concerned in the present case may rely on Directive 79/7 as having direct effect for their benefit in any dispute with the state concerning the application to them of s. 36(4)(d) or s. 37(5) of the 1975 Act. Furthermore, 'in the absence of appropriate measures for the implementation of [art. 4.1 of Directive 79/7] women are entitled to be treated in the same manner and to have the same rules applied to them as men who are in the same situation since, where the Directive has not been implemented, those rules remain the only valid point of reference': *Borrie Clarke* v. *Chief Adjudication Officer* [1987] ECR 2865 at p. 2881, para. 13.

(7)   A provision such as s. 36(4)(d) or s. 37(5) of the 1975 Act, which disqualifies a person who has attained pensionable age from receiving SDA or ICA unless she was entitled to it immediately before attaining that age, does not constitute 'the determination of pensionable age for the purposes of granting old-age and retirement pensions' within the meaning of art. 7(1)(a). If either such discriminatory provision is to fall within the authority conferred by art. 7(1)(a), it must fall within the words 'and the possible consequences thereof for other benefits.' Thus in the end the outcome of this appeal is likely to depend on the meaning of those eight words and their applicability (if any) to sections 36(4)(d) and 37(5) of the 1975 Act.

(8)   No one has sought to argue before this Court that legislation by a member state has to include an explicit election to disapply Directive 79/7 in

an identified respect if it is to benefit from the liberty conferred by art. 7(1)(a) of the Directive.

*The proper approach to the construction of art. 7(1)(a)*

It will be necessary to approach the construction of art. 7(1)(a), and in particular the phrase 'and the possible consequences thereof for other benefits', from a Community point of view. In *R.* v. *Henn* [1981] AC 850 at p. 904, Lord Diplock warned of the danger of an English Court applying English canons of statutory construction to 'the interpretation of the Treaty or, for that matter, of Regulations and Directives' and of disregarding relevant decisions of the European Court. As he put it (at p. 905):

> The European Court, in contrast to English courts, applies teleological rather than historical methods to the interpretation of the Treaties and other Community legislation. It seeks to give effect to what it conceives to be the spirit rather than the letter of the Treaties; sometimes, indeed, to an English judge, it may seem to the exclusion of the letter.

(As to the need to apply a purposive construction, see also *Pickstone* v. *Freemans plc* [1989] AC 66 at p. 112D *per* Lord Keith of Kinkel and at pp 125H and 128C *per* Lord Oliver of Aylmerton.)

Following the Community approach to the construction of art. 7(1)(a) of Directive 79/7, five points are in my opinion clear.

First, the concept of 'granting old age and retirement pensions and the possible consequence thereof for other benefits' expressed in art. 7(1)(a) must be given an independent meaning, unaffected by variable national criteria which depend upon the manner in which each member state chooses to arrange its social security legislation.

Secondly, the phrase 'possible consequence' in art. 7(1)(a), being part of a derogation from individual rights conferred by Directive 79/7, must be construed strictly.

Thirdly, in considering a derogation such as this, the Court should have in mind the aim of the Community authorities in view of which the derogation was included.

Fourthly, the phrase 'possible consequences' must be construed in accordance with the general principle of Community law known as 'the principle of proportionality', which requires that a derogation from an individual right conferred by a Council Directive remains within the limits of what is appropriate and necessary for achieving the aim in view.

Fifthly, it is for the national court to determine consistently with the four propositions set out above, whether in any given case the principle of proportionality has been observed by a member state which has sought to invoke the derogation permitted by art. 7(1)(a).

The first of these propositions is, I think, self-evident, but Mr Advocate-General Mayras put the point felicitously in his Opinion in *Sotgiu* v. *Deutsche Bundespost* [1974] ECR 153 at p. 169 as follows:

... it should be noted that where powers of their own have been conferred on Community institutions, the primacy, the direct effect and the necessity for a uniform application of the rules laid down by these bodies cannot admit of criteria of interpretation which would permit each Member State to fashion to its own taste, that is, to extend or limit the scope of such Community rules.

As authority for the second of these propositions, I refer again to the *Sotgiu* case. There the European Court had to consider points of interpretation arising under art. 48(4) of the EEC Treaty and arts 7(1) and (4) of Regulation 1612/68 of the Council which are designed to secure freedom of movement for workers within the Community. However, by virtue of art. 48(4) of the Treaty, these provisions were not applicable to 'employment in the public service', so that the extent of the exception had to be defined. In the course of giving its judgment, the European Court said (at p. 162):

Taking account of the fundamental nature, in the scheme of the Treaty, of the principles of freedom of movement and equality of treatment of workers within the Community, the exceptions made by art. 48(4) cannot have a scope going beyond the aim in view of which this derogation was included.

The interests which this derogation allows Member States to protect are satisfied by the opportunity of restricting admission of foreign nationals to certain activities in the public service.

In referring in this passage to 'the aim and view of which this derogation was included', the Court was, in my opinion, plainly referring to the aim which the community legislators had in view in including the derogatory provision, art. 48(4). By parity of reasoning, I think that in construing art. 7(1)(a) of Directive 79/7, this Court is entitled and bound to have regard to the aim which the Community legislators had in view in including this derogatory provision and in particular the words 'and the possible consequences thereof for other benefits.'

As to the third proposition set out above, the need to apply a purposive construction has been recently illustrated in the observations of Lord Keith of Kinkel and Lord Oliver of Aylmerton in *Pickstone* v. *Freemans plc* [1989] AC 66 at pp. 112D, 125H and 128C.

As authority for the fourth and fifth of the propositions set out above, I refer to the decision of the European Court in *Johnston* v. *Chief Constable of the Royal Irish Constabulary* [1987] 1 QB 129. In that case, Mrs Johnston complained to the industrial tribunal of Northern Ireland that she had been unlawfully discriminated against by the Chief Constable of the Royal Ulster Constabulary by not renewing her full-time contract of employment with the Constabulary full-time Reserve, following his policy decision not to appoint women to full-time positions. That policy had been initiated because the Chief Constable had decided that all male police officers were to carry firearms when carrying out their regular duties, but that if women were armed, they might become a more frequent target for assassination, their firearms would fall into the hands of their assailants, the public would not welcome their carrying firearms and, if armed, they would be less effective in the social field. The discrimination was said to be contrary to Council Directive 76/207 of 9 February 1976 on the implementation of the principle of equal treatment for men and women as regards access to employment, vocational training and promotion and working conditions ('the Equal Treatment Directive').

It was submitted that such reasons were covered by an exception contained in art. 2(2) of the Directive. In the course of dealing with this point, the European Court dealt with this point as follows (at p. 151):

36. As regards the question whether such reasons may be covered by art. 2(1) of the directive, it should first be observed that *that provision, being a derogation from an individual right laid down in the directive, must be interpreted strictly*. However, it must be recognised that the context in which the occupational activity of members of an armed police force are carried out is determined by the environment in which that activity is carried out. In this regard, the possibility cannot be excluded that in a situation characterised by serious internal disturbances the carrying of firearms by policewomen might create additional risks of their being assassinated and might therefore be contrary to the requirements of public safety.

37. In such circumstances, the context of certain policing activities may be such that the sex of police officers constitutes a determining factor for carrying them out. If that is so, a member state may therefore restrict such tasks, and the training leading thereto, to men. In such a case, as is clear from art. 9(2) of the directive, the member states have a duty to assess periodically the activities concerned in order to decide whether, in the light of social developments, the derogation from the general scheme of the directive may still be maintained.

38. It must also be borne in mind that, in determining the scope of any derogation from an individual right such as the equal treatment of men and women provided by the directive, *the principle of proportionality, one of the general principles of law underlying the Community legal order, must be observed. That principle requires that derogations remain within the limits of what is appropriate and necessary for achieving the aim in view* and requires the principle of equal treatment to be reconciled as far as possible with the requirements of public safety which constitute the decisive factor as regards the context of the activity in question.

39. By reason of the division of jurisdiction provided for in art. 177 of the EEC Treaty, it is for the national court to say whether the reasons on which the Chief Constable based his decision are in fact well founded and justify the specific measure taken in Mrs Johnston's case. *It is also for the national court to ensure that the principle of proportionality is observed* and to determine whether the refusal to renew Mrs Johnston's contract could not be avoided by allocating the women duties which, without jeopardising the aims pursued, can be performed without firearms.

(The emphases in this passage have been added).

In para. 44 of its judgment, the European Court observed that art. 2(3) of the Equal Treatment Directive, which contained another exception to the general principles of the Directive must, like art. 2(2), be 'construed strictly.' In para. 52 it further observed:

> The derogation from the principle of equal treatment which, as stated above, is allowed by art. 2(2) constitutes only an option for the member states. It is for competent national court to see whether that option has been exercised in provisions of national law and to construe the content of those provisions. The question whether an individual may rely upon a provision of the directive in order to have a derogation laid down by national legislation set aside only if that derogation went beyond the limits of the exceptions permitted by art. 2(2) of that directive ...

The 'principle of proportionality', which is reflected in para. 38 of the *Johnston* judgment and is of considerable importance in the present case, is summarised thus by the learned editors of *Halsbury's Laws of England* (4th Edition) Vol. 51 (1986), para. 2.296, the notes to which cite a large number of supporting authorities:

> The principle of proportionality requires that the means used to attain a given end should be no more than what is appropriate and necessary to attain that end; in other words, persons may be obliged only to make the least sacrifice consonant with achieving the objective sought. In order to establish whether a provision of Community law is compatible with the principle of proportionality, it is necessary to establish whether the means it employs to achieve its aim correspond to the importance of the aim and whether those means are necessary in order to attain it. Whether a measure is disproportionate or not is not necessarily determined by reference to the individual position of any one particular group of operators. The principle of proportionality applies also to national measures.

It is common ground that any national legislature, in exercising the limited freedom or 'option' conferred on it by art. 7(1)(a) of the Directive, must do so within the limits imposed by the principle of proportionality.

The application of that principle in a case such as the present, in my judgment in effect involves the consideration of two separate, albeit closely connected, questions: First, is the aim of the relevant provisions of the national law in question justified, having regard to Community law? Secondly, do the derogations from the individual rights conferred by the Directive which are effected by provisions exceed the limits of what is appropriate and necessary to achieve that aim? The answers to these questions must partly depend on the meaning of the relevant Community legislation. Since such legislation must be given a purposive interpretation, the aim of the Community legislators must be relevant both in the process of construction and in applying the principle of proportionality.

I proceed to consider the meaning of art. 7(1)(a) of Directive 79/7 and in particular its second limb 'and the possible consequences thereof for other benefits', the addition of which, as we know from the *travaux préparatoires*, was proposed by the United Kingdom.

*The meaning of art. 7(1)(a)*

To dispose of one preliminary matter, I accept the submission of Mr Lester that the word 'possible' in the phrase 'possible consequences' is merely an acknowledgement that the effects of the difference in pensionable ages may differ between member states, since they may organise their social security schemes in different ways, so that a consequential adjustment required in one state may not be required in another; the use of the word 'possible' does not weaken the requirements of strict interpretation and proportionality in construing the phrase 'and the possible consequences thereof for other benefits.'

The right conferred on member states by art. 7(1)(a) is exercisable subject to the obligations imposed by arts 7(2) and 8. Under art. 7(2) they are obliged periodically to examine matters excluded under art. 7(1) to ascertain in the light of social developments whether there is justification for maintaining the relevant exclusions. Under art. 8 they are obliged to inform the Commission of their reasons for maintaining any existing provisions on such matters and of the possibility of reviewing them at a later date. We have been told that the United Kingdom, along with other member states, periodically informs the Commission of such progress.

Subject to these obligations, the aim of the first limb of art. 7(1)(a) was clearly to confer on member states the option at their discretion to differentiate between men and women in defining age qualifications in relation to *old age and retirement benefits*, notwithstanding the general prohibitions against sex discrimination contained in the earlier provisions of the directive.

The aim of the second limb was, in my judgment, to absolve member states from infringement of the Directive 79/7 in cases where people's rights, other than rights to old age and retirement pensions, are necessarily affected as a result of the fixing of a different pensionable age for men and women for the purposes of granting old age or retirement pensions. As the European Court said in its judgment in *Beets-Proper* v. *Van Lanschot Bankiers* [1986] ECR 773 (para. 37), in the course of commenting on art. 7(1)(a) and the earlier judgment of that Court in *Burton* v. *British Railways Board* [1982] ECR 555:

> The Court thus acknowledged that benefits linked to a national scheme which lays down a different pensionable age for men and women may lie outside the ambit of the afore-mentioned obligation.

*Burton* was a case in which the European Court ruled that there was no breach of the principle of equal treatment where an employer made access to voluntary redundancy available only during the five years preceding the minimum pensionable age fixed by the national security legislation. (The authority of that decision is now doubtful, for reasons appearing later in this judgment.)

In his Opinion in *Marshall* v. *Southampton & South West Hampshire Area Health Authority* [1986] ECR 723 at p. 730, Mr Advocate-General Sir Gordon Slynn described the second limb of art. 7(1)(a) as 'dealing with other benefits under State schemes which are geared to the pensionable age fixed by the Member States.'

However, it does not follow that any 'link' or 'gearing' will suffice. If a member state is to rely on that second limb, a sufficiently strong causative link must, in my judgment, be shown to exist between the (permitted) discriminatory provisions relating to old-age or retirement pensions and the relevant discriminatory provisions relating to other benefits which are sought to be justified; the very word 'consequences' presupposes cause and effect. Mr Commissioner Monroe, in his decision in *Thomas*, in a passage adopted by Mr Commissioner Hallett in his decision in *Cooze*, said this:

> I have reached the conclusion that it is not sufficient to escape the directive simply to gear a different benefit to the differential pensionable ages if the resulting differential between sexes in that benefit cannot be shown to have some objective link with pensionable age. If it were it would make it all too easy to evade the provisions of the directive ... I have reached the conclusion that something more is needed than the mere reference to pensionable age with its inherent element of discrimination. There must be some objective link with the differentiation in pensionable ages.

I agree, but would go a little further in characterising the nature of that objective link. Construing the phrase 'and the possible consequences thereof for other benefits' strictly and in accordance with the principle of proportionality, I conclude that it gives member states authority to prescribe or retain different age limits for men and women when defining the qualifications for entitlement to benefits other than old-age and retirement benefits *only when this is a necessary consequence of their having defined the qualifications for entitlement to old-age or retirement benefits by reference to different age limits for men and women only in a manner which is appropriate to meet this necessity.* The need to avoid illogicality, unfairness or absurdity may well give rise to necessity in this context, but, as Mr Lester submitted, I find it difficult to envisage other circumstances when the necessity will arise.

It is for the member state itself to decide whether it wishes to avail itself of the option conferred by either limb of art. 7(1)(a) of Directive 79/7. In my judgment, however, it is for the national court (not the member state itself) to decide whether any purported exercise of such option falls within the ambit of the authority conferred by the article, in particular the principle of proportionality: (see the *Johnston* case (*supra*), para 39 quoted above). This,

I conceive, is what Mr Commissioner Monroe and Mr Commissioner Hallett had in mind in referring to the nature of the necessary link as being 'objective.'

*Do sections 36(4)(d) and 37(5) of the 1975 Act fall within the liberty conferred on Member States by the second limb of art. 7(1)(a) of Directive 79/7?*

While, in construing art. 7(1)(a), it is right to take into account the aim of the Community legislators, it is also right to take into account the aim of Parliament in enacting sections 36(4)(d) and 37(5) of the 1975 Act when this Court considers whether these two subsections fall within the liberty conferred on member states by the second limb of the article. For this purpose it will, in my judgment, be legitimate to have regard (*inter alia*) to the White Paper *Social Security Provision for Chronically Sick and Disabled People* HC 276: see for example *Pickstone* v. *Freemans plc* [1989] AC 66. I shall refer to this as 'the White Paper.'

Paragraph 56 of the White Paper demonstrates the intention of Parliament that SDA (there referred to as 'non-contributory invalidity pension') was to be available 'to people of working age who would have been entitled to contributory invalidity pension had they satisfied the contribution conditions and who would ordinarily have been breadwinners but for their disablement.' Paragraph 60 shows the intention that ICA was to be available for 'those of working age who would be breadwinners in paid employment but for the need to stay at home and act as unpaid attendants for people who are severely disabled and need care.'

Mr Plender, on behalf of the Secretary of State, explained that the 1975 Act makes provision for a range of benefits and allowances payable on the occurrence of specified risks, either (a) to replace the income lost on the occurrence of the risk, or (b) to meet the additional costs incurred as a result of the consequence. Benefits to replace income include unemployment benefit and sickness benefit (s. 14); (contributory) invalidity pension (s. 15(1)); statutory sick pay (s. 15A); invalidity allowance (s. 16(1)); maternity allowance (s. 22); widow's allowance (s. 24); SDA (s. 36); ICA (s. 37) and retirement benefits for the aged (sections 28-30 and 39). Allowances to meet costs include maternity grants (s. 21); child's special allowance (s. 31); death grant (s. 32); attendance allowance (s. 35); mobility allowance (s. 37A); and guardian's allowance (s. 38).

ICA and SDA, along with other social security benefits designed to replace income as distinct from allowances to meet costs, are tied by the wording of the 1975 Act to pensionable age. In his submission, however, ICA and SDA and other benefits designed to replace income are tied to pensionable age not only in a linguistic sense, but also in a logical or functional sense, on the principle that the income falling to be replaced is income lost by reason of the occurrence of the insured risk during working life - in other words is income which would otherwise be earned while the claimant is of working age.

In the case of all such benefits, Mr Plender submitted, it is necessary to prescribe some upper age limit for termination of the working age; otherwise the benefits would cease to be income-replacement benefits. For this purpose, he said, Parliament has found it necessary to devise a means of distinguishing between those persons of working age and those not of working age in a simple and administratively workable manner by reference to 'actual patterns of employment', and the appropriate way to do this has been by reference to 'pensionable age.' This, in opening the appeals, he described as the 'nutshell' of the Secretary of State's submission.

However, he went on to submit that within the statutory scheme applicable in Great Britain, the link between the determination of pensionable age for retirement pensions and the different treatment of men and women by the 1975 Act in relation to income replacement benefits (including SDA and ICA) is fortified by three other factors.

First, the Social Security (Credits) Regulations (SI 1975 No 336) provide that recipients of income-replacement benefits, including ICA and SDA, should receive credits for contributions to retirement pensions; it would only be appropriate to give such credits to persons under pensionable age. Secondly, in the exceptional case where a benefit continues to be payable after retirement, the amount of the income-replacement benefit is, by virtue of the Overlapping Benefits Regulations, reduced by the amount of any retirement pension received or of any occupational pension received in the case of a man over 60. Thirdly, the amount of SDA and ICA has been tied to 'category C' retirement pensions.

I will deal first with these three other factors. As to the first two, the particular Regulations referred to, albeit involving an element of sex discrimination, may themselves be justified by the second limb of art. 7(1)(a) of Directive 79/7. In my judgment, however, they do not assist the argument that sections 36(4)(d) and 37(5) of the 1975 Act are a necessary consequence of the legislature having defined the qualifications for entitlement to old-age and retirement benefits by reference to different age limits for men and women. As to the third, on which some stress has been laid,

> Category C pensions were a response to political pressure to help those who were uninsured under the pre-1948 schemes and, being over pensionable age when the 1946 Act came into effect, had not had the chance to establish eligibility to a pension under this legislation. They were to receive a non-contributory flat-rate pension of 60 per cent of the basic contributory pension, with the exception of married women who were to get a similar proportion of the contributory pension for a dependent wife. It was considered inappropriate to pay the same amount as those who had contributed fully to the National Insurance Fund.

(*Ogus and Barendt: The Law of Social Security*, 3rd ed. 1988, p. 225.)

Paragraphs 56 and 60 of the White Paper show that, in specifying the same amounts for non-invalidity pension (now SDA) and ICA as those applicable for category C pensions, Parliament had in mind the following considerations:

> It is palpably wrong to deny altogether basic benefit as of right to people who because of severe disablement have not been able to establish themselves as contributors in the insurance scheme. At the same time, it would be inconsistent with the maintenance of the contributory basis of that scheme and inequitable in comparison with the treatment of those already over pension age - particularly those who have no or reduced pensions and are just as disabled as those under pension age - to pay non-contributory invalidity pension at the full contributory rates to people under pension age.

There is thus a tenuous link between SDA and ICA on the one hand and pensionable age on the other hand in the sense that Parliament, in fixing the uniform *rate* for SDA and ICA, has had in mind the aim of achieving broad fairness (a) as between those over pensionable age and those under that age, and (b) as between those who have contributed and those who have not. But I cannot see how this by itself renders the differentiation of ages between men and women, in specifying the qualifications for SDA and ICA, a consequence of the differentiation between them in the qualifications for old-age and retirement benefits.

I now revert to the main theme of the Secretary of State's case as advanced by Mr Plender. It was accepted on his behalf that in due course it may well be right to change pensionable age to a common age for men and women, notwithstanding the liberty conferred by art. 7(1) of Directive 79/7, and that such a change might affect female and male working patterns. (The differentiation, it seems, was originally made in deference to the expressed wishes of women's organisations: (see *Ogus & Barendt: The Law of Social Security*, 3rd ed. 1988, p. 255). However, it is said, until such change is made, ICA and SDA, along with other income replacement benefits, must necessarily be tied to pensionable age though the precise configuration of the bond will vary according to the nature of the benefit.

SDA and ICA are benefits intended to provide protection against the risk of what is described in Directive 79/7 as 'invalidity.' Their aim is wholly or in part to replace the income which disabled people or those caring for invalids, as the case may be, would have been in a position to earn but for the relevant invalidity. The 'target group' (the phrase used in argument before us) at whom the benefits are aimed comprises those persons who would or could be breadwinners but for the invalidity.

This being so, I have no difficulty in accepting that it is appropriate and necessary for our legislation (a) to identify with a sufficient degree of accuracy and administrative workability the 'target group', and (b) for this purpose to specify a minimum age which a person must attain before he or she can qualify for SDA or ICA, and a minimum 'cut-off' age after which he or she cannot become eligible to receive either benefit. It would simply not be practical to determine in the case of each individual elderly carer or disabled person whether he or she would be working but for the disability or care. (It appears scarcely logical, on the other hand, that under ss 36 and 37 a person having once qualified to receive either benefit can remain eligible to receive it even after attaining the 'cut-off' age; but this is an illogicality which does not concern us.) In the end the question for this Court is, I think, whether our legislation relating to old-age and relevant benefits makes it appropriate and necessary for Parliament, when designating the cut-off age for SDA and ICA purposes, to follow the concept of 'pensionable age', with its concomitant discrimination between men and women, rather than designating a uniform age.

Mr Plender more than once submitted that the policy behind the cut-off provisions in the two ss 36 and 37 is 'to identify with a sufficient degree of accuracy and administrative workability the portion of the population which is of working age.' However, the 'target group' could have been readily identified with a sufficient degree of accuracy by designating a uniform age for men and women. And, while it may be administratively convenient to make the cut-off age for SDA and ICA purposes the same as 'pensionable age', it has not, I think, been suggested that a uniform cut-off age would render our SDA and ICA legislation administratively unworkable. (Section 37A(5) of the 1975 Act, which provides for an upper age limit of 65 for mobility allowance except for those already entitled to it when they attain that age, demonstrates that it is administratively quite simple to have a common age.)

Ultimately therefore, in my judgment, the Secretary of State's case has to rest on the propositions forcefully advanced by Mr Plender that, in the case of SDA and ICA, (i) the statutory presumed working life must coincide as closely as possible with fact; (ii) in fact women, like men, tend to retire at pensionable age; and (iii) the United Kingdom, in accordance with the principle of proportionality, is entitled to set the cut-off point for SDA and ICA purposes at the respective ages when the greatest number of men and women do in fact retire, in view of the State's pensionable age.

Mr Lester and Mr Rowland did not accept the factual assumptions on which these propositions are based and, in my judgment, justifiably both because of the inconclusive nature of the statistics placed before us, and also for another reason. In an important and relevant recent judgment in *Barber* v. *Guardian Royal Exchange Assurance Group* [1990] 2 All ER 660, the European Court has held that it is contrary to art. 119 of the EEC Treaty to impose an age condition which differs according to sex in respect of pensions paid under a contracted-out scheme, even if the difference between the pensionable age for men and that for women is based on the one provided for by the national statutory scheme: see para. 32.

[I interpolate that in his Opinion in *Barber*, Mr Advocate-General Walter Van Gerven had dealt fully with the *Burton* decision, suggesting that *Burton* had been wrongly decided in so far as it held that the retirement scheme in that case could not be regarded as discriminatory within the meaning of the Equal Treatment Directive, on the grounds that the difference between the benefits for men and those for women stemmed from the fact that the retirement scheme was tied to the pension scheme governed by the United Kingdom social security provisions : see in particular paras. 41-43. Though the European Court in its judgment did not expressly refer to *Burton*, in this respect it appears implicitly to have endorsed the Advocate-General's Opinion, so that the decision in *Burton* now appears to be of very doubtful authority.]

As Mr Lester pointed out, it is reasonable to suppose that the *Barber* decision will have wide repercussions on the working patterns of employed men and women in this country whose pension arrangements are made under contracted-out schemes.

Thus, even apart from the inconclusive nature of the statistics placed before us, the, as yet unknown, impact of the *Barber* decision is a further reason why, in my judgment, the sex discrimination involved in sections 36(4)(d) and 37(5) of the 1975 Act cannot be justified by reference to the assumed working life of a woman as opposed to a man. A general assumption of this kind, which takes no account of individual circumstances and made without adequate factual basis, in my judgment itself discriminates against women: compare the observations of Lawton LJ in *Skyrail Oceanic Ltd* v. *Coleman* [1981] ICR 864 at pp. 869-870.

No one disputes that *some* discrimination between men and women in the operation of SDA and ICA is rendered appropriate and necessary by Parliament's designation of different pensionable ages for men and women and will be permitted by the second limb of art. 7(1)(a). One good example was given in the course of argument. Without special appropriate provision designed to meet this anomaly, the Secretary of State might find himself obliged to allow a woman between 60 and 65 who qualifies for both pension and ICA to receive the full benefit of both which would be quite contrary to the purpose of ICA. This problem is dealt with by the Overlapping Benefits Regulations. Where she is also entitled to ICA, her total benefit is reduced. No one disputes that this provision is preserved from the scope of Directive 79/7 by the second limb of art. 7(1)(a). As Mr Commissioner Hallett put it in *Cooze* (para. 31), 'there is here a clear objective tie or link.' The provision is truly consequential upon the difference in pensionable ages for men and women.

Thus, the second limb of art. 7(1)(a) may well justify denying a woman of over 60 the benefit of SDA or ICA on the ground that, by reason of her earlier pensionable age, she is in actual receipt of a pension. Many women of

60, however, will not qualify for a state pension because they will not have paid or been credited with sufficient contributions. In my judgment, the mere fact that pensionable age is 60 for women cannot possibly render it necessary and appropriate to disqualify such women from the (non-contributory) benefits of SDA or ICA, when men of 60 would be eligible to receive such benefits if they satisfied the qualifying conditions. As Mr Rowland pointed out, the disqualifying provisions of ss 36(5)(d) and 37(6) of the 1975 Act go far further than they need to prevent mere overlapping. He gave us a striking example from the *Beard* case itself. Mrs Beard (like many other women may be after the *Marshall* case) was entitled to continue work after the age of 60. However, at the age of 60 1/4 she gave up work to look after her invalid mother. She did not qualify for a pension at 60 because she had not paid the necessary contributions and she would have liked to continue working if her home circumstances had not prevented her: see pp. 1 and 2 of the *Beard* bundle. The mere fact that a woman's pensionable age is 60 rather than 65 does not appear to be a logical and sufficient ground for the statutory scheme to deprive Mrs Beard of ICA when a man of similar age in similar circumstances would not be disqualified. The fact that ICA, SDA and retirement pensions are all earnings replacement benefits does not constitute an adequate justifications for designating a discriminatory upper age limit for ICA and SDA where no retirement pension is in fact paid.

The particular anomaly referred to in the last paragraph could no doubt be dealt with by amending legislation which exempted women who did not qualify for a state pension from the provisions of sections 36(4)(d) and 37(5) of the 1975 Act. In my judgment, however, even as so amended, these two subsections would not fall within the liberty given to the legislature of a member state by art. 7(1)(a). The onus must fall on the Secretary of State to show that the designation of different age limits for men and women, when defining the qualifications for entitlement to SDA and ICA, is a necessary consequence of Parliament's having defined the qualifications for entitlement to old-age and retirement benefits by reference to different age limits for men and women. For the reasons which I have given, I do not think this onus has been or can be discharged.

I make two observations in conclusion. First, it is obvious that the decision of this Court in this case relating to SDA and ICA may have implications as regards some or all of the other income replacement benefits mentioned above. Mr Rowland conducted us expertly through some of the legislation regarding those other benefits. However, I prefer to say nothing further in this judgment about these other benefits to which different considerations may or may not apply.

Secondly, it is no less obvious that the decision of this Court in this case must depend heavily on the proper construction of art. 7(1)(a). It would be possible for this Court to refer any possible questions of construction on this article to the European Court. Mr Lester indeed at our request helpfully produced a preliminary draft designed to identify possible questions which might be submitted, if necessary. However, the area of difference between the parties as to the construction of the article did not appear to be a large one. The dispute related more to its applicability to the two particular subsections of the 1975 Act in question. Counsel on both sides expressed the hope that this Court would not find it necessary to make any such reference for the purpose of reaching a decision on this appeal. If the case goes higher, their Lordships may consider a reference is advisable, but I, for my part, do not consider that it is so at this stage.

We have had the benefit of very detailed, careful and erudite arguments of Counsel for all parties to these appeals. In deference to these arguments, I have attempted in this judgment to deal fairly fully with what I conceive to be the principal points raised. In the end, however, for the reasons stated (which correspond quite closely with the reasons given by Mr Commissioner Hallett in the *Cooze* appeal), my conclusion is that the inclusion of the admittedly discriminatory provisions of ss 36(4)(d) and 37(5) of the 1975 Act is not justified by art. 7(1)(a) of Directive 79/7.

Accordingly, I would dismiss the Secretary of State's appeals in the cases of Mrs Thomas, Mrs Cooze, Mrs Beard and Mrs Murphy. I would allow the appeal of Mrs Morley and would remit the matter to Mr Commissioner Morcom to make the further necessary findings of fact and give the appropriate decision in the light of such findings.

SIR DENYS BUCKLEY: I entirely agree with the judgment delivered by Slade LJ and would be content to say no more, but the principle of proportionality to which he has referred is a somewhat novel concept to English lawyers. I think it may be useful for me to add something on that topic in my own words.

Article 1 of Directive 79/7 makes clear that the purpose of that Directive is to procure the progressive implementation of the principle of equal treatment for men and women in the field of social security, and art. 2 indicates that the men and women to whom the Directive is to apply are those described as 'the working population.'

Article 5 of the Directive, read without reference to art. 7, contains a mandatory provision that every member state shall abolish any laws, regulations and administrative provisions which are contrary to the principle of equal treatment for men and women, thus conferring individual rights to equal treatment on members of the working population. Article 7, however, contains a relaxing provision modifying the mandatory character of art. 5 so as to permit any member state to fix ages at which men and women may respectively become entitled to draw old-age pensions and retirement pensions which discriminate between the sexes. This article is consequently in the nature of a derogation from the rights conferred by art. 5.

In setting out in this way what I take to be the effect of arts 1, 2, 5 and 7 of Directive 79/7 I have purposely not used the precise language of the Directive, hoping in that way to clarify what believe to be its effect.

Article 7 permits any member state, which avails itself of the power to exclude from the scope of the Directive any domestic law, regulation or provision, to do so in whatever way it chooses, provided that the way in which it does so is within the scope of the power conferred by art. 7(1); but whether the way in which the member state seeks to avail itself of the power is within the ambit of the power must clearly, in my judgment, be determined not by reference to the law of that member state but by reference to European Community law, and must involve the application of the principle of proportionality, as well as that of strict construction, as those principles are recognised in European Community law. See in this connection European Communities Act 1972, s. 3(1).

In reliance upon art. 7 of the Directive the United Kingdom has enacted, and has not abolished or amended, the statutory provisions set out under the heading 'Relevant UK statutory provisions' early in Slade LJ's judgment. What we have to determine is whether enacting and maintaining in force those provisions was and is within the competence of the British Parliament. If not, the five claimants are entitled to insist on equal treatment with men under the Directive.

Perhaps the most difficult part of this problem is to determine what is the precise effect of the last eight words of art. 7(1)(a). I agree with Slade LJ that the solution of this involved the principles of strict constructions and of proportionality as they are recognised and applied in the European Court.

At this stage two alternative courses of action present themselves. This Court could refer appropriately framed questions to the European Court to assist us in arriving at a proper conclusion on the construction of art. 7(1) of the Directive, or we can proceed to reach a conclusion without such assistance, but in the latter alternative we must proceed, as Slade LJ has said, 'from a Community point of view', by which I understand him to mean applying not English but Community law and principles of construction. For the reasons given by Slade LJ at the end of his judgment, I agree that in this case the latter alternative is preferable.

Helpful guidance on the principle of proportionality can be found in the judgment of the European Court in *Johnston* v. *Chief Constable of the Royal Ulster Constabulary* [1987] I QB 129. In that case the claimant, Mrs Johnston, complained that the Chief Constable had discriminated against her by refusing to renew her full-time contract of employment on the ground that her sex rendered her unsuitable to carry arms. This refusal was asserted to be contrary to a Council Directive (76/207) on the implementation of equal treatment between men and women as regards access to employment, vocational training, promotion and working conditions. At para. 38 of their judgment the European Court said:

> It must also be borne in mind that, in determining the scope of any derogation from an individual right such as the equal treatment of men and women provided for by the directive, the principle of proportionality, one of the general principles of law underlying the Community legal order, must be observed. That principle requires that derogations remain within the limits of what is appropriate and necessary for achieving the aim in view and requires the principle of equal treatment to be reconciled as far as possible with the requirements of public safety which constitute the decisive factor as regards the context of the activity in question.

In para. 39 of its judgment the Court indicated that it was for the national court to say whether the reasons on which the Chief Constable based his decision were in fact well founded and justified the course he took. 'It is also', they said, 'for the national court to ensure that the principle of proportionality is observed and to determine whether the refusal to renew Mrs Johnston's contract could not have been avoided' by adopting some other course.

In the instant case the prevailing and over-riding objective of Directive 79/1 is clearly stated in art. 1 as being the progressive implementation of the principle of equal treatment for men and women in matters of social security. Any law, rule or regulation promulgated or maintained in force by the British Parliament or authorities, which might operate unfavourably to the implementation of that objective, can only be countenanced if it is within the limits of what is 'appropriate and necessary for achieving the aim in view.' The end in view last-mentioned might appear to be the objective of the member state who has taken the action under the authority of art. 7, the propriety of which is assailed, but I do not think that can be right, for so to hold would make the member state the arbiter on the extent of its own power to derogate from the mandatory effect of art. 5 of the Directive. I conclude that the relevant 'aim in view' must be the objective which the European Community authorities must be taken to have had in view when promulgating art. 7(1): that is to say that we are thrown back to attempting to define the ambit of the power conferred by art. 7(1).

In my judgment, the presence of the word 'thereof' in art. 7(1)(a) is significant. When framing the language of art. 7(1)(a), the writer or legislator cannot be supposed to have known or speculated about the manner or term in which any member state might thereafter seek to avail itself of the power conferred upon it by the paragraph. It would consequently be unnatural to read 'thereof' as referring to any verbal formula or legislative device employed at a later date by any such member state. The word 'thereof' must accordingly, in my judgment, be read as referring to the act of determining pensionable ages for the purposes of granting old-age and retirement pensions and nothing more. I do not find it easy to suggest how the mere act of fixing pensionable ages, apart from any side-effects arising from the language employed in the context of the pension law of the particular member state, could have consequences for other benefits, but that circumstance would not, in my judgment, justify us in reading into art. 7(1)(a) a further substantive power to modify other benefits not consequentially but substantively. No such power can, I suggest, be spelt out of art. 7(1)(a).

Moreover, in my judgment, art. 7(1)(a) in terms preserves for every member state the right to exclude the mandatory effect of art. 5 only in respect of determining pensionable ages. It does not in terms preserve, as a separate and distinct right, a power to exclude other benefits from the effect of art. 5. Other benefits can be affected by art. 7(1)(a) only consequentially.

It seems to me, therefore, that the principle of proportionality comes into play in relation to art. 7(1)(a) only in respect of the problem whether a member state has, by the way in which it has introduced new pensionable ages, consequentially effected an excess derogation from the mandatory obligation under art. 5 to maintain and implement the principle of equal treatment. That principle is, in my judgment, the 'end in view' in relation to which the proportionality must be assessed.

I fully agree with Slade LJ that the use of the word 'consequences' in art. 7(1)(a) imports that there must be a causative link between any relevant provisions relating to pensionable ages and any relevant 'other benefits', and (to put it in my own words) that that link must be a convincing reason for holding that 'the other benefits' in question are affected in a relevant way which is in truth and necessarily a consequence of the provisions relating to pensionable ages.

I would not wish to be taken as necessarily assenting to the view that according to English principles of statutory construction it would be right to take the White Paper (HC 276) into consideration in this case, but I do not think that we know enough about how the European Court would view such a question for the purpose of assessing proportionality. Fortunately, none of this appears to me to bear upon my conclusion in this case.

I agree with Slade LJ when he says that the mere fact that pensionable age is 60 for women cannot possibly render it necessary and appropriate to disqualify such women from the benefits of SDA and ICA when men of 60 would be eligible to receive such benefits if they satisfied the qualifying conditions, and with what he goes on to say about the *Beard* case.

For these reasons and for those given by Slade LJ, I concur in the conclusions which he has reached and has stated at the end of his judgment. I also agree with the form of order he has proposed.

LORD JUSTICE STOCKER: I have had the opportunity of reading in draft both of the judgments of my Lords. I am wholly in agreement with them and therefore do not propose to add observations of my own.

# DOCUMENTATION

**1        BIBLIOGRAPHY**

**1.1      BOOKS AND REPORTS**

ATKINS, S., and HOGGETT, B., *Women and the Law* (1984).

BOURN, C., and WHITMORE, J., *Discrimination and Equal Pay* (1989).

BUCKLEY, M., and ANDERSON, M. (eds), *Women, Equality and Europe* (1988).

CARTER, A., *The Politics of Women's Rights* (1988).

CHIPLIN, B., and SLOANE, P., *Sex Discrimination in the Labour Market* (1976).

CREIGHTON, W.B., *Working Women and the Law* (1979), cited as CREIGHTON.

DAVIES, P., and FREEDLAND, M., *Labour Law. Texts and materials* (2nd ed. 1984),
        cited as DAVIES & FREEDLAND.

EDWARDS, J., *Positive Discrimination, Social Justice and Social Policy* (1987).

EDWARDS, S. (ed.), *Gender, Sex and the Law* (1985).

ELLIS, E., *Sex Discrimination Law* (1989).

GREGORY, J., *Sex, Race and the Law* (1987).

HEPPLE, B., *Equal Pay and the Industrial Tribunals* (1984).

HEPPLE, B., and O'HIGGINS, P., *Encyclopedia of Labour Relations Law*,
        cited as HEPPLE, *Encyclopedia.*

LEONARD, A.,
    -     *Judging Inequality. The effectiveness of the tribunal system in sex
          discrimination and equal pay cases* (1987).
    -     *Pyrrhic Victories. Successful sex discrimination and equal pay cases in the
          industrial tribunals 1980-84* (1987).

LESTER, A., and WAINWRIGHT, D., *Equal Pay for Work of Equal Value* (1984).

McCRUDDEN, C. (ed.), *Women, Employment and European Community Law* (1987),
        cited as McCRUDDEN.

McLEAN, S., and BURROWS, N. (eds), *The Legal Relevance of Gender* (1988).

MARTIN, J., and ROBERTS, C., *Women and Employment. A lifetime perspective*
        (1984).

MEEHAN, E., *Women's Rights at Work. Campaigns and policy in Britain and the United
        States* (1986).

O'DONOVAN, C., and SZYSZCZAK, E., *Equality and Sex Discrimination Law* (1988).

O'DONOVAN, C., *Sexual Divisions in Law* (1985).

OGUS, A., and BARENDT, E., *The Law of Social Security* (3rd ed. 1988).

PANNICK, D., *Sex Discrimination Law* (1985).

PHELPS BROWN, H.,
-    *The Inequality of Pay* (1977).
-    *Egalitarianism and the Generation of Inequality* (1988).

PRECHAL, S., and BURROWS, N., *Gender Discrimination Law of the European Community* (1990).

RIGHTS OF WOMEN EUROPE, *Women's Rights and the EEC* (1983).

ROBARTS, S., *Positive Action for Women* (1981).

RUBENSTEIN, M., *Equal Pay for Work of Equal Value* (1984).

SHARPE and ROBERTS, *Positive Action for Women. Changing the workplace* (1986).

SLOANE, P. (ed.), *Women and Low Pay* (1980).

TOWNSHEND-SMITH, R., *Sex Discrimination in Employment* (1989).

WILLBORN, S. L., *A Secretary and a Cook. Challenging women's wages in the courts of the United States and Great Britain* (1989).

ZABALZA, A., and TZANNATOS, Z., *Women and Equal Pay* (1985).


**1.2        ARTICLES AND REVIEWS**

ANON,
-    'Achieving Equal Opportunity through Positive Action', (1987) *EOR* No 14, p. 13.
-    'Equal Opportunities and Contract Compliance', (1986) *EOR* No 8, p. 9.
-    'Equal Value. The Union response', (1987) *EOR* No 11, p. 10.
-    'Equal Value. A Union update', (1988) *EOR* No 22, p. 9.

APPLEBY, G., and ELLIS, E., 'Formal Investigations. The Commission for Racial Equality and the Equal Opportunities Commission as Law Enforcement Agencies', (1984) *Public Law* 236.

ARNULL, A., 'Article 119 and Equal Pay for Work of Equal Value', (1986) 11 *European Law Review* 200.

ATKINS, S.,
-    'Social Security Act 1980 and the EEC Directive on Equal Treatment in Social Security Benefits', (1981) *Journal of Social Welfare Law* 16.
-    'The Home Responsibilities Provision in the New State Pension Scheme', (1980) *Journal of Social Welfare Law* 33.
-    'The Sex Discrimination Act 1975. The end of a decade', (1986) 24 *Feminist Review* 57.
-    'Women's Rights' in COOPER, J. and DHAVAN, R. (eds), *Public Interest Law* (1986).

BAILEY, S., 'Equal Treatment/Special Treatment. The dilemma of the dismissed pregnant employee', (1989) *Journal of Social Work Law* 85.

BEDDOE, R., 'Independent Experts?', (1986) *EOR* No 6, p. 13.

BINDMAN, G., 'Proving Discrimination. Is the burden too heavy?', *Law Guardian*, 17 December 1980.

BURROWS, N., 'The Promotion of Women's Rights by the European Economic Community', (1980) 17 *Common Market Law Review* 191.

BYRNE, P., and LOVENDUSKI, J.,
-   'The Equal Opportunities Commission', (1978) 1 *Women's Studies Int. Q.* 131.
-   'Sex Equality and the Law in Britain', (1978) 5 *Journal of Law and Society* 148.

CARR, J., *New roads to equality. Contract compliance for the UK?*, Fabian Society (1987).

CHIPLIN, CURRAN and PARSLEY, 'Relative Female Earnings in Great Britain and the Impact of Legislation', in P. SLOANE (ed.), *Women and Low Pay*, Macmillan (1980).

COLLINSON, D.L., 'Equal Value at Eagle Star', (1987) *EOR* No 11, p. 18.

COOTE, A., 'Equality and the Curse of the Quango', *New Statesman*, December 1978.

DAVIES, P.,
-   'European Equality Legislation, UK Legislative Policy and Industrial Relations', in McCRUDDEN, C. (ed.), *Women, Employment and European Equality Law* (1987).
-   'The Central Arbitration Committee and Equal Pay', (1980) *Current Legal Problems* 165.

DOCKSEY, C., 'The European Community and the Promotion of Equality', in McCRUDDEN, C. (ed.), *Women, Employment and European Equality Law* (1987).

FORMAN, J., 'The Equal Pay Principle Under Community Law. A commentary on article 119 EEC', in (1982) 1 *Legal Issues in European Integration* 17.

GREGORY, J.,
-   'Equal Pay and Sex Discrimination. Why women are giving up the fight', (1982) 10 *Feminist Review* 75.

HEPPLE, B.,
-   'Discrimination and Equality of Opportunity. Northern Ireland lessons', 10 *Oxford Journal of Legal Studies* 408.
-   'Judging Equal Rights', (1983) *Current Legal Problems* 71.
-   'The Judicial Process in Claims for Equal Pay and Equal Treatment in the United Kingdom', in McCRUDDEN, C. (ed.), *Women, Employment and European Equality Law* (1987).

HOSKYNS, C., 'Women's Equality and the European Community', (1985) 20 *Feminist Review*.

HOSKYNS, C., and LUCKHAUS, L., 'The European Community Directive on Equal Treatment in Social Security', (1989) 17 *Policy and Politics* 321.

JOWELL, J., 'The Enforcement of Laws against Sex Discrimination in England. Problems of institutional design', in RATNER R. (ed.), *Equal Employment Policy for Women* (1980).

LARSEN, 'Equal Pay for Women in the United Kingdom', (1971) 103 *International Labour Review* 1.

LOVENDUSKI, J., 'Implementing Equal Opportunities in the 1980s. An overview', (1989) 67 *Public Administration* 7.

LUCKHAUS, L.,
- 'Payment for Caring. A European solution', (1986) *Public Law* 526.
- 'Severe Disablement Allowance. The old dressed up as new', (1986) *Journal of Social Welfare Law* 153.
- 'Social Security. The equal treatment reforms', (1983) *Journal of Social Welfare Law* 325.
- 'Bridging Pensions. A question of difference', (1990) 19 *Industrial Law Journal* 148.
- 'The Social Security Directive. Its impact on part-time and unpaid work', in O'BRIEN, M., HANTRAIS, L., and MANGEN, S., *Women, Equal Opportunities and Welfare*, 11.
- 'Changing Rules, Enduring Structures', (1990) 53 *Modern Law Review* 655.

LUSTGARTEN, L., 'Problems of Proof in Employment Discrimination Cases', (1977) 6 *Industrial Law Journal* 212.

McCRUDDEN, C.,
- 'Comparable Worth. A common dilemma', (1986) 11 *Yale Journal of International Law* 396.
- 'Equal Pay for Work of Equal Value', (1983) 12 *Industrial Law Journal* 197.
- 'Institutional Discrimination', (1982) 2 *Oxford Journal of Legal Studies* 303.
- 'Legal Remedies for Discrimination in Employment', (1981) *Current Legal Problems* 211.
- 'Rethinking Positive Action', (1986) 15 *Industrial Law Journal* 230.

McINTOSH, 'Women at Work. A survey of employers', (1980) *Department of Employment Gazette* 1142.

MEEHAN, E.,
- 'Implementing Equal Opportunity Policies. Some British - American comparisons', *Politics*, vol 2, No 1, April 1982.
- 'Priorities of the Equal Opportunities Commission', (1983) 54 *Political Quarterly* 69.

NICKELL, 'Trade Unions and the Position of Women in the Industrial Pay Structure', (1977) 15 *British Journal of Industrial Relations* 192.

PANNICK, D.,
- 'Burden of Proof in Discrimination Cases', (1981) *New Law Journal* 895.
- 'Class Action and Discrimination Law', *New Community*, vol X, No 1, Summer 1982.

PIKE, M.,
- 'Segregation by Sex, Earnings Differentials and Equal Pay. An application of a job crowding model to UK data', (1982) 14 *Applied Economics* 503.
- 'The Employment Response to Equal Pay Legislation', (1985) 37 *Oxford Economic Papers* 304.

RENDEL, M., 'Law as an Instrument of Oppression or Reform', in CARLEN, P. (ed.), *The Sociology of Law*, University of Keele, Sociological Review Monograph (1976).

RUBENSTEIN, M.,
- 'The Equal Treatment Directive and UK Law', in McCRUDDEN, C. (ed.), *Women, Employment and European Equality Law* (1987).
- 'The Law of Sexual Harassment at Work', (1983) 12 *Industrial Law Journal* 1.

SACKS, V., 'The Equal Opportunities Commission - Ten Years On', (1986) 49 *Modern Law Review* 560.

SHRUBSHALL, V., 'Additional Protocol to the European Social Charter - Employment Rights', (1989) 18 *Industrial Law Journal* 39.

SNELL, M., 'The Equal Pay and Sex Discrimination Acts. Their impact on the workplace', (1979) 1 *Feminist Review* 37.

STEINER, 'Sex Discrimination under UK and EEC Law. Two plus four equals one', (1983) 32 *ICLQ* 39.

SZYSZCZAK, E.,
- 'Pay Inequalities and Equal Value Claims', (1985) 45 *Modern Law Review*, 139.
- 'The Equal Pay Directive and UK Law', in McCRUDDEN, C. (ed.), *Women, Employment and European Equality Law* (1987).

USHER, J., 'European Community Equality Law. Legal instruments and judicial remedies', in McCRUDDEN, C., *Women, Employment and European Equality Law* (1987).

WILLBORN, S., 'Theories of Employment Discrimination in the United Kingdom and the United States', (1986) 9 *Boston College International and Comparative Law Review* 243.

## 1.3     OTHER DOCUMENTS

ADVISORY CONCILIATION AND ARBITRATION SERVICE,
- Annual Reports.
- Job Evaluation (1979).

BOWEY, A., *Evaluation of the Role of Independent Experts in Equal Value Cases in Britain, 1984-88* (1989).

BYRE, A., *Indirect Discrimination* (1987).

CHAMBERS, G., and HORTON, C., *Promoting Sex Equality. The role of industrial tribunals* (1990).

COLLING, T., and DICKENS, L., *Equality Bargaining - Why Not?* (1989).

CONFEDERATION OF BRITISH INDUSTRY, *Equal Pay ... Making it Work: CBI Response to EOC Consultative Document* (1989).

DEPARTMENT OF EMPLOYMENT, *Equal Opportunities for Men and Women* (1973).

DICKENS, L., TOWNLEY, D., and WINCHESTER, D., *Tackling Sex Discrimination through Collective Bargaining. The impact of section 6 of the Sex Discrimination Act 1986* (1988).

EARNSHAW, *Sex Discrimination and Dismissal. A review of recent case law*, University of Manchester Institute of Science and Technology, Department of Management Sciences, Occasional Paper 8505 (1985).

EQUAL OPPORTUNITIES COMMISSION,
-    *Equal Treatment for Men and Women. Strengthening the Acts* (1988).
-    *Equalising the Pension Age*, EOC, Manchester (1978).
-    *Job Evaluation Schemes Free of Sex Bias* (1981).
-    *Legislating for Change?* (1986).
-    *Equal Pay ... Making it Work - A Review of the Equal Pay Legislation. Consultative Document*, EOC, Manchester (1989).
-    *Towards Equality. A casebook of decisions on sex discrimination and equal pay* (1989).

EQUAL OPPORTUNITIES COMMISSION FOR NORTHERN IRELAND, *A Casebook of Decisions on Sex Discrimination and Equal Pay* (1990).

GHOBADIAN and WHITE, *Job Evaluation and Equal Pay*, Department of Employment Research Paper No 58 (1987).

GRAHAM, C., and LEWIS, N., *The Role of ACAS Conciliation in Equal Pay and Sex Discrimination Cases* (1985).

GREGORY, J., *Trial by Ordeal. A study of people who lost equal pay and sex discrimination cases in the industrial tribunals during 1985 and 1986* (1989).

HAKIM, *Occupational Segregation*, Department of Employment Research Paper No 9 (1979).

HOME OFFICE, *Sex Discrimination. A guide to the Sex Discrimination Act 1975*.

JUSTICE, *Industrial Tribunals* (Chairman: Bob Hepple) (1988).

KREMER, *Women and Work in Northern Ireland, 1983-1988* (1988).

LEONARD, *The First Eight Years. A profile of applicants to the industrial tribunals under the Sex Discrimination Act 1975 and the Equal Pay Act 1970: who they were, their claims, their success, 1976-1983* (1986).

McGOLDRICK, *Equal Treatment in Occupational Pension Schemes*, EOC, Manchester (1984).

NORTHERN IRELAND DEPARTMENT OF ECONOMIC DEVELOPMENT, *Equality of Opportunity in Employment in Northern Ireland - Future Strategy Options. A Consultative Paper* (1986).

SNELL, GLUCKLICH and POVALL, *Equal Pay and Opportunities*, Department of Employment Research Paper No 20 (1981).

STANDING ADVISORY COMMISSION ON HUMAN RIGHTS, 'Religious and Political Discrimination and Equality of Opportunity in Northern Ireland', *Report on Fair Employment*, Cm 237, HMSO (1987).

TUC EQUAL RIGHTS DEPARTMENT, *Equal Pay for Work of Equal Value*, Briefing No 2 (March 1989).

TUC GENERAL COUNCIL, *Equal Pay ... Making it Work - EOC Consultative Document: Comments of the TUC General Council*, London, TUC (1989).

TURU,
- *Job Evaluation and 'Equal Value' - Similarities and Differences,* Technical Note No 104 (December 1987).
- *Independent Experts and their Reports,* Technical Note No 103 (June 1988).
- *Women and Job Evaluation,* A Report of an Action Research Project sponsored by the Equal Opportunities Commission (unpublished, 1988).

WHITE PAPER, *Equality for Women,* Cmnd 5724 (1974).

# 2        INFORMATION

## 2.1        USEFUL  ADDRESSES

**Equal  Opportunities  Commission**
Overseas House,
Quay Street,
Manchester,        M3 3HN

**Equal  Opportunities  Commission  for  Northern  Ireland**
Chamber of Commerce House,
22, Great Victoria Street,
Belfast       BT2 2BA
Northern Ireland

# INDEX

ACCESS
  — to benefits, facilities, services . . . . . . . . . . 71-73, 77, 149, 150, 154, 155,
         157, 206
  — to employment . . . . . . . . . . . . . . . . . . . . 71, 148, 154, 155
  — to promotion . . . . . . . . . . . . . . . . . . . . 71, 72, 77, 149, 204, 205
  — to training . . . . . . . . . . . . . . . . . . . . . . 71-73, 76, 77, 149, 150, 156, 157
ADVERTISEMENTS . . . . . . . . . . . . . . . . . . . . . 74, 75, 160, 161, 202, 203
AGE
  — limit . . . . . . . . . . . . . . . . . . . . . . . . . . 23, 483-487
  — retirement . . . . . . . . . . . . . . . . . . . . . 34, 59-61, 91-93, 95, 98, 142,
         148-150, 272, 347-355
AGENCY MONITORING . . . . . . . . . . . . . . . . . . 132
ANNULMENT . . . . . . . . . . . . . . . . . . . . . . . . . 114, 130, 131, 185, 186, 212
ARMED FORCES AND MILITARY CORPS . . . . . 36, 65, 138, 142, 143, 190, 191
ARBITRATION OFFICER . . . . . . . . . . . . . . . . . 124, 125, 140, 142, 143
ASYMMETRICAL PROTECTION . . . . . . . . . . . . 13, 146, 147
AUTHENTICITY . . . . . . . . . . . . . . . . . . . . . . . 62-64, 150
AUTOMATIC NULLITY . . . . . . . . . . . . . . . . . . 130, 131, 185, 186, 212, 213

BENEFITS
  — family . . . . . . . . . . . . . . . . . . . . . . . . . . 89
  — fringe . . . . . . . . . . . . . . . . . . . . . . . . . . 38
  — in general . . . . . . . . . . . . . . . . . . . . . . . 38, 72, 73, 77, 89-95
  — invalid care allowance . . . . . . . . . . . . . . . 92, 271
  — post-employment . . . . . . . . . . . . . . . . . . 39
  — unemployment . . . . . . . . . . . . . . . . . . . 89
BREADWINNER . . . . . . . . . . . . . . . . . . . . . . . 22, 96
BURDEN OF PROOF . . . . . . . . . . . . . . . . . . . . 111-113, 146, 379-387, 436-446

CASE LAW
  — equal pay . . . . . . . . . . . . . . . . . . . . . . . . 282-346
  — equality in social security . . . . . . . . . . . . . 500-523
  — equal treatment . . . . . . . . . . . . . . . . . . . 347-499
CLASS ACTIONS . . . . . . . . . . . . . . . . . . . . . . . 120, 121, 252, 253
CLERGY . . . . . . . . . . . . . . . . . . . . . . . . . . . . . 65, 159
CODE OF PRACTICE . . . . . . . . . . . . . . . . . . . . 86, 169-171
COHABITANT . . . . . . . . . . . . . . . . . . . . . . . . 97
COLLECTIVE AGREEMENTS . . . . . . . . . . . . . . 40, 130, 212, 213
COLLECTIVE REDRESS . . . . . . . . . . . . . . . . . . 132
COMMUNAL ACCOMMODATION . . . . . . . . . . . 66, 67, 163, 164
COMPARATOR . . . . . . . . . . . . . . . . . . . . . . . . 16, 41, 74, 148, 293-317, 470-475
COMPARISON
  — cross-industry . . . . . . . . . . . . . . . . . . . . 43
  — of groups . . . . . . . . . . . . . . . . . . . . . . . . 42
  — of terms . . . . . . . . . . . . . . . . . . . . . . . . 36, 37, 282-292
COMPENSATION . . . . . . . . . . . . . . . . . . . . . . 115-117, 130, 139, 140, 177,
         420-424
CONCILIATION . . . . . . . . . . . . . . . . . . . . . . . . 125, 176
CONDITIONS OF WORK . . . . . . . . . . . . . . . . . 75, 76, 82
CONSTITUTIONAL LAW . . . . . . . . . . . . . . . . . 9, 87
CONTEMPORANEOUS EMPLOYMENT . . . . . . . 41

CONTRACT
   — compliance . . . . . . . . . . . . . . . . . . . . . . . 132
   — of employment . . . . . . . . . . . . . . . . . . . . . 35
CONTRIBUTIONS
   — direct . . . . . . . . . . . . . . . . . . . . . . . . . . 89
   — by employee . . . . . . . . . . . . . . . . . . . . . . 38, 39, 89
   — by employer . . . . . . . . . . . . . . . . . . . . . . . 37, 38, 89
COSTS . . . . . . . . . . . . . . . . . . . . . . . . . . . . . . .113, 249, 250
COURTS AND TRIBUNALS . . . . . . . . . . . . . 101-125, 182, 183, 225-228,
                                             238-265
CRIMINAL SANCTIONS . . . . . . . . . . . . . . . . . . 120

DAMAGES . . . . . . . . . . . . . . . . . . . . . . . . . . . .115-117, 139, 140, 177, 420-424
DECENCY . . . . . . . . . . . . . . . . . . . . . . . . . . . . .62, 65, 150, 151
DECLARATION . . . . . . . . . . . . . . . . . . . . . . . . . .115, 139, 176
DEPENDANT . . . . . . . . . . . . . . . . . . . . . . . . . . . .97, 98
DETERMINING FACTOR . . . . . . . . . . . . . . . . . . 61-67, 98, 99, 150-152
DETRIMENT . . . . . . . . . . . . . . . . . . . . . . . . . . . .16, 28, 29, 72, 78, 149, 425-435,
                                             488-490
DIRECT DISCRIMINATION . . . . . . . . . . . . . . . 13-19, 146-148
DIRECT EFFECT
   — of Directives . . . . . . . . . . . . . . . . . . . . . . . 6-8
   — of EEC Treaty . . . . . . . . . . . . . . . . . . . . . . 6
DIRECTIVES
   — direct effect of . . . . . . . . . . . . . . . . . . . . . 6-8
   — on equality . . . . . . . . . . . . . . . . . . . . . . . . 6, 76, 89, 91-96
DISCRIMINATION
   — definition of . . . . . . . . . . . . . . . . . . . . . . . . 13, 17, 20
   — direct . . . . . . . . . . . . . . . . . . . . . . . . . . . .13-19, 146-148
   — by employee . . . . . . . . . . . . . . . . . . . . . . . 79, 80, 161, 162, 447-453
   — indirect . . . . . . . . . . . . . . . . . . . . . . . . . . .20-31, 318-325
   — instruction to discriminate . . . . . . . . . . . . . . 78, 161
   — intentional . . . . . . . . . . . . . . . . . . . . . . . . .14, 15, 29, 420-435, 470-475
   — practices . . . . . . . . . . . . . . . . . . . . . . . . . . 80, 160
   — pressure to discriminate . . . . . . . . . . . . . . . 78, 161
   — termination of discriminatory conduct . . . . . 114
   — by trade union . . . . . . . . . . . . . . . . . . . . . . 79, 80, 155, 161, 162
   — unintentional . . . . . . . . . . . . . . . . . . . . . . . 15, 356-378
DISMISSAL . . . . . . . . . . . . . . . . . . . . . . . . . . . .18, 72, 78, 149, 154, 155
DISPROPORTIONATE IMPACT . . . . . . . . . . . . . . 24-29, 388-406, 454-469,
                                             483-487
DOMESTIC EMPLOYEES . . . . . . . . . . . . . . . . . . 36, 71, 151
DRESS CODES . . . . . . . . . . . . . . . . . . . . . . . . . .19

ECONOMIC BENEFITS / MARKET FORCES . . . . 50, 51, 318-325
EDUCATION AND TRAINING . . . . . . . . . . . . . . 73, 76, 77, 149, 156, 157,
                                           370-375
EMPLOYEES
   — definition of . . . . . . . . . . . . . . . . . . . . . . . . 35, 69, 138, 187
   — discrimination by . . . . . . . . . . . . . . . . . . . . 79, 80, 161, 162, 447-453
   — domestic . . . . . . . . . . . . . . . . . . . . . . . . . . 36, 71
EMPLOYMENT
   — access to . . . . . . . . . . . . . . . . . . . . . . . . . . 71, 148, 154, 155
   — conditions of . . . . . . . . . . . . . . . . . . . . . . . 75, 76, 82
   — contract of . . . . . . . . . . . . . . . . . . . . . . . . . 35
   — offer of . . . . . . . . . . . . . . . . . . . . . . . . . . . 71, 72, 75, 148, 150, 152, 154,
                                           155
   — refusal of . . . . . . . . . . . . . . . . . . . . . . . . . . 71, 72, 75, 148, 154, 155
   — terms of . . . . . . . . . . . . . . . . . . . . . . . . . . .71, 75, 148, 150, 152, 154, 155

ENFORCEMENT . . . . . . . . . . . . . . . . . . . . . . 101-132, 146, 182, 183, 243, 244,
                                                      249, 250, 274, 275, 278, 293-305,
                                                      420-424, 436-446
ENFORCEMENT AGENCY . . . . . . . . . . . . . . . . 126-130
EQUAL OPPORTUNITIES COMMISSION . . . . . . 101, 125-130, 168-171, 173, 174,
                                                      177-181, 183, 184, 192-196
EQUAL PAY . . . . . . . . . . . . . . . . . . . . . . . . . .33-54, 136-143
    — case law . . . . . . . . . . . . . . . . . . . . . . . .282-346
    — components of . . . . . . . . . . . . . . . . . . . .37-39
    — equality of . . . . . . . . . . . . . . . . . . . . . . . 6, 13, 33-54, 136-139
    — enforcement of the principle . . . . . . . . . . . . 101-132
    — exceptions to equality of . . . . . . . . . . . . . 33-35
    — legislation . . . . . . . . . . . . . . . . . . . . . . .136-143, 221-265
    — legitimate reason . . . . . . . . . . . . . . . . . . 49-54, 137, 293-325, 338-346
    — personal scope . . . . . . . . . . . . . . . . . . . . .35, 36
    — proportionate . . . . . . . . . . . . . . . . . . . . . .49
EQUAL PAY CLAUSE . . . . . . . . . . . . . . . . . . . . 130, 136
EQUAL TREATMENT. . . . . . . . . . . . . . . . . . . . . 6, 13, 55-87, 144-220
    — case law . . . . . . . . . . . . . . . . . . . . . . . . .347-499
    — enforcement of principle . . . . . . . . . . . . . 101-132
    — exceptions . . . . . . . . . . . . . . . . . . . . . . . .55-67
    — legislation . . . . . . . . . . . . . . . . . . . . . . . .144-265
    — personal scope . . . . . . . . . . . . . . . . . . . . .69-71
    — special . . . . . . . . . . . . . . . . . . . . . . . . . .80-87
    — territorial scope . . . . . . . . . . . . . . . . . . . . 68, 153, 154
EQUALITY
    — officer. . . . . . . . . . . . . . . . . . . . . . . . . . .122-124
    — of opportunity . . . . . . . . . . . . . . . . . . . . .6, 13
    — of pay . . . . . . . . . . . . . . . . . . . . . . . . . . .6, 13, 33-54, 136-143, 282-346
    — in social security . . . . . . . . . . . . . . . . . . . 6, 13, 89-100, 266-279, 500-523
    — of treatment . . . . . . . . . . . . . . . . . . . . . . . 6, 13, 55-87, 144-220, 347-499
    — principle of . . . . . . . . . . . . . . . . . . . . . . . 13, 33, 55, 136-139
ESTABLISHMENT
    — different . . . . . . . . . . . . . . . . . . . . . . . . .42, 293-305
    — same. . . . . . . . . . . . . . . . . . . . . . . . . . . .41, 138
    — single-sex . . . . . . . . . . . . . . . . . . . . . . . .62, 67, 151, 162, 163, 217, 218
    — size of . . . . . . . . . . . . . . . . . . . . . . . . . . .33, 55, 199
EUROPEAN COURT OF JUSTICE . . . . . . . . . . . . 6-9
EVIDENCE
    — acquisition of . . . . . . . . . . . . . . . . . . . . . .107-111
    — prescribed forms . . . . . . . . . . . . . . . . . . . 107, 182, 183, 225-228
    — relevant evidence . . . . . . . . . . . . . . . . . . 108-110, 243, 244, 293-305,
                                                      439-446
    — statistical . . . . . . . . . . . . . . . . . . . . . . . . .25-27, 388-406, 483-487
EXCEPTIONS
    — to equality of pay . . . . . . . . . . . . . . . . . . .33-35
    — to equality in social security . . . . . . . . . . . 98, 99
    — to equality of treatment . . . . . . . . . . . . . . 55-67
EXCLUSION . . . . . . . . . . . . . . . . . . . . . . . . . .55, 78
EXCLUSION OF JUDICIAL REDRESS . . . . . . . . 121, 175, 185
EXPERT'S REPORT . . . . . . . . . . . . . . . . . . . . . .105-107

FACTORS . . . . . . . . . . . . . . . . . . . . . . . . . . . .48, 137
FAMILY BENEFITS . . . . . . . . . . . . . . . . . . . . . 89
FAMILY STATUS . . . . . . . . . . . . . . . . . . . . . . .17, 23
FRINGE BENEFITS . . . . . . . . . . . . . . . . . . . . . 38

GENUINE OCCUPATIONAL QUALIFICATION . . . . . . 61-63, 71, 72, 150-152, 155, 201,
                                                      202

HEAD OF HOUSEHOLD . . . . . . . . . . . . . . . . . . 22, 97
HEALTH AND SAFETY . . . . . . . . . . . . . . . . 33, 55-58, 82, 166, 476-482
HIRING . . . . . . . . . . . . . . . . . . . . . . . . . . . . . .74, 75
HOME WORKERS . . . . . . . . . . . . . . . . . . . . . . . .35, 70, 154
HOSPITALS . . . . . . . . . . . . . . . . . . . . . . . . . . .62, 66, 151
HUMAN RIGHTS . . . . . . . . . . . . . . . . . . . . . . . .4, 87
HYPOTHETICAL MALE . . . . . . . . . . . . . . . . . . 42

IDENTICAL WORK . . . . . . . . . . . . . . . . . . . . . . 43, 137, 138
IMPACT ON THE INDIVIDUAL . . . . . . . . . . . . . 28, 29
INDEPENDENT CONTRACTORS . . . . . . . . . . . . 35, 69, 138, 152, 153
INDIRECT DISCRIMINATION . . . . . . . . . . . . . . 20-31, 146, 147, 318-325
INFORMATION . . . . . . . . . . . . . . . . . . . . . . . . .110, 111
INJUNCTION . . . . . . . . . . . . . . . . . . . . . . . . . .129, 130, 180, 181
INSTRUCTION TO DISCRIMINATE . . . . . . . . . . 78, 161
INTERNATIONAL ORGANISATIONS . . . . . . . . . 4, 5
INVALID CARE ALLOWANCE . . . . . . . . . . . . . . 92, 271

JOB
— classification . . . . . . . . . . . . . . . . . . . . . 46
— description . . . . . . . . . . . . . . . . . . . . . . . . 75
— evaluation . . . . . . . . . . . . . . . . . . . . . . . 45-48, 140, 326-337
— title . . . . . . . . . . . . . . . . . . . . . . . . . . . 75
JUSTIFICATION OF DISCRIMINATION . . . . . . . 29-31, 50-54

LABOUR INSPECTORATE . . . . . . . . . . . . . . . . . 126
LEAVE
— parental . . . . . . . . . . . . . . . . . . . . . . . . . 82
LEGAL AID . . . . . . . . . . . . . . . . . . . . . . . . . . . 102, 113, 114, 127, 183
LEGISLATION . . . . . . . . . . . . . . . . . . . . . . . . .3, 10-12, 166, 167, 215-219
— equal pay . . . . . . . . . . . . . . . . . . . . . . . . 136-143, 221-265
— equality in social security . . . . . . . . . . . . . 266-279
— equal treatment . . . . . . . . . . . . . . . . . . . . 144-265
— protective . . . . . . . . . . . . . . . . . . . . . . . 18, 72, 78, 80-82
LEGITIMATE REASON . . . . . . . . . . . . . . . . . . . 49-54, 137, 293-325, 338-346
LEVELLING UP / DOWN . . . . . . . . . . . . . . . . . 54, 99, 100, 136-139, 274
LIKE WORK . . . . . . . . . . . . . . . . . . . . . . . . . . . 13, 36, 43, 44, 137, 138

MARKET FORCES . . . . . . . . . . . . . . . . . . . . . . . 50, 51, 318-325
MARITAL STATUS . . . . . . . . . . . . . . . . . . . . . . 17, 23, 62, 146, 147, 151,
                                                         470-475
MATERIAL DIFFERENCE . . . . . . . . . . . . . . . . . 49, 137
MATERNITY . . . . . . . . . . . . . . . . . . . . . . . . . . .80-82, 166
MEANS . . . . . . . . . . . . . . . . . . . . . . . . . . . . . .86
MIDWIVES . . . . . . . . . . . . . . . . . . . . . . . . . . . .66, 148, 149, 156, 159, 160
MOBILITY REQUIREMENT . . . . . . . . . . . . . . . . 23
MODELS . . . . . . . . . . . . . . . . . . . . . . . . . . . . . .63, 64

NATIONAL SECURITY . . . . . . . . . . . . . . . . . . . 33, 58, 59, 167, 168
NIGHT-WORK . . . . . . . . . . . . . . . . . . . . . . . . . .44, 51, 293-305
NON-EMPLOYED PERSONS . . . . . . . . . . . . . . . . 36, 71
NOTICE . . . . . . . . . . . . . . . . . . . . . . . . . . . . . .128, 129, 177-179, 229-237
NULLITY . . . . . . . . . . . . . . . . . . . . . . . . . . . . .114, 130, 131, 185, 186, 212

OBJECTIVE JUSTIFICATION . . . . . . . . . . . . . . . 29-31, 318-325, 388-410
OCCUPATIONAL SOCIAL SECURITY . . . . . . . . 6, 90, 95, 102, 277, 278
OFFER OF EMPLOYMENT . . . . . . . . . . . . . . . . . 71, 72, 75, 148, 150, 152

PARENTAL LEAVE . . . . . . . . . . . . . . . . . . . . . .82
PART-TIME WORK . . . . . . . . . . . . . . . . . . . . . .22, 51, 52, 100, 206,
                                                        338-346, 388-406, 454-469

PENSIONS
    — age . . . . . . . . . . . . . . . . . . . . . . . . . . . . . .91-93, 95, 347-355
    — dependency increase . . . . . . . . . . . . . . . . .97, 98
    — element of pay . . . . . . . . . . . . . . . . . . . . .37, 39, 40
    — invalidity . . . . . . . . . . . . . . . . . . . . . . . . . .93-95
    — occupational pension . . . . . . . . . . . . . . . .37, 39, 40, 60, 272, 274, 275, 278
    — retirement . . . . . . . . . . . . . . . . . . . . . . . .91-93, 95, 347-355
    — survivor . . . . . . . . . . . . . . . . . . . . . . . .95, 96
PERSONAL SERVICES . . . . . . . . . . . . . . . . . . .62, 151
PHYSICAL
    — attributes . . . . . . . . . . . . . . . . . . . . . . . . . .19, 24, 48, 63
    — education teachers . . . . . . . . . . . . . . . . . .66, 388-406
    — strength . . . . . . . . . . . . . . . . . . . . . . . . . .23
POLICE . . . . . . . . . . . . . . . . . . . . . . . . . . . . . .64, 157, 159
POSITIVE
    — action . . . . . . . . . . . . . . . . . . . . . . . . . . . .82-87, 155, 164-166, 207-208
    — action plan . . . . . . . . . . . . . . . . . . . . . . . . .120
    — enforcement order . . . . . . . . . . . . . . . . . . .119, 120, 139, 140, 177
POST-EMPLOYMENT BENEFITS . . . . . . . . . . . .39
PREGNANCY . . . . . . . . . . . . . . . . . . . . . . . . . . .17, 18, 23, 34, 80-82, 146, 166
PRESSURE TO DISCRIMINATE . . . . . . . . . . . . .78, 161
PRISON OFFICERS . . . . . . . . . . . . . . . . . . . . . . .62, 64, 65, 151, 159
PRIVACY . . . . . . . . . . . . . . . . . . . . . . . . . . . . . .62, 65, 150, 151
PRIVATE HOME . . . . . . . . . . . . . . . . . . . . . . . .62, 151
PROMOTION . . . . . . . . . . . . . . . . . . . . . . . . . . .71, 72, 77, 149, 204, 205
PROPORTIONATE PAY . . . . . . . . . . . . . . . . . . .49
PROTECTION
    — against dismissal . . . . . . . . . . . . . . . . . . . .18, 72, 78
    — in maternity . . . . . . . . . . . . . . . . . . . . . . .18, 80-82
PUBLIC SECTOR . . . . . . . . . . . . . . . . . . . . . . . .35, 70, 138, 148-152, 190-192

QUALIFICATION . . . . . . . . . . . . . . . . . . . . . . . .72, 73, 156

RECOMMENDATION . . . . . . . . . . . . . . . . . . . . .117-119, 177
RECRUITMENT
    — advertisements . . . . . . . . . . . . . . . . . . . . . .74, 75, 160, 161, 202, 203
    — methods . . . . . . . . . . . . . . . . . . . . . . . . . .74, 148, 201
    — selection . . . . . . . . . . . . . . . . . . . . . . . . . .71, 72, 75, 148, 154, 155, 201
    — terms . . . . . . . . . . . . . . . . . . . . . . . . . . . .71, 72, 148-150, 154, 155
RED CIRCLING . . . . . . . . . . . . . . . . . . . . . . . . .52, 53
REFUSAL OF EMPLOYMENT . . . . . . . . . . . . . . .71, 72, 75, 148
RELATION TO PAY . . . . . . . . . . . . . . . . . . . . . .76, 137, 148-150, 152
RELIGION . . . . . . . . . . . . . . . . . . . . . . . . . . . . .34, 59, 65, 159, 217, 218
REMEDIES . . . . . . . . . . . . . . . . . . . . . . . . . . . . .114-120, 128-130, 139, 140, 173,
                                                        174, 176-181
RETIREMENT AGE . . . . . . . . . . . . . . . . . . . . . .34, 59-61, 91-93, 95, 98, 142,
                                                        148-150, 272, 347-355
RETROSPECTIVE IMPLEMENTATION . . . . . . . .8, 9

SANCTIONS . . . . . . . . . . . . . . . . . . . . . . . . . . . .120
SECURITY
    — armed forces and military corps . . . . . . . . .36, 65, 138, 142, 143, 190, 191
    — national . . . . . . . . . . . . . . . . . . . . . . . . . . .33, 58, 59, 167, 168
    — police . . . . . . . . . . . . . . . . . . . . . . . . . . . .64, 157-159
    — prison officers . . . . . . . . . . . . . . . . . . . . . .62, 64, 65, 151, 159
    — social . . . . . . . . . . . . . . . . . . . . . . . . . . . .89-100

SELECTION ARRANGEMENTS . . . . . . . . . . . . 71, 72, 75, 148, 154, 155, 203, 204
SENIORITY . . . . . . . . . . . . . . . . . . . . . . . . . .24, 454-463
SEXUAL HARASSMENT . . . . . . . . . . . . . . . . . 19, 425-435, 447, 453, 488-490
SIMILAR WORK . . . . . . . . . . . . . . . . . . . . . . . .43, 44, 137, 138
SOCIAL ASSISTANCE . . . . . . . . . . . . . . . . . . . .91
SOCIAL SECURITY
    — case law . . . . . . . . . . . . . . . . . . . . . . . . .500-523
    — definition . . . . . . . . . . . . . . . . . . . . . . . .89-91
    — Directives . . . . . . . . . . . . . . . . . . . . . . . .6, 91-96, 500-523
    — enforcement of principle in . . . . . . . . . . . . 101-103
    — equality in . . . . . . . . . . . . . . . . . . . . . . . .6, 13, 89-100
    — exceptions . . . . . . . . . . . . . . . . . . . . . . . .98, 99
    — legislation . . . . . . . . . . . . . . . . . . . . . . . .266-279
    — problematic concepts . . . . . . . . . . . . . . . . 96-98
SOLE BREADWINNER . . . . . . . . . . . . . . . . . . . . .96, 97
SPECIAL LABOUR COURT OR TRIBUNAL . . . . . 122
SPECIAL TREATMENT . . . . . . . . . . . . . . . . . . . .80-87
SPECIALIZATION . . . . . . . . . . . . . . . . . . . . . . . .125
SPECIALIZED TRAINING . . . . . . . . . . . . . . . . . .125
STATISTICAL EVIDENCE . . . . . . . . . . . . . . . . . .25-27, 388-406, 483-487
STATUTORY SOCIAL SECURITY . . . . . . . . . . . .89-90
STRENGTH . . . . . . . . . . . . . . . . . . . . . . . . . . . .23
SUSPECT CRITERIA . . . . . . . . . . . . . . . . . . . . .21-24, 338-346, 388-406, 411-419, 454-469, 483-487

TERMINATION OF DISCRIMINATION . . . . . . . . 114
TERMS
    — of comparison . . . . . . . . . . . . . . . . . . . . . .36, 37
    — of employment . . . . . . . . . . . . . . . . . . . . . .71, 75, 148, 150, 152
TIME LIMITS . . . . . . . . . . . . . . . . . . . . . . . . . .121, 122, 139, 140, 184, 185
TRADE UNIONS . . . . . . . . . . . . . . . . . . . . . . . .79, 80, 85, 86, 155, 161, 162, 165, 166
TRAINING
    — access to . . . . . . . . . . . . . . . . . . . . . . . . . .71-73, 76, 77, 149, 150, 156, 157
    — bodies . . . . . . . . . . . . . . . . . . . . . . . . . . . .83, 149, 164, 219, 220
TREATY (EEC) . . . . . . . . . . . . . . . . . . . . . . . . .6, 30, 37-40, 52, 54, 61, 91, 131
TRIBUNALS . . . . . . . . . . . . . . . . . . . . . . . . . . .101-125, 182, 183, 225-228, 238-265

VALUE
    — equal . . . . . . . . . . . . . . . . . . . . . . . . . . . .13, 36, 44-48, 137, 138, 326-337
    — equivalent . . . . . . . . . . . . . . . . . . . . . . . . .13, 36
    — higher . . . . . . . . . . . . . . . . . . . . . . . . . . . .49
VICTIMIZATION . . . . . . . . . . . . . . . . . . . . . . . .31, 147, 148, 206

WEIGHTINGS . . . . . . . . . . . . . . . . . . . . . . . . . .48
WORK
    — collective agreement of . . . . . . . . . . . . . . . 40, 130, 212, 213
    — conditions of . . . . . . . . . . . . . . . . . . . . . . .75, 76, 82
    — contract of . . . . . . . . . . . . . . . . . . . . . . . . .35
    — done outside the jurisdiction . . . . . . . . . . . . 33, 55, 62, 151,
    — of equal value . . . . . . . . . . . . . . . . . . . . . . .13, 36, 44-48, 137, 138, 326-337
    — of equivalent value . . . . . . . . . . . . . . . . . . . 13, 36
    — of higher value . . . . . . . . . . . . . . . . . . . . . .49
    — hours of . . . . . . . . . . . . . . . . . . . . . . . . . . .23, 388-406, 464-469
    — identical work . . . . . . . . . . . . . . . . . . . . . . .43, 137, 138
    — like work . . . . . . . . . . . . . . . . . . . . . . . . . .13, 36, 43, 44, 137, 138

WORK continued
  — part-time . . . . . . . . . . . . . . . . . . . . . . 22, 51, 52, 100, 206, 338-346,
                                         388-406, 454-469
  — night-work . . . . . . . . . . . . . . . . . . . . . . 44, 51
  — relation to pay . . . . . . . . . . . . . . . . . . . . 76, 137, 148-150, 152
  — similar work . . . . . . . . . . . . . . . . . . . . . 43, 44, 137, 138
WORKER
  — domestic . . . . . . . . . . . . . . . . . . . . . . . 36, 71, 151
  — home . . . . . . . . . . . . . . . . . . . . . . . . . .35, 70, 154

# Venta y suscripciones • Salg og abonnement • Verkauf und Abonnement • Πωλήσεις και συνδρομές
## Sales and subscriptions • Vente et abonnements • Vendita e abbonamenti
### Verkoop en abonnementen • Venda e assinaturas

**BELGIQUE / BELGIË**

**Moniteur belge /
Belgisch staatsblad**
Rue de Louvain 42 / Leuvenseweg 42
B-1000 Bruxelles / B-1000 Brussel
Tél. (02) 512 00 26
Fax (02) 511 01 84

**Jean De Lannoy**
Avenue du Roi 202 / Koningslaan 202
B-1060 Bruxelles / B-1060 Brussel
Tél. (02) 538 51 69
Télex 63220 UNBOOK B
Fax (02) 538 08 41
Autres distributeurs/
Overige verkooppunten:

**Librairie européenne/
Europese boekhandel**
Rue de la Loi 244/Wetstraat 244
B-1040 Bruxelles / B-1040 Brussel
Tél. (02) 231 04 35
Fax (02) 735 08 60.
Document delivery:

**Credoc**
Rue de la Montagne 34 / Bergstraat 34
Bte 11 / Bus 11
B-1000 Bruxelles / B-1000 Brussel
Tél. (02) 511 69 41
Fax (02) 513 31 95

**DANMARK**

**J. H. Schultz Information A/S**
Herstedvang 10-12
DK-2620 Albertslund
Tlf. 43 63 23 00
Fax (Sales) 43 63 19 69
Fax (Management) 43 63 19 49

**DEUTSCHLAND**

**Bundesanzeiger Verlag**
Breite Straße 78-80
Postfach 10 05 34
D-50445 Köln
Tel. (02 21) 20 29-0
Telex ANZEIGER BONN 8 882 595
Fax 202 92 78

**GREECE/ΕΛΛΑΔΑ**

**G.C. Eleftheroudakis SA**
International Bookstore
Nikis Street 4
GR-10563 Athens
Tel. (01) 322 63 23
Telex 219410 ELEF
Fax 323 98 21

**ESPAÑA**

**Boletín Oficial del Estado**
Trafalgar. 27-29
E-28071 Madrid
Tel. (91) 538 22 95 -
Fax (91) 538 23 49

**Mundi-Prensa Libros, SA**
Castelló, 37
E-28001 Madrid
Tel. (91) 431 33 99 (Libros)
431 32 22 (Suscripciones)
435 36 37 (Dirección)
Télex 49370-MPLI-E
Fax (91) 575 39 98

Sucursal:

**Librería Internacional AEDOS**
Consejo de Ciento, 391
E-08009 Barcelona
Tel. (93) 488 34 92
Fax (93) 487 76 59

**Llibreria de la Generalitat
de Catalunya**
Rambla dels Estudis, 118 (Palau Moja)
E-08002 Barcelona
Tel. (93) 302 68 35
Tel. (93) 302 64 62
Fax (93) 302 12 99

**FRANCE**

**Journal officiel
Service des publications
des Communautés européennes**
26, rue Desaix
F-75727 Paris Cedex 15
Tél. (1) 40 58 77 01/31
Fax (1) 40 58 77 00

**IRELAND**

**Government Supplies Agency**
4-5 Harcourt Road
Dublin 2
Tel. (1) 66 13 111
Fax (1) 47 80 645

**ITALIA**

**Licosa SpA**
Via Duca di Calabria 1/1
Casella postale 552
I-50125 Firenze
Tel. (055) 64 54 15
Fax 64 12 57
Telex 570466 LICOSA I

**GRAND-DUCHÉ DE LUXEMBOURG**

**Messageries du livre**
5, rue Raiffeisen
L-2411 Luxembourg
Tél. 40 10 20
Fax 49 06 61

**NEDERLAND**

**SDU Overheidsinformatie**
Externe Fondsen
Postbus 20014
2500 EA 's-Gravenhage
Tel. (070) 37 89 911
Fax (070) 34 75 778

**PORTUGAL**

**Imprensa Nacional**
Casa da Moeda, EP
Rua D. Francisco Manuel de Melo, 5
P-1092 Lisboa Codex
Tel. (01) 69 34 14
Fax (01) 69 31 66

**Distribuidora de Livros
Bertrand, Ld.ª**

**Grupo Bertrand, SA**
Rua das Terras dos Vales, 4-A
Apartado 37
P-2700 Amadora Codex
Tel. (01) 49 59 050
Telex 15798 BERDIS
Fax 49 60 255

**UNITED KINGDOM**

**HMSO Books (Agency section)**
HMSO Publications Centre
51 Nine Elms Lane
London SW8 5DR
Tel. (071) 873 9090
Fax 873 8463
Telex 29 71 138

**ÖSTERREICH**

**Manz'sche Verlags-
und Universitätsbuchhandlung**
Kohlmarkt 16
A-1014 Wien
Tel. (1) 531 610
Telex 112 500 BOX A
Fax (1) 531 61-181

**SUOMI/FINLAND**

**Akateeminen Kirjakauppa**
Keskuskatu 1
PO Box 218
FIN-00381 Helsinki
Tel. (0) 121 41
Fax (0) 121 44 41

**NORGE**

**Narvesen Info Center**
Bertrand Narvesens vei 2
PO Box 6125 Etterstad
N-0602 Oslo 6
Tel. (22) 57 33 00
Telex 79668 NIC N
Fax (22) 68 19 01

**SVERIGE**

**BTJ AB**
Traktorvgen 13
S-22100 Lund
Tel. (046) 18 00 00
Fax (046) 18 01 25
30 79 47

**SCHWEIZ / SUISSE / SVIZZERA**

**OSEC**
Stampfenbachstraße 85
CH-8035 Zürich
Tel. (01) 365 54 49
Fax (01) 365 54 11

**BĂLGARIJA**

**Europress Klassica BK
Ltd**
66, bd Vitosha
BG-1463 Sofia
Tel./Fax 2 52 74 75

**ČESKÁ REPUBLIKA**

**NIS ČR**
Havelkova 22
CZ-130 00 Praha 3
Tel. (2) 235 84 46
Fax (2) 235 97 88

**MAGYARORSZÁG**

**Euro-Info-Service**
Európa Ház
Margitsziget
H-1138 Budapest
Tel./Fax 1 111 60 61
1 111 62 16

**POLSKA**

**Business Foundation**
ul. Krucza 38/42
PL-00-512 Warszawa
Tel. (22) 621 99 93. 628-28-82
International Fax&Phone
(0-39) 12-00-77

**ROMÂNIA**

**Euromedia**
65, Strada Dionisie Lupu
RO-70184 Bucuresti
Tel./Fax 0 12 96 46

**RUSSIA**

**CCEC**
9,60-letiya Oktyabrya Avenue
117312 Moscow
Tel./Fax (095) 135 52 27

**SLOVAKIA**

**Slovak Technical
Library**
Nm. slobody 19
SO-812 23 Bratislava 1
Tel. (7) 220 452
Fax : (7) 295 785

**CYPRUS**

**Cyprus Chamber of Commerce and
Industry**
Chamber Building
38 Grivas Dhigenis Ave
3 Deligeorgis Street
PO Box 1455
Nicosia
Tel. (2) 449500/462312
Fax (2) 458630

**MALTA**

**Miller distributors Ltd**
PO Box 25
Malta International Airport
LQA 05 Malta
Tel. 66 44 88
Fax 67 67 99

**TÜRKIYE**

**Pres Gazete Kitap Dergi
Pazarlama Dagitim Ticaret ve sanayi
AŞ**
Narlibaçhe Sokak N. 15
Istanbul-Cagaloğlu
Tel. (1) 520 92 96 - 528 55 66
Fax 520 64 57
Telex 23822 DSVO-TR

**ISRAEL**

**ROY International**
PO Box 13056
41 Mishmar Hayarden Street
Tel Aviv 61130
Tel. 3 496 108
Fax 3 648 60 39

**EGYPT/
MIDDLE EAST**

**Middle East Observer**
41 Sherif St.
Cairo
Tel/Fax 39 39 732

**UNITED STATES OF AMERICA /
CANADA**

**UNIPUB**
4611-F Assembly Drive
Lanham, MD 20706-4391
Tel. Toll Free (800) 274 4888
Fax (301) 459 0056

**CANADA**

Subscriptions only
Uniquement abonnements

**Renouf Publishing Co. Ltd**
1294 Algoma Road
Ottawa, Ontario K1B 3W8
Tel. (613) 741 43 33
Fax (613) 741 54 39
Telex 0534783

**AUSTRALIA**

**Hunter Publications**
58A Gipps Street
Collingwood
Victoria 3066
Tel. (3) 417 5361
Fax (3) 419 7154

**JAPAN**

**Kinokuniya Company Ltd**
17-7 Shinjuku 3-Chome
Shinjuku-ku
Tokyo 160-91
Tel. (03) 3439-0121

**Journal Department**
PO Box 55 Chitose
Tokyo 156
Tel. (03) 3439-0124

**SOUTH-EAST ASIA**

**Legal Library Services Ltd**
STK Agency
Robinson Road
PO Box 1817
Singapore 9036

**SOUTH AFRICA**

**Safto**
5th Floor, Export House
Cnr Maude & West Streets
Sandton 2146
Tel. (011) 883-3737
Fax (011) 883-6569

**AUTRES PAYS
OTHER COUNTRIES
ANDERE LÄNDER**

**Office des publications officielles
des Communautés européennes**
2, rue Mercier
L-2985 Luxembourg
Tél. 499 28-1
Télex PUBOF LU 1324 b
Fax 48 85 73/48 68 17